T0181981

Lecture Notes in Artificial Intelligence   12748

Subseries of Lecture Notes in Computer Science

More information about this subseries at http://www.springer.com/series/1244

Ido Roll · Danielle McNamara ·
Sergey Sosnovsky · Rose Luckin ·
Vania Dimitrova (Eds.)

Artificial Intelligence
in Education

22nd International Conference, AIED 2021
Utrecht, The Netherlands, June 14–18, 2021
Proceedings, Part I

 Springer

Editors
Ido Roll ⓘ
Technion – Israel Institute of Technology
Haifa, Israel

Sergey Sosnovsky ⓘ
Utrecht University
Utrecht, The Netherlands

Vania Dimitrova
University of Leeds
Leeds, UK

Danielle McNamara ⓘ
Arizona State University
Tempe, AZ, USA

Rose Luckin
London Knowledge Lab
London, UK

ISSN 0302-9743   ISSN 1611-3349   (electronic)
Lecture Notes in Artificial Intelligence
ISBN 978-3-030-78291-7   ISBN 978-3-030-78292-4   (eBook)
https://doi.org/10.1007/978-3-030-78292-4

LNCS Sublibrary: SL7 – Artificial Intelligence

This Springer imprint is published by the registered company Springer Nature Switzerland AG
The registered company address is: Gewerbestrasse 11, 6330 Cham, Switzerland

Preface

The 22nd International Conference on Artificial Intelligence in Education (AIED 2021), originally planned for Utrecht, the Netherlands, was held virtually during June 2021. AIED 2021 was the latest in a longstanding series of yearly international conferences for the presentation of high-quality research into ways to enhance student learning through applications of artificial intelligence, human computer interaction, and the learning sciences.

The theme for the AIED 2021 conference was "Mind the Gap: AIED for Equity and Inclusion." Over the past decades, racial and other bias-driven inequities have persisted or increased, diversity remains low in many educational and vocational contexts, and educational gaps have widened. Despite efforts to address these issues, biases based on factors such as race and gender persist. These issues have come to the forefront with recent crises around the world. In this conference, we reflected on issues of equity, diversity, and inclusion in regards to the educational tools and algorithms that we build, how we assess the efficacy and impact of our applications, theoretical frameworks, and the AIED society. The use of intelligent educational applications has increased, particularly within the past few years. As a community, development and assessment practices mindful of potential (and likely) inequities are necessary. Likewise, planned diversity, equity, and inclusion practices are necessary within the AIED society and home institutions and companies.

There were 168 submissions as full papers to AIED 2020, of which 40 were accepted as full papers (10 pages) with virtual oral presentation at the conference (an acceptance rate of 23.8%), and 66 were accepted as short papers (4 pages). Of the 41 papers directly submitted as short papers, 12 were accepted. Each submission was reviewed by at least three Program Committee (PC) members. In addition, submissions underwent a discussion period (led by a leading reviewer) to ensure that all reviewers' opinions would be considered and leveraged to generate a group recommendation to the program chairs. The program chairs checked the reviews and meta-reviews for quality and, where necessary, requested that reviewers elaborate their review. Final decisions were made by carefully considering both meta-review scores (weighed more heavily) and the discussions, as well as by rereading many of the papers. Our goal was to conduct a fair process and encourage substantive and constructive reviews without interfering with the reviewers' judgment.

Beyond paper presentations and keynotes, the conference also included the following:

- An Industry and Innovation track, intended to support connections between industry (both for-profit and non-profit) and the research community.
- A series of six workshops across a range of topics, including: empowering education with AI technology, intelligent textbooks, challenges related to education in AI (K-12), and optimizing human learning.

– A Doctoral Consortium track, designed to provide doctoral students with the opportunity to obtain feedback on their doctoral research from the research community.
– A Student Forum, funded by the Schmidt Foundation, that supported undergraduate students in learning about AIED, its past, present, and future challenges, and helped them make connections within the community. Special thanks go to Springer for sponsoring the AIED 2020 Best Paper Award. We also wish to acknowledge the wonderful work of the AIED 2020 Organizing Committee, the PC members, and the reviewers who made this conference possible. This conference was certainly a community effort and a testament to the community's strength.

April 2021

Ido Roll
Danielle McNamara
Sergey Sosnovsky
Rose Luckin
Vania Dimitrova

Organization

General Conference Chairs

Rose Luckin — University College London, UK
Vania Dimitrova — University of Leeds, UK

Program Co-chairs

Ido Roll — Technion - Israel Institute of Technology, Israel
Danielle McNamara — Arizona State University, USA

Industry and Innovation Track Co-chairs

Steve Ritter — Carnegie Learning, USA
Inge Molenaar — Radboud University, The Netherlands

Doctoral Consortium Track Co-chairs

Janice Gobert — Rutgers Graduate School of Education, USA
Tanja Mitrovic — University of Canterbury, New Zealand

Workshop and Tutorials Co-chairs

Mingyu Feng — WestEd, USA
Alexandra Cristea — Durham University, UK
Zitao Liu — TAL Education Group, China

Interactive Events Co-chairs

Mutlu Cukurova — University College London, UK
Carmel Kent — Educate Ventures, UK
Bastiaan Heeren — Open University of the Netherlands, the Netherlands

Local Co-chairs

Sergey Sosnovsky — Utrecht University, the Netherlands
Johan Jeuring — Utrecht University, the Netherlands

Proceedings Chair

Irene-Angelica Chounta — University of Duisburg-Essen, Germany

Publicity Chair

Elle Yuan Wang   Arizona State University, USA

Web Chair

Isaac Alpizar-Chacon   Utrecht University, the Netherlands

Senior Program Committee Members

Ryan Baker	University of Pennsylvania, USA
Tiffany Barnes	North Carolina State University, USA
Emmanuel Blanchard	IDÛ Interactive Inc., Canada
Christopher Brooks	University of Michigan, USA
Min Chi	BeiKaZhouLi, USA
Sidney D'Mello	University of Colorado Boulder, USA
Benedict du Boulay	University of Sussex, UK
Janice Gobert	Rutgers, USA
Peter Hastings	DePaul University, USA
Neil Heffernan	Worcester Polytechnic Institute, USA
Ulrich Hoppe	University of Duisburg-Essen, Germany
Judy Kay	The University of Sydney, Australia
H. Chad Lane	University of Illinois at Urbana-Champaign, USA
James Lester	North Carolina State University, USA
Noboru Matsuda	North Carolina State University, USA
Gordon McCalla	University of Saskatchewan, Canada
Bruce Mclaren	Carnegie Mellon University, USA
Agathe Merceron	Beuth University of Applied Sciences Berlin, Germany
Tanja Mitrovic	University of Canterbury, New Zealand
Inge Molenaar	Radboud University, the Netherlands
Roger Nkambou	Université du Québec à Montréal, Canada
Amy Ogan	Carnegie Mellon University, USA
Andrew Olney	University of Memphis, USA
Luc Paquette	University of Illinois at Urbana-Champaign, USA
Abelardo Pardo	University of South Australia, Australia
Zach Pardos	University of California, Berkeley, USA
Niels Pinkwart	Humboldt-Universität zu Berlin, Germany
Kaska Porayska-Pomsta	University College London, UK
Martina Rau	University of Wisconsin-Madison, USA
Ma. Mercedes T. Rodrigo	Ateneo de Manila University, Philippines
Jonathan Rowe	North Carolina State University, USA
Olga C. Santos	UNED, Spain
Sergey Sosnovsky	Utrecht University, the Netherlands
Erin Walker	Arizona State University, USA
Beverly Park Woolf	University of Massachusetts, USA

Kalina Yacef   The University of Sydney, Australia
Diego Zapata-Rivera   Educational Testing Service, USA

Program Committee Members

Laura Allen   University of New Hampshire, USA
Antonio R. Anaya   Universidad Nacional de Educacion a Distancia, Spain
Roger Azevedo   University of Central Florida, USA
Esma Aïmeur   University of Montreal, Canada
Michelle Banawan   Ateneo de Davao University, Philippines
Michelle Barrett   Edmentum, USA
Ig Bittencourt   Federal University of Alagoas, Brazil
Nigel Bosch   University of Illinois at Urbana-Champaign, USA
Anthony F. Botelho   Worcester Polytechnic Institute, USA
Jesus G. Boticario   UNED, Spain
Kristy Elizabeth Boyer   University of Florida, USA
Bert Bredeweg   University of Amsterdam, the Netherlands
Simon Buckingham Shum   University of Technology Sydney, Australia
Geiser Chalco Challco   ICMC/USP, Brazil
Maiga Chang   Athabasca University, Canada
Pankaj Chavan   IIT Bombay, India
Guanliang Chen   Monash University, Australia
Penghe Chen   Beijing Normal University, China
Heeryung Choi   University of Michigan, USA
Irene-Angelica Chounta   University of Duisburg-Essen, Germany
Andrew Clayphan   The University of Sydney, Australia
Keith Cochran   DePaul University, USA
Mark G. Core   University of Southern California, USA
Alexandra Cristea   Durham University, UK
Veronica Cucuiat   University College London, UK
Mutlu Cukurova   University College London, UK
Rafael D. Araújo   Universidade Federal de Uberlandia, Brazil
Mihai Dascalu   University Politehnica of Bucharest, Romania
Kristin Decerbo   Khan Academy, USA
Anurag Deep   IIT BOMBAY, India
Carrie Demmans Epp   University of Alberta, Canada
Diego Dermeval   Federal University of Alagoas, Brazil
Tejas Dhamecha   IBM, India
Barbara Di Eugenio   University of Illinois at Chicago, USA
Daniele Di Mitri   DIPF - Leibniz Institute for Research and Information
                                 in Education, Germany
Vania Dimitrova   University of Leeds, UK
Fabiano Dorça   Universidade Federal de Uberlandia, Brazil
Nia Dowell   University of California, Irvine, USA
Mingyu Feng   WestEd, USA
Rafael Ferreira Mello   Federal Rural University of Pernambuco, Brazil

Carol Forsyth	Educational Testing Service, USA
Reva Freedman	Northern Illinois University, USA
Kobi Gal	Ben Gurion University, Israel and University of Edinburgh, UK
Cristiano Galafassi	Universidade Federal do Rio Grande do Sul, Brazil
Dragan Gasevic	Monash University, Australia
Isabela Gasparini	UDESC, Brazil
Elena Gaudioso	UNED, Spain
Michail Giannakos	Norwegian University of Science and Technology, Norway
Niki Gitinabard	North Carolina State University, USA
Ashok Goel	Georgia Institute of Technology, USA
Alex Sandro Gomes	Universidade Federal de Pernambuco, Brazil
Art Graesser	University of Memphis, USA
Monique Grandbastien	Universite de Lorraine, France
Nathalie Guin	Université de Lyon, France
Gahgene Gweon	Seoul National University, South Korea
Rawad Hammad	University of East London, UK
Jason Harley	McGill University, Canada
Yusuke Hayashi	Hiroshima University, Japan
Bastiaan Heeren	Open University of the Netherlands, the Netherlands
Martin Hlosta	The Open University, UK
Tomoya Horiguchi	Kobe University, Japan
Sharon Hsiao	Arizona State University, USA
Stephen Hutt	University of Pennsylvania, USA
Paul Salvador Inventado	California State University, Fullerton, USA
Seiji Isotani	University of São Paulo, Brazil
Patricia Jaques	UNISINOS, Brazil
Srecko Joksimovic	University of South Australia, Australia
Akihiro Kashihara	The University of Electro-Communications, Japan
Sandra Katz	University of Pittsburgh, USA
Carmel Kent	Educate Ventures, UK
Simon Knight	University of Technology Sydney, Australia
Ken Koedinger	Carnegie Mellon University, USA
Kazuaki Kojima	Teikyo University, Japan
Emmanuel Awuni Kolog	University of Ghana Business School, Ghana
Amruth Kumar	Ramapo College of New Jersey, USA
Tanja Käser	EPFL, Switzerland
Susanne Lajoie	McGill University, Canada
Sébastien Lallé	The University of British Columbia, Canada
Andrew Lan	University of Massachusetts Amherst, USA
Jim Larimore	Riiid Labs, USA
Nguyen-Thinh Le	Humboldt-Universität zu Berlin, Germany
Blair Lehman	Educational Testing Service, USA
Sharona Levy	University of Haifa, Israel
Fuhua Lin	Athabasca University, Canada

Lei Shi	Durham University, UK
Sean Siqueira	Federal University of the State of Rio de Janeiro, Brazil
Caitlin Snyder	Vanderbilt University, USA
Trausan-Matu Stefan	Politehnica University of Bucharest, Romania
Angela Stewart	Carnegie Mellon University, USA
Thepchai Supnithi	NECTEC, Thailand
Pierre Tchounikine	University of Grenoble, France
K. P. Thai	Age of Learning, USA
Craig Thompson	The University of British Columbia, Canada
Armando Toda	University of São Paulo, Brazil
Richard Tong	Yixue Education Inc, China
Maomi Ueno	The University of Electro-Communications, Japan
Hedderik van Rijn	University of Groningen, the Netherlands
Kurt Vanlehn	Arizona State University, USA
Felisa Verdejo	Universidad Nacional de Educación a Distancia, Spain
Rosa Vicari	Universidade Federal do Rio Grande do Sul, Brazil
Elle Yuan Wang	Arizona State University, USA
Chris Wong	University of Technology Sydney, Australia
Simon Woodhead	Eedi, UK
Sho Yamamoto	Kindai University, Japan
Xi Yang	NCSU, USA
Bernard Yett	Vanderbilt University, USA
Ningyu Zhang	Vanderbilt University, USA
Qian Zhang	University of Technology Sydney, Australia
Guojing Zhou	University of Colorado Boulder, USA
Jianlong Zhou	University of Technology Sydney, Australia
Gustavo Zurita	Universidad de Chile, Chile

Additional Reviewers

Abdelshiheed, Mark
Afzal, Shazia
Anaya, Antonio R.
Andres-Bray, Juan Miguel
Arslan, Burcu
Barthakur, Abhinava
Bayer, Vaclav
Chung, Cheng-Yu
Cucuiat, Veronica
Demmans Epp, Carrie
Diaz, Claudio
DiCerbo, Kristen
Erickson, John
Finocchiaro, Jessica
Fossati, Davide

Frost, Stephanie
Gao, Ge
Garg, Anchal
Gauthier, Andrea
Gaweda, Adam
Green, Nick
Gupta, Itika
Gurung, Ashish
Gutiérrez Y. Restrepo, Emmanuelle
Haim, Aaron
Hao, Yang
Hastings, Peter
Heldman, Ori
Jensen, Emily
Jiang, Weijie

John, David
Johnson, Jillian
Jose, Jario
Karademir, Onur
Landes, Paul
Lefevre, Marie
Li, Zhaoxing
Liu, Tianqiao
Lytle, Nick
Marwan, Samiha
Mat Sanusi, Khaleel Asyraaf
Matsubayashi, Shota
McBroom, Jessica
Mohammadhassan, Negar
Monaikul, Natawut
Munshi, Anabil
Paredes, Yancy Vance
Pathan, Rumana
Prihar, Ethan
Rodriguez, Fernando

Segal, Avi
Serrano Mamolar, Ana
Shahriar, Tasmia
Shi, Yang
Shimmei, Machi
Singh, Daevesh
Stahl, Christopher
Swamy, Vinitra
Tenison, Caitlin
Tobarra, Llanos
Xhakaj, Franceska
Xu, Yiqiao
Yamakawa, Mayu
Yang, Xi
Yarbro, Jeffrey
Zamecnick, Andrew
Zhai, Xiao
Zhou, Guojing
Zhou, Yunzhan

International Artificial Intelligence in Education Society

Management Board

President
Rose Luckin   University College London, UK

President-Elect
Vania Dimitrova   University of Leeds, UK

Secretary/Treasurer
Bruce M. McLaren   Carnegie Mellon University, USA

Journal Editors
Vincent Aleven   Carnegie Mellon University, USA
Judy Kay   The University of Sydney, Australia

Finance Chair
Ben du Boulay   University of Sussex, UK

Membership Chair
Benjamin D. Nye   University of Southern California, USA

Publicity Chair

Manolis Mavrikis   University College London, UK

Executive Committee

Ryan S. J. d. Baker   University of Pennsylvania, USA
Min Chi   North Carolina State University, USA
Cristina Conati   The University of British Columbia, Canada
Jeanine A. Defalco   CCDC-STTC, USA
Vania Dimitrova   University of Leeds, UK
Rawad Hammad   University of East London, UK
Neil Heffernan   Worcester Polytechnic Institute, USA
Christothea Herodotou   The Open University, UK
Akihiro Kashihara   University of Electro-Communications, Japan
Amruth Kumar   Ramapo College of New Jersey, USA
Diane Litman   University of Pittsburgh, USA
Zitao Liu   TAL Education Group, China
Rose Luckin   University College London, UK
Judith Masthoff   Utrecht University, the Netherlands
Noboru Matsuda   Texas A&M University, USA
Tanja Mitrovic   University of Canterbury, New Zealand
Amy Ogan   Carnegie Mellon University, USA
Kaska Porayska-Pomsta   University College London, UK
Ma. Mercedes T. Rodrigo   Ateneo De Manila University, Philippines
Olga Santos   UNED, Spain
Ning Wang   University of Southern California, USA

Contents – Part I

Full Papers

RepairNet: Contextual Sequence-to-Sequence Network for Automated
Program Repair. 3
    Kumar Abhinav, Vijaya Sharvani, Alpana Dubey, Meenakshi D'Souza,
    Nitish Bhardwaj, Sakshi Jain, and Veenu Arora

Seven-Year Longitudinal Implications of Wheel Spinning
and Productive Persistence 16
    Seth A. Adjei, Ryan S. Baker, and Vedant Bahel

A Systematic Review of Data-Driven Approaches to Item
Difficulty Prediction 29
    Samah AlKhuzaey, Floriana Grasso, Terry R. Payne,
    and Valentina Tamma

Annotating Student Engagement Across Grades 1–12: Associations
with Demographics and Expressivity 42
    Nese Alyuz, Sinem Aslan, Sidney K. D'Mello, Lama Nachman,
    and Asli Arslan Esme

Affect-Targeted Interviews for Understanding Student Frustration 52
    Ryan S. Baker, Nidhi Nasiar, Jaclyn L. Ocumpaugh, Stephen Hutt,
    Juliana M. A. L. Andres, Stefan Slater, Matthew Schofield,
    Allison Moore, Luc Paquette, Anabil Munshi, and Gautam Biswas

Explainable Recommendations in a Personalized Programming
Practice System 64
    Jordan Barria-Pineda, Kamil Akhuseyinoglu, Stefan Želem-Ćelap,
    Peter Brusilovsky, Aleksandra Klasnja Milicevic, and Mirjana Ivanovic

Multilingual Age of Exposure. 77
    Robert-Mihai Botarleanu, Mihai Dascalu, Micah Watanabe,
    Danielle S. McNamara, and Scott Andrew Crossley

DiSCS: A New Sequence Segmentation Method for Open-Ended
Learning Environments 88
    James P. Bywater, Mark Floryan, and Jennifer L. Chiu

Interpretable Clustering of Students' Solutions
in Introductory Programming 101
    Tomáš Effenberger and Radek Pelánek

Adaptively Scaffolding Cognitive Engagement with Batch Constrained
Deep Q-Networks   113
  Fahmid Morshed Fahid, Jonathan P. Rowe, Randall D. Spain,
  Benjamin S. Goldberg, Robert Pokorny, and James Lester

Ordering Effects in a Role-Based Scaffolding Intervention for
Asynchronous Online Discussions   125
  Elaine Farrow, Johanna Moore, and Dragan Gašević

Option Tracing: Beyond Correctness Analysis in Knowledge Tracing   137
  Aritra Ghosh, Jay Raspat, and Andrew Lan

An Approach for Detecting Student Perceptions of the Programming
Experience from Interaction Log Data   150
  Jamie Gorson, Nicholas LaGrassa, Cindy Hsinyu Hu, Elise Lee,
  Ava Marie Robinson, and Eleanor O'Rourke

Discovering Co-creative Dialogue States During Collaborative Learning   165
  Amanda E. Griffith, Gloria Ashiya Katuka, Joseph B. Wiggins,
  Kristy Elizabeth Boyer, Jason Freeman, Brian Magerko,
  and Tom McKlin

Affective Teacher Tools: Affective Class Report Card and Dashboard   178
  Ankit Gupta, Neeraj Menon, William Lee, William Rebelsky,
  Danielle Allesio, Tom Murray, Beverly Woolf, Jacob Whitehill,
  and Ivon Arroyo

Engendering Trust in Automated Feedback: A Two Step Comparison
of Feedbacks in Gesture Based Learning   190
  Sameena Hossain, Azamat Kamzin,
  Venkata Naga Sai Apurupa Amperayani, Prajwal Paudyal,
  Ayan Banerjee, and Sandeep K. S. Gupta

Investigating Students' Reasoning in a Code-Tracing Tutor   203
  Jay Jennings and Kasia Muldner

Evaluating Critical Reinforcement Learning Framework in the Field   215
  Song Ju, Guojing Zhou, Mark Abdelshiheed, Tiffany Barnes,
  and Min Chi

Machine Learning Models and Their Development Process as Learning
Affordances for Humans   228
  Carmel Kent, Muhammad Ali Chaudhry, Mutlu Cukurova,
  Ibrahim Bashir, Hannah Pickard, Chris Jenkins, Benedict du Boulay,
  Anissa Moeini, and Rosemary Luckin

Predicting Co-occurring Emotions from Eye-Tracking and Interaction Data
in MetaTutor   241
    Sébastien Lallé, Rohit Murali, Cristina Conati, and Roger Azevedo

A Fairness Evaluation of Automated Methods for Scoring Text Evidence
Usage in Writing.   255
    Diane Litman, Haoran Zhang, Richard Correnti,
    Lindsay Clare Matsumura, and Elaine Wang

The Challenge of Noisy Classrooms: Speaker Detection During Elementary
Students' Collaborative Dialogue   268
    Yingbo Ma, Joseph B. Wiggins, Mehmet Celepkolu,
    Kristy Elizabeth Boyer, Collin Lynch, and Eric Wiebe

Extracting and Clustering Main Ideas from Student Feedback Using
Language Models   282
    Mihai Masala, Stefan Ruseti, Mihai Dascalu, and Ciprian Dobre

Multidimensional Team Communication Modeling for Adaptive Team
Training: A Hybrid Deep Learning and Graphical Modeling Framework   293
    Wookhee Min, Randall Spain, Jason D. Saville, Bradford Mott,
    Keith Brawner, Joan Johnston, and James Lester

A Good Start is Half the Battle Won: Unsupervised Pre-training
for Low Resource Children's Speech Recognition for an Interactive
Reading Companion   306
    Abhinav Misra, Anastassia Loukina, Beata Beigman Klebanov,
    Binod Gyawali, and Klaus Zechner

Predicting Knowledge Gain During Web Search Based on Multimedia
Resource Consumption   318
    Christian Otto, Ran Yu, Georg Pardi, Johannes von Hoyer,
    Markus Rokicki, Anett Hoppe, Peter Holtz, Yvonne Kammerer,
    Stefan Dietze, and Ralph Ewerth

Deep Performance Factors Analysis for Knowledge Tracing   331
    Shi Pu, Geoffrey Converse, and Yuchi Huang

Gaming and Confrustion Explain Learning Advantages for a Math Digital
Learning Game.   342
    J. Elizabeth Richey, Jiayi Zhang, Rohini Das, Juan Miguel Andres-Bray,
    Richard Scruggs, Michael Mogessie, Ryan S. Baker,
    and Bruce M. McLaren

Tackling the Credit Assignment Problem in Reinforcement
Learning-Induced Pedagogical Policies with Neural Networks.   356
    Markel Sanz Ausin, Mehak Maniktala, Tiffany Barnes, and Min Chi

TARTA: Teacher Activity Recognizer from Transcriptions and Audio...... 369
  Danner Schlotterbeck, Pablo Uribe, Abelino Jiménez, Roberto Araya,
  Johan van der Molen Moris, and Daniela Caballero

Assessing Algorithmic Fairness in Automatic Classifiers of Educational
Forum Posts.. 381
  Lele Sha, Mladen Rakovic, Alexander Whitelock-Wainwright,
  David Carroll, Victoria M. Yew, Dragan Gasevic, and Guanliang Chen

"Can You Clarify What You Said?": Studying the Impact of Tutee Agents'
Follow-Up Questions on Tutors' Learning 395
  Tasmia Shahriar and Noboru Matsuda

Classifying Math Knowledge Components via Task-Adaptive
Pre-Trained BERT 408
  Jia Tracy Shen, Michiharu Yamashita, Ethan Prihar, Neil Heffernan,
  Xintao Wu, Sean McGrew, and Dongwon Lee

A Multidimensional Item Response Theory Model for Rubric-Based
Writing Assessment... 420
  Masaki Uto

Towards Blooms Taxonomy Classification Without Labels............. 433
  Zichao Wang, Kyle Manning, Debshila Basu Mallick,
  and Richard G. Baraniuk

Automatic Task Requirements Writing Evaluation via Machine
Reading Comprehension 446
  Shiting Xu, Guowei Xu, Peilei Jia, Wenbiao Ding, Zhongqin Wu,
  and Zitao Liu

Temporal Processes Associating with Procrastination Dynamics 459
  Mengfan Yao, Shaghayegh Sahebi, Reza Feyzi Behnagh, Semih Bursali,
  and Siqian Zhao

Investigating Students' Experiences with Collaboration Analytics
for Remote Group Meetings.................................... 472
  Qi Zhou, Wannapon Suraworachet, Stanislav Pozdniakov,
  Roberto Martinez-Maldonado, Tom Bartindale, Peter Chen,
  Dan Richardson, and Mutlu Cukurova

"Now, I Want to Teach It for Real!": Introducing Machine Learning
as a Scientific Discovery Tool for K-12 Teachers 486
  Xiaofei Zhou, Jingwan Tang, Michael Daley, Saad Ahmad, and Zhen Bai

Better Model, Worse Predictions: The Dangers in Student
Model Comparisons   500
  Jaroslav Čechák and Radek Pelánek

Author Index   513

Contents – Part II

Keynotes

Scrutability, Control and Learner Models: Foundations for Learner-Centred
Design in AIED   3
    Judy Kay

Short Papers

Open Learner Models for Multi-activity Educational Systems   11
    Solmaz Abdi, Hassan Khosravi, Shazia Sadiq, and Ali Darvishi

Personal Vocabulary Recommendation to Support Real Life Needs   18
    Victoria Abou-Khalil, Brendan Flanagan, and Hiroaki Ogata

Artificial Intelligence Ethics Guidelines for K-12 Education: A Review
of the Global Landscape   24
    Cathy Adams, Patti Pente, Gillian Lemermeyer, and Geoffrey Rockwell

Quantitative Analysis to Further Validate WC-GCMS, a Computational
Metric of Collaboration in Online Textual Discourse   29
    Adetunji Adeniran and Judith Masthoff

Generation of Automatic Data-Driven Feedback to Students Using
Explainable Machine Learning   37
    Muhammad Afzaal, Jalal Nouri, Aayesha Zia, Panagiotis Papapetrou,
    Uno Fors, Yongchao Wu, Xiu Li, and Rebecka Weegar

Interactive Personas: Towards the Dynamic Assessment of Student
Motivation within ITS   43
    Ishrat Ahmed, Adam Clark, Stefania Metzger, Ruth Wylie, Yoav Bergner,
    and Erin Walker

Agent-Based Classroom Environment Simulation: The Effect of Disruptive
Schoolchildren's Behaviour Versus Teacher Control over Neighbours   48
    Khulood Alharbi, Alexandra I. Cristea, Lei Shi, Peter Tymms,
    and Chris Brown

Integration of Automated Essay Scoring Models Using Item
Response Theory   54
    Itsuki Aomi, Emiko Tsutsumi, Masaki Uto, and Maomi Ueno

Towards Sharing Student Models Across Learning Systems   60
  Ryan S. Baker, Bruce M. McLaren, Stephen Hutt, J. Elizabeth Richey,
  Elizabeth Rowe, Ma. Victoria Almeda, Michael Mogessie,
  and Juliana M. AL. Andres

Protecting Student Privacy with Synthetic Data from Generative
Adversarial Networks   66
  Peter Bautista and Paul Salvador Inventado

Learning Analytics and Fairness: Do Existing Algorithms Serve Everyone
Equally?   71
  Vaclav Bayer, Martin Hlosta, and Miriam Fernandez

Exploiting Structured Error to Improve Automated Scoring of Oral Reading
Fluency   76
  Beata Beigman Klebanov and Anastassia Loukina

Data Augmentation for Enlarging Student Feature Space and Improving
Random Forest Success Prediction   82
  Timothy H. Bell, Christel Dartigues-Pallez, Florent Jaillet, and
  Christophe Genolini

The School Path Guide: A Practical Introduction to Representation and
Reasoning in AI for High School Students   88
  Sara Guerreiro-Santalla, Francisco Bellas, and Oscar Fontenla-Romero

Kwame: A Bilingual AI Teaching Assistant for Online SuaCode Courses . . .   93
  George Boateng

Early Prediction of Children's Disengagement in a Tablet Tutor Using
Visual Features   98
  Bikram Boote, Mansi Agarwal, and Jack Mostow

An Educational System for Personalized Teacher Recommendation in K-12
Online Classrooms   104
  Jiahao Chen, Hang Li, Wenbiao Ding, and Zitao Liu

Designing Intelligent Systems to Support Medical Diagnostic Reasoning
Using Process Data   109
  Elizabeth B. Cloude, Nikki Anne M. Ballelos, Roger Azevedo,
  Analia Castiglioni, Jeffrey LaRochelle, Anya Andrews,
  and Caridad Hernandez

Incorporating Item Response Theory into Knowledge Tracing   114
  Geoffrey Converse, Shi Pu, and Suely Oliveira

Automated Model of Comprehension V2.0.   119
  Dragos-Georgian Corlatescu, Mihai Dascalu,
  and Danielle S. McNamara

Pre-course Prediction of At-Risk Calculus Students.   124
  James Cunningham, Raktim Mukhopadhyay,
  Rishabh Ranjit Kumar Jain, Jeffrey Matayoshi, Eric Cosyn,
  and Hasan Uzun

Examining Learners' Reflections over Time During Game-Based Learning. . .   129
  Daryn A. Dever, Elizabeth B. Cloude, and Roger Azevedo

Examining the Use of a Teacher Alerting Dashboard During
Remote Learning.   134
  Rachel Dickler, Amy Adair, Janice Gobert, Huma Hussain-Abidi,
  Joe Olsen, Mariel O'Brien, and Michael Sao Pedro

Capturing Fairness and Uncertainty in Student Dropout Prediction – A
Comparison Study.   139
  Efthyvoulos Drousiotis, Panagiotis Pentaliotis, Lei Shi,
  and Alexandra I. Cristea

Dr. Proctor: A Multi-modal AI-Based Platform for Remote Proctoring
in Education.   145
  Ahmed E. Elshafey, Mohammed R. Anany, Amr S. Mohamed,
  Nourhan Sakr, and Sherif G. Aly

Multimodal Trajectory Analysis of Visitor Engagement with Interactive
Science Museum Exhibits   151
  Andrew Emerson, Nathan Henderson, Wookhee Min, Jonathan Rowe,
  James Minogue, and James Lester

Analytics of Emerging and Scripted Roles in Online Discussions:
An Epistemic Network Analysis Approach.   156
  Máverick Ferreira, Rafael Ferreira Mello, Rafael Dueire Lins,
  and Dragan Gašević

Towards Automatic Content Analysis of Rhetorical Structure in Brazilian
College Entrance Essays   162
  Rafael Ferreira Mello, Giuseppe Fiorentino, Péricles Miranda,
  Hilário Oliveira, Mladen Raković, and Dragan Gašević

Contrasting Automatic and Manual Group Formation: A Case Study in a
Software Engineering Postgraduate Course.   168
  Giuseppe Fiorentino, Péricles Miranda, André Nascimento,
  Ana Paula Furtado, Henrik Bellhäuser, Dragan Gašević,
  and Rafael Ferreira Mello

Aligning Expectations About the Adoption of Learning Analytics in a
Brazilian Higher Education Institution   173
  Samantha Garcia, Elaine Cristina Moreira Marques,
  Rafael Ferreira Mello, Dragan Gašević, and Taciana Pontual Falcão

Interactive Teaching with Groups of Unknown Bayesian Learners   178
  Carla Guerra, Francisco S. Melo, and Manuel Lopes

Multi-task Learning Based Online Dialogic Instruction Detection
with Pre-trained Language Models   183
  Yang Hao, Hang Li, Wenbiao Ding, Zhongqin Wu, Jiliang Tang,
  Rose Luckin, and Zitao Liu

Impact of Predictive Learning Analytics on Course Awarding Gap of
Disadvantaged Students in STEM   190
  Martin Hlosta, Christothea Herodotou, Vaclav Bayer,
  and Miriam Fernandez

Evaluation of Automated Image Descriptions for Visually Impaired
Students   196
  Anett Hoppe, David Morris, and Ralph Ewerth

Way to Go! Effects of Motivational Support and Agents on Reducing
Foreign Language Anxiety   202
  Daneih Ismail and Peter Hastings

"I didn't copy his code": Code Plagiarism Detection with Visual Proof   208
  Samuel John and George Boateng

An Epistemic Model-Based Tutor for Imperative Programming   213
  Amruth N. Kumar

Long Term Retention of Programming Concepts Learned Using Tracing
Versus Debugging Tutors   219
  Amruth N. Kumar

Facilitating the Implementation of AI-Based Assistive Technologies for
Persons with Disabilities in Vocational Rehabilitation: A Practical Design
Thinking Approach   224
  Marco Kähler, Rolf Feichtenbeiner, and Susan Beudt

Quantifying the Impact of Severe Weather Conditions on Online Learning
During the COVID-19 Pandemic   229
  Ezekiel Adriel Lagmay and Ma. Mercedes T. Rodrigo

I-Mouse: A Framework for Player Assistance in Adaptive Serious Games . . .   234
Riya Lalwani, Ashish Chouhan, Varun John, Prashant Sonar,
Aakash Mahajan, Naresh Pendyala, Alexander Streicher,
and Ajinkya Prabhune

Parent-EMBRACE: An Adaptive Dialogic Reading Intervention   239
Arun Balajiee Lekshmi Narayanan, Ju Eun Lim, Tri Nguyen,
Ligia E. Gomez, M. Adelaida Restrepo, Chris Blais, Arthur M. Glenberg,
and Erin Walker

Using Fair AI with Debiased Network Embeddings to Support Help
Seeking in an Online Math Learning Platform   245
Chenglu Li, Wanli Xing, and Walter Leite

A Multimodal Machine Learning Framework for Teacher Vocal
Delivery Evaluation.   251
Hang Li, Yu Kang, Yang Hao, Wenbiao Ding, Zhongqin Wu,
and Zitao Liu

Solving ESL Sentence Completion Questions via Pre-trained Neural
Language Models   256
Qiongqiong Liu, Tianqiao Liu, Jiafu Zhao, Qiang Fang, Wenbiao Ding,
Zhongqin Wu, Feng Xia, Jiliang Tang, and Zitao Liu

DanceTutor: An ITS for Coaching Novice Ballet Dancers Using Pose
Recognition of Whole-Body Movements   262
Lurlynn Maharaj-Pariagsingh and Phaedra S. Mohammed

Tracing Embodied Narratives of Critical Thinking.   267
Shitanshu Mishra, Rwitajit Majumdar, Aditi Kothiyal, Prajakt Pande,
and Jayakrishnan Madathil Warriem

Multi-armed Bandit Algorithms for Adaptive Learning: A Survey   273
John Mui, Fuhua Lin, and M. Ali Akber Dewan

Paraphrasing Academic Text: A Study of Back-Translating Anatomy
and Physiology with Transformers   279
Andrew M. Olney

PAKT: A Position-Aware Self-attentive Approach for Knowledge Tracing . . .   285
Yuanxin Ouyang, Yucong Zhou, Hongbo Zhang, Wenge Rong,
and Zhang Xiong

Identifying Struggling Students by Comparing Online Tutor Clickstreams . . .   290
Ethan Prihar, Alexander Moore, and Neil Heffernan

Exploring Dialogism Using Language Models   296
    Stefan Ruseti, Maria-Dorinela Dascalu, Dragos-Georgian Corlatescu,
    Mihai Dascalu, Stefan Trausan-Matu, and Danielle S. McNamara

EduPal Leaves No Professor Behind: Supporting Faculty via a
Peer-Powered Recommender System   302
    Nourhan Sakr, Aya Salama, Nadeen Tameesh, and Gihan Osman

Computer-Supported Human Mentoring for Personalized and Equitable
Math Learning   308
    Peter Schaldenbrand, Nikki G. Lobczowski, J. Elizabeth Richey,
    Shivang Gupta, Elizabeth A. McLaughlin, Adetunji Adeniran,
    and Kenneth R. Koedinger

Internalisation of Situational Motivation in an E-Learning Scenario Using
Gamification.   314
    Philipp Schaper, Anna Riedmann, and Birgit Lugrin

Learning Association Between Learning Objectives and Key Concepts to
Generate Pedagogically Valuable Questions   320
    Machi Shimmei and Noboru Matsuda

Exploring the Working and Effectiveness of Norm-Model Feedback in
Conceptual Modelling – A Preliminary Report   325
    Loek Spitz, Marco Kragten, and Bert Bredeweg

A Comparative Study of Learning Outcomes for Online
Learning Platforms   331
    Francois St-Hilaire, Nathan Burns, Robert Belfer, Muhammad Shayan,
    Ariella Smofsky, Dung Do Vu, Antoine Frau, Joseph Potochny,
    Farid Faraji, Vincent Pavero, Neroli Ko, Ansona Onyi Ching,
    Sabina Elkins, Anush Stepanyan, Adela Matajova, Laurent Charlin,
    Yoshua Bengio, Iulian Vlad Serban, and Ekaterina Kochmar

Explaining Engagement: Learner Behaviors in a Virtual Coding Camp   338
    Angela E. B. Stewart, Jaemarie Solyst, Amanda Buddemeyer,
    Leshell Hatley, Sharon Henderson-Singer, Kimberly Scott, Erin Walker,
    and Amy Ogan

Using AI to Promote Equitable Classroom Discussions: The TalkMoves
Application   344
    Abhijit Suresh, Jennifer Jacobs, Charis Clevenger, Vivian Lai,
    Chenhao Tan, James H. Martin, and Tamara Sumner

Investigating Effects of Selecting Challenging Goals   349
    Faiza Tahir, Antonija Mitrović, and Valerie Sotardi

Modeling Frustration Trajectories and Problem-Solving Behaviors
in Adaptive Learning Environments for Introductory Computer Science.   355
   Xiaoyi Tian, Joseph B. Wiggins, Fahmid Morshed Fahid,
   Andrew Emerson, Dolly Bounajim, Andy Smith, Kristy Elizabeth Boyer,
   Eric Wiebe, Bradford Mott, and James Lester

Behavioral Phenotyping for Predictive Model Equity and Interpretability
in STEM Education.   361
   Marcus Tyler, Alex Liu, and Ravi Srinivasan

Teaching Underachieving Algebra Students to Construct Models Using a
Simple Intelligent Tutoring System   367
   Kurt VanLehn, Fabio Milner, Chandrani Banerjee, and Jon Wetzel

Charisma and Learning: Designing Charismatic Behaviors for Virtual
Human Tutors   372
   Ning Wang, Aditya Jajodia, Abhilash Karpurapu, and Chirag Merchant

AI-Powered Teaching Behavior Analysis by Using 3D-MobileNet and
Statistical Optimization   378
   Ruhan Wang, Jiahao Lyu, Qingyun Xiong, and Junqi Guo

Assessment2Vec: Learning Distributed Representations of Assessments
to Reduce Marking Workload.   384
   Shuang Wang, Amin Beheshti, Yufei Wang, Jianchao Lu, Quan Z. Sheng,
   Stephen Elbourn, Hamid Alinejad-Rokny, and Elizabeth Galanis

Toward Stable Asymptotic Learning with Simulated Learners.   390
   Daniel Weitekamp, Erik Harpstead, and Kenneth Koedinger

A Word Embeddings Based Clustering Approach for Collaborative
Learning Group Formation.   395
   Yongchao Wu, Jalal Nouri, Xiu Li, Rebecka Weegar, Muhammad Afzaal,
   and Aayesha Zia

Intelligent Agents Influx in Schools: Teacher Cultures, Anxiety Levels
and Predictable Variations   401
   R. Yamamoto Ravenor

WikiMorph: Learning to Decompose Words into
Morphological Structures   406
   Jeffrey T. Yarbro and Andrew M. Olney

Individualization of Bayesian Knowledge Tracing Through Elo-infusion   412
   Michael Yudelson

Self-paced Graph Memory Network for Student GPA Prediction and
Abnormal Student Detection   417
    Yue Yun, Huan Dai, Ruoqi Cao, Yupei Zhang, and Xuequn Shang

Using Adaptive Experiments to Rapidly Help Students   422
    Angela Zavaleta-Bernuy, Qi Yin Zheng, Hammad Shaikh, Jacob Nogas,
    Anna Rafferty, Andrew Petersen, and Joseph Jay Williams

A Comparison of Hints vs. Scaffolding in a MOOC with Adult Learners   427
    Yiqiu Zhou, Juan Miguel Andres-Bray, Stephen Hutt, Korinn Ostrow,
    and Ryan S. Baker

An Ensemble Approach for Question-Level Knowledge Tracing   433
    Aayesha Zia, Jalal Nouri, Muhammad Afzaal, Yongchao Wu, Xiu Li,
    and Rebecka Weegar

Industry and Innovation

Scaffolds and Nudges: A Case Study in Learning Engineering Design
Improvements   441
    Stephen E. Fancsali, Martina Pavelko, Josh Fisher, Leslie Wheeler,
    and Steven Ritter

Condensed Discriminative Question Set for Reliable Exam
Score Prediction   446
    Jung Hoon Kim, Jineon Baek, Chanyou Hwang, Chan Bae,
    and Juneyoung Park

Evaluating the Impact of Research-Based Updates to an Adaptive Learning
System   451
    Jeffrey Matayoshi, Eric Cosyn, and Hasan Uzun

Back to the Origin: An Intelligent System for Learning
Chinese Characters   457
    Jinglei Yu, Jiachen Song, Yu Lu, and Shengquan Yu

Doctoral Consortium

Automated Assessment of Quality and Coverage of Ideas in Students'
Source-Based Writing   465
    Yanjun Gao and Rebecca J. Passonneau

Impact of Intelligent Tutoring System (ITS) on Mathematics Achievement
Using ALEKS   471
    Rashmi Khazanchi

Designing and Testing Assessments and Scaffolds for Mathematics
Practices in Science Inquiry   476
  Joe Olsen and Janice Gobert

Contextual Safeguarding in Education: Bayesian Network Risk Analysis
for Decision Support   482
  Matthew Woodruff and Graham Feek

Author Index   487

Full Papers

RepairNet: Contextual Sequence-to-Sequence Network for Automated Program Repair

Kumar Abhinav[1], Vijaya Sharvani[2], Alpana Dubey[1(✉)], Meenakshi D'Souza[2], Nitish Bhardwaj[1], Sakshi Jain[1], and Veenu Arora[1]

[1] Accenture Labs, Bangalore, India
{k.a.abhinav,alpana.a.dubey,nitish.a.bhardwaj,
sakshi.c.jain,veenu.arora}@accenture.com
[2] IIIT, Bangalore, India
{vijaya.shravani,meenakshi}@iiitb.ac.in

Abstract. Compile-time errors can wreak havoc for programmers – seasoned and novice. Often developers spend a lot of time debugging them. An automated system to repair such errors can be a useful aid to the developers for their productivity. In this work, we propose a deep generative model, RepairNet, that automatically repairs programs that fail at compile time. RepairNet is based on sequence-to-sequence modeling and uses both code and error messages to repair the program. We evaluated the effectiveness of our system on 6,971 erroneous submissions for 93 programming tasks. RepairNet outperforms the existing state-of-the-art technique, MACER, with 17% relative improvement of repair accuracy. Our approach can fix 66.4% of the erroneous submissions completely and 14.2% partially.

Keywords: Program repair · Sequence modeling · Bug fixing

1 Introduction

The ever-changing computing world has led to continuous advancements in new programming paradigms. This evolution has created great opportunities for programmers who keep abreast with the advances. Based on studies done in [35,36], there is a massive shortage of programmers to meet the industry demand. These have made programming a promising career choice for many people. The number of people interested in learning programming has drastically increased [35]. Initiatives such as Udacity and Coursers attempt to meet this demand by providing Massive Open Online Courses (MOOCs) that are easily accessible to learners worldwide. While MOOCs have numerous advantages, their main downside is that they do not replicate an in-person learning environment. With thousands of learners often enrolled in a single course, it is impossible for faculty and teaching assistants to provide support similar to a classroom environment in a remote learning setup.

© Springer Nature Switzerland AG 2021
I. Roll et al. (Eds.): AIED 2021, LNAI 12748, pp. 3–15, 2021.
https://doi.org/10.1007/978-3-030-78292-4_1

Some of the courses require learners to work on programming tasks where one needs to write code for solving a specific problem, compile and run it on multiple test cases. However, proper syntax and semantics are overlooked during implementation, leading to compile-time errors. Debugging the errors requires time and effort even from seasoned programmers [1,22,34]. In a classroom setup, faculty or teaching assistants usually guide the students in overcoming such problems but such levels of engagement are not possible in MOOCs mainly due to lack of physical presence, scale, and learners living in different time zones. Hence, there is a need for intelligent and automated support to assist students in their programming tasks during the course.

Compile-time errors are first-level errors and relatively simple to address than run-time errors; however, we have observed that they can be misleading and may introduce additional errors for new programmers [22,34]. This gets accentuated for MOOC learners who are learning the language for the first time. We illustrate this issue with two examples. Figure 1 shows two erroneous programs with the error messages (and suggested fix by our approach). The compiler error messages appearing in these examples are not very informative for a novice programmer to fix the issues. For example, in Program (a) shown in Fig. 1, the compiler error message may mislead a new programmer as the fix suggested by the error message (i.e. expected ';' before '&&' token) will not resolve the error and in fact, introduce another error. Similarly in Program (b) shown in Fig. 1, applying the fix suggested by the compiler (i.e. adding ';' before $printf("unlucky");$') will not fix the error. The appropriate fixes for such scenarios are identified with program context and error together by an experienced (human) programmer.

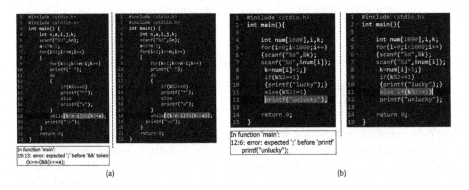

(a)   (b)

Fig. 1. Programs repaired by RepairNet. Applying fixes suggested by compiler messages in both the programs (a) and (b) might mislead the novice programmer.

In this paper, we propose a system that uses deep neural networks to provide program repair recommendations. There has been an increasing interest in the field of Natural Language Processing (NLP) and related techniques to solve common programming errors such as the use of incompatible operators and missing scope delimiters [2,9,14]. We present a learning-based technique to automatically generate fixes for erroneous submissions. Our approach uses a sequence-to-sequence generative model [30] to correct programming errors. We also propose a novel deep neural architecture, RepairNet, which incorporates both source code and error messages to repair the program. A key contribution of our approach is encoding error messages as an additional context within the model to fix the error.

We apply RepairNet on C programs written by students for 93 different programming tasks in an introductory programming course. These programs are available as part of the Prutor dataset [19]. Each of these tasks is vividly different and our network generalizes well to programs across these tasks. We evaluated our approach on the Prutor dataset using "repair accuracy" as a metric and compared it against state-of-the-art technique "MACER" [9]. With our approach, we have been able to repair 66.4% programs completely and 14.2% partially, a significant improvement when compared to "MACER". Our approach was able to fix the programs by considering source code and error messages, shown in Fig. 1, which was not possible by just using source code.

The remainder of this paper is structured as follows: Sect. 2 discusses the related work on automated program repair. In Sect. 3, we describe our approach for program repair followed by the evaluation methodology and results in Sect. 4. In Sect. 5, we discuss threats to the validity of our framework. Finally, Sect. 6 concludes with future work.

2   Related Work

There has been a growing interest in learning-based approaches to automatically repair erroneous programs [4, 8]. With the advancement in NLP and Deep Learning techniques [3, 31], there is an increased focus to fix programming errors by leveraging such techniques [2, 14]. Liu et al. [5] developed an automatic program repair tool, TBar, that systematically attempts to apply the fix patterns to bugs in a program. Endres et al. [16] proposed a template-based search algorithm, InFix, that repairs erroneous input data for novice programs. Bader et al. [20] proposed a tool, Getafix, based on a novel hierarchical agglomerative clustering algorithm, which summarizes a given set of fix commits into a hierarchy of fix patterns. Based on this hierarchy and a ranking technique, one can decide which fix pattern is most appropriate for a new occurrence of a bug category.

Chen et al. [6] developed a tool, SEQUENCER, which uses a sequence-to-sequence deep learning model that aims at automatically fixing bugs by generating one-line patches. Vasic et al. [7] proposed an approach that jointly learns to localize and repair a special class of errors called variable-misuse errors which are logical errors where programmers use an inappropriate identifier, possibly because of confusion in identifier names. Mesbah et al. [10] proposed a technique, DeepDelta, to learn patterns by extracting Abstract Syntax Tree (AST) changes between the failed and resolved snapshots of the code and provide them as abstracted features to a deep neural network.

Gupta et al. [13] proposed a deep reinforcement learning agent, called RLAssist, for syntactic error repair in programs. The policy of the agent is learned using the Asynchronous Advantage Actor-Critic (A3C) algorithm. Chhatbar et al. [9] proposed a technique, MACER, for fixing error based on modular segregation of the repair process into repair identification and repair application. MACER uses discriminative learning techniques such as multi-label classifiers and rankers to first identify the type of repair required and then apply the suggested repair. Hajipour et al. [14] proposed a deep generative framework, SampleFix, using variational auto-encoders to automatically correct common programming errors by learning the distribution over potential fixes and interacting with a compiler in an iterative procedure. Gupta et al. [2] proposed a sequence-to-sequence neural network to fix errors. While prior works in program repair purely apply sequence-to-sequence models to programs [2,14] or rely on the program's Abstract Syntax Tree (AST) representations [10,12], our approach uses a modified sequence-to-sequence model that incorporates error messages along with code tokens to fix the error. We compared some of the directly related work which leverage same dataset as ours (Prutor dataset [19]), DeepFix [2], RLAssist [13], SampleFix [14], TRACER [17] and MACER [9], to assess the effectiveness of our proposed architecture. The comparison of results is provided in Table 2. Our model, RepairNet, outperforms all these approaches in terms of repair accuracy. There has been a focus to consider error messages along with source code to fix the error by using traditional approaches such as Control Flow Graph [39], Genetic Programming [40] etc. To the best of our knowledge, ours is the first approach that uses source code and error messages in Deep Neural Network to fix the error.

3   Approach

We pose the problem of program repair as a sequence-to-sequence problem. RepairNet is a sequence-to-sequence generative model that aims at automatically fixing bugs in programs by generating potential fixes. A similar concept has been applied to Neural Machine Translation where the input is a sequence of words in one language and output is the same sequence translated to other language [29,30]. We use a many-to-many sequence model where the input is a sequence of tokens with a dynamic length, and the output is also a sequence with dynamic length.

The model architecture of RepairNet is shown in Fig. 2. A sequence-to-sequence model consists of two main components: (1) an encoder; and (2) a decoder. Both the encoder and the decoder are a variant of Recurrent Neural Network (RNN) in which layers are implemented using Long Short-Term Memory (LSTM) or Gated Recurrent Units (GRU) blocks [27]. The encoder processes the input sequence into a fixed representation that is fed into the decoder as a context vector. The decoder then decodes the processed information into an output sequence. Along with the input token sequence, we pass additional context information to the decoder by concatenating it with the input context. In Repair-Net, the additional context is the error message that is generated on compiling the program. Not all code tokens can be relevant while predicting the correct tokens to fix errors. The Attention Mechanism provides higher weights to the tokens which influence the output. The decoder module concatenates the context vector and error information to predict the correct token. The error message contains vital contextual information about what kind of error is present in the code. For each step in the target side, hidden units are obtained by combining the representation produced by the target LSTM at the previous timestep, the word representations at the current timestep, and the error embedding. The softmax layer predicts the correct token that will fix the error. We compute the cross-entropy over the softmax layer outputs at each timestep of the decoder and sum them over the output sequence to compute the loss function.

We discuss each component of our model separately below.

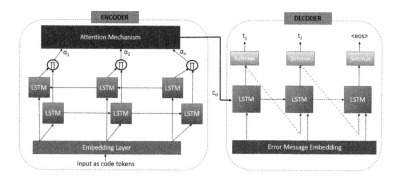

Fig. 2. RepairNet model architecture

1. **Encoder:** For an input sequence $(x_1, x_2, \cdots, x_n)$, the hidden unit at each time step h^t is given as

$$h^t = f(h^{t-1}, x^t) \qquad (1)$$

where f is a non-linear activation function (LSTM in our case).
We use a Bidirectional LSTM (BiLSTM) [25] as Encoder, which has proved to be effective in several applications such as speech recognition, machine translation etc. [26,27].
2. **Attention Layer:** Attention mechanism was introduced to address the limitation of modeling long dependencies and efficient usage of memory for computation [28]. The attention mechanism intervenes as an intermediate layer between the encoder and the decoder, with the objective of capturing the information from the sequence of tokens that are relevant to the contents of the sentence. Unlike the encoder-decoder model that uses the same context vector for every hidden state of the decoder, the attention mechanism computes a new vector c_t for the output word y_t at the decoding timestep t. The

context vector c_t is, then, computed as a weighted sum of hidden states

$$c_t = \sum_{j=1}^{n_x} \alpha_{tj} h_j \qquad (2)$$

where h_j is the hidden state of the input sequence x_j, α_{tj} is the weight of h_j for predicting y_t, and n_x is the number of hidden sequence. This vector is also called attention vector.

$$\alpha_{ij} = \frac{exp(e_{ij})}{\sum_{k=1}^{n} exp(e_{ik})} \qquad (3)$$

where $exp(e_{ij})$ is a parameterized alignment model which scores how well the inputs around position 'j' and the output at position 'i' match.

This context vector c_t is used by a learnable function to allow each output token y_t to pay "attention" to different encoder hidden states when predicting a token.

3. **Decoder:** The hidden states of the decoder network are initialized with the final states of the encoder network i.e. context vector c_t. The hidden state of the decoder at timestep t is computed as

$$h^t = g(h^{t-1}, x^t) \qquad (4)$$

where $g()$ is a non-linear activation function (LSTM in this case).

We also introduce the error message as one of the inputs to the decoder to generate the output y_t based on the context vector c_t and previous timestep output y_{t-1}. The decoder defines a probability over the output y (p_y) by decomposing the joint probability as follows:

$$p_y = \prod_{t=1}^{T} p(y_t | y_1, y_2, \cdots, y_{t-1}, c_t, e_t) \qquad (5)$$

$$p(y_t | y_1, y_2, \cdots, y_{t-1}, c, e_t) = q(y_{t1}, h_t, c_t, e_t) \qquad (6)$$

where $q()$ is a non-linear activation function (Softmax), h_t is the hidden unit activation and e_t is the error embedding vector at time step 't'.

Repair Strategy: RepairNet considers the program and error message to iteratively fix the error (as shown in Fig. 3). The program and error message are passed through the encoding layer. We treat a program as a sequence of tokens X and expect our network to produce another sequence Y such that Y is a repaired version of X. Program text consists of different kinds of tokens such as types, keywords, special characters (e.g., semicolons), functions, literals, and variables. These tokens are mapped to unique IDs. A program is broken down into several lines where each line comprises of a sequence of tokens. Each program is represented as $(l_1, s_1, e_1), (l_2, s_2, e_2), \cdots, (l_n, s_n, e_n)$ where n is the number of lines in program, l_i is the line number, s_i is the tokenized sequence for line l_i, and e_i is the error message encoding for line l_i.

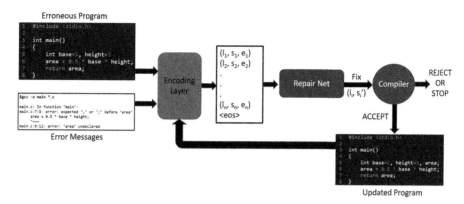

Fig. 3. RepairNet strategy to fix the error

The process of encoding a single line of program is shown in Fig. 4. Here, '*int temp* = 2;' is encoded as a vector $[3, 4, 10, 0, 9]$. A similar process is applied to all the lines of a program (Note: The vocabulary indices shown in the figure are just for explaining the concept). For each program, the encoding layer also generates a one-hot encoding vector of the error messages. For the lines having no error, we pass '0' as an encoded value for the error message. Embeddings of program token and error message are passed to the model, RepairNet. The model generates the potential fix $\hat{y} = (l_i, s'_i)$ using softmax probabilities. The fix is applied to the program by replacing s_i at l_i with s'_i. The updated program is then passed through the compiler which accepts or rejects the fix. If the potential fix reduces the number of errors and doesn't induce any new errors, then the fix is accepted, else it is rejected. After applying the fix on the input program, the updated program is passed to the network again to resolve other errors. The iteration continues until the network fixes all the errors, or the compiler rejects the fix, or a predefined number of iterations is reached. Our iterative repair strategy is similar to [2].

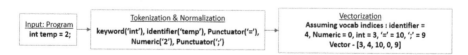

Fig. 4. Example of processing a single line of input program and converting it into vector representation

RepairNet learns error repair strategies from the training data that comprises several pairs of programs, where one program in the pair fails to compile and the other program in the pair is free of compilation errors. RepairNet can repair programs in which multiple lines require repairs, and such datasets are included in our experiments. With every such program pair, we also receive the error message generated by the compiler. Table 1 shows error messages mapped to corresponding error types present in our datasets and their occurrences. In our datasets, we have a total of 67 unique error messages. We have displayed (in Table 1) the top five error messages along with their frequency of occurrence listed in decreasing order. Even for the same type of error message, their representation in the compiler error message is different because of the inclusion of program-specific tokens such as identifiers, keywords, etc. in error messages. For example, errors reported by two different programs "8:9: error: 'i' undeclared (first use in this function) $for(i = 0; i < n; i++)$" and "error: '$count$' undeclared (first use in this function) $if(count == 0)$" fall in one category itself "variable not declared before it's use". We defined a template for each unique type of error messages present in our datasets. The mapping of error messages was performed based on the defined template. For instance, all error messages with 'variable declaration' being mapped to "Use of undeclared identifier _" (Error code - E1) (shown in Table 1).

4   Model Evaluation

4.1   Dataset

RepairNet recommends error fixes based on the programs submitted by students across different courses offered in MOOCs. To validate such a system, we use the publicly available dataset originally developed in the DeepFix [2] work. Below we describe the steps taken to create a training dataset for RepairNet from these submissions.

Raw Data Collection. The dataset consists of C programs written by students for 93 different programming tasks with 6,971 erroneous programs in an Introductory C programming course (CS1) at the Indian Institute of Technology Kanpur (IIT-K). These programs were collected using Prutor [19], a system that stores intermediate versions of programs written by students in addition to final submissions. The dataset is available at [38].

Data Preparation. We have two classes of programs in our dataset - programs that compile and programs that do not compile. A student may submit several erroneous programs. Among them, we pick a random sample of (P_e, P_c) program pairs along with the compiler error message M_c for P_e, where P_e is a version of a student's program which fails with at least one compiler error, P_c is a later version of the attempt by the same student which does not produce any compilation errors and M_c is the error message captured during the compilation of the program P_e.

4.2   Experiments and Results

In this section, we will discuss the experimental setup of our proposed architecture and evaluate the accuracy of the RepairNet model. We will experimentally compare the performance of our model with state-of-the-art approaches. The network consists of four layers of LSTM cells with 300 units in each layer. We apply the dropout [32] of 0.2 after each layer. The network is trained using the Adam optimizer [33] with batch size 30, learning rate 0.001, and gradient clipping 1. To encode the program into the network, we tokenized the programs and converted them into 50-dimensional vectors using the embedding layer. We also generated the one-hot encoding of the error message for each program. We applied 5-fold cross-validation to evaluate the performance of our model. We trained our model up to 40 epochs and selected the model with the best performance on the test set. We used PyTorch implementation of the sequence-to-sequence model [37] as a base setup and modified it's implementation for our architecture. Experiments were performed on a system with Intel i7 CPU and Nvidia GTX 1070 GPU.

We used repair accuracy as a metric to evaluate the performance of our model. Repair accuracy is defined as the fraction of fixes corrected out of all the errors. We measured repair accuracy for two types of fixes: a) complete fixes: programs that are completely fixed, and b) partial fixes: programs that are partially fixed. We compared our results with other state-of-the-art models for program repair on the Prutor dataset (as shown in Table 2). The experiments show that our approach, with 66.4% repair accuracy, outperforms the prior works significantly. We obtain a 17% relative improvement over the state-of-the-art approach "MACER" [9]. Table 2 captures the accuracy for both complete and partial program fixes for different models. We believe that the inclusion of error message as contextual information helped the model to perform significantly well in comparison with previous approaches. Error messages shown by the compiler play an important role in modeling the program repair as they can provide more contextual information about the type of error. We also computed the accuracy in fixing different types of error messages. Table 1 shows the accuracy of the top five error messages. We observed that the model performs quite well in fixing error messages 'Expected _ after expression' (E1) and 'Use of undeclared identifier _' (E2). The result indicates that RepairNet can effectively fix errors of diverse types.

Table 1. Top five error messages along with their frequency of occurrence and Repair Accuracy. The symbol _ is a placeholder for program-specific tokens such as identifiers, reserved keywords, punctuation marks, etc.

Error code	Error messages	Error count	Repair accuracy
E1	Expected _ after expression	4999	73.2%
E2	Use of undeclared identifier _	4709	82.4%
E3	Expected expression _	3818	51.2%
E4	Expected _ in _ statement specifier	720	57.6%
E5	Expression is not assignable	538	29.4%

Table 2. RepairNet results and comparison with prior work on the publicly available dataset. '-' indicates that results were not reported in the paper

Models	Complete fixes	Partial fixes
DeepFix [2]	27.0%	19%
RLAssist [13]	26.6%	18.8%
SampleFix [14]	45.3%	–
TRACER [17]	43.9%	–
MACER [9]	56.6%	–
RepairNet (without error message)	**44.6%**	**18%**
RepairNet (with error message)	**66.4%**	**14.2%**

4.3   Ablation Study on Model Architecture

We modified the sequence-to-sequence model to incorporate error messages to fix the error. In this section, we evaluate the effectiveness of our modifications to the model. For that, we built a similar sequence-to-sequence model using a Bidirectional LSTM network with attention mechanism. This network considers only the program tokens as input (without the error message). Program is represented as $(l_1, s_1), (l_2, s_2), \cdots, (l_n, s_n)$ where n is the number of lines in program, l_i is the line number, and s_i is the tokenized sequence for line l_i. We used the same network parameters as discussed in Sect. 4. We observed repair accuracy to be 44.6% for complete fixes and 18% for partial fixes for such a network. RepairNet introduces the error message along with the code tokens as input to the decoder. The network architecture for RepairNet is explained in Sect. 3. RepairNet fixes 66.4% of the erroneous submissions completely and 14.2% partially. The results are captured in Table 2. We observed 49% relative improvement for complete fixes by incorporating error messages into the network.

5   Threats to Validity

A threat to the external validity of our results is that we have evaluated our approach only on small programs obtained from an introductory C programming course, which might not be representative of other programming courses taught in different languages such as Python, Java, etc. However, as we have seen sequence-to-sequence model-based approaches working pretty well for any natural language which is less structured and much more ambiguous than programming languages; we believe that it should work on other programming languages as well. A threat to internal validity is that sometimes there could be multiple ways to fix the errors. However, our approach does not provide multiple options; it learns the potential fix from the data it has seen.

6 Conclusion

In this work, we considered the problem of automatically repairing programs based on the error messages and program token sequences. We proposed a novel generative sequence-to-sequence model that considers the error message as contextual information to repair the program. Our approach significantly outperforms prior approaches of completely fixing programs by 17%. The model also performed well in fixing individual error types as compared to prior approaches. RepairNet, with its automated program repair recommendations, can assist programmers - seasoned or novice, in learning new programming languages more efficiently. It can also be used by teaching assistants to assess student submissions even in a physical setting. Moreover, in the future, compilers can be augmented with such an approach to provide better recommendations to programmers. In future work, we will consider fixing other types of errors such as run-time errors and extend it for other programming languages.

References

1. Bhatia, S., Kohli, P., Singh, R.: Neuro-symbolic program corrector for introductory programming assignments. In: 2018 IEEE/ACM 40th International Conference on Software Engineering (ICSE), pp. 60–70. IEEE (2018)
2. Gupta, R., Pal, S., Kanade, A., Shevade, S.: DeepFix: fixing common C language errors by deep learning. In: Thirty-First AAAI Conference on Artificial Intelligence (2017)
3. Li, J., Galley, M., Brockett, C., Spithourakis, G.P., Gao, J., Dolan, B.: A persona-based neural conversation model. arXiv preprint arXiv:1603.06155 (2016)
4. Goues, C.L., Pradel, M., Roychoudhury, A.: Automated program repair. Commun. ACM **62**(12), 56–65 (2019)
5. Liu, K., Koyuncu, A., Kim, D., Bissyandé, T.F.: TBar: revisiting template-based automated program repair. In: Proceedings of the 28th ACM SIGSOFT International Symposium on Software Testing and Analysis, pp. 31–42 (2019)
6. Chen, Z., Kommrusch, S.J., Tufano, M., Pouchet, L.N., Poshyvanyk, D., Monperrus, M.: Sequencer: sequence-to-sequence learning for end-to-end program repair. IEEE Trans. Softw. Eng. (2019)
7. Vasic, M., Kanade, A., Maniatis, P., Bieber, D., Singh, R.: Neural program repair by jointly learning to localize and repair. arXiv preprint arXiv:1904.01720 (2019)
8. Yang, G., Min, K., Lee, B.: Applying deep learning algorithm to automatic bug localization and repair. In: Proceedings of the 35th Annual ACM Symposium on Applied Computing, pp. 1634–1641 (2020)
9. Chhatbar, D., Ahmed, U.Z., Kar, P.: MACER: a modular framework for accelerated compilation error repair. arXiv preprint arXiv:2005.14015 (2020)
10. Mesbah, A., Rice, A., Johnston, E., Glorioso, N., Aftandilian, E.: DeepDelta: learning to repair compilation errors. In: Proceedings of the 2019 27th ACM Joint Meeting on European Software Engineering Conference and Symposium on the Foundations of Software Engineering, pp. 925–936 (2019)
11. Koyuncu, A., et al.: iFixR: bug report driven program repair. In: Proceedings of the 2019 27th ACM Joint Meeting on European Software Engineering Conference and Symposium on the Foundations of Software Engineering, pp. 314–325 (2019)

12. Tarlow, D., et al.: Learning to fix build errors with Graph2Diff neural networks. arXiv preprint arXiv:1911.01205 (2019)
13. Gupta, R., Kanade, A., Shevade, S.: Deep reinforcement learning for syntactic error repair in student programs. In: Proceedings of the AAAI Conference on Artificial Intelligence, vol. 33, pp. 930–937 (2019)
14. Hajipour, H., Bhattacharya, A., Fritz, M.: SampleFix: learning to correct programs by sampling diverse fixes. arXiv preprint arXiv:1906.10502 (2019)
15. Gupta, R., Kanade, A., Shevade, S.: Deep learning for bug-localization in student programs. arXiv preprint arXiv:1905.12454 (2019)
16. Endres, M., Sakkas, G., Cosman, B., Jhala, R., Weimer, W.: InFix: automatically repairing novice program inputs. In: 2019 34th IEEE/ACM International Conference on Automated Software Engineering (ASE), pp. 399–410. IEEE (2019)
17. Ahmed, U.Z., Kumar, P., Karkare, A., Kar, P., Gulwani, S.: Compilation error repair: for the student programs, from the student programs. In: Proceedings of the 40th International Conference on Software Engineering: Software Engineering Education and Training, pp. 78–87 (2018)
18. Lee, J., Song, D., So, S., Oh, H.: Automatic diagnosis and correction of logical errors for functional programming assignments. In: Proceedings of the ACM on Programming Languages, vol. 2, no. OOPSLA, pp. 1–30 (2018)
19. Das, R., Ahmed, U.Z., Karkare, A., Gulwani, S.: Prutor: a system for tutoring CS1 and collecting student programs for analysis. arXiv preprint arXiv:1608.03828 (2016)
20. Bader, J., Scott, A., Pradel, M., Chandra, S.: Getafix: learning to fix bugs automatically. In: Proceedings of the ACM on Programming Languages, vol. 3, no. OOPSLA, pp. 1–27 (2019)
21. Pu, Y., Narasimhan, K., Solar-Lezama, A., Barzilay, R.: sk_p: a neural program corrector for MOOCs. In: Companion Proceedings of the 2016 ACM SIGPLAN International Conference on Systems, Programming, Languages and Applications: Software for Humanity, pp. 39–40 (2016)
22. McCauley, R., et al.: Debugging: a review of the literature from an educational perspective. Comput. Sci. Educ. **18**(2), 67–92 (2008)
23. Seo, H., Sadowski, C., Elbaum, S., Aftandilian, E., Bowdidge, R.: Programmers' build errors: a case study (at Google). In: Proceedings of the 36th International Conference on Software Engineering, pp. 724–734 (2014)
24. Monperrus, M.: Automatic software repair: a bibliography. ACM Comput. Surv. (CSUR) **51**(1), 1–24 (2018)
25. Schuster, M., Paliwal, K.K.: Bidirectional recurrent neural networks. IEEE Trans. Sig. Process. **45**(11), 2673–2681 (1997)
26. Graves, A., Jaitly, N., Mohamed, A.R.: Hybrid speech recognition with deep bidirectional LSTM. In: 2013 IEEE Workshop on Automatic Speech Recognition and Understanding, pp. 273–278. IEEE (2013)
27. Sundermeyer, M., Alkhouli, T., Wuebker, J., Ney, H.: Translation modeling with bidirectional recurrent neural networks. In: Proceedings of the 2014 Conference on Empirical Methods in Natural Language Processing (EMNLP), pp. 14–25 (2014)
28. Bahdanau, D., Cho, K., Bengio, Y.: Neural machine translation by jointly learning to align and translate. arXiv preprint arXiv:1409.0473 (2014)
29. Cho, K., et al.: Learning phrase representations using RNN encoder-decoder for statistical machine translation. arXiv preprint arXiv:1406.1078 (2014)
30. Sutskever, I., Vinyals, O., Le, Q.V.: Sequence to sequence learning with neural networks. In: Advances in Neural Information Processing Systems, pp. 3104–3112 (2014)

31. Vinyals, O., Kaiser, Ł., Koo, T., Petrov, S., Sutskever, I., Hinton, G.: Grammar as a foreign language. In: Advances in Neural Information Processing Systems, pp. 2773–2781 (2015)
32. Srivastava, N., Hinton, G., Krizhevsky, A., Sutskever, I., Salakhutdinov, R.: Dropout: a simple way to prevent neural networks from overfitting. J. Mach. Learn. Res. **15**(1), 1929–1958 (2014)
33. Kingma, D.P., Ba, J.: Adam: a method for stochastic optimization. arXiv preprint arXiv:1412.6980 (2014)
34. Denny, P., Luxton-Reilly, A., Tempero, E.: All syntax errors are not equal. In: Proceedings of the 17th ACM Annual Conference on Innovation and Technology in Computer Science Education, pp. 75–80 (2012)
35. Robins, A.V.: Novice programmers and introductory programming. In: Cambridge Handbooks in Psychology. The Cambridge Handbook of Computing Education Research, pp. 327–376 (2019)
36. Ottosson, S., Zaslavskyi, V.: Visualize what to be coded before programming. In: 2019 IEEE International Conference on Advanced Trends in Information Theory (ATIT), pp. 355–358. IEEE (2019)
37. https://github.com/pytorch/tutorials/blob/master/intermediate_source/seq2seq_translation_tutorial.py
38. https://bitbucket.org/iiscseal/deepfix/src/master/
39. Gopinath, D., Malik, M.Z., Khurshid, S.: Specification-based program repair using SAT. In: Abdulla, P.A., Leino, K.R.M. (eds.) TACAS 2011. LNCS, vol. 6605, pp. 173–188. Springer, Heidelberg (2011). https://doi.org/10.1007/978-3-642-19835-9_15
40. Le Goues, C., Nguyen, T., Forrest, S., Weimer, W.: GenProg: a generic method for automatic software repair. IEEE Trans. Softw. Eng. **38**(1), 54–72 (2011)

Seven-Year Longitudinal Implications of Wheel Spinning and Productive Persistence

Seth A. Adjei[1]([✉]), Ryan S. Baker[2], and Vedant Bahel[3]

[1] Northern Kentucky University, Highland Heights, KY 41099, USA
adjeis1@nku.edu
[2] University of Pennsylvania, Philadelphia, PA 19104, USA
[3] G H Raisoni College of Engineering, Nagpur, India

Abstract. Research in learning analytics and educational data mining has some-times failed to distinguish between wheel-spinning and more productive forms of persistence, when students are working in online learning system. This work has, in cases, treated any student who completes more than ten items on a topic without mastering it as being in need of intervention. By contrast, the broader fields of education and human development have recognized the value of grit and persistence for long-term outcomes. In this paper, we compare the longitudinal impact of wheel-spinning and productive persistence (completing many items but eventually mastering the topic) in online learning, utilizing a publicly available data set. We connect behavior during learning in middle school mathematics to a student's eventual enrollment (or failure to enroll) in college. We find that pro-ductive persistence during middle school mathematics is associated with a higher probability of college enrollment, and that wheel-spinning during middle school mathematics is not statistically significantly associated with college enrollment in either direction. The findings around productive persistence remain statistically significant even when controlling for affect and disengaged behavior.

Keywords: Wheel-spinning · Grit · Productive persistence · College enrollment

1 Introduction

Grit, the combination of persistence and passion, is important to both learning and life outcomes [11, 12]. The benefits of grit can span across several years [12]. Recent work has argued that the persistence component of grit is more important to student outcomes than passion [9]. Ultimately, the ability to work hard towards a goal – and not give up even in the face of serious challenge – appears to be a key part of life success.

At the level of courses and programs, the learning analytics literature recognizes the value of persistence. There has been considerable research on studying stopout/ dropout, quitting a course or program prior to completion. There has also been a proliferation of research on models that can detect that a learner is at risk of stopping or dropping out [10, 14, 19], as well as work on understanding the factors that lead students to stop out or drop out [29, 31, 35]. This work underpins the development of systems used to prevent

© Springer Nature Switzerland AG 2021
I. Roll et al. (Eds.): AIED 2021, LNAI 12748, pp. 16–28, 2021.
https://doi.org/10.1007/978-3-030-78292-4_2

stopout and dropout, which in many cases have led to better outcomes for learners, where they persevere to successful completion [2, 21, 33].

Curiously, however, the more micro aspects of the learning analytics literature – looking at student behavior within a problem set, for instance – have largely treated perseverance as a problem rather than as a strength. The term "wheel-spinning" has been applied to this behavior, viewing persistence as being the same thing as making no progress [4]. The initial definition of wheel-spinning proposed by Beck and Gong [4] treated any student who completed ten mathematics problems on a single skill without mastering the skill as wheel-spinning. This has continued as the most common definition of wheel-spinning (though some work has hand-labeled wheel-spinning – i.e. [20]); the preponderance of research on wheel-spinning has not differentiated between students who persevere but eventually succeed, and students who persevere and never succeed (i.e. [7, 13, 15]). However, Kai and colleagues [17] have noted that many students continue to make progress, and obtain mastery, even after completing ten problems. Käser and her colleagues [18] argue that a student should only be considered wheel-spinning if they are no longer making progress in terms of a knowledge model.

Following on work by Kai et al. [17], we adopt a different view on persistence during the learning process, separating persistence that ultimately leads to success (termed "productive persistence") from persistence that never does (which we term "wheel-spinning", somewhat in contrast to the use in [4]).

2   Research Questions

In this paper, we investigate the relationship between measures of learner persistence in the ASSISTments system, used in middle school, and a longitudinal outcome, college enrollment. We measure three indicators of persistence (or the lack thereof):

- Wheel-spinning: The student persists but never succeeds in mastering the skill
- Productive persistence: The student persists and eventually masters the skill
- Quitting: The student does not persist and quits the skill without mastery

We hypothesize that productive persistence will be associated with positive longitudinal outcomes, whereas wheel-spinning and quitting will be associated with negative longitudinal outcomes, albeit for different reasons.

3   The ASSISTments System

In this study, we examine the effects of learners' persistence on college enrollment within the ASSISTments learning system. ASSISTments [16] is a free online learning system that several thousand middle school teachers in the United States use to assign math homework to their students. On average, over 35,000 students across the United States use this system on a daily basis, solving approximately 323,000 questions a day.

The system provides sets of prepackaged questions or problems, called problem sets, grouped by math topics/skills. Each problem set is made up of a set of problems that are tagged with at least a single math skill, where the skills are sourced from the United

States Common Core State Standards for Mathematics. [8] Many of these problem sets, referred to as "skill builders", are mastery based, where the system continues giving the student problems until they demonstrate mastery. The mastery criterion (i.e. specific number of questions correct in a row required for mastery) is predetermined for each problem set, although it can be adjusted by the teacher. In general, the mastery criterion is 3 problems correct in a row. If a student completes ten problems on a skill without reaching mastery, the system asks them to take a break on the skill until the next day.

Many ASSISTments problems, including all skill builder problems, have features that allow students to seek help if they experience difficulties as they answer the questions. Figure 1 shows a sample problem presented in the ASSISTments tutor. The tutor gives students access to help-seeking features, including hints and scaffolding questions. Hints are short simple statements or clues about the question that help guide the student through the solution to the problem, for instance by explaining the knowledge component(s) required to solve the problem or providing the formula required to solve the problem. Hints become available in increasing order of specificity, with the final hints usually providing the answer to the question (referred to as the bottom-out hint.) Scaffolding questions [26] are created based on the original math problem. The original problem is broken down into smaller, less difficult steps, designed to be answered in a linear sequence. The answer to the final scaffold question is the answer to the main question. Within skill builders, for each main question, students are provided with both of these help features and can choose either. If a student seeks help on a question, the system can either (according to the teacher's preference) mark the question incorrect or give the student partial credit based on the number of help-seeking steps they sought [23, 30, 32]. Students' work within ASSISTments is logged, including the problem identifier, the correctness of the student's response, the type of help the student sought, the number of hints the student requested, as well as the time (in seconds) the student spent in answering the question.

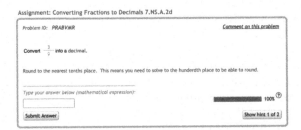

Fig. 1. A sample ASSISTments problem displayed in the tutor. The system presents the student an opportunity to ask for hints and to attempt the question multiple times.

4   Data

4.1   ASSISTments Log

In this paper, we analyze a publicly available ASSISTments dataset, the dataset used in the ASSISTments Longitudinal Data Challenge [25], selected because of the availability of longitudinal outcome data. The overall data set consisted of data from 1,709 students – we analyze the subset of students who completed skill-builder assignments. This smaller dataset was comprised of the problem response logs of 236 students who completed a total of 431 skill-builder assignments in the ASSISTments system. The logs were collected between the 2004 and 2007 school years. On average each student either started (and/or completed) 18 skill-builder assignments, generating a total of 25,159 logs across a total of 5,979 problems.

4.2 College Enrollment Data

College enrollment records were collected for the 236 students whose logs we examine in this paper (and for the rest of the students in the data set as well). Each student's enrollment record includes a binary feature that indicates whether they enrolled in college. This data was collected through the National Student Clearinghouse, a database on college enrollment, and made available to researchers through the ASSISTments Longitudinal Data Challenge. A full discussion of the collection of this data is given in [28]. Data was collected for college major and post-college job as well [25], but will not be analyzed in this paper due to the smaller sample size.

4.3 Affect and Behavior Data

The data set included estimates of students' affect and behavior as they answer the complete the mastery-based skill builders in ASSISTments. The affective states for which the data set had estimates are boredom, engaged concentration, confusion and frustration. The behavioral estimates are of two forms of students' disengagement as they complete the assignment: gaming the system and off-task behavior. These estimates were originally generated (see [24]) using a two-step process. In the first step, observers trained in the BROMP protocol and HART android app [22] recorded observations of student affect and disengaged behaviors for a small sample of students. In the second step of the process, the observations were used to create models inferring affect and disengaged behaviors from only problem logs. These models were then used to calculate estimates of students' affective and behavioral states for the unseen ASSISTments problem logs. Each affect and behavior estimate was scaled from 0 (0% probability) to 1 (100% probability) by the models.

5 Feature Generation

In order to study how persistence was associated with college enrollment, we created features from the ASSISTments log data to represent different aspects of persistence. The following sections describe each of the features in detail.

5.1 Mastery Speed

In the context of ASSISTments, Xiong et al. [34] defined mastery speed as the number of questions a student answers prior to achieving mastery of a skill. For instance, a student who obtains three right in a row on the 7th, 8th, and 9th problems in a mastery-based assignment will have a mastery speed of 9. (The student will not have achieved the mastery criterion prior to the 9th question) We calculated this feature for each student/assignment pair. A student who already knows a skill will achieve mastery (according to the system) by obtaining correct answers on the first 3 problems in a row. However, students can also be deemed to have mastered the skill if they answer the very first question in the assignment correctly without any help (i.e. hints or scaffolds). These students are deemed to have "tested out" of the assignment. In such cases, the mastery speed for such a student-assignment pair was counted as 1.

5.2 Wheel-Spinning

In this paper, we adopt a definition of wheel-spinning similar to the definition used by Kai and colleagues [17]. As ten problems completed (for persistent) and three-in-a-row correct (for mastery) match the operationalizations used in the ASSISTments system itself, we adopt these definitions. We define a student as wheel-spinning if they complete ten problems without reaching mastery and never reach mastery on that skill. If a student completes ten problems without reaching mastery but then masters the skill, we define them instead as a separate category, persistent-mastered. To reiterate, a student is deemed to be persistent in a skill builder assignment if they are unable to achieve mastery by the 10th question in the assignment – if their problem count for the given assignment is at least 10. The ASSISTments system generally stops the student from being presented with additional questions in an assignment on the same day if they have not mastered the skill by the 10th question (unless the 10th question is answered correctly after the 9th question was also answered correct). Whether or not they eventually master the skill determines whether they are treated as persistent-mastered or wheel-spinning.

5.3 Persistence-Related Features

We categorize students in terms of their mastery and persistence in terms of four behaviors, each of which is expressed in a data feature as the percentage of skills where the students demonstrated that behavior: *Persistent-Mastered*, *Wheel-Spinning*, *Quickly-Mastered*, and *Quit*, shown in Table 1. These features are also described below:

(i)   **Quickly-Mastered**: The percentage of assignments in which the student mastered the skill in ten or fewer problems.

(ii) **Persistent-Mastered**: The percentage of assignments in which the student attained mastery of the skill builder after more than ten problems (referred to as "productive persistence" in Kai et al. [17]).

(iii) **Wheel-Spinning**: The percentage of assignments in which the student completed more than ten problems and never attained mastery.

(iv) **Quit**: The percentage of assignments in which the student neither attained mastery nor was persistent – they quit working on the problem set prior to the tenth problem. Also referred to as "early stopout" [6].

Table 1. The four categories of persistence and success analyzed in this study.

	Persistent (> 10 problems)	Non-Persistent (≤ 0 problems)
Mastered	Persistent-Mastered	Quickly-Mastered
Did not master	Wheel-Spinning	Quit

5.4   Other Mastery-Related and Performance Features

In addition to the above-mentioned features, we examined the following high-level features to understand their interaction with college enrollment and better clarify our findings: the percentage of assignments in which the student was persistent (the student exceeded ten problems, irrespective of whether they achieved mastery or not), the percentage of assignments that the student mastered, and the average percent correct across all questions they were presented across all assignments.

5.5   Aggregation of Features

As stated earlier, on average each student completed 18 mastery-based assignments. In order to be able to compare the features across these assignments to college enrollment, we aggregated all the features described above such that each student record will have a single average value for each of the affect, behavior and ASSISTments-related features. For example, instead of using a single mastery speed for an assignment in our models, we used the average mastery speed across all assignments.

6   Analysis Plan

To research the effects of wheel-spinning on college enrollment, we conducted three analyses, much as in [28]. In the first analysis, we looked at the relationship between each of the features discussed above, taken individually, and college enrollment. For each feature, we conducted a two-sample two-tailed t-test, assuming equal variances, comparing the value of each feature between students who attended college and students who did not attend college – for example, was wheel-spinning more frequent among students who eventually attended college, or students who did not eventually attend college? Cohen's D effect sizes were used to assess the magnitude of the differences. Given that we ran 18 tests, a Benjamini & Hochberg [5] post-hoc control was used. Benjamini & Hochberg's procedure, a false discovery rate procedure, attempts to ensure that the overall rate of Type II false discoveries (non-effects treated as effects; false positives) remains at the 5% level. In doing so, Benjamini & Hochberg's procedure avoids the over-conservatism and inflated Type II error rate that the Bonferroni correction is known for, while avoiding the inflated Type I error rate that occurs when multiple tests are run and no post-hoc adjustment is used. Within the Benjamini & Hochberg correction, different tests are assigned different alpha values (which the p value must be below to reach statistical significance), based on both the overall number of tests run and the number of tests that have lower p values than the current test.

In the second analysis, we created a single logistic regression model which attempted to predict college enrollment using both persistence measures and affect and disengagement variables. We chose to use logistic regression because the outcome measure was binary (whether or not the student enrolled in college), and logistic regression is a particularly interpretable algorithm. Several variables came up non-significant (see below). Therefore, in the third analysis, we took the single logistic regression model from the second analysis, removed all non-significant variables, and re-ran the analysis. In these analyses, we again use a Benjamini & Hochberg post-hoc control.

Table 2. Features for Students who attended college (1, n = 136) and didn't attend college (0, n = 102)

Features (df = 234)	Enrolled in College	Mean	Std. Dev.	t-value	Cohen's D
Mastery Speed	0	**8.327**	**7.916**	**3.816**	0.514
	1	**13.05**	**10.320**	**(p < 0.001)**	
Persisted	0	**0.349**	**0.341**	**3.661**	0.489
	1	**0.533**	**0.407**	**(p < 0.001)**	
Percent Mastered	0	**0.601**	**0.345**	**4.911**	0.639
	1	**0.802**	**0.278**	**(p < 0.001)**	
Quickly Mastered	0	0.458	0.325	−1.831	0.157
	1	0.403	0.369	(p = 0.238)	
Persistent-Mastered	**0**	**0.143**	**0.253**	**5.227**	0.715
	1	**0.398**	**0.437**	**(p < 0.001)**	
Wheel-Spinning	0	0.136	0.274	−1.261	0.166
	1	0.092	0.253	(p = 0.208)	
Quit	**0**	**0.261**	**0.277**	**−5.568**	0.706
	1	**0.105**	**0.148**	**(p < 0.001)**	
Percent Correct	**0**	**0.739**	**0.165**	**2.614**	0.342
	1	**0.792**	**0.143**	**(p < 0.001)**	
Boredom	**0**	**0.176**	**0.087**	**−5.3811**	0.719
	1	**0.108**	**0.103**	**(p < 0.001)**	
Confusion	**0**	**0.030**	**0.045**	**−5.746**	0.716
	1	**0.006**	**0.016**	**(p < 0.001)**	
Concentration	0	0.691	0.078	0.601	0.081
	1	0.698	0.011	(p = 0.547)	

(continued)

Table 2. (*continued*)

Features (df = 234)	Enrolled in College	Mean	Std. Dev.	t-value	Cohen's D
Frustration	0	0.151	0.143	−1.346	0.181
	1	0.121	0.189	(p = 0.179)	
Gaming	0	0.139	0.166	−1.3607	0.178
	1	0.111	0.143	(p = 0.174)	
Off Task	0	0.227	0.093	−0.812	0.106
	1	0.218	0.078	(p = 0.418)	

7 Results

7.1 Single-Feature Analyses

As shown in Table 2, eight features were statistically significant predictors of college enrollment when taken individually, after post-hoc Benjamini & Hochberg correction. Students who enrolled in college had a higher proportion of being persistent in the face of difficulty and mastering difficult topics (Persistent Mastered) (M = 0.398) than students who did not enroll in college (M = 0.143), $t(233) = 5.227$, $p < 0.001$, D = 0.715. Students who enrolled in college were less likely to quit problem sets without reaching mastery (M = 0.261) than students who did not eventually enroll in college (M = 0.105), $t(233) = -5.568$, $p < 0.001$, D = 0.706. However, contrary to our initial hypothesis, wheel-spinning was not significantly different for students who enrolled in college than students who did not, $t(233) = -1.261$, $p = 0.208$; mastering problem sets quickly was also not statistically significantly different, $t(233) = -1.831$. In fact, students who enrolled in college actually took longer on average to master the problem sets they mastered (M = 13.05) than students who did not enroll (M = 8.327), $t(233) = 3.816$, $p < 0.001$, likely due to the difference in quitting early.

There were affective differences between students who enrolled in college versus those who did not enroll, broadly similar to the analyses of the super-set of this data set seen in [28]. Students who enrolled in college were statistically significantly less often bored and confused than students who did not enroll in college. Unlike that larger data set, however, students who enrolled in college did not game the system significantly more or less often than students who did not enroll in college.

7.2 Productive Persistence Models (Full Model)

Table 3 presents a logistic regression model that uses three of the four productive persistence features to predict college enrollment (the fourth, Quickly Mastered, is omitted due to collinearity), controlling for affect and disengaged behavior. We find that productive persistence is still a significant predictor of college enrollment, even after accounting for all the affect and behavior features ($p < 0.01$). However, quitting was no longer a significant predictor of enrollment once other features were controlled for. It is possible that boredom or confusion, both negatively associated with student outcomes, may have played a role both in why students quit and why they are less likely to enroll in college. Engaged concentration was marginally significantly positively associated with enrollment. Gaming the system, on the other hand, became significantly negatively associated with enrollment once other features were controlled for.

Table 3. Logistic regression model including both persistence features and affect and disengagement features. Significant features are in boldface, and marginally significant features are in italics. Alpha values from the Benjamini & Hochberg post-hoc control are included.

Feature	Coefficient	p-value (alpha value)	Odds Ratio	Risk Ratio
Persistent Mastered	**0.350**	**0.004 (0.006)**	**1.420**	**1.606**
Wheel-Spinning	0.308	0.105 (n/a)	1.361	1.678
Quit	−0.108	0.546 (n/a)	0.897	0.569
Boredom	**−0.927**	**0.020 (0.022)**	0.396	0.317
Confusion	**−2.709**	**0.006 (0.011)**	0.067	<0.001
Engaged Concentration	0.824	0.0279 (0.0278)	2.280	3.829
Frustration	0.164	0.395 (n/a)	1.178	1.390
Gaming	**−0.771**	**0.0096 (0.017)**	**0.463**	**0.263**
Off Task	0.148	0.674 (n/a)	1.159	1.449
Constant	−0.009	0.731 (n/a)	1.104	0.265

Table 4. Model for College Enrollment omitting non-significant predictors. Significant features are in boldface

Feature	Coefficient	p-value (alpha value)	Odds Ratio	Risk Ratio
Persistent Mastered	**0.323**	**0.0005 (0.01)**	**1.382**	**1.663**
Boredom	**−0.814**	**0.0224 (0.03)**	**0.443**	**0.426**
Confusion	**−2.813**	**0.0015 (0.02)**	**0.060**	**0.000**
Engaged Concentration	**0.686**	**0.0453 (0.05)**	**1.986**	**3.170**
Gaming	**−0.408**	**0.0347 (0.04)**	**0.665**	**0.472**
Constant	0.214	0.415 (n/a)	1.239	0.301

Finally, we removed the non-significant features from the model presented in Table 3 in order to examine whether the directionality and significance of the previously significant features remain the same as before. Engaged concentration goes from marginally significant to significant; the significance and directionality of the other features remains the same (See Table 4).

8 Discussion and Conclusions

In this paper, we compared behaviors associated with persistence in online learning, during middle school, to the longitudinal outcome of whether a student eventually enrolls in college: wheel-spinning (completing many items and never mastering the skill), productive persistence (completing many items and eventually mastering the skill), and quitting a skill (without mastery or completing a substantial number of items).

Of these three, only productive persistence is reliably associated with college enrollment after controlling for student affect and disengaged behaviors. Students who are productively persistent more often are more likely to enroll in college, years later. In fact, students who enroll in college were productively persistent in middle school mathematics almost three times as often, an effect size (Cohen's D) of 0.715, aligning to other research showing the importance of persistence for life outcomes [9, 11, 12].

By contrast, wheel-spinning is not statistically significantly associated with eventual college enrollment. This finding suggests that though struggling without success is an emotionally upsetting experience and is associated with lower amounts of positive engaged concentration [3], it may not be as problematic for students in the long-term as may have been thought. Students may find another way to learn the material they cannot succeed on in the learning system, perhaps asking a teacher, a parent, or fellow students, or perhaps learning it on their own later in the school year.

Quitting without persisting or reaching mastery is associated with statistically significantly lower probability of college enrollment, when taken on its own. However, when controlling for student affect and another form of disengaged behavior, quitting is no longer a statistically significant predictor. This finding suggests an important role for affect and/or disengagement in the processes that mediate between giving up on a problem set and eventual impact on outcomes. It is possible that either boredom or confusion may lead a student to quit a problem set, and the relationship between those two affective states and longer-term outcomes may be a more important factor than how often a student quit a problem set. As with wheel-spinning, students may find another way to learn this material. Better understanding these relationships will be an important area for future work.

Beyond this, this paper's findings suggest several additional directions for future work. Better understanding the intermediate steps between productive persistence in middle school online learning, and eventual outcomes, would likely be a valuable area for further investigation. Is the possible impact of productive persistence due to greater learning? Or is it because productive persistence in online learning correlates to persistence and grit in other contexts as well? Teasing out the degree to which productive persistence is important in itself, and the degree to which it is simply indicative of broader grit, will be a worthwhile question to answer.

At the same time, it may be worth looking further into the future, as has been done for affect [1, 27]. It is not feasible with the current data set – although both skill builder problem sets (needed to assess wheel-spinning and productive persistence according to our current definitions of each) and later longitudinal measures are available for the current data set, the overlap between these variables in insufficiently large to support analysis (i.e. the students who completed skill builders were generally not the same ones for whom later longitudinal measures were available). Investigating this issue will need to wait for another data set.

As a final theme, this paper shows the value of longitudinal data, linked to online learning data, for a variety of secondary analyses. The ASSISTments longitudinal data set has now been used in dozens of analyses beyond its initial intended analyses – at the time that data set was collected, the first paper on wheel-spinning in online learning had not yet been published. All too often, online learning researchers do not retain the information needed for longitudinal follow-up. We hope that this paper provides yet further justification encouraging researchers to retain this information.

References

1. Almeda, M.V.Q., Baker, R.S.: Predicting student participation in STEM careers: the role of affect and engagement during middle school. J. Educ. Data Min. **12**(2), 33–47 (2020)
2. Arnold, K.E., Pistilli, M.D.: Course signals at Purdue: using learning analytics to increase student success. In: Proceedings of the 2nd International Conference on Learning Analytics and Knowledge (2012)
3. Beck, J., Rodrigo, M.M.T.: Understanding wheel spinning in the context of affective factors. In: Trausan-Matu, S., Boyer, K.E., Crosby, M., Panourgia, K. (eds.) ITS 2014. LNCS, vol. 8474, pp. 162–167. Springer, Cham (2014). https://doi.org/10.1007/978-3-319-07221-0_20
4. Beck, J., Gong, Y.: Wheel-spinning: students who fail to master a skill. In: Chad Lane, H., Yacef, K., Mostow, J., Pavlik, P. (eds.) AIED 2013. LNCS (LNAI), vol. 7926, pp. 431–440. Springer, Heidelberg (2013). https://doi.org/10.1007/978-3-642-39112-5_44
5. Benjamini, Y., Hochberg, Y.: Controlling the false discovery rate: a practical and powerful approach to multiple testing. J. Roy. Stat. Soc.: Ser. B (Methodol.) **57**(1), 289–300 (1995)
6. Botelho, A.F., Varatharaj, A., Inwegen, E.G.V., Heffernan, N.T.: Refusing to try: characterizing early stopout on student assignments. In: Proceedings of the 9th International Conference on Learning Analytics & Knowledge (2019)
7. Botelho, A.F., Varatharaj, A., Patikron, T., Doherty, D., Adjei, S.A., Beck, J.E.: Developing early detectors of student attrition and wheel spinning using deep learning. IEEE Trans. Learn. Technol. **12**(2), 158–170 (2019)
8. CCSS-MA: Common Core State Standards for Mathematics, Washington, DC (2010)
9. Credé, M., Tynan, M.C., Harms, P.D.: Much ado about grit: a meta-analytic synthesis of the grit literature. J. Pers. Soc. Psychol. **113**(3), 492 (2017)
10. Dekker, G.W., Pechenizkiy, M., Vleeshouwers, J.M.: Predicting students drop out: a case study. In: Proceedings of the International Conference on Educational Data Mining (2009)
11. Duckworth, A.: Grit: The Power of Passion and Perseverance. Scribner, New York (2016)
12. Duckworth, A.L., Peterson, C., Matthews, M.D., Kelly, D.R.: Grit: perseverance and passion for long-term goals. J. Pers. Soc. Psychol. **92**(6), 1087 (2007)
13. Flores, R.M., Rodrigo, M.M.T.: Wheel-spinning models in a novice programming context. J. Educ. Comput. Res. **58**, 1101–1120 (2020). https://doi.org/10.1177/0735633120906063
14. Gardner, J., Brooks, C.: Student success prediction in MOOCs. User Model. User-Adap. Inter. **28**(2), 127–203 (2018). https://doi.org/10.1007/s11257-018-9203-z
15. Gong, Y., Beck, J.E.: Towards detecting wheel-spinning: future failure in mastery learning. In: Proceedings of the Second ACM Conference on Learning@ Scale (2015)
16. Heffernan, N.T., Heffernan, C.L.: The ASSISTments ecosystem: building a platform that brings scientists and teachers together for minimally invasive research on human learning and teaching. Int. J. Artif. Intell. Educ. **24**(4), 470–497 (2014). https://doi.org/10.1007/s40593-014-0024-x

17. Kai, S., Almeda, M.V., Baker, R.S., Heffernan, C., Heffernan, N.: Decision tree modeling of wheel-spinning and productive persistence in skill builders. J. Educ. Data Min. **10**(1), 36–71 (2018)
18. Käser, T., Klingler, S., Gross, M.:. When to stop? Towards universal instructional policies. In: Proceedings of the Sixth International Conference on Learning Analytics & Knowledge (2016)
19. Kloft, M., Stiehler, F., Zheng, Z., Pinkwart, N.: Predicting MOOC dropout over weeks using machine learning methods. In: Proceedings of the EMNLP 2014 Workshop on Analysis of Large Scale Social Interaction in MOOCs (2014)
20. Matsuda, N., Chandrasekaran, S., Stamper, J.C.: How quickly can wheel spinning be detected? In: Proceedings of the International Conference on Educational Data Mining (2016)
21. Milliron, M.D., Malcolm, L., Kil, D.: Insight and Action analytics: three case studies to consider. Res. Pract. Assess.ment **9**, 70–89 (2014)
22. Ocumpaugh, J., Baker, R.S., Rodrigo, M.M.T.: Baker Rodrigo Ocumpaugh monitoring protocol (BROMP) 2.0 technical and training manual. Teachers College, Columbia University and Ateneo Laboratory for the Learning Sciences, New York, NY and Manila, Philippines (2015)
23. Ostrow, K., Donnelly, C., Adjei, S., Heffernan, N.: Improving student modeling through partial credit and problem difficulty. In: Proceedings of the Second ACM Conference on Learning@ Scale. ACM (2015)
24. Pardos, Z.A., Baker, R.S., San Pedro, M.O., Gowda, S.M., Gowda, S.M.: Affective states and state tests: investigating how affect and engagement during the school year predict end-of-year learning outcomes. J. Learn. Anal. **1**(1), 107–128 (2014)
25. Patikorn, T., Baker, R.S., Heffernan, N.T.: ASSISTments longitudinal data mining competition special issue: a preface. J. Educ. Data Min. **12**(2), i–xi (2020)
26. Razzaq, L., Heffernan, N.: Scaffolding vs. Hints in the Assistment System. In: Ikeda, M., Ashley, K.D., Chan, T.-W. (eds.) ITS 2006. LNCS, vol. 4053, pp. 635–644. Springer, Heidelberg (2006). https://doi.org/10.1007/11774303_63
27. San Pedro, M.O., Ocumpaugh, J., Baker, R.S., Heffernan, N.T.: Predicting STEM and Non-STEM college major enrollment from middle school interaction with mathematics educational software. In: Proceedings of the International Conference on Educational Data Mining (2014)
28. San Pedro, M.O.Z., Baker, R., Bowers, A., Heffernan, N.: Predicting college enrollment from student interaction with an intelligent tutoring system in middle school. In: Proceedings of the 6th International Conference on Educational Data Mining (2013)
29. Tinto, V.: Leaving College: Rethinking the Causes and Cures of Student Attrition. University of Chicago Press, Chicago (1987)
30. Van Inwegen, E.G., Adjei, S.A., Wang, Y., Heffernan, N.T.: Using partial credit and response history to model user knowledge. In: Proceedings of the International Conference on Educational Data Mining (2015).
31. Wang, Y., Baker, R.: Grit and intention: why do learners complete MOOCs? Int. Rev. Res. Open Distrib. Learn. **19**(3) (2018)
32. Wang, Y., Heffernan, N.T., Beck, J.E.: Representing student performance with partial credit. In: Proceedings of the International Conference on Educational Data Mining (2010)
33. Whitehill, J., Williams, J., Lopez, G., Coleman, C., Reich, J.: Beyond prediction: first steps toward automatic intervention in MOOC student stopout. In: Proceedings of the International Conference on Educational Data Mining (2015)

34. Xiong, X., Li, S., Beck, J.E.: Will you get it right next week: predict delayed performance in enhanced ITS mastery cycle. In: Proceedings of the Florida Artificial Intelligence Research Symposium (2013)
35. Xiong, Y., Li, H., Kornhaber, M.L., Suen, H.K., Pursel, B., Goins, D.D.: Examining the relations among student motivation, engagement, and retention in a MOOC: A structural equation modeling approach. Glob. Educ. Rev. **2**(3), 23–33 (2015)

A Systematic Review of Data-Driven Approaches to Item Difficulty Prediction

Samah AlKhuzaey(✉), Floriana Grasso, Terry R. Payne,
and Valentina Tamma

University of Liverpool, Liverpool L69 3BX, UK
{S.Alkhuzaey,F.Grasso,T.R.Payne,V.Tamma}@liverpool.ac.uk

Abstract. Assessment quality and validity is heavily reliant on the quality of items included in an assessment or test. Difficulty is an essential factor that can determine items and tests' overall quality. Therefore, *item difficulty prediction* is extremely important in any pedagogical learning environment. Data-driven approaches to item difficulty prediction are gaining more and more prominence, as demonstrated by the recent literature. In this paper, we provide a systematic review of data-driven approaches to item difficulty prediction. Of the 148 papers that were identified that cover item difficulty prediction, 38 papers were selected for the final analysis. A classification of the different approaches used to predict item difficulty is presented, together with the current practices for item difficulty prediction with respect to the learning algorithms used, and the most influential difficulty features that were investigated.

Keywords: Difficulty prediction · Item difficulty · Question difficulty · Systematic review · Difficulty modelling · Difficulty estimation

1 Introduction

Student assessments are a fundamental component of any pedagogical learning environment. Assembling tests that contain items (i.e. questions) which measure the various types of skills of different levels of learners in a fair way is a challenging task. Teachers and item writers must ensure the consistent quality of assessment materials to provide objective and effective evaluation.

Assessment quality and validity is heavily reliant on the quality of items included in the test; therefore, significant effort and resources have been devoted to *item analysis tasks*. For item writers, item analysis is of great importance as it allows them to improve items' overall quality by eliminating non-functional items [30]. *Difficulty* is an essential factor that can determine the overall quality of items and tests, whereas *item difficulty* refers to the estimation of the skill or knowledge level needed by students to answer an item [13]. Thus, difficulty calibration is crucial in the assessment construction process; to provide equitable opportunities to all test takers in any assessment, the item selection process must be conducted according to the difficulty level of each item [34]. Designing

© Springer Nature Switzerland AG 2021
I. Roll et al. (Eds.): AIED 2021, LNAI 12748, pp. 29–41, 2021.
https://doi.org/10.1007/978-3-030-78292-4_3

unbalanced tests which contain arbitrary numbers of easy and difficult items can result in significant disadvantages to test takers who are affected by assessment-based decisions. For example, assessments that consist of mostly *easy* items will result in wrongly qualifying and certifying those less-than-competent test takers.

Traditional methods for obtaining an a priori estimation of difficulty rely on two methods [10,39]: i) pretesting and ii) experts' judgement. However, such approaches are frequently criticised in the literature for being costly, time-consuming, subjective and difficult to scale [6,20,29]. Therefore, a number of alternative methods have been considered to overcome these limitations.

In this paper, we will examine the item difficulty prediction literature with a special focus on data-driven approaches. To the best of our knowledge, there has been no such review, nor a summary of the empirical evidence established so far in this emerging research area. More specifically, the following research questions will be addressed:

RQ1: What AI-based computational models are currently developed to offer a priori difficulty prediction?
RQ2: What are the most investigated domains and item types?
RQ3: What are the influential features that were found to affect difficulty?

We provide a overview of the research on item difficulty estimation in Sect. 2. We then present the method by which the systematic review was conducted (Sect. 3), before discussing research questions and how they fit the literature within the review (Sect. 4). We then conclude in Sect. 5.

2   Background

The research on item difficulty estimation is extensive and well-established. Psychometricians, educational psychologists and linguists have long been studying the potential sources of difficulty in educational items. These fields have provided theoretical frameworks of cognitive processes involved in assessments. Furthermore, statistical methods and manual coding practices have been applied to extract features and explore the relationship between different variables. More recently however, AI techniques such as neural networks, natural language processing (NLP), expert systems and machine learning algorithms have transformed the field by applying unconventional concepts of non-linear modelling, linguistic pattern recognition and advanced predictive power. We present a classification of two opposing approaches to item difficulty prediction based on a comprehensive survey of the literature; that of *cognitive* and *systematic* approaches (Fig. 1).

Cognitive approaches include methods that address difficulty on the cognitive level by examining what cognitive abilities are required to answer an item correctly. These approaches are qualitative in nature and rely on pre-defined notions of difficulty, based on educational taxonomies or heuristic methods which define difficulty according to the perceptions of educators, item writers and/or learners. In contrast, *systematic approaches* focus on quantifying the concept of difficulty by employing more objective techniques found in statistical or data-driven

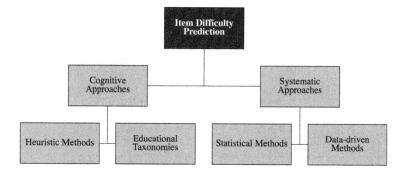

Fig. 1. Item difficulty prediction approaches

prediction models. Some of the most employed statistical methods are psychometric statistical models that analyse the relationship between difficulty and examinees' latent traits. Furthermore, basic statistical models (e.g. regression) have also been used to examine the relationship between difficulty and various variables [11,24,32,42]. Despite the fact that, in this approach, researchers were using data to draw conclusions, it is nonetheless heavily theory driven. Difficulty variables were either produced by experts or identified from previous theories in the literature. Moreover, feature extraction processes are typically conducted manually by domain experts in this type of investigation.

More recently, there has been a focus on employing data-driven approaches that represent an array of methods and techniques used to quantify and objectify the process of difficulty prediction. This line of investigation strives to eliminate or at least reduce any subjectivity caused by human intervention [21], and do not necessarily require domain experts to label or define difficulty features. Moreover, pre-testing the items to an appropriate sample will not be needed if automatic methods prove its validity. Hence, data-driven approaches (which include techniques such as NLP, rule-based and machine learning algorithms) are gaining more and more prominence [3,5,10,17,20,21,28].

In this paper, we provide a general overview of the broader field of item difficulty prediction in order to gain a full understanding of the research area. However, the scope of this review will only include data-driven approaches which incorporate computational models to model difficulty.

3 Review Method

This review's protocol is informed by the guidelines provided in [25], and is illustrated in Fig. 2. The search process was conducted manually using the following paper archives: IEEE[1], ACM Digital Library[2], ScienceDirect[3], Springer[4],

---

[1] https://ieeexplore.ieee.org/Xplore/home.jsp.
[2] https://dl.acm.org/.
[3] https://www.sciencedirect.com/.
[4] https://www.springer.com/.

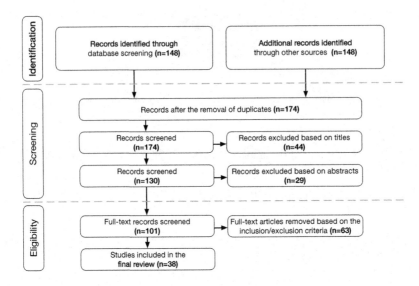

Fig. 2. The study selection process

and Elsevier[5]. Additional papers were included in the search by examining the 'related work' and the 'reference list' sections of each identified paper. Also, general and academic search engines such as Google search and Google Scholar were included to identify relevant papers. We also considered the citations to certain papers by using the 'cited by' option in Google Scholar to include papers which were not identified by the previous methods. The search process identified 148 papers which were screened in three stages: 1) title and abstract screening, 2) full-text screening, and 3) inclusion and exclusion criteria-based filtering. As a result, 38 papers were included for the final analysis.

Papers focusing on data-driven approaches to item difficulty prediction were included without constraints on publication year, paper type, domain or item type. Papers were excluded if they violated one or more of the following criteria:

– The paper is not written in English.
– The full text of the paper is not available.
– The proposed prediction model is not evaluated.
– The difficulty model is not data-driven. We exclude papers that predict difficulty based on heuristic, statistical or educational taxonomies approaches.
– The paper estimates difficulty *after* administrating the test. We only focus on methods which offer a priori prediction of difficulty in order to overcome limitations of traditional prediction methods.
– The items are not textual (i.e. containing images, graphs or formulas). We exclude these types of items as they require different analytical techniques compared to textual items.

---

[5] https://www.elsevier.com/.

- The paper does not address assessment items. For example, we exclude studies that predict the difficulty of questions in question answering communities such as Stack Overflow as this type of question differs completely from assessment questions with regard to their purpose, style and structure.
- The difficulty features are not extracted from items. We focus on difficulty features that are derived from items' structure, hence, we exclude features which are extracted from other data sources such as eLearning environments or sensors.
- The paper focuses on item classification based on features other than difficulty. For instance, we exclude papers that classify items based on question type.

The field of item difficulty estimation is an interdisciplinary one. Relevant fields such as educational assessment, psychology and computer science use different-yet synonymous terms to address the same tasks. Therefore, different combinations of search terms were assembled. As a result, the following combinations of keywords and operators were used:

> *Item difficulty prediction, Item difficulty estimation, Item difficulty modelling, Difficulty modelling, (item OR question) AND difficulty AND (estimation OR prediction OR modelling)*

A specific form was designed for the data extraction process given the objectives of this review, which included: *title, year of publication, method/approach, domain, item type, number of items, data, evaluation, participant, metrics, difficulty feature, results, paper type, publication venue and quality score.* Eight quality assessment criteria were adopted from [50], where *reporting quality, rigour* and *credibility* were the most frequently assessed dimensions in software engineering systematic reviews. The quality assessment process was conducted after reading the full text and after completing the data extraction with values assigned as Yes = 1, No = 0 and Partly = 0.5.

Included Papers: [1–6, 8–10, 12, 14–23, 26–29, 33, 35–38, 40, 41, 43–49]

4   Results and Discussion

4.1   RQ1: Data-Driven Item Difficulty Prediction

In this section, we address the question: *What AI-based computational models are currently developed to offer a priori difficulty prediction?* The computational models used in the prediction process could be discussed under two headings: *machine learning* and *rule-based modelling.* The majority of papers considered utilise machine learning algorithms such as neural networks and support vector machine (SVM) [14, 19–21, 38], with NLP being used to perform automatic extraction of difficulty features. Neural networks were some of the first data-driven methods to be implemented in the item difficulty prediction field. In 1995 they were used to predict the difficulty of reading comprehension items taking

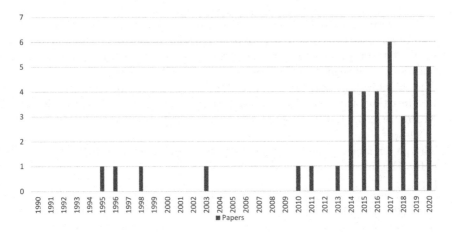

Fig. 3. Number of publications distributed by year

from a TOEFL test [37], with the aim of exploring an unconventional approach that could outperform statistical approaches. Rule-based algorithms were also used, but relied on hard-coded instructions which do not follow a pre-defined algorithm [15,36]. For this type of modelling, difficulty features were manually identified and extracted by experts, which were represented in the form of rules.

It is clear from Fig. 3, which depicts the number of publications over time, that publishing in this research area progressed through two different stages. The first wave of publications started in the mid-1990s by employing neural networks which, at the time, represented a novel approach for exploring non-linear relationships between item parameters and difficulty. Previous research had to this point only employed statistical approaches, which explains the relationships in a linear manner [8,9,12,37]. The second wave of studies started in 2010 as researchers began to explore different data-driven approaches to this problem, such as rule-based expert systems, support vector machine (SVM) and Naïve Bayesian models [4,22,35]. A steep increase in publications is noticeable from 2014 to 2020, especially in 2017, 2019 and 2020, suggesting a growing relevance of machine learning in the item difficulty research community.

In [21], a data-driven approach was employed to predict the difficulty of 30,000 reading comprehension items collected from a standard English test. The item, options and the reading passages were analysed for each item. Sentence representations were then extracted from the item components using a CNN-based architecture. Finally, the difficulty level was determined by aggregating the semantic representation of all items' components. In a different study, the authors investigated whether item difficulty correlates with the semantic similarity between item components [20]. To achieve this, they utilised word embeddings to construct the semantic space of learning materials and obtained the semantic vectors of item elements. The semantic similarity scores were used as an input to a SVM model to predict the difficulty of items collected from Entrance Exams in the social studies domain. This contrasts with [35], where a difficulty estimation approach was presented which attempted to estimate the difficulty of converting natural language sentences into First Order Logic (FOL) formulae. An expert system was then employed to estimate the difficulty level of exercises based on several parameters for measuring the complexity of the conversion process, such as the connectives of the FOL expressions.

In general, there are four key architectural components that item difficulty prediction models have in common, which represent four fundamental tasks:

Observed difficulty measurement: where the ground-truth difficulty is measured using psychometric models or labeled by experts for later comparison with the predicted difficulty.

Pre-processing: where textual data is prepared for use by removing irrelevant words and producing well-defined pieces of text.

Feature extraction: this is used to transform text into machine-processable representations. Various NLP techniques are used in this step such as Bag-of-Words, Word2vec and TF-IDF.

Prediction Model: the specified machine learning algorithm is used to analyse the data.

4.2   RQ2: Domains and Item Types

With respect to the question: *What are the most investigated domains and item types?* we found that the majority of papers on data-driven difficulty prediction are domain specific (Fig. 4). Language learning is the most frequently investigated domain [3,14,21,33], followed by Computer Science [17,35] and Medicine [18,26,38]. This contrasted with other domains, such as Mathematics and Social Studies, which appeared in a minority of cases [20,23]. The popularity of the language learning and medical domains could be explained by the existence of several standardised test-organisations that offer international and national language proficiency tests (e.g. TOELF or IELTS), and medical licensing examinations which require a massive number of frequently updated items. Difficulty calibration is considered a fundamental process in these types of tests as it ensures fairness and comparability of high-stakes exams, which are used to inform important decisions regarding certification and employment.

Domain-independent (i.e. *generic*) studies accounted for almost 27% of the publications that we examined. The main rationale for investigating domain-independent studies is the possibility of producing difficulty prediction frameworks that are generalisable, and that could be applied to other domains.

The types of item formats investigated included Multiple Choice Questions (MCQs), true/false questions, gap-filling, and factual items in addition to other types (Fig. 5). MCQs represented the majority of item types studied; due to the ability to explore different sources of difficulty by analysing the relationship between item components such as item stem, distractor and correct responses.

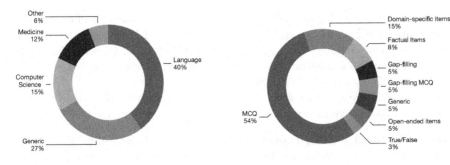

Fig. 4. Most investigated domains   **Fig. 5.** Most investigated item types

4.3   RQ3: Difficulty Features

The third question we investigated poses the question *What are the influential features that were found to affect difficulty?* Educational items are natural language phrases constructed by experts to assess a certain skill. When investigating the sources of difficulty in textual items, textual complexity plays an important role. The underlying theory is that more textually complex items require more advanced language proficiency skills in order to read, comprehend and correctly answer items. Therefore, linguistic features are considered the most obvious sources of difficulty when studying textual items. Recent studies on item difficulty prediction use NLP and text mining techniques to automatically extract syntactic and semantic features of items [4, 6, 7, 31, 40].

Linguistic features provide information regarding two levels of language: *syntactic* and *semantic*. The relationship between difficulty and linguistic variables have previously been extensively studied and focus mainly on syntactic features [9, 19, 35, 37]. More recently, researchers have started examining semantic-related factors by exploring semantic relevance and semantic similarity between item components (stem, distractor and correct answers) [20, 28, 38, 46].

Before discussing linguistic features in depth, it is worth mentioning a type of feature that was observed in four other studies [18, 22, 33, 37]. Psycholinguistic variables were examined to explore the affect of cognitive aspects of language on item difficulty. Such features are concerned with how words or sentences are constructed, processed and interpreted by the brain. For example, the Age of Acquistion (AOA) variable (which refers to the age at which a certain word is learned) was examined in two studies to evaluate its affect on difficulty. Other psycholinguistic features included word concreteness and word imageability.

Syntax-Based Features: Structure-level features refer to linguistic components that govern the textual structure of an item. This level of language typically incorporates syntactic, lexical and grammatical components. The main motivation behind analysing this type of feature is to determine the underlying characteristics which indicate the level of textual complexity and readability. Moreover, this source of difficulty is estimated by considering word- or sentence- level measures, achieved by counting words, sentences and syllables and examining the relationship between these textual components. Table 1 summarises the most common syntactic features. For example, [29] noted that the lexical frequency of the words was the best predictor of difficulty. Another study found that the part-of-speech (POS) count could accurately predict item difficulty [40]. Word count is the most common feature investigated; in many studies, it is referred to as *word frequency* or *word familiarity*, as both terms include counting the number of words to examine the frequency of the word or its familiarity. Word count can target special words types such as verbs, nouns, negation and named entities. Furthermore, some studies further examined the frequency of complex types of words which require advanced cognitive skills; for example, academic, complex and uncommon words. This is also the case for sentence-level analysis which utilises measures to count the number of sentences or special types of sentences (e.g. type of clause) to assess the complexity level of an item.

Table 1. Common syntax-based difficulty features

Syntactic difficulty feature	Studies
Word count	[2,3,5,6,9,10,12,18,33,37,40]
Frequency of complex words	[10,18,29,37]
Word length	[3–5,10,12,18,19,29,33]
POS count	[3,19,40]
Grammatical forms	[2,3,18,33,37]
Negation count	[10,18]
Verb variation	[3,10]
Sentence length	[3,4,18,19,21,33,38,43]
Sentence count	[5,10,18,33,37]
Type of clause	[10,18,33]

Another proxy of textual complexity is the word/sentence length [16,19]. It is believed that long words/sentences are more difficult to understand than shorter ones. Therefore, utilising measures to count the number of characters in a word or words in a sentence is very common in the literature. Separating content words from function words is the main purpose for using part of speech (POS) tagging measures. This distinction is necessary to identify content words which represent lexical meaning and function words that represent syntactic relations. Further analysis would incorporate POS counting to count the number of appearances of each POS tag (e.g. verbs, nouns and pronouns) in order to explore features like verb variation which increases text complexity.

Semantic-Based Features. The second type of features focus on the relationship between difficulty and semantic properties of an item or its components (see Table 2). Features that address this level of language were absent in many earlier studies. However, more recently there has been a recognition of the importance of deeper levels of analysis for examining sources of difficulty at the semantic level. *Semantic similarity* is the most investigated feature; both for considering the similarity between words or between item components. The latter includes the semantic relationship between item stem and distractors, distractors and correct responses, or between distractors. The intuition behind using such features is that highly semantically-related components increase the cognitive load on examinees when choosing the correct answer, resulting in an increase in difficulty level. For example, in gap filling items the semantic relatedness between the gap and its context is a significant factor which affects difficulty [4].

Table 2. Common semantic-based difficulty features

Semantic difficulty feature	Studies
Semantic similarity between words	[28]
Semantic similarity between options	[1, 20, 27]
Semantic similarity between item stem and options	[20, 38, 43]
Semantic similarity between context (i.e. learning material or passage) and item elements (stem, options and answer)	[3, 38, 49]

It is worth mentioning that recent publications have utilised ontology-based measures to measure semantic similarity between items' components [26, 27, 44–46]. Ontologies have been increasingly utilised because they provide means to describe semantic relations of domain knowledge in a formal, structured and machine-processable format. Therefore, several ontology-based metrics have been developed in the literature by considering the relationship between concepts, predicates and individuals in the ontology. For example, word popularity on a semantic level can be determined by counting the number of object properties which are linked to an individual from other individuals [46].

5   Conclusion

In this paper, we have provided a systematic literature review on data-driven item difficulty prediction, and presented a classification which distinguishes between cognitive and systematic approaches to item difficulty prediction. The review establishes the data-driven approaches as a recent trend, that has emerged to overcome limitation of previous methods. The majority of the reviewed papers were domain- and item-specific. Furthermore research also suggests that linguistic features play a major role in determining items' difficulty level.

The reviewed papers failed to identify specific data-driven approaches that are able to provide generic frameworks that can be applicable across multiple domains and item types. This would have served as a first step towards providing automatic, reliable and objective evaluation methods to automatically validate items with regard to difficulty. This is the objective of our future research.

References

1. Alsubait, T., Parsia, B., Sattler, U.: Generating multiple choice questions from ontologies: lessons learnt. In: Keet, C.M., Tamma, V.A.M. (eds.) Proceedings of 11th International Workshop on OWL: Experiences and Directions (OWLED 2014). CEUR Workshop Proceedings, vol. 1265, pp. 73–84 (2014)
2. Aryadoust, V.: Predicting item difficulty in a language test with an adaptive neuro fuzzy inference system. In: 2013 IEEE Workshop on Hybrid Intelligent Models and Applications (HIMA), pp. 43–50. IEEE (2013)
3. Beinborn, L., Zesch, T., Gurevych, I.: Predicting the difficulty of language proficiency tests. Trans. Assoc. Comput. Linguist. **2**, 517–530 (2014)
4. Beinborn, L., Zesch, T., Gurevych, I.: Candidate evaluation strategies for improved difficulty prediction of language tests. In: Proceedings of the Tenth Workshop on Innovative Use of NLP for Building Educational Applications, pp. 1–11 (2015)
5. Benedetto, L., Cappelli, A., Turrin, R., Cremonesi, P.: Introducing a framework to assess newly created questions with natural language processing. In: Bittencourt, I.I., Cukurova, M., Muldner, K., Luckin, R., Millán, E. (eds.) AIED 2020. LNCS (LNAI), vol. 12163, pp. 43–54. Springer, Cham (2020). https://doi.org/10.1007/978-3-030-52237-7_4
6. Benedetto, L., Cappelli, A., Turrin, R., Cremonesi, P.: R2de: a NLP approach to estimating IRT parameters of newly generated questions. In: Proceedings of the 10th International Conference on Learning Analytics & Knowledge, pp. 412–421 (2020b)
7. Bilotti, M.W., Ogilvie, P., Callan, J., Nyberg, E.: Structured retrieval for question answering. In: Proceedings of the 30th Annual International ACM SIGIR Conference on Research and Development in Information Retrieval, pp. 351–358 (2007)
8. Boldt, R.F.: GRE analytical reasoning item statistics prediction study. ETS Res. Rep. Series **1998**(2), 1–23 (1998)
9. Boldt, R.F., Freedle, R.: Using a neural net to predict item difficulty. ETS Res. Rep. Series **1996**(2), 1–19 (1996)
10. Choi, I.C., Moon, Y.: Predicting the difficulty of EFL tests based on corpus linguistic features and expert judgment. Lang. Assess. Q. **17**(1), 18–42 (2020)
11. Crisp, V., Grayson, R.: Modelling question difficulty in an a level physics examination. Res. Papers Educ. **28**(3), 346–372 (2013)
12. Fei, T., Heng, W.J., Toh, K.C., Qi, T.: Question classification for e-learning by artificial neural network. In: Fourth International Conference on Information, Communications and Signal Processing, 2003 and the Fourth Pacific Rim Conference on Multimedia. Proceedings of the 2003 Joint, vol. 3, pp. 1757–1761. IEEE (2003)
13. Franzen, M.: Item difficulty. Encycl. Clin. Neuropsychol. 100 (2011)
14. Gao, Y., Bing, L., Chen, W., Lyu, M.R., King, I.: Difficulty controllable generation of reading comprehension questions. arXiv preprint arXiv:1807.03586 (2018)
15. Grivokostopoulou, F., Hatzilygeroudis, I., Perikos, I.: Teaching assistance and automatic difficulty estimation in converting first order logic to clause form. Artif. Intell. Rev. **42**(3), 347–367 (2013). https://doi.org/10.1007/s10462-013-9417-8
16. Grivokostopoulou, F., Perikos, I., Hatzilygeroudis, I.: Estimating the difficulty of exercises on search algorithms using a neuro-fuzzy approach. In: 2015 IEEE 27th International Conference on Tools with Artificial Intelligence (ICTAI), pp. 866–872. IEEE (2015)
17. Grivokostopoulou, F., Perikos, I., Hatzilygeroudis, I.: Difficulty estimation of exercises on tree-based search algorithms using neuro-fuzzy and neuro-symbolic

approaches. In: Hatzilygeroudis, I., Palade, V., Prentzas, J. (eds.) Advances in Combining Intelligent Methods. ISRL, vol. 116, pp. 75–91. Springer, Cham (2017). https://doi.org/10.1007/978-3-319-46200-4_4

18. Ha, V., Baldwin, P., Mee, J., et al.: Predicting the difficulty of multiple choice questions in a high-stakes medical exam. In: Proceedings of the 14th Workshop on Innovative Use of NLP for Building Educational Applications, pp. 11–20 (2019)

19. Hoshino, A., Nakagawa, H.: Predicting the difficulty of multiple-choice close questions for computer-adaptive testing. Nat. Lang. Process. Appl. **46**, 279 (2010)

20. Hsu, F.Y., Lee, H.M., Chang, T.H., Sung, Y.T.: Automated estimation of item difficulty for multiple-choice tests: an application of word embedding techniques. Inf. Process. Manage. **54**(6), 969–984 (2018)

21. Huang, Z., et al.: Question difficulty prediction for reading problems in standard tests. In: AAAI, pp. 1352–1359 (2017)

22. Hutzler, D., David, E., Avigal, M., Azoulay, R.: Learning methods for rating the difficulty of reading comprehension questions. In: 2014 IEEE International Conference on Software Science, Technology and Engineering, pp. 54–62. IEEE (2014)

23. Khodeir, N.A., Elazhary, H., Wanas, N.: Generating story problems via controlled parameters in a web-based intelligent tutoring system. Int. J. Inf. Learn. Technol. **35**(3), 199–216 (2018)

24. Khoshdel, F., Baghaei, P., Bemani, M.: Investigating factors of difficulty in c-tests: a construct identification approach. Int. J. Lang. Test. **6**(2), 113–122 (2016)

25. Kitchenham, B.A., Charters, S.: Guidelines for performing systematic literature reviews in software engineering. Technical Report EBSE 2007–001, Keele University and Durham University Joint Report (07 2007)

26. Kurdi, G., et al.: A Comparative Study of Methods for a Priori Prediction of MCQ Difficulty. Semantic Web - Interoperability, Usability, Applicability (2020)

27. Lin, C., Liu, D., Pang, W., Apeh, E.: Automatically predicting quiz difficulty level using similarity measures. In: Proceedings of the 8th International Conference on Knowledge Capture, pp. 1–8 (2015)

28. Lin, L.H., Chang, T.H., Hsu, F.Y.: Automated prediction of item difficulty in reading comprehension using long short-term memory. In: 2019 International Conference on Asian Language Processing (IALP), pp. 132–135. IEEE (2019)

29. Loukina, A., Yoon, S.Y., Sakano, J., Wei, Y., Sheehan, K.: Textual complexity as a predictor of difficulty of listening items in language proficiency tests. In: Proceedings of COLING 2016, the 26th International Conference on Computational Linguistics: Technical Papers, pp. 3245–3253 (2016)

30. Mitra, N., Nagaraja, H., Ponnudurai, G., Judson, J.: The levels of difficulty and discrimination indices in type a multiple choice questions of pre-clinical semester 1 multidisciplinary summative tests. Int. e-J. Sci. Med. Educ. (IeJSME) **3**(1), 2–7 (2009)

31. Narayanan, S., Kommuri, V.S., Subramanian, N.S., Bijlani, K., Nair, N.C.: Unsupervised learning of question difficulty levels using assessment responses. In: Gervasi, O., et al. (eds.) ICCSA 2017. LNCS, vol. 10404, pp. 543–552. Springer, Cham (2017). https://doi.org/10.1007/978-3-319-62392-4_39

32. Ozuru, Y., Rowe, M., O'Reilly, T., McNamara, D.S.: Where's the difficulty in standardized reading tests: The passage or the question? Behav. Res. Methods **40**(4), 1001–1015 (2008)

33. Pandarova, I., Schmidt, T., Hartig, J., Boubekki, A., Jones, R.D., Brefeld, U.: Predicting the difficulty of exercise items for dynamic difficulty adaptation in adaptive language tutoring. Int. J. Artif. Intell. Educ. **29**(3), 342–367 (2019)

34. Parry, J.R.: Ensuring fairness in difficulty and content among parallel assessments generated from a test-item database. Online Submission (2020). https://doi.org/10.13140/RG.2.2.32537.03689
35. Perikos, I., Grivokostopoulou, F., Hatzilygeroudis, I., Kovas, K.: Difficulty estimator for converting natural language into first order logic. In: Intelligent Decision Technologies, pp. 135–144. Springer (2011). https://doi.org/10.1007/978-3-642-22194-1_14
36. Perikos, I., Grivokostopoulou, F., Kovas, K., Hatzilygeroudis, I.: Automatic estimation of exercises' difficulty levels in a tutoring system for teaching the conversion of natural language into first-order logic. Exp. Syst. **33**(6), 569–580 (2016)
37. Perkins, K., Gupta, L., Tammana, R.: Predicting item difficulty in a reading comprehension test with an artificial neural network. Lang. Test. **12**(1), 34–53 (1995)
38. Qiu, Z., Wu, X., Fan, W.: Question difficulty prediction for multiple choice problems in medical exams. In: Proceedings of the 28th ACM International Conference on Information and Knowledge Management, pp. 139–148 (2019)
39. Rust, J., Golombok, S.: Modern Psychometrics: The Science of Psychological Assessment. Routledge (2014)
40. Sano, M.: Automated capturing of psycho-linguistic features in reading assessment text. In: Annual Meeting of the National Council on Measurement in Education, Chicago, IL (2015)
41. Seyler, D., Yahya, M., Berberich, K.: Knowledge questions from knowledge graphs. In: Proceedings of the ACM SIGIR International Conference on Theory of Information Retrieval, pp. 11–18 (2017)
42. Stiller, J., et al.: Assessing scientific reasoning: a comprehensive evaluation of item features that affect item difficulty. Assess. Eval. High. Educ. **41**(5), 721–732 (2016)
43. Susanti, Y., Tokunaga, T., Nishikawa, H., Obari, H.: Controlling item difficulty for automatic vocabulary question generation. Res. Pract. Technol. Enhanced Learn. **12**(1), 1–16 (2017). https://doi.org/10.1186/s41039-017-0065-5
44. Vinu, E.V., Alsubait, T., Sreenivasa Kumar, P.: Modeling of item-difficulty for ontology-based MCQs. CoRR abs/1607.00869 (2016)
45. Vinu, E.V., Sreenivasa Kumar, P.: A novel approach to generate MCQs from domain ontology: considering DL semantics and open-world assumption. J. Web Semant. **34**, 40–54 (2015)
46. Vinu, E.V., Sreenivasa Kumar, P.: Automated generation of assessment tests from domain ontologies. Semant. Web **8**(6), 1023–1047 (2017)
47. Vinu, E.V., Sreenivasa Kumar, P.: Difficulty-level modeling of ontology-based factual questions. arXiv preprint arXiv:1709.00670 (2017)
48. Xue, K., Yaneva, V., Runyon, C., Baldwin, P.: Predicting the difficulty and response time of multiple choice questions using transfer learning. In: Proceedings of the Fifteenth Workshop on Innovative Use of NLP for Building Educational Applications, pp. 193–197 (2020)
49. Yeung, C.Y., Lee, J.S., Tsou, B.K.: Difficulty-aware distractor generation for gap-fill items. In: Proceedings of the The 17th Annual Workshop of the Australasian Language Technology Association, pp. 159–164 (2019)
50. Zhou, Y., Zhang, H., Huang, X., Yang, S., Babar, M.A., Tang, H.: Quality assessment of systematic reviews in software engineering: a tertiary study. In: Proceedings of the 19th International Conference on Evaluation and Assessment in Software Engineering, pp. 1–14 (2015)

Annotating Student Engagement Across Grades 1–12: Associations with Demographics and Expressivity

Nese Alyuz[1]([⊠]), Sinem Aslan[1], Sidney K. D'Mello[2], Lama Nachman[1], and Asli Arslan Esme[1]

[1] Intel Labs, Intel Corporation, Santa Clara, USA
{nese.alyuz.civitci,sinem.aslan,lama.nachman,
asli.arslan.esme}@intel.com
[2] University of Colorado Boulder, Boulder, USA
sidney.dmello@colorado.edu

Abstract. Digital learning technologies that aim to measure and sustain student engagement typically use supervised machine learning approaches for engagement detection, which requires reliable "ground-truth" engagement annotations. The present study examined associations between student demographics (age [grade], gender, and ethnicity) and the reliability of engagement annotations based on visual behaviors. We collected videos of diverse students ($N = 60$) from grades 1–12 who engaged in one-hour online learning sessions with grade-appropriate content. Each student's data was annotated by three trained coders for behavioral and emotional engagement. We found that inter-rater reliability (IRR) for behavioral engagement was higher for older students whereas IRRs for emotional engagement was higher for younger students. We also found that both rotational head movements and facial expressivity decreased with age, and critically, rotational head movements mediated the effects of grade on behavioral IRR; there was no mediation for emotional IRR. There were no effects of gender or ethnicity on IRR. We discuss the implications of our findings for annotating engagement in supervised learning models for diverse students and across grades.

Keywords: Student engagement · Inter-rater Reliability (IRR) · Demographics · Expressivity

1 Introduction

The relationship between engagement and learning can be summarized as: "a student who is engaged is primed to learn; a student who is disengaged is not" [1]. And although there are different perspectives on defining engagement [2–4], it is generally acknowledged that engagement is a multi-componential construct [2, 5], consisting of: (1) Behavioral engagement (learners' participation during the learning task - e.g., effort, persistence); (2) emotional engagement (learners' affective states during the learning task); (3) cognitive engagement (learners' cognitive investment in the learning task).

© Springer Nature Switzerland AG 2021
I. Roll et al. (Eds.): AIED 2021, LNAI 12748, pp. 42–51, 2021.
https://doi.org/10.1007/978-3-030-78292-4_4

Given the importance of engagement to learning and the ever-increasing use of technology in classrooms [6], there has been an increasing research on developing technologies to promote learner engagement over the last two decades [1]. Such efforts require reliable measurement of engagement, a challenging endeavor. In contrast to traditional measurement approaches (e.g., self-reports, experience sampling methods, observational methods, and academic and behavior records) [1], advanced technologies leverage machine learning for automated engagement monitoring [7–10]. Such models are typically trained using a supervised approach where student data are collected and annotated by trained human-expert coders to obtain ground-truth labels [11, 12]. Due to the subjective nature of engagement labelling [13], data annotation requires multiple coders to label the same data. This enables the use of inter-rater reliability as a metric to evaluate the "subjectivity" of engagement labeling. This metric also provides a constraint on model performance in that the models are as good as the labels used to train them. As reviewed below, whereas there has been an increased interest in population validity [14] – ensuring that the models yield equitable performance across different subgroups (demographics) – considerably less research has investigated the influence of demographics on the reliability of the ground-truth labels used to train the models. To address this gap, this paper focuses on understanding the reliability of engagement annotations across different demographics (i.e., age, gender, ethnicity).

1.1 Background and Related Work

There have been several studies investigating various machine learning methods to detect student engagement in technology-mediated learning environments (see [5] for a review). Despite of this ever-increasing interest, previous research has mostly focused on providing results for participant-level validity [5], ensuring that the same participant is not represented in both the training and test sets.

In the literature, a limited number of studies explored issues related to population validity (i.e., generalizability to new student populations) [14]. Most of these explorations have been around understanding cross-cultural differences: In [15], the researchers studied engagement with Cognitive Tutor across three Latin American countries and found out that there are differences in student engagement, collaboration, and needs across different cultures. In [16], the researchers developed machine learning models for detecting student carelessness in Cognitive Tutor and evaluated generalizability of these detectors between Philippine high school and US middle school and concluded that they were generalizable. As opposed to [16], researchers in [17] identified that the detectors developed for help-seeking behavior was not transferable across Costa Rica, the Philippines, and the US.

In addition to cross-cultural generalizability, there have been some studies focusing on generalizing over other demographic attributes. For example, in [14] automatic detectors were developed to infer learning-related affective states using log files when the students were using the mathematics ASSISTments system. In a case study, the researchers investigated inter-group differences among urban, suburban, and rural students to evaluate whether they could achieve population validity across these three groups. They concluded that population validity was difficult to accomplish in some cases. In addition to these relatively small-scale studies investigating generalizability, researchers [18] recently trained sensor-free affect detection models with the data from 69,174 students who used an online mathematics platform throughout a school year. Leveraging platform usage and demographics information (such as grade, gender, ethnicity, lunch status etc.), the researchers clustered the students to evaluate generalizability of the model across different clusters. They concluded that the improvement obtained with cluster-based models over the generic ones were limited, and the sensor-free models were generalizable.

1.2   Current Study and Research Questions

As evident from the literature review, the results on generalizability of engagement models are mixed. Furthermore, all studies focus on the accuracy of the trained models across subgroups, which makes it difficult to identify causes of a lack of generalizability. Taking a different approach, we focus on demographic influences on one of the core ingredients of the models – the reliability of the engagement annotations or ground truth labels used to train the underlying models.

Towards this end, we collected a gender-balanced multi-modal dataset, covering a widespan of age groups (grades 1 to 12) and varied ethnicities. Considering how an expert would assess engagement of a student in real-time and in an unobtrusive manner, we focused on the two components of engagement that are observable from visual features: (1) Behavioral engagement addresses student involvement in a learning task and was characterized as On-Task vs. Off-Task; and (2) emotional engagement, assessing student affect during the learning task as Satisfied [content], Bored, or Confused. We did not consider cognitive engagement (i.e., investment in the learning process) since it is more of an internal state (e.g., involving deep processing, focused attention) that is less well-defined perceptible visual correlates [5].

We focus on three demographics: ethnicity as the socio-cultural context impacting emotional development of children [19], students' age since expressive behaviors of emotions evolve over time as children mature [19], and students' gender since related research suggest that gender has an effect on how expressive behaviors are expressed or inhibited [20]. Our first research question pertained to associations between age, gender, and ethnicity and the inter-rater reliability (IRR) of coding behavioral and emotional engagement. For our second research question, we investigated the influence of students' behavioral expressions (rotational head movements and changes in facial expressions) on both IRR measures. We also investigated if behavioral expressions mediated the influence of demographics on the IRR measures.

2   Methods

2.1   Data Collection

We collected data from 60 diverse gender-balanced (50% female) students from different grade levels (grades 1–12) and ethnicities (30 Asian, 5 Indian, 25 Caucasian) in Canada (the ethnicities reflect the demographics of the region). Students (in groups of 6–8 individuals) attended learning sessions in a lab setting arranged by the research team. The lab had a large table around which laptops dedicated to individual students were positioned. There was a moderator who provided preliminary instructions to students on how to use the educational content platform and addressed any questions emerged during the sessions. The students individually engaged with online educational content customized for their grades using their assigned laptops. The online content was preselected by an educational researcher to match each grade level. It included instructional videos on Math topics (e.g., addition, subtraction, solving equations, fractions) and related assessment exercises on the platform. There was a total of nine learning sessions with 6–8 participants per session, and each session consisted of two 30-min blocks with a ten-minute break in between. In total, we collected 60 h of data, with a one-hour learning session per student. We collected audiovisual data of the student from the laptop's webcam and screen capture of the educational content (showing both the content and the student interactions). These were incorporated into a single video stream (synchronized and concatenated side-by-side) for engagement annotation.

2.2 Annotation Procedure and Computing Inter-rater Reliability

We employed six coders trained with Human-Expert Labeling Process (HELP) [12] to annotate the data for engagement. The trained coders were randomly divided into two groups of three, and the groups were assigned to label either behavioral or the emotional engagement. Coders could also provide a *Can't Decide* label if they could not decide on a specific behavioral/emotional label; and a *Not Available* label if the student was not present or the learning session had not started yet. Each coder was asked to label the entire dataset (either for behavioral or emotional labels, depending on the assigned group) using the students' videos, accompanying audio recordings, and the screen capture. The coders viewed the videos and identified *segments* based on observed state changes (e.g., student switching from being Confused to being Bored). This was done in lieu of using pre-defined segments with pre-defined durations, and each segment was defined by the start and end times of the identified state. Note that we only provided operational definitions of the engagement states and no additional prescriptive instructions (e.g., yawning means boredom) were given to avoid any bias.

After labeling was completed, we processed each set of segment-wise annotations with varied durations provided by multiple coders. First, *instances* of fixed length were defined using a sliding window of 8 s over an entire video with 50% overlaps (window length and overlap amount are adopted from [21]). Then, instance-wise labels for each video were assigned per coder, by checking the corresponding segment label provided by that coder. In case of different labels (i.e., multiple segments) intersecting the span of an instance, the overlaps between the segments and the instance were calculated and the label with the longer overlap was assigned as the instance-wise label for that coder. Converting segment-wise labels into corresponding instance-wise labels enabled us to obtain time-aligned sequences of labels (provided by multiple coders), which were necessary for inter-rater reliability calculations. In total, 188,967 instances (obtained from three coders for the entire 60 h of data) were considered in inter-rater reliability analysis, where reliability was computed per student and the overall measure was obtained by averaging over students. Due to the presence of highly imbalanced label distributions (as expected and subsequently confirmed), we utilized Gwet's First-Order Agreement

Coefficient (AC1) as the inter-rater reliability metric, considering its robustness with data imbalance [22].

2.3 Video Analytics

We processed each video using a facial behavior analysis tool called OpenFace [23]. We computed two metrics: (1) *Rotational head movement*, to measure how much the head rotates as an indicator of overall motion; and (2) *expressivity*, to measure how expressive the face is in an instance. For rotational head movement, we utilized frame-level rotational pose estimates for three axes provided by OpenFace, computed the standard deviation (across frames of an entire video) for each axis, and then obtained the average standard deviation across the three axes. For expressivity, we utilized the frame-level classification outputs for facial action units (AUs; e.g., brow lowerer), where the output is 1 if the face is classified as having a specific AU, and 0 otherwise. For each frame, we first computed a frame-wise expressivity value by averaging the classification outputs over all AUs (18 in total) per frame and then computing the average over all frames of the entire video as a general measure of expressivity.

3   Results and Discussion

3.1   Descriptives

The distribution of student demographics (i.e., grade, gender, ethnicity) is shown in Fig. 1. The distributions of post-processed engagement annotations collected from multiple coders (i.e., instance-wise labels pooled over multiple coders) are given in Fig. 2. We found that students were perceived largely as On-Task (90.6% of the time they were present) and mostly content (71.5% satisfied) and sometimes bored (16.7%); confusion was relatively infrequent (4.5%). We did not compare differences in engagement labels across demographics due to differences in content across grades and because it is not germane to our main research question on inter-rater reliability.

3.2   Inter-rater Reliability (IRR) Measures

The inter-rater reliability measures for different grade levels and ethnicities are shown in Fig. 3. IRRs for Behavioral engagement ($M = .95, SD = .07$) was significantly larger (paired-samples $t(59) = 14.9, p < .001$) than the IRR for Emotional engagement ($M = .60, SD = .16$). Importantly, behavioral and emotional IRR scores were not correlated ($r = -.09, p = .45$).

We regressed behavioral and emotional IRR measures on grade (continuous variable), gender (categorical with female as reference group), and Ethnicity (with Asian as the reference group). We found (See Table 1) that grade was significantly associated with higher IRR for behavioral engagement, but lower IRR for emotional engagement. There were no gender or ethnicity effects.

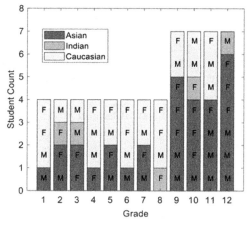

Fig. 1. Distribution of students across different grades, ethnicities, and genders (gender: F: Female, M: Male).

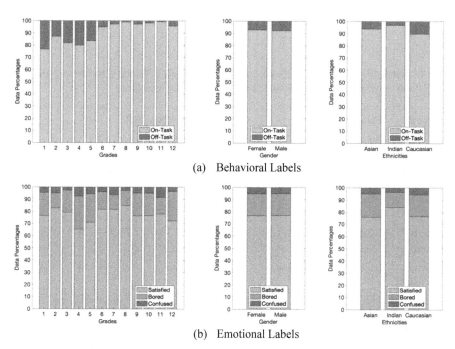

(a) Behavioral Labels

(b) Emotional Labels

Fig. 2. Distribution of all instance-wise labels pooled over multiple coders considering different grades (left), gender (middle), and ethnicities (right) for (a) behavioral and (b) emotional engagement states.

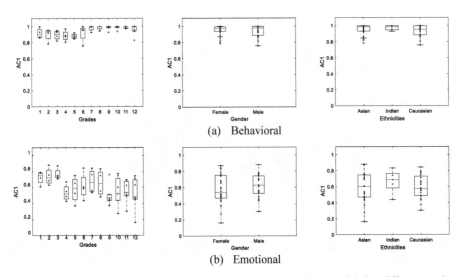

(a) Behavioral

(b) Emotional

Fig. 3. Inter-rater reliability measures (AC1) among multiple coders considering different grades (left), gender (middle), and ethnicities (right) for (a) behavioral and (b) emotional engagement states.

Table 1. Standardized coefficients (beta), confidence intervals (CI), and significance values (p) for the linear regression model predicting inter-rater reliability measures.

Predictors	Behavioral IRR			Emotional IRR		
	Beta	95% CI	p	Beta	95% CI	p
(Intercept)	0.05	−0.32–0.42	**<0.001**	−0.11	−0.52–0.29	**<0.001**
Grade	0.57	0.34–0.79	**<0.001**	−0.45	−0.70−−0.20	**0.001**
Gender [Male]	−0.13	−0.56–0.31	0.565	0.31	−0.16–0.79	0.195
Ethnicity [Indian]	0.48	−0.33–1.29	0.241	0.36	−0.53–1.25	0.416
Ethnicity [Caucasian]	−0.07	−0.54–0.40	0.762	−0.18	−0.70–0.34	0.491

3.3 Video Analytics

Regression analyses indicated that grade-level was significantly negatively associated with rotational head movement and expressivity and there were no gender or ethnicity effects (see Table 2).

We hypothesized that the higher IRRs for behavioral engagement achieved for older students might be due to the lower rotational head movements for these students. To test this hypothesis, we conducted a causal mediation analysis (with 1000 bootstrapped samples) testing whether rotational head movement mediated the relationship between grade and behavioral IRR. The results are summarized in Fig. 4. We found that grade

Table 2. Standardized coefficients (beta), confidence intervals (CI), and significance values (p) for the linear regression models for rotational head movement and expressivity measures.

Predictors	Rotational head movement			Expressivity		
	Beta	95% CI	p	Beta	95% CI	p
(Intercept)	0.17	−0.17–0.51	**<0.001**	0.02	−0.40–0.44	**<0.001**
Grade	−0.66	−0.86–−0.45	**<0.001**	−0.39	−0.65–0.13	**0.004**
Gender [Male]	−0.26	−0.66–0.14	0.199	0.24	−0.26–0.73	0.346
Ethnicity [Indian]	−0.29	−1.03–0.46	0.442	−0.41	−1.33–0.52	0.481
Ethnicity [Caucasian]	−0.03	−0.47–0.40	0.884	−0.24	−0.78–0.30	0.375

negatively predicted rotational head movement ($\beta_1 = -0.66$, p < 0.001), which in turn, negatively predicted behavioral IRR ($\beta_2 = -0.67$, p < 0.001). The bootstrapped unstandardized indirect effect ($\beta_1 \times \beta_2 = 0.008$ with a 95% confidence interval of 0.004 to 0.010) was significant (p < .001), thereby confirming our hypothesis. For emotional engagement IRR, we hypothesized that the lower IRR for higher grade students could be due to lower expressivity among these students. However, expressivity was not a significant (p = 0.200) mediator of the relationship between grade and emotional IRR.

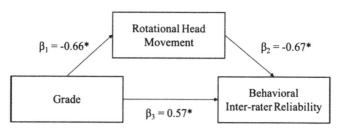

Fig. 4. Standardized regression coefficients for the relationship between grade and Behavioral inter-rater reliability as mediated by the rotational head movement.

4   General Discussion

We explored associations between demographics (i.e., grade, gender, ethnicity) and inter-rater reliability (IRR) of assessments of behavioral and emotional engagement by trained coders. We found that behavioral IRRs increased with age, but emotional IRRs decreased with age. We also found that younger students were more active and expressive than their older counterparts, which partly explained grade-level differences in behavioral IRRs. Neither gender nor ethnicity predicted IRRs.

Like all studies, ours has limitations. Although other demographics information (i.e., gender, ethnicity) did not predict IRR, our analysis was limited to a dataset of 60 students. Moreover, although the students had different ethnic origin, they were residents of the same country. Therefore, there is a need to replicate our findings with larger and more diverse datasets. For such a large-scale study, qualitative methods should be additionally considered to obtain a deeper understanding of the coders' perspectives on assessing engagement, as well as for identifying demographic factors related to expressions of engagement. We also focused on a 1:1 math learning in a lab setting. The research should be expanded to take into account different learning contexts (e.g., different topics, educational games, group work) and in more authentic learning environments (e.g., students' homes).

Our findings suggest that age has a critical role for engagement measurement. One major implication is that age should be considered when developing engagement detection models. We hypothesize that models adapted for different target groups (e.g., different age cohorts) could automatically focus on group-specific behavioral patterns, which will in turn improve model accuracies. We expect this improvement to be apparent for models considering the visual modality based on the significant association between grade and behavioral patterns (i.e., rotational head movement). Further research needs to be conducted to evaluate the impact of age on accuracies of engagement models and to validate the potential improvement of age-informed models.

Acknowledgements. Sidney D'Mello was supported by the Institute of Education Sciences (IES R305C160004), Intel research, and the National Science Foundation (NSF DRL 2019805). The opinions expressed are those of the authors and do not represent views of the funding agencies.

References

1. D'Mello, S.K.: Improving Student Engagement in and with Digital Learning Technologies (in press)
2. Fredricks, J.A., Blumenfeld, P.C., Paris, A.H.: School engagement: potential of the concept, state of the evidence. Rev. Educ. Res. **74**(1), 59–109 (2004)
3. Reeve, J., Tseng, C.-M.: Agency as a fourth aspect of students' engagement during learning activities. Contemp. Educ. Psychol. **36**(4), 257–267 (2011)
4. Pekrun, R., Linnenbrink-Garcia, L.: Academic emotions and student engagement. In: Christenson, S., Reschly, A., Wylie, C. (eds.) Handbook of Research on Student Engagement, pp. 259–282. Springer, New York (2012). https://doi.org/10.1007/978-1-4614-2018-7_12
5. D'Mello, S., Dieterle, E., Duckworth, A.: Advanced, analytic, automated (AAA) measurement of engagement during learning. Educ. Psychol. **52**(2), 104–123 (2017)
6. Madden, M., Lenhart, A., Duggan, M., Cortesi, S., Gasser, U.: Teens and technology (2005)
7. Pardos, Z.A., Baker, R.S., San Pedro, M.O., Gowda, S.M., Gowda, S.M.: Affective states and state tests: investigating how affect throughout the school year predicts end of year learning outcomes. In: Proceedings of the Third International Conference on Learning Analytics and Knowledge, pp. 117–124 (2013)
8. Bosch, N., et al.: Automatic detection of learning-centered affective states in the wild. In: Proceedings of the 20th International Conference on Intelligent User Interfaces, pp. 379–388 (2015)

9. Chen, Y., Bosch, N., D'Mello, S.: Video-Based Affect Detection in Noninteractive Learning Environments. International Educational Data Mining Society (2015)

10. Salmeron-Majadas, S., et al.: Filtering of spontaneous and low intensity emotions in educational contexts. In: Conati, C., Heffernan, N., Mitrovic, A., Verdejo, M. (eds.) AIED 2015. LNCS (LNAI), vol. 9112, pp. 429–438. Springer, Cham (2015). https://doi.org/10.1007/978-3-319-19773-9_43

11. Ocumpaugh, J.: Baker Rodrigo Ocumpaugh monitoring protocol (BROMP) 2.0 technical and training manual. Technical Report. New York, NY: Teachers College, Columbia University. Manila, Philippines: Ateneo Laboratory for the Learning Sciences (2015)

12. Aslan, S., et al.: Human expert labeling process (HELP): towards a reliable higher-order user state labeling process and tool to assess student engagement. Educ. Technol. **57**, 53–59 (2017)

13. Siegert, I., Böck, R., Wendemuth, A.: Inter-rater reliability for emotion annotation in human–computer interaction: comparison and methodological improvements. J. Multimodal User Interf. **8**(1), 17–28 (2013). https://doi.org/10.1007/s12193-013-0129-9

14. Ocumpaugh, J., Baker, R., Gowda, S., Heffernan, N., Heffernan, C.: Population validity for educational data mining models: a case study in affect detection. Br. J. Educ. Technol. **45**(3), 487–501 (2014)

15. Ogan, A., et al.: Collaboration in cognitive tutor use in Latin America: field study and design recommendations. In: Proceedings of the SIGCHI Conference on Human Factors in Computing Systems, pp. 1381–1390 (2012)

16. San Pedro, M.O.C.Z., Baker, R., Rodrigo, M.M.T.: Detecting carelessness through contextual estimation of slip probabilities among students using an intelligent tutor for mathematics. In: Biswas, G., Bull, S., Kay, J., Mitrovic, A. (eds.) AIED 2011. LNCS (LNAI), vol. 6738, pp. 304–311. Springer, Heidelberg (2011). https://doi.org/10.1007/978-3-642-21869-9_40

17. Soriano, J.C.A., et al.: A cross-cultural comparison of effective help-seeking behavior among students using an ITS for math. In: Cerri, S.A., Clancey, W.J., Papadourakis, G., Panourgia, K. (eds.) ITS 2012. LNCS, vol. 7315, pp. 636–637. Springer, Heidelberg (2012). https://doi.org/10.1007/978-3-642-30950-2_98

18. Jensen, E., Hutt, S., D'Mello, S.K.: Generalizability of Sensor-Free Affect Detection Models in a Longitudinal Dataset of Tens of Thousands of Students. International Educational Data Mining Society (2019)

19. Saarni, C.: Emotional competence and effective negotiation: the integration of emotion understanding, regulation, and communication. In: Aquilar, F., Galluccio, M. (eds.) Psychological and Political Strategies for Peace Negotiation, pp. 55–74. Springer, New York (2011). https://doi.org/10.1007/978-1-4419-7430-3_4

20. Brody, L.R.: Gender differences in emotional development: a review of theories and research. J. Pers. **53**(2), 102–149 (1985)

21. Aslan, S., et al.: Investigating the impact of a real-time, multimodal student engagement analytics technology in authentic classrooms. In: Proceedings of the 2019 CHI Conference on Human Factors in Computing Systems, pp. 1–12 (2019)

22. Gwet, K.L.: Handbook of Inter-Rater Reliability: The Definitive Guide to Measuring the Extent of Agreement Among Raters. Advanced Analytics, LLC (2014)

23. Baltrusaitis, T., Zadeh, A., Lim, Y.C., Morency, L.P.: Openface 2.0: facial behavior analysis toolkit. In: 2018 13th IEEE International Conference on Automatic Face & Gesture Recognition (FG 2018), pp. 59–66 (2018)

Affect-Targeted Interviews for Understanding Student Frustration

Ryan S. Baker[1]([⊠]), Nidhi Nasiar[1], Jaclyn L. Ocumpaugh[1], Stephen Hutt[1],
Juliana M. A. L. Andres[1], Stefan Slater[1], Matthew Schofield[1], Allison Moore[2],
Luc Paquette[3], Anabil Munshi[2], and Gautam Biswas[2]

[1] Graduate School of Education, University of Pennsylvania, Philadelphia, USA
rybaker@upenn.edu
[2] Vanderbilt University, Nashville, USA
[3] University of Illinois at Urbana-Champaign, Champaign, USA

Abstract. Frustration is a natural part of learning in AIED systems but remains relatively poorly understood. In particular, it remains unclear how students' perceptions about the learning activity drive their experience of frustration and their subsequent choices during learning. In this paper, we adopt a mixed-methods approach, using automated detectors of affect to signal classroom researchers to interview a specific student at a specific time. We hand-code the interviews using grounded theory, then distill particularly common associations between interview codes and affective patterns. We find common patterns involving student perceptions of difficulty, system helpfulness, and strategic behavior, and study them in greater depth. We find, for instance, that the experience of difficulty produces shifts from engaged concentration to frustration that lead students to adopt a variety of problem-solving strategies. We conclude with thoughts on both how this can influence the future design of AIED systems, and the broader potential uses of data mining-driven interviews in AIED research and development.

Keywords: Frustration · Mixed methods · Affect detection · Attitudes · Self-regulated learning

1 Introduction

Frustration is a natural part of learning, both in the context of AIED systems and more broadly, and yet it remains relatively poorly understood. Some articles have argued that frustration is a negative part of the learning experience, and should be eliminated [1, 2]. Other accounts have argued that frustration is necessary for an appropriate feeling of challenge and retention of knowledge over time (e.g. [3]). Indeed, the relationship between frustration and learning is unclear, with studies finding both negative associations [4, 5], and positive associations [6]. One study's results suggest that it is frustration's duration that matters for learning, not its overall rate of occurrence [7]. Theoretical accounts even disagree about whether frustration is properly understood as a single, discrete affective state, with arguments that there are multiple types of frustration -- some even pleasurable

© Springer Nature Switzerland AG 2021
I. Roll et al. (Eds.): AIED 2021, LNAI 12748, pp. 52–63, 2021.
https://doi.org/10.1007/978-3-030-78292-4_5

[8] -- or that frustration can be meaningfully split into whether it is germane or extraneous to the learning task [9]. By contrast, other researchers have argued that confusion and frustration interact with learning in many of the same ways [7]. Hence, it is fair to say that the field of AIED -- and educational psychology more broadly -- is confused about frustration. Many of us even appear to be frustrated about frustration.

In particular, it is poorly understood how frustration interacts with the broader ongoing experience of participating in an AIED learning activity. We know that frustration precedes disengagement and tends to be relieved by disengaged behavior [10]. We know that frustration precedes help-seeking or on-task conversation with other students and can be relieved by those behaviors [11]. We know that frustration varies by learning activity [5] but what we do not know looms large. Researchers have argued that frustration is associated with the experience of difficulty [12, 13], but can we better understand how? How does frustration interact with a student's shifting perspective on whether a learning system is interesting or helpful (cf. [14])? And finally, there is some evidence that frustration is tied to self-regulated learning processes and learning strategy [15], but it is not yet fully clear how.

Although the majority of the past studies on frustration in AIED systems are quantitative, some of the attempts to more deeply understand frustration have leveraged qualitative or even introspective methods [8]. However, it has thus far been challenging to study frustration qualitatively, as out-of-context retrospective descriptions of a frustration experience may no longer have full access to the context or phenomenological experience that accompanies frustration (see review of the memory limitations surrounding retrospective interviews in Huber and Power [16]). Indeed, meta-analyses suggest that naturalistic frustration during learning is not always a particularly frequent or lengthy experience, D'Mello's [17] meta-analysis finds that frustration is rarer than any other commonly-studied affective state except surprise, and other research has shown that a typical occurrence of frustration lasts an average of 8–40 s [18, 19]. Thus, a randomly-timed set of interviews would not be expected to capture a particularly large proportion of frustration experiences. Spontaneous self-report in time diaries [20] can capture the context surrounding a specific experience of frustration, but have limited scope for follow-up questions and rely heavily on participant initiative. Artificially-induced frustration [21] may differ from genuine frustration in key fashions – for instance, the stimuli used to create frustration within this methodology may not be representative of the contexts where frustration naturally emerges.

To better study frustration, we adopt a novel mixed-methods approach, using affect detection to drive qualitative research. In this approach, a suite of automated affect detectors is integrated into a learning system. When an event of interest occurs – in this case, a transition from a different affective state to frustration, or a student experiencing sustained frustration over a significant period of time – a message is sent to a qualitative researcher present in the classroom, who can conduct an immediate, timely interview. This approach to mixed methods differs from the most common uses of mixed methods in education, which typically involve using both qualitative and more traditional quantitative methods (such as survey instruments or tests) to triangulate a research question, qualitative methods to explain quantitative findings, or using qualitative analysis to identify behaviors for further quantitative study (e.g. [22]). Instead, we use a quantitative method – automated detection of affect – in support of a qualitative method – field interviews. As such, this method can increase the time-efficiency and cost-efficiency of using qualitative methods to study relatively rare events.

2   Methods

2.1   Betty's Brain

Betty's Brain is an open-ended, computer-based learning system that uses a learning-by-teaching paradigm to teach complex scientific processes [23]. Betty's Brain asks students to teach a virtual agent (Betty) about scientific phenomena (e.g., climate change, ecosystems, thermoregulation) by constructing concept maps that demonstrate the causal relationships involved (see Fig. 1)

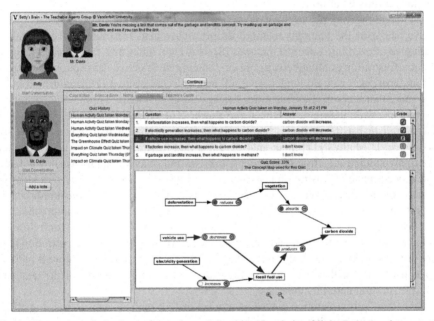

Fig. 1. Screenshot of viewing quiz results and checking the chain of links Betty used to answer a quiz question

The learning process required by Betty's Brain necessitates high levels of self-regulation. As students construct their map, they must navigate through multiple hyper-media information sources where they can read about a variety of subthemes. They choose how often to test Betty's knowledge, and they may elect to interact with a virtual mentor agent (an experienced teacher named Mr. Davis) if they are having trouble teaching Betty. Because of these design factors, strong self-regulated learning behaviors are crucial for succeeding within Betty's Brain.

These pedagogical agents (Betty and Mr. Davis) provide a social framework for the gradual internalization of effective learning behaviors, and an emphasis on self-regulatory feedback that has been demonstrated to improve these behaviors among students who use Betty's Brain [23]. Prior research [24] has explored the relationships between students' cognitive and affective experiences in Betty's Brain and emphasized how automated affect detector models can be beneficial for providing students with personalized guidance that respond to their affective-cognitive states during learning.

2.2 Study Design

This study uses data from 93 sixth graders who used Betty's Brain during the 2016–2017 school year during their science classes in an urban public school in Tennessee. Data were collected over the course of seven school days. Students and their parents completed a consent form prior to the study. On the first day of the study, students completed a 30–45-min paper-based pre-test that measured knowledge of scientific concepts and causal relationships. On day 2, students participated in a 30-min training session that familiarized them with the learning goals and user interface of the software. Following the pre-test and training, students used the Betty's Brain software on days 2 through 6, for approximately 45–50 min each session, using concept maps to teach Betty about the causal relationships involved in the process of climate change. On day 7, students completed a post-test that was identical to the pre-test, in order to assess changes in knowledge based on working with Betty's Brain for the week.

As students interacted with Betty's Brain, automatic detectors of educationally relevant affective states [25] and behavioral sequences [24], already embedded in the software, identified key moments in the students' learning processes, either from specific affective patterns or theoretically aligned behavioral sequences. This detection was then used to prompt student interviews. The affect detection used logistic regression or step regression to recognize affect from behavior patterns, and was normed using classroom observations [25].

Interviewers were signaled through a field research app, Quick Red Fox (QRF), which integrates with Betty's Brain events and allows users to record metadata related to each event (in this case, timestamps and which student was being interviewed). A prioritization algorithm was used to select which student should be interviewed in instances where multiple students displayed interesting patterns at roughly the same time. In addition to prioritizing rarer affective sequences (e.g., sustained frustration), prioritization was also given to students who had not yet been interviewed (or who had not been recently interviewed). If interviewers were not comfortable interrupting a student, for any reason, they could skip the prompt within the app, and receive another recommendation from QRF.

Interviewers attempted to take a helpful but non-authoritative role when speaking with students. Interviews were open ended and occurred without a set script; however, they often asked students what their strategies were (if any) for getting through the system. As new patterns and information emerged in these open-ended interviews, questions designed to elicit information about intrinsic interest (e.g., "What kinds of books do you like to read and why?" or "What do you want to be when you grow up?") were added.

Overall, however, students were encouraged to provide feedback about their experience with the software and talk about their choices as they used the software.

2.3 Interview Coding

A total of 358 interviews were conducted and recorded during this study. Audio files were collated and stored on a secure file management system available only to the research team members. Three members of the research team manually transcribed the interviews, having agreed upon formatting and style. Metadata, including timestamps and recording IDs, were preserved, but student-level information was de-identified (i.e., each student was assigned an alphanumeric identifier, used across data streams).

The code development process followed the recursive, iterative process used in [26] that includes seven stages: conceptualization of codes, generation of codes, refinement of the first coding system, generation of the first codebook, continued revision and feedback, coding implementation, and continued revision of the codes [26]. The conceptualization of codes included a review of related literature to capture meaningful experiences relevant to the study's research questions. Using grounded theory [27], a method that is appropriate for the kind of open-ended interviews where students are being asked to interpret their own experiences, we worked with the lead interviewer (the 3rd author) to identify categories that were (1) relevant to both affective theory (i.e. [28]) and self-regulated learning theory (e.g. [29]) and (2) likely to saliently emerge in the interviews. A draft lexicon and multiple criteria were generated for a coding system to help identify these constructs.

This coding scheme was iteratively refined, allowing us to identify relevant subcategories as they emerged from initial analyses, until the entire research team had reached a shared understanding of the criteria and constructs being examined. Following the production of a coding manual, external coders simultaneously coded with the 5th author to reach acceptable inter-rater reliability before coding all of the transcripts. All codes had Cohen's kappa > 0.6, and the average Cohen's kappa across codes was 0.80 -- see Table 1 for details. Throughout the coding, external coders met and clarified any concerns with the codebook authors to avoid misinterpretation or miscoding of the data. A total of 12 interview codes were developed from the interview data; however, we prioritized first coding for experiences involving difficulty (Diff), resource helpfulness (Help), interestingness (Int), and strategic use of resources (Strat) based on the perceived frequency of these experiences and their relevance to the affective experience of frustration. As these qualitative codes are not mutually exclusive, a single interview may be coded under multiple categories.

2.4 Affect Sequence Calculation

Once the interview data from Betty's Brain was fully labeled, we calculated each affective pattern's prevalence within each student's log files, looking not just at which patterns triggered a specific interview but all patterns present in the 80 s (four affective transitions) immediately before the interview. For each twenty-second period, we labeled it with the most likely (highest probability) affective state. Prior to comparing detector outputs to determine which affective state was most likely, the offset of each detector was mathematically adjusted so that the distribution of the predicted affective states matched the proportions of each affective state within the data originally used to develop the detectors. This step was taken to control for biases potentially introduced through the practice of re-sampling rarer classes, used in the original detector development [25].

Table 1. The coding scheme used for the interviews.

Code	N	Description, Example
Difficult (Diff)	165	Negative evaluations, confusion, or frustration while interacting with the platform. Ex. "I am reading the science book again but I don't get it." $\kappa = .911$
Helpfulness (Help)	51	Utility of within-game resources in learning, improvement, and positive evaluations of the resources. Ex. "I like how you put in the dictionary all the things that could help you with the – this, 'cause I have no idea." $\kappa = .643$
Interestingness (Int)	11	Interestingness of within-game resources in learning and a continued desire to use the platform. Ex. "Everything I do [in Betty's Brain] interests me, you get one question right or everything right." $\kappa = .726$
Strategic Use (Strat)	205	Indicates a plan for interacting with the platform, notes changes in strategy or interaction with the platform based on experiences. Ex. " I'm just doing one section at a time…one section at a time that I tell Betty to take a test on it…and then I do it in the next section to see if she gets a 100 or if she gets one question wrong I go back and see." $\kappa = .911$

In our analyses, we focus on three types of affect patterns that have been previously examined in [30]. Each involved a sequence of either three or four 20-s log-file clips. First, we looked at sequences that mirror the two cycles outlined by D'Mello and Graesser [28] the ENG-CON-DEL-ENG cycle (a student goes from engaged, to confused, to delighted, to engaged again) and the ENG-CON-FRU-BOR cycle (going from engaged, to confusion, to frustration, and boredom). For the purposes of this study, we have limited the analysis to 80 s (four-clip) versions of these cycles.

Next, we considered transitions between two states. For these analyses, we looked for a student having at least two consecutive clips with the same affective state predictions before transitioning to a second state (e.g., ENG-ENG-BOR or CON-CON-FRU). These durations allow us to explore the potential effect that a longer duration (two or more steps) of any given antecedent might have on the subsequent steps in a sequence. Thus, we are able to explore the possibility that affective states of a longer duration (more than one successive step) might be influencing the results seen for sequences involving multiple transitions without testing all possible durations.

Finally, we consider sustained instances of two affective states that seemed to be driving the other patterns of statistical significance in this study. These are operationalized as 4-clip sequences (BOR-BOR-BOR-BOR and DEL-DEL-DEL-DEL), which we compare to sustained off-task behavior (OFF-OFF-OFF-OFF).

2.5 Identifying and Studying Relationships

Calculating the relationships between affect sequences and interview codes would ideally involve statistical significance testing but doing so is infeasible for two reasons. First, the number of affect sequences and interview codes being studied is sufficiently large that studying their combination would require a much larger data set than is feasible for interview data, for even a very liberal false discovery rate post-hoc control. This could be controlled for by selecting a much smaller number of affective sequences in advance. However, doing so would miss the opportunity to explore the space of affective sequences, a still incompletely-understood area. A second limitation, even stronger, is that many of the interview codes and affective sequences are rare within the data set, requiring even more data to be able to capture the relationships between them.

Instead, we look for the largest magnitudes of relationship, looking at the relative differences in frequency of an affective sequence when an interview code is present or absent. This provides a set of potentially interesting relationships to investigate in further detail. Having found the largest-magnitude relationships, we examine the transcripts of the interviews to understand the relationships better, presented below. Pseudonyms were assigned to participants using http://random-name-generator.info/ which generates names based on the frequencies within all U.S. census data, ignoring local community or subgroup variation, and ignoring the actual gender or age of the student.

3 Results

The top five strongest associations between affective sequences and specific interview codes were [helpful, sustained FRU], [helpful, BOR-- > FRU], [difficult, ENG-- > FRU], [interesting, BOR-- > ENG], [strategic, ENG-- > FRU]. Table 2 shows the magnitude of the relationships between these affective sequences and interview codes. In examining the interviews in detail, we were able to better understand many of these relationships.

Strategic: ENG- > FRU and *Difficulty: ENG- > FRU.*

Many of the same interviews that immediately followed ENG-FRU affect transitions involved reports of both difficulty and strategic behavior.

Several students seemed to transition from engaged to frustrated when they experienced difficulty and did not understand the system's feedback. For example, Gretchen said, "I change one thing and then I go back to the clues on those things and then I'm yeah. My head hurts... He keeps giving me zeros even though I on yesterday I got a percent when I know this there... I don't even know what correct is."

Gretchen responded to her frustration by trying different approaches, such as taking notes -- "I know it's very good to take his clues... Sometimes I had trouble with sea ice so I would go to sea ice now change and thing that was put in the ice and then you see

Table 2. The five strongest associations between affective sequences and interview codes

Interview code	Affective sequence	Pct Code when affect	Pct Code when~affect	Pct affect when code	Pct affect when~code	Relative Diff (by Code)
Helpful	SusFRU	66.7%	13.4%	4.5%	0.4%	12.4x
Helpful	BOR-> FRU	50.0%	13.7%	2.3%	0.4%	6.2x
Difficult	ENG-> FRU	83.3%	44.8%	3.5%	0.6%	6.0x
Interesting	BOR-> ENG	12.5%	2.3%	12.5%	2.3%	5.5x
Strategic	ENG-> FRU	83.3%	53.9%	2.9%	0.7%	4.2x

that's not the thing and then you would have to come in for what he's...So whatever I do like I go back to...", to which the interviewer responded "Yeah that's that's one way to keep a note."

Willard adopted a different strategy: "So I'm focusing on one subject and taking a quiz. Sometimes I think I'm not going...", to which the interviewer responded "But now you've got that. Yeah but things that want to test it. OK. So, you'll work from this quiz." and Willard responded, "Yeah it's [inaudible], so whatever he doesn't you know that's wrong."

Another student, Shawn, also adopted a different strategy. Shawn expressed his frustration -- "I keep getting them wrong and I don't really know what I'm doing [inaudible] trying to learn a bit more about it" -- but adopted a strategic response to the situation: "I've been trying to fix my links."

Helpful: Sustained FRU

Two of the three cases where sustained frustration occurred had student reports of the system being helpful. These students experienced sustained frustration, but then experienced breakthroughs -- even eureka moments -- after that sustained frustration. The system's features were helpful, but the students' own strategies also played a role.

In one example, Jason tells the interviewer "I haven't done too well but it helped me know a lot of things I have wrong and I still have a few areas to [inaudible]. I think I'm making progress...".

Jason expresses his frustration -- matching the detector assessment -- "I feel like I kind of skimmed a little on the science book. And reading it again and it's like wait, I don't remember reading that and then I add it to the concept map... We have like I have something that like connects something that's not supposed to even though overall it should do that. Then it's like messing me up... I suspect I'm still missing something, and I need to add something on."

But later, Jason explains the strategy he is using, and how it helps the system help him: "I was having trouble finding what was wrong so then I tried to make more specific quizzes and... it's helped me understand more. Because I'm pretty sure I fixed this." When prompted, by the interviewer, "Yeah? Are you using them more frequently now or?" Jason responds, "Yes."

Helpful: BOR- > FRU

Looking at this relationship shows the limitation of this method. In this case, the fairly large difference in relative magnitude came down to the very limited number of cases of BOR- > FRU, only 2, one of which coincided with helpful. The resulting interview demonstrates boredom, frustration, and helpfulness, but it appears they may coincide due to the interviewer's choice of questions rather than a genuine interrelationship.

Early in the interview, Shirley indicates frustration: "Because when I do shortcuts I get it wrong when I'm pretty sure it was right so I'm trying to fix this shortcut..." -- later she discusses her lack of interest in the topic -- in response to the interviewer's question "Is it the sort of thing that you like to do generally?" the student responds "After school I usually read... I like to read fanfiction... Anime. A lot of anime."

She discusses with the interviewer when Mr. Davis is helpful within the system, in response to a specific question on what is helpful. First, the interviewer asks, "So tutorial this morning help?", to which the student responds "Yeah." Then the interviewer asks "Yeah okay, is there anything else you figured out the last day or so help?", and Shirley responds "I figured out that with my quiz result, if I get something wrong I let [Mr. Davis] try to figure out why I got it." -- but these questions and responses are not connected to the immediate context of the interview.

4 Discussion and Conclusions

In this paper, we have used a novel multi-method approach to better understand the student perceptions surrounding the experience of frustration while learning from Betty's Brain. In this approach, automated detectors were used to identify affective transitions involving frustration (and sustained frustration) while using Betty's Brain, in real-time, and then field researchers conducted in-the-moment interviews with students experiencing those affective patterns. The interviews were coded for experiences of difficulty, perceptions of helpfulness, perceptions of interestingness, and use of strategic behaviors. We then distilled the top five sequences of affect that were most associated with a difference in the frequency of specific interview codes and analyzed cases where these affective sequences and interview codes co-occurred.

Through this analysis process, we found patterns that provided insights on the "why" and "what next" of frustration. Students who went from experiencing engaged concentration to frustration often reported both experiencing difficulty and using strategic behavior to resolve it. It may be possible to leverage this pattern, a productive response to experiencing difficulty, to better support students. These findings suggest that if a student goes from engaged to frustrated when encountering difficulty, but does not adopt a strategic behavior (which can be automatically detected as well [24, 31]), it may be appropriate for the learning system to offer recommendations of learning strategies. However, the best strategy may vary from case to case. Gretchen, Willard, and Shawn all adopted different learning strategies in response to the combination of frustration and difficulty. Jason's experience shows that the right system support can help resolve frustration -- even sustained frustration. Therefore, a learning system such as Betty's Brain may be able to use an approach such as reinforcement learning [32] to identify which strategy to recommend to which student, using the qualitative findings presented here to drive the design of learning strategy supports.

At the same time, Shirley's example -- where an affective state and interview code coincided due to the interviewer's choice of questions rather than a more useful overlap -- shows that there are still limitations to our method to be worked out. Another limitation is seen in our method's speed. Our method successfully focused interviewer time on key events of interest and facilitated the collection of interviews involving relatively rare events. However, the coding required afterwards was time-intensive, and is still ongoing for additional interview codes. It may be possible to improve the method -- to address both these limitations – by following interviews with an immediate end-of-day round of interview data coding, while the interview experience is still fresh in the field researchers' minds. This would also support the possibility of using this method not just for research, but for fast-paced iterative design.

Our next steps, therefore, are to use these findings to refine Betty's Brain. In that work, we will study the potential of Quick Red Fox -- with some procedural adjustments -- to enhance our process for rapid iterative design. At the same time, we will continue to study the rich data set we have obtained for further insights on student affect and perceptions. Overall, we believe these results demonstrate the potential of integrating data mining and qualitative research in new ways, facilitating the process of better understanding learners and improving learning experiences.

References

1. Grawemeyer, B., Wollenschlaeger, A., Santos, S.G., Holmes, W., Mavrikis, M., Poulovassilis, A.: Using Graph-based Modelling to explore changes in students' affective states during exploratory learning tasks. In: Proceedings of the International Conference on Educational Data Mining, pp. 382–383 (2017)
2. DeFalco, J.A., et al.: Detecting and addressing frustration in a serious game for military training. Int. J. Artif. Intell. Educ. **28**(2), 152–193 (2018)
3. Sottilare, R., Goldberg, B.: Designing adaptive computer-based tutoring systems to accelerate learning and facilitate retention. Cogn. Technol. **17**(1), 19–33 (2012)
4. Forbes-Riley, K., Rotaru, M., Litman, D.: The relative impact of student affect on performance models in a spoken dialogue tutoring system. User Model. User-Adap. Inter. **18**, 11–43 (2007)
5. D'Mello, S.K., Lehman, B., Person, N.: Monitoring affect states during effortful problem solving activities. Int. J. Artif. Intell. Educ. **20**(4), 361–389 (2010)
6. Pardos, Z.A., Baker, R.S., San Pedro, M.O.C.Z., Gowda, S.M., Gowda, S.M.: Affective states and state tests: investigating how affect and engagement during the school year predict end of year learning outcomes. J. Learn. Anal. **1**(1), 107–128 (2014)
7. Liu, Z., Pataranutaporn, V., Ocumpaugh, J., Baker, R.: Sequences of frustration and confusion, and learning. In: Proceedings of the International Conference on Educational Data Mining (2013)
8. Gee, J.P.: Good video games+ good learning: Collected essays on video games, learning, and literacy. Peter Lang Pub Incorporated, Bern, Switzerland (2007)
9. Richey, J.E., et al.: More confusion and frustration, better learning: the impact of erroneous examples. Comput. Educ. **139**, 173–190 (2019)
10. Sabourin, J., Rowe, J.P., Mott, B.W., Lester, J.C.: When off-task is on-task: the affective role of off-task behavior in narrative-centered learning environments. In: Biswas, G., Bull, S., Kay, J., Mitrovic, A. (eds.) AIED 2011. LNCS (LNAI), vol. 6738, pp. 534–536. Springer, Heidelberg (2011). https://doi.org/10.1007/978-3-642-21869-9_93

11. Baker, R.S., Moore, G.R., Wagner, A.Z., Kalka, J., Salvi, A., Karabinos, M., Yaron, D.: The dynamics between student affect and behavior occurring outside of educational software. In: Proceedings of the International Conference on Affective Computing and Intelligent Interaction, pp. 14–24 (2011)
12. Valitutti, A.: Action decomposition and frustration regulation in the assisted execution of difficult tasks. In: Proceedings of the AIED 2009 Workshops, Brighton, UK (2009)
13. Miller, M.K., Mandryk, R.L.: Differentiating in-game frustration from at-game frustration using touch pressure. In: Proceedings of the 2016 ACM International Conference on Interactive Surfaces and Spaces, pp. 225–234 (2016)
14. McCuaig, J., Pearlstein, M., Judd, A.: Detecting learner frustration: towards mainstream use cases. In: Aleven, V., Kay, J., Mostow, J. (eds.) ITS 2010. LNCS, vol. 6095, pp. 21–30. Springer, Heidelberg (2010). https://doi.org/10.1007/978-3-642-13437-1_3
15. Buono, S., Zdravkovic, A., Lazic, M., Woodruff, E.: The effect of emotions on self-regulated-learning (SRL) and story comprehension in emerging readers. Front. Educ. **5**, 218 (2020)
16. Huber, G.P., Power, D.J.: Retrospective reports of strategic-level managers: guidelines for increasing their accuracy. Strateg. Manag. J. **6**(2), 171–180 (1985)
17. D'Mello, S.: A selective meta-analysis on the relative incidence of discrete affective states during learning with technology. J. Educ. Psychol. **105**(4), 1082 (2013)
18. D'Mello, S., Graesser, A.: The half-life of cognitive-affective states during complex learning. Cogn. Emot. **25**(7), 1299–1308 (2011)
19. Botelho, A.F., Baker, R., Ocumpaugh, J., Heffernan, N.: Studying affect dynamics and chronometry using sensor-free detectors. In: Proceedings of the 11th International Conference on Educational Data Mining, pp. 157–166 (2018)
20. Lazar, J., Bessiere, K., Ceaparu, I., Robinson, J., Shneiderman, B.: Help! I'm lost: user frustration in web navigation. IT Soc. **1**(3), 18–26 (2003)
21. Taylor, B., Dey, A., Siewiorek, D., Smailagic, A.: Using physiological sensors to detect levels of user frustration induced by system delays. In: Proceedings of the 2015 ACM International Joint Conference on Pervasive and Ubiquitous Computing, pp. 517–528 (2015)
22. Canossa, A., Drachen, A., Sørensen, J.R.M.: Arrrgghh!!! blending quantitative and qualitative methods to detect player frustration. In: Proceedings of the 6th International Conference on Foundations of Digital Games, pp. 61–68 (2011)
23. Leelawong, K., Biswas, G.: Designing learning by teaching agents: the Betty's Brain system. Int. J. Artif. Intell. Educ. **18**(3), 181–208 (2008)
24. Munshi, A., Rajendran, R., Ocumpaugh, J., Biswas, G., Baker, R., Paquette, L.: Modeling learners' cognitive and affective states to scaffold SRL in open-ended learning environments. In: Proceedings of the 25th Conference on User Modeling, Adaptation, and Personalization, pp. 131–138 (2018)
25. Jiang, Y., et al.: Expert feature-engineering vs. deep neural networks: which is better for sensor-free affect detection? In: Proceedings of the International Conference on Artificial Intelligence in Education, pp. 198–211. Springer, Cham (2018)
26. Weston, C., Gandell, T., Beauchamp, J., McAlpine, L., Wiseman, C., Beauchamp, C.: Analyzing interview data: the development and evolution of a coding system. Qual. Sociol. **24**(3), 381–400 (2001)
27. Charmaz, K.: The grounded theory method: an explication and interpretation. Contemp. Field Res. 109–126 (1983)
28. D'Mello, S., Graesser, A.: Dynamics of affective states during complex learning. Learn. Instr. **22**(2), 145–157 (2012)
29. Winne, P.H., Hadwin, A.F.: Studying as self-regulated engagement in learning. In: Hacker, D., Dunlosky, J.,Hillsdale, G.A. (eds.) Metacognition in Educational Theory and Practice, Erlbaum, pp. 277–3048 (1998)

30. Andres, J.M.A.L., et al.: Affect sequences and learning in Betty's Brain. In: Proceedings of the 9th International Learning Analytics and Knowledge Conference, pp. 383–390 (2019)
31. Azevedo, R., Gašević, D.: Analyzing multimodal multichannel data about self-regulated learning with advanced learning technologies: issues and challenges. Comput. Hum. Behav. **96**, 207–210 (2019)
32. Chi, M., VanLehn, K., Litman, D., Jordan, P.: Empirically evaluating the application of reinforcement learning to the induction of effective and adaptive pedagogical strategies. User Model. User-Adap. Inter. **21**(1), 137–180 (2011)

Explainable Recommendations in a Personalized Programming Practice System

Jordan Barria-Pineda[1][(⊠)] , Kamil Akhuseyinoglu[1] , Stefan Želem-Ćelap[2] ,
Peter Brusilovsky[1] , Aleksandra Klasnja Milicevic[2] ,
and Mirjana Ivanovic[2]

[1] University of Pittsburgh, Pittsburgh, PA, USA
jab464@pitt.edu
[2] University of Novi Sad, Novi Sad, Serbia

Abstract. This paper contributes to the research on explainable educational recommendations by investigating explainable recommendations in the context of personalized practice system for introductory Java programming. We present the design of two types of explanations to justify recommendation of next learning activity to practice. The value of these explainable recommendations was assessed in a semester-long classroom study. The paper analyses the observed impact of explainable recommendations on various aspects of student behavior and performance.

Keywords: Educational recommender systems · Explanations

1 Introduction

The popularity of recommender systems in everyday-life activities encouraged researchers from several areas to explore the applications of recommender technologies to education [8,20]. Over the years, this stream of research gradually expanded to cover a variety of recommendation types from recommending a discussion thread, to suggesting the next problem to solve, to recommending courses to take [7]. It can be observed, however, that a recent major trend in the field of recommender systems – explainable recommendations – is currently underrepresented in educational recommender systems. Our work attempts to bridge this gap by exploring explainable recommendations specifically adapted to an educational context, where the main reason to recommend content is the learner's knowledge state, rather than taste or interests. We present a design of knowledge-based recommendations augmented with visual and verbal explanations. These technologies were integrated into an online personalized practice system and explored a semester-long study in a classroom context. The study examined how students use recommendations and explanations and assessed the impact of these technologies on various aspects of the educational process.

© Springer Nature Switzerland AG 2021
I. Roll et al. (Eds.): AIED 2021, LNAI 12748, pp. 64–76, 2021.
https://doi.org/10.1007/978-3-030-78292-4_6

2   Related Work

Over the last decade, explainable recommendations emerged as a major trend in the area of recommender systems [15]. Tintarev and Masthoff [19] define explanations as *"item descriptions that help the user to understand the qualities of the item well enough to decide whether it is relevant to them or not"*. Research has shown that presenting explanations to users can increase the persuasiveness of the recommended items as well as users' trust and satisfaction with the recommender system [10,14]. While being popular in domains where recommendations are based on interests and taste such as movies or songs [15], explainable recommendations remain understudied in the online learning domain.

One of the challenges of transferring explanation approaches accumulated in the area of traditional recommender systems [10,15] to the area of educational recommendations is the different nature of these recommendations, which are typically based on the learner's knowledge state rather than user interests or taste. Given this, explanations of educational recommendations have to be designed afresh rather than re-used from the taste-based domains. At the same time, the "knowledge-based" nature of educational recommendations offers a new opportunity. *Learner models* that are used for generating educational recommendations carry a much higher explanation potential than *user profiles* applied by traditional recommender systems [9]. While user profiles are notoriously hard for users to understand or control [2], the long history of AI-Ed research on *open learner models* (OLM) demonstrates that learner models could serve as a means to understand and control the behavior of adaptive educational systems [4,5]. Moreover, OLMs have shown their effectiveness in facilitating navigation and supporting metacognitive processes of planning, monitoring, and reflection [5].

We believe that the large body of OLM research offers an excellent starting ground for the design of explainable educational recommendations. Moreover, as argued by [6,17] insights learned from OLM research can be used for a broader goal to improve interpretability in AI-driven educational systems. Yet to complete the task, a layer of visual or verbal explanations should be built on the top of OLM to produce explainable recommendations. The work in this direction is at the very beginning and we could cite only a few motivating cases. Putnam and Conati [16] investigated the value of having explanations for automatically generated hints in an Intelligent Tutoring System (ITS). Barria-Pineda et al. [3] and Abdi et al. [1] were the first to explore the effects of using an OLM as the basis of justifying learning content recommendations. Most recently Zhou et al.[21] found that explaining the decisions of an ITS to students could improve the student-system interaction in terms of their engagement and autonomy.

3   Java Personalized Programming Practice System

To explore the value of explainable recommendations in online learning, we implemented content recommendations for Java Personalized Programming Practice System (JP^3). JP^3 is an online personalized system offering students in introductory Java programming courses to practice their skills using several types of interactive learning content. The system is designed as a non-mandatory practice and self-assessment tool that each student could use for individual needs. In this section, we present the design of content recommendations in JP³ and the mechanism for generating recommendations, and their explanations.

3.1 Explainable Recommendations in JP³

JP³ provides access to three types of Java learning content: worked examples, challenges - faded examples where students have to complete missing parts of the code [12], and short coding problems [22]. The learning content in JP³ is grouped into topics (e.g., variables, if-else, etc.) that follow the chronological order of the course. To start practicing, the student has to select one of the topics as the current goal. After opening a topic, the student can see the list of available practice content for this topic along with *personalized guidance* for choosing the most appropriate activity (Fig. 1). The personalized guidance is based on a concept-level overlay model of student's Java knowledge. The model is built by observing student behavior in the system and represents the probability of students knowing each Java concept. To make this learner model "open" to

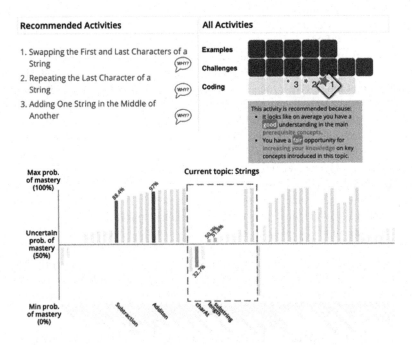

Fig. 1. Visualization for *Strings* topic in JP³ with recommended content shown as a list (left) and with stars. The learner mouses over the top recommendation and JP³ (1) highlights in the OLM the estimated knowledge of concepts linked to this item (see bar chart) and (2) shows a verbal explanation (see yellow box). (Color figure online)

the student, it is visualized as a bar chart on the bottom part of the activity selection interface. Each bar depicts one concept. The height and the color of the bar indicate the estimated mastery of this concept: the higher and the greener is the bar, the higher is the mastery estimation; whilst the lower (below the origin) and the redder is the bar, the lowest is the estimated mastery. Concepts are arranged along the x-axis following the order of topics where they are introduced. Concepts introduced in the current topic are emphasized by a dashed rectangle.

The personalized guidance is offered by recommendations and explanations. Recommendations suggest the three most relevant learning activities in the topic given the current state of the learner model. Recommendations are provided as a ranked list on the left and also in navigation support form as stars of different sizes placed over the recommended activities. As explained in the next section, the recommendation approach favors activities that combine sufficient levels of prerequisite knowledge (concepts to be learned in earlier topics) with a good opportunity to master target knowledge (concepts introduced in the topic).

Explanations are offered in visual and verbal form. Following Tintarev and Masthoff's guidelines for explanations of recommendations [18], explanations attempt to increase the *transparency* of the recommendation process. Given the nature of JP^3 recommendations, both types of explanations focus on highlighting the balance between prerequisite and target knowledge associated with an activity. **Visual explanations** are provided when student mouses over an activity cell by highlighting names and bars of concepts that can be practiced through this activity. The visualization stresses whether the student has sufficient prerequisite knowledge to attempt the activity and how much this activity could improve the target knowledge. As we see in Fig. 1, the top recommended problem (large star) pointed by the mouse involves five concepts. Two prerequisite concepts (*addition* and *subtraction*) to be learned in the earlier topics are already mastered making the student ready to attempt the problem. At the same time, three target concepts (*substring*, *charAt*, *length*) are not yet well-learned making the problem a good opportunity to improve this knowledge.

Verbal explanations attempt to convey the same idea of readiness and relevance through natural language (yellow box on the right of Fig. 1). A typical explanation was composed of two sentences where the first explains the system's assessment of the prerequisite knowledge for the examined activity while the second assesses its learning opportunity. To stress how positive is each part of the assessment, the focus keyword of each part (e.g., good, fair) is marked by the green color of different intensity. The darker the green is, the more positive is the assessment. Our original intention was to make verbal explanations accessible along with visual explanations on mouse-over, however, we were concerned that it will make it hard to examine the usage of each type separately. To support our study needs, we implemented two ways to access verbal explanations: *explanations on mouse-over* (*expOnMouseover*) where verbal explanations were presented along with visual by mousing-over the recommended activity in the grid and *explanations on-click* (*expOnClick*) where verbal explanations were accessed by clicking on *why* icon next to the recommended activity in the list.

3.2   The Implementation of Explainable Recommendations

Knowledge Modeling: JP^3 uses an ontology of Java concepts as the core for its knowledge representation. Each learning content item in JP^3 is linked to the ontology concepts automatically using a concept parser [13]. A Bayesian Network [11] is used to maintain a probabilistic overlay student model for these concepts. The network was initially trained with data collected through JP^3 in earlier classroom studies. The knowledge estimates are seeded based on students' performance in the pretest. Every time a student attempted a challenge or a problem while practicing with JP^3, the system updated the probability estimates related to the concepts linked to that activity. Simply, the probability estimates increase when the student's answer was correct and decreased otherwise.

Recommendation Approach: JP^3 content recommendation algorithm maximizes the balance between the opportunity to improve knowledge of target concepts and the necessity of sufficient knowledge on prerequisite concepts that are needed to solve the activity correctly. A concept associated with an activity is labeled as a prerequisite if it is expected to be mastered in the chronologically earlier topics and as a target if it is the topic where the concept is first introduced. The recommendation algorithm uses the concept-level knowledge estimates taken from the student model and generates content recommendations according to the following rules: (1) only non-completed activities are recommended; (2) examples have recommendation priority when they introduce a new concept that has not been practiced before; (3) for challenges and problems, a recommendation score is calculated using the Eq. 1,

$$\text{rec score}_{ij} = \frac{1}{NW} \left(\sum_p w_p * \theta_{pj} + \sum_t w_t * (1 - \theta_{tj}) \right) \tag{1}$$

where p represents the prerequisite concepts and t represents the target concepts associated with activity i. θ_{pj} and θ_{tj} are the knowledge estimates of student j for both types of concepts. w denotes the topic-level importance of the concepts (either p or t) calculated by the *tf-idf* approach (i.e., the more unique a concept in a topic, the higher its importance) and W is the sum of the weights for the associated concepts (both prerequisite and target ones). Finally, N denotes the total number of concepts associated with activity i. Learning activities are sorted based on these scores and top-3 items are recommended to the learner.

Verbal Explanations: To generate verbal explanations for recommendations, we calculate the average proficiency for both the top three prerequisite and target concepts ($\bar{\theta}_p$ and $\bar{\theta}_t$). Based on these proficiency estimations, we generate short paragraphs for each part of the verbal explanations. Table 1 presents samples of verbal explanations for several thresholds. The thresholds and wording were selected to offer a qualitative explanation of numerical values and were not used to drive the recommendation process. A recommended example was justified by stating that *"it presents concept(s) that are new to you (e.g. concept_name)"*.

Table 1. Rules for generating explanations for educational recommendations

Verbal explanation template for prerequisite concepts	$\theta_p \geq .6$	$\theta_p \geq .75$	$\theta_p \geq .95$
It looks like on average, you have a ... understanding in the main prerequisite concepts.	good	proficient	excellent
Verbal explanation template for target concepts	$\theta_t \leq .6$	$\theta_t \leq .4$	$\theta_t \leq .2$
You have a ... opportunity for increasing your knowledge on key concepts introduced in this topic.	fair	good	excellent

4 Study

To assess the impact of explainable educational recommendations, we performed a semester-long classroom study. The study was conducted with 86 undergraduate students taking a Java Programming course at a European university. After taking an online pretest designed to assess their prior knowledge, each student was given access to the JP^3. The use of JP^3 was non-mandatory, so there was no penalty to those who did not use the system. In contrast, to encourage JP^3 use, 10% extra credit was added to their final course grade if they viewed at least 80% examples, solved at least 70% of challenges, and 60% of coding problems. At the end of the term, an online post-test (isomorphic to the pretest) was taken. Pretest scores show that a high proportion of students had an medium level of proficiency in Java, given that the median grade in the pretest was 5 out of 10.

Students were randomly assigned to one of two explanatory treatments described in Sect. 3.1: *expOnMouseover* ($n = 45$) or *expOnClick* ($n = 41$). Student actions in JP^3 were logged. The logs included content openings, problem solving attempts, mouse-overs (with duration) on recommended and non-recommended activities, and access to verbal explanations on-click. As the summary of activities shows (Table 2), on average, students opened and attempted a large fraction of available learning activities.

Table 2. Summary of students' activity in JP^3 (Mean(SD))

	Number of mouse-overs	Mouse-overs' duration (sec)	Explanations' clicks	Activities opened	Activities attempted	Activities solved
Coding (n=46)	37.3(27.3)	1.42(.31)	2.98(2.19)	19.5(13.3)	13.7(10.3)	8.1(7.7)
Challenges (n=76)	53.5(37.1)	1.34(.36)	3.18(1.98)	33.2(12.7)	30(11.9)	28.4(11.4)
Examples (n=55)	39.3(30.1)	1.36(.31)	4.86(3.05)	25.4(11.1)	22.3(8.7)	20.5(8.12)

4.1 Value of Recommendations

To assess the impact of recommendations on engagement, we contrasted student engagement with recommended and non-recommended activities on two levels:

(1) attempting the learning activity once it is opened (*conversion rate*) and (2) keep working on the activity after the first attempt until solving it correctly (*persistence rate*). To reliably assess the impact of recommendations, we considered (1) topics with more than 6 activities and (2) students' actions until more than 3 activities left to be completed in a topic to eliminate cases where students had *no other choice* than to select a recommended item.

We fit a series of mixed-linear models to predict conversion and persistence rates by using the pretest score, the type of learning activity (recommended or non-recommended) and the interaction (*int*) between these two variables as independent variables. We add student ids as a random effect. In this and following analyses we use common notation to report significance levels of variables within models: $p < .05 \rightarrow *$, $p < .01 \rightarrow **$, $p < .001 \rightarrow ***$. We found a significant model for the conversion rate in coding problems ($p < .001$), which revealed that the probability of attempting a problem once it is opened depends on the starting knowledge of the student measured by the pre-test ($\beta_{int} = -.025*$). We also found significant main effects ($\beta_{pretest} = .04***, \beta_{rec} = .13*$). More exactly, low-pretest learners exhibited significantly higher conversion rates on recommended items while high-pretest students demonstrated higher chances of attempting non-recommended ones. On one hand, it indicates that students with lower domain knowledge relied considerably on system recommendations when selecting content to practice. On the other hand, it hints that JP^3 underestimated the knowledge of high-pretest students since a considerable proportion of their Java learning happened before the course and was not accurately modeled. No significant model was found for conversion on challenges and examples. Conversion rates were uniformly very high for all students indicating that they were less picky when selecting low-effort activities.

We found similar results when checking the impact of recommendations on the *success rate* of attempted coding problems (i.e., where conversion was reported). We fit the same model as used for conversion rates, but including success rate as the dependent variable ($p < .05$). We found a significant interaction between pretest and the presence of recommendation ($\beta = -.016*$) . We also found significant main effects ($\beta_{pretest} = .018*, \beta_{rec} = .13**$). The data shows that learners with lower pretest exhibited much higher success rates when working on recommended coding problems while for students with high pretest scores there was almost no difference. A similar model for challenges ($p < .001$) failed to reveal an impact of recommendations. The only factor that affected the success rate of students was the pretest ($\beta = .03***$) – high-pretest students exhibited higher success rates with challenges.

For *persistence rate*, only pretest acted as a significant predictor ($\beta = 0.08**$) for the model ($p < .001$) – the higher the pretest, the more persistent students are in coding problems, regardless if they were recommended or not. No significant model was found for explaining persistence on challenges and examples.

4.2   Value of Explanations

The first step of assessing the value of explanations is to examine whether they were used or not. As Table 2 shows, on-click explanations were requested for about 16% of attempted activities, which is a considerable usage. To assess whether students were "processing" mouse-over explanations for recommended content as well, we contrasted the duration of mouse-overs on recommended and non-recommended activities. For this analysis, we excluded "short" mouse-overs (<1 s), which were likely generated "on passing" and provided too little time to pay attention to either visual or verbal explanations. We found that students took on average more time on mousing over recommended items than non-recommended ones, which suggests that they paid attention to explanations of recommended activities ($p < .001$). Moreover, we found that this difference was lower for $expOnClick$ who can only check visual explanations on mouse-over ($M_{diff} = .051$) and higher for $expOnMouseover$ ($M_{diff} = .181$), who receive both explanation types on mouse-over. A greater additional time spent by $expOnMouseover$ students ($p = .033$) hints that they paid attention to both verbal and visual explanations.

Next, we checked whether inspection of explanations (measured as the mean duration of mouse-overs on learning content) was associated with adoption of either recommended or non-recommended activities. We fit two multiple regression models: (a) $predictors$: pretest score and mouse-overs' duration on recommended items, $outcome$: percentage of the total items accessed by the learner which were recommended ones; and (b) $predictors$: pretest score and mouse-overs' duration on non-recommended items, $outcome$: percentage of the total items accessed by the learner which were non-recommended ones. For (a), we found that both pretest score ($\beta = -2.01^*$) and mean mouse-over duration on recommended activities ($\beta = 31.8^*$) were significant predictors of commitment with these type of items ($F(2, 58) = 10.93$, $adj.R^2 = .25$, $p < .001$). Similarly, for (b) we found that pretest score ($\beta = 2.09^*$) and average mouse-over duration on non-recommended activities ($\beta = -37.19^*$) were correlated with the adoption of non-recommended content for practicing ($F(2, 58) = 6.78$, $adj.R^2 = .16$, $p = .002$). The data shows that the ability to examine explanations of recommended problems increases student's motivation to attempt these problems. On the other hand, the ability to inspect explanations of non-recommended problems decreases learner's chances to attempt those items. These results also reiterate that low-pretest students chose to work more on recommended content, in contrast to high-pretest students who decided to perform a self-guided exploration of the content instead. We did not find any influence of mouse-over duration on challenges or examples.

To assess if the difference in how to access explanations in the $expOnClick$ group influenced students' engagement with the learning activities, we analyzed if the number of clicks performed by a learner correlated with students' engagement in working on JP[3]. We divided students into low and high "explanation requesters", according to the median of explanations' clicks (considering the three types of learning content). We found that these two different groups significantly differ on the number of attempts on coding problems ($p < .01$), where high explanation requesters exhibited a much higher average number of attempts on coding problems ($Med = 33$) than low explanation requesters ($Med = 20$).

4.3 Students' Work in JP³ and Course Performance

To assess the educational value of practicing with JP^3, we examined the correlation between the work of students within JP^3 and their performance in the course throughout the term. In this study, we had access to two classroom test scores that evaluated students' performance (*Test1* in the first half and *Test2* in the second half of the course), and the post-test scores that were not graded. To prepare data, we counted the number of successful and failed attempts on learning activities and calculated the average success rate per week. To account for the regularity of practice performance, we calculated the skewness of the distribution of weekly success/failure attempts. We repeated the same calculations for the number of sessions in JP^3 per week. Skewness can tell us if the work/performance of students was concentrated at the start (positive skewness) or the end (negative skewness) of the course. In our multiple regression models, we added pretest scores to control for the prior knowledge. We performed a step-wise feature selection process for each prediction model. While we considered these metrics for all the types of learning content, only performance on coding problems added predictive power to the models, while variables related to work on challenges and examples did not. It is consistent with the fact that, given the incentives for getting extra-credit and the lower efforts associated with completing challenges and examples, all learners achieved a uniformly high completion level at the end of the term.

We first predicted scores in *Test1* and found a significant overall model ($F(3, 42) = 6.328$, $adj.R^2 = .26$, $p < .001$) where average success rate was the only significant predictor ($\beta = .44^{***}$). Second, we fitted a model to predict *Test2* scores and results indicated a significant model ($F(3, 41) = 5.616$, $adj.R^2 = .24$, $p = .003$) with only pretest-score as a significant predictor ($\beta = .44$) among other predictors. Finally, we predicted post-test scores ($F(3, 52) = 8.018$, $adj.R^2 = .28$, $p < .001$) and found that pretest scores ($\beta = .36^*$), skewness of incorrect coding attempts ($\beta = -.58^*$) and average success rate ($\beta = .2^*$) were significant predictors of post-test scores.

5 Summary and Discussion

In this paper, we presented the design of an online programming practice system JP^3 augmented with explainable recommendations of learning content to practice. The recommendations were generated by optimizing the balance between the current level of prerequisite knowledge and the opportunity of practicing new concepts. As input, the explainable educational recommender module uses the state of student knowledge of Java concepts estimated by a student model based on the observable student performance. Explanations were generated in two different forms (see Fig. 1): (1) visual explanation through a concept-level OLM which showed the estimations of the learner's knowledge on the concepts associated with each learning item (2) verbal explanation describing the balance between prerequisites and potential for new knowledge acquisition (only for recommended content). We also presented a semester-long study where JP³ was used as a learning support tool for an intermediate programming class. Our goal was to investigate how recommendations and explanations affect different aspects of student work with the learning content in a free practice mode.

Our data showed that students invested their time to access and inspect the explanations of the recommendations. The average time spent on mousing over activities was significantly higher for recommended activities than for non-recommended ones. Moreover, students in the *expOnMouseover* group exhibited longer mouse-overs on recommended items than *expOnClick* learners, since the first group was able to observe both visual and verbal explanations when mousing over recommended activities and needed more time to process it.

By examining the effect of recommendations on student behavior, we observed that recommendations affected student selection and engagement with high-effort (coding problems) and low-effort activities (challenges and examples) differently. While for low-effort activities, learners' behavior was not influenced significantly by the recommendations, the *conversion* for coding problems (making at least one attempt on an opened problem) was significantly and positively influenced by the presence of a recommendation. This effect seems to be mediated by the students' prior knowledge. As we observed, low-pretest students, exhibited a higher level of trust in the recommendations and the willingness to work with recommended problems. Moreover, we found that students with lower prior knowledge achieved a higher success rate on solving recommended coding problems than on non-recommended ones. These results indicate a better match of recommended problems to student knowledge. In contrast, students with a higher level of starting knowledge exhibited higher conversion rates on non-recommended problems. This situation might be explained by the fact that the learner model was initialized using results of a relatively small 10-problem pretest that underestimated the knowledge of students with a high level of proficiency in Java. Given the transparent OLM, these students might have noticed that the recommendations were generated using an incomplete model and preferred to select the content to practice themselves. In this sense, the explanations still achieved their goal to help students in selecting the right content to practice, in this case, revealing that recommended content is not adequate and helping them to make their own choice with OLM-based visualization.

On top of the effect of recommendations, we also observed that inspection of the explanations affected student engagement with learning content. The more time students spent while mousing over the recommended activities, the more they were willing to open them. In contrast, the more time student spent on inspecting visual explanations for non-recommended activities, the less they were inclined to open them. In this aspect, student behavior was also influenced by their starting level of knowledge. The students with high pre-test scores exhibited lower ratios of engagement with the recommended activities. This behavior is likely to have the same roots as discussed above for conversion data.

By putting together all these results, we can conclude that explainable recommendations can support students working with a programming practice system, most noticeably affecting the learners who are novices in programming and have the highest need for help in choosing activities to practice. The presence of recommendations and explanations could increase student engagement with knowledge-relevant learning content leading to a higher success rate and an increased opportunity to learn. In turn, it was exactly the success rate in problem-solving within JP^3 that impacted students' knowledge progress throughout the term, as it was positively correlated with student performance on intermediate evaluations and also on the post-test at the end of the class. Altogether, our explainable recommendation approach has the potential to positively impact students activity within JP^3 by pushing them to practice more, focusing on the most appropriate high-effort learning materials, and at the same time providing them with the opportunity for reflecting on the appropriateness of the content for supporting each step of their learning.

However, this study has several limitations. In particular, we were not able to reliably track student work with visual and verbal explanations using logs, as we use only mouse-over time as a proxy of attention. In the future, we need to better assess the impact of explanations by running studies where visual attention of students can be captured (e.g. eye-tracking controlled study). Also, more efforts are needed to define strategies that could make recommendations more relevant and useful for learners with higher initial levels of knowledge.

References

1. Abdi, S., Khosravi, H., Sadiq, S., Gasevic, D.: Complementing educational recommender systems with open learner models. In: Proceedings of the Tenth International Conference on Learning Analytics and Knowledge, LAK 2020, New York, NY, USA, pp. 360–365. ACM (2020)
2. Ahn, J.W., Brusilovsky, P., Grady, J., He, D., Syn, S.Y.: Open user profiles for adaptive news systems: help or harm? In: the 16th International Conference on World Wide Web, WWW 2007, pp. 11–20. ACM (2007)
3. Barria Pineda, J., Brusilovsky, P.: Making educational recommendations transparent through a fine-grained open learner model. In: Workshop on Intelligent User Interfaces for Algorithmic Transparency in Emerging Technologies at the 24th ACM Conference on Intelligent User Interfaces, IUI 2019, vol. 2327. CEUR (2019)
4. Bull, S.: There are open learner models about!. IEEE Trans. Learn. Technol. **13**(2), 425–448 (2020)
5. Bull, S., Kay, J.: SMILI: a framework for interfaces to learning data in open learner models, learning analytics and related fields. Int. J. Artif. Intell. Educ. **26**(1), 293–331 (2016)
6. Conati, C., Porayska-Pomsta, K., Mavrikis, M.: AI in education needs interpretable machine learning: lessons from open learner modelling. arXiv preprint arXiv:1807.00154 (2018)

7. Drachsler, H., Verbert, K., Santos, O., Manouselis, N.: Panorama of recommender systems to support learning. In: Ricci, F., Rokach, L., Shapira, B. (eds.) Recommender Systems Handbook, pp. 421–451. Springer, Boston (2015). https://doi.org/10.1007/978-1-4899-7637-6_12

8. Erdt, M., Fernández, A., Rensing, C.: Evaluating recommender systems for technology enhanced learning: a quantitative survey. IEEE Trans. Learn. Technol. **8**(4), 326–344 (2015)

9. Gauch, S., Speretta, M., Chandramouli, A., Micarelli, A.: User profiles for personalized information access. In: Brusilovsky, P., Kobsa, A., Nejdl, W. (eds.) The Adaptive Web. LNCS, vol. 4321, pp. 54–89. Springer, Heidelberg (2007). https://doi.org/10.1007/978-3-540-72079-9_2

10. Gedikli, F., Jannach, D., Ge, M.: How should I explain? A comparison of different explanation types for recommender systems. Int. J. Hum. Comput. Stud. **72**(4), 367–382 (2014)

11. Hosseini, R.: Program construction examples in computer science education: from static text to adaptive and engaging learning technology. Doctoral dissertation (2018)

12. Hosseini, R., Akhuseyinoglu, K., Petersen, A., Schunn, C.D., Brusilovsky, P.: PCEX: interactive program construction examples for learning programming. In: Proceedings of the 18th Koli Calling International Conference on Computing Education Research, pp. 5:1–5:9. ACM (2018)

13. Hosseini, R., Brusilovsky, P.: JavaParser: a fine-grain concept indexing tool for Java problems. In: The First Workshop on AI-Supported Education for Computer Science (AIEDCS 2013), pp. 60–63 (2013)

14. Kulesza, T., Stumpf, S., Burnett, M., Yang, S., Kwan, I., Wong, W.K.: Too much, too little, or just right? Ways explanations impact end users' mental models. In: Proceedings of IEEE Symposium on Visual Languages and Human-Centric Computing, VL/HCC, pp. 3–10 (2013)

15. Nunes, I., Jannach, D.: A systematic review and taxonomy of explanations in decision support and recommender systems. User Model. User-Adap. Inter. **27**(3–5), 393–444 (2017)

16. Putnam, V., Conati, C.: Exploring the need for explainable artificial intelligence (XAI) in intelligent tutoring systems (ITS). In: Joint Proceedings of the ACM IUI 2019 Workshops Co-located with the 24th ACM Conference on Intelligent User Interfaces (ACM IUI 2019), Los Angeles, USA, 20 March 2019 (2019)

17. Rosé, C.P., McLaughlin, E.A., Liu, R., Koedinger, K.R.: Explanatory learner models: why machine learning (alone) is not the answer. Br. J. Edu. Technol. **50**(6), 2943–2958 (2019)

18. Tintarev, N., Masthoff, J.: Designing and evaluating explanations for recommender systems. In: Ricci, F., Rokach, L., Shapira, B., Kantor, P. (eds.) Recommender Systems Handbook, 2nd edn, pp. 479–510. Springer, Boston (2010). https://doi.org/10.1007/978-0-387-85820-3_15

19. Tintarev, N., Masthoff, J.: Evaluating the effectiveness of explanations for recommender systems: methodological issues and empirical studies on the impact of personalization. User Model. User-Adap. Inter. **22**(4–5), 399–439 (2012)

20. Verbert, K., et al.: Context-aware recommender systems for learning: a survey and future challenges. IEEE Trans. Learn. Technol. **5**(4), 318–335 (2012)

21. Zhou, G., Yang, X., Azizsoltani, H., Barnes, T., Chi, M.: Improving student-system interaction through data-driven explanations of hierarchical reinforcement learning induced pedagogical policies. In: Proceedings of the 28th ACM Conference on User Modeling, Adaptation and Personalization, UMAP 2020, New York, NY, USA, pp. 284–292. ACM (2020)
22. Zingaro, D., Cherenkova, Y., Karpova, O., Petersen, A.: Facilitating code-writing in PI classes. In: Proceeding of the 44th ACM Technical Symposium on Computer Science Education, SIGCSE 2013, New York, NY, USA, pp. 585–590. ACM (2013)

Multilingual Age of Exposure

Robert-Mihai Botarleanu[1], Mihai Dascalu[1,2(✉)], Micah Watanabe[3],
Danielle S. McNamara[3], and Scott Andrew Crossley[4]

[1] University Politehnica of Bucharest, 313 Splaiul Independentei, 060042 Bucharest, Romania
robert.botarleanu@stud.acs.upb.ro, mihai.dascalu@cs.pub.ro
[2] Academy of Romanian Scientists, Str. Ilfov, Nr. 3, 050044 Bucharest, Romania
[3] Department of Psychology, Arizona State University, PO Box 871104, Tempe,
AZ 85287, USA
{micah.watanabe,dsmcnama}@asu.edu
[4] Department of Applied Linguistics/ESL, Georgia State University, Atlanta, GA 30303, USA
scrossley@gsu.edu

Abstract. The ability to objectively quantify the complexity of a text can be a useful indicator of how likely learners of a given level will comprehend it. Before creating more complex models of assessing text difficulty, the basic building block of a text consists of words and, inherently, its overall difficulty is greatly influenced by the complexity of underlying words. One approach is to measure a word's Age of Acquisition (AoA), an estimate of the average age at which a speaker of a language understands the semantics of a specific word. Age of Exposure (AoE) statistically models the process of word learning, and in turn an estimate of a given word's AoA. In this paper, we expand on the model proposed by AoE by training regression models that learn and generalize AoA word lists across multiple languages including English, German, French, and Spanish. Our approach allows for the estimation of AoA scores for words that are not found in the original lists, up to the majority of the target language's vocabulary. Our method can be uniformly applied across multiple languages though the usage of parallel corpora and helps bridge the gap in the size of AoA word lists available for non-English languages. This effort is particularly important for efforts toward extending AI to languages with fewer resources and benchmarked corpora.

Keywords: Natural language processing · Age of acquisition · Age of exposure · Multilingual

1 Introduction

The quantification of textual complexity is a crucial step toward better understanding the relations between text comprehension, the reader, and the nature of the text. Words are the fundamental building blocks of texts, and thus analysis of word complexity in a text can provide insight into the difficulties that readers might have in understanding certain documents. However, many of the tools used to estimate word complexity are created specifically for the English language. While simple measures such as number of characters in syllables can be easily identified regardless of the language, other measures

© Springer Nature Switzerland AG 2021
I. Roll et al. (Eds.): AIED 2021, LNAI 12748, pp. 77–87, 2021.
https://doi.org/10.1007/978-3-030-78292-4_7

of word complexity can only be measured by examining the relations between words and how words are used within the context of the language. Creating new tools to measure word complexity in multiple languages can aid in the crafting of better online instruction materials and techniques as well as interventions for a broader range of students. This is an important objective, particularly for under-resourced countries and languages.

Numerous approaches to quantifying word complexity have been proposed. These range from simple surface-level measurements, such as the number of syllables or characters, to measurements such as a word's frequency in a corpus or the number of synonyms for a given word. Previous studies have demonstrated detrimental impacts of complex words on reading comprehension. People tend to spend more time focusing on ambiguous or infrequent terms [1], which directly impacts reading speed. Certain words are more easily learned by L2 speakers [2] and various measures of word complexity are employed in evaluating of the complexity of phrases and texts [3].

"Age of Acquisition" (AoA) is an indicator of a word's complexity from the perspective of language learning. AoA is an estimate of the average age an average language learner acquired a given word. Word lists of AoA scores are typically collected using adults' estimates of when they learned the word [4]. The production of AoA lists is costly, time-consuming, and reflects adults' memories of word learning, and not the actual process of word learning. Like AoA, Age of Exposure (AoE) [5] is also an estimate of the average age that an average language learner acquires a given word. However, AoE scores are derived from a machine learning model that is trained on increasingly large corpora of texts, which simulates the process of learning a language to provide an automated measure of word complexity.

Age of Exposure is an extension of the Word Maturity model created by Landauer et al. [6]. In the Word Maturity model, Latent Semantic Analysis [7] was used to generate word vectors on increasingly larger, cumulative, corpora of texts. By performing Procrustes rotation between the vector spaces given by the LSA word vectors, one is then able to measure the cosine distance between the representation of a word at a given step in the trajectory and the final, "adult", representation. In AoE, Latent Dirichlet Allocation (LDA) [8] is used instead of LSA [6]; LDA affords better estimates of polysemy, with lower computational costs. In addition, AoE also introduces additional statistical features extracted from the learning trajectories.

While AoA and AoE scores are related to measures of reading comprehension and writing skill, the majority of published lists of AoA scores are for English words, and previous iterations of the AoE model have only been trained on English text corpora [6]. Thus, the aim of this study is to expand on the AoE models by providing a method of directly estimating the AoE scores from the learning trajectories, generated using unsupervised language models of words in English, German, French and Spanish AoA word lists. We investigate the similarities between these word lists and show that our method can generalize accurate AoA estimations for different languages, allowing for the creation of approximate AoA word lists on the entirety of a language's (known) vocabulary. The differences between the distributions of AoA scores in different languages are expected to impact the performance of modeled learning trajectories; however, our method shows that simulated word learning trajectories generated by applying unsupervised language models on multi-lingual corpora can capture similarities as well as differences between the word learning processes in those languages. We thus aim to answer the following research questions: a) Are AoA word lists in different languages sufficiently similar to afford using the same statistical modeling technique? and b) Can we estimate, within reasonable error, the AoA scores for words in a language automatically and how do these models relate in terms of the features used?

2 Method

2.1 Corpora

To perform the iterative model training necessary to estimate learning trajectories, we required a corpus that was both sufficiently large and also similar between languages. To this end, selected the "ParaCrawl" [9] dataset which provides documents that are aligned between various languages (i.e., they are equivalent through translation), extracted from a large number of webpages. Of these, we used three aligned corpora, English-German (en-de), English-French (en-fr), and English–Spanish (en-es).

In order for the trained models to estimate learning trajectories for various languages, the texts in the corpora must present sufficient variety in terms of complexity. One means of evaluating text complexity, independent of the AoA, is to use an automatic readability formula such as the Flesch Reading Ease [10], which uses simple surface-statistics of the structure of an English text to estimate its difficulty. By plotting the distributions of the Flesch Reading Ease scores across the three corpora we selected, we observed a uniform distribution of readability on the English documents in the dataset (see Fig. 1). Some of the documents exceed the 0–100 range that Flesch defined in the original paper; however, this possibly resulted from the documents being automatically crawled from webpages resulting in syntax errors (i.e., sentences not terminated properly or whitespaces between words missing). Nevertheless, the three corpora present relatively uniform distributions with the majority of texts being located in the 50–75 range. Given that the Flesch Reading Ease formula was constructed for English, applying it directly to directly to the other three languages is not uniformly reliable. We elected, instead, to assume that the aligned texts had readability levels similar to their English counterparts.

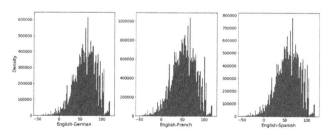

Fig. 1 Flesch Reading Ease distributions for the English dataset

In the AoE paradigm, language models are trained on increasingly larger subsections of a corpus. This is intended to simulate the way in which humans are exposed to more texts (or discourse) as they learn to speak, read, and write. In our experiments, we elected to split each of the three corpora into 20 different stages. Each stage included all of the texts in the previous ones, with the final model being trained on the entirety of the corpus of a language. In Fig. 2, the progression of the size of the three corpora as language acquisition is simulated has been plotted. All three are large, with the English-German corpus having 813,223 documents in the first stage and 16,264,448 documents in the final stage; English–Spanish 1,099,364 in the first and 21,987,267 documents in the final stage; and English-French 1,568,709 in the first and 31,374,161 documents in the final stage. Here, a "document", means a pair of aligned texts in two languages. We also considered two different orders for the documents: an arbitrary ordering and one based on Flesch Reading Ease, with the most readable texts being *seen* first, with the least readable ones being left for the latter stages.

Our model simulates the manner in which humans are exposed to language, starting by reading simpler texts and increasing difficulty as their language mastery improves; nevertheless, this approach does not consider other channels for language learning (e.g., dialogue with other people, video and audio entertainment, writing). In the context of the Word Maturity and AoE models, word acquisition is modeled as the growth of the simulated vocabulary when the model is presented with increasingly more text. The simulated learning trajectories take a simplified view of human language learning because they do not take into account individual differences (e.g., personal interests, different educational systems) and are intended to model the average level of language exposure a language speaker might encounter solely by reading texts.

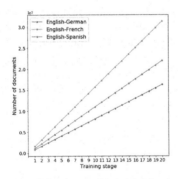

Fig. 2 Number of documents in each of the three corpora

AoE scores are correlated with AoA scores because they are assumed to reflect the language learning process. Thus, in order to estimate AoE word scores, we trained statistical regression models that required training and evaluation data – namely AoA word lists. We selected an AoA word list per language: English [4], French ([11], Spanish [12], and German ([13]. The three word lists varied in size (English: 30,121; French: 1,493; Spanish: 7,039: German: 3,200); however, our approach assumed that the model follows the same learning process for all languages (which is likely incorrect but necessary for the current analysis). To assess the viability of this assumption, we performed automatic word-to-word translations and measured the correlations between the English word list and the others. While not all the words could be automatically matched, the majority were, and we were able to confirm their correlation using Spearman Rank Correlations: English-German $r = 0.681$, English-French $r = 0.594$ and English–Spanish $r = 0.682$.

The distributions for the four AoA lists are provided in Fig. 3. The English word list scores are the closest to a normal distribution, while the Spanish scores appear almost bimodal. The ranges of the distributions also differ, with some English word scores exceeding 20, while the maximum Spanish scores are 11, and the German and French scores are approximately 15. In addition to their relative sizes, these differences in the distributions can impact attempts to train regression models to predict AoA scores.

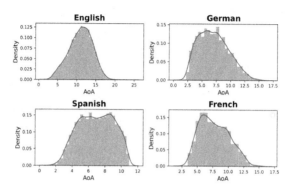

Fig. 3 Distribution plots for the four AoA word lists

2.2 Modeling Learning Trajectories

To model learning trajectories, we trained Word2Vec [14] language models utilizing the cumulatively increasing corpora, as outlined previously in Sect. 2.1. Of the two variants of Word2Vec, we chose to use the skip-gram architecture wherein the Word2vec model is used to predict context words for a given target term. Our choice of using Word2Vec instead of LDA as used in the first version of AoE was motivated by the inherent geometrical properties of the word vectors it produces. Word2Vec maps words into a multi-dimensional vector space wherein arithmetic operations between the vectors are used to represent semantic and syntactic relationships between words. As such, this method was a more a natural fit in the incremental training algorithm used to model learning trajectories. Specifically, the Word2Vec model could then be evaluated as it evolved (i.e., as it was exposed to more texts) by comparing intermediate vector spaces to the mature one.

Specifically, we utilized word embedding vectors of size 300, with a context window of 5 and trained each model for 50 epochs. Because the models were trained on incrementally increasing portions of each corpus, the final, "mature", model was assumed to contain the most accurate word embeddings. With this in mind, the intermediate models offer snapshots into what Word2Vec was able to model at each "learning" step. Measuring the discrepancy between an intermediate word representation and its final, mature one can be done using cosine similarity. We trained our models in stages. Hence, there were 19 intermediate model similarities to the mature representation, which formed the learning trajectories. Prior to measuring the cosine similarity, we performed a Procrustes alignment of the vector space represented by the intermediate word embeddings to the mature vector space. An illustration of these learning trajectories is provided in Fig. 4, which shows the cosine similarities of the intermediate models to the mature one for the English texts of the *English to German* corpus. Each of the learning trajectories is colored on a gradient from blue-to-red based on word frequencies in the corpus. These evolutions are consistent with the ones from the first model of AoE [5], but are more fine-grained with smoother evolutions.

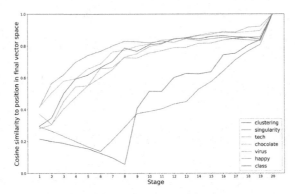

Fig. 4 Example of learning trajectories for the English to German corpus

Via these illustrations, we observed that some words, such as "tech" and "singularity", have noticeably steeper learning trajectories. Others, such as "happy" and "chocolate", have relatively good cosine similarities from the earliest stages, suggesting that the intermediate model's representations of those terms are closer to the mature model representation. In terms of AoA, we can consider "happy" as having a low age of acquisition, with "clustering" being acquired later. In comparison to the AoE trajectories, the ones we generated showed a monotonic increase, which is expected from the fact that the Word2Vec model trained at a certain stage uses all the documents on which the previous intermediate stages were trained, in addition to its own portion.

Similarly, we explore the learning trajectories for words in different languages (see Fig. 5). While some common words, namely "dog" and "red", appear to have similar trajectories in the four languages, we can observe differences. Namely, in Spanish, the word for "class" (i.e., "clase") seems to be learned far more quickly than in other languages. Consequentially, the AoA score for the Spanish word "clase" is somewhat lower (3.84) than its translations in other languages (English "class": 4.95, French "classe": 4.92, German: no equivalent in word list). Similarly, the Spanish AoA score for "virus" is 8.16, while the English word list has it at 9.5 and the German word list at 9.65. The process of learning words differs from language to language, especially in the case of specialized terms. These are a few randomly chosen examples; however, the presence of differences in the trajectories modeled by AoE that are also reflected in AoA word lists suggests that our trajectories resemble aspects of human word acquisition and capture, at least partially, differences between word learning in different languages.

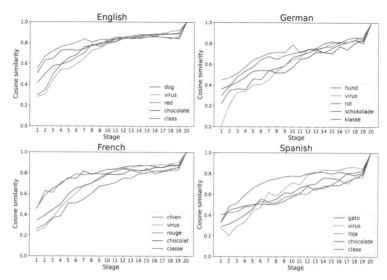

Fig. 5 Learning trajectories for different languages

From these learning trajectories, we extracted several features that described both the relations between a word and the rest of the vocabulary and the learning process for that word. These features can be split into two groups:

- **Mature Model Features:** the cosine similarities between the word embeddings of a term and other words in the vocabulary. These include the 1st, 2nd and 3rd highest cosine similarities to words in the vocabulary and their average, as well as the number of words that have a cosine similarity of at least 0.3 to the term and their average cosine similarity.
- **Learning Trajectory Features:** the 19 intermediate model cosine similarities, their average and its 1-complement, the index of the first intermediate model that achieves a cosine similarity above a certain threshold (from 0.3 to 0.7 in 0.05 increments) and the slope of the best fitting line on the plots shown in Fig. 4 and its inverse value.

Through these features, we aimed to capture a combination of vocabulary knowledge and information about the learning trajectories. These features were then used as predictor variables in order to train regression models to predict AoE word scores.

2.3 Regression Models

For each word, 39 features were generated from the learning trajectories and the mature word embeddings. Of these features, 9 are continuous (being cosine similarities) and the remainder are ordinal. Performing a variance inflation factor analysis of multicollinearity, using a threshold of 5 would reduce these features to 6. However, we found that our models, which are non-linear, perform better when multicollinearity-based pruning of features was not used. For standardizing the input features, we utilized z-score normalization prior to training the models.

Given the limited number of features generated, as well as the relatively small number of data points (i.e., 1,493 to 30,121 terms), we elected to evaluate the models using Random Forest Regression and Support Vector Regression (SVR). For Random Forest Regression, we used 50 estimator trees. For SVR, we found that the best results were produced using a radial basis function kernel, with $\varepsilon = 0.2$, $C = 1$, and with γ set to inverse of the number of features multiplied by the variance of the feature matrix.

3   Results

We measured the performance across 10 cross-validation folds and report both the mean absolute error and the mean R^2 coefficient for the test splits. For each of the three corpora, namely English-German (en-de), English-French (en-fr), and English–Spanish (en-es), we performed four experiments: one per language and one per document ordering criteria (i.e., arbitrary ordering and ordered by their Flesch Reading Ease). These results are provided in Table 1; consistently throughout all experiments, ordering ensures a more predictive model than the consideration of texts in a random order.

Table 1 Cross-validation results for predicting AoA scores

Corpus	Language	Ordering	Random Forest		Support Vector Regressor	
			MAE	R^2	MAE	R^2
EN-DE	English	Arbitrary	1.95	0.34	1.94	0.35
		Sorted	1.87	0.39	**1.85**	**0.40**
	German	Arbitrary	1.67	0.27	1.84	0.18
		Sorted	**1.67**	**0.28**	1.84	0.19
EN-ES	English	Arbitrary	1.97	0.33	1.97	0.34
		Sorted	1.88	0.39	**1.87**	**0.40**
	Spanish	Arbitrary	1.53	0.16	1.56	0.14
		Sorted	1.44	0.25	**1.41**	**0.27**
EN-FR	English	Arbitrary	2.02	0.31	2.02	0.31
		Sorted	1.90	0.37	**1.89**	**0.38**
	French	Arbitrary	1.82	0.12	1.75	0.14
		Sorted	1.67	0.21	1.65	**0.24**

The first observation is that the ordering the documents by their English Flesch Readability Score seems to bring an improvement of performance in all cases. This strengthens our hypothesis that the Readability Score as measured on the English document offers a reasonable proxy for its foreign-language counterpart. Additionally, English results are consistent between the three corpora and do not appear to be correlated to the size of each corpus in terms of the number of documents (see Fig. 2).

The AoA word lists differed in the range of possible AoA scores. Hence, comparing the results between languages using the mean absolute error does not provide a good estimate of model performance. The R^2 coefficient, on the other hand, shows that the English models have a much better performance, while the other languages tend yield results in the 0.24–0.28 range. One immediate explanation for this might be that the English word list is much larger than the others, which translates into more sample points for training the regression models. Additionally, the English word list is the most normally distributed of the four (see Fig. 3), which may also help explain the better performance of the models trained on the English data. While the German and Spanish results are similar, the French results are slightly lower. These results may be attributed to there being words in the French word list and their relatively non-normal distribution.

For the SVR models with radial basis functions, extracting feature importance directly is not possible because the data is projected into another dimensional space. For the Random Forest Regressors, feature importance can be extracted by measuring the impurity (i.e., the Gini importance); however, this method has been shown to be biased towards features with high cardinalities [15]. Thus, a better alternative for our case was to use permutation importance.

While we did find variance in terms of the order of the top features, the most important ones were always those in the "Learning Trajectory Features" category (see Sect. 2.2). Statistical information about the learning trajectories (i.e., slope, average) or the values of the points of the learning trajectories (i.e., the cosine similarities between intermediate models and the mature model) were found to have higher feature importance scores than the Mature Model Features, across all languages and ordering criteria. This aligned with our expectations because the learning trajectories were intended to simulate the way in which humans acquire new words in their vocabulary.

4 Conclusions

This study explores the possibility of estimating AoA scores for multiple languages, through a simulation of human word acquisition. Statistical features generated from the learning trajectories were then used to train regressors capable of predicting AoA scores. Expanding on the work done in the AoE model [5], we applied Word2Vec on incrementally increasing corpora of texts, and then generated features based on the resulting learning trajectories. AoA score regressors were trained, achieving reasonable results, with R^2 coefficients ranging from 0.27 to 0.40 on word lists for four languages: Spanish, German, French and English. The post-training feature importance analyses confirmed that the generated features from the learning trajectories were rated as being the most relevant by the regressors. Additionally, empirical observations reveal that our simulated learning trajectories captured differences in word acquisition between languages that are also present in AoA word lists, with certain words having lower AoA scores in one language (e.g., Spanish) than in the others – this corresponds to less steep learning trajectories for that particular language. Our approach can be uniformly applied for any language and has strong potential to help bridge the gap in word complexity research for non-English languages.

Our approach of automatically estimating AoE scores opens up the possibility of expanding existing word lists. Generalizing from the regression training data (i.e., the human-sourced AoA lists) allows us to estimate AoE scores for the entirety of the English, German, French and Spanish vocabularies that were present in the corpora during training (i.e., over 40,000 words for each language). Having access to more complete AoA lists can positively impact research on textual complexity and reading comprehension. Comparisons between learning trajectories of words in different languages, as shown in Fig. 5, highlight notable differences in word acquisition that could form the basis of better L2 learning systems through the creation of curriculums that take multicultural lingual differences into account.

The principal limitations of our method relate to the distributions of the scores in the AoA word lists used to train the regressors, as well as the cardinality of the AoA lists. Our results indicate that the English word list, which is normally distributed and has a large number of terms, leads to better regression results with higher R^2 coefficients. Training the language models is also a limiting factor because it is a computationally expensive process. For each language, we trained 20 Word2Vec models on up to 31,374,161 documents, for 50 epochs each. A possible avenue of research would be to explore the possibility of using smaller datasets and to find a criterion for selecting adequate documents. When choosing the "Para Crawl" dataset, we looked at the distribution of Flesch Reading Ease scores on the corpora to ensure that a sufficient range of complexity existed in the texts; however, other methods might allow for the targeted selection of documents in order to not use the entire dataset. Another avenue of research would be to explore the use of different language models. In addition to previously used methods, namely LSA and LDA, temporal word embedding models [16, 17] can be used to model diachronic changes in vocabulary and could be applied to the cumulatively increasing language exposure corpus used to simulate human learning.

This study illustrates the potential of machine learning to inform measures of word complexity across different languages. The ability to predict word complexity enhances teachers' and researchers' capacity to develop instructional materials for a broader range of students, and for particular student abilities. For example, research on AoA scores has demonstrated processing advantages for phrases consisting of low-AoA words compared to high-AoA words [18]. Thus, texts might be modified by replacing words with low-AoA or high-AoA synonyms (e.g., "the dog ate my homework" *versus* "the dog devoured my essay"). Providing students with personalized materials is critical for learning because the readability of texts is partially influenced by the difficulty of words in relation to students' vocabulary, prior knowledge, and reading skills. Mulilingual AoE provides a potential means to enhance foreign language learning materials by focusing on the aspects that are either easier or harder to understand by students of different cultures. Because our method is applied uniformly across languages, it can be readily used in multilingual textual complexity applications and can help bring research in non-English languages to parity.

Acknowledgements. This research was supported by a grant of the Romanian National Authority for Scientific Research and Innovation, CNCS – UEFISCDI, project number TE 70 *PN-III-P1-1.1-TE-2019-2209*, ATES – "Automated Text Evaluation and Simplification", the Institute of Education Sciences (R305A180144 and R305A180261), and the Office of Naval Research (N00014-17-1-2300; N00014-20-1-2623). The opinions expressed are those of the authors and do not represent views of the IES or ONR.

References

1. Rayner, K., Duffy, S.A.: Lexical complexity and fixation times in reading: effects of word frequency, verb complexity, and lexical ambiguity. Memory Cogn. **14**(3), 191–201 (1986)
2. Rosa, K.D., Eskenazi, M.: Effect of word complexity on L2 vocabulary learning. In: 6th Workshop on Innovative Use of NLP for Building Educational Applications, pp. 76–80. ACL, Portland, Oregon (2011)
3. Maddela, M., Xu, W.: A word-complexity lexicon and a neural readability ranking model for lexical simplification. arXiv preprint, arXiv:1810.05754 (2018)
4. Kuperman, V., Stadthagen-Gonzalez, H., Brysbaert, M.: Age-of-acquisition ratings for 30,000 English words. Behav. Res. Methods **44**(4), 978–990 (2012)
5. Dascalu, M., McNamara, D.S., Crossley, S.A., Trausan-Matu, S.: Age of exposure: a model of word learning. In: 30th AAAI Conference on Artificial Intelligence, pp. 2928–2934. AAAI Press, Phoenix, AZ (2016)
6. Landauer, T.K., Kireyev, K., Panaccione, C.: Word maturity: a new metric for word knowledge. Sci. Stud. Reading **15**(1), 92–108 (2011)
7. Landauer, T.K., Dumais, S.T.: A solution to Plato's problem: the Latent Semantic Analysis theory of acquisition, induction and representation of knowledge. Psychol. Rev. **104**(2), 211–240 (1997)
8. Blei, D.M., Ng, A.Y., Jordan, M.I.: Latent dirichlet allocation. J. Mach. Learn. Res. **3**(4–5), 993–1022 (2003)
9. Esplà-Gomis, M., Forcada, M.L., Ramírez-Sánchez, G., Hoang, H.: ParaCrawl: Web-scale parallel corpora for the languages of the EU. In: Machine Translation Summit XVII Volume 2: Translator, Project and User Tracks, pp. 118–119. ACL, Dublin, Ireland (2019)
10. Flesch, R.: A new readability yardstick. J. Appl. Psychol. **32**(3), 221–233 (1948)
11. Ferrand, L., Bonin, P., Méot, A., Augustinova, M., New, B., Pallier, C., Brysbaert, M.: Age-of-acquisition and subjective frequency estimates for all generally known monosyllabic French words and their relation with other psycholinguistic variables. Behavior Res. Methods **40**(4), 1049–1054 (2008)
12. Alonso, M.A., Fernandez, A., Díez, E.: Subjective age-of-acquisition norms for 7,039 Spanish words. Behavior Res. Methods **47**(1), 268–274 (2015)
13. Birchenough, J.M., Davies, R., Connelly, V.: Rated age-of-acquisition norms for over 3,200 German words. Behavior Res. Methods **49**(2), 484–501 (2017)
14. Mikolov, T., Chen, K., Corrado, G., Dean, J.: Efficient estimation of word representation in vector space. In: Workshop at ICLR, Scottsdale, AZ (2013)
15. Altmann, A., Toloşi, L., Sander, O., Lengauer, T.: Permutation importance: a corrected feature importance measure. Bioinformatics **26**(10), 1340–1347 (2010)
16. Yao, Z., Sun, Y., Ding, W., Rao, N., Xiong, H.: Dynamic word embeddings for evolving semantic discovery. In: 11th ACM International Conference on Web Search and Data Mining, pp. 673–681. ACM, Marina Del Rey, CA, USA (2018)
17. Di Carlo, V., Bianchi, F., Palmonari, M.: Training temporal word embeddings with a compass. In: AAAI Conference on Artificial Intelligence, vol. 33, pp. 6326–6334, Honolulu, Hawaii, USA (2019)
18. Arnon, I., McCauley, S.M., Christiansen, M.H.: Digging up the building blocks of language: age-of-acquisition effects for multiword phrases. J. Memory Lang. **92**, 265–280 (2017)

DiSCS: A New Sequence Segmentation Method for Open-Ended Learning Environments

James P. Bywater[1]([✉]) [iD], Mark Floryan[2] [iD], and Jennifer L. Chiu[2] [iD]

[1] James Madison University, Harrisonburg, VA, USA
bywatejx@jmu.edu
[2] University of Virginia, Charlottesville, VA, USA
{mrf8t,jlc4dz}@virginia.edu

Abstract. Open-ended learning environments afford students opportunities to explore, manipulate, and test concepts, and have the potential to provide students with feedback and support by leveraging the log data generated by them. However, within open-ended contexts, student log data is often noisy and identifying periods of meaningful activity is difficult. This paper introduces a new sequence mining method to overcome this challenge. The Differential Segmentation of Categorical Sequences (DiSCS) algorithm finds segments within a sequence of actions that are maximally or near-maximally different from their immediate neighbors. Segments are then clustered to reveal common periods of student activity. We examine the performance of this method under a variety of conditions to find how well DiSCS can identify where different states of simulated activity start and end. We report that when provided with only the observed actions, DiSCS is able to identify the hidden states of simulated student activity with strong and very strong associations. This strong performance is robust across a variety of contexts including those where observed actions are noisy or common to multiple states. We discuss the implications and limitations of this method for open-ended learning environments.

Keywords: Sequence mining · Segmentation · Open-ended learning environments

1 Introduction

Open-ended learning environments use the affordances of technology to create opportunities for students to explore, manipulate, and test concepts and knowledge [1]. Open-ended learning environments are designed to engage students with ill-structured tasks and typically involve computer-based games, simulations, visualizations, design, or experimentation tools [2–4]. However, implementing open-ended learning environments in classrooms presents challenges for teachers [2, 5, 6]. For example, to provide effective guidance to students using design-based learning environments, teachers need to understand and notice the different design strategies that each student takes [7]. Given that each student will likely have a unique solution instead of one "right" answer, and their paths to that solution are likely to differ, noticing these design strategies for each student can be complex and challenging [8, 9].

© Springer Nature Switzerland AG 2021
I. Roll et al. (Eds.): AIED 2021, LNAI 12748, pp. 88–100, 2021.
https://doi.org/10.1007/978-3-030-78292-4_8

Various ways to document or capture student's learning behaviors within open-ended learning environments include think-alouds [10] or reflections [11]. These methods are typically labor intensive, usually implemented in undergraduate or professional settings [12], and have limited applicability to precollege classroom settings. Given the computer-based nature of open-ended learning environments, students can be provided with automated guidance by leveraging log data of students' actions within the environment. As a result, various research investigates applying data mining techniques to log data to provide insight into students' learning behaviors. Within open-ended learning environments, microlevel student interaction data [13] from a variety of contexts such as coding tasks [14], inquiry tasks [15, 16], and iterative design tasks [17, 18] have been used to identify and support a broad range of constructs including metacognitive states [19, 20], inquiry or design strategies [15, 16, 18] and problem-solving [17].

However, while there are numerous sequential data mining techniques used to analyze student interaction data [21], less attention has been given to applying these methods to open-ended design-based contexts, and especially with real, noisy, open-ended classroom data. Many challenges with classroom data remain, particularly when segmenting sequences into meaningful periods of student activity [13]. To improve this important area of data mining this paper introduces and describes a new sequential data mining method for segmenting noisy student activity from open-ended learning environments. The Differential Segmentation of Categorical Sequences (DiSCS) algorithm uses dynamic programming and genetic techniques to find segments within an individual student's sequence of actions that are maximally or near-maximally different from segments that are their immediate neighbors. Clustering techniques then group segments and reveal common periods of activity within an individual student's sequence, or across the sequences of multiple students. This makes it possible to identify different phases of activity and when they start and stop. To examine the performance of this method, this paper addresses the following research questions:

1. To what degree is DiSCS able to identify optimal segmentation when using classroom data?
2. What is the strength and robustness of the association between states identified by DiSCS and simulated hidden states?

2 Sequence Mining

The field of educational data mining is broadly defined as developing and applying computer algorithms to detect patterns in educational data that would be difficult to do otherwise [22]. These algorithms can be used at the national, institutional, or classroom levels, with the latter often referred to as fine-grained or microlevel analysis [13]. Microlevel techniques include a variety of knowledge tracing strategies [23], time-series analyses [24], or the development of 'evidence models' or sensors for the constructs of interest [25]. To different degrees, these techniques combine deductive expert knowledge with inductive knowledge found using a variety of data mining methods.

Within educational settings, microlevel (i.e., student interaction level) sequential log data are commonly analyzed using process or pattern mining. This approach looks for the presence of specific ordered patterns of interactions or keystrokes within a sequence, or for the frequency of the most commonly occurring patterns. However, with noisy educational data, sequential pattern mining algorithms such as the Sequential Pattern Mining (SPAM) [26] algorithm and the Generalized Sequential Pattern (GSP) [27] mining algorithm often find large numbers of frequent patterns that make it difficult to identify which patterns are important or meaningful [19]. Furthermore, students are known to use different microlevel pathways to achieve similar goals or performance. While some studies have identified sequential patterns that characterize high and low achieving students [28], or found patterns that are different between periods of increasing and decreasing performance [19], any set of specific patterns identified this way are likely to be incomplete and problematic to use for instructional feedback [29]. Therefore, when examining sequences for phases of inquiry or design behavior, techniques that place less emphasis on the temporal ordering of microlevel actions and which take a more holistic approach may be more appropriate.

An alternative approach involves segmenting sequences and examining each segment holistically. These approaches can overcome some of the problems highlighted above, however, rules for when to cut a sequence into segments can also create their own problems. In contexts where students complete a series of small finite tasks or levels, segmentation has occurred at the start and end of each of these tasks [30]. However, this approach has limited applicability to open-ended learning contexts given that these settings are inherently less prescriptive. Within open-ended learning settings, segmentation has been performed by examining concurrent performance data and creating segments corresponding to periods of increasing and decreasing performance scores [19]. However, during phases of student activity, performance scores may fluctuate as students investigate the positive and negative impact of different factors, thus segmenting on a performance basis has limited applicability. An alternative approach has been to set a temporal resolution and use the timestamps of the dataset to segment after a fixed time period (e.g., every minute [18] or every 20-s [31]). However, to avoid slicing distinct periods of activity into unrepresentative segments this approach requires that the chosen duration is set much shorter than the expected length of periods of activity. Other heuristics for segmenting sequences, such as using periods of inactivity, risk conflating meaningful transitions in learning behavior with less meaningful transitions such as bathroom breaks, the end of class, or an unreliable internet connection.

For data from open-ended learning settings, there is still a need for a method to segment a sequence of student actions that is based on differences between phases of those actions. That is, there is not yet a method that determines how best to segment a sequence by comparing, holistically, the segments themselves. This paper introduces such a method.

3   Differential Segmentation of Categorical Sequences (DiSCS)

The DiSCS algorithm takes a *categorical sequence* and splits it into *segments* so that each of the segments is as *different* from its immediate neighbors as possible. In effect, it finds the most distinct segments within a sequence of categories (see Fig. 1 for a simple example).

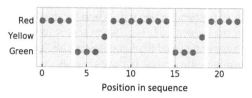

Fig. 1. In this simple example, DiSCS splits a sequence into five distinct segments separated by vertical white lines.

3.1 Optimization Function

More specifically, DiSCS splits an individual student's sequence of L time-ordered, categorical actions into m non-overlapping, contiguous segments such that the average of all the differences between neighboring segments is maximized. The difference between a given pair of neighboring segments is measured by finding the difference between the proportions of the actions in the neighboring segments. The paired z-scores for each of the actions is then found and averaged. That is, if $A = \{a_1, a_2, \ldots, a_k\}$ is the set of possible categorical actions and $S = \{s_1, s_2, \ldots, s_L\}$, $s_i \in A$ is the time-ordered sequence of these actions, the algorithm splits S into m non-overlapping, contiguous segments $\{C_1, C_2, \ldots, C_m\}$ where $C_1 = \{s_1, s_2, \ldots, s_{l_1}\}$, $C_2 = \{s_{l_1+1}, s_{l_1+2}, \ldots, s_{l_2}\}$, etc. Given that both the number of segments, m, and the positions at which the segments end, $l_1, l_2, \ldots, l_{m-1}$, can vary, DiSCS adjusts these parameters to maximize the average of the differences between all the pairs of neighboring segments, i.e., it averages the difference between C_j and C_{j+1} for j from 1 to $m - 1$.

The difference between a given pair of segments C_j and C_{j+1}, Z_j, is measured by first finding the proportion of each action for the segments, P_j and P_{j+1}, where $P_j = \{p_{1j}, p_{2j}, \ldots, p_{kj}\}$ and p_{ij} is the count of action a_i in segment C_j divided by n_j, the total number of actions in segment C_j. Then, the paired-sample z-test statistic, z_{ij}, is calculated for each of the k pairs of corresponding proportions, i.e. p_{ij} and $p_{i(j+1)}$,

$$z_{ij} = \frac{p_{ij} - p_{i(j+1)}}{\sqrt{p_{pooled}\left(1 - p_{pooled}\right)\left(\frac{1}{n_j} + \frac{1}{n_{j+1}}\right)}}. \tag{1}$$

The difference between a given pair of segments C_j and C_{j+1}, Z_j, is calculated by averaging the absolute values of z_{ij}, i.e.,

$$Z_j = \frac{\sum_{i=1}^{k} |z_{ij}|}{k}, \tag{2}$$

and an overall score for the differences between all the $m - 1$ pairs of neighboring segments in the sequence, Z, is calculated by averaging each of the values of Z_j, i.e.,

$$Z = \frac{\sum_{j=1}^{m-1} Z_j}{m - 1}. \tag{3}$$

Given that the optimal number of segments, m, is not known, we evaluate Z for values of m from 2 (i.e., the smallest possible number of segments) to a value much higher than the number of segments expected. While the maximum possible value of m is equal to the length of the sequence, L, (i.e., when segments consist of only one action per segment), given the computational burden of testing all these values, it is possible to use a heuristic for determining this value. For example, as we explain later, in this paper we test m up to three standard deviations above the expected number of segments, but other heuristic such as $L/3$ or $L/4$ would likely be sufficient.

Therefore, by varying the parameter m between 2 and M (either L or an alternative heuristic) and the end positions, l_1, l_2, ..., l_{m-1}, of the segments to all their possible combinations, DiSCS maximizes Z, i.e.,

$$\underset{2 \leq m \leq M}{\mathrm{argmax}} \left(\underset{l_1, l_2, ..., l_{m-1}}{\mathrm{argmax}} \left(\frac{\sum_{j=1}^{m-1} Z_j}{m-1} \right) \right) \tag{4}$$

In this form, our optimization function tends to favor small numbers of long segments. This is because the initial segmentation tends to capture the largest differences within a sequence and averaging in subsequent segmentations typically lowers the average. In order to adjust for this tendency, we introduce a smoothing variable, t, which has the effect of favoring larger numbers of segments, or smaller grain-size segments of student actions. The final optimization function can therefore be written as:

$$\underset{2 \leq m \leq M}{\mathrm{argmax}} \left(\underset{l_1, l_2, ..., l_{m-1}}{\mathrm{argmax}} \left(\frac{\sum_{j=1}^{m-1} Z_j}{m-1+t} \right) \right). \tag{5}$$

3.2 Algorithm

While it is possible to find the optimal solution described above using a brute-force approach, the number of calculations required to test all the possible values of the parameters m, l_1, l_2, ..., l_{m-1}, with m up to a maximum M, on a sequence of length L, is proportional to L^M. Therefore, DiSCS uses two different optimization techniques (a genetic and a dynamic programing algorithm) to find solutions more quickly, and takes the best result from each approach. The code for each of these algorithms is available at the DiSCS code repository [32]. While this approach has the advantage of differentially segmenting categorical sequences quickly, it introduces the possibility of finding only local-maxima and may report non-optimal parameter values which could be particularly problematic when analyzing noisy classroom data. This potential problem is investigated in research question 1.

3.3 Clustering

After segmenting a sequence, DiSCS clusters the segments. This step is intended to help identify similarities in the design behaviors across all students and examine the proportion of actions that are typical of that cluster. To do this, we used k-means clustering with the distance measure set to the Euclidean distance between the proportions of actions within each segment. We repeated the k-means clustering 100 times for every possible value of the total number of clusters, each time calculating the average silhouette width [33] to measure of the quality of the clustering. The clustering with the largest average silhouette width was selected. Segments that were in the same cluster were then given the same arbitrary label. For example, the final DiSCS output for the simple example given in Fig. 1 would create two clusters, one for segments where the observations are 'red' and another for segments with 'green' and 'yellow'.

4 Optimality of DiSCS

The first research question that this paper addresses is the degree to which DiSCS is able to identify optimal segmentation when using noisy classroom data. To do this we compared DiSCS segmentations with brute-force optimal segmentations under conditions that allow for a timely brute-force result (i.e., when the maximum number of segments tested, M, is 5).

4.1 Method

Context. The classroom data used for this investigation was obtained from 75 environmental science high school students who worked in 38 small groups (typically pairs) in their regular classroom setting to complete a design activity over multiple days. The design activity consisted of a series of scaffolded design challenges related to building a house that consumed no net energy over a year while still meeting cost, size, and aesthetic constraints. Students used an open-ended CAD environment called Energy3D [34] that enabled them to build and test different building designs that incorporate solar panels. Embedded tools could be used to examine energy gains and losses under various conditions and help students understand concepts such as energy transfer. The high school was located in the Eastern United States, two of the classes were 'honors' classes and three 'regular' level classes, and the school demographics were 34% Black, 9% Hispanic, and 45% White students with 45% of students receiving free or reduced lunch.

Data Collection. Student action data was collected while students were engaged with the design activity. Examples of the types of actions recorded were "edit roof", "add a solar panel", "change the tilt of the solar panel", and "do annual energy analysis". For each of the 38 small groups, one sequence of action data was collected containing all the actions performed by that group throughout the duration of the design activity. The sequences were long (mean = 379; standard deviation = 245) and included up to 42 different actions.

Analysis. To assess the degree to which the genetic and the dynamic programing algorithms used by DiSCS were able to find the optimal segmentation, we compared the maximum optimization function parameter values (see Eq. 5) for these algorithms with the guaranteed maximum value found by the brute-force algorithm. This analysis was conducted with the sequence of actions recorded by each group of students.

4.2 Results

When considered separately, the genetic algorithm reported maxima that were on aver-age 0.2% smaller than brute-force, and the dynamic programming algorithm reported maxima that were on average 0.4% smaller. This indicates that both algorithms provide near optimal solutions. However, this result is improved when following the approach used by DiSCS and selecting the best performing result from these two algorithms. In this case, the maxima were on average only 0.03% smaller than the actual maxima found using the brute-force algorithm. This indicates that while sub-optimal, using an approach that uses both a genetic algorithm and a dynamic programming algorithm, and takes the best of the two solutions generated provides very near optimal solutions.

5 Strength and Robustness of DiSCS

The second research question that this paper addresses relates to the strength and robust-ness of the association between states identified by DiSCS and simulated hidden states. To do this we examined the strength of the association and considered how well this strength is maintained under different input conditions.

5.1 Method

To explore the strength and robustness of DiSCS, we conducted a simulation study where stochastically created sequences were generated, segmented with DiSCS, and the association between the segment clusters and the hidden states of the original sequence calculated.

Sequence Generation. We used a hidden Markov model to stochastically generate the sequences used in the simulation study. The hidden states represent simulated phases of inquiry or design activity that students may be engaged in and the probability that the student transitions to a different phase is represented by p. Different hidden states were modeled to have multiple equally likely observable actions including an action that was common to all hidden states (see Fig. 2).

Analysis. For each sequence of observable actions generated, we also recorded the corresponding sequence of hidden states. For example, for the sequence of observations $\{a_1, a_1, a_2, b_2, b_2, b_1, a_1, a_2\}$ we would also record the hidden states $\{A, A, A, B, B, B, A, A\}$. The sequence of observations was segmented and clustered with DiSCS and the association between the clusters and the hidden states calculated. See Fig. 3 for a summary of the workflow.

Given that both the labels of the hidden states and the labels of the DiSCS clusters were nominal categorical values, we used the Cramér's V statistic [35] to measure the association between DiSCS output and the hidden states. As with other measures of association or correlation, $0 \leq V \leq 1$, with one corresponding to a perfect association, and zero for no association between the labels. Values for Cramér's V between 0.6 and 0.8 are considered to be strong associations and values between 0.8 and 1.0 are considered to be very strong [36].

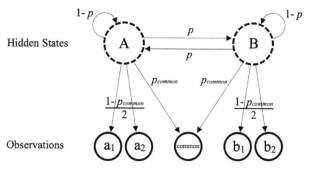

Fig. 2. A hidden Markov model used to generate simulated sequences of student actions. This model shows the case when two hidden states (A and B) each have two observable actions (a_1 and a_2, b_1 and b_2) and a common observable action.

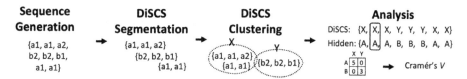

Fig. 3. Workflow for the simulation study.

Trials. To understand the robustness of the association, we calculated Cramér's V under different input conditions. First, we examined the impact of sequence length, by testing each of the values, $L = \{25, 50, 75, 100, 150, 200, 300, 400\}$. We did this keeping the number of hidden states $= 3$, the number of action observations per state $= 2$, transition probability, $p = 0.1$, the probability of a common action observed, $p_{common} = 0$, and the DiSCS smoothing variable, $t = 3$. For this and other trails in this study, the maximum number of segments that DiSCS optimized over was set to three standard deviations above the expected number of segments i.e., $Lp + 3\sqrt{Lp(1 - p)}$. For each value we repeated the test 20 times and recorded the value of Cramér's V each time. Second, we repeated the first trial but changed the number of hidden states from 3 to 2, then to 4. Third, we repeated the first trial again, but changed the number of action observations per state from 2 to 4, then 6. The results from these trials are shown in Fig. 4.

The next set of trials examined the impact of adjusting the sequence generation probabilities p and p_{common}. We examined the impact of different transition probabilities by testing each of the values, $p = \{0, 0.05, 0.1, 0.15, 0.2, 0.25\}$ while keeping the sequence length, $L = 200$, the number of hidden states $= 3$, the number of action observations per state $= 2$, the probability of a common action observed, $p_{common} = 0$, and the DiSCS smoothing variable, $t = 3$. Again, for each value we repeated the test 20 times and recorded the value of Cramér's V each time. Then we repeated this trial, but instead testing each of the values $p_{common} = \{0, 0.05, 0.1, 0.15, 0.2, 0.25\}$ while keeping the transition probability, $p = 0.1$. The results from these trials are shown in Fig. 5.

Lastly, to examine the impact of the DiSCS smoothing variable, we tested each of the values, $t = \{3, 6, 9, 12, 15, 18, 21, 24, 27, 30\}$ while keeping the sequence length, L

$= 200$, the number of hidden states $= 3$, the number of action observations per state $=$ 2, the transition probability, $p = 0.1$, and the probability of a common action observed, $p_{common} = 0$. Again, for each value we repeated the test 20 times and recorded the value of Cramér's V each time. We repeated this trial with the transition probability, $p = 0.05$. The results from these trials are shown in Fig. 6.

5.2 Results

When varying the sequence length, L, strong or very strong associations occurred for most values tested. However, this strength decreased as the sequences became longer. The lines for different numbers of hidden states are close together indicating that changing the number of hidden states has little impact on V for all sequence lengths. This is not the case for the number of actions per state which has a dramatic effect on V, especially for small L (see Fig. 4).

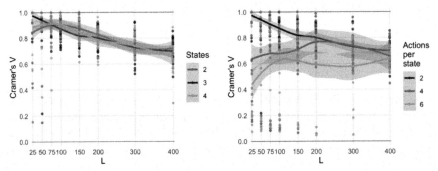

Fig. 4. The impact on association, V, of sequence length, L, using sequences with 2, 3 and 4 hidden states (left) and 2, 4 and 6 actions per state (right). Loess lines with standard errors are shown.

When varying the sequence generation probabilities, p and p_{common}, strong or very strong associations also occurred for most values tested. This strength decreased steadily as these probabilities increased, with larger decreases occurring when the transition probability, p, increases than when p_{common} increases (see Fig. 5).

When varying the DiSCS smoothing variable, t, very strong associations occurred for all values tested. This strength was most stable for when $p = 0.05$, and improved slightly at larger t values when $p = 0.1$. This indicates that when phases of design activity are expected to change about every 10 actions, adjusting t to larger values improved DiSCS performance, but that when phases of design activity are longer, or change less frequently, adjusting t will have minimal impact on DiSCS performance (see Fig. 6).

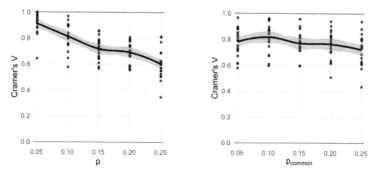

Fig. 5. The impact on association, V, of the sequence generation probabilities, p and p_{common}. Loess lines with standard errors are shown.

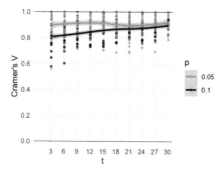

Fig. 6. The impact on association, V, of different values of the DiSCS smoothing variable, t, at two values of the transition probability, p. Loess lines with standard errors are shown.

6   Limitations

Results demonstrate that DiSCS is a strong and robust technique for segmenting sequences of categorical actions such as those commonly found in open-ended learning environments. For example, with sequences with up to 4 hidden states, strong or very strong associations were found. Strong or very strong associates were also found with up to 4 actions per state, up to very high transition probabilities, (at $p = 0.25$ transitions are expected to occur every 4 actions), and when the probability of common actions is also high. However, our simulation testing indicated important limitations. For example, as might be expected, it is clear that performance decreases with larger sequences, and when larger numbers of states and actions make the task more difficult. When sequences are larger than 400, we recommend that DiSCS results are used with caution unless transitions are expected to occur less often that once every 20 actions (equivalent to $p < 0.05$).

7   Implications

DiSCS offers a novel method for educational data mining that can provide insight into student activity within open-ended learning environments. The algorithm provides an efficient and robust method of segmenting categorical sequences of student activity from recorded log data. DiSCS might be used in combination with other measures (e.g., performance, learning gains from pretest to posttest) to determine patterns of actions that correspond to better student performances or learning [28], or that indicate students need help or support. By providing a more efficient method of finding meaningful segments of learning activity, DiSCS works towards being able to provide targeted feedback to learners in open-ended learning environments [17]. Python functions that perform DiSCS segmentation and clustering with either one or multiple lists of categorical actions are available at the DiSCS code repository [32].

Acknowledgments. This material is based upon work supported by the National Science Foundation under Grant No. (NSF DRL-1503170). Any opinions, findings, and conclusions or recommendations expressed in this material are those of the author(s) and do not necessarily reflect the views of the National Science Foundation.

References

1. Land, S.: Cognitive requirements for learning with open-ended learning environments. Educ. Tech. Res. Dev. **48**(3), 61–78 (2000)
2. Hannafin, M., Hill, J., Land, S., Lee, E.: Student-centered, open learning environments: research, theory, and practice. In: Spector, J Michael, Merrill, M David, Elen, Jan, Bishop, M. J. (eds.) Handbook of Research on Educational Communications and Technology, pp. 641–651. Springer, New York (2014). https://doi.org/10.1007/978-1-4614-3185-5_51
3. de Jong, T., Linn, M., Zacharia, Z.: Physical and virtual laboratories in science and engineering education. Science **340**(6130), 305–308 (2013)
4. Young, J.: Technology-enhanced mathematics instruction: a second-order meta-analysis of 30 years of research. Educ. Res. Rev. **22**, 19–33 (2017)
5. Kolodner, J., et al.: Problem-based learning meets case-based reasoning in the middle-school science classroom: putting learning by design into practice. J. Learn. Sci. **12**(4), 495–547 (2003)
6. Moore, T., Stohlmann, M., Wang, H., Tank, K., Glancy, A., Roehrig, G.: Implementation and integration of engineering in K-12 STEM education. In: Engineering in Pre-college Settings: Synthesizing Research, Policy, and Practices, pp. 35–60. Purdue University Press (2014)
7. Crismond, D., Adams, R.: The informed design teaching and learning matrix. J. Eng. Educ. **101**(4), 738–797 (2012)
8. Purzer, S., Moore, T., Baker, D., Berland, L.: Supporting the implementation of the Next Generation Science Standards (NGSS) through research: engineering (2014)
9. Wang, H., Moore, T., Roehrig, G., Park, M.: STEM integration: teacher perceptions and practice. J. Pre-Coll. Eng. Educ. Res. **1**(2), 2 (2011)
10. Gero, J., Tang, H.-H.: The differences between retrospective and concurrent protocols in revealing the process-oriented aspects of the design process. Des. Stud. **22**(3), 283–295 (2001)
11. Chen, H., Cannon, D., Gabrio, J., Leifer, L., Toye, G., Bailey, T.: Using wikis and weblogs to support reflective learning in an introductory engineering design course. Hum. Behav. Des. **5**, 95–105 (2005)
12. Cross, N.: Design cognition: results from protocol and other empirical studies of design activity. In: Eastman, C., Newstatter, W., McCracken, M. (eds.) Design Knowing and Learning: Cognition in Design Education, pp. 79–103. Elsevier, Oxford (2001)

13. Fischer, C., et al.: Mining big data in education: affordances and challenges. Rev. Res. Educ. **44**(1), 130–160 (2020)
14. Blikstein, P.: Using learning analytics to assess students' behavior in open-ended programming tasks. In: Proceedings of the 1st International Conference on Learning Analytics and Knowledge, pp. 110–116 (2011)
15. Gobert, J.D., Sao Pedro, M., Baker, R., Toto, E., Montalvo, O.: Leveraging educational data mining for real-time performance assessment of scientific inquiry skills within microworlds. J. Educ. Data Min. **4**(1), 104–143 (2012)
16. Käser, T., Schwartz, D.L.: Modeling and analyzing inquiry strategies in open-ended learning environments. Int. J. Artif. Intell. Educ. **30**(3), 504–535 (2020). https://doi.org/10.1007/s40 593-020-00199-y
17. Xing, W., et al.: Automatic assessment of students' engineering design performance using a Bayesian network model. J. Educ. Comput. Res. **59**, 230–256 (2020)
18. Vieira, C., Goldstein, M., Purzer, Ş, Magana, A.: Using learning analytics to characterize student experimentation strategies in the context of engineering design. J. Learn. Anal. **3**(3), 291–317 (2016)
19. Kinnebrew, J., Loretz, K., Biswas, G.: A contextualized, differential sequence mining method to derive students' learning behavior patterns. J. Educ. Data Min. **5**(1), 190–219 (2013)
20. Taub, M., Azevedo, R.: Using sequence mining to analyze metacognitive monitoring and scientific inquiry based on levels of efficiency and emotions during game-based learning. J. Educ. Data Min. **10**(3), 1–26 (2018)
21. Bogarín, A., Cerezo, R., Romero, C.: Survey on educational process mining. Wiley Interdiscip. Rev. Data Min. Knowl. Discov. **8**(1), e1230 (2018)
22. Romero, C., Ventura, S.: Data mining in education. Wiley Interdiscip. Rev. Data Min. Knowl. Discov. **3**(1), 12–27 (2013)
23. Pelánek, R.: Bayesian knowledge tracing, logistic models, and beyond: an overview of learner modeling techniques. User Model. User-Adap. Interact. **27**(3), 313–350 (2017)
24. Xie, C., Zhang, Z., Nourian, S., Pallant, A., Hazzard, E.: A time series analysis method for assessing engineering design processes using a CAD tool. Int. J. Eng. Educ. **30**(1), 218–230 (2014)
25. Shute, V.: Stealth assessment in computer-based games to support learning. Comput. Games Instr. **55**(2), 503–524 (2011)
26. Ayres, J., Flannick, J., Gehrke, J., Yiu, T.: Sequential pattern mining using a bitmap representation. In: Proceedings of the Eighth ACM SIGKDD International Conference on Knowledge Discovery and Data Mining, pp. 429–435 (2002)
27. Srikant, R., Agrawal, R.: Mining sequential patterns: generalizations and performance improvements. In: Apers, P., Bouzeghoub, M., Gardarin, G. (eds.) EDBT 1996. LNCS, vol. 1057, pp. 1–17. Springer, Heidelberg (1996). https://doi.org/10.1007/BFb0014140
28. Martinez, R., Yacef, K., Kay, J., Al-Qaraghuli, A., Kharrufa, A.: Analysing frequent sequential patterns of collaborative learning activity around an interactive tabletop. In: 4th International Conference on Educational Data Mining, pp. 111–120 (2011)
29. Bannert, M., Reimann, P., Sonnenberg, C.: Process mining techniques for analysing patterns and strategies in students' self-regulated learning. Metacogn. Learn. **9**(2), 161–185 (2013). https://doi.org/10.1007/s11409-013-9107-6
30. Bouchet, F., Harley, J., Trevors, G., Azevedo, R.: Clustering and profiling students according to their interactions with an intelligent tutoring system fostering self-regulated learning. J. Educ. Data Min. **5**(1), 104–146 (2013)
31. DeFalco, J., et al.: Detecting and addressing frustration in a serious game for military training. Int. J. Artif. Intell. Educ. **28**(2), 152–193 (2018)
32. DiSCS code repository. https://github.com/jpbywater/DiSCS

33. Rousseeuw, P.: Silhouettes: a graphical aid to the interpretation and validation of cluster analysis. J. Comput. Appl. Math. **20**, 53–65 (1987)
34. Xie, C., Schimpf, C., Chao, J., Nourian, S., Massicotte, J.: Learning and teaching engineering design through modeling and simulation on a CAD platform. Comput. Appl. Eng. Educ. **26**(4), 824–840 (2018)
35. Cramer, H.: Mathematical Methods of Statistics. Princeton University Press, Princeton (1946)
36. Rea, L., Parker, R.: Designing and Conducting Survey Research: A Comprehensive Guide, 4th edn. Jossey-Bass, San Francisco (2014)

Interpretable Clustering of Students' Solutions in Introductory Programming

Tomáš Effenberger$^{(\boxtimes)}$ and Radek Pelánek

Masaryk University, Brno, Czech Republic
tomas.effenberger@mail.muni.cz, pelanek@fi.muni.cz

Abstract. In introductory programming and other problem-solving activities, students can create many variants of a solution. For teachers, content developers, or applications in student modeling, it is useful to find structure in the set of all submitted solutions. We propose a generic, modular algorithm for the construction of interpretable clustering of students' solutions in problem-solving activities. We describe a specific realization of the algorithm for introductory Python programming and report results of the evaluation on a diverse set of problems.

1 Introduction

Learning environments often provide problem-solving activities, where students construct solutions that are automatically evaluated for correctness while still allowing for multiple approaches. We focus on introductory programming in Python, but similar types of problems are common in computer science education (e.g., regular expressions, SQL), mathematics (geometry constructions, logic proofs), or physics (gravity, electrical circuits).

Even for a simple problem, there may be many solutions; see Fig. 1 for a specific illustration for introductory programming. All these programs passed functionality tests, yet they differ significantly in their style and quality. Online learning environments collect a large number of solutions, and it is not feasible to analyze all of them manually. It is thus useful to use machine learning techniques to uncover structure in the solution set, particularly to cluster similar solutions.

Such clustering has several use cases. To teachers, it provides a summary of students' approaches, examples of poor style, or inspiration for class discussion [6]. The understanding of students' solutions is also valuable for content authors; the clustering can reveal that a problem is solved in an unexpected way, which is helpful for guiding revisions and the development of new content [13]. Another application is automating feedback to students [17,18]. If we are able to find sufficiently coherent clusters, we can use the same feedback message for the whole cluster. Clustering can also be used to improve student models since the cluster into which a solution belongs provides additional information about the student's state beyond the commonly used answer correctness and response time. For example, a solution to a programming problem can contain evidence of a misconception or insufficient understanding of some programming concepts.

I. Roll et al. (Eds.): AIED 2021, LNAI 12748, pp. 101–112, 2021.
https://doi.org/10.1007/978-3-030-78292-4_9

```
    def count_a(text):         def count_a(text):         def count_a(text):
 a    x = 0                  b    n = 0                  c    x = text.count('a') \
      for i in range(len(text)):    for i in text:               + text.count('A')
          if text[i] == "A" or \         if i == 'a' or \        return x
             text[i] == "a":                i == 'A':
             x += 1                         n += 1
      return x                   return n
```

```
    def count_a(text):         def count_a(text):         def count_a(text):
 d    count = 0              e    text = text.upper()    f    count = 0
      for i in text.lower():      count = 0                   for i in text:
          if i == "a":            for letter in text:             if i == "a" or i == "A":
              count += 1              if letter == "A":               count = count + 1
      return count                    count += 1              return count
                                  return count
```

Fig. 1. Examples of students' solutions to the following programming problem: *"Write a function that counts the occurrences of letters 'a' and 'A' in a text."*

Clustering of students' solutions has been tackled before, even specifically for the introductory programming [3,5,21]. Yet, no algorithm was developed that would lead to a small number of *interpretable* clusters, as needed for many of the outlined use cases. Consider, for instance, feedback writing. Having a guarantee that all solutions in the cluster contain `for` and `if`, and do not contain `ord` can save you from manually inspecting all the solutions.

Previously proposed algorithms that consider interpretability are based on some notion of exact matching (e.g., equivalence after canonicalization), which leads to hundreds of small clusters [6,9,14]. With so many clusters, the complete clustering is not well-interpretable, even if the individual clusters are. Another substantial limitation of these previous attempts is that they were evaluated on just 3 or 4 similar problems, and it is not at all clear how well they would generalize beyond them.

Outside of the educational domain, several interpretable clustering algorithms have been proposed. They describe clusters using either branches in a decision tree [2,4,15], frequent patterns [19], or the most relevant features in matrix decomposition [8]. These algorithms cannot be used off-the-shelf for clustering students' solutions since they are not designed to utilize varying importance of solution's features, e.g., the occurrence of recursion vs. addition.

In this paper, we formulate the problem of interpretable clustering of students' solutions in terms of desirable properties of such clustering. We then propose a generic algorithm to solve this problem, describe its specific realization for introductory programming in Python and report the results it gives for a diverse set of problems.

2   Interpretable Clustering Problem

The general aim of interpretable clustering of students' solutions is to compute clusters of solutions that are useful for the intended applications where the interpretability is indispensable. To facilitate interpretability, the output should consist of not just the clusters of solutions but also their succinct description.

An example of such description is "`for, if, or, no [i]`" for solutions that use `for`, `if`, and `or` and do not use indexing. Although the utility of a clustering depends on the specific application, we can formulate three general key properties of any interpretable clustering: homogeneity, interpretability, and coverage.

Homogeneity. Each cluster should be compact, i.e., the solutions within the cluster should be similar to each other. In addition, the clusters should be well separated from each other, i.e., the solutions from different clusters should be dissimilar. These two requirements apply to non-interpretable clustering as well, and many metrics to quantify them have already been proposed, e.g., variance ratio, Xie-Beni index, and Silhouette coefficient [16]. Many of these metrics define homogeneity as the ratio between within-cluster compactness and between-clusters separability. Compactness can be measured, for instance, as the average distance between two points in the cluster and the separability as the distance from the cluster centroid to the closest centroid of another cluster.

Interpretability. Each cluster should be accompanied by a succinct description. These descriptions should provide insight into students' approaches and facilitate the writing of useful feedback applicable to all solutions in the cluster. Some applications require *perfect recall* of the descriptions, meaning that the description applies to all solutions in the cluster. Without perfect recall, the description could easily mislead the user to write feedback that does not make sense for some of the solutions. This condition is also referred to as *strong interpretability* or *1-interpretability* [19]. Ideally, the description should apply *only* to the solutions in the cluster being described *(perfect precision)*. We may, however, trade off precision for improvement in other criteria.

Coverage. Each cluster should cover a reasonable portion of the solutions. Consequently, a small number of clusters should be sufficient to cover a vast majority of the solutions. For most applications, we do not need to have complete coverage—it is sufficient to cover all the typical solutions and report the rest as atypical. The appropriate number of clusters depends on the application; in our experience, 4 to 8 clusters are appropriate for writing feedback and providing insight to authors.

3   Interpretable Clustering Algorithm

In this section, we describe an algorithm that solves the interpretable clustering problem. The proposed algorithm is flexible—it can be applied to any problem type just by specifying appropriate features, and it can be adapted to different use cases by adjusting parameters that determine focus on individual criteria (homogeneity, interpretability, and coverage). Thus it constitutes a good starting point against which to compare more complex or specialized approaches.

In the description of the algorithm, we use the following terminology: *feature* is a property of a solution (e.g., usage of a concept like `if` or `nested loops`), *clause* is a single feature with an optional quantifier (e.g., `many if`, `no elif`),

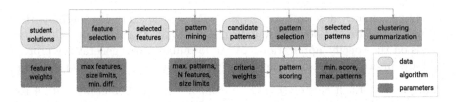

Fig. 2. Overview of the proposed interpretable clustering algorithm.

pattern is a conjunction of multiple clauses, and *label* is a short, possibly imprecise description of the pattern.

The input to the algorithm is a set of students' solutions to a given problem, represented in the form of a feature matrix. The features should be interpretable properties of the solutions, such as `recursion`. The algorithm describes the clusters by patterns over these interpretable features. In the final stage, the patterns are converted to short labels by omitting less important clauses.

The algorithm consists of four stages (Fig. 2), which are to a large degree independent and can be individually improved—or even approached in a distinctively different way than in our proposal. The four stages are:

1. **feature selection:** For the given problem, we select a small set of important, relevant, and distinct features.
2. **pattern mining:** Combining the selected features, we generate a set of candidate patterns that capture a large portion of the solutions, with the preference for short patterns with important features.
3. **pattern selection:** We score each candidate pattern with respect to its homogeneity, interpretability, and coverage. We then select the pattern with the highest score, remove matching solutions and repeat. We stop once we have enough patterns, or earlier if there is no pattern with a high score.
4. **clustering summarization:** We summarize each cluster by a short label derived from the pattern, together with a few examples of specific solutions from the given cluster.

A useful tool for understanding, implementing, and improving the algorithm is the feature matrix visualization with a column for each solution and a row for each feature (Fig. 3). If we cluster the solutions according to the selected feature patterns, we can see homogeneity and coverage of individual clusters at a glance.

3.1   Feature Selection

Different problem types need different features. For regular expressions problems, individual letters might be sufficient, while for programming problems, letters would be useless. Instead, we can extract keywords and compute statistics such as the number of variables from the abstract syntax tree of the program [7,17,20]. A completely different set of features can be obtained by similarity analysis, e.g.,

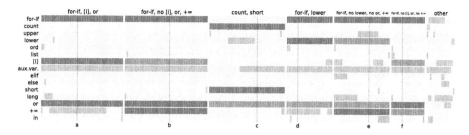

Fig. 3. Clustered feature matrix for the problem *Count A* with highlighted solutions a–f from Fig. 1. Each column corresponds to one solution, each row to one feature. Color hue denotes presence of features in solutions. Darker colors denote features in the corresponding pattern. (Color figure online)

edit distances to other solutions [12,21], or dynamic analysis, e.g., variable values sequences [6,9].

Many of these features might be useful for non-interpretable clustering, but only the ones that are interpretable by themself are suitable for the interpretable clustering. The more comprehensive and interpretable features, the better the output of the clustering algorithm, which is why some authors hand-crafted very specific features such as shape of the memoization array for dynamic programming problems [14], or whether a given sorting function is in-place [20].

Our algorithm can utilize domain knowledge about importance (interpretability) of the features in the form of *feature weights*. Instead of setting them manually, the weights can also be estimated from the data, e.g., based on the prevalence of the feature in the solutions.

If we define the features and their weights for a *problem type*, then only a fraction of these features might be relevant for any *specific problem*. Therefore, in the first stage, we select a set of useful features for the given problem. We use a greedy approach: considering one feature at a time, starting with the feature with the highest weight, we select the feature unless it is either extremely rare, used in nearly all solutions, or too similar to one of the already selected features. To measure the similarity between two features, we use the Jaccard coefficient (ratio of intersection and union) of the sets of solutions containing these features.

To illustrate the feature selection, let us consider the *Count A* problem (Fig. 1). The algorithm—assuming thresholds discussed later in Sect. 4.1—selects 15 features that are listed in Fig. 3. It skips 10 rare features, e.g., `recursion`, which was used in only 4 out of 240 solutions. It also skips 6 features too similar to other already selected, e.g., `if`, which closely coincides with more specific `for-if`.

3.2   Pattern Mining

The next step is to generate frequent patterns using the selected features. In contrast to the well-known apriori algorithm and other general pattern mining techniques [10], we take into account the interpretability of the patterns by preferring fewer clauses and important features (i.e., features with high weights). Our approach is similar to the depth-first *tree projection algorithm* for mining frequent itemsets [1], using feature weights for the ordering of the features.

We generate the candidate patterns recursively, starting from an empty pattern. For each feature and each possible quantifier, we try to extend the parent pattern by one clause (quantified feature). We then check whether the extended pattern is sufficiently frequent (i.e., whether there are enough solutions that match the pattern) while simultaneously not too similar to the parent pattern (i.e., whether there are enough solutions that match the parent pattern but not the extended pattern). If both conditions are met, we include the extended pattern into the candidate set and search for more specific patterns recursively.

The search tree can differ a lot between problems, so it is impossible to have a single set of universal thresholds. We circumvent this issue by *iterative deepening*: we start with tight thresholds, run the search and iteratively loosen the thresholds until we find a sufficient number of patterns (e.g., 1000).

We introduce two additional modifications that increase the interpretability of the generated patterns. First, we increase the thresholds on the pattern inclusion in proportion to the length of the pattern, expressing the preference for shorter patterns. Second, we increase the number of considered features in each iteration (*iterative broadening*), expressing the preference for important features.

3.3   Pattern Selection

To select patterns, we use a greedy approach known as *sequential covering* [11]. In each iteration, we score all candidate patterns, select the best, and remove matching solutions. This process is repeated until we select a prespecified number of patterns or until there is no pattern with a score above a prespecified threshold. Instead of using a constant threshold for the minimum score, we can increase it in each iteration; this is useful when the problems are diverse: starting with a low threshold ensures that at least some patterns are selected, while increasing it after each iteration avoids selecting an excessive number of patterns.

Pattern scoring reflects the desirable properties of homogeneity, interpretability, and coverage. We operationalize these properties using scores with a value between 0 and 1; a higher value is better. In the following discussion, we highlight the high-level idea and rationale behind each part of the scoring function. We also briefly mention specific formulas used in our realization of the algorithm.

Homogeneity consists of two aspects—*hard* and *soft*—which are averaged. *Hard homogeneity* is the degree to which *all* solutions in the cluster share some features (or their absence). Hard homogeneity is closely related to interpretability and actionability of clusters since exact matches are easy to understand and act upon (e.g., in feedback). We quantify hard homogeneity as the sum of weights of the shared features, normalized by the sum of weights of all relevant features selected for the problem. *Soft homogeneity* is the degree to which solutions in the cluster are similar and differentiated from other clusters. Soft homogeneity also applies to non-interpretable clustering, but the standard measures like Silhouette coefficient [16] must be adapted to work with an incomplete clustering.

We quantify soft homogeneity as $\max(0, 1 - D_{in}/D_{out})$, where D_{in} is the mean distance from a solution within the cluster to the centroid, and D_{out} is the mean distance from a solution outside the cluster to the centroid.

Interpretability considers four properties of the pattern; the interpretability score is the product of the individual criteria. The pattern should be *short* (long patterns are harder to interpret) and contain features that are *important* and *positive* (negative clauses are harder to interpret). The fourth aspect is *precision*, which expresses the preference to avoid "false positives," i.e. solutions matching the pattern that are already assigned to one of the previous patterns. Specifically, the length score is b^{L-1}, where L is the number of clauses and $b = 0.95$; the importance score is the average of the maximum and mean feature weights, normalized by the maximum weight over all selected features; the positivity score is $1 - c \cdot$ (proportion of positive clauses), using $c = 0.5$; and the precision is the ratio of the number of solutions in the cluster to the number of all solutions matching the pattern.

Coverage is based on the size of the cluster. A straightforward approach would be to make the coverage score equal to the relative size r of the cluster. However, it is more important to distinguish clusters of the sizes 3% and 6% than clusters of sizes 53% and 56%, so it is preferable to use a nonlinear scoring function. We use a simple, one-parametric piecewise linear function. Specifically, the coverage score is $\frac{1-k}{k}r$ for $r < k$ and $\frac{k}{1-k}r + 1 - \frac{k}{1-k}$ for $r \geq k$, using $k = 0.2$.

Overall Score. To combine these three criteria into a single score, we take their harmonic mean. The harmonic mean is more sensitive to the lowest value than the arithmetic mean, which better suits the requirement that all three criteria should be reasonably satisfied—even perfect coverage cannot make up for poor interpretability. If one of the criteria is more important for the considered use case, *weighted* harmonic mean can be used.

3.4   Clustering Summarization

Finally, it is useful to provide a short description of each cluster, as the full patterns are sometimes too long. A basic step is to remove implied features (e.g., `for-if` implies `if`). We can also simplify patterns by omitting some less important clauses. For example, negative clauses like `no import` are only informative if the feature appears in many solutions; otherwise, the user is likely to assume that the feature is not used unless specifically mentioned in the pattern.

4   Application to Python Programming

We have developed a proof-of-concept implementation of the algorithm and applied it to introductory Python programming data. The data come from an online learning environment `umimeprogramovat.cz`, which is used by both high school and university students. The environment offers quite a standard interface for solving programming problems: students see a problem statement and a sample testing data, write the code inside the browser, and after each submission, their solution is evaluated on hidden tests. If the submitted program is incorrect, the student can improve it and submit again. In this work, we consider only the correct solutions (i.e., the solutions that passed the tests).

The problems in the environment cover most topics typically included in the first university programming course (CS1). The simplest problems are one-line programs, such as writing a logic condition. The most difficult ones can still be solved with up to 15 lines of code but involve non-trivial concepts like lists and nested loops and take an average student around 15 min. The number of collected solutions ranges from 80 to 550 per problem.

4.1 Methodology and Setting

We have developed the algorithm iteratively using 11 problems (2 358 solutions). We have manually labeled a subset of solutions from these problems to clarify the desirable output of individual stages and perform experiments to refine the algorithm and find reasonable values for parameters. After this design phase, we reached the algorithm as described above. Then, we tested the algorithm on 11 new problems (2 598 solutions) without any change to the algorithm, parameter values, or feature weights. The number of problems may seem small, but our dataset is actually much more diverse than the datasets used in previous work [6,9,14], which contain just 3 or 4 similar problems.

The algorithm requires specification of features relevant for a given problem type, together with their weights. We automatically extract about 100 features from the abstract syntax tree. Most features correspond directly to a node in the abstract syntax tree (e.g., `for`, `if`), but a few are derived from relationships between multiple nodes (e.g., `recursion`, `for-if`). In addition, we use features `short` and `long` for programs that are below the first or above the last quartile in the number of lines for a given problem.

To set the feature weights, we used a semi-automatic approach. We started with weights estimated by a heuristic based on how soon and how frequently the feature appears in students' solutions (considering the ordering of problems in the learning environment), and then we manually adjusted some of the weights according to our experience with feedback writing.

To set values for other parameters, we used the training set of 11 problems. The advantage of the modular approach is that individual stages are largely independent, and thus each parameter can be set by analyzing inputs and outputs of a single stage. Using this approach, we reached the following setting:

- *feature selection*: max. 20 features, rel. size limit 0.02, min. difference 0.1,
- *pattern mining*: max. 1000 patterns; $12 + i$ features and relative size limit $0.09 - 0.01 \cdot i$ in the i-th iteration ($i \in 1, 2, \ldots, 8$),
- *pattern scoring*: unit weights in the harmonic mean; coverage score function with $k = 0.2$, length score base $b = 0.95$, positivity effect $c = 0.5$,
- *pattern selection*: max. 10 patterns, min. score $0.05 \cdot i$ in the i-th iteration.

4.2   Results

Figure 4 contains a compact overview of the obtained clusters for the 22 problems. The problems are displayed in the same order in which they appear in the learning environment, i.e., approximately from easier to more difficult. The problems used for training are marked by an asterisk.

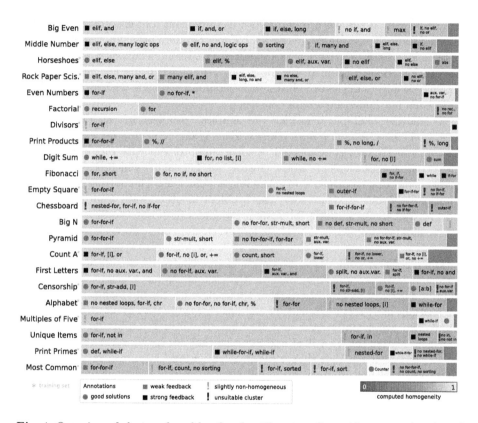

Fig. 4. Overview of clusters found by the algorithm, together with a manual rating of their quality. The gray rectangles correspond to the remaining unclustered solutions. (Color figure online)

Each rectangle represents one cluster: width corresponds to coverage, color to computed homogeneity, and the label can be used for basic assessment of cluster interpretability. For each cluster, we created a detailed report—complete patterns and a sample of solutions belonging to the cluster. Based on these reports, we manually classified each cluster into one of five categories: *good solutions* (a homogeneous set of solutions that do not require feedback), *strong feedback* (a set of solutions for which we can provide clear and useful advice that is applicable to all of them), *weak feedback* (similar to strong feedback, but the feedback is rather a hint or a suggestion), *slightly non-homogeneous* (the cluster makes sense, but is not completely homogeneous), and *unsuitable cluster* (highly non-homogeneous or hard to interpret).

Overall, the results show that the algorithm can generate useful and interpretable clusters. For many clusters, we can provide strong feedback, e.g., in the *Count A* problem, there is a large "`for-if,or,[i]`" cluster (Fig. 1a) for which we can provide the following feedback: *"This problem can be solved more elegantly without indexing."* Negative clauses are often indicative of useful feedback, especially if the feature in question is important and used by most of the other solutions. For example, in the *Rock Paper Scissors* problem, the 3rd cluster contains long solutions that use many nested `if`s. Useful feedback is to show how the solution to such problem can be greatly simplified using logical operators. Similarly, students in the 6th cluster write complicated code without `elif`; they might even not know this useful construct.

As another example, consider the simplest problem in the dataset: *Big Even* (*"Write a function that returns True if the larger of the two numbers is even."*) Students were expected to solve this problem with one line of code. These compact solutions are in the cluster "`no if, and,`" which is slightly non-homogeneous due to presence of a few longer solutions. The output of the algorithm reveals that students solve the problem in other ways than anticipated and provides useful impulse for system designers (e.g., for the development of new, scaffolded problems). The three largest clusters also afford clear and useful feedback.

The algorithm sometimes produces clusters that are not sufficiently homogeneous or satisfactory. This is mostly the case of the last clusters. These cases could be partially resolved by further tinkering with the algorithm parameters, but partially it is a consequence of the basic greedy strategy used in the algorithm. The problematic cases are distributed relatively uniformly among the training and test set, i.e., it is not the case that we have overfitted the training set, but rather a sign that some problems would require a more tuned or improved algorithm. However, for some cases, it would be challenging to provide a high-quality interpretable clustering even for a human expert.

5   Discussion

The central aim of this work is to highlight the issue of *interpretability* in the context of clustering of students' solutions in problem-solving activities. For this purpose, we propose a generic, modular algorithm and demonstrate its application to data from introductory Python programming. The algorithm is able to produce useful, interpretable, and actionable clusters—they provide useful insight for content authors and allow efficient distribution of feedback to students.

The limitation of the presented work is that it is based solely on qualitative evaluation by the algorithm authors. The algorithm also contains quite a few choices and parameters. Although our experience suggests that the approach is reasonably robust and we have not observed any significant degradation of performance on the test set, the setting of the algorithm parameters needs further exploration. Since the presented algorithm is able to produce reasonable clusters, it provides a good starting point for a search for improved versions. These improvements can take the form of better parameter optimization, but also of non-greedy alternatives to individual stages or even significantly different approaches. Another important direction for future work is the exploration of the generalizability of the proposed algorithm to other problem-solving activities.

References

1. Agarwal, R.C., Aggarwal, C.C., Prasad, V.V.V.: A tree projection algorithm for generation of frequent item sets. J. Parallel Distrib. Comput. **61**(3), 350–371 (2001)
2. Basak, J., Krishnapuram, R.: Interpretable hierarchical clustering by constructing an unsupervised decision tree. IEEE Trans. Knowl. Data Eng. **17**(1), 121–132 (2005)
3. Blikstein, P., Worsley, M., Piech, C., Sahami, M., Cooper, S., Koller, D.: Programming pluralism: using learning analytics to detect patterns in the learning of computer programming. J. Learn. Sci. **23**(4), 561–599 (2014)
4. Dasgupta, S., Frost, N., Moshkovitz, M., Rashtchian, C.: Explainable k-means clustering: theory and practice. In: XXAI Workshop. ICML (2020)
5. Gao, L., Wan, B., Fang, C., Li, Y., Chen, C.: Automatic clustering of different solutions to programming assignments in computing education. In: Proceedings of the ACM Conference on Global Computing Education, pp. 164–170 (2019)
6. Glassman, E.L., Scott, J., Singh, R., Guo, P.J., Miller, R.C.: OverCode: visualizing variation in student solutions to programming problems at scale. ACM Trans. Comput. Hum. Interact. (TOCHI) **22**(2), 1–35 (2015)
7. Glassman, E.L., Singh, R., Miller, R.C.: Feature engineering for clustering student solutions. In: Proceedings of the First ACM Conference on Learning@ Scale Conference, pp. 171–172 (2014)
8. Greene, D., Cunningham, P.: Producing accurate interpretable clusters from high-dimensional data. In: Jorge, A.M., Torgo, L., Brazdil, P., Camacho, R., Gama, J. (eds.) PKDD 2005. LNCS (LNAI), vol. 3721, pp. 486–494. Springer, Heidelberg (2005). https://doi.org/10.1007/11564126_49
9. Gulwani, S., Radiček, I., Zuleger, F.: Automated clustering and program repair for introductory programming assignments. ACM SIGPLAN Not. **53**(4), 465–480 (2018)
10. Han, J., Cheng, H., Xin, D., Yan, X.: Frequent pattern mining: current status and future directions. Data Min. Knowl. Discov. **15**(1), 55–86 (2007)
11. Han, J., Kamber, M., Pei, J.: Data Mining Concepts and Techniques. The Morgan Kaufmann Series in Data Management Systems, 3rd edn., vol. 5, no. 4, pp. 83–124 (2011)
12. Huang, J., Piech, C., Nguyen, A., Guibas, L.: Syntactic and functional variability of a million code submissions in a machine learning MOOC. In: AIED 2013 Workshops Proceedings Volume, vol. 25 (2013)
13. Joyner, D., et al.: From clusters to content: using code clustering for course improvement. In: Proceedings of the 50th ACM Technical Symposium on Computer Science Education, pp. 780–786 (2019)

14. Kaleeswaran, S., Santhiar, A., Kanade, A., Gulwani, S.: Semi-supervised verified feedback generation. In: Proceedings of the 2016 24th ACM SIGSOFT International Symposium on Foundations of Software Engineering, pp. 739–750 (2016)
15. Liu, B., Xia, Y., Yu, P.S.: Clustering through decision tree construction. In: Proceedings of the Ninth International Conference on Information and Knowledge Management, pp. 20–29 (2000)
16. Liu, Y., Li, Z., Xiong, H., Gao, X., Wu, J.: Understanding of internal clustering validation measures. In: 2010 IEEE International Conference on Data Mining, pp. 911–916. IEEE (2010)
17. Nguyen, A., Piech, C., Huang, J., Guibas, L.: Codewebs: scalable homework search for massive open online programming courses. In: Proceedings of the 23rd International Conference on World Wide Web, pp. 491–502 (2014)
18. Piech, C., Huang, J., Nguyen, A., Phulsuksombati, M., Sahami, M., Guibas, L.: Learning program embeddings to propagate feedback on student code. In: Proceedings of Machine Learning Research, Lille, France, 07–09 July 2015, vol. 37, pp. 1093–1102. PMLR (2015)
19. Saisubramanian, S., Galhotra, S., Zilberstein, S.: Balancing the tradeoff between clustering value and interpretability. In: Proceedings of the AAAI/ACM Conference on AI, Ethics, and Society, pp. 351–357 (2020)
20. Taherkhani, A., Korhonen, A., Malmi, L.: Automatic recognition of students' sorting algorithm implementations in a data structures and algorithms course. In: Proceedings of the 12th Koli Calling International Conference on Computing Education Research, pp. 83–92 (2012)
21. Yin, H., Moghadam, J., Fox, A.: Clustering student programming assignments to multiply instructor leverage. In: Proceedings of the Second (2015) ACM Conference on Learning@ Scale, pp. 367–372 (2015)

Adaptively Scaffolding Cognitive Engagement with Batch Constrained Deep Q-Networks

Fahmid Morshed Fahid[1]($\boxtimes$) , Jonathan P. Rowe[1] , Randall D. Spain[1],
Benjamin S. Goldberg[2] , Robert Pokorny[3], and James Lester[1]

[1] North Carolina State University, Raleigh, NC 27695, USA
{ffahid,jprowe,rdspain,lester}@ncsu.edu
[2] U.S. Army CCDC - STTC, Orlando, FL 32826, USA
benjamin.s.goldberg.civ@mail.mil
[3] Intelligent Automation Inc., Rockville, MD 20855, USA

Abstract. Scaffolding student engagement is a central challenge in adaptive learning environments. The ICAP framework defines levels of cognitive engagement with a learning activity in terms of four different engagement modes—Interactive, Constructive, Active, and Passive—and it predicts that increased cognitive engagement will yield improved learning. However, a key open question is how best to translate the ICAP theory into the design of adaptive scaffolding in adaptive learning environments. Specifically, should scaffolds be designed to require the highest levels of cognitive engagement (i.e., Interactive and Constructive modes) with every instance of feedback or knowledge component? To answer this question, in this paper we investigate a data-driven pedagogical modeling framework based on batch-constrained deep Q-networks, a type of deep reinforcement learning (RL) method, to induce policies for delivering ICAP-inspired scaffolding in adaptive learning environments. The policies are trained with log data from 487 learners as they interacted with an adaptive learning environment that provided ICAP-inspired feedback and remediation. Results suggest that adaptive scaffolding policies induced with batch-constrained deep Q-networks outperform heuristic policies that strictly follow the ICAP model without RL-based tailoring. The findings demonstrate the utility of deep RL for tailoring scaffolding for learner cognitive engagement.

Keywords: Deep reinforcement learning · Cognitive engagement · ICAP · Adaptive learning environments

1 Introduction

Adaptive learning environments provide scaffolding in the form of hints, feedback and remediation to improve learning experiences. Scaffolds offer temporary support to students as they learn, which is gradually faded as students gain knowledge and achieve mastery. Designing effective scaffolds is challenging. Determining how and when to deliver scaffolding in different situations is critical to enabling effective learning experiences [22]. A key factor in adaptive scaffolding is the cognitive engagement of learners. Chi and Wylie [7] describe *cognitive engagement* as an "active learning" process

© Springer Nature Switzerland AG 2021
I. Roll et al. (Eds.): AIED 2021, LNAI 12748, pp. 113–124, 2021.
https://doi.org/10.1007/978-3-030-78292-4_10

that involves higher-order thinking (e.g., analyzing, synthesizing, evaluating). Ideally, adaptive scaffolding is designed to optimize students' cognitive engagement, and by extension, enhance learning outcomes.

The ICAP framework provides a taxonomy for categorizing different modes of cognitive engagement: Interactive, Constructive, Active, and Passive [7]. ICAP predicts that learning activities requiring higher levels of cognitive engagement (e.g., peer dialogue, writing a summary) yield improved learning outcomes compared to activities that involve lower levels of cognitive engagement (e.g., listening passively, highlighting text). There is strong evidence in support of the ICAP theory, and it has been used to guide the design of lesson plans [6] and adaptive learning technologies [20], but it is less clear how to translate ICAP into the design of individual scaffolds. High levels of cognitive engagement require time and student motivation. A direct translation of ICAP may not be optimal for every scaffold and knowledge component in an adaptive learning environment. This raises a natural question: should ICAP be operationalized by *adaptively* scaffolding cognitive engagement, eliciting higher-order thinking at key moments with the aim of enhancing overall learning outcomes, and, if so, how should we devise models for adaptively scaffolding cognitive engagement?

Recent years have seen growing interest in using reinforcement learning (RL) to devise policies for scaffolding student learning in adaptive learning environments [5, 8]. Deep RL, which combines RL and deep neural networks, has shown particular promise for this task [1–3, 31]. Several studies have shown that deep RL techniques yield effective pedagogical models in adaptive learning environments [3, 15]. However, previous work has not systematically investigated methods for adaptively scaffolding cognitive engagement with deep RL techniques.

In this paper, we introduce a data-driven pedagogical modeling framework based on batch constrained deep Q-networks, a type of deep RL method, to induce policies for scaffolding cognitive engagement in adaptive learning environments. The policies drive ICAP-based feedback and remediation following instructional videos and embedded assessments in a learning environment for training operational command skills. The policies are induced using interaction log data from 487 learners as they engaged with the adaptive learning environment. We compare scaffolding policies induced with batch constrained deep Q-networks with heuristic policies that strictly follow the ICAP model without RL-based tailoring.

2   Related Work

RL provides a natural framework for inducing data-driven scaffolding models to improve student learning experiences. Wang conducted a study with 30 students learning software development concepts in a dialogue-based tutoring system and found that an RL-based teaching assistant was able to learn from its teaching experience and continuously improve its teaching strategies online [29]. Georgila and colleagues [10] found that RL-based models fostered increased confidence among learners through adaptive scaffolding to support the development of interpersonal skills. Their results suggest that the induced policies matched, or outperformed heuristic scaffolding models designed by human experts. Similar findings have been reported in other studies and learning environments investigating RL-based pedagogical models [23, 33].

Over the past several years, deep RL techniques have shown significant promise for inducing scaffolding policies in adaptive learning environments. For example, Wang and colleagues [30] found that adaptively scaffolding student learning in a narrative-centered learning environment for middle school microbiology using deep RL models trained with simulated students outperformed baseline methods. Additional work has investigated offline deep RL methods, where RL models are trained with previously collected data rather than simulations to induce scaffolding policies. For example, Aziz-soltani and colleagues [4] found that inferring immediate rewards using Gaussian process estimation to train offline deep RL-based pedagogical models can significantly improve learning gains in students. To date, deep RL techniques have not been used to induce policies for adaptively scaffolding cognitive engagement with ICAP-inspired feedback and remediation in adaptive learning environments.

The ICAP framework predicts that as students become more actively engaged with learning materials, moving from passive to active to constructive to interactive behaviors, their learning will increase. Support for the ICAP framework has been found in a number of studies [18, 20, 32]. Mitrovic et al. [20] found that using interactive visualization and prompts to enforce constructive engagement in a video-based learning environment led to high levels of confidence and lower levels of frustration during the learning episode compared to students who engaged in passive learning behaviors. Few studies have investigated how adaptive ICAP-inspired scaffolding applied at a step-based or micro-loop level in adaptive learning environments supports student learning [26].

3 Dataset

To induce data-driven pedagogical models for delivering ICAP-inspired feedback and remediation, we utilize log data collected from an online study involving 487 learners (54% male, 42% female) recruited through Amazon Mechanical Turk who interacted with an adaptive learning environment for training operational command skills. The learning environment was built using the Generalized Intelligent Framework for Tutoring (GIFT), an open-source domain-independent framework for designing, deploying, and evaluating adaptive learning technologies [25]. The learning environment includes a series of instructional videos that cover core concepts and principles associated with operational command. Following each video, learners answered a series of multiple-choice questions. An incorrect response to a question prompted the learning environment to deliver ICAP-inspired feedback and remediation that required the learner to either (1) passively re-read a transcription of the video that was just presented in the lesson video, (2) re-read the transcription of the video and actively highlight the portion of text that answered the recall question that was just missed, or (3) re-read the video transcription and constructively summarize the answer to the question in their own words. The learning environment did not have built-in support for the interactive mode of engaging with feedback and remediation, so that component of ICAP was omitted. The active and constructive remediation prompts included expert highlighting/summaries that asked students to self-evaluate the accuracy of their responses. The learning environment also included a "no remediation" prompt that provided learners with a simple feedback message stating they incorrectly answered the question.

After completing a remediation exercise, learners were presented again with the previously attempted question. If they answered the question correctly, then they advanced to the next question or video lesson. Learners continued to receive remediation, potentially of different types, until they correctly answered the question. The learning environment utilized a random policy to determine the type of ICAP-inspired remediation learners received each time they missed a question (irrespective of their number of attempts), although a software error caused passive and no remediation instances to be under-sampled.

In all, learners completed 39 embedded assessments, which were distributed across four units that typically take 1–2 h in total to complete. The adaptive learning environment also included a set of web-based surveys designed to collect demographic information and a set of pre- and post-test items that measured student learning as a result of completing the course.

The resulting dataset included a total of 4,998 instances of ICAP-inspired feedback and remediation. On average, learners received 10 instances of remediation while completing the course ($SD = 12.7; min = 1, max = 113$). Table 1 summarizes the distribution of remediation instances encountered throughout the course. A paired t-test showed that the pre-test scores ($M = 4.18, SD = 2.30, min = 0, max = 11$) and the post-test scores ($M = 8.32, SD = 2.96, min = 0, max = 12$) were significantly different ($p < 0.001$), implying the adaptive learning environment improved knowledge of operational command concepts and skills among the participants.

Table 1. Distribution of ICAP-based remediation instances.

Remediation	Total	Chapter 1	Chapter 2	Chapter 3	Chapter 4
None	470 (9.40%)	155 (3.10%)	141 (2.82%)	141 (2.82%)	33 (0.66%)
Passive	445 (8.90%)	145 (2.90%)	136 (2.72%)	127 (2.54%)	37 (0.74%)
Active	2074 (41.50%)	684 (13.65%)	587 (11.74%)	639 (12.79%)	166 (3.32%)
Constructive	2009 (40.20%)	626 (12.53%)	606 (12.12%)	611 (12.22%)	166 (3.32%)

4   Adaptive Scaffolding with Batch Constrained Deep Q-Networks

In this section, we present a deep RL framework for creating policies to scaffold cognitive engagement in adaptive learning environments. Specifically, we describe our deep RL-based pedagogical model architecture, our approach to formalizing adaptive scaffolding as a Markov decision process, and a pair of metrics for evaluating policies for the delivering ICAP-inspired feedback and remediation.

4.1   Deep RL-Based Pedagogical Model Architecture

To devise data-driven policies for adaptively scaffolding students' cognitive engagement, we used deep Q learning, a type of RL technique that leverages deep neural network-based function approximation to represent the values of input states [21]. Q-learning is a model-free RL algorithm where the goal is to learn an optimal policy π^* based on the optimal action-value function $Q^*(s, a)$ estimated from sample data without use of an explicit model of the task environment [27]. Starting from state $s \in \mathbb{S}$ and taking action $a \in \mathbb{A}$ while getting reward $r \in \mathbb{R}$, the Q values are defined as the expected cumulative reward following a policy π that generates a set of actions at each successive state. To reduce extrapolation errors often seen in offline RL, we utilized batch constrained deep Q-networks [9].

Deep Q-networks (DQNs) follow an off-policy learning approach that involves iteratively sampling from a finite experience buffer to greedily estimate Q values according to the Bellman equation. A loss function (Eq. 1) is defined to train a deep neural network to estimate the model's Q-values:

$$Loss(\theta) = \mathbb{E}[(y - Q(s, a; \theta))^2] \tag{1}$$

where θ represents the set of weights in the neural network.

A variant of DQNs is the *Double DQN*, which uses two separate networks to reduce overestimation bias in the DQN by separating the action selection and action evaluation components of the model [11]. This provides improved stabilization and convergence while the model is trained. In Double DQNs, two neural networks with identical architectures are used, namely, the target network ($\overline{\theta}$) and the online network (θ). The online network is trained on every iteration while the target network is frozen for a fixed number of iterations. During training, the online network is used to select the next action $a' \in \mathbb{A}$ based on the next state $s' \in \mathbb{S}$, and the target network is used to evaluate the Q value of the action:

$$y = r + \gamma Q(s', argmax_{a' \in \mathbb{A}} Q(s', a'; \theta); \overline{\theta}) \tag{2}$$

where $\gamma \in [0, 1]$ is the discount factor that controls the contribution of future rewards.

DQNs are often used with an *experience replay buffer* to keep track of a finite set of recent training observations [21]. During training, transitions are sampled from the buffer randomly. Prioritized experience replay [24] prioritizes the sampling of transitions based upon the current temporal difference errors. This additional priority makes the network more data efficient [12] by ensuring quick convergence. Priority is calculated as follows:

$$t_{priority} = \left|\{r + \gamma Q(s', argmax_{a' \in \mathbb{A}} Q(s', a'; \theta); \overline{\theta})\} - \{Q(s, a; \theta)\}\right|^\omega \tag{3}$$

Here, $t_{priority}$ is the priority of a transition t and ω is a hyperparameter.

In batch RL, also known as offline RL, the experience replay buffer remains fixed. This approach is often necessary in RL applications in adaptive learning environments, where a training corpus is collected from students prior to employing RL, and additional data collection is not feasible during the RL process. With limited data, DQNs often suffer from divergence issues due to extrapolating Q values outside of the data distribution. Batch constrained DQNs restrict such extrapolation errors by only allowing actions that are evident in the available data using a probabilistic sampling technique [9]:

$$y = r + \gamma Q(s', argmax_{a' | (a'|s') / max_{\hat{a}} \pi_b(\hat{a}|s') > \tau} Q(s', a'; \theta); \overline{\theta}) \tag{4}$$

Here, π_b is the policy used to collect the data and τ is a probability threshold.

Deep neural networks within batch constrained DQNs can be implemented using different neural architectures. In this work, we implement two commonly used architectures: fully connected (FC) layers and long short-term memory (LSTM) layers. In FC layers, each neuron is a perceptron that calculates a weighted sum of the input units to produce an output value through an activation function. All inputs are connected to all neurons in the first layer, all of the output of the first layer is fully connected to input neurons of the second layer, and so on until the final output layer.

LSTMs are a specialized version of recurrent neural networks that use long term temporal dependencies to avoid common issues in neural networks such as the vanishing and exploding gradient problems [13]. An LSTM unit consists of a memory cell state and three gates: a forget gate, an input gate, and an output gate. These pieces together control the flow of information during model training. Notably batch constrained DQNs with LSTM networks support sequential input representations, which enables them to keep track of (and forget) previous inputs and hidden states.

4.2 States, Actions and Reward

To formalize the task of inducing a policy for scaffolding cognitive engagement in an adaptive learning environment, we defined a Markov decision process, which involves controlling a set of actions $\mathbb{A}$ based on some state $s \in \mathbb{S}$ to optimize the accumulation of reward $r \in \mathbb{R}$. Markov decision process provide a standardized mathematical representation for RL tasks. We define the state ($\mathbb{S}$), action ($\mathbb{A}$) and reward ($\mathbb{R}$) components of the Markov decision process as follows.

State ($\mathbb{S}$). We devise the state representation by extracting 31 features from learners' log data, which are divided into 3 groups: (1) survey features, (2) video playback features, and (3) remediation engagement features. The survey features include gender, age, education level, content familiarity, domain interest, and pre-test score on a content knowledge assessment. Four video playback features are extracted: time spent on the last video, average time spent on videos, whether learners received automated feedback about their time spent on the last video, and time spent on the feedback. Twenty remediation features are extracted: the previous type of remediation delivered, the total number of remediation instances delivered for each ICAP category, the average time spent engaged in the remediation activity, the average time spent on all previous remediation activities, and features reflecting how long learners spent answering the recall questions. We normalize each feature to range between [0,1] to improve stability when training the DQNs. Batch constrained DQNs require a discrete state space to calculate the probability of each state-action pair. Therefore, we cluster the set of state-action pairs into 5 groups using k-means clustering. We visually select the number of clusters using the distortion elbow method [17]. These clusters are used when sampling for the batch constrained DQN action probabilities.

Action ($\mathbb{A}$). At each pedagogical decision point (i.e., after a missed question), there are 4 possible actions (i.e., ICAP-based remediations) that can be selected: constructive (re-read the video transcription and summarize), active (re-read the video transcript and highlight relevant section), passive (re-read the video transcript), or no remediation.

Reward ($\mathbb{R}$). Each participant completed a 12-item pre- and post-test to assess content knowledge about operational command concepts. We use learners' pre- and post-test scores to calculate normalized learning gains (NLG) associated with each sequence of ICAP-inspired remediation instances [19]. Note that, for each student, we will only have a single NLG value at the end of their episode, which is the delayed reward [4]. Our reward value is a real number and ranges between 0 to 100.

4.3 Evaluation Metrics

In batch constrained DQNs, the optimal policy (π^*) usually has a significantly different distribution of state-action pairs than the behavioral policy (π_b) that was used to collect the training data. Performing RL policy evaluation with data collected under a different policy is known as *off-policy evaluation* [28]. We use two evaluation metrics, Expected Cumulative Reward and Doubly Robust.

Expected cumulative reward (ECR) computes the average expected reward associated with a particular policy π beginning at the initial state $s_i \in \mathbb{S}$ in a given dataset D of the RL task. Specifically, ECR reports the average Q value over all initial states as follows:

$$ECR(D) = \frac{1}{N} \sum_{i=1}^{N} \max_{a \in \mathbb{A}} Q(s_i, a) \tag{5}$$

where N is the total number of episodes and s_i is an initial state for the ith episode.

Doubly Robust (DR) evaluation [14] is an alternative technique that combines the low variance of importance sampling estimation and the low biases of model-based estimation into a single metric according to the following equation:

$$DR(D) = \frac{1}{N} \sum_{i=1}^{N} \sum_{t=0}^{\infty} \gamma^t \prod_{l=0}^{t} \frac{\pi(a_l|s_l)}{\pi_b(a_l|s_l)} \left(R_t^i - Q\left(s_t^i, a_t^i\right) \right) + \gamma^t \prod_{l=0}^{t-1} \frac{\pi(a_l|s_l)}{\pi_b(a_l|s_l)} V(s_t^i) \tag{6}$$

The Q function and the value function (V) are based on a given policy π. Doubly Robust provides unbiased estimates if a model is accurate and/or provides low variance estimates if the behavior policy is known.

5 Results and Discussion

To devise deep RL-based policies for adaptively scaffolding cognitive engagement, we created pedagogical models with batch constrained double DQNs (BCQs) using prioritized experience replay buffers. All models and analyses were implemented in Python using the Scikit-learn and Keras packages with Tensorflow backend. We select $\tau = 10\%$ for the batch constrained hyperparameter because the training data contains 8.9% passive remediations and 9.4% no remediations, resulting in any τ greater than 12% never applying constrained sampling and any value below 8% always enforcing random sampling. We use $\omega = 0.5$ as our priority exponent following prior work [12] and use $\gamma = 0.95$

with a minibatch size of 128. We copy the parameters from the online network to the target network every 100 epochs. All models are trained for 20,000 epochs, repeated 5 times with different random seeds. We do not split our dataset into a training and testing set for validation as it is not necessary in batch RL [28].

We compare two alternative neural network architectures in the BCQ models: FC networks and LSTM networks. The FC BCQ models utilize four fully connected layers with 128 units per layer using ReLU activation functions. The LSTM BCQ models utilize 3 LSTM layers and a fully connected layer at the end, each with 128 units using ReLU activation functions. The output layer always uses a linear activation function to output Q values. For both architectures, a learning rate of 0.001 was utilized with the Adam optimizer [16] and L2 regularization.

For both BCQ models we explore three types of input: input with only the current state (FC-1 or LSTM-1), input with the current state and the previous state (FC-2 or LSTM-2), and input with the current state and previous two states (FC-3 or LSTM-3). In the FC BCQ models, the input states are concatenated and encoded as a single observation. In LSTM BCQ, the input states are provided sequentially.

We include three baseline models for the purpose of comparison in our analyses. All baseline models use a similar architecture as the FC BCQ models, but instead of following a greedy approach to action selection based upon the Bellman equation during model training (i.e., select the action with the maximum Q value in the next state), each baseline model takes a predetermined action while learning the Q functions as follows:

$$y = r + \gamma Q(s', a^{base}; \overline{\theta}) \tag{7}$$

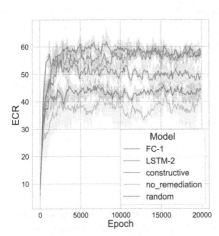

Fig. 1. Comparison between BCQ and ICAP-inspired baseline models.

Here a^{base} is a constructive remediation for the constructive baseline model, and a^{base} is no remediation for the no remediation baseline model. For the random baseline, a^{base} involves selecting an ICAP-inspired remediation according to a random policy. We select these baselines to serve as heuristic-based models that strictly follow ICAP without RL-based tailoring. τ is set to 0 for the baseline models.

We investigated the learning curves of different models based upon their ECR values. We found LSTM-2 BCQ performs slightly better than the LSTM-1 and LSTM-3 models, whereas little difference was observed between the three FC BCQ models. Based upon these findings, we focus our remaining analyses on FC-1 and LSTM-2.

As shown in Fig. 1, FC-1 and LSTM-2 both perform better than the three baseline models that strictly follow ICAP-inspired heuristics. Among the baselines, we observe that a random policy yields the lowest ECR and a constructive policy yields the highest.

To investigate the models' behavior after they converge to a stable policy, we examined their performance during the last 2000 training epochs (10% of the total training). Results are shown in Fig. 2. We observed that FC-1 and LSTM-2 scored higher than all other baselines in terms of both the ECR and DR evaluation metrics. Running a pairwise Tukey HSD test reveals significant differences ($p\text{-}value < 0.001$) between all models except between FC-1 and LSTM-2 for both the ECR and DR metrics. These results suggest there are no observed significant differences between the FC-1 BCQ and LSTM-2 BCQ models, but both significantly outperform all of the baselines.

Next, we examined the number of times each type of ICAP-inspired remediation was selected by the different models. Once again, we use the last 2000 epochs for this analysis. For FC-1, we find that the most frequently selected action is Constructive ($M = 2195, SD = 573$), with Active being the second most frequent ($M = 1183, SD = 450$) and Passive being the third ($M = 962, SD = 674$). (All pairwise comparison p-values are less than 0.05). For LSTM-2, there are no significant differences observed between the number of Active ($M = 1041, SD = 555$), Passive ($M = 1041, SD = 618$) and No Remediation ($M = 1003, SD = 566$) actions. However, both models recommend Constructive remediation significantly more often than other types of remediation ($p = 0.001$).

To interpret these results, it is useful to revisit our original research question: should ICAP be operationalized by *adaptively* scaffolding cognitive engagement, and, if so, how should we devise models for adaptively scaffolding cognitive engagement? In this analysis, higher ECR and DR values suggest a remediation policy has the potential to yield increased student normalized learning gains. Our findings indicate that the constructive heuristic policy performs the same or better than the no remediation and random policies, respectively (Fig. 1 and Fig. 2). This is consistent with the ICAP model; feedback and remediation that elicits higher cognitive engagement yields higher learning gains than policies that elicit lower or randomized cognitive engagement. Upon comparison with adaptive ICAP-inspired remediation policies (i.e., FC-1 BCQ and LSTM-2 BCQ), we find that the adaptive policies perform better than the non-adaptive constructive policy on the ECR and DR metrics (Fig. 1 and Fig. 2). This suggests that a deep RL-based adaptive approach to operationalizing ICAP to design scaffolding policies has promise for promoting increased learning compared to non-adaptive scaffolding policies. Notably, we see that the adaptive policies select constructive remediation more frequently than other types, which is further consistent with ICAP (Fig. 2).

There are limitations of the work. Most notably, the ECR and DR metrics are calculated from our existing dataset, which was collected according to a random policy. It is possible that the distribution of our data may differ from the true distribution when deep RL-based remediation policies are implemented in a run-time setting. This highlights the importance of future work implementing adaptive ICAP-inspired remediation policies at run-time and evaluating their impact on student learning outcomes. Despite these limitations, the results point toward the potential for improving student learning outcomes by combining ICAP with RL-based tailoring using batch constrained DQNs.

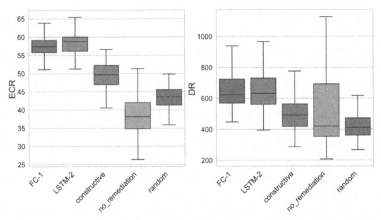

Fig. 2. Performance comparison between BCQ and baseline models during the last 2,000 training epochs.

6   Conclusions and Future Work

Scaffolding cognitive engagement is a key challenge in adaptive learning environments. The ICAP framework predicts that increased cognitive engagement will yield improved learning, but it is unclear how to best translate the guidance provided by this theory into the design of scaffolding in adaptive learning environments. We utilized batch constrained deep Q-networks to induce policies for presenting learners with ICAP-inspired scaffolding in an adaptive learning environment. Empirical analysis of converged RL policies indicates that batch constrained deep Q-networks yield adaptive scaffolding policies that outperform heuristic-based policies which exclusively select constructive scaffolding, no scaffolding, or scaffolding at random. Policies induced with batch constrained deep Q-networks also select constructive scaffolding more frequently than active, passive, or no scaffolding. These results (1) support the ICAP framework, and (2) suggest that adaptively scaffolding cognitive engagement using deep RL-induced policies shows promise for optimizing student learning outcomes.

There are several promising directions for future work. First, future research should investigate the impact of additional reward and state features in deep RL-based policies to identify their impact on student learning and engagement. Second, it will be instructive to examine how multimodal data such as video-based analysis of student engagement can be used to augment RL-induced policies for scaffolding student engagement. Finally, it will be important to evaluate the RL policies by implementing them in a run-time learning environment and investigating their impact on student learning outcomes.

Acknowledgements. The research described herein has been sponsored by the U.S. Army Research Laboratory under cooperative agreement W911NF-15-2-0030. The statements and opinions expressed in this article do not necessarily reflect the position or the policy of the United States Government, and no official endorsement should be inferred.

References

1. Ai, F., Chen, Y., Guo, Y., Zhao, Y., Wang, Z., Fu, G.: Concept-aware deep knowledge tracing and exercise recommendation in an online learning system. In: Proceedings of the 12th International Conference on Educational Data Mining, pp. 240–245 (2019)
2. Sanz Ausin, M., Maniktala, M., Barnes, T., Chi, M.: Exploring the impact of simple explanations and agency on batch deep reinforcement learning induced pedagogical policies. In: Bittencourt, I.I., Cukurova, M., Muldner, K., Luckin, R., Millán, E. (eds.) AIED 2020. LNCS (LNAI), vol. 12163, pp. 472–485. Springer, Cham (2020). https://doi.org/10.1007/978-3-030-52237-7_38
3. Ausin, M.S., Azizsoltani, H., Barnes, T., Chi, M.: Leveraging deep reinforcement learning for pedagogical policy induction in an intelligent tutoring system. In: Proceedings of the 12th International Conference on Educational Data Mining, pp. 168–177 (2019)
4. Azizsoltani, H., Jin, Y.: Unobserved is not equal to non-existent: using Gaussian processes to infer immediate rewards across contexts. In: Proceedings of the 28th International Joint Conference on Artificial Intelligence, pp. 1974–1980 (2019). https://doi.org/10.24963/ijcai.2019/273
5. Chi, M., VanLehn, K., Litman, D.: Do micro-level tutorial decisions matter: applying reinforcement learning to induce pedagogical tutorial tactics. In: Aleven, V., Kay, J., Mostow, J. (eds.) ITS 2010. LNCS, vol. 6094, pp. 224–234. Springer, Heidelberg (2010). https://doi.org/10.1007/978-3-642-13388-6_27
6. Chi, M.T.H., et al.: Translating the ICAP theory of cognitive engagement into practice. Cogn. Sci. **42**(6), 1777–1832 (2018). https://doi.org/10.1111/cogs.12626
7. Chi, M.T.H., Wylie, R.: The ICAP framework: Linking cognitive engagement to active learning outcomes. Educ. Psychol. **49**(4), 219–243 (2014). https://doi.org/10.1080/00461520.2014.965823
8. Doroudi, S., Aleven, V., Brunskill, E.: Where's the reward? Int. J. Artif. Intell. Educ. **29**(4), 568–620 (2019). https://doi.org/10.1007/s40593-019-00187-x
9. Fujimoto, S., Meger, D., Precup, D.: Off-policy deep reinforcement learning without exploration. In: Proceedings of the 36th International Conference on Machine Learning, pp. 2052–2062 (2019)
10. Georgila, K., Core, M.G., Nye, B.D., Karumbaiah, S., Auerbach, D., Ram, M.: Using reinforcement learning to optimize the policies of an intelligent tutoring system for interpersonal skills training. In: Proceedings of the 18th International Conference on Autonomous Agents and Multiagent Systems, pp. 737–745. IFAAMAS, Richland (2019). https://dl.acm.org/doi/abs/10.5555/3306127.3331763
11. Van Hasselt, H., Guez, A., Silver, D.: Deep reinforcement learning with double q-learning. In: Proceedings of the 30th AAAI Conference on Artificial Intelligence, pp. 2094–2100 (2016)
12. Hessel, M., et al.: Rainbow: combining improvements in deep reinforcement learning. In: Proceedings of the 32nd AAAI Conference on Artificial Intelligence, pp. 3215–3222 (2018)
13. Hochreiter, S., Schmidhuber, J.: Long short-term memory. Neural Comput. **9**(8), 1735–1780 (1997). https://doi.org/10.1162/neco.1997.9.8.1735
14. Jiang, N., Li, L.: Doubly robust off-policy value evaluation for reinforcement learning. In: Proceedings of the 33rd International Conference on Machine Learning, pp. 652–661 (2016)
15. Ju, S., Zhou, G., Barnes, T., Chi, M.: Pick the moment: identifying critical pedagogical decisions using long-short term rewards. In: Proceedings of the 13th International Conference on Educational Data Mining, pp. 126–136 (2020)
16. Kingma, D.P., Ba, J.: Adam: a method for stochastic optimization. arXiv preprint arXiv:1412.6980 (2014)

17. Kodinariya, T.M., Makwana, P.R.: Review on determining number of cluster in K-Means clustering. Int. J. Adv. Res. Comput. Sci. Manag. Stud. **1**(6), 90–95 (2013)
18. Lim, J., et al.: Active learning through discussion: ICAP framework for education in health professions. BMC Med. Educ. 19(1), Article 47 (2019). https://doi.org/10.1186/s12909-019-1901-7
19. Marx, J.D., Cummings, K.: Normalized change. Am. J. Phys. **75**(1), 87–91 (2007). https://doi.org/10.1119/1.2372468
20. Mitrovic, A., Gordon, M., Piotrkowicz, A., Dimitrova, V.: Investigating the effect of adding nudges to increase engagement in active video watching. In: Isotani, S., Millán, E., Ogan, A., Hastings, P., McLaren, B., Luckin, R. (eds.) AIED 2019. LNCS (LNAI), vol. 11625, pp. 320–332. Springer, Cham (2019). https://doi.org/10.1007/978-3-030-23204-7_27
21. Mnih, V., et al.: Human-level control through deep reinforcement learning. Nature **518**(7540), 529–533 (2015). https://doi.org/10.1038/nature14236
22. van de Pol, J., Volman, M., Oort, F., Beishuizen, J.: The effects of scaffolding in the classroom: support contingency and student independent working time in relation to student achievement, task effort and appreciation of support. Instr. Sci. **43**(5), 615–641 (2015). https://doi.org/10.1007/s11251-015-9351-z
23. Sawyer, R., Rowe, J., Lester, J.: Balancing learning and engagement in game-based learning environments with multi-objective reinforcement learning. In: André, E., Baker, R., Hu, X., Rodrigo, M.M.T., du Boulay, B. (eds.) AIED 2017. LNCS (LNAI), vol. 10331, pp. 323–334. Springer, Cham (2017). https://doi.org/10.1007/978-3-319-61425-0_27
24. Schaul, T., Quan, J., Antonoglou, I., Silver, D.: Prioritized experience replay. arXiv preprint arXiv:1511.05952 (2015)
25. Sottilare, R.A., Brawner, K.W., Goldberg, B.S., Holden, H.K.: The generalized intelligent framework for tutoring (GIFT). US Army Research Laboratory–Human Research & Engineering Directorate (ARL-HRED), Orlando (2012)
26. Spain, R., Rowe, J., Goldberg, B., Pokorny, R., Lester, J.: Enhancing learning outcomes through adaptive remediation with GIFT. In: Proceedings of the Interservice/Industry Training, Simulation and Education Conference. Paper No. 19275 (2019)
27. Sutton, R.S., Barto, A.G.: Reinforcement Learning: An Introduction, 2nd edn. MIT Press, Cambridge (2018)
28. Thomas, P., Brunskill, E.: Data-efficient off-policy policy evaluation for reinforcement learning. In: Proceedings of the 33rd International Conference on Machine Learning, pp. 2139–2148 (2016)
29. Wang, F.: Reinforcement learning in a POMDP based intelligent tutoring system for optimizing teaching strategies. Int. J. Inf. Educ. Technol. **8**(8), 553–558 (2018). https://doi.org/10.18178/ijiet.2018.8.8.1098
30. Wang, P., Rowe, J., Min, W., Mott, B., Lester, J.: High-fidelity simulated players for interactive narrative planning. In: Proceedings of the 27th International Joint Conference on Artificial Intelligence, pp. 3884–3890 (2018). https://doi.org/10.24963/ijcai.2018/540
31. Wang, P., Rowe, J.P., Min, W., Mott, B.W., Lester, J.C.: Interactive narrative personalization with deep reinforcement learning. In: Proceedings of the 26th International Joint Conference on Artificial Intelligence, pp. 3852–3858 (2017). https://doi.org/10.24963/ijcai.2017/538
32. Wiggins, B.L., Eddy, S.L., Grunspan, D.Z., Crowe, A.J.: The ICAP active learning framework predicts the learning gains observed in intensely active classroom experiences. AERA Open. **3**(2), 1–14 (2017). https://doi.org/10.1177/2332858417708567
33. Zhou, G., Yang, X., Azizsoltani, H., Barnes, T., Chi, M.: Improving student-system interaction through data-driven explanations of hierarchical reinforcement learning induced pedagogical policies. In: Proceedings of the 28th ACM Conference on User Modeling, Adaptation and Personalization, pp. 284–292. ACM, New York (2020). https://doi.org/10.1145/3340631.3394848

Ordering Effects in a Role-Based Scaffolding Intervention for Asynchronous Online Discussions

Elaine Farrow[1]([⊠]) ⓘ, Johanna Moore[1] ⓘ, and Dragan Gašević[2] ⓘ

[1] School of Informatics, University of Edinburgh, Edinburgh, UK
{Elaine.Farrow,J.Moore}@ed.ac.uk
[2] Faculty of Information Technology, Monash University, Melbourne, Australia
Dragan.Gasevic@monash.edu

Abstract. A common scaffolding approach in computer-supported collaborative learning is the assignment of specific roles to the participants in online asynchronous discussions. Previous work has demonstrated how this type of scaffolding can result in student contributions of greater depth and quality. However, since students necessarily experience the roles in varying orders, it is important to consider whether the ordering impacts the outcome. This paper addresses the issue by examining a scaffolding intervention that was deployed in an asynchronous online discussion forum, where students were assigned to lead the discussion in one thread as the 'expert' and to participate in other threads by asking questions. A network analytic approach was used to visualise and quantify several potential ordering effects within the intervention. The constructs of cognitive presence and cognitive engagement, from the Community of Inquiry and the ICAP frameworks, were used together to measure the depth and quality of the discussion contribution expressed in each message. The analysis confirmed that the contributions made while the student was in the 'expert' role scored significantly higher for both constructs, but found that the order in which students took on each role had little impact on the quality of their contributions to other threads. This result contrasts with earlier work on single-duty roles that found an advantage in being assigned certain roles early in the discussion, and suggests that instructors should feel confident in rotating more complex user roles between students.

Keywords: Online discussion · Scaffolding · Critical thinking · Student engagement · Learning analytics · Community of inquiry · Cognitive presence · Cognitive engagement · Epistemic network analysis

This work was supported in part by the EPSRC Centre for Doctoral Training in Data Science, funded by the UK Engineering and Physical Sciences Research Council (grant EP/L016427/1) and the University of Edinburgh.

I. Roll et al. (Eds.): AIED 2021, LNAI 12748, pp. 125–136, 2021.
https://doi.org/10.1007/978-3-030-78292-4_11

1   Introduction

Asynchronous online discussion forums are a common feature in virtual learning environments. Stand-alone discussion platforms such as Piazza[1] are also used to manage students' questions, in both online and classroom-based courses. The discussions that take place in these forums can help to build a sense of community among learners [6] – particularly important when in-person interaction was severely restricted due to a global pandemic. Time-stamped transcripts of the messages that are exchanged can also be used to inform research into how effective learning takes place through discussion.

Research in computer-supported collaborative learning (CSCL) has shown that participation in asynchronous discussions can be beneficial to participants, giving them opportunities to increase the depth of their own cognitive engagement through collaborative knowledge construction [12–14] as well as fostering social belonging [6]. However, in order to achieve these benefits, it is often necessary to provide explicit guidance in the form of scaffolding [11,15,18]. Prior work [26] suggests that when students are assigned a role that requires them to summarise the contributions of others, there is a positive effect on their breadth of listening while they are 'in-role', but the effect is not sustained afterwards. Other studies [7,21] have suggested that the timing of role assignment can impact outcomes, with earlier assignment seen as more beneficial for some roles.

The depth and quality of student participation in asynchronous online discussions has been examined and quantified using many different theoretical frameworks (*e.g.* Bloom's Taxonomy [2], the SOLO taxonomy [1], The Community of Inquiry framework (CoI) [13,14], and the Interactive-Constructive-Active-Passive (ICAP) framework [3]). Of these, only CoI was designed specifically for the online context. Most previous studies have focused on a single framework, while a few have used a combination of two or more in order to provide a richer, multi-dimensional analysis of the data [8,9,19,22].

The specific type of scaffolding intervention considered in this work is an approach centred on assigning 'roles' to discussion participants. The study presented here investigated how the effect of the role-based scaffolding was moderated by the order in which participants experienced the different roles. Messages were classified using both the *phases of cognitive presence* from CoI and the *modes of cognitive engagement* in ICAP.

2   Background

2.1   The Community of Inquiry Framework

The Community of Inquiry (CoI) framework defines three 'presences' that support learning in an online community: *social presence*, *teaching presence*, and *cognitive presence* [14]. Of these, cognitive presence is considered to be the most fundamental to educational success. Discussions are expected to progress through

---

[1] https://piazza.com.

its four phases (*Triggering Event, Exploration, Integration,* and *Resolution*) over time (Table 1), and the phases have been used as a measure of the depth and quality of student participation in asynchronous discussions [8,9]. In the ideal case, a discussion would start with a *Triggering Event* that defines the problem, move through an *Exploration* phase where new ideas are considered, then bring some of those ideas together in the *Integration* phase, and finally achieve consensus on a solution in the *Resolution* phase. In reality, progression through the phases is seldom linear. Many discussions do not reach the *Resolution* phase.

Table 1. The four CoI phases of cognitive presence in ascending order, plus the *Other* label, which can be used where a message does not display any cognitive presence.

Short label	Phase of cognitive presence	Example behaviour
TRIG	Triggering Event	Asking a question or posing a problem
EXP	Exploration	Exchanging ideas
INT	Integration	Integrating ideas and constructing meaning
RES	Resolution	Reaching consensus or suggesting a new hypothesis
OTH	*Other*	Commenting with no sign of cognitive presence

2.2 The ICAP Framework

The ICAP framework [4] has been used widely, in classroom-based studies as well as online. It defines four modes of cognitive engagement, based on observable student behaviours: **I**nteractive, **C**onstructive, **A**ctive, and **P**assive. Each mode represents a qualitatively different type of knowledge growth. Interventions and activities that targeted the higher modes of cognitive engagement were shown to achieve greater learning gains. Several recent studies adapted and expanded the original framework [8,9,25,28] in the context of asynchronous online discussions. The *Constructive* and *Active* modes were each subdivided and messages of *Affirmation* were treated separately (Table 2).

3 Research Question

Previous studies have shown how external scripts such as assigned roles can help students to develop skills relating to collaboration and social knowledge construction [7,11,21,24,27]. However, there is some evidence that the effects may not persist after the intervention has ended [26]. Some roles have been shown to be particularly beneficial to those who take them on (*e.g.* 'summarizer' [21]). Other single-duty roles have been shown to be detrimental to learning (*e.g.* 'source-searcher' [7]) when used in isolation. It is therefore seen to be important to rotate single-duty roles among students and to consider the use of composite roles that combine several lower-level duties [15,27]. The timing of role assignment has also been seen to impact learning outcomes [7]. There is thus a need for research into potential ordering effects within role-based interventions, since participants necessarily experience the roles in varying orders.

Table 2. The extended set of ICAP modes of cognitive engagement in descending order, plus the *Off-task* label, used for messages displaying no cognitive engagement.

Short label	Mode of cognitive engagement	Example behaviour
I	Interactive	As for **C1**, in response to earlier message content
C1	Constructive Reasoning	Displaying explanation or reasoning about the current topic
C2	Constructive Extending	Introducing new content to the discussion
F	Affirmation	Affirming what was said in an earlier message
A1	Active Targeted	Referencing specific previous content
A2	Active General	Showing other signs of being engaged with content
P	Passive	Reading messages without responding
O	*Off-task*	Commenting with no relation to the topic/ course

Earlier studies looked at the effects of role assignments using a single measure of the quality of knowledge construction [21], sometimes in combination with final exam scores [7]. Recent work has shown the benefits of integrating insights from multiple frameworks for analysing aspects of student participation in asynchronous discussion tasks [8,9,19,22]. The research question addressed in the present study was therefore:

RQ: *How do ordering effects between roles affect the depth and quality of student contributions to an asynchronous discussion task, as measured by both the CoI phases of cognitive presence and the ICAP modes of cognitive engagement?*

4   Method

4.1   Description of the Data

The role-based scaffolding intervention examined in this study was deployed in a credit-bearing distance-learning course in Software Engineering over six course offerings (2008–2011). The discussion task accounted for 10% of the course grade and helped students to develop their own research questions. Two complex user roles were defined, with students expected to take on both roles during the task.

- *Research Expert*: prepare and upload a presentation about a relevant research paper of their choice, then lead a discussion on its content on a dedicated thread in the discussion forum; and
- *Practising Researcher*: contribute to discussions about other students' presentation topics.

Both roles thus incorporated duties defined in earlier work as 'summarizer', 'source searcher', and 'theoretician' [7,21,27]. The *Research Expert* role additionally required the student to undertake 'moderator' and 'topic leader' duties.

The discussion task ran during weeks 3–6 of each course offering. Every student was expected to take on the *Research Expert* role once and the *Practising Researcher* role several times. Approximately one-third of the students took on the *Research Expert* role in each of the first three weeks of the task. The discussions that followed were asynchronous and ranged from 3 days to 27 days in duration. The median thread duration was 13 days. All discussion threads remained open until the end of the task. It was thus very common for a student to contribute to one or more threads as a *Practising Researcher* at the same time as they were acting as the *Research Expert* in their own thread.

In order to examine possible ordering effects in the present study, we considered two different ways of grouping messages by time, and another metric derived from those and intended to capture role order more directly (Table 3).

- **Thread Week**: The week within the discussion task when the message thread was started – even though the message itself may have been posted later. This allowed us to assess whether message quality changed when more time was available to contribute to a thread before the task ended.
- **Expert Week**: The week within the discussion task when the student who wrote the message started a discussion thread in the role of *Research Expert*. This allowed us to compare messages from students who experienced the *Research Expert* role at different times during the course.
- **Role Order**: The label *BeforeExpert*, *WhileExpert*, or *AfterExpert*, based on whether the Thread Week for the message was earlier, in the same week, or in a later week, compared with the Expert Week. This allowed us to assess the effects of role ordering more directly.

Table 3. Labels assigned to messages in threads where students A, B, C, and D took on the *Research Expert* role in the first, second, second, and third week, respectively.

Thread	Student	Thread Week	Expert Week	Role Order
Expert-A	B	1	2	*BeforeExpert*
Expert-B	C	2	2	*WhileExpert*
Expert-D	A	3	1	*AfterExpert*

Our analysis focused on the messages sent by students while they were in the *Practising Researcher* role, for two reasons: we wanted to distinguish potential role ordering effects from the large effect of the role assignment intervention itself [9,15]; and each student was only the *Research Expert* once. We excluded 9 messages that were sent by participants who never took on the *Research Expert* role, leaving 891 messages from 84 threads (Tables 4 and 5).

Each message was assigned one label from each theoretical framework, based on its textual content. Two expert coders labelled the messages with the CoI phases of cognitive presence (Table 1), achieving high levels of agreement (98.1%

Table 4. Counts of unique participants, threads, and messages.

Week	Thread Week		Expert Week	
	Threads	Messages	Participants	Messages
1	32	352	26	346
2	30	288	30	312
3	22	251	22	233
Total	84	891	78	891

Table 5. Message counts in the Role Order groups.

	BeforeExpert	WhileExpert	AfterExpert	Total
Messages	310	304	277	891

agreement, Cohen's $\kappa = 0.974$). A second pair of independent coders assigned labels from the extended set of ICAP modes of cognitive engagement (Table 2), achieving 'substantial' inter-annotator agreement (Cohen's $\kappa = 0.623$) [17].

For the purposes of the present study, the *Interactive* and *Constructive Reasoning* labels were combined together and only *Constructive Reasoning* was used. The primary difference between them is that a message can only be labelled as *Interactive* if it is a direct response to the substantive content of a previous message (Table 2). While *Interactive* messages were relatively common for a *Research Expert*, there were limited opportunities for a *Practising Researcher* to interact in such a way during the discussion task presented in this study.

4.2 Epistemic Network Analysis

Epistemic Network Analysis (ENA) [23] is a network analytic approach that is designed for analysing the *connections between* small sets of concepts in a densely connected network. It allows sub groups to be compared both visually and statistically, and has been widely used in studies of online discussions [16,29] in general, and specifically for the constructs of cognitive presence and social presence in a Community of Inquiry [10,19,20].

Co-occurrences of labels in the data are used to construct a high-dimensional concept network. The *conversation* parameter defines which connections are included in the analysis. The network is projected down onto the two most informative dimensions, while maintaining the mathematical relationships between concepts, using *singular value decomposition*. The relative positions of the concept nodes in the resulting *projection space* makes the space itself interpretable, because concepts that share a pattern of connections will tend to be located close together [23]. A single point in the projection space represents the weighted mean of the connections in one sub-network, defined by the *unit of analysis* parameter. For example, this could be all the messages in a thread.

In the present study, we set the conversation parameter to be a single message. This meant that the only connections included in the network were the pairs of labels from the two theoretical frameworks: one label from the CoI phases of cognitive presence and one from the ICAP modes of cognitive engagement. We first grouped the messages by student and thread, so that all the messages sent by the same student in a single thread were aggregated together. As we looked at the order-based groupings in turn, the messages were aggregated further.

To become familiar with the general associations between the individual CoI phases of cognitive presence and the ICAP modes of cognitive engagement in this data set, we first explored the overall mean network based on all the messages sent in both roles. Noting the locations of the nodes in the overall mean network allowed us to interpret the space in terms of the framework constructs. The same projection space was subsequently reused for the analyses of messages sent by *Practising Researchers*, broken down by each of the different groupings (Thread Week, Expert Week, and Role Order). The messages were aggregated by student, thread, and group to create the data points for each network. We used Mann-Whitney tests to determine whether pairs of groups were significantly different along either of the two axes of the projection space.

5 Results

Figure 1 shows the average ENA network across all messages. The framework constructs are shown using their short labels (Tables 1 and 2) to reduce visual clutter. The X axis accounts for 21.7% of the variance in the data and the Y axis accounts for 20.2%. The X axis primarily distinguishes between the early phases (*Triggering Event* and *Exploration*) and the later (*Integration*) phase of cognitive presence, while the Y axis distinguishes linearly between the three highest ICAP modes of cognitive engagement. The direct effect of the role assignment intervention is clearly visible. The points representing messages sent by students in the *Research Expert* role are all found toward the upper left of the plot, in the vicinity of the *Constructive Reasoning* (**C1**) node. In contrast, the messages sent by those in the *Practising Researcher* role are dispersed throughout the projection space, with the group mean near the centre of the plot.

Figure 2 shows the projection networks comparing messages sent by *Practising Researchers*, aggregated by Thread Week, Expert Week, and Role Order. These networks all use the same projection space as Fig. 1. The axes account for slightly less of the variance in the data: 21.1% for the X axis, and 20.1% for the Y axis. In each case, the group means appear close together, indicating that any differences are small. A series of Mann-Whitney tests showed that there were no statistically significant differences at the $\alpha = 0.05$ level between any of the Thread Week values in Fig. 2(a). In addition, *ExpertWeek1* and *ExpertWeek2* were not significantly different from each other in Fig. 2(b). The small difference seen between *ExpertWeek2* and *ExpertWeek3* along the Y axis was not considered significant after Bonferroni correction. However, *ExpertWeek3* was significantly different at the $\alpha = 0.05$ level along the Y axis (V2) from *ExpertWeek1* ($U = 24809.00$, $p = 0.0007$, $r = 0.18$). This indicates that students who

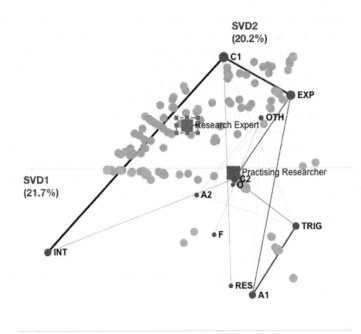

Fig. 1. ENA network constructed by aggregating the label co-occurrences within the messages sent by each student in each thread across both user roles. The positions of the black nodes indicate the locations of each framework construct in the two-dimensional projection space. Edge thickness indicates connection frequency. The pale blue and pale red points indicate the weighted mean of each student's messages: blue for *Practising Researchers* and red for *Research Experts*. Group means are shown as squares in darker blue and red respectively, labelled with the relevant user role. (Color figure online)

were in the last group to take on the *Research Expert* role tended to contribute to other threads at a lower level, as measured by the ICAP modes of cognitive engagement, compared to their counterparts in the first group. The effect size is small [5]. There was no significant difference along the X axis.

Considering the effect of Role Order in Fig. 2(c), a series of Mann-Whitney tests confirmed that, after Bonferroni correction, the only statistically significant difference between the groups was between the *AfterExpert* group and the the *BeforeExpert* group along the Y axis ($U = 29967.00$, $p = 0.0094$, $r = 0.13$). This indicates a small effect size for Role Order, corresponding to a tendency for students to demonstrate higher levels of the ICAP modes of cognitive engagement in threads that were started in the week(s) after their own expert thread, compared with the threads that were started in the week(s) before their own.

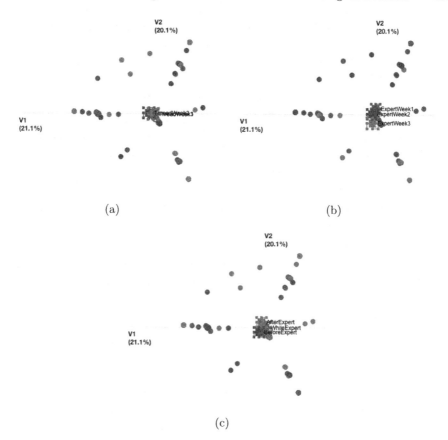

Fig. 2. ENA networks constructed using the messages sent in the *Practising Researcher* role, grouped by (a) Thread Week, (b) Expert Week, and (c) Role Order, in addition to student and thread. The points are coloured according to the relevant group: (a) the week within the task when the thread started; (b) the week within the task when the message author started acting as *Research Expert*; (c) the Role Order label. In both (a) and (b), week 1 is shown in red, week 2 in blue, and week 3 in purple. In (c), *BeforeExpert* is shown in blue, *WhileExpert* is in red, and *AfterExpert* is in purple. Group means are labelled and shown as squares in the appropriate colour. (Color figure online)

6   Discussion

The results of this study confirmed the ability of a role-based scaffolding intervention to effect positive change, as seen in previous work [9,15] where messages sent by students in the *Research Expert* role achieved greater depth on both the CoI and ICAP frameworks, compared with those sent by students in the *Practising Researcher* role. However, there was little evidence of ordering effects. No significant differences were found between the message threads that were started in the first week of the activity compared to those in the final batch, despite the much longer time available for students to develop a deeper discussion.

The students in the present study were always assigned to a role, and these were composite roles that incorporated several of the low-level single-duty roles investigated in previous work. We noted a small effect where the group of students who were last to take on the *Research Expert* role demonstrated lower cognitive engagement in their contributions to other threads. One explanation for this could be that the effort of leading their own thread in the final week, while also ensuring that they had fulfilled the participation requirements, led to shallower engagement. Another potential explanation is the timing effect found in prior work [7], where a cohort that began without roles and had them assigned later performed worse than a cohort that had roles from the beginning. It is possible that the group who took on the *Research Expert* role last did not fully engage with the *Practising Researcher* role earlier.

A small effect was also found in the analysis of Role Order. Students in the *Practising Researcher* role, contributing to threads that started in the weeks after their own *Research Expert* thread started, scored higher on the ICAP modes of cognitive engagement. This could be because those students had time to devote to asking deeper questions, having finished with their own presentation. It could also be because they had learned from the experience of being in the *Research Expert* role and used this knowledge in later situations [7].

Since the discussion task in the present study only ran for four weeks, we were not able to discover any longer-term effects on behaviour. Analysis of discussions that took place over a longer period could produce different results, as participants grow in confidence and develop their skills, or perhaps become disengaged. The nature of the discussion task meant that students were often managing both roles in parallel: leading their own thread as a *Research Expert*, while at the same time contributing to other threads as a *Practising Researcher*. More specific instructions were given to participants in the later course offerings regarding the minimum contribution expected from students in the *Practising Researcher* role. The present study did not distinguish between those cases.

7   Conclusion

In the role-based scaffolding intervention presented in this study, the effects of role order were found to be small – especially in the context of the large primary effect of the intervention in improving student contributions according to two separate measures of depth and quality. This result suggests that instructors should feel confident in assigning complex roles and rotating them between students, without being afraid that a particular ordering might lead to disadvantage. Since the discussion task in the present study was relatively short in duration, future work should look at behaviour over the longer term, and in particular at examples where students repeat a similar style of task over time. It would also be valuable to directly contrast the use of single-duty roles with composite roles like those used here.

References

1. Biggs, J.B., Collis, K.F.: Evaluating the Quality of Learning: The SOLO Taxonomy (Structure of the Observed Learning Outcome). Academic Press, New York. Educational psychology (1982)
2. Bloom, B.S., Krathwohl, D.R., Masia, B.B.: Taxonomy of Educational Objectives: The Classification of Educational Goals. Handbook 1, Cognitive Domain. Longman Group Ltd., London (1956)
3. Chi, M.T.H., Bassok, M., Lewis, M.W., Reimann, P., Glaser, R.: Self-explanations: how students study and use examples in learning to solve problems. Cogn. Sci. **13**(2), 145–182 (1989)
4. Chi, M.T.H., Wylie, R.: The ICAP framework: linking cognitive engagement to active learning outcomes. Educ. Psychol. **49**(4), 219–243 (2014)
5. Cohen, J.: A power primer. Psychol. Bull. **112**(1), 155–159 (1992)
6. Dawson, S.: A study of the relationship between student social networks and sense of community. Educ. Technol. Soc. **11**(3), 224–238 (2008)
7. De Wever, B., Van Keer, H., Schellens, T., Valcke, M.: Roles as a structuring tool in online discussion groups: the differential impact of different roles on social knowledge construction. Comput. Hum. Behav. **26**(4), 516–523 (2010)
8. Farrow, E., Moore, J., Gašević, D.: Dialogue attributes that inform depth and quality of participation in course discussion forums. In: Proceedings of the Tenth International Conference on Learning Analytics & Knowledge, pp. 129–134. LAK 2020. ACM, New York (2020)
9. Farrow, E., Moore, J., Gašević, D.: A network analytic approach to integrating multiple quality measures for asynchronous online discussions. In: Proceedings of the 11th International Conference on Learning Analytics & Knowledge, LAK 2021. ACM, New York (2021)
10. Ferreira, R., Kovanović, V., Gašević, D., Rolim, V.: Towards combined network and text analytics of student discourse in online discussions. In: Penstein Rosé, C., et al. (eds.) AIED 2018. LNCS (LNAI), vol. 10947, pp. 111–126. Springer, Cham (2018). https://doi.org/10.1007/978-3-319-93843-1_9
11. Fischer, F., Kollar, I., Stegmann, K., Wecker, C.: Toward a script theory of guidance in computer-supported collaborative learning. Educ. Psychol. **48**(1), 56–66 (2013)
12. Garrison, D.R.: E-Learning in the 21st Century: A Framework for Research and Practice, 2nd edn. Routledge, New York (2011)
13. Garrison, D.R.: Thinking Collaboratively: Learning in a Community of Inquiry. Routledge, New York (2016)
14. Garrison, D.R., Anderson, T., Archer, W.: Critical inquiry in a text-based environment: computer conferencing in higher education. Internet High. Educ. **2**(2), 87–105 (2000)
15. Gašević, D., Adesope, O., Joksimović, S., Kovanović, V.: Externally-facilitated regulation scaffolding and role assignment to develop cognitive presence in asynchronous online discussions. Internet High. Educ. **24**, 53–65 (2015)
16. Gašević, D., Joksimović, S., Eagan, B.R., Shaffer, D.W.: SENS: network analytics to combine social and cognitive perspectives of collaborative learning. Comput. Hum. Behav. **92**, 562–577 (2019)
17. Landis, J.R., Koch, G.G.: The measurement of observer agreement for categorical data. Biometrics **33**(1), 159–174 (1977)

18. Radkowitsch, A., Vogel, F., Fischer, F.: Good for learning, bad for motivation? A meta-analysis on the effects of computer-supported collaboration scripts. Int. J. Comput.-Supp. Collab. Learn. **15**(1), 5–47 (2020)
19. Rolim, V., Ferreira, R., Lins, R.D., Găsević, D.: A network-based analytic approach to uncovering the relationship between social and cognitive presences in communities of inquiry. Internet High. Educ. **42**, 53–65 (2019)
20. Rolim, V., Ferreira Leite De Mello, R., Kovanovic, V., Gasevic, D.: Analysing social presence in online discussions through network and text analytics. In: Proceedings - IEEE 19th International Conference on Advanced Learning Technologies, ICALT 2019, pp. 163–167 (2019)
21. Schellens, T., Van Keer, H., De Wever, B., Valcke, M.: Scripting by assigning roles: does it improve knowledge construction in asynchronous discussion groups? Int. J. Comput.-Supp. Collab. Learn. **2**(2), 225–246 (2007)
22. Schrire, S.: Knowledge building in asynchronous discussion groups: going beyond quantitative analysis. Comput. Educ. **46**(1), 49–70 (2006)
23. Shaffer, D.W., Collier, W., Ruis, A.R.: A tutorial on epistemic network analysis: analyzing the structure of connections in cognitive, social, and interaction data. J. Learn. Anal. **3**(3), 9–45 (2016)
24. Strijbos, J.W., Weinberger, A.: Emerging and scripted roles in computer-supported collaborative learning. Comput. Hum. Behav. **26**(4), 491–494 (2010)
25. Wang, X., Wen, M., Rosé, C.P.: Towards triggering higher-order thinking behaviors in MOOCs. In: Proceedings of the Sixth International Conference on Learning Analytics & Knowledge, pp. 398–407. LAK 2016. ACM, New York (2016)
26. Wise, A.F., Chiu, M.M.: The impact of rotating summarizing roles in online discussions: effects on learners' listening behaviors during and subsequent to role assignment. Comput. Hum. Behav. **38**, 261–271 (2014)
27. Wise, A.F., Saghafian, M., Padmanabhan, P.: Towards more precise design guidance: specifying and testing the functions of assigned student roles in online discussions. Educ. Technol. Res. Dev. **60**(1), 55–82 (2012)
28. Yogev, E., Gal, K., Karger, D., Facciotti, M.T., Igo, M.: Classifying and visualizing students' cognitive engagement in course readings. In: Proceedings of the Fifth Annual ACM Conference on Learning at Scale, pp. 1–10. ACM, New York (2018)
29. Zhang, S., Liu, Q., Cai, Z.: Exploring primary school teachers' technological pedagogical content knowledge (TPACK) in online collaborative discourse: an epistemic network analysis. Br. J. Educ. Technol. **50**(6), 3437–3455 (2019)

Option Tracing: Beyond Correctness Analysis in Knowledge Tracing

Aritra Ghosh[1], Jay Raspat[2], and Andrew Lan[1(✉)]

[1] University of Massachusetts Amherst, Amherst, USA
andrewlan@cs.umass.edu
[2] Pittsburgh, PA, USA

Abstract. Knowledge tracing refers to a family of methods that estimate each student's knowledge component/skill mastery level from their past responses to questions. One key limitation of most existing knowledge tracing methods is that they can only estimate an *overall* knowledge level of a student per knowledge component/skill since they analyze only the (usually binary-valued) correctness of student responses. Therefore, it is hard to use them to diagnose specific student errors. In this paper, we extend existing knowledge tracing methods beyond correctness prediction to the task of predicting the exact option students select in multiple choice questions. We quantitatively evaluate the performance of our option tracing methods on two large-scale student response datasets. We also qualitatively evaluate their ability in identifying common student errors in the form of clusters of incorrect options across different questions that correspond to the same error.

1 Introduction

Knowledge tracing (KT) [9] refers to a family of student modeling methods that estimate student mastery levels on knowledge components/skills/concepts from their past responses to questions/items and predict their future performance. These estimates and predictions can be used to i) provide feedback to students on their progress, especially in intelligent tutoring systems [44] and ii) drive personalization, i.e., selecting the action that each learner should take next to maximize their learning outcomes [10,28,36]. Many different KT methods have been developed, ranging from hidden Markov model-based Bayesian knowledge tracing methods [21,33,46], factor analysis-based methods such as learning factor analysis [5], performance factor analysis [34], and the item Difficulty, student ability, skill, and student skill practice history (DAS3H) method [7], to deep learning-based methods [15,31,32,35,45,47]. These methods have enjoyed various degrees of success; some of these methods, including most Bayesian knowledge tracing and factor analysis-based methods, exhibit excellent interpretability while other, deep learning-based methods trade off interpretability for excellent predictive accuracy on students' future performance.

This work is supported by the National Science Foundation under grant IIS-1917713. We also thank the reviewers for their constructive feedback.

I. Roll et al. (Eds.): AIED 2021, LNAI 12748, pp. 137–149, 2021.
https://doi.org/10.1007/978-3-030-78292-4_12

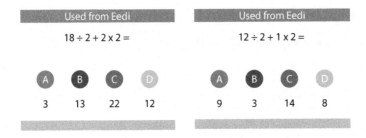

Fig. 1. Some distractor options in well-designed MCQs are potentially capable of capturing typical student errors. Option C in both questions here correspond to the error of not mastering the order of operations and always working left to right.

However, one key limitation of these KT methods is that they operate exclusively on (usually binary-valued) response data that indicates whether a student responds to a question correctly or not. Therefore, they can only estimate students' *overall* mastery level on each knowledge component. However, not all incorrect responses are equal: there can be numerous incorrect ways to answer a math question [27], caused by different underlying errors. Studies have shown that only a fraction of incorrect answers generated by students can be anticipated and explained by cognitive models integrated into intelligent tutoring systems [24,36,41], teachers [11], and numerical simulations [11,37]. Typical underlying errors include having a "buggy rule" [4], exhibiting a certain misconception [12,13,38], or a general lack of knowledge on certain knowledge components [2]. Since it is hard to diagnose such student errors from correctness data alone, we need to develop KT methods that analyze full student responses.

Some datasets, including the large-scale Eedi[1] [43] and EdNet[2] [8] datasets, contain the exact options students select on multiple choice questions (MCQs); this option data provides us with an opportunity to extend existing KT methods to analyze specific student option selections rather than their answer correctness. In an ideal situation, well-designed MCQs should have well-crafted incorrect distractor options that each corresponds to one or more typical student errors; Figure 1 shows an example from the Eedi dataset for two questions on the subject brackets, indices, division, multiplication, addition, subtraction (BIDMAS). Option C in both questions correspond to the same error of not fully mastering "order of operations" and always working left to right. However, manually identifying these errors is an unscalable and labor-intensive process since most existing MCQs do not come with consistent labels on the error(s) underlying each incorrect option. Therefore, it is important to explore whether we can develop KT methods to identify errors each incorrect option corresponds to and potentially diagnose student errors automatically. These methods would then be useful through i) informing teachers to communicate with students to understand the source of their errors, ii) enabling the development of automated

---

[1] https://eedi.com/projects/neurips-education-challenge.
[2] https://github.com/riiid/ednet.

feedback [19], and iii) enabling the design of alternative instructional approaches such as asking students to criticize erroneous examples [1].

1.1 Contributions

In this paper, we develop option tracing (OT), a KT framework that uses the exact option each student selects on each question as both input and predicted output. We extend several existing KT methods to the OT setting, including a long short-term memory (LSTM) network-based method, deep knowledge tracing (DKT) [35], a graph convolutional network-based method, graph-based interaction model for knowledge tracing (GIKT) [45], and an attention network-based method, attentive knowledge tracing (AKT) [15]. We emphasize that the goal of this paper is **NOT** to compare all KT methods; instead, our goal is to study how can we generalize them to analyze student option selections in MCQs. Therefore, we only study some representative methods. We conduct the following experiments on the Eedi and EdNet datasets: First, we quantitatively evaluate our OT methods under both the collaborative filtering (CF) setup (introduced by the NeurIPS 2020 Education Challenge [43]) and the typical KT setup on the task of option prediction. Second, we qualitatively demonstrate the interpretability exhibited by our OT framework using clustering algorithms to group incorrect options across multiple questions into clusters of shared underlying errors. Results show that the learned clusters match up with those manually identified by a domain expert to some degree. Therefore, OT can potentially offer a *bottom-up* approach for error identification by extracting student errors from actual data instead of the typical *top-down* approach of anticipating errors before seeing data. Our implementation will be publicly available at https://github.com/arghosh/OptionTracing.

2 Related Work

The options students select in MCQs can be regarded as a type of *categorical data*, which has previously been studied in both the item response theory (IRT) and recommender systems research communities. However, in both cases, most prior works focus on the case where the categories are *ordered*. In IRT research, polytomous IRT-based models [25, 26, 30] are used to model students' responses with multiple ordered categories, such as letter grades and partial credits. In recommender systems research, neural collaborative filtering (NCF)-based methods are used to model star ratings provided by users on items [20]. There are relatively few models for *unordered* categorical data such as the nominal response model (NRM) from the IRT research community, which has been applied to the analysis of MCQs [40, 42].

3   Data and Problem Setup

The Eedi dataset contains the responses of more than 100,000 students to 27,613 MCQs across 389 labeled subjects, totaling over 15 million responses over the course of more than a year. Each response corresponds to the exact option a student selected on each question (among four options, {A,B,C,D}). We will also use a small subset of the Eedi data where we have access to the exact question (in the form of images) for quantitative analysis; this dataset contains the responses of more than $4,900$ students to 948 questions, totaling in over 1.3 million responses. The EdNet dataset contains the responses of more than 700,000 students to 13,169 MCQs across 189 labeled subjects, totaling over 95 million responses over the course of more than two years.

We use two experimental setups for evaluation purposes. First, in the CF setup, the task is to predict each student's responses to a subset of questions that they responded to, given their responses to other questions (possibly in the future). Popular methods for this setup are neural collaborative filtering (NCF) [20] and graph convolutional networks (GCN) [3,23]. Second, in the KT setup for evaluating KT methods, the task is to predict each student's responses to future questions based on their entire past response history.

3.1   Problem Setup

Each student's performance record consists of a sequence of responses to questions assigned at a series of discrete time steps. For student i at time step t, we denote the combination of the question that they answered, the set of subjects this question covers, their binary-valued response correctness, the option they chose, and the correct option to this question as a tuple, $(q_t^i, \{s_{t,j}^i\}_{j=1}^{n_t^i}, r_t^i, y_t^i, c_t^i)$, where $q_t^i \in \mathbb{N}^+$ is the question index, $s_{t,j}^i \in \mathbb{N}^+$ denotes the index of the jth subject, $j \in 1, \ldots, n_t^i$ since each question can be tagged with multiple subjects, $r_t^i \in \{0,1\}$ is the response correctness (1 corresponds to a correct response), $y_t^i \in \{A, B, C, D\}$ is the option the student selected, and $c_t^i \in \{A, B, C, D\}$ is the correct option for this question. In the CF setup, we associate a mask variable $m_t^i \in \{0,1\}$ with each time step, where 1 represents that the timestep is part of the training set. This variable helps us to mask out responses we need to predict when we compute the training loss. Given observed responses $\{(q_t^i, \{s_{t,j}^i\}_{j=1}^{n_t^i}, r_t^i, y_t^i, c_t^i)\}_{t:m_t^i=1}$, the task is to predict the exact options students select on questions in the test set, i.e., $y_{t'}^{i'}$ for $(t', i') : m_t^i = 0$. In the KT setup, we observe each student's entire history of responses to questions; thus, given their past history up to time $t-1$ as $\{(q_\tau^i, \{s_{\tau,j}^i\}_{j=1}^{n_\tau^i}, r_\tau^i, y_\tau^i, c_\tau^i)\}_{\tau=1}^{t-1}$, our goal is to predict y_t^i at the current time step, t. Under these notations, existing KT methods focus on predicting response correctness, r_t^i.

4   Methodology

In this section, we detail our OT methods for both the CF and KT setups. Before delving into the individual methods, we start with a set of unified modules that apply to all methods in this paper. The question embedding module E_q : $q \rightarrow \mathbb{R}^d$ transforms the question index q_t^i to a d-dimensional, learnable real-valued vector in $\mathbb{R}^d$. Similarly, the response embedding module $E_r : r \rightarrow \mathbb{R}^d$ transforms the response correctness r_t^i to $\mathbb{R}^d$ and the option embedding module $E_o : \{A, B, C, D\} \rightarrow \mathbb{R}^d$ transforms the correct option c_t^i and the chosen option y_t^i to vectors in $\mathbb{R}^d$. We do not use separate embeddings for every question-option (q, o) pair since that leads to overfitting in our experiments; instead, the $2d$-dimensional embedding for (q, o) is obtained using $[E_q(q) \oplus E_o(o)]$ where $\oplus$ is the concatenation operator. The subject embedding module $E_s : s \rightarrow \mathbb{R}^d$ transforms the subject index to $\mathbb{R}^d$. Since each question may be tagged with several subjects, we define the final subject embedding as $E_s(\{s_{t,j}^i\}_{j=1}^{n_t^i}) = \sum_{j=1}^{n_t^i} E_s(s_{t,j}^i)$. Some of the methods (such as NCF) use a user embedding module $E_u : i \rightarrow \mathbb{R}^d$ that transforms the student index to $\mathbb{R}^d$. For simplicity, we use the same d-dimensional vector for all embedding modules; however, the dimensions of each module can be different. We train all model parameters, denoted as Θ, which contains the embeddings listed here and other model parameters specific to each individual method, by minimizing the negative log-likelihood of the selected options as

$$\underset{\Theta}{\text{minimize}} \quad -\sum_{i=1}^{|\text{Students}|} \sum_{t=1}^{|\text{Sequence}_i|} \sum_{o \in \{A,B,C,D\}} \mathbb{1}[y_t^i = o] \log p(o|q_t^i; \Theta),$$

where $\mathbb{1}$ is the indicator function. Since the options are unordered categories, the resulting loss function corresponds to the common cross-entropy loss [16].

4.1   Option Prediction Under the CF Setup

NCF. NCF is one of the most popular CF methods for user-item interaction data. In the option prediction task, students correspond to users and questions corresponds to items. The input for NCF at time step t for student i, $\mathbf{x}_t^i$, is

$$\mathbf{x}_t^i = [E_q(q_t^i) \oplus E_u(i) \oplus E_s(\{s_t^i\})].$$

Predictive probabilities $p(y_t^i = o)$ over four options $o \in \{A, B, C, D\}$ are calculated using the softmax function [16],

$$\mathbf{z}_t^i = f(\mathbf{x}_t^i) \in \mathbb{R}^4, \quad p(y_t^i = o|\mathbf{x}_t^i) = [\text{softmax}(\mathbf{z}_t^i)]_o, \quad \hat{y}_t^i = \underset{o \in \{A,B,C,D\}}{\text{argmax}} [\mathbf{z}_t^i]_o,$$

where $f(\cdot)$ denotes a feed-forward, fully-connected neural network and $[]_o$ refers to the oth entry of a vector. In NCF, the model parameters are the weights and biases in the feed-forward neural network $f(\cdot)$; this prediction module is shared by the subsequent methods.

PO-BiDKT. The main drawback of NCF is that the student embedding is static and not updated as students answer more questions and their knowledge states evolve. Recurrent neural networks, and in particular LSTM-type models are capable of modeling evolving knowledge as hidden states [35]. However, we cannot directly use methods such as DKT in the CF setup since the student's responses at some time steps in their response sequence are not observed. Therefore, we use the following method to handle evolving knowledge states using recurrent networks with missing observations. The input at each time step is given by

$$\mathbf{x}_t = [\mathrm{E}_q(q_t^i) \oplus \mathrm{E}_o(c_t^i) \oplus \mathrm{E}_s(\{s_t^i\}) \oplus \left(\mathrm{E}_o(y_t^i) \odot m_t^i\right) \oplus \left(\mathrm{E}_l(r_t^i) \odot m_t^i\right)], \quad (1)$$

where $\odot$ denotes the element-wise multiplication between two vectors. We mask the option embeddings and response correctness embeddings using m_t^i for time steps where we do not observe them but still use the question embedding as input. We also extend the base LSTM module in DKT to a bi-directional LSTM (Bi-LSTM) [17]. Here, we compute two latent knowledge states using two separate LSTM modules, the forward state $\overrightarrow{\mathbf{h}}_t$ that summarizes the student's past response history and the backward state $\overleftarrow{\mathbf{h}}_t$ that summarizes the student's future response history at time step t as

$$\overrightarrow{\mathbf{h}}_{t+1} = \text{Forward LSTM}(\overrightarrow{\mathbf{h}}_t, \mathbf{x}_t), \quad \overleftarrow{\mathbf{h}}_{t-1} = \text{Backward LSTM}(\overleftarrow{\mathbf{h}}_t, \mathbf{x}_t).$$

The final latent knowledge state is the concatenation of the two states as $\mathbf{h}_t = [\overrightarrow{\mathbf{h}}_t \oplus \overleftarrow{\mathbf{h}}_t]$. The parameters include two sets of parameters for the forward and backward LSTMs in addition to the parameters for the fully connected network $f(\cdot)$. We call this method partially observed bi-directional DKT, or PO-BiDKT. The output to the prediction module is computed using

$$\mathbf{z}_t^i = f([\mathbf{h}_t^i \oplus \mathrm{E}_q(q_t^i) \oplus \mathrm{E}_o(c_t^i) \oplus \mathrm{E}_s(\{s_t^i\})]) \in \mathbb{R}^4. \quad (2)$$

GCN-Augmented PO-BiDKT (BiGIKT). In our datasets, each question is tagged with a few subjects by question designers or domain experts. These subject tags provide important information on how these questions are related since we expect questions from the same subject to have some shared features. GCNs excel at formulating these relations and learning from graph-structured data. Since we can represent the question-subject association matrix using a bipartite graph, (loosely) following GIKT [45], we connect GCNs with PO-BiDKT to jointly learn question and subject embeddings using the structure imposed by the subject tags. In this method, we use hierarchical representations of subjects and questions: starting with initial subject and question embeddings $\mathrm{E}_s(s_t^i)$ and $\mathrm{E}_q(q_t^i)$, the first layer GCN embedding for the jth subject and the second layer GCN embedding for the ith question are computed as

$$\mathbf{s}_j^1 = \tanh\left(\mathbf{W}_s^s \mathrm{E}_s(s_j) + \frac{\sum_{i \in N_j^s} \mathbf{W}_s^q \mathrm{E}_q(q_i)}{|N_j^s|}\right), \quad \mathbf{q}_i^2 = \tanh\left(\mathbf{W}_q^q \mathrm{E}_q(q_i) + \frac{\sum_{j \in N_i^q} \mathbf{W}_q^s \mathbf{s}_j^1}{|N_i^q|}\right),$$

where N_j^s (N_i^q) denotes the set of questions (subjects) associated with subject (question) s_j (q_i) and $\mathbf{W}_s^s$, $\mathbf{W}_s^q$, $\mathbf{W}_q^s$ and $\mathbf{W}_q^q$ are learnable parameter matrices. The hyperbolic tangent (tanh) non-linearity operate entry-wise on vectors. We replace the subject embeddings $E_s(s_t^i)$ and the question embedding $E_q(q_t^i)$ in the base Bi-LSTM (Eq. 1 and Eq. 2) with these GCN-based embeddings. The model parameters of this method include the GCN weight parameter matrices in addition to the Bi-LSTM parameters.

4.2   Option Prediction Under the KT Setup

In the KT setup, we predict future responses using only past responses and assume that every past student response is observed. We extend several existing neural network-based KT methods for the option prediction task.

DKT. We apply a simple modification to the DKT method [35] to extend it to i) predict options instead of response correctness and ii) handle questions that are tagged with multiple subjects (the original DKT method assumes that each question is tagged with a single subject). We use

$$\mathbf{x}_t = [E_q(q_t^i) \oplus E_o(c_t^i) \oplus E_s(\{s_t^i\}) \oplus E_o(a_t^i) \oplus E_l(r_t^i)]$$

as the input to the DKT LSTM input module. The student's hidden knowledge states are computed using the LSTM model as $\mathbf{h}_{t+1} = \text{LSTM}(\mathbf{h}_t, \mathbf{x}_t)$. The predictive probabilities of selecting each option are computed using

$$\mathbf{z}_t^i = f([\mathbf{h}_t^i \oplus E_q(q_t^i) \oplus E_o(c_t^i) \oplus E_s(\{s_t^i\})]) \in \mathbb{R}^4, \; \hat{y}_t^i = \underset{o \in \{A,B,C,D\}}{\text{argmax}} \; [\mathbf{z}_t^i]_o.$$

DKVMN. Instead of using LSTMs to model latent knowledge state transitions, the dynamic key-value memory network (DKVMN) method uses a key-value memory network to retrieve and update knowledge at every time step using an external memory module as $\mathbf{h}_{t+1} = \text{MemoryModule}(\mathbf{h}_t, \mathbf{x}_t)$; refer to [47] for details. We use the same input and output structure for the DKVMN memory module as that for DKT.

AKT. We also adapt AKT, an attention network-based, state-of-the-art KT method for the option prediction task. AKT computes a query, a key, and a value vector for each time step, and then uses the similarity between the query and key vectors at different time steps to attend to questions in the past and use their corresponding value vectors to retrieve acquired knowledge in the past. We compute the query, key, and value vectors as $\mathbf{q}_t = \mathbf{W}^Q \mathbf{n}$, $\mathbf{k}_t = \mathbf{W}^K \mathbf{n}$, and $\mathbf{v}_t = \mathbf{W}^V[E_l(r_t^i) \oplus E_q(q_t^i) \oplus E_o(y_t^i) \oplus E_o(c_t^i)]$ respectively, where $\mathbf{W}^Q$, $\mathbf{W}^K$, and $\mathbf{W}^V$ are the query, key, and value projection matrices and $\mathbf{n} = [E_q(q_t^i) \oplus E_s(\{s_t^i\}) \oplus E_o(c_t^i)]$. The retrieved latent knowledge state is then computed as $\mathbf{h}_t = g\left(\sum_{\tau < t} \alpha_{t,\tau} \mathbf{v}_\tau\right)$, where g is another feedforward network and $\alpha_{t,\tau}$ is the normalized attention score between the query at the current time step t and the key at a past time step τ. For AKT, we employ the exponential decay module to compute the attention scores [15] and then compute the output using the attention-weighted value $\mathbf{h}_t^i$ and a fully connected network $f(\cdot)$.

Table 1. Performance of all methods under the CF (top half) and KT (bottom half) setups on both datasets. Best results are in **bold**.

Model	Option prediction				Correctness prediction	
	Accuracy		Average Macro F_1 Score		Accuracy	
	Eedi	EdNet	Eedi	EdNet	Eedi	EdNet
NCF	64.75 ± 0.02	67.24 ± 0.01	0.2824 ± 0.002	0.2552 ± 0.001	72.6 ± 0.03	71.49 ± 0.01
PO-BiDKT	65.87 ± 0.01	**69.42 ± 0.01**	**0.3283 ± 0.001**	**0.3260 ± 0.001**	75.18 ± 0.01	**75.21 ± 0.02**
BiGIKT	**66.16 ± 0.02**	69.29 ± 0.02	0.3261 ± 0.001	0.3168 ± 0.001	**75.62 ± 0.02**	75.07 ± 0.01
DKT	65.95 ± 0.44	68.03 ± 0.09	0.313 ± 0.008	0.2887 ± 0.005	74.7 ± 0.34	73.19 ± 0.06
DKVMN	**66.03 ± 0.49**	68.01 ± 0.1	**0.3152 ± 0.007**	0.2842 ± 0.005	**74.75 ± 0.3**	73.02 ± 0.06
AKT	65.91 ± 0.47	**68.44 ± 0.09**	0.3139 ± 0.007	**0.3062 ± 0.004**	74.65 ± 0.31	**73.6 ± 0.06**

5   Experiments

Experimental Setup. In addition to the option prediction task, we also evaluate all methods under the standard, binary-valued response correctness prediction task. We do not need to use a separate set of methods; instead, we can simply replace the final output layer of the option predictor module ($f : \cdot \to \mathbb{R}^4$) with an output layer that consists of a single node ($f : \cdot \to \mathbb{R}^1$) for all OT methods; the resulting loss function corresponds to standard binary cross entropy loss. For option prediction, we use both accuracy and macro F_1 score as evaluation metrics. For correctness prediction, we use accuracy as the only evaluation metric which aligns with the option prediction task. We compute the F_1 score for each question-option pair individually and average across all such pairs. This metric treats every option in every question equally, thus magnifying the impact of options that are rarely selected. For reference, on the Eedi and EdNet datasets, the selection probabilities across options for an average question (from most frequent to least frequent) are 57%, 25%, 11%, 7% and 66%, 20%, 10%, 4%, respectively. For option prediction, a random classifier has an average macro F_1 score and an accuracy score of 0.25 on both of these datasets, while a majority class classifier has an average macro F_1 score (accuracy) of 0.184 (57%) and 0.205 (66%) on the Eedi and EdNet datasets, respectively.

Training and Testing. We perform standard k-fold cross-validation (with $k = 5$) for all methods on both datasets. Under the CF setup, on average 20% of the time steps (for each student) are randomly chosen as the held out test set, 20% of time steps are randomly chosen as the validation set, and the other 60% are chosen as the training set to train all methods. Under the KT setup, all time steps for a randomly chosen 20% of students are used as the test set, and the validation and training sets are constructed similarly.

Network Architectures and Hyper-Parameters. Since the datasets are large, we do minimal hyper-parameter tuning and set most of the values to their default values for all the methods; exploratory experiments found that evaluation results are robust across most parameter values. We set the question, subject, option, response embedding dimension for all methods to $d \in \{32, 64\}$ for the

CF setup and $d \in \{64, 128\}$ for the KT setup. We use the Adam optimizer [22] to train all models with a batch size of 64 students to ensure that an entire batch can fit into the memory of our machine (equipped with one NVIDIA Titan X GPU). For all methods, we set the learning rate to $10^{-4}/10^{-3}$ for the Eedi/EdNet dataset and run all the methods for 200 epochs and perform early stopping based on the loss on the validation set. We set the latent knowledge state ($\mathbf{h}_t$) dimension to 256/512 for all methods under CF/KT setup. For NCF, we select the user embedding dimension as $d = 256$.

Results and Discussion. Table 1 lists the performance of all OT methods for both the CF and KT setups for both the option prediction and correctness prediction tasks, on both datasets; we report the averages as well as the standard deviations across the five folds. We observe a significant dropoff ($\sim 10\%$) in the accuracy metric on the option prediction task compared to the correctness prediction task, which is as expected since there are four categories to predict (A, B, C, D) instead of two categories (correct/incorrect). As a result of this difference, the correctness prediction task can be seen as a sub-task in the option prediction task by computing the probability a student selects the correct option. The performance of different methods are also quite consistent across all cases.

We observe that recurrent neural network-based methods such as PO-BiDKT perform significantly better than NCF in all cases. This observation suggests that even in a CF setup for model evaluation, methods that take the evolving nature of student knowledge into account are still more effective than popular CF methods that do not account for these temporal dynamics. Overall, we observe that the performance gains on the option prediction task provided by complex model architectures are marginal. This observation suggests that more work needs to be done on the option prediction task to understand the dynamics behind students' decisions to select a specific incorrect option, which motivates our exploration in Sect. 5.1. In the KT setup, we observe that DKVMN performs best on the Eedi dataset while AKT performs best on the EdNet dataset. This observation suggests that complex neural network architectures such as attention modules are more beneficial when a large amount of training data is available.

In both setups, we observe that the F_1 scores are low for all methods; despite clearly not simply predicting the most frequent option, the performance of these methods leaves significant room for improvement due to class imbalance. Possible approaches to improve prediction accuracy for options that are rarely selected include oversampling them [6]; however, since a student's responses to different questions are not independent data points, how these methods can be applied to the option tracing task is not immediately clear.

5.1 Clustering Incorrect Options

To qualitatively evaluate our option tracing methods, we attempt to group incorrect options across multiple questions into clusters and examine whether question-option pairs in the same cluster correspond to the same underlying error. To this end, we train a modified version of PO-BiDKT on the Eedi dataset [43]; we learn an embedding module $E_{q,o}(q, o) : q \times o \rightarrow \mathbb{R}^d$ for

Table 2. Incorrect option clustering quality for a subset of questions in the Eedi dataset using errors labeled by a domain expert. 1 in both metrics indicates perfect clustering.

Metric	Adjusted rand index	Fowlkes-Mallows index
Score	0.372	0.455

each question-option pair. Then, we compute the option selection probabilities using the latent knowledge state h_t^i and the question-option pair embeddings as $p(o|q_t^i) = \frac{f(h_t^i)^T E_{q,o}(q_y^i, o)}{\sum_{o'} f(h_t^i)^T E_{q,o}(q_y^i, o')}$. This modification suffers a small drop in predictive performance but encodes information in the question-option pair embeddings for us to cluster them and search for common student errors.

We selected all incorrect options ($31 \times 3 = 63$) in questions on subject 33 (BIDMAS) where question images are released on the smaller subset of the Eedi dataset; see [43] for details. A domain expert manually labeled each option based on which error likely resulted in the student selecting it, resulting in a total of 14 high-level errors (errors that cannot be named are excluded), each corresponding to multiple options across different questions; further splitting them into finer-grained errors results in clusters that are not meaningful. We perform k-means clustering [29] on the learned question-option pair embeddings and compare them to the "ground truth" option clusters provided by the expert.

Due to spatial constraints, we only report quantitative results on clustering quality using two commonly used metrics: The adjusted Rand index [39] and the Fowlkes-Mallows index [14]; the former has a range of $[-1, 1]$ while the latter has a range of $[0, 1]$, with 1 corresponding to perfect clustering.

Table 2 lists these metrics on the learned question-option pair embeddings based on the ground truth expert labeling. Overall, the clustering performance is acceptable but not excellent. We observe that some errors such as "sign error in calculation involving negative numbers" have relatively easy-to-identify corresponding option clusters (5 out of 8 options labeled by the expert as corresponding to that error are put into the same cluster). On the other hand, some options such as $69D$ and $293C$ (the left half of Fig. 1) correspond to the same error but are not grouped into the same cluster. One possible explanation is that students may not consistently demonstrate an error, as found in prior research [41]; among students who selected $69D$, only 51% selected $293C$ while 34% of them selected the correct option, $293B$. Therefore, further work is required to study whether more robust KT methods and clustering algorithms can identify error clusters more effectively. Nevertheless, our approach produces a starting point to reduce the effort for domain experts to manually label errors and provides them a way to do it under data-driven support.

6   Conclusions and Future Work

Analyzing the exact options students select across multiple choice questions has the potential to uncover their error modes and help teachers to provide targeted feedback to improve learning outcomes. In this paper, we proposed a set of methods to extend common knowledge tracing methods that analyze only the correctness of students' responses to questions to analyze the exact options they select on multiple choice questions. We validated these methods with quantitative experiments on two large-scale datasets in terms of their ability to predict the options students select on each question and qualitative experiments in terms of clustering incorrect options according to underlying errors. There are many avenues for future work. First, we need to develop methods that are aware of the evolving nature of student errors. One possible approach is to develop methods that can explicitly account for the recurrence of past errors, such as using a neural copy mechanism [18]; these methods may help us track students' progress in correcting their errors. Second, low F_1 scores for the option prediction task suggest that it is much more challenging than the typical correctness prediction task in knowledge tracing literature and thus deserves more attention.

References

1. Adams, D.M., et al.: Using erroneous examples to improve mathematics learning with a web-based tutoring system. Comput. Hum. Behav. **36**, 401–411 (2014)
2. Anderson, J.R., Jeffries, R.: Novice LISP errors: undetected losses of information from working memory. Hum.-Comput. Interact. **1**(2), 107–131 (1985)
3. Berg, R., Kipf, T.N., Welling, M.: Graph convolutional matrix completion. arXiv preprint arXiv:1706.02263 (2017)
4. Brown, J.S., Burton, R.R.: Diagnostic models for procedural bugs in basic mathematical skills. Cogn. Sci. **2**(2), 155–192 (1978)
5. Cen, H., Koedinger, K., Junker, B.: Learning factors analysis – a general method for cognitive model evaluation and improvement. In: Ikeda, M., Ashley, K.D., Chan, T.-W. (eds.) ITS 2006. LNCS, vol. 4053, pp. 164–175. Springer, Heidelberg (2006). https://doi.org/10.1007/11774303_17
6. Chawla, N.V., Bowyer, K.W., Hall, L.O., Kegelmeyer, W.P.: SMOTE: synthetic minority over-sampling technique. J. Artif. Intell. Res. **16**, 321–357 (2002)
7. Choffin, B., Popineau, F., Bourda, Y., Vie, J.J.: DAS3H: modeling student learning and forgetting for optimally scheduling distributed practice of skills. In: Proceedings of the International Conference on Educational Data Mining, pp. 29–38 (2019)
8. Choi, Y., et al.: EdNet: a large-scale hierarchical dataset in education. In: Bittencourt, I.I., Cukurova, M., Muldner, K., Luckin, R., Millán, E. (eds.) AIED 2020. LNCS (LNAI), vol. 12164, pp. 69–73. Springer, Cham (2020). https://doi.org/10.1007/978-3-030-52240-7_13
9. Corbett, A., Anderson, J.: Knowledge tracing: modeling the acquisition of procedural knowledge. User Model. User-Adapt. Interact. **4**(4), 253–278 (1994). https://doi.org/10.1007/BF01099821
10. Doroudi, S., Aleven, V., Brunskill, E.: Where's the reward? Int. J. Artif. Intell. Educ. **29**(4), 568–620 (2019). https://doi.org/10.1007/s40593-019-00187-x
11. Erickson, J.A., Botelho, A.F., McAteer, S., Varatharaj, A., Heffernan, N.T.: The automated grading of student open responses in mathematics. In: Proceedings of the International Conference on Learning Analytics & Knowledge, pp. 615–624 (2020)

12. Feldman, M.Q., Cho, J.Y., Ong, M., Gulwani, S., Popović, Z., Andersen, E.: Automatic diagnosis of students' misconceptions in K-8 mathematics. In: Proceedings of the CHI Conference on Human Factors in Computing Systems, pp. 1–12 (2018)
13. Feng, J., Zhang, B., Li, Y., Xu, Q.: Bayesian diagnosis tracing: application of procedural misconceptions in knowledge tracing. In: Isotani, S., Millán, E., Ogan, A., Hastings, P., McLaren, B., Luckin, R. (eds.) AIED 2019. LNCS (LNAI), vol. 11626, pp. 84–88. Springer, Cham (2019). https://doi.org/10.1007/978-3-030-23207-8_16
14. Fowlkes, E.B., Mallows, C.L.: A method for comparing two hierarchical clusterings. J. Am. Stat. Assoc. **78**(383), 553–569 (1983)
15. Ghosh, A., Heffernan, N., Lan, A.S.: Context-aware attentive knowledge tracing. In: Proceedings of the ACM SIGKDD International Conference on Knowledge Discovery & Data Mining, pp. 2330–2339 (2020)
16. Goodfellow, I., Bengio, Y., Courville, A.: Deep Learning. MIT Press, Cambridge (2016)
17. Graves, A., Mohamed, A.R., Hinton, G.: Speech recognition with deep recurrent neural networks. In: Proceedings of the IEEE International Conference on Acoustics, Speech and Signal Processing, pp. 6645–6649 (2013)
18. Gu, J., Lu, Z., Li, H., Li, V.O.: Incorporating copying mechanism in sequence-to-sequence learning. arXiv preprint arXiv:1603.06393 (2016)
19. Gusukuma, L., Bart, A.C., Kafura, D., Ernst, J.: Misconception-driven feedback: results from an experimental study. In: Proceedings of the ACM Conference on International Computing Education Research, pp. 160–168 (2018)
20. He, X., Liao, L., Zhang, H., Nie, L., Hu, X., Chua, T.S.: Neural collaborative filtering. In: Proceedings of the International Conference on World Wide Web, pp. 173–182 (2017)
21. Khajah, M., Huang, Y., González-Brenes, J., Mozer, M., Brusilovsky, P.: Integrating knowledge tracing and item response theory: a tale of two frameworks. In: Proceedings of the International Workshop on Personalization Approaches in Learning Environments, vol. 1181, pp. 7–15 (2014)
22. Kingma, D.P., Ba, J.: Adam: a method for stochastic optimization. In: Proceedings of the International Conference on Learning Representations (2015)
23. Kipf, T.N., Welling, M.: Semi-supervised classification with graph convolutional networks. arXiv preprint arXiv:1609.02907 (2016)
24. Koedinger, K.R., Corbett, A., et al.: Cognitive tutors: technology bringing learning sciences to the classroom. In: The Cambridge Handbook of the Learning Sciences, pp. 61–77 (2006)
25. Lan, A.S., Studer, C., Baraniuk, R.G.: Matrix recovery from quantized and corrupted measurements. In: IEEE International Conference on Acoustics, Speech and Signal Processing, pp. 4973–4977, May 2014
26. Lan, A.S., Studer, C., Waters, A.E., Baraniuk, R.G.: Tag-aware ordinal sparse factor analysis for learning and content analytics. In: Proceedings of the 6th International Conference on Educational Data Mining, pp. 90–97, July 2013
27. Lan, A.S., Vats, D., Waters, A.E., Baraniuk, R.G.: Mathematical language processing: automatic grading and feedback for open response mathematical questions. In: Proceedings of the ACM Conference on Learning at Scale, pp. 167–176 (2015)
28. Lindsey, R., Shroyer, J., Pashler, H., Mozer, M.: Improving students' long-term knowledge retention through personalized review. Psychol. Sci. **25**(3), 639–647 (2014)
29. Lloyd, S.: Least squares quantization in PCM. IEEE Trans. Inf. Theory **28**(2), 129–137 (1982)

30. Ostini, R., Nering, M.L.: Polytomous Item Response Theory Models, No. 144, Sage (2006)

31. Pandey, S., Karypis, G.: A self attentive model for knowledge tracing. In: Proceedings of the International Conference on Educational Data Mining, pp. 384–389, July 2019

32. Pandey, S., Srivastava, J.: RKT: relation-aware self-attention for knowledge tracing. arXiv preprint arXiv:2008.12736 (2020)

33. Pardos, Z.A., Heffernan, N.T.: Modeling individualization in a Bayesian networks implementation of knowledge tracing. In: De Bra, P., Kobsa, A., Chin, D. (eds.) UMAP 2010. LNCS, vol. 6075, pp. 255–266. Springer, Heidelberg (2010). https://doi.org/10.1007/978-3-642-13470-8_24

34. Pavlik Jr., P., Cen, H., Koedinger, K.: Performance factors analysis-a new alternative to knowledge tracing. In: Proceedings of the International Conference on Artificial Intelligence in Education (2009)

35. Piech, C., et al.: Deep knowledge tracing. In: Proceedings of the Conference on Advances in Neural Information Processing Systems, pp. 505–513 (2015)

36. Ritter, S., Anderson, J.R., Koedinger, K.R., Corbett, A.: Cognitive tutor: applied research in mathematics education. Psychon. Bull. Rev. **14**(2), 249–255 (2007). https://doi.org/10.3758/BF03194060

37. Selent, D.A.: Creating systems and applying large-scale methods to improve student remediation in online tutoring systems in real-time and at scale. Ph.D. thesis, Worcester Polytechnic Institute (2017)

38. Smith III, J.P., DiSessa, A.A., Roschelle, J.: Misconceptions reconceived: a constructivist analysis of knowledge in transition. J. Learn. Sci. **3**(2), 115–163 (1994)

39. Steinley, D.: Properties of the Hubert-arable adjusted rand index. Psychol. Methods **9**(3), 386 (2004)

40. Thissen, D., Steinberg, L.: A taxonomy of item response models. Psychometrika **51**(4), 567–577 (1986)

41. VanLehn, K.: Bugs are not enough: empirical studies of bugs, impasses and repairs in procedural skills. J. Math. Behav. (1982)

42. Wang, F., et al.: Neural cognitive diagnosis for intelligent education systems. Pro. AAAI Conf. Artif. Intell. **34**, 6153–6161 (2020)

43. Wang, Z., et al.: Diagnostic questions: the NeurIPS 2020 education challenge. arXiv preprint arXiv:2007.12061 (2020)

44. Woolf, B.P.: Building Intelligent Interactive Tutors: Student-Centered Strategies for Revolutionizing E-learning. Morgan Kaufmann (2010)

45. Yang, Y., et al.: GIKT: a graph-based interaction model for knowledge tracing. In: Hutter, F., Kersting, K., Lijffijt, J., Valera, I. (eds.) ECML PKDD 2020. LNCS (LNAI), vol. 12457, pp. 299–315. Springer, Cham (2021). https://doi.org/10.1007/978-3-030-67658-2_18

46. Yudelson, M.V., Koedinger, K.R., Gordon, G.J.: Individualized Bayesian knowledge tracing models. In: Lane, H.C., Yacef, K., Mostow, J., Pavlik, P. (eds.) AIED 2013. LNCS (LNAI), vol. 7926, pp. 171–180. Springer, Heidelberg (2013). https://doi.org/10.1007/978-3-642-39112-5_18

47. Zhang, J., Shi, X., King, I., Yeung, D.Y.: Dynamic key-value memory networks for knowledge tracing. In: Proceedings of the International Conference on World Wide Web, pp. 765–774, April 2017

An Approach for Detecting Student Perceptions of the Programming Experience from Interaction Log Data

Jamie Gorson[✉], Nicholas LaGrassa, Cindy Hsinyu Hu, Elise Lee,
Ava Marie Robinson, and Eleanor O'Rourke

Northwestern University, Evanston, IL, USA
{jgorson,nick.lagrassa,cindyhu2023,eliselee,
avarobinson2021}@u.northwestern.edu, eorourke@northwestern.edu

Abstract. Student perceptions of programming can impact their experiences in introductory computer science (CS) courses. For example, some students negatively assess their own ability in response to moments that are natural parts of expert practice, such as using online resources or getting syntax errors. Systems that automatically detect these moments from interaction log data could help us study these moments and intervene when the occur. However, while researchers have analyzed programming log data, few systems detect pre-defined moments, particularly those based on student perceptions. We contribute a new approach and system for detecting programming moments that students perceive as important from interaction log data. We conducted retrospective interviews with 41 CS students in which they identified moments that can prompt negative self-assessments. Then we created a qualitative codebook of the behavioral patterns indicative of each moment, and used this knowledge to build an expert system. We evaluated our system with log data collected from an additional 33 CS students. Our results are promising, with F1 scores ranging from 66% to 98%. We believe that this approach can be applied in many domains to understand and detect student perceptions of learning experiences.

Keywords: CS education · Detection systems · Self-assessment

1 Introduction

While programming skills are increasingly important for 21st century learners, many students struggle in introductory computer science (CS) courses [24,32]. Recent studies suggest that this struggle may be exacerbated by students' self-perceptions; students often believe that they do not belong [30,48,54], are not capable of succeeding [13,19,34], or are performing poorly in CS [21,26,31,32]. In this paper, we focus on one aspect of student self-perceptions: negative self-assessments. In our previous work, we found that students frequently assess their own programming ability, using moments that occur during the programming

© Springer Nature Switzerland AG 2021
I. Roll et al. (Eds.): AIED 2021, LNAI 12748, pp. 150–164, 2021.
https://doi.org/10.1007/978-3-030-78292-4_13

process as signals of whether they are performing well [21,22]. However, many of the moments that students see as negative performance indicators are natural parts of expert practice; for example, many students believe that spending time planning and struggling with syntax errors are signs of low ability [28,41,52]. Students who negatively self-assess more frequently also tend to have lower self-efficacy [22], which can influence persistence and performance in CS [31,37].

While our previous survey studies have established the prevalence of negative self-assessments in CS [21,22], we have a limited understanding of the programming moments that prompt negative self-assessments. If we could detect these moments as they arise during the programming process, we would be able to study them more directly. Furthermore, if such a detection system were automated, we could study these moments using a significantly larger sample of data, as manually detecting them is labor-intensive. An automated detection system would also enable the development of real-time feedback interventions, which provide messages to students at key moments. This type of intervention has been shown to be effective in mediating student perceptions in other contexts [11,39] and can scale to meet the increasing demand in CS.

Interaction log data collected from programming environments may be useful for automatically detecting self-assessment moments, since researchers have successfully leveraged this type of data to analyze student programming process [7–9], predict student performance [1,9,23,38,42], and build automated feedback interventions [14,35]. However, most of these prior systems use bottom-up methods to identify behavioral patterns in interaction data, rather than using top-down approaches to detect pre-defined programming moments like struggling with syntax errors, an example of the self-assessment moments. Systems that use top-down approaches, such as cognitive tutors [2,3,10], generally require models of expert practice. However, researchers are not experts in understanding how students perceive the programming process, and thus we would need to elicit this knowledge from students to create such a model in this domain.

To address these challenges, we contribute an approach called *retrospective-enabled perception recognition* for designing systems that detect student perceptions of the programming process. In this approach, the designer uses retrospective interviews [16] to elicit student perceptions of programming moments, and then builds a qualitative codebook that describes the behavioral patterns indicative of each moment. This codebook is used to inform the design of an expert system. We used our approach to design an automated detector for eight self-assessment moments based on retrospective interviews with 41 CS students. We evaluated the performance of our system using data collected from an additional 33 students, comparing the automatically detected moments to those manually labelled by the authors. Our results are promising, with F1 scores ranging from 66% to 98%. We also present an analysis of our systems' incorrect decisions, enabled by the transparency of the expert system approach. Our detection system has the potential to facilitate future studies of self-assessment moments and support interventions that provide real-time feedback. Our findings also suggest that the *retrospective-enabled perception recognition* approach can be used to design detection systems for student perceptions in other contexts in the future.

2   Background

2.1   Student Self-perceptions in CS

Computing education researchers have found that students often have negative perceptions about themselves and their experiences in CS. For example, when student perceptions of a programming session do not align with their expectations, students sometimes have negative emotional reactions even after successfully solving problems [25]. Additionally, students who have community-oriented goals often perceive that they can not meet these goals in computing careers [29]. Studies also show that many students perceive that they do not belong in computer science, often because they belong to a group that is underrepresented in the field [15,18,36,48,53]. These negative perceptions have been shown to correlate with students' self-efficacy [4,25,26,54], or the belief in one's ability to accomplish a task or achieve mastery in a specific domain [5,6,47]. Self-efficacy has a direct impact on student learning outcomes [45] and often correlates with student performance in CS courses [33,43,55].

In this paper, we focus on students' perceptions of programming experiences that prompt them to negatively assess their ability. CS1 students assess their programming ability frequently [21,26], and often think they are performing poorly when they encounter programming moments essential to the programming process [21,22]. Our recent survey study with 214 CS students from three universities identified 13 programming moments which cause many students to negatively self-assess, even though the moments are also natural parts of expert practice [28,41,52]. For example, some students report that they feel like the are performing poorly when they use online documentation to look up syntax, stop to think about their solution, and spend time planning [22]. We also found that students who negatively self-assess in response to more of these moments tend to have lower self-efficacy. However, we do not know how these moments arise or when they occur in students' programming process.

2.2   Analyzing Programming Interaction Log Data

Researchers have explored many methods for interpreting log data collected from programming environments. This interaction data is used for two primary purposes: to produce new knowledge from a bottom-up analysis of student interactions, and to perform top-down detection of programming moments.

Many researchers take data-driven approaches to study the student programming process [7,8,20,51] and to evaluate or predict student performance [1,9,23,38,42,55]. Initially, most of this work analyzed compilation logs [23,51], but more recently, researchers have leveraged machine learning techniques to identify patterns in interaction log data. For example, Blikstein et al. clustered students based on their problem-solving pathways to study how they progressed through programming assignments [9]. Berland et al. also used clustering techniques to study tinkering and how programming behaviors change across stages of the problem [7]. These studies used a bottom-up approach, analyzing data to find patterns organically rather than building hand-architected models to identify preconceived moments of interest.

Some researchers have used interaction log data and expert knowledge of the programming process to identify pre-defined moments through top-down approaches. Expert systems, a common technique, reason about student interactions based on models of expert decision-making processes. For example, cognitive tutors like the LISP tutor [44] use expert systems to provide relevant feedback. Marwan et al. used a similar approach to analyze program states to identify milestones in student progress while solving problems [35]. Koskal et al., however, demonstrated how challenging it can be to build systems that detect pre-defined programming moments [27]. The authors set out to develop a system to automatically detect the stages in the *design recipe* [17], a scaffolded process for solving programming problems. However, they found that the fuzzy design recipe stages were hard to automatically detect from low-level log data due to the wide variation in student behaviors during each stage [27].

While previous studies show promise in deriving indicators of student behavior and process from low-level data, existing approaches do not yet explore how to use log data to automatically detect moments based on student perceptions. Expert systems are designed to model expert knowledge, but researchers are not experts in understanding how students perceive the programming process. As a result, we need an approach for eliciting this knowledge from students. We contribute a new approach for designing systems that use interaction log data to detect programming moments that students perceive as meaningful.

3   Retrospective-Enabled Perception Recognition

The main contribution of this paper is our approach for detecting student perceptions of the programming experience from interaction log data. In this section, we describe our new approach and present the methods we used to build a system to detect moments when students may negatively self-assess while programming.

To enable our system, we designed extensions to collect interaction log data from two programs: jGRASP [12] (an IDE often used in introductory Java courses) and Chrome (a commonly used web browser). We chose these two programs because they account for a large portion of student interactions with the computer while programming. Each extension collects time-series data in a JSON format for a number of user actions and events, which allows us to keep track of student behavior and the state of the IDE. Our jGRASP extension, built in collaboration with the jGRASP development team, captures all keystrokes, cursor movements, console messages, and interactions with buttons and windows. Our Chrome tool captures all navigation on websites, including the URLs and scrolling behavior while viewing a page. During the data collection process, we iterated on the events and actions collected by the extensions as we learned more about the behaviors associated with each moment. For example, after looking at the data, we realized that student scrolling patterns revealed important information about their behavior, so we added this to our extensions.

3.1   Phase 1: Retrospective Interviews

We conducted retrospective interviews during Phase 1 to capture student perceptions of the programming experience. We recruited 41 participants from a large
public university in the United States. At the time of the study, all participants
enrolled in a second-semester introductory CS course (CS2), a requirement for
CS majors, were eligible to participate. We recruited students with emails sent
by the professor of the course. The study took place virtually through Zoom.
Students provided consent to participate and were compensated for their time.

The goal of the interview was to gather examples of self-assessment moments
naturally occurring during programming sessions, along with participants' perceptions of those moments. When a participant joined the Zoom call, the
researcher installed the Chrome and jGRASP extensions on the student's computer. Then the researcher provided a short review of how to use jGRASP to
ensure a baseline level of familiarity with the development environment. We
asked the student to work on one of three similar programming problems while
sharing their screen, and told them to work on the problem like they would a
homework assignment. During this part of the interview, the researcher turned
the student's video and microphone off and did not interrupt them to reduce the
effect of the lab environment on their behavior as much as possible.

After 30 min of programming, we conducted a retrospective interview [16]. We
gave the student a list describing a subset of the self-assessment moments from
Gorson & O'Rourke [22] (see examples in Table 1). We chose to only include the
moments that occur during the programming process, like *changing approaches*,
and not general reflections, like *spending a long time on a problem*, because we
were more likely to be able to determine when they will happen. Finally, the
student and researcher watched a screen recording of the programming session
and the student identified each time one of those moments occurred. Below in
Fig. 1, we provide an example of the self-assessment moments that were labelled
in the retrospective interview for one participant.

Table 1. Negative self-assessment moments detected by our expert system.

Moments *and detailed descriptions*
Using resources to look up syntax *from the web or other sources*
Using resources to research an approach *from the web or other sources*
Changing approaches *to try a new approach for solving the programming problem*
Writing a plan *in the comments or notes to outline future programming steps*
Getting simple errors *are usually compiler errors due to oversights or typos*
Getting Java errors *are usually runtime errors due to conceptual mistakes*
Struggling with errors *while trying to fix or debug the errors*
Stopping to think *while implementing a solution*

Fig. 1. The self-assessment moments that occured in one participant interview.

3.2   Phase 2: Qualitative Analysis

The goal of Phase 2 was to develop a qualitative codebook that the researchers could use to identify negative self-assessment moments independently, without additional knowledge of student perceptions. Identifying moments such as using resources may appear straightforward, however students' perceptions of these moments are quite nuanced. For example, in our prior work students reported different reactions when using resources to look up syntax versus using resources to research how to solve the problem [21,22]. While it is relatively easy to determine when a student is viewing a website or a course resource, determining the purpose of its use is more difficult. In addition, it is critical to identify each use of a resource, because a student who references the same resource multiple times will have a different experience than a student who uses multiple resources for different purposes. We therefore use a detailed qualitative codebook to capture the nuances discovered through the retrospective interview process.

To develop this codebook, we qualitatively analyzed the retrospective interviews. After conducting the first 20 interviews, we compiled a list of all student-labeled moments. From that list, we distilled a set of representative behaviors for each moment and wrote an initial draft of the codebook. The codebook includes a high-level definition of each moment and a set of heuristics that describe the behavioral patterns indicative of each moment. We then re-watched the first twenty interviews and iterated on the behavioral descriptions for each moment until two researchers could accurately and consistently label all of the moments.

As an example, we describe how we identify *struggling with errors* using our codebook. We defined three levels of behavioral indicators for this moment: strong, medium, and weak. If a student exhibits a strong indicator, such as running code in an attempt to fix a bug three times in a row without succeeding, we would label this as *struggling with errors*. If there is no strong indicator, but there are two medium indicators, such as using resources after getting an error, we would also label this as *struggling with errors*. Finally, while weak indicators, such as a slower pace of typing, are not enough to label the moment on their own, the researchers use them to strengthen their confidence in the decisions.

3.3   Phase 3: Codebook Verification

In Phase 3, we first tested the codebook using data from an additional 21 interviews. After each new interview, two authors watched the screen recording of the programming session and used the codebook to label the self-assessment moments. Then, the researchers compared their decisions to the participant's labels in the retrospective interview as member-checks of the labelling scheme [49]. When there were misalignments between a participant's labels and the researchers' labels that could not be explained by the participant misusing or missing a label, the researchers adjusted the description of that moment to incorporate the newly observed behavior. This iterative process continued until the researchers did not need to make changes for five consecutive interviews in which the moment was present. At that point, we considered the codebook for that moment to have reached saturation [40,46]. Of the 12 moments that we asked student to label during the retrospective interview, we were able to reach saturation for eight (see Table 1). Most of the moments for which we did not reach saturation occurred at the beginning of the programming session, such as *writing a plan before implementation*. At this point, students generally interact less with the computer, making it more difficult to identify these moments.

3.4   Phase 4: Implementation of the Detection System

In Phase 4, we built an expert system to detect self-assessment moments using the heuristics in our qualitative codebook. Our system has two stages: data transformation and decision-making. In the data transformation stage, we parse through each event captured in the interaction log data, recreating the programming session and recording around 100 human-authored metrics into a knowledge base. Together the metrics provide a comprehensive snapshot of the state of the programming process. For example, one metric captures the number of lines that a student pastes from a resource into their code. In the decision-making stage, we analyze the metrics at each log event to determine if any of the self-assessment moments occurred. We use two different styles of heuristic algorithms, either if-then rules when there is less ambiguity in the decision-making process (e.g. *getting simple errors*), or fuzzy logic [56] when many metrics need to be considered in parallel (e.g. *using resources to look up syntax*). For example, we use fuzzy logic to increase our confidence that a student is using a resource to look up syntax if they paste either one or two lines of code from the resource.

As a concrete example, consider the strong indicator for the *struggling with errors* moment, when a student runs the code in an attempt to fix a bug three times in a row. One metric for this indicator calculates whether the student is working on the same error across multiple compilations. This metric keeps track of the number of the errors in the console and the names of the errors. After each compile, we use this information (along with some additional details about code edits) to evaluate if the student is still working on the same bug.

We chose an expert system because retrospective data is time-intensive to collect. It is impractical to collect enough student-labeled data to serve as ground-truth for machine learning algorithms. Additionally, data-driven approaches often produce features that are not human-interpretable, making it difficult to understand their decisions and limitations. With an expert system, we can trace the decision process and ensure that the system is making logical choices.

4   Evaluation of the System

4.1   Methods

We evaluated our system by comparing the automatically detected moments to those manually labelled by the authors. While researchers can make mistakes in labeling, this data is the most reliable item of comparison, as participant-labelled data is often inconsistent due to differing interpretations of the moments and participant attention spans. We collected data from programming sessions with 33 additional students from the same university and CS2 course as our initial interviews. The setting and procedure were the same, with the exception of the retrospective interview, which was excluded. To establish the reliability of the researcher-assigned labels, two authors independently labelled the same seven interviews, or 21% of this data set, achieving 82% agreement. Those authors then authors independently labelled the remainder of the data.

One challenge in evaluating this system is establishing a way to compare moment timing between the researchers and the machine. When manually labelling the moments, the researchers picked a timeslot from non-overlapping ten-second windows (e.g., 0–10, 10–20). When comparing the system's results to the researcher-labelled set, we used an additional fifteen-second buffer on both sides of the ten-second window because the start time of a moment can be difficult to determine and might fall on the border of a window. We marked a machine detection as correct if the timestamp assigned to a label was within this forty-second window. We used a slightly larger buffer to more accurately represent two of the moments. For *changing approaches*, we used a two-minute buffer instead of a fifteen-second buffer because this moment often takes places over a few minutes, and we did not have a way to consistently identify matching start times. For *struggling with errors*, the researchers identified the start and end time for the error cycle in which the participant struggled. We deemed a system-identified label as correct if the system chose any time within the error-cycle boundaries. While both of these windows are larger, they reflect the context of these moments and the system's ability to identify these moments accurately.

After running our system on the log data from our evaluation data set, we further analyzed its performance by looking at each false positive and false negative result. The authors reviewed each case and categorized the reason for the false detection by watching the screen recording of the moment and consulting the codebook. During this process, we identified a number of instances when the researchers mislabeled moments, and also noted the limitations of our system.

4.2   Findings

Our results in Table 2 show that we had very high F1 scores for some moments, such as *getting simple errors*, and lower but still reasonable F1 scores for others, such as *writing a plan*. While precision and recall are both important, high precision matters most for interventions to ensure that real-time messages are delivered in response to true moments, and recall is most important for studies to ensure that relevant moments are not missed. The data also shows that the moments arise at varying levels of frequency; *getting simple errors* and *stopping to think* were most frequent, while *writing a plan* and *using resources to research an approach* only occurred occasionally. Our system tended to perform worse for less frequent moments, likely because our codebook and system were developed using fewer observations. However, the frequency of a moment does not necessarily indicate its importance. While we do not yet know how each moment

Table 2. Results from our evaluation of the detection system

Moment	Precision	Recall	F1 score	Count	Human errors
Using resources to look up syntax	82.0%	86.1%	84.0%	128	2
Using resources to research approach	66.7%	66.7%	66.7%	21	1
Changing approaches	73.1%	73.1%	73.1%	26	8
Writing a plan	60.0%	75.0%	66.7%	15	0
Getting simple errors	99.1%	97.7%	98.4%	213	13
Getting Java errors	90.3%	90.3%	90.3%	31	2
Struggling with errors	69.2%	90.0%	78.3%	26	5
Stopping to think	79.1%	75.3%	77.2%	159	15

influences student self-efficacy, some of the less frequent moments may have a stronger impact on student experiences than the more frequent ones.

One benefit of our approach is that our system's decisions are transparent and can be assessed using our qualitative codebook. This enabled us to conduct an analysis on our system's false positives and false negatives. First, our analysis revealed many human errors in labeling, showing how challenging it is for humans to accurately label this type of data and highlighting the value of an automated system. Our analysis also revealed trends that provide direction for improving the system. For example, 10% of the system's incorrect decisions occured because the researcher and system disagreed about the timing of a moment. When we designed the codebook, we focused on describing the heuristics to determine whether a moment occurred, rather than the exact start time for every moment. As a result, our system had less information to help it choose start times. Many of these moments occur over a period of multiple minutes, and therefore detection within a wider range of times could be acceptable. In the future, we would suggest either developing heuristics for determining start times during the qualitative analysis or changing the evaluation to allow the system to select any time point during the moment, as we did for *struggling with errors*.

Our analysis of the system's incorrect decisions also revealed that particular metrics were difficult to encode. For example, our system was not always able to determine when a student had resolved a particular error, which is crucial to detecting the *struggling with errors* moment. This can be quite complex, as students exhibit a wide variety of behaviors when debugging. Another challenge we encountered is that our system does not always have enough information to determine the student's purpose for using resources when it knows a *using resources* moment occurred, resulting in a lower recall for *using resources to research an approach*. Even though our metrics generally provided enough guidance for the researcher, without human intuition or contextual understanding, the system was less accurate in interpreting the variety of ways that students use resources. With more development time, we could increase the accuracy of detection for both of these moments, but it would require significant effort to fully model all potential behaviors. While it is likely not possible to fully capture the variance in student behavior in our models, our relatively high detection accuracy and our concrete ideas for improvement show that this is a viable approach.

5   Conclusions

In this paper, we present a new approach for designing systems that detect student perceptions of the programming process, called *retrospective-enabled perception recognition*. We apply this approach to develop an expert system to detect programming moments that prompt students to negatively self-assess, building on expertise gained through retrospective interviews with 41 CS2 students. We evaluated our system with programming session data collected from an additional 33 CS2 students, finding that our system achieve F1 scores ranging from 66% to 98% for the eight self-assessment moments.

While we are encouraged by our system's performance, this work has a number of limitations. First, our evaluation relies on researcher-assigned labels. While we verified the labeling process through a formal qualitative analysis, researcher labels may not perfectly represent student perceptions. Additionally, while we believe the *retrospective-enabled perception recognition* approach can be applied to other problems, more research is needed to understand how our expert system generalizes. We developed and tested our system with students from just one course and university, and our observations of student programming sessions occurred in a lab setting. Furthermore, students worked on a limited set of problems in one programming language. As a result, additional work is needed to understand whether our system will generalize to a more naturalistic setting, more diverse problems, and other programming languages.

While our results are promising, our models could likely be improved with additional techniques for interpreting interaction log data. For example, natural language processing could help our system understand the semantics of comments and web-page content, which the researchers used when labelling the moments. Additionally, the success of this expert system suggests that this problem may be a good fit for machine teaching, an approach that empowers experts to guide machines in learning to make decisions [50]. Future work should explore whether the knowledge of student perceptions derived from the retrospective interviews can inform a machine teaching algorithm and increase our ability to detect student perceptions accurately.

Through *retrospective-enabled perception recognition*, we contribute a new approach for combining qualitative methods and expert system design to detect learning moments that students perceive as meaningful, which could generalize to a number of problems and contexts. Furthermore, our system for detecting negative self-assessment moments has the potential to enable new studies and interventions that were not previously possible. In future work, we hope to use this system to study the relationship between student behaviors, perceptions of the programming process, and self-assessments. We also hope to develop real-time feedback interventions to help students re-frame self-assessment moments and improve self-efficacy.

Acknowledgement. This work was supported by NSF Grant IIS-1755628. Thank you to Delta Lab.

References

1. Ahadi, A., Lister, R., Haapala, H., Vihavainen, A.: Exploring machine learning methods to automatically identify students in need of assistance. In: Proceedings of the Eleventh Annual International Conference on International Computing Education Research - ICER 2015, pp. 121–130. ACM Press, Omaha (2015). https:// doi.org/10.1145/2787622.2787717. http://dl.acm.org/citation.cfm?doid=2787622. 2787717
2. Anderson, J.R., Conrad, F.G., Corbett, A.T.: Skill acquisition and the LISP tutor. Cogn. Sci. **13**(4), 467–505 (1989)
3. Anderson, J.R., Corbett, A.T., Koedinger, K.R., Pelletier, R.: Cognitive tutors: lessons learned. J. Learn. Sci. **4**(2), 167–207 (1995)
4. Bandura, A.: Self-efficacy mechanism in human agency. Am. Psychol. **37**(2), 122 (1982)
5. Bandura, A.: Self-Efficacy: The Exercise of Control. Macmillan, New York (1997)
6. Bandura, A.: Self-efficacy. In: The Corsini Encyclopedia of Psychology, pp. 1–3. Wiley Online Library (2010)
7. Berland, M., Martin, T., Benton, T., Petrick Smith, C., Davis, D.: Using learning analytics to understand the learning pathways of novice programmers. J. Learn. Sci. **22**(4), 564–599 (2013)
8. Blikstein, P.: Using learning analytics to assess students' behavior in open-ended programming tasks. In: Proceedings of the 1st International Conference on Learning Analytics and Knowledge, pp. 110–116. ACM (2011). http://dl.acm.org/ citation.cfm?id=2090132
9. Blikstein, P., Worsley, M., Piech, C., Sahami, M., Cooper, S., Koller, D.: Programming pluralism: using learning analytics to detect patterns in the learning of computer programming. J. Learn. Sci. **23**(4), 561–599 (2014)
10. Corbett, A.: Cognitive computer tutors: solving the two-sigma problem. In: Bauer, M., Gmytrasiewicz, P.J., Vassileva, J. (eds.) UM 2001. LNCS (LNAI), vol. 2109, pp. 137–147. Springer, Heidelberg (2001). https://doi.org/10.1007/3-540-44566-8_14
11. Corbett, A.T., Anderson, J.R.: Locus of feedback control in computer-based tutoring: impact on learning rate, achievement and attitudes. In: Proceedings of the SIGCHI Conference on Human Factors in Computing Systems, pp. 245–252. ACM (2001)
12. Cross, J.H., Hendrix, D., Umphress, D.A.: JGRASP: an integrated development environment with visualizations for teaching Java in CS1, CS2, and beyond. In: 34th Annual Frontiers in Education, FIE 2004, pp. 1466–1467. IEEE Computer Society (2004)
13. Cutts, Q., Cutts, E., Draper, S., O'Donnell, P., Saffrey, P.: Manipulating mindset to positively influence introductory programming performance. In: Proceedings of the 41st ACM Technical Symposium on Computer Science Education, pp. 431–435. ACM (2010). http://dl.acm.org/citation.cfm?id=1734409
14. Edwards, S., Li, Z.: Towards progress indicators for measuring student programming effort during solution development. In: Proceedings of the 16th Koli Calling International Conference on Computing Education Research - Koli Calling 2016,

pp. 31–40. ACM Press, Koli (2016). https://doi.org/10.1145/2999541.2999561. http://dl.acm.org/citation.cfm?doid=2999541.2999561

15. Ehrlinger, J., Dunning, D.: How chronic self-views influence (and potentially mislead) estimates of performance. J. Pers. Soc. Psychol. **84**(1), 5 (2003)

16. Ericsson, K.A., Simon, H.A.: Protocol Analysis: Verbal Reports as Data. MIT Press, Cambridge (1984)

17. Felleisen, M., Findler, R.B., Flatt, M., Krishnamurthi, S.: How to Design Programs. MIT Press, Cambridge (2001)

18. Fisher, A., Margolis, J.: Unlocking the clubhouse: the Carnegie Mellon experience. ACM SIGCSE Bull. **34**(2), 79–83 (2002). http://dl.acm.org/citation.cfm?id=543836

19. Flanigan, A.E., Peteranetz, M.S., Shell, D.F., Soh, L.K.: Exploring changes in computer science students' implicit theories of intelligence across the semester. In: Proceedings of the Eleventh Annual International Conference on International Computing Education Research, ICER 2015, Omaha, Nebraska, USA, pp. 161–168. Association for Computing Machinery, New York (2015). https://doi.org/10.1145/2787622.2787722

20. Fuchs, M., Heckner, M., Raab, F., Wolff, C.: Monitoring students' mobile app coding behavior data analysis based on IDE and browser interaction logs. In: 2014 IEEE Global Engineering Education Conference (EDUCON). pp. 892–899. IEEE, Istanbul, April 2014. https://doi.org/10.1109/EDUCON.2014.6826202. http://ieeexplore.ieee.org/document/6826202/

21. Gorson, J., O'Rourke, E.: How do students talk about intelligence? An investigation of motivation, self-efficacy, and mindsets in computer science. In: Proceedings of the 2019 ACM Conference on International Computing Education Research - ICER 2019, pp. 21–29. ACM Press, Toronto ON, Canada (2019). https://doi.org/10.1145/3291279.3339413. http://dl.acm.org/citation.cfm?doid=3291279.3339413

22. Gorson, J., O'Rourke, E.: Why do CS1 Students Think They're Bad at Programming? Investigating Self-efficacy and Self-assessments at Three Universities. In: Proceedings of the 2020 ACM Conference on International Computing Education Research, pp. 170–181 (2020)

23. Jadud, M.C.: Methods and tools for exploring novice compilation behaviour. In: Proceedings of the Second International Workshop on Computing Education Research, Canterbury, United Kingdom, ICER 2006, pp. 73–84. Association for Computing Machinery, New York (2006). https://doi.org/10.1145/1151588.1151600

24. Kinnunen, P., Simon, B.: Experiencing programming assignments in CS1: the emotional toll. In: Proceedings of the Sixth International Workshop on Computing Education Research, pp. 77–86. ACM (2010)

25. Kinnunen, P., Simon, B.: CS majors' self-efficacy perceptions in CS1: results in light of social cognitive theory. In: Proceedings of the Seventh International Workshop on Computing Education Research, pp. 19–26. ACM (2011)

26. Kinnunen, P., Simon, B.: My program is ok - am I? Computing freshmen's experiences of doing programming assignments. Comput. Sci. Educ. **22**(1), 1–28 (2012). https://doi.org/10.1080/08993408.2012.655091. http://www.tandfonline.com/doi/abs/10.1080/08993408.2012.655091

27. Köksal, M.F., Başar, R., Üsküdarlı, S.: Screen-replay: a session recording and analysis tool for DrScheme. In: Proceedings of the Scheme and Functional Programming Workshop, Technical Report, California Polytechnic State University, CPSLO-CSC-09, vol. 3, pp. 103–110. Citeseer (2009)

28. LaToza, T.D., Venolia, G., DeLine, R.: Maintaining mental models: a study of developer work habits. In: Proceeding of the 28th International Conference on Software Engineering - ICSE 2006, p. 492. ACM Press, Shanghai (2006). https://doi.org/10.1145/1134285.1134355. http://portal.acm.org/citation.cfm?doid=1134285.1134355

29. Lewis, C., Bruno, P., Raygoza, J., Wang, J.: Alignment of goals and perceptions of computing predicts students' sense of belonging in computing. In: Proceedings of the 2019 ACM Conference on International Computing Education Research - ICER 2019, pp. 11–19. ACM Press, Toronto (2019). https://doi.org/10.1145/3291279.3339426. http://dl.acm.org/citation.cfm?doid=3291279.3339426

30. Lewis, C.M., Anderson, R.E., Yasuhara, K.: "I Don't Code All Day": fitting in computer science when the stereotypes don't fit. In: Proceedings of the 2016 ACM Conference on International Computing Education Research, ICER 2016, Melbourne, VIC, Australia, pp. 23–32. Association for Computing Machinery, New York (2016). https://doi.org/10.1145/2960310.2960332

31. Lewis, C.M., Yasuhara, K., Anderson, R.E.: Deciding to major in computer science: a grounded theory of students' self-assessment of ability. In: Proceedings of the Seventh International Workshop on Computing Education Research, pp. 3–10. ACM (2011)

32. Lishinski, A., Yadav, A., Enbody, R.: Students' emotional reactions to programming projects in introduction to programming: measurement approach and influence on learning outcomes. In: Proceedings of the 2017 ACM Conference on International Computing Education Research - ICER 2017, pp. 30–38. ACM Press, Tacoma, Washington (2017). https://doi.org/10.1145/3105726.3106187. http://dl.acm.org/citation.cfm?doid=3105726.3106187

33. Lishinski, A., Yadav, A., Good, J., Enbody, R.: Learning to program: gender differences and interactive effects of students' motivation, goals, and self-efficacy on performance. In: Proceedings of the 2016 ACM Conference on International Computing Education Research, pp. 211–220. ACM Press (2016). https://doi.org/10.1145/2960310.2960329. http://dl.acm.org/citation.cfm?doid=2960310.2960329

34. Loksa, D., Ko, A.J., Jernigan, W., Oleson, A., Mendez, C.J., Burnett, M.M.: Programming, problem solving, and self-awareness: effects of explicit guidance. In: Proceedings of the 2016 CHI Conference on Human Factors in Computing Systems, pp. 1449–1461. ACM Press (2016). https://doi.org/10.1145/2858036.2858252. http://dl.acm.org/citation.cfm?doid=2858036.2858252

35. Marwan, S., Gao, G., Fisk, S., Price, T.W., Barnes, T.: Adaptive immediate feedback can improve novice programming engagement and intention to persist in computer science. In: Proceedings of the 2020 ACM Conference on International Computing Education Research, pp. 194–203. ACM, Virtual Event New Zealand, August 2020. https://doi.org/10.1145/3372782.3406264. https://dl.acm.org/doi/10.1145/3372782.3406264

36. Master, A., Cheryan, S., Meltzoff, A.N.: Computing whether she belongs: stereotypes undermine girls' interest and sense of belonging in computer science. J. Educ. Psychol. 108(3), 424 (2016)

37. Miura, I.T.: The relationship of computer self-efficacy expectations to computer interest and course enrollment in college. Sex Roles 16(5–6), 303–311 (1987). https://doi.org/10.1007/BF00289956. http://link.springer.com/10.1007/BF00289956

38. Munson, J.P., Zitovsky, J.P.: Models for early identification of struggling novice programmers. In: Proceedings of the 49th ACM Technical Symposium on Computer Science Education, pp. 699–704 (2018)
39. O'Rourke, E., Haimovitz, K., Ballweber, C., Dweck, C., Popović, Z.: Brain points: a growth mindset incentive structure boosts persistence in an educational game. In: Proceedings of the SIGCHI Conference on Human Factors in Computing Systems, pp. 3339–3348. ACM (2014)
40. O'Reilly, M., Parker, N.: 'Unsatisfactory Saturation': a critical exploration of the notion of saturated sample sizes in qualitative research. Qual. Res. **13**(2), 190–197 (2013). https://doi.org/10.1177/1468794112446106. http://journals.sagepub.com/doi/10.1177/1468794112446106
41. Perscheid, M., Siegmund, B., Taeumel, M., Hirschfeld, R.: Studying the advancement in debugging practice of professional software developers. Softw. Qual. J. **25**(1), 83–110 (2017). https://doi.org/10.1007/s11219-015-9294-2. http://link.springer.com/10.1007/s11219-015-9294-2
42. Piech, C., Sahami, M., Koller, D., Cooper, S., Blikstein, P.: Modeling how students learn to program. In: Proceedings of the 43rd ACM Technical Symposium on Computer Science Education, pp. 153–160. ACM (2012)
43. Ramalingam, V., LaBelle, D., Wiedenbeck, S.: Self-efficacy and mental models in learning to program. In: ACM SIGCSE Bulletin, vol. 36, pp. 171–175. ACM (2004)
44. Reiser, B.J., Anderson, J.R., Farrell, R.G.: Dynamic student modelling in an intelligent tutor for LISP programming. IJCAI **85**, 8–14 (1985)
45. Relich, J.D., Debus, R.L., Walker, R.: The mediating role of attribution and self-efficacy variables for treatment effects on achievement outcomes. Contemp. Educ. Psychol. **11**(3), 195–216 (1986)
46. Saunders, B., et al.: Saturation in qualitative research: exploring its conceptualization and operationalization. Qual. Quant. **52**(4), 1893–1907 (2018). https://doi.org/10.1007/s11135-017-0574-8. http://link.springer.com/10.1007/s11135-017-0574-8
47. Schunk, D.H.: Self-efficacy, motivation, and performance. J. Appl. Sport Psychol. **7**(2), 112–137 (1995). https://doi.org/10.1080/10413209508406961. https://www.tandfonline.com/doi/full/10.1080/10413209508406961
48. Shapiro, J.R., Williams, A.M.: The role of stereotype threats in undermining girls' and women's performance and interest in STEM fields. Sex Roles **66**(3–4), 175–183 (2012). https://doi.org/10.1007/s11199-011-0051-0. http://link.springer.com/10.1007/s11199-011-0051-0
49. Shenton, A.K.: Strategies for ensuring trustworthiness in qualitative research projects. Educ. Inf. **22**(2), 63–75 (2004). https://doi.org/10.3233/EFI-2004-22201. https://www.medra.org/servlet/aliasResolver?alias=iospress&doi=10.3233/EFI-2004-22201
50. Simard, P.Y., et al.: Machine teaching: a new paradigm for building machine learning systems. arXiv preprint arXiv:1707.06742 (2017)
51. Soloway, E., Bonar, J., Ehrlich, K.: Cognitive strategies and looping constructs: an empirical study. Commu. ACM **26**(11), 853–860 (1983). https://doi.org/10.1145/182.358436. https://dl.acm.org/doi/10.1145/182.358436
52. Sonnentag, S.: Expertise in professional software design: a process study. J. Appl. Psychol. **83**(5), 703 (1998)
53. Steele, C.M., Aronson, J.: Stereotype threat and the intellectual test performance of African Americans. J. Pers. Soc. Psychol. **69**(5), 797 (1995)

54. Veilleux, N., Bates, R., Allendoerfer, C., Jones, D., Crawford, J., Floyd Smith, T.: The relationship between belonging and ability in computer science. In: Proceedings of the 44th ACM Technical Symposium on Computer Science Education, pp. 65–70. ACM (2013)
55. Watson, C., Li, F.W., Godwin, J.L.: No tests required: comparing traditional and dynamic predictors of programming success. In: Proceedings of the 45th ACM Technical Symposium on Computer Science Education, pp. 469–474 (2014)
56. Zadeh, L.A.: Fuzzy logic. Computer **21**(4), 83–93 (1988)

Discovering Co-creative Dialogue States During Collaborative Learning

Amanda E. Griffith[1]([✉]), Gloria Ashiya Katuka[1], Joseph B. Wiggins[1],
Kristy Elizabeth Boyer[1], Jason Freeman[2], Brian Magerko[2], and Tom McKlin[3]

[1] University of Florida, Gainesville, FL 32607, USA
{amandagriffith,gkatuka,jbwiggi3,keboyer}@ufl.edu
[2] Georgia Institute of Technology, Atlanta, GA 30332, USA
{jason.freeman,magerko}@gatech.edu
[3] The Findings Group, Decatur, GA 30030, USA
tom@thefindingsgroup.org

Abstract. Many important forms of collaborative learning are co-creative in nature. AI systems to support co-creativity in learning are highly underinvestigated, and very little is known about the dialogue mechanisms that support learning during collaborative co-creativity. To address this need, we analyzed the structure of collaborative dialogue between pairs of high school students who co-created music by writing code. We used hidden Markov models to analyze 68 co-creative dialogues consisting of 3,305 total utterances. The results distinguish seven hidden states: three of the hidden states are characterized by conversation, such as social, aesthetic, or technical dialogue. The remaining four hidden states are characterized by task actions including code editing, accessing the curriculum, running the code successfully, and receiving an error when running the code. The model reveals that immediately after the pairs ran their code successfully, they often transitioned into the aesthetic or technical dialogue state. However, when facing code errors, learners were unlikely to transition into a conversation state. In the few cases where they did transition to a conversation state, this transition was almost always to the technical dialogue state. These findings reveal processes of human co-creativity and can inform the design of intelligent co-creative agents that support human collaboration and learning.

Keywords: Collaborative learning · Dialogue · Co-creativity

1 Introduction

There is growing interest in using artificial intelligence (AI) to support collaborative learning. AI companions have the potential to improve learners' collaborative skills by, for example, encouraging "deep thinking" and initiative taking [10]. AIs have been developed for applications ranging from emotional learning companions that support elementary school children learning to code [14] to

I. Roll et al. (Eds.): AIED 2021, LNAI 12748, pp. 165–177, 2021.
https://doi.org/10.1007/978-3-030-78292-4_14

discussing Jane Austen books with lifelong learners [16]. AIs to support collaborative learning are underinvestigated, even though collaborative learning has been shown to increase learner interest in solving problems during online tutoring [2], decrease learner boredom [2], and improve critical thinking skills [8]. Researchers have begun to uncover features of strong collaboration, including gaze synchronization [22], the importance of proximity [4], and semantic similarity [21]. Substantial work has investigated collaborative processes with a variety of data sources including eye tracking [5,22], motion sensors [4,5,18], dialogue analysis [3,21], and speech features [24].

Research on the dialogue of collaboration has focused on detecting when students are off-task [3], supporting inquiry learning by analyzing the role of questions in collaborative computational modeling [23], and predicting problem-solving modes to support adaptive tutoring [19]. Research on collaborative learning within groups has used conversational agents to facilitate productive conversations [6] and dialogue features to identify trouble during collaboration [9].

Most research on virtual agents in collaborative learning has involved agents in a tutor or support role, but some work with agents as partners to human learners has demonstrated benefits including significantly higher levels of shared understanding, progress monitoring, and feedback [20]. Research on agents as partners has also investigated support for human-computer co-creation, a type of collaborative creativity in which responsibility for an artifact is shared between the human and computer [11]. To move toward systems that support collaborative co-creation during learning, we need to build an understanding of the dialogue mechanisms that characterize this process.

To address this need, this work makes a step toward characterizing the dialogue modes learners tend to enter as they engage in co-creative dialogue. We examined dialogue and system interactions between pairs of high school students learning to code through remixing musical samples. Using a hidden Markov model, we distinguished seven states, three characterized by conversation and four characterized by task actions. The model suggests that learners engaged in two types of discourse—aesthetic and technical—during this co-creative process. The *aesthetic* discourse pertains to musical style, taste, and expression, while the *technical* discourse pertains to writing code and task objectives. By modeling co-creative dialogue, we can move toward intelligent support of human collaboration and toward intelligent co-creative agents that support learning.

2   Methods

This work analyzes a corpus of textual student-student dialogue collected between November 2019 and March 2020 during computer science classes from eight public high schools in two districts in the southern United States, consisting of a total of 140 participants. More than half of the schools had a student population of majority (>50%) Caucasian students; one school was majority Black; two schools had a substantial (>25%–35%) Latinx population; one school had a substantial Asian population. All students were in grades 10–12 (15–18 years old). Teachers placed the students into dyads, and students were placed at a distance in separate rooms or different areas of the same room to facilitate their communication through the textual chat interface (Fig. 1). Students collaborated synchronously for an average of 48 min to remix musical samples and create an original song or ringtone. Some participants, 9 pairs, split their work across two class days. We included only the first day's dialogue for these pairs because concatenating two separate dialogues would change the natural beginning, middle, and end of the sequences; whereas including both dialogues for a pair would unevenly weight their patterns while training the hidden Markov models.

2.1 Learning Environment for Computational Music Remixing

This study was conducted in the EarSketch learning environment, an online interface for developing computational music (Fig. 1). In prior studies, students that used EarSketch had significant positive results related to content knowledge and attitudes towards computing, especially in currently underrepresented groups in computing [13]. The EarSketch interface includes a code editor for Python or JavaScript and a digital audio workstation that allows users to access the music they have written [7]. The interface also features a content manager with samples (sound clips) that can be used to create music, as well as a curriculum tab that provides helpful resources associated with the class. Both students had access to all of the tools allowing both to contribute to the code simultaneously. In this study, the interface included a chat box to communicate with their partner. We logged all students' textual dialogue, all changes made in the code editor, all items accessed in the curriculum tab, and the results of the students running their scripts (such as successes or errors).

2.2 Dialogue Tagging

In cleaning the dataset, we removed two sessions that contained exclusively off-task, joking, offensive, or gibberish content. The remaining textual dialogue corpus includes 68 sessions (136 students) and 3305 utterances, with a mean of 48 utterances per session ($SD = 35$, $Min = 4$, and $Max = 214$). We developed and applied a dialogue act taxonomy that included 16 labels, which three independent annotators applied with a kappa of 0.76, *substantial*, agreement [12]. Among the 16 original labels, 10 occurred with greater than 5% probability in the hidden states within the HMM reported here, and one more label appeared in an example excerpt in this paper's discussion section. These 11 relevant dialogue act labels are shown in Table 1.

2.3 Analyses

After compiling the lists of sequential observation symbols that represent the collaborative interactions, we implemented an HMM to analyze the learners' interactions and model the co-creative sequences [17]. We chose this method

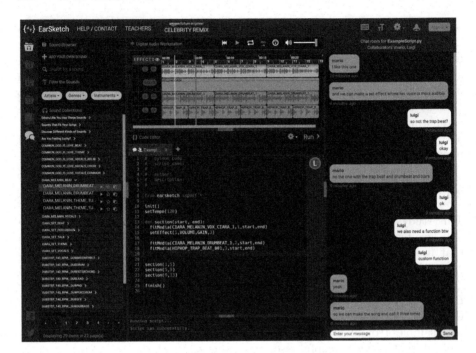

Fig. 1. The modified EarSketch environment with chat window used during the study.

because we were interested in the hidden discourse states. In an HMM, observable events such as textual messages and coding actions are represented by sequences of *observation symbols*. Influences upon those observation sequences are referred to as hidden states, and in an HMM each hidden state is characterized by its *emission distribution*, a probability distribution over observation symbols. Once the model is learned, every observation is modeled as having been "generated" by a hidden state, and each hidden state has a set of transition probabilities that indicates how likely the model is to either continue in that state or transition to another state.

The observation symbols are the labeled dialogue and task actions in this model. There are 23 distinct possible observation symbols—19 dialogue act tags, of which 16 are represented in Table 1, and the following actions:

- **curriculum** - The student accessed the curriculum or moved between lessons.
- **edit** - Any consecutive insertion or removal of characters in the code editor.
- **success** - Each time the script was run successfully.
- **error** - Each time the script was run and any type of error was received.

We represented each of the 68 collaborative dialogues as a sequence of these observation symbols and trained an HMM on these sequences. We did not model time between actions, nor did we model which of the two students performed each action.

Table 1. Taxonomy of co-creative dialogue act labels. Tags that occurred with less than 5% probably in all hidden states and that do not appear in the examples presented in this paper are not included in this table.

Dialogue act label	Relative frequency in Corpus	Description	Examples
Statement (**Stmnt**)	17.14%	Utterance of info or explanation, or something that exists in the coding workspace	*well we also have to make a loop*
Social (**Soc**)	14.11%	A general salutation, off-task comment, or display of remorse. Plays some social function not captured in the other tags	*how are you?*
Proposal (**P**)	12.32%	An assertion of creativity, related to code or music, for the partner to consider.	*we should do some beats in the background*
Directive (**Dir**)	11.55%	An utterance used to set task responsibilities for each or a single partner	*We should focus on the custom function first*
Confusion (**Con**)	10.41%	Seeking help, expressing confusion, lack of knowledge, or uncertainty	*What are those variables for?*
Acknowledgement (**Ack**)	6.35%	Accepting the content of the previous utterance or series of utterances	*yeah*
Passing Responsibility (**PR**)	6.17%	Passing creative or technical choice to partner	*Do you know what sounds you would like to use?*
Proposal Acceptance (**ProposalAccept**)	5.67%	Accepting a partner's addition or assertion to the co-creative mental model shared by both partners	*yeah jazzand dubstep sounds fine*
Positive Feedback (**PosFdbk**)	5.29%	Positive response relating to something the partner accomplished within the scope of the task	*I liked the piano thing you did*
Directive Acceptance (**DirAccept**)	3.97%	Response to a partner accepting the dictation of flow or direction of project	*ok i will figure out a makebeat*
Non-positive Feedback (**NPosFdbk**)	2.29%	Non-positive response relating to something incorrectly done by the partner within the scope of the task	*it doesnt sound as good as i thought it would*

3 Results

To select the best number of hidden states, we used leave-one-out cross validation and compared the average Akaike information criterion (AIC) score for each number of hidden states [1]. We compared models using 4–9 states, finding that the best AIC scores were consistently found for six and seven states. We then trained ten models for both six and seven states and compared the best models using log likelihood. The best models from each were nearly identical. One of the dialogue states for the six-state model split to become two dialogue states in the seven-state model, with the rest of the states remaining the same. We opted to move forward with the 7-state HMM.

The HMM analysis revealed that collaborative sessions contained the following seven hidden states (see Fig. 2) which we interpreted as follows:

- **Social Dialogue:** In the this state, observation symbols are heavily (79%) *social* dialogue acts. Around 90% of sessions begin in this state.
- **Aesthetic Dialogue:** In the *Aesthetic Dialogue* state, *proposal* and *proposal acceptance* dialogue acts, which involve assertions and acceptances of creativity, constitute (51%) of observation symbols. The dialogue that belongs to this state usually involves discussing some aspect of the music.
- **Curriculum:** The observation symbols from this state were almost exclusively (91%) from students accessing the curriculum.
- **Code Editing:** The observation symbols from this state are almost entirely (99%) code editing.
- **Technical Dialogue:** The dialogue acts that characterized this state involved *statement, directive, confusion, acknowledgement,* and *directive acceptance.* The dialogue that belongs to this state usually involves discussion of code features or task requirements.
- **Code Runs Successfully:** Mostly characterized by students running the code successfully, this state involves some *positive feedback* (6%) and *statement* (5%) dialogue acts.
- **Runs Code with Error:** Mostly characterized by students receiving an error when running the code, this state involves some *confusion* (8%), *statement*(5%), and *directive*(5%) dialogue acts.

This model revealed three distinct states of conversation that occur in these co-creative interactions: *Social Dialogue, Aesthetic Dialogue,* and *Technical Dialogue.* The *Social Dialogue* state usually occurs at the beginning of the interaction, but can occur throughout and usually includes some rapport building and off-task discussions. Utterances in the *Aesthetic Dialogue* state usually involved discussing different aspects of the music such as instruments, tempo, genre, and even what artist to emulate. Utterances in the *Technical Dialogue* state were typically about task requirements and code. This model also revealed four hidden states focused on coding: *Curriculum, Code Editing, Code Runs Successfully,* and *Runs Code with Error.* The sessions never begin in the *Curriculum* state, and no other states consistently lead to it. Every state, excluding the *Social Dialogue* state, has a significant chance to lead to the *Code Editing* state, and 21.3%

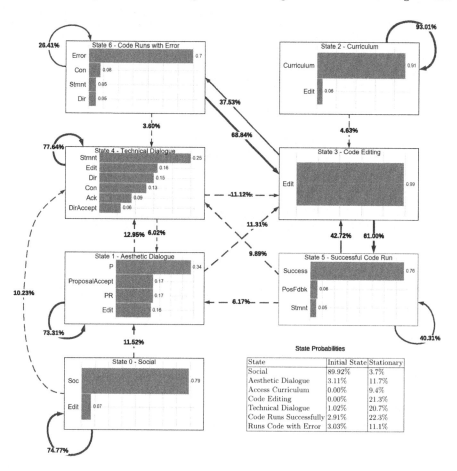

Fig. 2. The co-creative dialogue states' emission and transition probabilities.

of the actions occur in this state. This percent does not represent how much elapsed time learners spent editing the code, because we combined sequences of consecutive edits into a single *edit* observation symbol. *Code Editing* transitions to a *Success* or an *Error* state 98.53% of the time. The states the *Successful Code Run* state is likely to transition to are *Code Editing* (42.72%), *Technical Dialogue* (9.89%), and *Aesthetic Dialogue* (6.17%). The other state *Code Runs with Error* is most likely to transition to is *Code Editing* (68.84%), and the only other state is *Technical Dialogue* (3.60%).

4   Discussion

4.1   Dialogue States

These results revealed ways in which co-creative dyads moved among collaborative dialogue states characterized by conversation and task actions. Of the

Table 2. Excerpt 1: Learner conversation transitioning from Aesthetic (State 1) to Technical (State 4) Dialogue State. Each dialogue state was determined automatically using the HMM presented in this work.

State	Action	User	Text
1	PR	**Student 1**	what you want to do
1	P	**Student 2**	lets do dubstep cause its fire
1	PA	**Student 1**	i feel you
4	C	**Student 1**	what did she say how many variables
4	STMNT	**Student 2**	3
4	D	**Student 1**	ok lets do this
4	C	**Student 2**	ngl im kinda lost already so im sorry
4	C	**Student 1**	i dont know what to do
4	C	**Student 2**	me either ima ask for help

seven hidden states identified by the HMM, three were composed primarily of dialogue acts. *Social Dialogue* was the most likely state for students to start in, primarily composed of greetings and off-task dialogue. This is a typical feature of collaborative dialogue, prefacing discussion with periods of rapport building in which the partners become more familiar with each other [15]. After leaving this initial *Social Dialogue* state, we found that the conversation was nearly twice as likely to move directly to the *Aesthetic Dialogue* state (60%) as to the *Technical Dialogue* state (31%). In the *Aesthetic Dialogue* state, students brainstorm and exchange dialogue related to the musical piece they are constructing. The *Technical Dialogue* is where students begin planning how to accomplish their creative goals. In the excerpt in Table 2, the students set their goal of creating a dubstep song and then debate how they would accomplish that in their code. While the transitions can move from either the *Technical Dialogue* state to the *Aesthetic Dialogue* state or vice versa, the transitions from *Aesthetic Dialogue* to *Technical Dialogue* were much more likely, 12.95% versus 6.02%, than the reverse. This observation suggests most pairs tend to decide on what they want to make before they move on to making it.

4.2   The Debugging Process and the Conversation It Inspires

The remaining four states are mostly focused on actions in the interface: reading the curriculum and tutorials on code constructs (state 2), editing the code (state 3), encountering coding errors (state 6), and successfully compiling code (state 5). The transitions between states 3, 5, and 6 demonstrate the movement between collaborative states that occur during debugging, and they offer insights about how co-creative conversations unfold. The editing state (state 3) primarily transitioned to the compile states (Error or Success), with no transitions to any of the dialogue states. After entering the success state, students were most likely to go back to the editing state, but they also sometimes transitioned back

Table 3. Excerpt 2: Learners' successful code compilation (state 5) leading to Technical (state 4) and Aesthetic Dialogue (state 1). Each dialogue state was determined automatically using the HMM presented in this work

State	Action	User	Text
5	success	**Student 1**	
4	ACK	**Student 2**	oh
4	STMNT	**Student 1**	ohh its because they are 2 second each
4	STMNT	**Student 2**	each measure isnt exactly 2 s
4	STMNT	**Student 2**	its a little longer i think
4	STMNT	**Student 1**	but when another is added to the 30 it becomes exactly 2 s longer
4	STMNT	**Student 2**	measure 15 is at 28.5 s
4	success	**Student 2**	
1	P	**Student 1**	we can use a combination of sounds
1	P	**Student 2**	we should just leave it at 31
1	P	**Student 2**	i think that will be fine
1	PA	**Student 1**	yeah
	...	...	...
5	success	**Student 2**	
1	edit	**Student 1**	\n
1	P	**Student 2**	we should put like a synth or something to that effect
1	P	**Student 2**	add some like futuristic noises or airhorns or something

into the *Technical Dialogue* or *Aesthetic Dialogue* states. Table 3 illustrates this transition.

The *Success* state seems to be an inflection point in the co-creative process, in which the group may start to renegotiate some of the creative aspects of their code. In contrast, the *Error* state only transitions to *Editing* or *Technical Dialogue* suggesting partners who encounter errors focus on resolving their problems rather than discussing new ideas (*Aesthetic Dialogue*).

4.3   Implications for Co-creative Agents in Education

The findings of this research provide insights for modeling co-creative discourse, which can inform the design of AI to support learning based on human co-creative interactions. For example, after the initial rapport-building phase, human pairs in our study usually moved on to establish aesthetic details, such as what kind of artifact they wanted to create or what elements to use, before they transitioned to discussing the technical implementation of how to create the artifact, as seen in the excerpt in Table 2. Additionally, certain milestones, such as completing a subtask or running the code successfully if it is a coding artifact, can be an opportunity to renegotiate or confirm aesthetic or technical decisions, as shown in the excerpt in Table 3. In contrast, when students encountered an issue, they usually continued with task-based actions, and any dialogue that occurred after was usually technical in nature and directly addressed the problem, as shown in the excerpt in Table 4. This finding suggests that a co-creative AI or collaboration support system should address the need for immediate focus on debugging before attempting to resume any aesthetic conversation. On the

Table 4. Excerpt 3: Learners having a compilation error (state 6) and transitioning to *Technical Dialogue* (state 4). Each dialogue state was determined automatically using the HMM presented in this work

State	Action	User	Text
6	error	**Student 1**	Unknown Identifier
3	edit	**Student 1**	;
6	error	**Student 1**	Unknown Identifier
4	NPosFdbk	**Student 1**	bruh
4	C	**Student 1**	whats the error
4	error	**Student 2**	Unknown Identifier
4	STMNT	**Student 2**	vairable or function not defined makes sense
4	STMNT	**Student 2**	variable*
3	edit	**Student 2**	\n
6	D	**Student 1**	try fixing it idk what to do
6	error	**Student 1**	Unknown Identifier
6	DA	**Student 2**	okay

other hand, because dialogue can be such a powerful mechanism for identifying and resolving errors, an intelligent collaboration support system could foster productive dialogue in these instances where our data suggest learners may not engage in dialogue without scaffolding. This work could improve the design of AIED systems by identifying distinct phases of co-creative collaboration and identifying productive and unproductive patterns co-creative dialogues. These findings may inform co-creative agents inspired by human co-creativity that can support the different phases of collaboration.

5   Conclusion and Future Work

Co-creativity is important for many collaborative learning contexts, and understanding dialogue around these processes is important for supporting collaborative learning. In a study with 136 high school learners in 68 pairs co-creating music through programming, we analyzed learners' dialogue moves and contextual actions with a hidden Markov model. We uncovered three distinct dialogue states that included social, aesthetic, and technical dialogue. When the students successfully ran their script, they transitioned into either aesthetic or technical dialogue, suggesting a renegotiation or planning phase. When the students encountered a coding error, they almost always returned to the code editing state and rarely transitioned to a conversational state. When they did transition to a conversational state, they only transitioned to *Technical Dialogue*. These findings revealed insights into co-creativity during learning and provide initial direction for developing co-creative agents for education.

The results point to several important directions for future work. For example, it is important not only to investigate what humans do during co-creativity, but how those actions are associated with outcomes. Such a research direction will identify not only what strategies are natural, but which strategies are most effective. Another direction for continuing this research is to examine the hidden states from the perspective of each student. Understanding these states from the perspective of each partner can inform the creation of agents as partners. Moving forward, we need to add co-creative AI to the ranks of pedagogical agents and other adaptive supports that are supporting learners in increasingly complex domains. These technologies have the potential to support engagement and learning for diverse students learning challenging material.

Acknowledgements. This work is supported by the National Science Foundation through the grants DRL-1814083 and DRL-1813740. Any opinions, findings, and conclusions or recommendations expressed in this material are those of the author(s) and do not necessarily reflect the views of the National Science Foundation.

References

1. Akaike, H.: A new look at the statistical model identification. IEEE Trans. Autom. Control **19**(6), 716–723 (1974)
2. Arroyo, I., Wixon, N., Allessio, D., Woolf, B., Muldner, K., Burleson, W.: Collaboration improves student interest in online tutoring. In: André, E., Baker, R., Hu, X., Rodrigo, M.M.T., du Boulay, B. (eds.) AIED 2017. LNCS (LNAI), vol. 10331, pp. 28–39. Springer, Cham (2017). https://doi.org/10.1007/978-3-319-61425-0_3
3. Carpenter, D., et al.: Detecting off-task behavior from student dialogue in game-based collaborative learning. In: Bittencourt, I.I., Cukurova, M., Muldner, K., Luckin, R., Millán, E. (eds.) AIED 2020. LNCS (LNAI), vol. 12163, pp. 55–66. Springer, Cham (2020). https://doi.org/10.1007/978-3-030-52237-7_5
4. Chng, E., Seyam, M.R., Yao, W., Schneider, B.: Using motion sensors to understand collaborative interactions in digital fabrication labs. In: Bittencourt, I.I., Cukurova, M., Muldner, K., Luckin, R., Millán, E. (eds.) AIED 2020. LNCS (LNAI), vol. 12163, pp. 118–128. Springer, Cham (2020). https://doi.org/10.1007/978-3-030-52237-7_10
5. Dich, Y., Reilly, J., Schneider, B.: Using physiological synchrony as an indicator of collaboration quality, task performance and learning. In: Penstein Rosé, C., et al. (eds.) AIED 2018. LNCS (LNAI), vol. 10947, pp. 98–110. Springer, Cham (2018). https://doi.org/10.1007/978-3-319-93843-1_8
6. Dyke, G., Adamson, D., Howley, I., Rose, C.P.: Enhancing scientific reasoning and discussion with conversational agents. IEEE Trans. Learn. Technol. **6**(3), 240–247 (2013)
7. Freeman, J., Magerko, B., Verdin, R.: EarSketch: a web-based environment for teaching introductory computer science through music remixing. In: The 46th ACM Technical Symposium on Computer Science Education, SIGCSE 2015, p. 5. Association for Computing Machinery, New York (2015)
8. Gokhale, A.A.: Collaborative learning enhances critical thinking **7**(1), 22–30 (1995)

9. Goodman, B.A., Linton, F.N., Gaimari, R.D., Hitzeman, J.M., Ross, H.J., Zarrella, G.: Using dialogue features to predict trouble during collaborative learning. User Model. User-Adapt. Interact. **15**(1), 85–134 (2005). https://doi.org/10.1007/s11257-004-5269-x

10. Howard, C., Jordan, P., Di Eugenio, B., Katz, S.: Shifting the load: a peer dialogue agent that encourages its human collaborator to contribute more to problem solving. Int. J. Artif. Intell. Educ. **27**(1), 101–129 (2017). https://doi.org/10.1007/s40593-015-0071-y

11. Kantosalo, A., Toivanen, J., Xiao, P., Toivonen, H.: From isolation to involvement: adapting machine creativity software to support human-computer co-creation. In: The Fifth International Conference on Computational Creativity, vol. 2014, pp. 1–7 (2014)

12. Landis, J.R., Koch, G.G.: The measurement of observer agreement for categorical data. Biometrics **33**(1), 159–174 (1977)

13. Magerko, B., et al.: EarSketch: a steam-based approach for underrepresented populations in high school computer science education. ACM Trans. Comput. Educ. (TOCE) **16**(4), 1–25 (2016)

14. Morales-Urrutia, E.K., Ocaña Ch., J.M., Pérez-Marín, D., Pizarro-Romero, C.: Promoting learning and satisfaction of children when interacting with an emotional companion to program. In: Bittencourt, I.I., Cukurova, M., Muldner, K., Luckin, R., Millán, E. (eds.) AIED 2020. LNCS (LNAI), vol. 12164, pp. 220–223. Springer, Cham (2020). https://doi.org/10.1007/978-3-030-52240-7_40

15. Ogan, A., Finkelstein, S., Walker, E., Carlson, R., Cassell, J.: Rudeness and rapport: insults and learning gains in peer tutoring. In: Cerri, S.A., Clancey, W.J., Papadourakis, G., Panourgia, K. (eds.) ITS 2012. LNCS, vol. 7315, pp. 11–21. Springer, Heidelberg (2012). https://doi.org/10.1007/978-3-642-30950-2_2

16. Parde, N., Nielsen, R.D.: AI meets Austen: towards human-robot discussions of literary metaphor. In: Isotani, S., Millán, E., Ogan, A., Hastings, P., McLaren, B., Luckin, R. (eds.) AIED 2019. LNCS (LNAI), vol. 11626, pp. 213–219. Springer, Cham (2019). https://doi.org/10.1007/978-3-030-23207-8_40

17. Rabiner, L., Juang, B.: An introduction to hidden Markov models. IEEE ASSP Mag. **3**(1), 4–16 (1986)

18. Radu, I., Tu, E., Schneider, B.: Relationships between body postures and collaborative learning states in an augmented reality study. In: Bittencourt, I.I., Cukurova, M., Muldner, K., Luckin, R., Millán, E. (eds.) AIED 2020. LNCS (LNAI), vol. 12164, pp. 257–262. Springer, Cham (2020). https://doi.org/10.1007/978-3-030-52240-7_47

19. Rodríguez, F.J., Boyer, K.E.: Discovering individual and collaborative problem-solving modes with hidden Markov models. In: Conati, C., Heffernan, N., Mitrovic, A., Verdejo, M.F. (eds.) AIED 2015. LNCS (LNAI), vol. 9112, pp. 408–418. Springer, Cham (2015). https://doi.org/10.1007/978-3-319-19773-9_41

20. Rosen, Y.: Computer-based assessment of collaborative problem solving: exploring the feasibility of human-to-agent approach. Int. J. Artif. Intell. Educ. **25**(3), 380–406 (2015). https://doi.org/10.1007/s40593-015-0042-3

21. Samoilescu, R.-F., Dascalu, M., Sirbu, M.-D., Trausan-Matu, S., Crossley, S.A.: Modeling collaboration in online conversations using time series analysis and dialogism. In: Isotani, S., Millán, E., Ogan, A., Hastings, P., McLaren, B., Luckin, R. (eds.) AIED 2019. LNCS (LNAI), vol. 11625, pp. 458–468. Springer, Cham (2019). https://doi.org/10.1007/978-3-030-23204-7_38

22. Schneider, B., Pea, R.: Toward collaboration sensing. Int. J. Comput.-Supp. Collab. Learn. **9**(4), 371–395 (2014). https://doi.org/10.1007/s11412-014-9202-y

23. Snyder, C., Hutchins, N.M., Biswas, G., Emara, M., Yett, B., Mishra, S.: Understanding collaborative question posing during computational modeling in science. In: Bittencourt, I.I., Cukurova, M., Muldner, K., Luckin, R., Millán, E. (eds.) AIED 2020. LNCS (LNAI), vol. 12164, pp. 296–300. Springer, Cham (2020). https://doi.org/10.1007/978-3-030-52240-7_54

24. Viswanathan, S.A., VanLehn, K.: Using the tablet gestures and speech of pairs of students to classify their collaboration. IEEE Trans. Learn. Technol. **11**(2), 230–242 (2018)

Affective Teacher Tools: Affective Class Report Card and Dashboard

Ankit Gupta[2], Neeraj Menon[2], William Lee[1], William Rebelsky[1],
Danielle Allesio[1], Tom Murray[1], Beverly Woolf[1], Jacob Whitehill[2],
and Ivon Arroyo[1,2(✉)]

[1] University of Massachusetts Amherst, Amherst, USA
{williamlee,wrebelsky,allessio,tmurray,bev,ivon}@cs.umass.edu
[2] Worcester Polytechnic Institute, Worcester, USA
{agupta6,nsmenon,jrwhitehill,iarroyo}@wpi.edu

Abstract. While using online learning software, students demonstrate many reactions, various levels of engagement, and emotions (e.g. confusion, excitement, frustration). Having such information automatically accessible to teachers (or digital tutors) can aid in understanding how students progress and suggest when and who needs further assistance. We developed the Affective Teacher Tools, a report card and dashboard that present teachers measures of students' engagement and affective states as they use an online tutoring system, MathSpring.org, which supports students as they practice mathematics problem-solving at the middle school level. We conducted two development and research studies – one that assesses teachers perception of the affective report card and a second study that assesses a live affective dashboard, which senses students' affect and performance in a live class that is using MathSpring. We use computer vision techniques to measure students' engagement and affective states from their facial expressions while they use the tutoring system. In this paper, we summarize both the report card and affective dashboard, the research studies and results, and we also discuss implications, and future planned experiments for the next phase of this research.

Keywords: Teaching · Affect · Engagement · Design · Intelligent tutoring systems

1 Introduction

As students engage with online learning technologies, they often demonstrate a wide variety of reactions, dependent on a combination of their motivation, mood, and background knowledge. Students experience various levels of engagement and might express emotions such as confusion, excitement, frustration, anxiety, and many more. Engagement and different affective states of students can be tightly correlated with their learning gains on many learning tasks, such as math problem solving and concept understanding [2,7]. Having such engagement and affective information accessible to teachers (or digital tutors) can aid

© Springer Nature Switzerland AG 2021
I. Roll et al. (Eds.): AIED 2021, LNAI 12748, pp. 178–189, 2021.
https://doi.org/10.1007/978-3-030-78292-4_15

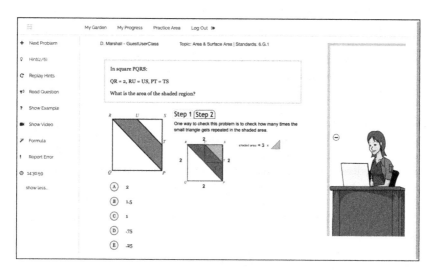

Fig. 1. The MathSpring tutoring system. Multimedia hints are available from the "Hints" button on the left, as well as Worked-out examples and Tutorials. Jane (right) is an affective agent who emphasizes the importance of putting in effort.

in understanding students' progress, and suggest when and who needs further assistance, which eventually improves students' learning outcomes.

MathSpring.org (Fig. 1) is a web-based online tutoring system designed to aid students' learning of mathematical problem-solving strategies [1], aligned to the Common Core Standards, the national mathematics curricula in the USA. However, just like with many other teaching tools, students' success and advancement also depends on teachers' effective lesson plans, and teacher's ability to support students during and after they use MathSpring. This is the main reason why we created MathSpring's Teacher Tools, a portal where students can log in to configure the material that students will receive the next time they log in, and inspect students' performance on math Problems and curricular areas. Teachers need to understand and gain insights of their students' progress, in order to obtain valuable information that they could feed back to their teaching strategies. One challenge is that today's curriculum of test scores and assignments do not generally translate to real-time understanding of students' progress. Even further, it hypothesized it would be ideal if teachers could have a snapshot of students affective profiles. We consequently developed the Affective Teacher Tools to support teachers with two main goals: a) to collect students' "just-in-time" affective and engagement states as they solve mathematical problems in MathSpring and b) to provide teachers with real-time information to understand the progress of their students over time. Ultimately, teachers would gain insights into their students' motivation, interests, attention and effort, *in addition* to their cognitive progress towards mastering mathematics concepts. By monitoring and capturing students' affective and engagement states, these constructs could help teachers realize whether their lesson plans are helping the students grow and strengthen their engagement, whether they need to re-teach or reinforce certain concepts.

Using an iterative design approach, we conducted two studies to understand how to design and implement Affective Teacher Tools that would benefit teachers and in turn students of MathSpring. First, we present the Affective Report Card of the Teacher tools, a series of asynchronous reports that summarize each students' effort and emotions reported and expressed within MathSpring, as a complement to their performance in mathematical problem solving. We present a final analysis of ten (10) teachers' perceptions of these tools after three rounds of iterative feedback from senior mathematics teachers and an interface designer, which led to a final improved design. Second, we present a Facial Expression-Augmented Teacher Dashboard, an addition to MathSpring's Teacher Tools to identify students' affective states and provide nuanced information to teachers, in real-time, as students are using MathSpring. We present results from a usability study with four (4) math teachers, which revealed promising results about its usefulness. Finally, we discuss our planned experiments for the next phase of this research.

2   Related Work

2.1   Affect-Aware Intelligent Tutoring System

A growing body of literature has analyzed user affect and expressions while interacting with online learning systems [2, 4, 5, 8, 14–17]. Student affect is measured and modeled using techniques such as self-reports of how they are feeling [15], human ratings [2], log data [5], facial expression recognition [17], and a combination of them [8]. As facial expression recognition advances as part of computer vision and machine learning research efforts, a subset of literature has analyzed student affect within learning environments, using various facial expression analysis techniques [4, 6, 8, 14]. For example, Bosch et al. [4] analyzed videos of students interacting with an educational physics game and used computer vision techniques to detect students' affect from facial expressions and body movements. Whitehill et al. [14] developed machine-learning based detectors of engagement from students' facial expressions. While various studies have been conducted on estimating students' knowledge and affect, not enough research has been done to transform this collected (raw) data into meaningful information that is more relatable to teachers, parents and other stakeholders. We conducted research that captures student performance and detects students' facial expressions to generate a live dashboard for teachers to use in the classroom while their students are using the MathSpring.org tutoring system.

2.2   Affective Learning Analytics

A variety of research has analyzed how dashboards and digital gradebooks can support teachers. Bienkowski, Feng and Means [3] discussed how student data are important for educators to plan and apply actionable teaching strategies. Understanding this data and relationships within the data would help educators to make faster decisions to support their students, and serve as a form of feedback to inform teachers how effective their lesson plans have been. However, teachers are often overwhelmed and do not have the time to analyze any collected student data. Hence, teachers need ease of understanding of complex relationships within the data without the need of performing any data analysis, for instance at the item level, such as Heffernan et al. [10], who created a dashboard for teachers to receive feedback about their students' performance in math problems, so that teachers can identify students who need additional help, or material that needs to be re-taught. Innovative efforts by Holstein and colleagues [11] consisted of wearable glasses that provide teachers with live information about how their students are behaving and performing during class time. Other dashboards have provided teachers with information about collaborating students interacting via chat or alike, as they use learning technologies [13]. All of these efforts have proved to be effective at providing teachers information about their students. Our main research question though regarded understanding both the feasibility and interest of teachers in obtaining affective information about their students both in an asynchronous way (report card) and in a synchronous way (live dashboard), supporting teachers in their ability to understand students' affective states.

3   Affective Report Card

Menon [12] designed an initial prototype of a Cognitive and Affective Report Card in MathSpring. The prototype consists of multiple functions and capabilities to allow teachers to: 1) visualize individual students' performance and affect and 2) analyze group performance to spot strengths and weaknesses at the class level, 3) to spot engagement styles and profiles of their students that go beyond the mere correctness of answers. Using an iterative design approach, Menon went through three phases of development.

3.1   Method to Develop the Affective Report Card

An initial prototype was designed using best practices and researcher's expertise, providing information about problem solving and estimations of student ability in Common Core Math Skill areas. The MathSpring team learned a few lessons after an informal evaluation with mathematics teachers (N = 4). One of the key lessons learned was that teachers wanted to see how their students had been doing over time so that they could track their evolving knowledge (mastery), so that teachers may realize how well their lesson plans are working.

The team further took the lessons learned from those teachers and applied them to improve the user interface and visualization of the Affective Report Card. A new set of teachers (N = 10) participated in a 3-day MathSpring Professional Development workshop during the summer of 2018 to evaluate the improvement, which allowed teachers to learn which students might be falling

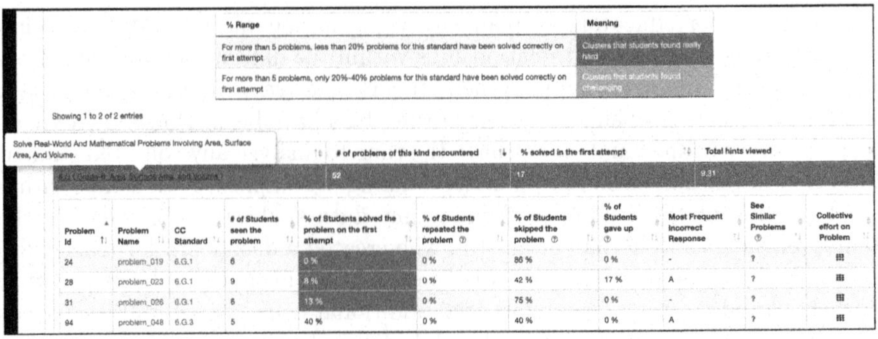

Fig. 2. Students performance in math problems, aggregated across all students in the class. Highlighted lines show Common Core Areas that are troublesome for students in the class. Opening the accordion reveals all problems seen by students for the Common Core Cluster, the percent correct responses, and much more. Clicking on the last column gives an effort chart (GIVEUP, SOF, etc.) for all students in the class who have encountered that math problem. Hovering over items reveals more information, e.g. an image of the problem.

behind and how students might be progressing over time. Teachers were able to see where and how their students might have fallen short as a class, both at the class level and broken down by Math Common Core Areas (e.g., most frequently incorrect answer of specific mathematical questions) Fig. 2, and also at the traditional per problem, per student level. The importance of realizing these details was to enable teachers to pinpoint which students needed additional remediation or identify which lesson plans needed improvement.

With the help of a HCI designer and a senior math teacher, the MathSpring team implemented a final design. An important attribute debuted was the "Emotion Chart." This chart is a visualization of students' subjective self-reports of their frustration, excitement, interest, and confidence while they were solving mathematical problems in MathSpring. Students are asked to report this information every 5 problems or 8 min, whichever comes first, as they are working in MathSpring, in between math problems (their work is not interrupted for this). Students are also invited to report for their reasons why they feel a certain way. Importantly, students can dismiss the emotion report window if they are not willing to report how they are feeling. From the Teacher Tools perspective, an "Emotion Chart" design makes this information available to teachers, as it arrives into the MathSpring servers. When chosen by the teacher, the asynchronous "Per Student" report shows the four different emotions in four separate bar graphs (see two emotions reported in Fig. 3), in addition to math performance information and engagement "effort" information. The result of a survey to teachers was that 91% of the N=10 interviewed teacher participants found the affective information in the bar graphs as somewhat or very useful. One of the participating teachers commented that the emotional aspects of the students are essential

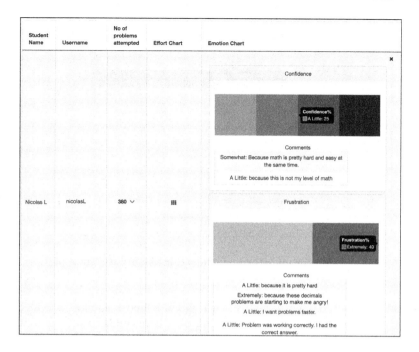

Fig. 3. Reported emotions for an individual student, in the per student report.

because seeing merely the accuracy of their answers "... doesn't always give us a good picture of a student's understanding."

Another feature was considered as useful, was the so-called "effort chart" visualization. Represented as stacked bar visualization, it was used to depict the effort excerpted by students on math problems, and their associated emotional states (Fig. 4). This effort stacked bar allows the teacher to see important details about how individual students are engaging with the material, including: 1) the percentage of problems answered correctly the first attempt (SOF), 2) percentage of problems that were skipped (SKIP), 3) the percentage of problems where the student gave up (GIVEUP), and 4) the percentage of problems where the student quick-guessed the answer of the problem (GUESS), among others. One teacher commented that the usefulness of the effort stacked bar is not just insight, but that teachers "... could use this information for conferencing with students." That specific teacher went ahead to run a small research project with his class about the benefit of conferencing with students about their behavior in MathSpring, using these visualizations (unpublished).

This same chart is presented at the class level, see the last "Collective Effort Per Problem" column of Fig. 2. All 10 teachers in the study considered this specific feature to be somewhat or very useful also, as it allows to understand how all students in the class have engaged with a specific math problem. All teachers perceived one feature called "Similar Problems" as very useful, which would allow them to find math problems that were "similar" to the current question that

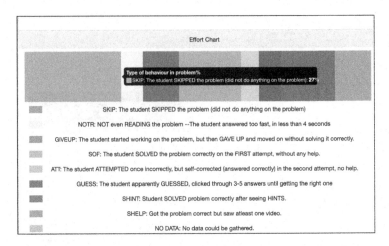

Fig. 4. Effort for an individual student, in the per student report.

students might be having difficulty with. Open ended responses revealed that the "Similar Problems" button, consisting of a hyper-link to problems related to the same standard in the Massachusetts Comprehensive Assessment System Web Portal (MCAS), was very useful to them, because it provides teachers with other math problems they could provide their students, after identifying that they were weak in a specific area. This would provide additional opportunities to practice and boost their confidence in that CC standard area.

4   Teacher Dashboard to Inform Teachers

The second effort is a Facial Expression-Augmented Teacher Dashboard. It seeks to enhance information provided to the teachers through MathSpring's Teacher Tools while students are using MathSpring. The dashboard captures student performance and detects students' facial expressions (smiles, nose wrinkles and frowns), which highlight students' emotion and engagement, using a deep learning model for facial expression detection. Instead of the intelligent tutor performing an intervention (e.g., have the character talk to the student) this information is shown to teachers in order to support them to understand what is going on, juxtaposing the state of knowledge and corresponding affect of students. This helps teachers understand students' states of mind, as they are using Math-Spring. This information is presented back to the teachers so they might act, altering their instruction or interaction with each student in a personalized way. Figure 6 shows the Teacher Dashboard highlighting students' facial action units gestures (AU4, AU9, and AU12 or facial expression, Frown, Nose wrinkle, and Smile) during the student's live session. When clicking on a student tile in Fig. 6, further detail on the student is presented, as shown in Fig. 7.

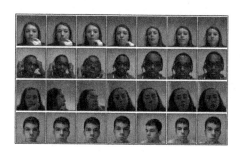
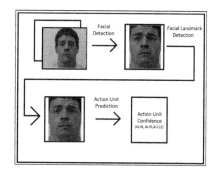

Fig. 5. Evolution of facial expressions of students using MathSpring (left). The facial expression detection pipeline (right)

4.1   Method to Develop the Teacher Dashboard

Gupta [9] developed a pipeline to build a model for recognizing facial expressions (Fig. 5). Specifically, multiple convolutional neural networks were trained to detect the presence and intensity of three action units for smile, nose wrinkle and frown (AU4, AU9, and AU12, respectively).

Face detection is first performed using a pre-trained Single Shot Multibox Detector (SSD) based on the MobileNetV1. Essentially, each image goes through the SSD in which a bounding box of a potential face is computed. Next, after a foreground face has been identified, features representing facial landmarks of eyebrows, eyes, nose, and mouth are extracted. Particularly, the face extraction model was trained using a dataset of 35K face images labeled with 68 face landmark points. The open-source libraries face-api.js and Tensorflow.js were used for the detection and extraction. In the facial expression prediction phase, a fully connected neural network was trained using the features identified from the extraction model. The input of the model is a $[24 \times 1]$ vector containing the attributes corresponding to the facial landmarks of eyebrows, eyes, nose, and mouth. The output contains a $[3 \times 1]$ vector containing the prediction of the confidence of the 3 facial action units.

The accuracy of the detector under cross-validation, testing over 20% of the data, was high (82%, 79% and 70% for smile, nose wrinkle and frown, respectively) with AUCs of 0.8, 0.76 and 0.69. The final AU detector was deployed in the front-end of MathSpring (Fig. 6). As teachers click on a student card, they can see further detail (Fig. 7). The student effort pie chart provides the concentration for the different efforts observed by the students on various mathematics problems. It provides an analysis of the students' performance during each session. Along with it, the student detail page also provides the last 5 mastery and efforts depicting the student's performance during the last 5 problems (Fig. 7). It also provides teachers with information about topics on which students have currently worked.

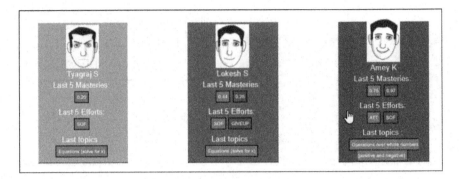

Fig. 6. The Teachers' Dashboard provides a snapshot of the class, with student expressions, recent topics visited, recent effort on problems (e.g. GIVEUP means a student has moved on without answering a problem, SOF means the student has correctly solved a question on the first attempt, and "mastery" is the probability that the student knows/masters the topic.

4.2 Usability Study for the Teacher Dashboard

A live video of the dashboard, as it was being used by MathSpring students as part of a class, was shown to four (N = 4) senior math teachers who are users of MathSpring, and had experience with its use in the classroom (without the Dashboard). They completed a qualitative/quantitative 11-question survey that captured teachers' critical views, suggestions regarding the new development, and perceptions of usefulness, after seeing a captured video of the Dashboard change and update, while a class of actual students was using MathSpring. The survey contains questions that capture teachers' view about various aspect of the dashboard, the facial gestures component in particular, and the impact of it in their understanding of students' current states while they solve problems on MathSpring platform. For instance, the two first questions were: "Do you think this dashboard could be useful for you as a teacher in the classroom, as students use MathSpring?" and "Does the facial expression in the dashboard seem to provide useful information or not? Please explain." The 11-questions asked for perceptions and feedback about every detail in the dashboard.

The usability study showed promising results from teachers, who rated the information as very useful in general, with a majority of positive answers for all questions. Most teachers found the detailed information on the students informative and meaningful. When asked about how valuable they thought it is on a scale of zero to five(zero being least valuable and 5 being most valuable), they responded with three and above(3+). One of the teachers mentioned that the live dashboard seems to be a "great way to monitor students when not having direct access to them" during distance learning. The tile representation of simplified faces of the live students together in one place was appreciated by all teachers (Fig. 6). Another teacher mentioned that the new facial expression depiction on the live dashboard was a "nice and quick" way of understanding the students'

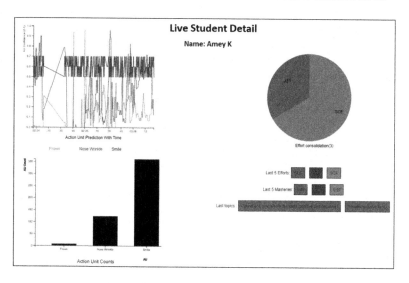

Fig. 7. When clicking on a student tile in Fig. 6, further detail on the student comes up. The left charts show that this student has smiled very frequently (appears relaxed). The charts to the right show student performance on math problems. The pie chart shows the frequency of recent behaviors on problems by students (this student recently solved 65% of problems correctly on first attempt (SOF), and solved incorrectly but self-corrected 35% of the time (ATT).

comfort level while they solved problems. Participant teachers also described it as a useful tool to detect students who "express a lack of confidence" so that they can focus on them further.

5   Summary and Future Work

In summary, we showed that teachers believe they would benefit from the Affective Report Card and Affective Dashboard. Teachers found the abilities to drill-down into the details of their students' recent progress and affective states as important in order to identify what leads to students' progress or hindrance. Such drill-down serves as a form of feedback to teacher's strategies, lesson plans, and which students to focus on further. In general, the feedback received from teachers was encouraging, as they perceived these Affective Teacher Tools, which supplement affective and cognitive data from students, could help them understand students further and personalize their response to students as well.

Using an iterative design approach, we built multiple improved prototypes that involved teachers feedback. Another round of improvements will be carried out, taking into account teachers' feedback, including an important suggestion from teachers to combine the information currently present in the Affective Report Card and show it in combination with the Dashboard. This would allow juxtaposing facial expressions with students recent reports of how they feel and why, which should provide very valuable information for teachers to assess the situation of each student. Another major component of the next phase of this research is a larger scale study with more teachers, using the Affective Teacher Tools, in full, with their own students.

References

1. Arroyo, I., Woolf, B.P., Burelson, W., Muldner, K., Rai, D., Tai, M.: A multimedia adaptive tutoring system for mathematics that addresses cognition, metacognition and affect. Int. J. Artif. Intell. Educ. **24**(4), 387–426 (2014). https://doi.org/10.1007/s40593-014-0023-y
2. Baker, R.S., D'Mello, S.K., Rodrigo, M.M.T., Graesser, A.C.: Better to be frustrated than bored: the incidence, persistence, and impact of learners' cognitive-affective states during interactions with three different computer-based learning environments. Int. J. Hum.-Comput. Stud. **68**(4), 223–241 (2010)
3. Bienkowski, M., Feng, M., Means, B.: Enhancing teaching and learning through educational data mining and learning analytics: an issue brief, October 2012. http://archvie2.cra.org/ccc/files/docs/learning-analytics-ed.pdf
4. Bosch, N., D'mello, S.K., Ocumpaugh, J., Baker, R.S., Shute, V.: Using video to automatically detect learner affect in computer-enabled classrooms. ACM Trans. Interact. Intell. Syst. (TiiS) **6**(2), 1–26 (2016)
5. Corrigan, S., Barkley, T., Pardos, Z.: Dynamic approaches to modeling student affect and its changing role in learning and performance. In: Ricci, F., Bontcheva, K., Conlan, O., Lawless, S. (eds.) UMAP 2015. LNCS, vol. 9146, pp. 92–103. Springer, Cham (2015). https://doi.org/10.1007/978-3-319-20267-9_8
6. D'Mello, S., Dieterle, E., Duckworth, A.: Advanced, analytic, automated (AAA) measurement of engagement during learning. Educ. Psychol. **52**(2), 104–123 (2017)
7. D'Mello, S., Lehman, B., Pekrun, R., Graesser, A.: Confusion can be beneficial for learning. Learn. Instr. **29**, 153–170 (2014)
8. Grafsgaard, J.F., Wiggins, J.B., Vail, A.K., Boyer, K.E., Wiebe, E.N., Lester, J.C.: The additive value of multimodal features for predicting engagement, frustration, and learning during tutoring. In: Proceedings of the 16th International Conference on Multimodal Interaction, pp. 42–49 (2014)
9. Gupta, A.: Live Performance and Emotional Analysis of MathSpring Intelligent Tutor System Students. Master's thesis, Worcester Polytechnic Institute (2020)
10. Heffernan, N., Heffernan, C.: The ASSISTments ecosystem: building a platform that brings scientists and teachers together for minimally invasive research on human learning and teaching. Int. J. Artif. Intell. Educ. **24**, 470–497 (2014). https://doi.org/10.1007/s40593-014-0024-x
11. Holstein, K., McLaren, B.M., Aleven, V.: Student learning benefits of a mixed-reality teacher awareness tool in AI-enhanced classrooms. In: Penstein Rosé, C., et al. (eds.) AIED 2018. LNCS (LNAI), vol. 10947, pp. 154–168. Springer, Cham (2018). https://doi.org/10.1007/978-3-319-93843-1_12
12. Menon, N.: Improving User Interface and User Experience of MathSpring Intelligent Tutoring System for Teachers. Master's thesis, Worcester Polytechnic Institute (2018)
13. Van Leeuwen, A., Rummel, N., Van Gog, T.: What information should CSCL teacher dashboards provide to help teachers interpret CSCL situations? Int. J. Comput.-Support. Collab. Learn **14**, 261–289 (2019). https://doi.org/10.1007/s11412-019-09299-x

14. Whitehill, J., Serpell, Z., Lin, Y.C., Foster, A., Movellan, J.R.: The faces of engagement: automatic recognition of student engagement from facial expressions. IEEE Trans. Affect. Comput. **5**(1), 86–98 (2014)

15. Wixon, M., Arroyo, I.: When the question is part of the answer: examining the impact of emotion self-reports on student emotion. In: Dimitrova, V., Kuflik, T., Chin, D., Ricci, F., Dolog, P., Houben, G.-J. (eds.) UMAP 2014. LNCS, vol. 8538, pp. 471–477. Springer, Cham (2014). https://doi.org/10.1007/978-3-319-08786-3_42

16. Woolf, B., Burleson, W., Arroyo, I., Dragon, T., Cooper, D., Picard, R.: Affect-aware tutors: recognising and responding to student affect. Int. J. Learn. Technol. **4**(3–4), 129–164 (2009)

17. Zatarain-Cabada, R., Barrón-Estrada, M.L., Camacho, J.L.O., Reyes-García, C.A.: Affective tutoring system for Android mobiles. In: Huang, D.-S., Jo, K.-H., Wang, L. (eds.) ICIC 2014. LNCS (LNAI), vol. 8589, pp. 1–10. Springer, Cham (2014). https://doi.org/10.1007/978-3-319-09339-0_1

Engendering Trust in Automated Feedback: A Two Step Comparison of Feedbacks in Gesture Based Learning

Sameena Hossain[✉], Azamat Kamzin[✉],
Venkata Naga Sai Apurupa Amperayani[✉], Prajwal Paudyal,
Ayan Banerjee[✉], and Sandeep K. S. Gupta[✉]

Arizona State University, Tempe, AZ 85281, USA
{shossai5,akamzin,vamepray,ppaudyal,abanerj3,Sandeep.Gupta}@asu.edu
http://www.impact.lab.asu.edu

Abstract. Advances in AI and Visual Recognition have paved the pathway for cutting edge research in Gesture Recognition. While automated feedback is able to open doors for newer opportunities in gesture based learning and practice, the effectiveness of these feedback as compared to manual feedback remains as a question in the minds of the users. For learners of American Sign Language (ASL), automated feedback generated by an application often causes a sense of apprehension because: a) learners are unaware of the automated feedback generation process, and b) learners fear that they can not trust the automated feedback as it may not be as good as the manual feedback. We use an ASL learning application that provides fine grained explainable feedback and follow a two step process to present a comparison between the automated feedback and the manual feedback provided by experts.

Keywords: Automated feedback · Gesture based learning · Inclusion

1 Introduction

Appropriate feedback is known to enhance learning outcomes and much research has been conducted in support of this theory. In recent years ample research has been done as well to support enhancement in computer aided learning with the help of automated feedback. In a pandemic situation like Covid-19, computer aided learning can become most beneficial. Automated feedback-based applications can also help in regular times as they take away the perils of scheduling conflicts and can provide users with self-paced learning opportunities at their convenience. However, for a less conventional learning modality, like gesture based learning, there is not enough research done to provide such help. Automated feedback in gesture based learning applications can enhance learning opportunities in the field of assistive technologies [1,22], combat training [13,24], medical surgery [14], performance coaching [21] or applications facilitating Deaf and Hard of Hearing (DHH) education [17,18].

© Springer Nature Switzerland AG 2021
I. Roll et al. (Eds.): AIED 2021, LNAI 12748, pp. 190–202, 2021.
https://doi.org/10.1007/978-3-030-78292-4_16

Real time immediate feedback is known to enhance learning by providing better engagement with learners, as is seen in a classroom environment with teachers. Applications with automated feedback, are essentially designed to mimic the prompt feedback provided by teachers in a classroom. Advances in AI [2,10] has enabled these feedbacks to be fine grained and detailed. However, there is a distrust and confusion, in the minds of the users [11], about the generation and effectiveness of these automated feedbacks [19]. Even with pre-set rubrics and lack of objectivity, manual feedback remains the gold standard in learning since we associate learning with classrooms and human teachers [4].

In this paper, we engender trust by employing a second level expert who evaluates the quality of the feedback unaware of whether the feedback was automated or manual. We present the second level expert with two feedback choices and record the percentage of manual vs automated feedback chosen by the expert.

1.1   Related Work and Motivation

A review of the related work has motivated us to undertake this comparison based research. We discuss them in the following sub-sections.

Evaluation of Automated Feedback of an ASL Learning Application.
Formative assessment has been a heavily researched area for a very long time. Formative assessment allows learners to know about their mistakes that can build towards their overall understanding of the topic. This manual fine grained feedback mechanism is what has built a long standing trust on the manual feedback by a teacher. Hence, in recent years, this learning theory has been implemented in automated feedback research [8,23,27]. Realtime formative automated feedback offers finer details about evaluation. Automated feedback should instruct learners as to how the application has arrived at the result of the evaluation [26]. Research has shown that the explainability of feedback increases their acceptability [17]. Much research has also been done on the learners' preferences between automated and manual feedback [12,19]. However, very few research work has attempted to evaluate the automated formative feedback on the basis of expert evaluation. To increase user trust in automated feedback, this experiment utilizes the concept level feedback generated by *ASLHelp* and compares it with the formative manual feedback, based on expert evaluation. Using *ASLHelp*, novice ASL learners can view ASL gestures executed by experts, learn and practice them. The application as a part of CSAVE framework [6], is deployed at the author's university and is being used by novice ASL learners.

Potential Extendibility of Automated Gesture Based Feedback.
Research on automated feedback in the field of gesture based applications is still in its infancy. Most research efforts that have been made, focus on the application of the methods of gesture recognition in different areas of learning and practice [3]. This underexplored field of research remains underserved by lesser participation from users like Deaf and Hard of Hearing (DHH) individuals, mostly due to lack of trust. Australian researchers have explored design space

for visual-spatial learning system with feedback, but they were for Auslan sign users and mainly focused on the feedback on location of the sign being executed [5] and only studied learners' preferences for the presentation of the automated feedback [20]. Some research in ASL has shown promise in the field by introducing lexical details [7] and explainability in feedback generation [17,18] to enhance learning and build trust. Unlike traditional learning applications, gesture based applications are multimodal. Hence, errors that are present in an execution need to be tied directly to the specific component involved in the execution. There were very few research attempts to compare automated feedback on gesture execution with manual feedback from experts. For ASL Learners research has shown that students prefer visual feedback on their gesture execution [7], but no such research attempts were made to compare feedbacks in the field of physiotherapy, combat training or dance performance. There were no research attempt to compare gesture based automated feedbacks with manual feedbacks on the basis of studied expert opinion. In this experiment, we use *ASLHelp*, that generates explainable automated feedback based on the correctness of the location, movement and handshape in an ASL gesture. We use the same components as rubric for manual expert feedback and present a comparison between the two feedbacks based on expert opinion. The feedback generation in *ASLHelp* is modeled based on the expert execution of the gestures. This experiment will allow for designing automated feedback comparable to manual feedback and extend its usage to other gesture based training, e.g. robot assisted military combat [13,24], rehabilitation therapy for diseases like Parkinson's or Alzheimer's [1,22], heavy equipment operators [9], or for applications in coaching in performance arts [21]. Comparable automated feedback can not only help learning while social distancing but will also help individuals who are affected by a long period of inactivity and isolation with the required training that they would need to get back to their field of work.

1.2   Challenges

Challenge 1: Subjectivity. For a fair comparison between manual and automated feedback, we need to ensure that manual feedback follow the same structure as the automated feedback. *Solution*: In order to reduce subjectivity, we express an ASL gesture as a grammar based combination of concepts. This allows the generation of concept level formative feedback for a erroneous gesture execution.

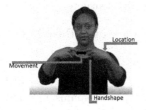

Fig. 1. Concepts in ASL

Fig. 2. Novice Learner Execution

Concept Level Formative Feedback: *ASLHelp* provides formative feedback for an "incorrect" response utilizing a context free grammar based representation of ASL gestures in terms of location, handshape and movement concepts as shown in Fig. 1. This allows learners to understand what they are evaluated on and attempts to build trust between the user and the machine [8,23,27]. For example, if the signer uses the correct handshapes for both hands and the location of the hands are also correct, but the movement of the right hand is incorrect, *ASLHelp* will generate a feedback like- *"Location is correct, Handshape is correct, Movement of the right hand is incorrect"*. For our experiment, we ensured that the expert evaluators follow the same structure of evaluation to give feedback based on the location, movement and handshape. A preset structure or rubric reduces subjectivity and allows for a fair comparison.

Challenge 2: Method of Comparison. In order to compare expert manual with automated feedback, the evaluation of both feedback techniques has to be performed by another ASL expert unaware of the source of feedback and the purpose of the experiment. *Solution*: We utilize a two step evaluation method. The first step involves three experts who review the recorded gesture executions of the novice learners and provide manual feedback. Automated feedback is also generated for the same videos using *ASLHelp*. Both manual and automated feedback are compared for each video. All feedback are recorded for use in the second step, as shown in Fig. 3.

In the second step, we use a *fourth* expert who is unaware of the previous step and the purpose of the experiment. The expert is presented with two feedback choices for each gesture (from the pool of recorded automated and manual feedback) for that video and is asked to choose a feedback that is appropriate for the corresponding video, as shown in the inset of Fig. 3.

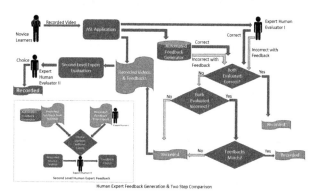

Fig. 3. Two step comparison of automated feedback with manual feedback

2   Method of Experiment

To implement the solutions discussed in Sect. 1, we collected recorded video data from experts and novice learners, collected feedback on the novice learners' videos from experts and *ASLHelp* to perform the two step evaluation process. Details of these steps are discussed in the following subsections:

2.1   Data

We have collected data sets from two different sources: Expert Data sets from *SignSavvy* website [15] and a novice learner data set with video recordings from first time ASL Learners. The novice data set consists of gesture videos from first time ASL learners using *ASLHelp*. Students learned the ASL gestures by watching expert videos on *SignSavvy*. The videos were recorded by users themselves while using the application in practice mode. Videos were collected from 26 learners, each performing 6 generic ASL terms. There were no restrictions on the light conditions, distance to the camera or on the position of the user while recording (standing or sitting down) as shown in Fig. 2. We recognize that while expert videos are recorded in ideal conditions with proper lighting and positioning, self recorded videos from students are not recorded in ideal condition with different items in their background and heterogenous camera use.

2.2   *ASLHelp* Feedback

ASLHelp is a self paced American Sign Language learning application. It provides context based explainable feedback to faciliate higher learning outcomes. It was deployed and used by novice ASL learners at the author's university. Users are able to perform two activities using *ASLHelp*: 1) learn ASL gestures (performed by experts) for everyday words, 2) test their knowledge by performing gestures of a given word that they have learnt. It compares expert gesture execution with learner's self recorded video and checks them for correctness. The process of comparison has the following components:

Grammar Expression of Gesture: *ASLHelp* uses the three modalities of ASL proposed by Stokoe: *location* of the sign, *movement*, and *handshape* [25] as shown in Fig. 1. Each gesture in ASL starts with an initial *handshape*, initial *location* of the palm and ends with a final *handshape* and final *location* of the palm. In between the initial *handshape*, *location* and final *handshape* and *location*, there is also a unique *movement* of the palm. These three components are unique concepts of a gesture since each of the *handshapes*, *locations* and *movements* have a specific meaning that make these gestures meaningful to ASL speakers. Recognition in *ASLHelp* is designed based on these three unique modalities of ASL gestures. We define *gesture expressions* in terms of these concepts (*handshape*, *location* and *movement*) and represent them using context free grammar.

We consider the *Concept Set*, Γ, where $\Gamma = \Gamma_H \bigcup \Gamma_L \bigcup \Gamma_M$. Here, Γ_H is the set of handshapes, Γ_L is the set of locations and Γ_m is the set of movements.

So, regular expression GE:

$$Handshapes(H) \rightarrow \Gamma_H \qquad\qquad\qquad (1)$$
$$Locations(L) \;\; \rightarrow \Gamma_L$$
$$Movements(M) \rightarrow \Gamma_M$$
$$GE \qquad\quad \rightarrow GE_{Left}GE_{Right}$$
$$GE_x \qquad \rightarrow H|\emptyset, \quad where, \; x \in Right, Left$$
$$GE_x \qquad \rightarrow HL$$
$$GE_x \qquad \rightarrow HLMHL$$

ASL learners are able to get automated feedback based on the correctness of these components. The correctness is determined by comparing learner's execution to the execution of an expert. To compare, *keypoints* are obtained from both the expert execution and learner execution. *Keypoints* are the body parts that are tracked frame by frame throughout the video. Keypoint estimation is necessary to identify the location, movement and handshape of the gesture execution. Keypoints for eys, nose, shoulder, elbows and wrists are collected using PoseNet [16].

Location Recognition: *ASLHelp* considers *start* and *end* locations of the hand position for pose estimation using the PoseNet model. This model identifies wrist joint positions frame by frame from a video of ASL gesture execution in a 2D space for key points. The two axes namely X-axis (the line that connects the two shoulder joints) and Y-axis (perpendicular to the x-axis) are drawn based on the shoulders of the learner as a fixed reference. We divide the video canvas into 6 different sub-sections called buckets. Then, as the learner executes any given sign, the location of both the wrist joints is tracked for each bucket resulting in a vector of length 6. This same procedure is followed for the expert executions, and a cosine based comparison is done between the two vectors.

Movement Recognition: The hand movement type is considered by capturing the movement of the hands with respect to time from its start to the end of the sign which is required for making comparisons. The Dynamic Time Warping technique is used for extracting frame by frame distance matrices with synchronization for the difference in speed or delayed start/stop times of the learner. This uses Z-normalization on the time-series for the difference in the size of the frame, distance of the learner from the camera and size of the learner relative to the tutor to some extent. DTW tries to get an optimal match for every data point in the sequence with any data point of the corresponding sequence. If segmental DTW distance between a learner's recording and a tutorial was higher than the threshold for each arm section, then a movement-based feedback is provided.

Handshape Recognition: ASL signs differ semantically only by the shape or orientation of the hands. To ensure focused hand shape comparisons and recognitions a tight crop of each of the hands is required. In *ASLHelp* this is done using the wrist position for different videos: a) Depending upon the orientation of the hands, the size of the crop was made very large relative to the learner's body and, b) The distance of the learner from the camera for the quality of the crop depending on the learner either being closer to or farther from the camera. The wrist location obtained, is used as a guide to auto-crop these hand-shape images. During recognition time, hand-shape images from each hand are extracted automatically from a learner's recording. Then 6 images for each hand are passed separately through the CNN and the softmax layer is obtained and are concatenated together. Similar processing is done on the expert video to obtain a vector of the same length. Then a cosine similarity is calculated on the resultant vector.

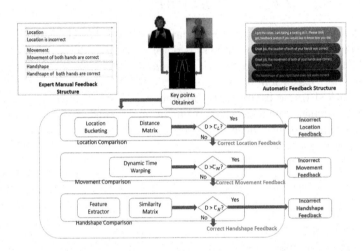

Fig. 4. Feedback generation process of *ASLHelp*

Automated Feedback: Based on the similarities between the recognized gesture components of experts and learners, *ASLHelp* provides appropriate feedback as shown in the inset og Fig. 4. This similarity is determined based on a threshold τ, pre-decided (based on expert opinion) for each of the components: τ_L for *location*, τ_M for *movement* and τ_H for *handshape*. For example, using a distance matrix, D, for *location* comparison, if learner's execution is completely dissimilar to the execution of the expert, we would get a value of 1 and if it is exactly like the expert's, we would get a value of 0. τ_L is pre-decided based on an acceptable range of dissimilarity with the expert execution, that would deem the learner's execution correct. If $D < \tau_L$, the feedback on location would be correct and if $D > \tau_L$, the feedback on location would be incorrect. Similar process is used to pre-decide τ_H and τ_M to generate appropriate feedback (Fig. 4).

2.3 Expert Manual Feedback

As mentioned in Sect. 1 to reduce the subjectivity of the manual feedback, we used a pre-set rubric for the feedbacks from the experts. We use the similar structure used in *ASLHelp* as the concepts used in evaluation make these feedback formative and also explanatory to the learner. An expert feedback also consists of evaluation based on the *location* of the sign, *movement* and *handshape*. Experts use their knowledge of the gesture to evaluate the learners execution as correct or incorrect. If the *location* of the sign is far off, the feedback for location is incorrect, whereas if the *movement* in the same execution is correct, the feedback on movement would be correct (inset of Fig. 4). Feedback based on the incorrect *movement* and *handshape* of the right or left-hand is also provided.

2.4 Two Step Evaluation

As a solution to the *Method of Comparison*, as mentioned in Sect. 1, we follow a two step evaluation process by the experts. First step is to perform a one to one comparison with automated feedback and the critical second step with choice options from the pool of recorded feedbacks from the first step.

First Step: The first step is to compare *ASLHelp* and expert feedback for the same videos. The feedbacks are compared to check whether the feedbacks match Fig. 3. Based on the comparison, there can be six combinations:

C_A & C_E, I_A & C_E, C_A & I_E, I_A & I_E with $F_A \cap F_E = F_A$ or F_E, I_A & I_E with $F_A \cap F_E = F_M$, I_A & I_E with $F_A \cap F_E = \emptyset$

where for *ASLHelp*, Correct feedback is C_A and incorrect is I_A. For experts, correct feedback is C_E and incorrect is I_E. F_A represents *ASLHelp* feedback, F_E is expert feedback and F_M is one or more matched feedback. All feedback is analyzed and recorded to be used in the second step.

Second Step: Another expert is brought in, who is unaware of the first step and the comparison process and second level of evaluation is performed using the same videos. The expert is provided with two feedback choices and asked to choose which is correct for the video. The feedback choices are provided from recorded feedback from *ASLHelp* and experts in the first step. Second level expert choice is then recorded and analyzed.

3 Results and Analysis

We show the execution results of the two step expert opinion based evaluation process to compare automated and manual expert feedback. The first step is a one to one comparison between automated and manual feedback for 154 novice learner videos. The second step utilizes expert opinion to evaluate the appropriateness of the feedbacks from the first step.

3.1 First Step: *Automated vs. Manual*

We collected 3 componential 154 feedbacks each from *ASLHelp* and expert Evaluators. As mentioned in the previous section, correct feedback for all 3 components from *ASLHelp* is labeled C_A, from experts as C_E. Feedback with any incorrect component was labeled I; I_A for *ASLHelp* and I_E for expert. Results from C_A & C_E and I_A & I_E with $F_A \cap F_E = F_A$ or F_E are most interesting to us, because these two combinations present the results when both feedback match exactly (100% match), regardless of the videos being labeled correct or incorrect.

Table 1. Combinations of feedback matching with results

Feedback matching	Total	Percent
100% match (C_A & C_E and I_A & I_E with $F_A \cap F_E = F_A$ or F_E)	57	36.25%
$\geq$66% match (I_A & C_E and C_A & I_E)	123	78.87%
$\geq$33% match (I_A & I_E with $F_A \cap F_E = F_M$)	152	98.70%
no match (I_A & I_E with $F_A \cap F_E = \emptyset$)	2	1.29%

For the 3 componential feedback the categories for matching would be 100%, 66%, 33% or no match. Table 1 shows that for 57 of the videos there was a 100% feedback match. A 66% match represents only 1 mismatch between the feedbacks in the detailed feedback category. We find that 78.87% of the times the feedbacks have only one mismatch, 98.70% of the times they agree on atleast one component of the feedback and only 1.29% of the times there is no match between them as shown in Table 1. Figure 5 shows that while the automated and manual feedbacks for *location* and *movement* match each other respectively 79.22% and 76.62% of the times, there are more disagreements for *handshape*, (59.74% match). Figure 6 shows that automated feedback is identifying gestures to be correct on all three components 58.44% of the times while manual feedback is identifying the same gestures to be correct on all components 76.62% of the times. We further isolated the results for matched feedbacks for each of the gestures, by three components, two components and one component matching (as shown in the Figs. 7, 8, 9).

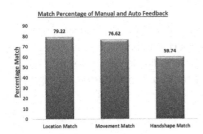

Fig. 5. Feedback on individual concepts

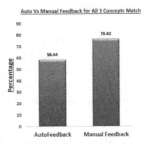

Fig. 6. Feedback on all three concepts combined

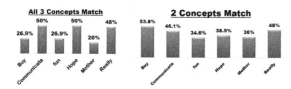

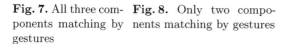

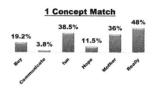

Fig. 7. All three components matching by gestures   **Fig. 8.** Only two components matching by gestures   **Fig. 9.** Only one component matching by gestures

3.2 Second Step: *Second Level Expert*

In this step, automated and manual feedback from first step are evaluated based on an expert opinion. Figure 10 shows that 59.09% of the times the expert agreed with the manual feedback and 40.91% of the times they agreed with the *ASLHelp*.

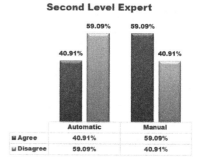

Fig. 10. Second Level Expert

3.3 Analysis of the Results

The results in the first step reflect that automated and manual feedback matches about 1/3 of the time. The matching is brought down significantly by the mismatched feedbacks for *handshape*. Automated and manual feedback matches most of the time on the *location* and *movement* components. The disparity in the *handshape* feedback could be the result of two very different conditions that novice and expert videos are recorded in, and applications ability to identify finer details in a handshape execution. Given the imperfect conditions, heterogeneous modes of recording and backgrounds with various objects in the videos of novice learners, *handshape* of the gesture may not be as clear as the *handshape* in expert videos that are recorded in near perfect condition with no obstructive objects. This result is indicative of a required improvement in the *handshape* recognition mechanism of *ASLHelp*. In second step, expert has agreed with the manual feedback more times than with automated feedback. This agrees with the findings in the first step and is reflective of the fact that manual evaluation is less sensitive than *ASLHelp*. However, expert has also chosen the automated feedback 40.91% of the times over the manual feedback reflecting that nearly half of the time *ASLHelp* feedback was more appropriate. The comparison between feedbacks for all three components being identified as correct (Fig. 6) also shows that *ASLHelp* is able to pick up on finer details in the videos than experts and hence can contribute to better performance in execution of the gesture; which we believe would add value to the extendibility of such automated feedback to various other gesture based learning applications in different fields.

4 Lessons Learned on Feedback

Through the findings of this experiment, we learn that more than half of the times expert opinion favors manual feedback over automated feedback on appropriateness. This can be the result of more forgiving nature of manual evaluation considering "approaches to be correct" as "correct", where as *ASLHelp* only considers which is precisely as correct. However, the findings are also indicative of higher levels of recognition mechanism that is required. For automated feedback to be comparable with manual feedback, a sound recognition of finer details is required- specially in the field of gesture based learning. We posit that ensuring finer recognition combined with adaptability for expert modulation of margin of error, can advance automated feedback to a comparable level of manual feedback.

5 Conclusion and Future Work

For computer based learning applications in all modalities to be considered useful, the reliability of the feedback generated by an application is of great importance. We know from numerous research in the field that automated feedback should provide feedback that is not only explanatory to the learner, but also instructive enough so that it can help improve learner's performance, just as a physiotherapist, a combat trainer, a performance coach or an interpreter would do. Through this experiment, we have demonstrated a two step evaluation process that can be applied successfully to compare automated feedback with expert manual feedback based on expert opinion. Analyzing the results from this experiment, we have seen that some gestures were easier to reproduce for learners than others, similarly automated and manual feedbacks for those gestures matched more times than others. Further research into this to calibrate the recognition and feedback process to match the difficulty level of the gesture may lead to interesting new insights.

References

1. Alwardat, M., et al.: Effectiveness of robot-assisted gait training on motor impairments in people with Parkinson's disease: a systematic review and meta-analysis. Int. J. Rehabil. Res. **41**, 1 (2018). https://doi.org/10.1097/MRR.0000000000000312
2. Banerjee, A., Lamrani, I., Hossain, S., Paudyal, P., Gupta, S.K.S.: AI enabled tutor for accessible training. In: Bittencourt, I.I., Cukurova, M., Muldner, K., Luckin, R., Millán, E. (eds.) AIED 2020. LNCS (LNAI), vol. 12163, pp. 29–42. Springer, Cham (2020). https://doi.org/10.1007/978-3-030-52237-7_3
3. Banerjee, A., Lamrani, I., Paudyal, P., Gupta, S.: Generation of movement explanations for testing gesture based co-operative learning applications. In: 2019 IEEE International Conference On Artificial Intelligence Testing (AITest), pp. 9–16. IEEE (2019)

4. Davis, F.D., Bagozzi, R.P., Warshaw, P.R.: User acceptance of computer technology: a comparison of two theoretical models. Manage. Sci. **35**(8), 982–1003 (1989)
5. Ellis, K., Fisher, J., Willoughby, L., Barca, J.: A design science exploration of a visual-spatial learning system with feedback (2016)
6. Hossain, S., Banerjee, A., Gupta, S.K.S.: Personalized technical learning assistance for deaf and hard of hearing students. In: Workshop on Artificial Intelligence for Education, AAAI 2020. New York, USA (2020)
7. Huenerfauth, M., Gale, E., Penly, B., Pillutla, S., Willard, M., Hariharan, D.: Evaluation of language feedback methods for student videos of American sign language. ACM Trans. Access. Comput. **10**(1) (2017). https://doi.org/10.1145/3046788
8. Irons, A.: Enhancing Learning Through Formative Assessment and Feedback. Routledge (2007)
9. Jiang, Q., Liu, M., Wang, X., Ge, M., Lin, L.: Human motion segmentation and recognition using machine vision for mechanical assembly operation. Springerplus **5**(1), 1–18 (2016). https://doi.org/10.1186/s40064-016-3279-x
10. Kamzin, A., Amperyani, A., Sukhapalli, P., Banerjee, A., Gupta, S.: Concept embedding through canonical forms: a case study on zero-shot asl recognition. In: ICPR 2020, p. 8 (2021)
11. Kamzin, A., Paudyal, P., Banerjee, A., Gupta, S.K.: Evaluating the gap between hype and performance of AI systems (2020)
12. Matsumura, S., Hann, G.: Computer anxiety and students' preferred feedback methods in EFL writing. Mod. Lang. J. **88**(3), 403–415 (2004)
13. McFarland, T.: Military robots: mapping the moral landscape [book reviews]. IEEE Technol. Soc. Mag. **35**(2), 23–25 (2016)
14. Min, H., Morales, D., Orgill, D., Smink, D., Yule, S.: Systematic review of coaching to enhance surgeons' operative performance. Surgery 158 (2015). https://doi.org/10.1016/j.surg.2015.03.007
15. MotionSavvy (2016). http://www.motionsavvy.com/. Accessed 15 Nov 2016
16. Papandreou, G., et al.: Towards accurate multi-person pose estimation in the wild. In: Proceedings of the IEEE Conference on Computer Vision and Pattern Recognition, pp. 4903–4911 (2017)
17. Paudyal, P., Banerjee, A., Gupta, S.: On evaluating the effects of feedback for sign language learning using explainable AI. In: Proceedings of the 25th International Conference on Intelligent User Interfaces Companion, pp. 83–84. IUI 2020, Association for Computing Machinery, New York (2020). https://doi.org/10.1145/3379336.3381469
18. Paudyal, P., Lee, J., Kamzin, A., Soudki, M., Banerjee, A., Gupta, S.: Learn2sign: explainable AI for sign language learning. In: CEUR Workshop Proceedings, vol. 2327. CEUR-WS (2019)
19. Perretta, J., Weimer, W., DeOrio, A.: Human vs. automated coding style grading in computing education. In: 2019 ASEE Annual Conference and Exposition (2019)
20. Phan, H.D., Ellis, K., Dorin, A., Olivier, P.: Feedback strategies for embodied agents to enhance sign language vocabulary learning. In: IVA 2020. Association for Computing Machinery, New York (2020). https://doi.org/10.1145/3383652.3423871
21. Riley, M., Ude, A., Atkeson, C., Cheng, G.: Coaching: an approach to efficiently and intuitively create humanoid robot behaviors. In: 2006 6th IEEE-RAS International Conference on Humanoid Robots, pp. 567–574 (2006)
22. Salichs, M.A., Encinar, I.P., Salichs, E., Castro-González, Á., Malfaz, M.: Study of scenarios and technical requirements of a social assistive robot for Alzheimer's dis-

ease patients and their caregivers. Int. J. Soc. Robot. **8**(1), 85–102 (2015). https://doi.org/10.1007/s12369-015-0319-6

23. Santamaría Lancho, M., Hernández, M., Sánchez-Elvira Paniagua, Á., Luzón Encabo, J.M., de Jorge-Botana, G.: Using semantic technologies for formative assessment and scoring in large courses and MOOCs. J. Interactive Media Educ. **2018**(1) (2018)

24. Sharkey, N.E.: The evitability of autonomous robot warfare. Int. Rev. Red Cross **94**(886), 787–799 (2012). https://doi.org/10.1017/S1816383112000732

25. Stokoe Jr., W.C.: Sign language structure: an outline of the visual communication systems of the American deaf. J. Deaf Stud. Deaf Educ. **10**(1), 3–37 (2005)

26. Zhang, Z.V., Hyland, K.: Student engagement with teacher and automated feedback on l2 writing. Assess. Writ. **36**, 90–102 (2018)

27. Zhu, M., Liu, O.L., Lee, H.S.: The effect of automated feedback on revision behavior and learning gains in formative assessment of scientific argument writing. Comput. Educ. **143**, 103668 (2020)

Investigating Students' Reasoning in a Code-Tracing Tutor

Jay Jennings[✉] and Kasia Muldner[✉]

Department of Cognitive Science, Carleton University, Ottawa, Canada
{jayjennings,kasiamuldner}@cunet.carleton.ca

Abstract. Code tracing involves stepping through a program in order to predict its output. In the present study ($N = 45$), we used the think-aloud protocol to gain insight into students' cognitive processes as they used a computer tutor to study code-tracing examples and work on code-tracing problems, using either a high-scaffolding or a reduced-scaffolding tutor interface. For the cognitive processes, we included both self-explanation and reading behaviors, relying on a qualitative coding to analyze the transcripts. Our results shed light on how different levels of assistance provided by a computer tutor impact student reasoning during code-tracing activities.

Keywords: Code tracing · Verbal protocols · Qualitative analysis · Programming education

1 Introduction

Programming involves writing instructions using a programming language that tell a computer how to accomplish a specific task. Learning to program presents a variety of challenges [21] because students must master not only the syntax and semantics of a programming language, but also a new way to think and problem solve [30]. Thus, support for this process is needed. To date, work has focused on program generation, for instance by providing feedback on solution attempts [29], assistance through hints [20] and worked examples of similar programs [27], gamification [24], and adaptive activity selection [10]. However, program generation is only one of four key skills students must master [32]. We focus on designing support for the foundational skill of code tracing.

Code tracing involves predicting the output of a program by simulating the high-level steps a computer would take while executing the program and how values of program variables change as a result [8]. Code tracing improves students' ability to write programs [1] and debug them (i.e., find errors in programs). Moreover, code tracing is hypothesized to support the development of appropriate mental models [1]. A mental model is an internal representation of how something works – typically this representation is highly abstracted. In the context of programming, a relevant mental model is the notional machine, an abstraction of a computer that helps students predict how the computer will

© Springer Nature Switzerland AG 2021
I. Roll et al. (Eds.): AIED 2021, LNAI 12748, pp. 203–214, 2021.
https://doi.org/10.1007/978-3-030-78292-4_17

execute their program [3]. Students have various misconceptions related to the notional machine [22]; one broad one is that the computer can reason about the intentions of the programmer and adapt accordingly [18]. In general, novices have difficulty reasoning about the logical flow of a program [15], tracing programs to predict their output [25], and building correct mental models [11], to name a few examples. Many students fail to code trace at all [8].

Given the importance of the code-tracing skill, some work has investigated how to foster it with animation tools showing the execution of a program, similar to a debugging tool. For instance, Hosseini et al. [12] provided students with visualizations of code traces, including plain-English explanations of program segments. The animations showed a visual trace of the program as well as the stack frame with values of variables. As a second example, Sorva et al. [23] designed a visual animation system capable of code tracing. To evaluate the system, they interviewed 11 students to gain insight into their perceptions of the visual animations. PL-Tutor [17] is another system that uses visual animations to illustrate the process of code tracing. The tutor provided a visualization of program execution and Python namespaces, stacks and frames, encouraging students to be constructive by entering variable values into the interface.

As described above, one approach to help students learn to code trace involves animation tools. An alternative approach is more basic, by placing the responsibility on the student to produce the code trace (typically with some scaffolding for the process). To illustrate, Baymen and Mayer [1] reported that providing basic written examples of worked-out code traces significantly improved students' performance on a code generation task compared to a control group that was not provided with the examples. More recently, Cunningham et al. [8] recorded how students code-traced short programs using paper-and-pencil. Their qualitative analysis identified methods that successful students used (e.g., keeping track of variables using an adhoc table). However, many students did not code trace effectively (e.g., traced incorrect variables, only partially traced), indicating that scaffolding for the process is needed.

In summary, there are a number of approaches available for assisting code-tracing activities. We adopted the basic, non-animation approach in the present work. Our target population corresponds to students who are not computer science majors and who are enrolled in a programming class. This scenario is becoming increasingly more common as the broad value of programming is recognized and so programming classes are required for all students regardless of their major, as is the case in our department. Given our target population, we wanted to abstract away technical terms like namespaces and frames that are not required for understanding code tracing. Our goal was to design a tutor that mimicked what successful students did when they code traced on paper because that activity had potential to be more familiar than a debugging-type interface. These considerations were inspired by our experiences in the classroom, which highlighted that students were not comfortable having to learn an additional technology (a visual debugger) but were willing to try and code trace on paper. Thus, we created an initial prototype of a code-tracing tutor that aimed to mimic

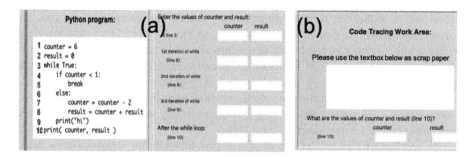

Fig. 1. Code-tracing problem interface for (a) high-scaffolding (HS) tutor and (b) fragment of the reduced-scaffolding (RS) tutor (not shown is the program, which is the same as the one shown in the left panel of (a))

paper and pencil activities. The tutor is not an intelligent tutoring system yet, as we wanted to evaluate what works and what doesn't before adding more complex functionality. Given that prior research involving code-tracing tutors has focused on outcomes from code-tracing activities, work is needed to gain insight into student reasoning *during* code tracing with a tutor and how tutor design choices impact that reasoning. To address this gap, we collected and analyzed data on how students reason with two different versions of our code-tracing tutor: a reduced and high-scaffolding interface. Before describing the study, we describe the tutor and these interfaces.

1.1   Code-Tracing Tutor and Prior Results

The code-tracing tutor we developed provides both code-tracing examples for students to study and code-tracing problems to solve (problems and examples are shown on separate screens) [14]; the programming language is Python. Following the precedent set by prior work [26], the tutor does not provide instruction on Python basics or the code-tracing procedure because the expectation is that students had previously received a lesson on these elements. The design of the example interface was based on work investigating students' code tracing on paper [8], where a popular method successful code tracers used corresponded to tracking variables as a program executes using a table format. We used this format in the design of the example interface (not shown here due to space limitations but the table format in the example was based on the one shown in Fig. 1(a), except the table cells were filled in). The example also included a high-level explanation of the program in plain English, motivated by prior work showing such explanations are associated with learning [16].

For the problem-solving interface, students were asked to predict the output of a program by code tracing it. We designed two alternative interfaces: high scaffolding (HS) and reduced scaffolding (RS). Both versions showed the Python program (Fig. 1a, left) and asked participants to predict what the program printed in the last line (Fig. 1a and 1b, bottom right). Both versions also provided immediate feedback on that final entry, by coloring the entry green or red, for correct vs. incorrect, respectively. However, in the HS interface, students had to input the intermediate solution steps into the code-tracing table, row by row (see Fig. 1(a); they received feedback for correctness on these entries and could not move on to the next row until the solutions for the current row were correct. In contrast, for the RS interface, students were provided with a free-form text box (see Fig. 1(b), middle), that they could use in any way they wished to track their code traces for the intermediate steps.

We evaluated the two versions of the problem-solving interface in a prior study [14]. Our original hypothesis was that students would learn more from the HS interface, as previous work suggested students did not code trace effectively without guidance [8]. However, the results showed that students learned *less* from the HS interface than the RS interface, which was unexpected. We hypothesized that the RS group might be self-explaining more (i.e., producing inferences beyond the instructional materials), because they had to produce code traces with less guidance than the HS condition. In other domains, self-explanation has been shown to be highly beneficial for learning [5] and so if we had evidence of it occurring we could substantiate that hypothesis. In our prior work, however, we did not collect students' reasoning to explain how they learned with each version of the tutor. To address this limitation, we conducted the present study.

2   Present Study

The high-level goal of the present study was to obtain data on students' reasoning patterns during code-tracing activities involving problems and examples. We therefore used a think-aloud methodology from prior work [7,9,13], and asked participants to verbalize their thoughts as they worked with their assigned tutor. We subsequently transcribed and analyzed the verbalizations (details below). This approach has the advantage of providing process data on how students are reasoning and thus insight into their code-tracing approaches.

We focused on two types of reasoning in our analysis: *reading* and *self-explanation*. Reading in our study corresponded to verbalizing the text in the interface (e.g., program, its explanation) with little or no changes. In contrast, self-explanation involves generating inferences that go beyond the instructional materials. While both reading and self-explanation are needed during instructional activities, self-explanation is particularly beneficial for learning [5]. We had the following research question:

Does the level of assistance (i.e., scaffolding) in the tutor interface influence patterns of self-explanation, reading, and comprehension?

To address this question, we used a between-subjects design[1], where some students interacted with the HS tutor and others with the RS tutor. Given prior results that students learned less from the HS interface [14], we hypothesized

---

[1] A between-subjects design was used because the high potential for order effects rendered a within-subject design not suitable.

that its design inadvertently reduced self-explanation. Due to the novelty of our context (code tracing), we did not have specific predictions related to reading behaviours within the tutor and comprehension.

2.1 Participants and Procedure

The participants were university students ($N = 45$) recruited using SONA (an online participant recruitment tool) and social media. Participants were compensated either with course credit or $20. As the tutor is designed for novice programmers, to be eligible, participants must not have taken more than one university programming class.

All sessions were conducted individually over Zoom; each session lasted no more than 1.5 h. After providing consent, participants studied an online Power-Point presentation that provided key foundations on variables, conditionals and loops, as well as two brief videos on code tracing. Participants could go through the presentation at their own pace. They then filled in a questionnaire (not analyzed here and so not described) and were given a warm-up think-aloud exercise to prepare them for the main phase of the study. Participants were shown a screen shot of the tutor interface they would be using and were walked through its functionality by the experimenter. Participants then worked with one of the two versions of the tutor (reduced or high scaffolding) to solve two code-tracing problems; each problem was preceded by one example displayed on a separate screen, that showed a similar problem and its step-by-step solution. As participants studied the examples and worked on the problems, they were asked to verbalize their thoughts and these verbalizations were audio recorded.

2.2 Qualitative Coding: Method

Recordings of participants' verbalizations were transcribed, segmented, and analyzed using the procedure in [4]. An initial coding scheme was developed that contained the target themes, including self-explanation of code-tracing constructs, as well as reading and comprehension. The protocols were segmented at the construct level and a single code was applied to each segment (i.e., codes did not overlap). Two researchers independently coded an initial subset of the protocols, meeting to discuss disagreements after each protocol was coded and compared; the coding scheme was updated based on these discussions to clarify and expand the target concepts. After using this process for six protocols, saturation was reached (i.e., coding scheme stabilized). The finalized coding scheme (see Table 1) included the original constructs related to self-explanation, reading, and comprehension, but refined to make their definitions clear.

The two researchers then independently coded 20% of the remaining protocols. Inter-rater agreement was very good as assessed by Cohen's kappa (.89, $p < .001$; pure agreement calculated by percentage of ratings in agreement was equal to 90%); disagreements were discussed but did not require further adjustments to the coding scheme. Given the high agreement, the primary author coded the remaining protocols (this approach is standard).

Table 1. The target constructs coded for in the transcripts (SE = self-explanation).

SE: general	Other self-explanations that go over and beyond the instructional materials
SE: flow of execution	Verbalizations about the flow of control in a program (e.g., *'now it goes back to the top of the loop'*)
SE: updating variable	Verbalizations related to substituting and/or updating variables by their values (e.g., *'so count is count plus one, so 2 plus 1 is 3'*)
Unevidenced variable substitution (UVS)	Verbalization of the value a variable has without rationale for how it was generated
Reading: program	Reading of the program without adding anything new content or explaining
Reading: CT Table	Reading the code-tracing (CT) table
Reading: explanation	Reading the code-tracing explanation provided in the two examples, without adding new content
Reading: other	Reading any other part of the interface
Comprehension: confusion	Statements expressing confusion about the material
Comprehension: 'I got it'	Statements relating to understanding something
Other	Other verbalizations (e.g., *'I'm looking at the program'*)

3   Results

To answer our research question, we used the results from the qualitative coding (see Table 1), namely self-explanation instances (*flow of execution, variable substitution, general*), reading instances (*program, explanation, CT table*), unevidenced variable substitution (UVS), and comprehension instances (*confusion, 'I got it'*) - see Table 1 for a description of each construct. For each participant, we extracted the total count of each instance (i.e., construct), for each example (E1 and E2) and problem (P1 and P2). Since all participants saw the same two examples and two problems, referred to as *activities* below, in the same sequence (E1-P1-E2-P2), we could analyze trends across activities for the target constructs, as well as interactions between instructional activity and condition. All but two participants finished the four activities (two participants did not start problem 2).

The mean number of each construct for each of the four activities are shown in Figs. 2 and 3. These figures highlight that patterns of self-explanation, reading, and comprehension did change over time and were affected by condition (high-scaffolding, *HS* vs. reduced scaffolding, *RS*). To analyze this further, we conducted a series of mixed ANOVAs for each dependent variable, with two factors: condition (a two level between-subjects factor corresponding to the level of assistance, HS and RS) and instructional activity (a within-subjects factor; unless stated otherwise, this factor had four levels, corresponding to the four activities,

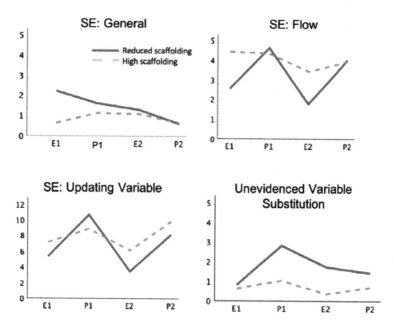

Fig. 2. Mean number of self-explanation (SE) instances in each condition, including *SE: general, SE: flow,* and *SE: updating variable,* as well as *Unevidenced Variable Substitution* (UVS); solid line = Reduced Scaffolding (RS), dashed line = High Scaffolding (HS), legend shown top-left panel; E1 and E2 = examples; P1 and P2 = problems

E1, P1, E2, P2). Sphericity violations were corrected using Greenhouse-Geisser. Of primary interest is the interaction between condition and instructional activity, as it informs on whether students' reasoning patterns for the target construct were affected by condition. Intuitively, if this were the case, the shape of the line graph would be different in the two conditions.

To analyze this formally, we followed up significant and marginal interactions with trend analyses - we report the highest significant polynomial related to the interaction. Note that a significant result in this context indicates that the form of the pattern across the four activities depends on the condition.

Self-Explanation (SE)-Related Results: We begin with the results for the three self-explanation constructs (see Fig. 2). The interaction between condition and instructional activity was significant or marginal for each of the three constructs (*SE: general:* $F(3, 123) = 2.9$, $p = .04$, $\eta_p^2 = .07$; *SE: flow:* $F(3, 123) = 2.9$, $p = .038$, $\eta_p^2 = .07$ *SE: updating variable:* $F(2.1, 86.8) = 2.3$, $p = .10$, $\eta_p^2 = .05$). We now present the follow up trend analyses and results.

For *SE: general,* follow-up polynomial contrasts indicated a significant linear trend for the condition × instructional activity interaction ($p = .02$). As illustrated in Fig. 2, participants in the RS condition exhibited more of these self-explanations for the first example than the HS condition and in general these explanations followed a linear downward trend. In contrast, the HS condition produced few such explanations for the first example, then increased that

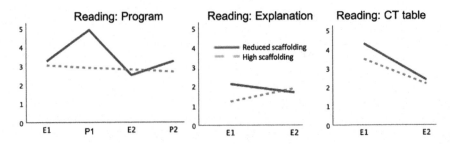

Fig. 3. Mean number of reading instances in each condition, including *reading program*, *reading explanation*, and *reading code-tracing (CT) table*; solid line = Reduced Scaffolding (RS), dashed line = High Scaffolding (HS), legend shown top-left panel; E1 and E2 = examples; P1 and P2 = problems

number while solving the first problem, and plateaued for the last example and problem.

The follow-up polynomial contrasts for the other two types of explanations (*SE: flow* and *SE: updating variable*) indicated a significant cubic trend for the interaction term ($p = .02$ and $p = .04$, respectively). For flow explanations, participants in the HS condition exhibited a generally consistent linear trend (≈ 4.5 explanations throughout) as compared to the RS condition (who varied from approximately 2.5 explanations for the examples to 4.5 in the problems). For updating variable values, the cubic trend was more pronounced for the RS group, see Fig. 2, bottom left.

While studying examples and solving problems, participants sometimes verbalized variable values without providing an explicit explanation, and that was captured by the *unevidenced variable substitution* construct (UVS). As shown in Fig. 2, bottom right, the pattern of this construct is different between the conditions over the course of the instructional activities (condition × instructional activity: $F(1.4, 55.9) = 2.4$, $p = .08$, $\eta_p^2 = .06$; the follow-up trend analysis reported a significant quadratic trend for the condition × instructional activity interaction ($p < .01$). While the number of UVS instances stayed fairly constant for the HS condition (.6 to .7), in the RS condition the pattern was different (i.e., in problem 1 the total was higher and although the mean decreased slightly in example 2 and problem 2, it stayed higher than the HS condition).

Reading-Related Results: We next analyzed if condition and instructional activity influenced reading behaviors (see Fig. 3). We begin with the *reading program* construct that corresponded to participants reading the Python program. There was a marginal interaction between condition and instructional activity, $F(3, 123) = 2.4$, $p = .07$, $\eta_p^2 = .06$. As illustrated in Fig. 3 (left), reading behavior for the HS group did not change much across the four activities. In contrast, the RS group read the program more in the first problem than participants in the HS condition. This interpretation is supported by the significant cubic trend for the condition × instructional activity interaction, $p = .02$.

The other two reading constructs (*reading explanation* and *reading CT table*) were only relevant in the context of the two examples and so the within-subject variable in the analysis includes two levels (example 1, example 2). (Note that trend analysis in this case is not applicable as there are only two levels). As shown in Fig. 3 (middle), there was a marginal interaction between condition and activity for explanation reading, $F(1, 43) = 2.7$, $p = .10$, $\eta_p^2 = .06$. Specifically, the RS group read the explanation more than the HS group for example 1, but for example 2, both conditions had a similar mean number of explanation reads. Also as shown in Fig. 3 (right), there was little difference between the conditions for the *read: CT table* construct, $F(1, 43) = .2$, $p = .64$, $\eta_p^2 < .01$.

Comprehension-Related Results: There were few instances of comprehension monitoring (confusion, 'I got it' - one or fewer), and differences between conditions were minimal and not significant. In general, there was more comprehension monitoring verbalizations, such as, *'That makes sense'* for the examples than in the problems and these decreased from 1.1 verbalizations in example 1 to 0.5 in problem 2; confusion exhibited a similar pattern.

4 Discussion

The target activity in the present work was code tracing. To date, work on how students reason during this activity is lacking, making it challenging to design assistance for it. Our work takes a step in filling this gap by investigating students' reasoning during code tracing through qualitative analysis of think-aloud transcripts. Thus, we take a process-based approach: we focus on the behaviours during the activities rather than the outcomes, because we wanted to obtain data on how tutor design impacted student reasoning behaviours.

One of the constructs we extracted from the transcripts was self-explanation (adapted to the present code-tracing domain), because work in various domains has shown it to be highly beneficial to learning [2,6,19,28,31]. Our prior evaluation of the two code-tracing tutor interfaces used here showed that the HS interface produced less learning compared to the RS interface [14] but in that study we did not collect data on how students were reasoning. We tentatively predicted that we would find more self-explanation in the RS interface; this hypothesis was also based on the fact that this interface provided less guidance and so could be a catalyst for self-explanation. The results from the study presented here, however, presented a more complex narrative. Broadly speaking, there was more variability between instructional activities (examples and problems) and assistance level in a given interface than anticipated, in terms of the frequency of explanations related to the flow of execution and updating variable values in the RS condition, as compared to the HS condition; this was particularly evident for the flow of execution explanations. While the HS condition remained fairly stable in terms of the number of flow of execution explanations regardless of context (example vs. problem), the RS condition produced fewer explanations when studying the examples but a similar number when solving the problem. Since the RS group had to do more independent problem solving as they had less guidance, they may have learned the flow principles and so did not need to produce explanations for them during example studying as frequently.

One of the self-explanations we analyzed corresponded to updating variable values. A related construct that we also extracted from the transcripts was unevidenced variable substitution (UVS), where participants would verbalize a value for a variable without articulating where the value came from. Prior to running the present study, we considered the possibility that we would see more of this construct in the HS interface, due to students guessing values to enter into the CT table (since the interface provided immediate feedback for correctness, and since the values tended to be in a limited range, guessing was possible). We did indeed see this behavior, but in general this guessing behavior was not common. What we did see in the transcripts and log files was evidence of students typing their code traces into the interface textboxes and then verbalizing only parts of them. This was particularly the case for the RS group, who had a textbox in their interface to keep track of code traces. The UVS pattern for this group followed a quadratic trend (as compared to a more linear one in the HS group); this quadratic trend for the RS group was driven by the higher number of the UVS construct during problem 1 solution generation, potentially reflecting greater effort invested in solving the problem because less assistance was available for it as compared to the HS group.

As far as the reading construct, the trend analysis identified a difference in reading patterns, highlighting that participants in the RS condition had higher program-reading frequency when solving the first problem. Note that this did not mean they read more of the program, because the segmentation was done at the construct level (so a participant could, for instance, read a line from a program, write a line in their code-tracing work area, self-explain, return to the program and read another line, and so on). Anecdotally, this switching between salient areas was common, and so this finding may be reflecting that participants referred to the program more in the RS condition when doing their code tracing. Code tracing without reference to the program is not possible (unless the program is memorized, but that was unlikely here) and so this finding points to a limitation in the HS interface that could explain why in the prior study it was not as effective as the RS interface [14]. In particular, the HS interface may have inadvertently encouraged a formulaic approach to calculating variable values that did not involve reference to the program.

To summarize, our work provides insight into students' self-explanation and reading behaviors recorded while students worked with a code-tracing tutor to study examples and solve problems. One implication of our work is that interface scaffolding resulted in more consistent self-explanation patterns. What is not yet clear, however, is how this translates to learning, a question we plan to tackle next. We also plan to apply sequence mining to analyze if condition impacts sequences of actions in each version of the tutor (e.g., is there more switching between the code tracing table and program areas?) and to investigate what types of traces participants produced in the RS interface textbox. We also plan to continue working on the design of the code-tracing tutor, including how to improve it so that all students benefit from interacting with it. While space limitations prevented us from describing this here, there was a lot of individual variability in terms of how students used the tutor (e.g., high standard deviations for many of the dependent variables). This points to the need for adaptive support to tailor assistance to students needs - another future avenue we plan to explore.

References

1. Bayman, P., Mayer, R.: Using conceptual models to teach basic computer programming. J. Educ. Psychol. **80**, 291–298 (1988)
2. Bisra, K., Liu, Q., Nesbit, J.C., Salimi, F., Winne, P.H.: Inducing self-explanation: a meta-analysis (2018)
3. Boulay, B.: Some difficulties of learning to program. J. Educ. Comput. Res. **2**, 57–73 (1986)
4. Chi, M.: Quantifying qualitative analyses of verbal data: a practical guide. J. Learn. Sci. **6**, 271–315 (1997)
5. Chi, M.T.H., Bassok, M., Lewis, M., Reimann, P., Glaser, R.: Self-explanations: how students study and use examples in learning to solve problems. Cogn. Sci. **13**, 145–182 (1989)
6. Chi, M.T.H., Leeuw, N., Chiu, M., LaVancher, C.: Eliciting self-explanations improves understanding. Cogn. Sci. **18**, 439–477 (1994)
7. Cowan, J.: The potential of cognitive think-aloud protocols for educational action-research. Act. Learn. High. Educ. **20**(3), 219–232 (2019)
8. Cunningham, K., Blanchard, S., Ericson, B., Guzdial, M.: Using tracing and sketching to solve programming problems: replicating and extending an analysis of what students draw. In: Proceedings of the 2017 ACM Conference on International Computing Education Research (2017)
9. Ericsson, A.: Valid and non-reactive verbalization of thoughts during performance of tasks towards a solution to the central problems of introspection as a source of scientific data. J. Conscious. Stud. **10**(9–10), 1–18 (2003)
10. Fabic, G.V.F., Mitrovic, A., Neshatian, K.: Adaptive problem selection in a mobile python tutor. In: Adjunct Publication of the 26th Conference on User Modeling, Adaptation and Personalization, pp. 269–274 (2018)
11. Hertz, M., Jump, M.: Trace-based teaching in early programming courses. In: SIGCSE 2013 (2013)
12. Hosseini, R., Sirkiä, T., Guerra, J., Brusilovsky, P., Malmi, L.: Animated examples as practice content in a Java programming course. In: Proceedings of the 47th ACM Technical Symposium on Computing Science Education, SIGCSE 2016, pp. 540–545. Association for Computing Machinery, New York (2016)
13. Jaspers, M.W., Steen, T., Van Den Bos, C., Geenen, M.: The think aloud method: a guide to user interface design. Int. J. Med. Informatics **73**(11–12), 781–795 (2004)
14. Jennings, J., Muldner, K.: When does scaffolding provide too much assistance? a code-tracing tutor investigation. Int. J. Artif. Intell. Educ., 1–36 (2020). https://doi.org/10.1007/s40593-020-00217-z
15. Lam, M.S.W., Chan, E., Lee, V., Yu, Y.T.: Designing an automatic debugging assistant for improving the learning of computer programming. In: ICHL (2008)
16. Lopez, M., Whalley, J., Robbins, P., Lister, R.: Relationships between reading, tracing and writing skills in introductory programming. In: ICER 2008 (2008)

17. Nelson, G.L., Xie, B., Ko, A.J.: Comprehension first: evaluating a novel pedagogy and tutoring system for program tracing in CS1. In: Proceedings of the 2017 ACM Conference on International Computing Education Research, pp. 2–11 (2017)
18. Pea, R.: Language-independent conceptual "bugs" in novice programming. J. Educ. Comput. Res. **2**, 25–36 (1986)
19. Rittle-Johnson, B., Loehr, A.M., Durkin, K.: Promoting self-explanation to improve mathematics learning: a meta-analysis and instructional design principles. ZDM **49**(4), 599–611 (2017). https://doi.org/10.1007/s11858-017-0834-z
20. Rivers, K., Koedinger, K.: Data-driven hint generation in vast solution spaces: a self- improving python programming tutor. Int. J. Artif. Intell. Educ. **27**(1), 37–64 (2017)
21. Robins, A.V., Rountree, J., Rountree, N.: Learning and teaching programming: a review and discussion. Comput. Sci. Educ. **13**(2), 137–172 (2003)
22. Sorva, J.: Notional machines and introductory programming education. ACM Trans. Comput. Educ. **13**, 8:1–8:31 (2013)
23. Sorva, J., Lönnberg, J., Malmi, L.: Students' ways of experiencing visual program simulation. Comput. Sci. Educ. **23**(3), 207–238 (2013)
24. Tahir, F., Mitrovic, A., Sotardi: investigating the effects of gamifying SQL-tutor. In: Proceedings of the 28th International Conference on Computers in Education (2020)
25. Vainio, V., Sajaniemi, J.: Factors in novice programmers' poor tracing skills. ACM SIGCSE Bull. **39**(3), 236–240 (2007)
26. VanLehn, K., et al.: The Andes physics tutoring system: five years of evaluations. In: AIED (2005)
27. Weber, G., Brusilovsky, P.: ELM-ART: an adaptive versatile system for web-based instruction. Int. J. Artif. Intell. Educ. (IJAIED) **12**, 351–384 (2001)
28. Weerasinghe, A., Mitrovic, A.: Facilitating deep learning through self-explanation in an open-ended domain. Int. J. Knowl.-Based Intell. Eng. Syst. **10**(1), 3–19 (2006)
29. Weragama, D., Reye, J.: Analysing student programs in the PHP intelligent tutoring system. Int. J. Artif. Intell. Educ. **24**, 162–188 (2014)
30. Wing, J.M.: Computational thinking. Commun. ACM **49**, 33–35 (2006)
31. Wylie, R., Chi, M.T.: 17 the Self-explanation Principle in Multimedia Learning. The Cambridge Handbook of Multimedia Learning, p. 413 (2014)
32. Xie, B., et al.: A theory of instruction for introductory programming skills. Comput. Sci. Educ. **29**(2–3), 205–253 (2019)

Evaluating Critical Reinforcement Learning Framework in the Field

Song Ju, Guojing Zhou, Mark Abdelshiheed, Tiffany Barnes, and Min Chi[✉]

Department of Computer Science, North Carolina State University,
Raleigh, NC 27695, USA
{sju2,gzhou3,mnabdels,tmbarnes,mchi}@ncsu.edu

Abstract. Reinforcement Learning (RL) is learning what action to take next by mapping *situations* to *actions* so as to maximize cumulative rewards. In recent years RL has achieved great success in inducing effective pedagogical policies for various interactive e-learning environments. However, it is often prohibitive to identify the *critical* pedagogical decisions that actually contribute to desirable learning outcomes. In this work, by utilizing the RL framework we defined *critical decisions* to be those states in which the agent has to take the optimal actions, and subsequently, the *Critical policy* as carrying out optimal actions in the critical states while acting randomly in others. We proposed a general *Critical-RL framework* for identifying critical decisions and inducing a Critical policy. The effectiveness of our Critical-RL framework is empirically evaluated from two perspectives: whether optimal actions *must* be carried out in critical states (*the necessary hypothesis*) and whether only carrying out optimal actions in critical states is as effective as a fully-executed RL policy (*the sufficient hypothesis*). Our results confirmed both hypotheses.

Keywords: Critical decisions · Reinforcement learning · ITS

1 Introduction

Intelligent Tutoring Systems (ITSs) have been shown to be effective for improving student learning. Most ITSs are adaptive instructional systems in that tutor decides what to do next. For example, the tutor can elicit the solution to the next step from the students with prompting and support or without. At each step, the ITS records its success or failure and may give feedback (e.g. correct/incorrect signals) and hints (suggestions for what to do next) automatically or on-demand. Alternatively, the tutor can choose to tell students the solution to the next step directly. Each of these tutor decisions will affect the students' subsequent actions and performance, and some may be more *impactful* than others. *Pedagogical policies* are used for the agent (tutor) to decide what action to take next in the face of alternatives.

Reinforcement Learning (RL) offers one of the most promising approaches to data-driven decision-making. RL algorithms are designed to induce effective

I. Roll et al. (Eds.): AIED 2021, LNAI 12748, pp. 215–227, 2021.
https://doi.org/10.1007/978-3-030-78292-4_18

policies that determine the best action for an agent to take in any given situation to maximize a cumulative reward. In recent years, RL, especially Deep RL, has achieved superhuman performance in several complex games [1,31,32]. However, different from the classic game-play situations where the ultimate goal is to make the agent effective, in human-centric tasks such as ITSs, the ultimate goal is for the agent to make the *student-system interactions* more productive and fruitful. Several researchers have studied the application of existing RL algorithms to improve the effectiveness of interactive e-learning environments such as ITSs [7,10,22,25–28,30,33,40,43]. While promising, relatively little work has been done to analyze, interpret, explain, or generalize RL-induced policies. While traditional hypothesis-driven, cause-and-effect approaches offer clear conceptual and causal insights that can be evaluated and interpreted, RL-induced policies especially Deep RL-induced ones, are often referred to as black-box models. This raises a major open question: *How can we identify the critical system pedagogical decisions that are linked to student learning outcomes?*

In this work, by utilizing the RL framework, we defined *critical decisions* to be those states in which the agent has to take the optimal actions and subsequently defined *Critical policy* as carrying out optimal actions in the critical states while acting randomly in others. We proposed a general *Critical-RL framework* for identifying critical decisions and inducing a Critical policy. In our prior work, we evaluated the effectiveness of our Critical-RL framework using simulations and our results showed that by carrying out critical decisions only, our Critical policy can be as effective as a fully executed RL policy. In this work, we *empirically* evaluate the Critical-RL framework in a classroom setting. To confirm whether the identified critical decisions are indeed critical, we argue that our identified critical decisions and induced Critical policy should satisfy two conditions.

First, they should satisfy the *Necessary Hypothesis* stating that it is *necessary* to carry out optimal actions in critical states otherwise the performance would suffer. To validate it, we compared two policies: Critical-optimal (Critical$_{opt}$) vs. Critical-suboptimal (Critical$_{sub}$). Both policies would carry out random actions in non-critical states and the only difference is that in critical states, Critical$_{opt}$ takes optimal actions while Critical$_{sub}$ takes suboptimal actions. As expected, our results showed that the former was indeed significantly more effective than the latter. Second, our induced Critical policy should satisfy the *Sufficient Hypothesis* stating that carrying out optimal actions in the critical states is *sufficient*. In other words, only carrying out optimal actions in critical states is as effective as a fully-executed RL policy. To validate it, we compared the Critical$_{opt}$ policy with a Full RL policy which takes optimal actions in every state. Our results showed that no significant difference was found between them.

In this work, we focus on pedagogical decisions at two levels of granularity: *problem* and *step*. More specifically, our tutor will first make a problem-level decision and then make step-level decisions based on the problem-level decision. For the former, our tutor first decides whether the next *problem* should be a worked example (WE), problem solving (PS), or a faded worked example (FWE). In WEs, students observe how the tutor solves a problem; in PSs students solve the problem themselves; in FWEs, the students and the tutor *co-construct* the solution. Based on the problem-level decision, the tutor then makes step-level decisions on whether to elicit the next solution step from the student or to show it to the student directly. We refer to such decisions as *elicit/tell* decisions. If WE is selected, an all-tell step policy will be carried out; if PS is selected, an all-elicit policy will be executed; finally, if FWE is selected, the tutor will decide whether to elicit or tell a step based on the corresponding induced step-level policy. While much of the prior work has relied on hand-coded or RL-induced pedagogical policies on these decisions, there is no well-established theory or widely accepted consensus on how WE vs. PS. vs. FWE can be best used and how they may impact students' learning. As far as we know, no prior research has investigated *when it is critical to give WE vs. PS vs. FWE*. In this work, by empirically confirming that our identified critical decisions and Critical policy satisfy the two hypotheses, we argue that the proposed Critical-RL framework sheds some light on identifying the moments that offering WE, PS, or FWE can make a difference.

2   Related Work

2.1   Applying RL to ITSs

Prior work has shown that RL can induce effective pedagogical policies for Intelligent Tutoring Systems [2,3,6,11,14,21,38]. For example, Shen et al. [29] applied an offline RL approach, value iteration, to induce a pedagogical policy with the goal of improving students' learning performance. Empirical evaluation results suggested that the RL policy can improve certain learners' performance as compared to a random policy. Mandel et al. [14] applied a partially observable Markov decision process (POMDP) to induce a pedagogical policy that aims to maximize students' learning gain. The effectiveness of the POMDP policy was evaluated by comparing it with an expert policy, and a random policy, on both simulated students and real students. Results showed that the POMDP policy significantly outperformed the other two. Wang et al. [38] applied a variety of Deep RL (DRL) approach to induce pedagogical policies aims at improving students' normalized learning gain in an educational game. Simulation evaluation results suggested that the DRL policies were more effective than a linear model-based RL policy. Finally, Zhou et al. [41] applied Hierarchical Reinforcement Learning (HRL) to induce a pedagogical policy to improve students' normalized learning gain. The HRL policy makes decisions first at the problem level and then at the step level. In a classroom study, the HRL policy was compared with two step level policies: DQN and random. Results showed that the HRL policy was significantly more effective than the other two.

In sum, prior work suggests that employing RL-induced pedagogical policies can improve the effectiveness of ITSs. However, despite this effectiveness, RL policies often make a lot of fine-grained decisions in training. For example, the HRL policy induced by Zhou et al. [41] can make over 400 decisions in 12 training problems. Therefore, it can be difficult to identify and study the origin of this fine-grained decision-making style of RL policies.

2.2   Identifying Critical Decisions

Recent advances in computational neuroscience have enabled researchers to simulate and study the decision-making mechanisms of humans and animals through computational approaches [13,15,19,24,34]. A number of works showed that RL-like learning and decision-making processes exist in humans/animals and we humans use immediate reward and Q-value to make decisions [13,15]. In RL, the Q-value is defined as the expected cumulative reward for taking an action a at state s and following the policy until the end of the episode. Therefore, the difference of Q-values between two actions reflects the magnitude of difference in the final outcomes. Motivated by research in human and animal behaviors, a lot of RL work has applied Q-value difference to measure the importance of a state and decide when to give advice in a simulated environment called the "Student-Teacher" framework [8,9,36,44]. In this framework, a "student" agent learns from the interaction with the environment, while a "teacher" agent provides action suggestions to accelerate the learning process. Their research question is not what to advise but when to advise, especially with a limited budget of advice. Results showed that the Q-value difference approach is significantly better than baseline strategies such as random advising and early advising. Overall, prior studies explored the problem of when to give advice in simulated environments. They showed that Q-value difference is an accurate heuristic function to estimate the importance of a state. However, they have not considered the immediate rewards and have not validated their findings on human students.

2.3   WE, PS and FWE

A variety of studies have explored the effectiveness of WE, PS, FWE, and their various combinations [16,17,20,23,37,39,42]. For example, Mclaren et al. compared WE-PS pairs with PS-only in a study [17] and WE-only, PS-only and WE-PS pairs in another study [16]. Overall, results suggested that studying WE can be as effective as doing PS, but students spend less time on WE. For FWE-involved studies, Renkl et al. [23] compared WE-FWE-PS with WE-PS pairs. Results showed that the WE-FWE-PS condition significantly outperformed the WE-PS condition, and there is no significant time-on-task difference between them. Similarly, Najar et al. [20] compared adaptive WE/FWE/PS with WE-PS pairs and found the former is significantly more effective than the latter. In summary, prior studies have demonstrated that adaptively alternating amongst WE, PS, and FWE is more effective than hand-coded expert rules in terms of improving student learning. However, it is still not clear which alternating is critical to the student learning outcome.

3   Method

3.1   Critical Deep Q-Network

To determine whether a state is critical, our Critical-RL framework considers both short-term reward (immediate reward) and long-term reward (Q-value difference). For the former, we consider the amount of the immediate rewards over all possible actions to determine the criticalness of a state. One of the primary challenges is that *on most ITSs we only have delayed rewards, and immediate rewards are often not available.* The most appropriate rewards to use in ITSs are student learning performance, which is typically delayed until the entire trajectory is complete. This is due to the complex nature of learning, which makes it difficult to assess students' knowledge level moment by moment, and more importantly, many instructional interventions that boost short-term performance may not be effective over the long term. To tackle this issue, we apply a Deep Neural Network-based approach called InferNet [4] to infer the immediate rewards from delayed rewards. Prior work has evaluated the effectiveness of inferred rewards, and results showed that inferred immediate rewards can be as effective as real immediate rewards in our application. Therefore, we think the *inferred* immediate rewards from InferNet are reliable to be considered as short-term rewards in our Critical-RL framework. More specifically, we apply the elbow method on the distribution of the inferred immediate rewards to determine two thresholds: one is a positive reward threshold above which the agent should pursue and the other is a negative reward threshold below which the agent should avoid. If any action on a state can lead to an inferred immediate reward either higher than the positive threshold or lower than the negative one, it should be critical.

To get the long-term rewards, our Critical-RL framework used Deep Q-Network (DQN). In recent years, DQN has shown a strong ability to handle complicated tasks, such as robot control and video game playing [18]. DQN approximates the Q-value function using deep neural networks following the Bellman equation. In the original DQN, the Q-values are calculated based on the assumption that the agent takes the optimal action in every state. However, in our Critical-RL framework, the **Critical policy** takes optimal actions only in the critical states, and takes random action in the non-critical states. To accommodate this difference, we modify the original Bellman equation:

$$Q(s,a) = \begin{cases} r + \gamma max Q(s',a') & s' \text{ is critical} \\ r + \gamma mean Q(s',a') & s' \text{ is non-critical.} \end{cases} \tag{1}$$

In Eq. 1, when the state s' is critical, its value function is the max Q-value of the optimal action while when it is non-critical, its value function is the mean Q-value over all the available actions. To induce the Critical-DQN policy, during each iteration in training, our algorithm first calculates the Q-value difference $\Delta(Q)$ for all states in the training dataset, where $\Delta(Q) = \max_a Q(s,a) - \min_a Q(s,a)$. Then the median of the differences is defined as a threshold. If the $\Delta(Q)$ of a state is greater than the threshold, it is critical; otherwise, it is non-critical. After the critical states have been determined, the algorithm follows Eq. 1 to update the Q-values. Then in the next iteration, the updated Q-values are applied to determine a new median threshold to update the critical states recursively. This process will repeat until convergence. Once the Critical-RL policy is induced, for any given state we calculate its Q-value difference and compare it with the corresponding median threshold. If the Q-value difference is larger than the threshold, the state is critical.

3.2 Hierarchical RL Policy Induction

Our tutor can make both problem-level decisions (WE/PS/FWE) and step-level decisions (elicit/tell). With the two levels of granularity, we extended the existing flat-RL algorithm to Hierarchical RL (HRL), which aims to induce an optimal policy to make decisions at different levels. Most HRL algorithms are based upon an extension of Markov Decision Processes (MDPs) called Discrete Semi-Markov Decision Processes (SMDPs). Different from MDPs, SMDPs have an additional set of complex activities [5] or options [35], each of which can invoke other activities recursively, thus allowing the hierarchical policy to function. The *complex* activities are distinct from the primitive actions in that a complex activity may contain multiple *primitive* actions. In our applications, WE, PS, and FWE are complex activities while elicit and tell are primitive actions. For HRL, learning occurs at multiple levels. A global learning generates a policy for the complex level decisions and local learning generates a policy for the primitive level decisions in each complex activity. More importantly, the goal of local learning is not inducing the optimal policy for the overall task, but the optimal policy for the corresponding complex activity. Therefore, our HRL approach learns a global problem level policy to make decisions on WE/PS/FWE and learns a local step level policy for each problem to choose between elicit/tell. More specifically, both problem and step level policies were learned by recursively using DQN or Critical-DQN to update the Q-value function until convergence.

4 Policy Induction

Training Corpus: Our training dataset contains a total of 1,148 students' interaction logs collected over six semesters' classroom studies (16 Fall to 19 Spring). During the studies, all students used the same tutor, followed the same general procedure, studied the same training materials, and worked through the same training problems. The components for RL induction are defined as follows:

State: From the student-system interaction logs, 142 features were extracted to represent the student learning state, which can be categorized into five groups: *Autonomy*(10) features describe the amount of work done by the student; *Temporal*(29) features are the time-related information during tutoring; *Problem Solving*(35) features indicate the context of the problem itself; *Performance*(57) features denote student's performance, and *Student Action*(11) features record the student behavior information. **Action:** Our tutor can make both problem and step-level decisions. There are two actions (elicit/tell) at the step level and three actions (WE/PS/FWE) at the problem level. **Reward:** There's no immediate reward during tutoring and the delayed reward is the students' Normalized Learning Gain (NLG), which measures their learning gain irrespective of their incoming competence. NLG is defined as $\frac{posttest - pretest}{\sqrt{1 - pretest}}$, where 1 is maximum score for both pre- and post-test.

Three Policies: We induced a standard DQN policy as the Full policy to carry out optimal actions in all states. Note that our prior work showed that the Full policy significantly outperformed the expert-designed policy on improving students' learning performance [12]. In this work, we induced a Critical-DQN policy to identify critical states. The $Critical_{opt}$ policy would carry out optimal actions in critical states but the $Critical_{sub}$ policy would take sub-optimal actions with minimum Q-value. In non-critical states, both of them acted randomly.

5 Empirical Experiment

Participants: This study was given to students as a homework assignment in an undergraduate Computer Science class in the Spring of 2020. Students were told to complete the study in one week and they will be graded based on demonstrated effort rather than learning performance. 164 students were randomly assigned into three conditions: $N = 58$ for $Critical_{opt}$, $N = 55$ for $Critical_{sub}$ and $N = 51$ for Full. Due to preparation for final exams and the length of study, 129 students completed the study. In addition, 14 students were excluded from our subsequent statistical analysis in which 8 students performed perfectly in the pre-test and 6 students worked in groups. The final group sizes were $N = 37$ for $Critical_{opt}$, $N = 39$ for $Critical_{sub}$ and $N = 39$ for Full. A Chi-square test on the relationship between students' condition and their completion rate found no significant difference among the conditions: $\chi^2(2) = 0.167$, $p = 0.92$.

Pyrenees Tutor: Our tutor is a web-based ITS teaching probability. It covers ten major principles of probability, such as the Additional Theorem, De Morgan's Theorem, and Bayes Rule. The Pyrenees tutor provides step-by-step adaptive instructions, immediate feedback, and on-demand hints to prompt students' learning. More specifically, help in Pyrenees tutor is provided via a sequence of increasingly specific hints, in which the last hint tells the student exactly what to do next.

Procedure and Grading: In the classroom study, students were required to complete 4 phases: 1) pre-training, 2) pre-test, 3) training on Pyrenees tutor, and 4) post-test. During the **pre-training** phase, all students studied the domain principles through a probability textbook, reviewed some examples, and solved certain training problems. Students then took a **pre-test** which contained 14 probability problems. The textbook was not available at this phase and students were not given feedback on their answers, nor were they allowed to go back to earlier questions. This was also true for the post-test. During **training**, students in all three conditions received the same 12 problems in the same order on Pyrenees tutor. The minimal number of steps needed to solve each problem ranged from 20 to 50, which included defining variables, applying principles, and solving equations. Each domain principle was applied at least twice in the 12 problems, and all of the students could access the textbook during this phase. Finally, all of the students completed a **post-test** with 20 problems: 14 of the problems were isomorphic to the pre-test, and the remaining six were non-isomorphic complicated problems. The pre- and post-test were graded in a double-blind manner by experienced graders. All scores are normalized in the range of 0 to 1.

6   Results

We will report our results based on the two hypotheses. For the Necessary Hypothesis, we compare Critical$_{opt}$ vs. Critical$_{sub}$ conditions and for the Sufficient Hypothesis, we compare Critical$_{opt}$ vs. Full conditions.

6.1   Necessary Hypothesis (Critical$_{opt}$ vs. Critical$_{sub}$)

Table 1 shows the comparisons between Critical$_{opt}$ (in gray) vs. Critical$_{sub}$. The left four columns show the mean and standard deviation (SD) of their learning performance, percentage of critical states and tutor decisions with the corresponding pairwise t-test results. No significant difference was found between the two conditions on pre-test: $t(112) = 0.56$, $p = .57$, $d = 0.13$. The result suggests that the two conditions are balanced in terms of incoming competence.

Table 1. Results of necessary hypothesis: Critical$_{opt}$ vs. Critical$_{sub}$

Learning performance				
	Critical$_{opt}$	Critical$_{sub}$	Pairwise T-test result	Full
Pre	0.75 (0.18)	0.72 (0.20)	$t(112) = 0.56$, $p = .570$, $d = 0.13$	0.70(0.19)
Iso Post	0.89 (0.16)	0.86 (0.16)	$t(112) = 0.81$, $p = .420$, $d = 0.18$	0.84(0.20)
Full Post	0.82 (0.19)	0.78 (0.19)	$t(112) = 0.99$, $p = .320$, $d = 0.23$	0.75(0.20)
Iso NLG	0.70 (0.36)	0.40 (0.85)	$t(112) = 2.27$, $p = .025^*$, $d = 0.52$	0.56(0.40)
Full NLG	0.41 (0.39)	0.01 (1.25)	$t(112) = 2.18$, $p = .031^*$, $d = 0.49$	0.18(0.55)
Time	94.5 (35.1)	78.1 (26.7)	$t(112) = 2.30$, $p = .023^*$, $d = 0.52$	91.5(31.7)
Percentage of critical states				
Prob-Level	46.9 (23.4)	31.5 (17.6)	$t(112) = 3.69$, $p < .001^*$, $d = 0.84$	38.4(12.4)
Step-Level	60.2 (20.1)	45.3 (26.0)	$t(112) = 2.42$, $p = .017^*$, $d = 0.55$	62.1(34.0)
Tutor decisions				
PS	3.56 (1.85)	2.38 (1.41)	$t(112) = 3.60$, $p < .001^*$, $d = 0.81$	3.32(0.81)
WE	2.54 (1.87)	5.13 (1.51)	$t(112) = -7.27$, $p < .001^*$, $d = 1.65$	5.24(1.19)
FWE	3.90 (2.00)	2.49 (1.34)	$t(112) = 4.01$, $p < .001^*$, $d = 0.91$	1.43(1.10)
Elicit	83.3 (49.2)	44.0 (30.6)	$t(112) = 4.37$, $p < .001^*$, $d = 0.99$	33.2(35.1)
Tell	82.9 (50.3)	55.4 (35.2)	$t(112) = 3.06$, $p = .003^*$, $d = 0.69$	29.8(28.3)

Improvement Through Training: To measure the improvement students gained through the ITS training, we compared their pre-test and isomorphic post-test scores. A repeated measures analysis showed that both conditions scored significantly higher in the post-test than in the pre-test: $F(1, 38) = 13.68$, $p = .0004$, $\eta = 0.392$ for $\text{Critical}_{\text{opt}}$ and $F(1, 38) = 11.5$, $p = .0011$, $\eta = 0.362$ for $\text{Critical}_{\text{sub}}$. It suggests that our ITS indeed helps students learning regardless of the pedagogical policies deployed.

Learning Performance: To investigate students' learning performance between the two conditions, we compared their isomorphic NLG (calculated based on Pre- and Iso Post-test) and full NLG (based on Pre- and Full Post-test). The full post-test contains six additional multiple-principle problems. Pairwise t-tests showed that $\text{Critical}_{\text{opt}}$ scored significantly higher than $\text{Critical}_{\text{sub}}$ on both the isomorphic NLG: $t(112) = 2.27$, $p = .025$, $d = 0.52$ and the full NLG: $t(112) = 2.18$, $p = .031$, $d = 0.49$. The results showed that the $\text{Critical}_{\text{opt}}$ policy is more effective than the $\text{Critical}_{\text{sub}}$ policy. It supports our hypothesis that different actions in the critical states can make a significant difference, so optimal actions *must* be made in critical states.

Time on Task and Percentage of Critical States: A pairwise t-test analysis revealed that $\text{Critical}_{\text{opt}}$ spend significantly more time (measured in minutes) than $\text{Critical}_{\text{sub}}$ in the training phase: $t(112) = 2.30$, $p = .023$, $d = 0.52$. The middle section in Table 1 presents the percentage of critical states (both problem and step level) each condition experienced. Pairwise t-test showed that $\text{Critical}_{\text{opt}}$ experienced significantly more critical states than $\text{Critical}_{\text{sub}}$ on both problem level: $t(112) = 3.69$, $p < .001$, $d = 0.84$ and step level: $t(112) = 2.42$, $p = .017$, $d = 0.55$. This suggests that the $\text{Critical}_{\text{opt}}$ policy is more likely to lead students to the critical intersections that make a difference.

Tutor Decisions: We investigated the number of different types of actions students received during training, as shown in the lower section of the Table 1. *Note that for step level decisions, we only considered the elicits and tells in the FWEs.* For the problem level, $\text{Critical}_{\text{opt}}$ received significantly more PS: $t(112) = 3.60$, $p < .001$, $d = 0.81$, more FWE: $t(112) = 4.01$, $p < .001$, $d = 0.91$ and fewer WE: $t(112) = -7.27$, $p < .001$, $d = 1.65$ than $\text{Critical}_{\text{sub}}$. For the step level, the former also received significantly more elicit: $t(112) = 4.37$, $p < .001$, $d = 0.99$ and more tell: $t(112) = 3.06$, $p = .003$, $d = 0.69$ than $\text{Critical}_{\text{sub}}$. The results indicate that the $\text{Critical}_{\text{sub}}$ policy prefers WEs while the $\text{Critical}_{\text{opt}}$ policy prefers PSs and FWEs.

6.2   Sufficient Hypothesis ($\text{Critical}_{\text{opt}}$ vs. Full)

In the Sufficient Hypothesis, we expect no significant difference in learning performance between the $\text{Critical}_{\text{opt}}$ and Full conditions. To align the analysis, we still focus on the three aspects as above (learning performance, critical states, tutor decisions). To save space, the statistics of the Full condition were shown in the rightmost column in Table 1. A pairwise t-test showed that there is no significant difference between $\text{Critical}_{\text{opt}}$ (2nd column in gray) vs. Full (last column) on the pre-test score: $t(112) = 1.18$, $p = .24$, $d = 0.27$. This suggests again that our random assignment indeed balanced students' incoming competence.

Improvement Through Training: A repeated measures analysis using test-type (pre-test and isomorphic post-test) as factors and test score as dependent measure showed that similar to Critical$_{opt}$, Full scored significantly higher in isomorphic post-test than in pre-test: $F(1, 36) = 11.0$, $p = .0015$, $\eta = 0.363$.

Learning Performance: The pairwise t-tests showed that there is no significant difference between the Critical$_{opt}$ and Full conditions on the two learning metrics, isomorphic NLG: $t(112) = 1.00$, $p = .32$, $d = 0.23$, full NLG: $t(112) = 1.24$, $p = .217$, $d = 0.29$. It implied that only carrying out optimal actions in critical states can be as effective as a fully-executed policy.

Furthermore, to determine whether these null results are significant, that is, the Critical$_{opt}$ is indeed perform as effective as Full, we calculated the effect size on all the comparisons and we found that they are all not statistically significant in that $\beta < 0.8$. On the other hand, across all the comparisons, Critical$_{opt}$ was slightly better than the Full. This result suggests that if we have enough population samples, the former can outperform the latter.

Time on Task and Percentage of Critical States: A pairwise t-test analysis revealed that the Critical$_{opt}$ condition spend a similar amount of time as the Full condition in the training phase: $t(112) = 0.42$, $p = .678$, $d = 0.10$. Pairwise t-tests showed that the Critical$_{opt}$ condition has significantly more critical states than the Full condition in the problem level: $t(112) = 2.02$, $p = .046$, $d = 0.46$ but no difference in the step level: $t(112) = -0.29$, $p = .769$, $d = 0.07$. The result suggests that the optimal actions in the non-critical states could reduce the chance of entering critical states.

Tutor Decisions: For the problem level, the Critical$_{opt}$ condition received significantly more FWE: $t(112) = 6.91$, $p < .001$, $d = 1.59$, fewer WE: $t(112) = -7.50$, $p < .001$, $d = 1.72$ decisions than the Full condition, but no difference on PS: $t(112) = 0.72$, $p = .472$, $d = 0.17$. For the step level, the Critical$_{opt}$ condition received significantly more elicit: $t(112) = 5.50$, $p < .001$, $d = 1.26$ and more tell: $t(112) = 5.83$, $p = .003$, $d = 1.34$ than the Full condition. The results suggest that the random actions in non-critical states could lead the RL policy to give more FWE and fewer WE in critical states.

7   Conclusion

In this study, we evaluated the effectiveness of the Critical-RL framework in identifying critical decisions through an empirical classroom study. Specifically, we compared the Critical$_{opt}$ policy with two baseline policies: a Critical$_{sub}$ policy and a Full policy. The comparisons are based upon two hypotheses: 1) optimal actions must be carried out in critical states (the Necessary Hypothesis), 2) only carrying out optimal actions in critical states can be as effective as the fully-executed policy (the Sufficient Hypothesis). The result shows that in terms of students' learning performance, 1) the Critical$_{opt}$ condition significantly outperforms the Critical$_{sub}$ condition; 2) more importantly, the former performs as effective as the Full condition. It suggests that our Critical-RL framework indeed identifies the critical decisions and satisfies the two hypotheses that 1) taking optimal actions in the identified critical states is significantly more effective than taking suboptimal actions; 2) only taking optimal actions during the critical moments can be as effective as taking optimal actions in every moment.

Acknowledgements. This research was supported by the NSF Grants: #1726550, #1651909, and #2013502.

References

1. Andrychowicz, M., Baker, B., et al.: Learning dexterous in-hand manipulation. arXiv preprint arXiv:1808.00177 (2018)
2. Ausin, M.S., Azizsoltani, H., Barnes, T., Chi, M.: Leveraging deep reinforcement learning for pedagogical policy induction in an intelligent tutoring system. In: EDM (2019)
3. Sanz Ausin, M., Maniktala, M., Barnes, T., Chi, M.: Exploring the impact of simple explanations and agency on batch deep reinforcement learning induced pedagogical Policies. In: Bittencourt, I.I., Cukurova, M., Muldner, K., Luckin, R., Millán, E. (eds.) AIED 2020. LNCS (LNAI), vol. 12163, pp. 472–485. Springer, Cham (2020). https://doi.org/10.1007/978-3-030-52237-7_38
4. Ausin, M.S., Maniktala, M., Barnes, T., Chi, M.: Tackling the credit assignment problem in reinforcement learning-induced pedagogical policies with neural networks. In: AIED (2021)
5. Barto, A.G., Mahadevan, S.: Recent advances in hierarchical reinforcement learning. Discret. Event Dyn. Syst. **13**(1–2), 41–77 (2003). https://doi.org/10.1023/A:1022140919877
6. Beck, J., Woolf, B.P., Beal, C.R.: Advisor: a machine learning architecture for intelligent tutor construction. In: AAAI/IAAI, pp. 552–557 (2000)
7. Chi, M., VanLehn, K., Litman, D., Jordan, P.: Empirically evaluating the application of reinforcement learning to the induction of effective and adaptive pedagogical strategies. User Model. User-Adap. Inter. **21**(1–2), 137–180 (2011). https://doi.org/10.1007/s11257-010-9093-1
8. Clouse, J.A.: On integrating apprentice learning and reinforcement learning. Ph.D. thesis (1996)
9. Fachantidis, A., Taylor, M.E., Vlahavas, I.P.: Learning to teach reinforcement learning agents. Mach. Learn. Knowl. Extract. **1**, 21–42 (2017)
10. Iglesias, A., Martínez, P., Aler, R., Fernández, F.: Reinforcement learning of pedagogical policies in adaptive and intelligent educational systems. Knowl.-Based Syst. **22**(4), 266–270 (2009)
11. Ju, S., Zhou, G., Azizsoltani, H., Barnes, T., Chi, M.: Identifying critical pedagogical decisions through adversarial deep reinforcement learning. In: EDM (2019)
12. Ju, S., Zhou, G., Barnes, T., Chi, M.: Pick the moment: identifying critical pedagogical decisions using long-short term rewards. In: EDM (2020)
13. Li, J., Daw, N.D.: Signals in human striatum are appropriate for policy update rather than value prediction, **31** (2011)

14. Mandel, T., Liu, Y.E., Levine, S., Brunskill, E., Popovic, Z.: Offline policy evaluation across representations with applications to educational games. In: AAMAS, pp. 1077–1084 (2014)
15. McClure, S.M., Laibson, D.I., Loewenstein, G., Cohen, J.D.: Separate neural systems value immediate and delayed monetary rewards. Science **306**, 503–507 (2004)
16. McLaren, B.M., Isotani, S.: When is it best to learn with all worked examples? In: Biswas, G., Bull, S., Kay, J., Mitrovic, A. (eds.) AIED 2011. LNCS (LNAI), vol. 6738, pp. 222–229. Springer, Heidelberg (2011). https://doi.org/10.1007/978-3-642-21869-9_30
17. McLaren, B.M., Lim, S.J., Koedinger, K.R.: When and how often should worked examples be given to students? New results and a summary of the current state of research. In: CogSci, pp. 2176–2181 (2008)
18. Mnih, V., et al.: Human-level control through deep reinforcement learning. Nature **518**, 529–533 (2015)
19. Morris, G., Nevet, A., Arkadir, D., Vaadia, E., Bergman, H.: Midbrain dopamine neurons encode decisions for future action. Nat. Neurosci. **9**(8), 1057–1063 (2006)
20. Najar, A.S., Mitrovic, A., McLaren, B.M.: Adaptive support versus alternating worked examples and tutored problems: which leads to better learning? In: Dimitrova, V., Kuflik, T., Chin, D., Ricci, F., Dolog, P., Houben, G.-J. (eds.) UMAP 2014. LNCS, vol. 8538, pp. 171–182. Springer, Cham (2014). https://doi.org/10.1007/978-3-319-08786-3_15
21. Narasimhan, K., Kulkarni, T., Barzilay, R.: Language understanding for text-based games using deep reinforcement learning. arXiv preprint arXiv:1506.08941 (2015)
22. Rafferty, A.N., Brunskill, E., et al.: Faster teaching via POMDP planning. Cogn. Sci. **40**(6), 1290–1332 (2016)
23. Renkl, A., Atkinson, R.K., Maier, U.H., Staley, R.: From example study to problem solving: smooth transitions help learning. J. Exp. Educ. **70**(4), 293–315 (2002)
24. Roesch, M.R., Calu, D.J., Schoenbaum, G.: Dopamine neurons encode the better option in rats deciding between different delayed or sized rewards. Nat. Neurosci. **10**(12), 1615–1624 (2007)
25. Rowe, J., Mott, B., Lester, J.: Optimizing player experience in interactive narrative planning: a modular reinforcement learning approach. In: Tenth Artificial Intelligence and Interactive Digital Entertainment Conference (2014)
26. Rowe, J.P., Lester, J.C.: Improving student problem solving in narrative-centered learning environments: a modular reinforcement learning framework. In: Conati, C., Heffernan, N., Mitrovic, A., Verdejo, M.F. (eds.) AIED 2015. LNCS (LNAI), vol. 9112, pp. 419–428. Springer, Cham (2015). https://doi.org/10.1007/978-3-319-19773-9_42
27. Shen, S., Ausin, M.S., Mostafavi, B., Chi, M.: Improving learning & reducing time: a constrained action-based reinforcement learning approach. In: UMAP (2018)
28. Shen, S., Chi, M.: Aim low: correlation-based feature selection for model-based reinforcement learning. In: EDM (2016)
29. Shen, S., Chi, M.: Reinforcement learning: the sooner the better, or the later the better? In: Proceedings of the 2016 Conference on User Modeling Adaptation and Personalization, pp. 37–44. ACM (2016)
30. Shen, S., Mostafavi, B., Lynch, C., Barnes, T., Chi, M.: Empirically evaluating the effectiveness of POMDP vs. MDP towards the pedagogical strategies induction. In: Penstein Rosé, C., et al. (eds.) AIED 2018. LNCS (LNAI), vol. 10948, pp. 327–331. Springer, Cham (2018). https://doi.org/10.1007/978-3-319-93846-2_61
31. Silver, D., et al.: Mastering the game of go with deep neural networks and tree search. Nature **529**(7587), 484–489 (2016)

32. Silver, D., Hubert, T., Schrittwieser, J., et al.: A general reinforcement learning algorithm that masters chess, shogi, and go through self-play. Science **362**(6419), 1140–1144 (2018)
33. Stamper, J.C., Eagle, M., Barnes, T., Croy, M.: Experimental evaluation of automatic hint generation for a logic tutor. In: Biswas, G., Bull, S., Kay, J., Mitrovic, A. (eds.) AIED 2011. LNCS (LNAI), vol. 6738, pp. 345–352. Springer, Heidelberg (2011). https://doi.org/10.1007/978-3-642-21869-9_45
34. Sul, J.H., Jo, S., Lee, D., Jung, M.W.: Role of rodent secondary motor cortex in value-based action selection. Nat. Neurosci. **14**(9), 1202–1208 (2011)
35. Sutton, R.S., Precup, D., Singh, S.: Between MDPs and semi-MDPs: a framework for temporal abstraction in reinforcement learning. Artif. Intell. **112**(1–2), 181–211 (1999)
36. Torrey, L., Taylor, M.E.: Teaching on a budget: agents advising agents in reinforcement learning. In: International conference on Autonomous Agents and Multi-Agent Systems, AAMAS 2013, pp. 1053–1060 (2013)
37. Van Gog, T., Kester, L., Paas, F.: Effects of worked examples, example-problem, and problem-example pairs on novices' learning. Contemp. Educ. Psychol. **36**(3), 212–218 (2011)
38. Wang, P., Rowe, J., Min, W., Mott, B., Lester, J.: Interactive narrative personalization with deep reinforcement learning. In: Proceedings of the Twenty-Sixth International Joint Conference on Artificial Intelligence (2017)
39. Zhou, G.: Big, little, or both? Exploring the impact of granularity on learning for students with different incoming competence. In: CogSci (2019)
40. Zhou, G., et al.: Towards closing the loop: bridging machine-induced pedagogical policies to learning theories. In: EDM (2017)
41. Zhou, G., Azizsoltani, H., Ausin, M.S., Barnes, T., Chi, M.: Hierarchical reinforcement learning for pedagogical policy induction. In: Isotani, S., Millán, E., Ogan, A., Hastings, P., McLaren, B., Luckin, R. (eds.) AIED 2019. LNCS (LNAI), vol. 11625, pp. 544–556. Springer, Cham (2019). https://doi.org/10.1007/978-3-030-23204-7_45
42. Zhou, G., Price, T.W., Lynch, C., Barnes, T., Chi, M.: The impact of granularity on worked examples and problem solving. In: CogSci, pp. 2817–2822 (2015)
43. Zhou, G., Yang, X., Azizsoltani, H., Barnes, T., Chi, M.: Improving student-tutor interaction through data-driven explanation of hierarchical reinforcement induced pedagogical policies. In: UMAP. ACM (2020)
44. Zimmer, M., Viappiani, P., Weng, P.: Teacher-student framework: a reinforcement learning approach. In: AAMAS Workshop Autonomous Robots and Multirobot Systems (2013)

Machine Learning Models and Their Development Process as Learning Affordances for Humans

Carmel Kent[1](✉), Muhammad Ali Chaudhry[2], Mutlu Cukurova[2], Ibrahim Bashir[1], Hannah Pickard[3], Chris Jenkins[3], Benedict du Boulay[4], Anissa Moeini[1], and Rosemary Luckin[2]

[1] EDUCATE Ventures, London, UK
[2] UCL Knowledge Lab, University College London, London, UK
[3] ZISHI, OSTC Group, London, UK
[4] University of Sussex, Brighton, UK

Abstract. This paper explores the relationship between unsupervised machine learning models, and the mental models of those who develop or use them. In particular, we consider unsupervised models, as well as the 'organisational co-learning process' that creates them, as learning affordances. The co-learning process involves inputs originating both from the human participants' shared semantics, as well as from the data. By combining these, the process as well as the resulting computational models afford a newly shaped mental model, which is potentially more resistant to the biases of human mental models. We illustrate this organisational co-learning process with a case study involving unsupervised modelling via commonly used methods such as dimension reduction and clustering. Our case study describes how a trading and training company engaged in the co-learning process, and how its mental models of trading behavior were shaped (and afforded) by the resulting unsupervised machine learning model. The paper argues that this kind of co-learning process can play a significant role in human learning, by shaping and safeguarding participants' mental models, precisely because the models are unsupervised, and thus potentially lead to learning from unexpected or inexplicit patterns.

Keywords: Learners' mental models · Unsupervised machine learning · Co-learning process

1 Introduction

It is well established in the learning literature that presenting learners with a simplified model of whatever is to be understood is a helpful step in learning [1]. One example of these simplified models is the use of "notional machines" in teaching about programs, computers and programming [2]. The programming teacher offers analogies such as "a variable is like a box" or possibly draws a simplified diagram of how a loop in a program works. Of course, learners' consequent mental models will not normally exactly match

© Springer Nature Switzerland AG 2021
I. Roll et al. (Eds.): AIED 2021, LNAI 12748, pp. 228–240, 2021.
https://doi.org/10.1007/978-3-030-78292-4_19

the simplified model that was presented, but they are normally influenced by it, and such simplified models also help towards a better understanding of the more complex truth from which the simplified model has been derived. The use of simplified models can assist organisations as well as individuals in learning new material, as well as about themselves. In the case of managers engaging in self-understanding of their organisation [3], machine learning (ML) techniques applied to organisational data can act as a mirror back to them and thus to the organisation [4]. In this respect, unsupervised learning methods play a particular role as they are more likely to reveal factors that the managers were not explicitly aware of. This paper extends on a preliminary work [5], and its main contribution is not in the modelling itself, but rather in the theoretical postulation that ML models, generated by unsupervised methods, can be used as learning affordances to support the development of the mental models of the managers in an organisation. For clarity in what follows, we are not concerned here with how the managers' changed mental models diffused through the organisation, but with the fact that something changed in the mental models of those managers.

The ZISHI/OSTC company trades in "futures"[1] and is a training company largely for university graduates, who join the company to learn the art of trading. The senior training managers who were leading this work in ZISHI, and were also interviewed in this study, are interchangeably referred to throughout this paper as either managers, trainers or experts. In order for them to support their learners (during and after two months of formal training), and to design mentoring/training tools for them, they needed first to understand what did trading actually look like in their own context, after years of nurturing tacit mental models. The trainers certainly had a strong sense that different traders traded in different ways and had developed a partial typology of trading behaviors: for example, some traders preferred to work in volatile markets, others in more stable markets. Based on this implicit mental model, trainers might suggest different markets to individual traders based on this preference. However, the typology had not been reified within the company and had remained largely tacit.

In an attempt to define 'learning', [6] (adapted from [7]) states that learning is *"a process that leads to change, which occurs as a result of experience and increases the potential for improved performance and future learning"* (p. 3). Therefore, in order to help the company better understand its traders' behavior and maintain a culture of learning and change [8], we used unsupervised ML methods to arrive at four multidimensional profiles of trading behavior. In parallel, we asked the company to generate its own, till then largely tacit [9], trading behavior profiles into written descriptions. We were then able to compare these data-driven profiles with the company's self-generated profiling. After comparison and validation, the data-driven profiles (being validated as a refinement of the original mental profiling model) were used as the basis of a predictive decision support tools for hiring and mentoring, both tools are out of the scope of this paper.

We term the process of crafting the four behavioral profiles using ML methods a 'co-learning process', since this is a process combined of human 'supervision' in some of its stages, where the experts' semantics guides the analysis, and is unsupervised in

---

[1] Futures are derivative financial contracts that obligate the parties to transact an asset at a predetermined future date and price.

other stages, where the modeling is being guided purely by the data patterns. In that sense, it embodies some of the notions of connectivism [10] or extended minds [11], where learning is not considered as residing within a single learner, but rather stems from the continuous interactions between learners, their organisation, and artefacts such as data.

This paper is organised into five sections. The next section focuses on the distinction between unsupervised ML models and mental models. Section 3 describes the ways in which unsupervised ML methods were used as potential learning affordances. Section 4 compares the resulting ML model with the company's original mental model. Section 5 concludes and summarises our findings.

2   Unsupervised ML Models and Mental Models

Raw data are not independent, contextless, self-sufficient repositories of meaning [12]. Contextualised modeling of data, using statistical methods and, particularly, ML, creates possibilities for assigning existing semantics to the models, as well as for creating new semantics, which in turn, can be used as **"learning affordances"**. The concept of affordance describes the complementary relationship between an environment and what it offers or provides to the actors within it [13]. The process of data modeling, which we refer to here as a "learning affordance", can start from a phase of feature engineering, in which the existing semantics can be attached to the raw data to shape it in a contextualised way. Later the process can generate (or rather bring to the surface) new hidden or implicit meanings, using methods such as unsupervised ML. In the unsupervised learning phase, hidden statistical relationships, or other statistical constructs (such as distributions) will emerge, to be interpreted via the stakeholders' original mental models (which are based on expectations, projections, cognitive biases, and emotions), as well as generating new inferences and new assumptions. This can be an iterative process, in which the unsupervised model will be reviewed, new hypotheses raised, and the model tweaked and refined to serve an augmented purpose. Its purpose, as we will suggest in this paper, can be to support individual or organisational learning, by externalising and simplifying existing mental models of the world they are learning about.

This paper argues that the model generated by unsupervised methods provides a learning affordance, not just because it simplifies, corrects and highlights different aspects of an existing mental model, but also because it can enable the creation of a new semantics and a new language to revise that mental model. The ML model is generated by a process, which by itself can be considered as a learning affordance in the sense that it offers a useful dialogical entity between knowledge existing in human minds, and the patterns arising from the data, and by means of that – might cancel out mutual biases, and open new opportunities for learning.

In many senses, supervised ML and reinforcement algorithms inherently include in them the aspiration to mimic some specific human behavior and to optimise on the basis of human observations. Unsupervised learning, on the other hand, can reveal factors and behaviors that human guidance might have been preventing us from seeing. In an analogy to human learning, a child might learn purely from observing (even if the scene is to some extent orchestrated by an adult human), and not always by following an adult deliberately pointing out (i.e., supervising), rewarding or punishing (i.e., reinforcing) to guide her. Unsupervised ML algorithms, such as clustering, dimension reduction or association techniques, are designed without a top-down supervision component, and in many respects, the only human intervention will be expressed prior to the algorithm itself, in the form of feature engineering. Thus, unsupervised algorithms are more about identification than recognition, are freer to observe the data, and are freer to learn [14]. For an example about the usage of unsupervised learning to learn and reveal see [15].

2.1 Mental Models

In order for us humans to make best use of the redundant sensory observations that we collect to build up our own mental models [16], our cognitive systems must make those models accessible to our future everyday perception. Mental models are perceived as internal representations of the environment that provide a conceptual framework for describing, explaining, and predicting future system states. These models should be "simple" (the parsimony principle for mental models, for example [17]), so that we will be able to use them to efficiently and quickly detect any new associations involved in learning. The mainstream cognitive psychology literature stresses that our brain is doing a profoundly difficult job in doing so [16]. It should deduce probabilistic links about our world and detect suspicious outliers, all by accessing and linking prior knowledge structures and schemas [18]. In this paper, we present a case study through which the process of creating the unsupervised ML models, as well as the models themselves are used to form, externalise and then articulate knowledge and, via that, making the learning more effective [19, 20].

An organisation is typically a complex entity with many communicative channels connecting between the learning processes of its individuals and its whole culture [21]. A ML model, whether developed through supervised or unsupervised methods, will always be a simplification from a particular point of view on this complexity. This simplification and loss of detail is also a strength that enables new insights; and even more so when the "point of view" on the complexity is less determined by prior expectations, such as occurs with unsupervised methods.

The word 'model' is used in this paper to refer to different concepts interchangeably (sometimes deliberately). A 'mental model' is "produced through cognition by individuals to create a representation or structure of a phenomenon or solution to a problem" [16, 22]. 'To model' is a verb describing the process that individuals undertake when they create, or retrieve existing mental models in order to solve problems [22]. A 'computational model' in this paper refers to unsupervised ML models, and the 'co-learning' process refers to a collaborative and connectivist process of developing the computational model.

Mental models help us explain and predict how learners interact with the world, and how they explain, understand, solve anticipated events, and communicate (see Fig. 1 below from [22]). While mental models are internal structures [16], they can be exteriorised [23] when triggered by interaction with a domain system [24] such as robotics [22]. Our suggestion here is that unsupervised computational models can also offer an externalisation trigger. This allows for an observable effect of the initial internalisation of a mental model by the learners. By that, it can serve as a learning affordance, and the learning outcome can be observed through a change in learners' language (for example by used concepts), and their ability to explain, predict and diagnose, as emphasised in [22] 'transitory mental model' (see the Fig. 1 below), and as we will show in the results section.

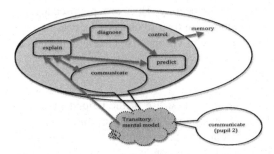

Fig. 1. Mental model mode: diagram of functionality [22]

One of the atomic units of mental models are concepts, along with their role in language and communication [17]. Effective learning is strongly associated with developing a clear definition of concepts, including the meaningful relations between them [25]. Human reasoning and decision making are further based on this initial storage of concepts, which is one kind of mental representation. In an effective process of learning, the mental model will be stored [26] in the long-term memory of an individual, serving later as a schema [27], or a script [28]. Once the model has been created, it exists independently of its sources [29]. Visualisations, images and text can serve as mental affordances [30] or as we term them – learning affordances – by assisting with the functionality of short-term memory [31], reducing cognitive load, and therefore assisting learning. Our proposition is that unsupervised ML models can do that too, for example, by simplifying and reducing the number of the used dimensions.

One characteristic of mental models is that they are not immutable entities that remain invariant across (or even within) students [22]. Since they are subjective, they can lead to misconceptions [32, 33]. They are channeled and processed through human long-term memory, which is essentially faulty, and thus they are not immune to biases and changes over time. Computational models, on the other hand, are more robust in that sense, as they are anchored on observed evidence and are externalised by statistical statements. In their work defining 'mental affordances', [30] specifies the three criteria for 'something' to be a mental affordance: (1) mental affordances are opportunities for mental action; (2) mental affordances are perceptible; and (3) the perception of a mental affordance involves the potentiation of the mental action that is afforded [30]. We raise the suggestion that unsupervised ML models can serve as a special kind of a mental affordance: a learning affordance. In Sect. 3 below we show how an unsupervised computational model serves as an opportunity for learning, how it is perceptible and that its perception involves the potentiation of learning.

2.2   Some Criticisms of ML

Criticisms are continually raised about the role of ML in the context of its focus on prediction rather than explanation [34]. Many have argued that the use of ML in the learning sciences often lacks a theoretical basis [35, 36] and that it is often undertaken with "one eye closed to the peculiarities of the data" [37]. The latter is specifically challenging in the learning sciences domain, as many central constructs (such as 'learning' and 'collaboration') are often ambiguous in their operationalisation, which makes it a hard pre-requisite for supervised ML algorithm to work effectively. Many scholars have strongly argued that modeling should start with certain educational goals in mind (e.g., student learning outcomes), that are measurable [38, 39]. Here we show how the unsupervised approach help learning in a more open-ended manner by helping a learning organisation to make tacit into explicit and to adjust their long-held beliefs.

3   The Co-learning Process: Learning About Trading Behavior

The next subsections list the stages in which the unsupervised model was produced within our case study. This is essentially a very typical data mining process, but it illustrates the various ways in which the organisational co-learning process serves as a learning affordance. In particular, how it opens opportunities for mental action in a tangible way [30]. In being a 'co-learning' process, where the company's expert trainers were engaged as designing partners and experts of their domain, each phase afforded them a different interaction with the data, and subsequently - learning opportunities, as described below. Figure 2 below summarises the main stages, showing where human semantics (of the experts) is playing an active role, when it is being guided by the data, and how new semantics is produced at the end of the pipeline. This dialogical interchange confronts the two (potentially differently biased) sources of knowledge, and by that potentially minimise the risks of a biased decision making (which by itself affords a new learning opportunity). Nevertheless, other mechanisms (out of the scope of this paper) such as ethical auditing, should also take place to minimise this risk further.

During the first phases, inputs such as experience and data guide the process, while the last two phases are unsupervised. The result is a parsimonious model, which affords new learning opportunities, that would potentially shape the mental model of the organisation (i.e., act as a learning affordance).

Knowledge Elicitation. During the knowledge elicitation phase, we triangulated evidence from the behavioral finance literature (to use empirical evidence about potential indicators for successful trading behaviors) with the domain experts' tacit semantics. This has 'supervised' our feature engineering and resulted in the domain experts' externalisation of their existing mental model of the traders types (see Table 2 below).

Data Integration. The complexity, inconsistencies and time associated with problem solving typically grow with the number of modalities or sources of information that need to be considered [40]. The resulting integrated data, while revealing an integrated semantics, is certainly one way in which computational models can be used as an affordance. In our case study, we used data from several data sources, such as clickstream

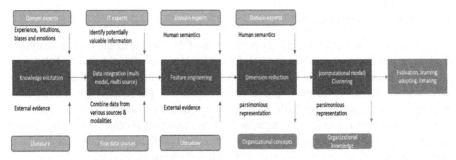

Fig. 2. A typical data mining process, resulting in an unsupervised model. The Blue rectangles represent the phases of the computing process. The light blue rectangles are semantic inputs going into the process. The Orange rectangles are outputs that go back to the organisation and potentially act as learning affordances. (Color figure online)

from a trading software, various market characteristics, and internal reports for 2017–2018. As technically challenging and subject to the subjectivity of data sources the data integration phase is, its serendipitous nature opens new opportunities for learning.

Feature Engineering. A typical feature engineering process is yet another opportunity for the human semantics to inflict itself and 'supervise' the modeling, while still allowing the set of statistical relationships to orchestrate a model without obvious human interference. At the end of this phase, we were left with a list of 35 features of traders' behavior. Some features were as simple as the number of specific types of action that a trader makes in a typical month, such as the number of amendments and cancellations of orders. Other features were more 'engineered', such as the proportion of their trading in larger markets, and the proportion of the market they covered.

Dimension Reduction. The parsimonious representation of a mental model makes it more accessible to short term memory retrieval, while also making it more vulnerable to flawed heuristics [17]. Dimension reduction is one way in which unsupervised ML offers some economy, and therefore removes some of the cognitive load related to high-dimensioned models. From the computational side as well, the 'curse of high dimensionality' is a term used to describe the challenges introduced by the presence of a vast number of variables, resulting in a performance degradation [41]. In our case study, we used principal component analysis (PCA) on our 35 behavioral features and 480 traders' data, after log-transforming the variables to make the distributions near-normal, and making sure that none of the variables were highly correlated with others. The PCA resulted in four main factors accounting for 83.37% of the total variance, which were then reviewed with the domain experts. The strongest factor was shown to cover elements of how active the trader is (quantifying the number of actions they initiated), the second was related to trading style (specifically, whether traders show the tendency to focus narrowly on a small number of markets, or whether they tend to widen their focus to cover a large number of markets, with less focus on each). The third factor covered the types of products they were typically traded (in terms of a product's properties such as liquidity and volatility), and the fourth factor was focused on the overall volume of their trading. As will be shown in Sect. 4, the introduction of these four dimensions into the organisational culture offered parsimony and a higher level of abstraction in the evolved mental model of trading behavior.

Clustering. Cluster analysis is a technique used to identify naturally occurring groups in a dataset, here used to profile trading behavior. In our case, the clustering was carried out to challenge the existing profiling mental model of traders, that the company has been using in order to design a tailored training and mentoring programs. We deliberately did not add to the clustered features any feature having a direct relationship to performance measures (such as profit). The purpose was to make salient data patterns that were purely behavioral, to support formative feedback from mentors. The technical details of the carried K-means cluster analysis are detailed in the appendix.

4   Results: Mental Models of Trading Behavior

To validate our hypothesis that the unsupervised model had affected the mental model of the training managers in the organisation, we interviewed two of the most senior ones. The interview questions, as well as the themes we followed in the analysis were based on the 'transitory mental model' [22] dimensions, such as the models' effects on language, prediction, diagnosis and supporting learners. Below are the main findings. In the interview the managers were asked to compare the mental model created within the company prior to our analysis, with the computational model created by that analysis (see Tables 2 and 3 respectively in the appendix).

The Main Differences Between the Two Models: The main difference noted was that the first model was *"subjective"*, in the sense that it had been derived from long experience of being traders and trainers, whereas the second model was *"objective"*, in the sense that it had emerged from the trading data. A related difference was in the number of profiles. The managers felt that they could have composed their mental model with more than the five profiles that they did, but chose not to so, as they had no easy way to determine what would be a sufficient set to cover the field. By contrast, arriving at four profiles rather than some other number was driven by the usual needs for parsimony vs. coverage of the data in unsupervised ML. Another important difference was that the second model more clearly articulated *"how engaged a trader is"* compared to the first model as it brought to the fore issues around order activity and diversity. This highlighted the fact that there were few tools available to managers to measure engagement with the data available to them.

The Main Commonalities Between the Two Models: One managers suggested that *"both models very much focus on the markets [and] the types of markets, and the characteristics of the markets in terms of what the individuals seem to prefer and pay particular attention to volatility and product diversity"*. An indirect issue is that neither model in itself indicates how best to train a particular type of trader, but the insight that training and mentoring could, in principle, be adapted in such a way indicated a shift in perception.

The ML Model's Effect on the Managers' Views on Trading and Training: On the positive side, it was noted that the ML model was able to show up similarities and differences between mixes of trader behavior in the various company offices across the world. It was also noted that the co-learning process had demonstrated the value of the company's data. One manager noted the value of the ML model in supporting both recruitment and mentoring, in a way that was not really possible with the initial model. In terms of recruiting, the ML model opened up the possibility of consciously improving the diversity of trading styles within the company as part of its overall risk management strategy. On the negative side, *"One disadvantage would be the potential for assumptions and first impressions to be derived from cluster categorisation before a mentor has really... had a chance to work closely with and get to know a trader"* and might also have a similar downside in recruitment. An interesting observation was made about the possibility that the ML profiles might become too rigid and constraining, and the need to update it when markets change.

The ML Model's Effect on the Managers's Language: Several ideas emerged with regard to language and concepts. From one manager, *"the key thing for me... was about behaviors, and how traders' behaviors [our emphasis] with the markets"*. This contrasts with the former focus on performance, typically profit and loss. For the other manager, *"the most obvious change is recognition that traders can be grouped by certain factors, other than their start date, and that they don't have to be considered as individual entities at all time[s]."* This manager also pointed out the consequence of the objectivity of the data, *"Due to the mentality of traders and analysts, and generally all departments within ZISHI/OSTC, I think there is a stronger propensity for people to acknowledge and factor in advice when it originates from a data led approach."*. The ML model has resulted in greater clarity, *"Both models, but certainly the newer one, separate volume and position size as separate factors. I think evidencing this is important as a common incorrect assumption is that a bigger position equates to higher volume. This teamed with the concept of complexity really broadens the criteria on which a traders' activity is 'judged'."* Note that the term *"complexity"* itself, which is now used routinely within the company, derived from the unsupervised modeling process.

The ML model also helped to extend the manager's thinking about the evolution of a trader's behavior with experience, *"The concept and likelihood of a trader gravitating from one cluster to another over time, which has been mentioned in the analysis, but perhaps not in the new model cluster descriptions is one aspect I think mentors and decision makers internally either need to accept as a possibility or on the other scale accept isn't as straightforward as they assume."*

The ML Model's Effect on the Managers' Ability to 'Diagnose' or 'Predict': One manager anticipated that, *"having a data fed model gives a mentor more confidence to forward plan, anticipate and react quicker to the obstacles and barriers that each trader may face when progressing. It also adds greater weight to your case when presenting why you think a trader needs more time/resources to develop than a higher-level decision-making body may invoke. It also has the ability to make communicating and justifying a mentor's approach and 'diagnosis' to others easier. This could even be as simple as having the reassurance that the same language and concepts are being used."*

Are There Any Other Changes, Not Already Noted, the Managers Have Noticed in Themselves and in Their Colleagues: One manager explained that, *"This type of insight, ... does open our eyes to who we have as a workforce and who traders are and how you can really look at performance."* The other pointed out that: *"there is a growing recognition that pairing the right mentor and mentee could be an important part of getting it right – although still somewhat in its infancy. From my own perspective I'm certainly more conscious of the fact that certain characteristics, or even whole clusters, that are considered to result in less profitable performance within ZISHI/OSTC might actually suit alternative trading environments which work under different parameters.... I certainly think it's made me consider if dependent on cluster characteristics, and very much linked to this is product mix, if risk parameters need to be adapted for the different clusters, even at a very junior stage of a career."*

In summary, the main affordance for the training managers and trainees is that the profiles derived by unsupervised ML created a handy, bias-fencing shorthand to encapsulate a large number of low-level behavioral variables. These behavioral variables are usually not directly observable by the managers themselves before the modelling, and developing a mental model would typically take significant cognitive effort and time. In addition, the fact that those models were unsupervised has afforded the trainers a sense of validation, as well as of standardisation across the company's different international locations. The unsupervised model and the concepts arising from the modeling changed the language within the company. New concepts such as *"complexity"*, *"cluster"*, and *"trading style"* were introduced and diffused across the company. Lastly, the new model opened up new dialogues about the shift of focus from performance onto behavior, about helping traders mobilise between profiles as part of their progress. It also opened up the possibility for more targeted recruitment and mentoring, as well as for potentially better matching traders to types of markets or mentors. The managers also identified a potential risk of trainers using the clusters as too simplified or rigid, and mentioned the need for awareness, and re-modeling.

5 Conclusions

The main rationale for using unsupervised ML models is that they can expose unexpected patterns, and therefore adds data-driven semantics to the existing semantics of human experts. Of course, that does not come without challenges and dangers. In this paper, we have used a case study of a trading and training company managers which reflected on the comparison between their own mental model, and a computational model produced by a co-learning process. We suggest that unsupervised models can be referred to as learning affordances, as they have the potential of reducing the complexity of a highly-dimensional behavior, floating inexplicit or unexpected patterns, introducing new concepts to the company's language and generally affecting its learning. For example, the company's training managers were now able to discuss how traders can be encouraged to move between different clusters of behavior and how their behavior might relate to performance. The model was an outcome of a collaborative modeling process, which suggests that it was itself a learning affordance. In our case it has enabled a space and time for a continuous interaction between the experts' tacit knowledge, their own various mental models and data modeling. The method used in this case study should be generalisable to other unsupervised methods and to organisations that have accumulated a large amount of untapped behavioral data.

Appendix A: Technical Details of the Cluster Analysis

Can be found at https://tinyurl.com/336dje9n.

References

1. Seel, N.M.: Model-based learning: a synthesis of theory and research. Educ. Tech. Res. Dev. **65**(4), 931–966 (2017). https://doi.org/10.1007/s11423-016-9507-9
2. du Boulay, B., O'Shea, T., Monk, J.: The black box inside the glass box: presenting computing concepts to novices. Int. J. Man Mach. Stud. **14**(3), 237–249 (1981)
3. Marsick, V.J., Watkins, K.E.: Demonstrating the value of an organisation's learning culture: the dimensions of the learning organisation questionnaire. Adv. Dev. Hum. Resour. **5**(2), 132–151 (2003)
4. Echeverria, V., Martinez-Maldonado, R., Buckingham Shum, S.: Towards collaboration translucence: giving meaning to multimodal group data. In: Proceedings of the CHI Conference on Human Factors in Computing Systems, pp. 1–16 (2019)
5. Kent, C., et al.: On how unsupervised learning can shape minds: a very brief overview. In: Proceedings of the 11th International Conference on Learning Analytics and Knowledge (2021)
6. Ambrose, S., Bridges, M., DiPietro, M., Lovett, M., Norman, M.: How Learning Works: 7 Research-Based Principles for Smart Teaching. Jossey-Bass, San Francisco (2010)
7. Mayer, R.E.: The Promise of Educational Psychology. Teaching for Meaningful Learning, vol. 2. Merrill Prentice Hall, Upper Saddle River (2002). https://doi.org/10.1002/pfi.4930420410
8. Watkins, K.E., Kim, K.: Current status and promising directions for research on the learning organisation. Hum. Resour. Dev. Q. **29**(1), 15–29 (2018)
9. Nonaka, I., Takeuchi, H.: The Knowledge Creating Company. Oxford University Press, Oxford (1995)
10. Siemens, G.: Connectivism: a learning theory for the digital age. Int. J. Instr. Technol. Distance Learn. (IRRODL) **2**(1), 3–10 (2005)
11. Smart, P.R., Engelbrecht, P.C., Braines, D., Hendler, J.A., Shadbolt, N.R.: The Extended Mind and Network-Enabled Cognition. School of Electronics and Computer Science, University of Southampton, Southampton, UK (2008)
12. Fjørtoft, H., Lai, M.K.: Affordances of narrative and numerical data: a social-semiotic approach to data use. Stud. Educ. Eval. 100846 (2020)
13. Gibson, J.J.: The Ecological Approach to Visual Perception, Classic Psychology Press, New York (2014)
14. Amershi, S., Conati, C.: Combining unsupervised and supervised classification to build user models for exploratory learning environments. JEDM J. Educ. Data Min. **1**(1), 18–71 (2009)
15. Zhang, N., Biswas, G., Dong, Y.: Characterizing students' learning behaviors using unsupervised learning methods. In: André, Elisabeth, Baker, Ryan, Hu, Xiangen, Rodrigo, Ma Mercedes T., du Boulay, Benedict (eds.) AIED 2017. LNCS (LNAI), vol. 10331, pp. 430–441. Springer, Cham (2017). https://doi.org/10.1007/978-3-319-61425-0_36

16. Johnson-Laird, P.N.: Mental Models: Towards a Cognitive Science of Language, Inference, and Consciousness, No. 6. Harvard University Press, Cambridge (1983)
17. Holyoak, K.J., Morrison, R.G. (eds.): The Cambridge Handbook of Thinking and Reasoning, vol. 137. Cambridge University Press, Cambridge (2005)
18. Barlow, H.B.: Unsupervised learning. Neural Comput. **1**(3), 295–311 (1989)
19. Bransford, J.D., Brown, A.L., Cocking, R.R.: How People Learn: Brain, Mind, Experience, and School (Expanded Edition). The National Academies Press, Washington, DC (2000)
20. Sawyer, R.K. (ed.): The Cambridge Handbook of the Learning Sciences. Cambridge University Press, Cambridge (2005)
21. Marsick, V.J., Watkins, K.E.: Facilitating Learning Organisations. Gower, Brookfield (1999)
22. Edwards-Leis, C.E.: Challenging learning journeys in the classroom: using mental model theory to inform how pupils think when they are generating solutions (2012)
23. Barker, P., van Schaik, P., Hudson, S., Meng Tan, C.: Mental models and their role in the teaching and learning of human-computer interaction. In: Ottman, T., Tomek, I. (eds.) Proceedings of ED-MEDIA/ED-TELECOM 1998, 10th World Conference on Educational Multimedia and Hypermedia, vol. 1. Association for the Advancement of Computing in Education, Charlottesville (1998)
24. Carroll, J.M., Olson, J.R.: Mental models in human-computer interaction. In: Helander, M. (ed.) Handbook of Human-Computer Interaction, pp. 45–65. Elsevier Science Publishers, Amsterdam (1988)
25. Ausubel, D.P.: Educational Psychology: A Cognitive View. Holt, Rinehart & Winston, New York (1968)
26. Bucciarelli, M.: How the construction of mental models improves learning. Mind Soc. **6**(1), 67–89 (2007)
27. Anderson, R.C.: The notion of schemata and the educational enterprise: general discussion of the conference. In: Anderson, R.C., Spiro, R.J., Montague, W.E. (eds.) Schooling and the Acquisition of Knowledge. Lawrence Erlbaum, Hillsdale (1977/1984)
28. Preece, J., Rogers, Y., Sharp, H., Benyon, D., Holland, S., Carey, T.: Human Computer Interaction. Addison Wesley, Boston (1994)
29. Barker, P.G.: Mental models and network pedagogy. In: Conference Proceedings of EN-ABLE 1999, International Conference EVITech. Helskinki University, Finland (1999)
30. McClelland, T.: The mental affordance hypothesis. Mind **129**(514), 401–427 (2020)
31. Henderson, L., Tallman, J.: Stimulated recall and mental models. Scarecrow Press, Inc., Lanham (2006)
32. Vosniadou, S., Brewer, W.F.: Mental models of the earth: a study of conceptual change in childhood. Cogn. Psychol. **24**(4), 535–585 (1992). https://doi.org/10.1016/0010-0285(92)900 18-W
33. Franco, C., Colinvaux, D.: Grasping mental models. In: Gilbert, J.K., Boulter, C.J. (eds.) Developing models in science education, pp. 93–118. Springer, Dordrecht (2000). https://doi.org/10.1007/978-94-010-0876-1_5
34. Vaughan, J.W., Wallach, H.: A human-centered agenda for intelligible machine learning. In: Machines We Trust: Getting Along with Artificial Intelligence (2020)
35. Nelson, L.K.: Computational grounded theory: a methodological framework. Sociol. Methods Res. **49**, 3–42 (2017). https://doi.org/10.1177/0049124117729703
36. Penuel, W.R., Shepard, L.A.: Assessment and teaching. In: Gitomer, D.H., Bell, C.A. (eds.) Handbook of Research on Teaching, 5th edn, pp. 787–850. American Educational Research Association, Washington, DC (2016)
37. Radford, J., Joseph, K.: Theory in, theory out: the uses of social theory in machine learning for social science. arXiv:2001.03203 (2020)

38. Hamilton, L., Halverson, R., Jackson, S., Mandinach, E., Supovitz, J., Wayman, J.: Using student achievement data to support instructional decision making (NCEE 2009-4067). National Center for Education Evaluation and Regional Assistance, Institute of Education Sciences, U.S. Department of Education, Washington, DC (2009). http://ies.ed.gov/ncee/wwc/public ations/practiceguides/
39. Mandinach, E.B., Schildkamp, K.: Misconceptions about data-based decision making in education: an exploration of the literature. Stud. Educ. Eval. 100842 (2020)
40. Rapp, D.N.: Mental models: theoretical issues for visualisations in science education. In: Gilbert, J.K. (ed.) Visualisation in Science Education, pp. 43–60. Springer, Dordrecht. (2005). https://doi.org/10.1007/1-4020-3613-2_4
41. Han, J., Pei, J., Kamber, M.: Data Mining: Concepts and Techniques. Elsevier, Amsterdam (2011)

Predicting Co-occurring Emotions from Eye-Tracking and Interaction Data in MetaTutor

Sébastien Lallé[1]([✉]), Rohit Murali[1], Cristina Conati[1], and Roger Azevedo[2]

[1] The University of British Columbia, Vancouver, BC, Canada
lalles@cs.ubc.ca
[2] University of Central Florida, Orlando, FL, USA
roger.azevedo@ucf.edu

Abstract. Emotions in Intelligent Tutoring Systems (ITS) are often modeled as single affective states, however there is evidence that emotions co-occur during learning, with implications for affect-aware ITS that need to have a comprehensive understanding of a student's affective state to react accordingly. In this paper we broaden the evidence that emotions co-occur in an educational context, and present a first attempt to predict these co-occurrences from data, using the MetaTutor ITS as a test-bed. We show that *boredom+frustration*, as well as *curiosity+anxiety*, frequently co-occur in MetaTutor, and that we can predict when these emotions co-occur significantly better than a baseline using eye-tracking and interaction data. These findings provide a first step toward building affect-aware ITS that can adapt to these complex co-occurring affective states.

Keywords: Co-occurring emotions · Eye-tracking · Logs · Classification

1 Introduction

There is extensive evidence that emotions can influence how well students learn from Intelligent Tutoring Systems (ITS), e.g., [1, 2], driving extensive efforts to design affect-aware ITS that can adapt to students' emotions, with results showing that such adaptation can increase learning [3, 4]. Delivering affect-aware adaptation requires detecting the student's emotional state at some level, and there is extensive evidence on the feasibility of predicting affective valence [5, 6] or single emotions [3, 7–12] assuming that one emotion is relevant at a time. There is also preliminary work showing that several pairs of emotions can co-occur simultaneously [13–17], suggesting that affect-aware adaptation in ITS could be further refined by being able to detect when students are experiencing multiple emotions. This existing work, however, has looked at different sets of emotions in different ITS, making it difficult to draw generalizable conclusions and calling for further research in this direction.

In this work, we contribute to this research in three ways. First, we provide further evidence on the presence of co-occurring emotions during learning. Specifically, we look at the same emotions investigated by [14] in a MOOC, in the context of a different ITS,

© Springer Nature Switzerland AG 2021
I. Roll et al. (Eds.): AIED 2021, LNAI 12748, pp. 241–254, 2021.
https://doi.org/10.1007/978-3-030-78292-4_20

MetaTutor [18], and found different co-occurring emotions, suggesting that emotion co-occurrence depends in part on the target learning environments.

Second, we show the feasibility of predicting when emotions co-occur in MetaTutor, as a first step toward building affect-aware ITS that can more comprehensively capture students' affective states during learning. To the best of our knowledge, this is the first attempt to predict multiple emotions in ITS, as well in affective computing at large.

Third, our predictive models leverage both interaction and eye-tracking data. These two data sources have shown promising results for affect detection when used in isolation, but they have never been compared and/or combined, thus our results provide novel insights of the value of these data sources for affect detection.

2   Related Work

Different affective frameworks have been leveraged to study the role of emotions in ITS [19]. One is the 6 Ekman's universal emotions [20] (*joy, sadness, surprise, disgust, anger, fear*) that can be identified from distinctive facial expressions. The Ekman's emotions however do not capture the more subtle emotions that students typically experience in learning situations. To overcome this issue, Pekrun [21, 22] identified several "academic emotions" that he showed can influence learning outcomes. These retain *joy, sadness, surprise, anger* from the Ekman, and add *pride, hope, gratitude, enjoyment, relief, curiosity, anxiety, boredom, frustration, confusion, shame, hopelessness*. Baker et al. [23] proposed a smaller set of 5 academic emotions in their BROMP framework in order to make it easier to code these emotions in learning situations, whereas identifying all of the Pekrun's emotions can be challenging. The BROMP set retains *curiosity, boredom, frustration* and *confusion* from Pekrun, and add *engagement*.

Several studies have provided evidence for the value of delivering affect-aware personalization based on academic emotions in an ITS (see overview in [24]). While in these studies the affective interventions were driven by the detection of a single emotion at a time, there is also evidence that students experience co-occurring emotions in ITS. Some work provides evidence [1, 16, 25], without further details on which these emotions are. Four studies have focused on identifying which specific pairs of emotions co-occur together. Two of these studies [15, 17] examined the same ITS that we target in this paper, MetaTutor. Harley et al. [15] examined the co-occurrences of the Ekman's emotions, where the emotions were detected via off-the-shelf software based on videos of students' faces collected during the study that generated the data we use in this paper. They found no pair of emotions that co-occur in more than 3% of the face measurements, likely because the Ekman's emotions are fairly uncommon in learning situations. Sinclair et al. [17] looked at a small subset of the Pekrun's emotions with MetaTutor (only *enjoyment, curiosity, pride, frustration, boredom*), and showed that *boredom+frustration* co-occur. We extend this work by considering all Pekrun's emotions to gain a more comprehensive understanding of which emotions co-occur in MetaTutor. Dillon et al. [14] studied Pekrun's emotions in a Statistics MOOC. Like Sinclair [17], they found that *boredom+frustration* co-occur, and they identified several other pairs of co-occurring negative emotions, indicating that it is worthwhile to look at the full Pekrun set. Bosch et al. [13] investigated the BROMP emotions in a Python tutor and found, like Dillon et al. [14], that *confusion+frustration* co-occur. They found none of the other pairs of negative emotions identified in [14], even when they fully overlapped with the BROMP emotions (e.g., *confusion+boredom*). In contrast, they found a pair of co-occurring positive emotions, *curiosity+engagement* which other work could not identify because engagement only appears in the BROMP set. These results show overall that while some emotion co-occurrences may generalize across ITS, most pairs identified so far depend on the target ITS, calling for further analysis to better understand the mechanisms at play.

Extensive work has been done in ITS to predict student emotions, but only focused on predicting one emotion at a time, rather than co-occurring emotions (see overview in [19]). It should be noted that, while some of these works predict several emotions, they do not predict when they co-occur together, as we do here.

We focus on interaction data and eye-tracking data to detect multiple emotions because there is initial evidence that each source in isolation can help detect individual emotions in a non-intrusive way. Namely, interaction data is one of the most used sources for affective user modeling in ITS due to the simplicity of its collection. For example interaction data was used to predict the five BROMP emotions in several ITS fostering science inquiry [8], medical training [26], and algebra [10]. Other work predicted subsets of the Pekrun's academic emotions in an ITS for microbiology [9] and algebra [11]. Eye-tracking has been used less extensively than interaction data for affect detection in ITS, but with encouraging results. Namely, eye-tracking has been leveraged in MetaTutor to predict emotion valence [5], as well as separate occurrences of boredom and curiosity [7]. In non-educational settings eye-tracking has also been used to predict boredom [27] and confusion [28].

We extend this work by examining the value of combining both interaction and eye-tracking data to predict co-occurring emotions. While there has been work on combining other data sources for affect prediction [26, 29], to the best of our knowledge the only other attempt to combine eye-tracking and interaction data was done in a non-educational setting, to predict confusion in a visualization interface [28]. Eye-tracking and interaction data were also used to predict other non-affective states such as mind wandering [30] and learning gains [31].

3   MetaTutor and User Study

MetaTutor [18], shown in Fig. 1, is an ITS that delivers content about the circulatory system via a hypermedia of text (Fig. 1D) and diagrams (Fig. 1E) and includes mechanisms to support Self-Regulated Learning (SRL). Students are given the overall goal of learning about the human circulatory system (Fig. 1A), and they can set subsequent learning subgoals (Fig. 1B) as they proceed through the material. 12 SRL processes fully described in [18] (e.g., setting subgoals, taking notes) are supported via the SLR palette (Fig. 1G), which students can access on their own initiative or when stimulated by one of 4 pedagogical agents (Fig. 1F). Students can also go in full-screen mode to focus solely on the text and diagram (Fig. 1D+E) and hide the rest of the interface.

The data used in this paper derives from a study designed to investigate the SRL processes used by students while working with MetaTutor [18]. The study involved

79 university students who were given 90 min to learn as much as possible about the circulatory system using MetaTutor. The participant's gaze was tracked with a Tobii T60 eye tracker. At regular intervals of about 14 min during learning with MetaTutor, students were prompted to report if they currently felt any of the Pekrun's emotions, by completing an Emotions and Value (EV) Questionnaire [18, 32], which listed an item of the form "<u>Right now</u> I feel X" for each emotion (e.g., "*Right now I feel bored*"). Both the instructions and the items clearly asked the students to report the emotions that they were actually feeling at the time of the EV report. Each item is rated on a 5-point Likert scale ranging from 1 ("strongly disagree") to 5 ("strongly agree"), capturing the student's self-perceived confidence in feeling or not feeling that emotion. We use the EVs generated from this study to investigate emotion co-occurrence in MetaTutor.

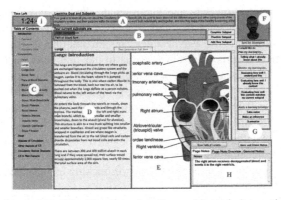

Fig. 1. Screenshot of the MetaTutor interface and its main interactive areas.

4   Evidence for Co-occurring Emotions

The study generated 395 EVs. We consider that an emotion occurs at the time of a given EV if the student self-reports a high confidence in feeling it, namely gives a rating of 4 or 5 to the corresponding EV item. 2.2% of the EVs were removed as outliers because they included a number of occurring emotions beyond 2 st. dev. (i.e., more than 5 emotions). Figure 2 shows the distribution over the remaining 386 EVs for the number of emotions that co-occurred in each report (M = 2.1, SD = 1.6). Overall two or more emotions co-occurred in more than 80% of the EV reports. To understand which specific emotions co-occur the most, we compute the lift score [33] of each pair of emotions E1, E2, which captures the likelihood that the emotions co-occur together over the likelihood that they each occur individually. A Lift score above 1 indicates that the pair of emotions co-occur more frequently than expected by chance [33], thus we use this threshold to identify co-occurring pairs (as in [13]), and found the following outcomes.

(i)   The most commonly occurring pairs (Lift scores ranging from 1.4 to 2.3) consist of positive emotions (*pride+hope, pride+enjoyment, curiosity+enjoyement, curiosity+hope*, and *curiosity+pride*) which appear in between 16% and 28% of all EV reports. Interestingly, none of these pairs, nor other pairs of positive emotions, were found by Dillon et al. [14] who analyzed the Pekrun emotions in a MOOC. On the other hand, Bosch and D'Mello [13] investigated only two positive emotions (curiosity and engagement) in an ITS for Python, and found that they co-occur. Together, these results suggest that the presence of positive pairs depends on the target learning environments.

(ii) There is one pair with mixed valence, a*nxiety+curiosity* occurring in 12% of all EV (Lift = 1.26). No other work in the literature has found pairs with mixed valence, including [14] that did collect both anxiety and curiosity in a MOOC. This shows that while mixed valence pairs are not common, they can occur depending on the target ITS, possibly indicating a conflicting emotional state that can be the target of specific adaptive interventions (see Sect. 4).

(iii) There is one pair with negative valence, *boredom+frustration,* occurring in 15% of all EV (Lift = 1.85). This pair was also found by Sinclair et al. [17] when they looked at a subset of the Pekrun's emotions (including *boredom, frustration* and 3 positive ones) using our same dataset and clustering of EVs to detect co-occurrences. The pair was also found by [14] in a different learning environment, thus these results together provide evidence that this is a relevant combination of negative emotions in learning, which might warrant specific pedagogical interventions, as discussed next.

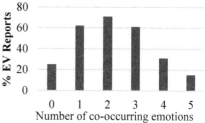

Fig. 2. Distribution (in %) of the number of occurring emotions per EV report.

Implications for Personalization. Positive affective states can be used to make personalized pedagogical decisions such as to detect what a student appreciates or provide empathic feedback [4, 34, 35]. However, this personalization could be delivered regardless of whether the student experiences one or several positive emotions. This is not the case for the negative and mixed valence pairs we found, for which their co-occurrence could drive very different personalization than single occurrences, as follows.

Boredom+frustration (**Bo+Fr**): Students who are just *bored* typically could benefit from immediate support geared toward reducing boredom (e.g. shifting to a new activity) since previous work has shown that boredom hinders learning, and that students generally do not overcome boredom on their own in learning situations [2, 36]. In contrast, students who are just *frustrated* may not need any personalized help yet, as previous work has shown that overcoming frustration on one's own can increase learning [2, 37]. However, the *co-occurrence of frustration and boredom* may indicate that the student is failing to overcome their frustration and is getting bored instead, with the persistence of these two states hindering learning [38]. This would indicate that now is the right time for personalized support that reduces the source of frustration.

Anxiety+Curiosity (**An+Cu**): Students who are *anxious* may benefit from support that has been proposed in educational psychology, such as self-calming or anxiety-reducing techniques [39, 40]. Students who are just *curious* do not require any dedicated support. Experiencing *both emotions* is less concerning that solely being anxious, as curiosity toward the learning content is already very positive, and the student may just be anxious about his capacity to master it. In that case simple encouraging feedback meant to build up the student confidence may be sufficient to reduce the anxiety.

In the next section, we will examine the feasibility of predicting the occurrence of both Bo+Fr and An+Cu, so as to drive the aforementioned forms of personalization.

5   Machine Learning Setup

We define the prediction of each pair of co-occurring emotions (Bo+Fr and An+Cu) as a separate 4-class classification task, with classes: None (no emotion occurred), either one of the emotions occurs without the other, the two emotions co-occurred (Both). As stated in the introduction, we use interaction and eye-tracking data for this prediction task. Due to software errors or tracking/calibration issues, we obtained valid data for 325 EV for the interaction dataset, and for 270 EV for the eye-tracking dataset. Table 1 shows the class distribution in each dataset for each of the co-occurrence pairs.

Table 1. Size (in %) of the classification classes in the interaction and the eye-tracking dataset.

Class	Bo+Fr				An+Cu			
	None	Bo	Fr	Both	None	An	Cu	Both
Interaction	40.13	22.46	14.15	23.08	21.85	14.15	36.00	28.00
Eye-Tracking	39.26	24.44	13.70	22.59	22.59	15.19	34.07	28.15

As described in Sect. 4, EVs were generated at regular intervals (~14 min). To predict whether our target pairs of emotion co-occur in a given EV r, we leverage all data collected between the appearance of r and the submission of the previous EV (or the start of the session for the first EV). For each of these time intervals we compute a battery of eye-tracking features and interaction features.

Eye-Tracking Features. The Tobii eye tracker provides data on user gaze patterns (Gaze from now on) and on the distance of the user's head from the screen (Head Distance from now on). We use EMDAT [41], an eye tracking data analysis toolkit, to derive from this data the features listed in Table 2, which were previously used to detect emotion valence [5], and curiosity and boredom in isolation during interaction with MetaTutor [7], and thus are good candidates for our classification task.

For gaze, EMDAT generates features based on various summary statistics (e.g., rate, mean) on user *fixations* (gaze maintained at one point on the screen), and *saccades* (quick eye movement between two fixations), both over the whole interface (Table 2a), as well as over specific areas of interest (AOI) defined over the nine regions of the MetaTutor interface shown in Fig. 1 (Table 2b). For Head Distance, EMDAT generates a set of summary statistics suitable for describing fluctuations of this measure over the course of the interaction with MetaTutor, namely *min, max, mean,* and *std. dev.,* as well as the distance at the beginning and end of the time interval (Table 2c).

Interaction Features. We leverage features that have been previously used to predict student learning and engagement with MetaTutor [42], and examine whether they can be predictive of co-occurring emotions as well. These features capture students' interaction with the learning content (shown in Table 3a), and their engagement with the 12 SRL strategies supported by MetaTutor (Table 3b). The content features in Table 3a aim to summarize how students allocated their time on the available pages of content, qualified based on whether they are relevant or not to the current active goal, as well as whether they are in standard or fullscreen mode. The SRL features summarize how many times the students use each of the SRL strategies, to capture to what extent the students self-regulated their learning (first 2 rows in Table 3b). The last 2 rows are specific to usage of the most used SRL strategies, note taking and subgoal planning.

Table 2. Set of eye-tracking features considered for classification.

a) Overall Gaze Features (19)	- Fixation rate, Mean & Std. deviation of fixation duration - Mean, Std. dev. of saccade length and saccade duration & Longest saccade - Mean, Std. deviation, Min & Max of saccade speed - Mean, Rate & Std. deviation of relative & relative saccade angles - Ratio between total fixation duration and total saccade duration
b) AOI Gaze Features for each AOI (135)	- Fixation rate, Longest fixation, Time to first & last fixation in AOI - Proportion of time, Proportion of fixations in AOI - Prop. of transitions from this AOI to every AOI
c) Head Distance Features (6)	- Mean, Std. dev., Max., Min. of head distance, - Head distance at the *first* and *last fixation* in the time intervals

To investigate the value of the feature sets described above for our classification task, we tested 3 standard machine learning algorithms available in the *sklearn* Python library [43]: Logistic regression (LR), Random Forest (RF), and Support-Vector Machine (SVM). We chose these classifiers because they have been extensively used for affect detection on datasets similar to ours in terms of size (i.e., small), without concluding evidence as for which one is the best (see [19, 44]). As a baseline, we use a probabilistic stratified classification algorithm (the sklearn's 'stratified' Dummy Classifier) that makes predictions simply based on the distribution it sees in the training set.

Table 3. Set of interaction features considered for classification

a) Content Features (17)	- Total time spent on all pages, and on pages relevant/irrelevant for the active subgoals - Total time spent on pages in default/fullscreen mode, on all/relevant/irrelevant pages - Total time spent on pages with no active subgoal - Proportion of relevant/irrelevant pages accessed overall, and for the active subgoals - Number of opened images
b) SRL Features (25)	- Number of SRL strategy usage (per SRL strategy) - Total, Mean number of SRL strategies used on pages relevant to active subgoals - Total time spent taking/reading notes, Number of notes taken/read/changed - Time spent adding/changing subgoals, Number of subgoals set/changed/completed

We trained classifiers on each of the eye-tracking and interaction feature sets, as well as over the combination of all features, resulting in a total of 4 (algorithms) × 3 (feature sets) = 12 classifiers. All classifiers were trained and evaluated with 10-runs-8-folds stratified nested cross-validation (CV) over students, meaning that all data for a given student are either in the training or in the test set. Stratification ensures that the class distribution in the folds is similar to that in the whole dataset. Due to the high number of features in our dataset, we used a PCA procedure (using sklearn's IncrementalPCA) with a batch size of 120 to reduce our feature dimensions by 80%. We apply the SMOTE algorithm [45] to oversample all minority classes so as to obtain a balanced training set. We performed hyper-parameter tuning through grid search with predefined parameter ranges via sklearn's GridSearchCV. The PCA, SMOTE and grid-search were all applied only on the train data, at the inner loop of the nested CV, to prevent data contamination. The trained classifiers were then tested on the test set at the outer loop of nested CV, and the performance of each classifier was averaged across the 8 folds, and then over the 10 runs. We report prediction performance in terms of: *overall accuracy* (number of correct predictions/number of datapoints) and *class accuracy* (for each class: number of correctly identified data points/number of datapoints in this class). These metrics provide an intuitive way to assess the practical usefulness of the models, and we dully compare them against the baseline in Sect. 6 to account for the skewed datasets. The code is available at https://github.com/rohit49plus2/AIED21/.

6   Classification Results

To identify which classifiers yield the best predictive performance, we ran a MANOVA for each pair of emotions (Bo + Fr and An + Cu) with:

- *All accuracy metrics* averaged over the 10 runs of CV as the dependent variables;
- *Algorithms* (4 levels, incl. the baseline) and *feature sets* (3 levels) as the factors.

For each emotion pair, the corresponding MANOVA reveals a significant main effect of algorithms ($F_{9,2317} = 73$, $p < .0000$ for Bo + Fr, $F_{9,2317} = 69$, $p < .0000$ for An + Cu) and of feature sets ($F_{6,1904} = 42$, $p < .0000$ for Bo + Fr, $F_{6,1904} = 25$, $p < .0000$ for An + Cu).

Main Effect of Algorithms. Post-hoc univariate ANOVAs show a main effect of algorithms on all accuracy metrics for both Bo + Fr and An + Cu. *T*-tests pairwise comparisons ran for each main effect, with Holm adjustments for multiple comparisons [46], indicate that SVM generally does not perform better than the baseline, therefore we do not discuss it further. The accuracy metrics of RF, LR, and the baseline averaged over feature sets is shown in Fig. 3, with a (*) indicating accuracy statistically significantly better than baseline.

RF significantly outperforms the baseline for both pairs of emotions in terms of overall accuracy, however RF and LR alternate in achieving the best predictions on individual class accuracies. LR is the winning classifier on 5 of the 8 class accuracy metrics, but clearly underperforms for *Acc_None* (for Bo + Fr) and for *Acc_Curiosity*, where RF outperforms the baseline instead. Therefore, these results suggest that combining both RF and LR in an Ensemble fashion might be valuable to maximize all class accuracies.

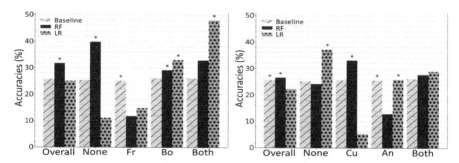

Fig. 3. All accuracy metrics for RF, LR and the baseline, for Bo + Fr (left) and An + Cu (right)

Interestingly, the only class that we could not predict is *Acc_Frustration*, in contrast with previous work showing that frustration can be predicted from interaction data [9, 10, 26]. This could be because frustration is the minority class in our dataset, accounting for only ~14% of the datapoints (Table 1). Thus even if we attempted to overcome this class imbalance with SMOTE, we might just need more data to detect frustration.

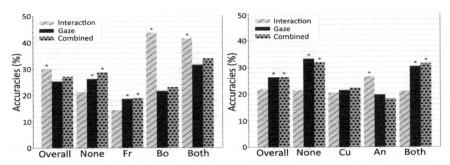

Fig. 4. All accuracy metrics across the feature sets, for Bo + Fr (left) and An + Cu (right)

Main Effect of Feature Sets. Post-hoc univariate ANOVAs show a main effect of feature sets on all dependent measures except *Acc_Frustration*, and *Acc_Both* for Bo + Fr, where all feature sets perform equally well. For the accuracy metrics with a main effect, we performed Holm-adjusted *t*-test pairwise comparisons, resulting in the statistically significant differences with the baseline indicated a star (*) in Fig. 4.

Figure 4 shows that Interaction and Eye-Tracking alternate as the best feature sets. In particular, Interaction generates substantially higher class accuracy for *Acc_Boredom* and *Acc_Anxiety*, showing that action patterns can capture useful signals when these emotions occur in isolation. Eye-Tracking on the other hand is the best at detecting when no emotion occurs (Acc_None for both pairs), as well as in terms of *Acc_Curiosity* and *Acc_Both* for An+Cu.

Although the above findings indicate that Eye-tracking and Interaction complement each other to reach the best class accuracies, the Combined feature sets never improves the prediction performance over the single feature sets. This suggests that there could be ways to take advantage of both feature sets by combining them in a different way than we did in this paper, for instance by using Ensembling approaches to fuse the Eye-Tracking and Interaction classifiers.

As a summary, Table 4 shows the peak accuracy obtained by the best combination of algorithm and feature set. Accuracies are mostly in the 25–50% range, with the exception of the very high 81.1% for *Acc_Boredom*. Albeit low, our levels of accuracy is not unusual even for binary classification tasks with single emotions [7, 9, 11]. It should also be noted that due to the small size of our datasets, we did not extensively fine-tune our classifiers or leverage more elaborated ML techniques. Thus our results provide a proof of concept that 4-class classification of co-occurring emotion pairs is possible, albeit a difficult task in general, and they should be considered lower bounds of what could be achieved with more data and more research on classifiers for these predictions.

Table 4. Peak accuracy obtained by the best combination of classifiers and feature set.

Bo+Fr	Classifier	Feature set	Peak acc	An+Cu	Classifier	Feature set	Peak acc
Acc_Overall	RF	Interaction	33.7	Acc_Overall	LR	Eye	27.1
Acc_None	RF	Interaction	46.4	Acc_None	LR	Eye	48.1
Acc_Bo	LR	Interaction	81.1	Acc_An	LR	Interaction	51.7
Acc_Fr	RF	Interaction	25.7	Acc_Cu	RF	Eye	39.5
Acc_Both	LR	Eye	49.51	Acc_Both	LR	Eye	35.8

7 Conclusion

This paper investigates the co-occurrences of students' emotions in MetaTutor, an ITS that scaffolds self-regulated learning, and the feasibility of predicting these co-occurrences from eye-tracking and interaction data. This research is driven by findings showing the value of tailoring pedagogical interventions to student emotions and by the lack of work on tailoring these interventions to co-occurring emotions, despite existing evidence that they do arise in ITS.

We extend this evidence by showing that emotions co-occur very frequently in MetaTutor, and make two contributions by examining these co-occurrences. First, we found several pairs of positive emotions, as well as a pair of mixed valence emotions, that were not identified in previous work looking at the same emotions in different ITS. This shows that it is important to further examine when and why emotions co-occur, depending on the target ITS. Second, we discuss how detecting two specific pairs of co-occurring emotions, *boredom+frustration* and *curiosity+anxiety*, can drive more precise affect-aware support in ITS than if these emotions were modelled as single states.

We show that both eye-tracking and interaction data used in isolation can predict the co-occurrence of the two emotion pairs significantly better than a baseline, and that they complemented each other depending on the target class, without one being better than the other. However, feature fusion of these two data sources does not improve performance over the individual sources, calling for further investigation on how to leverage both data sources together. To the best of our knowledge, our results are the first to target the prediction of co-occurring emotions in ITS, and to combine eye-tracking and integration data for affect prediction.

Altogether, our work is a first step toward building affect-aware ITS that can provide pedagogical interventions targeting co-occurring emotions Future work should be focused on investigating ways to improve the performance of our classifiers, either by collecting larger dataset, by using other ML techniques (including deep learning models which could be enabled by a larger dataset), and by using ensemble modelling to fuse eye-tracking and interaction predictors. Future work should also investigate the value of tailoring pedagogical interventions to single versus co-occurring emotions in ITS.

Acknowledgements. This paper is based upon work funded by the National Science Foundation (#DRL-1431552) and the Natural Sciences and Engineering Research Council (#22R01881).

References

1. Wortha, F., Azevedo, R., Taub, M., Narciss, S.: Multiple negative emotions during learning with digital learning environments–Evidence on their detrimental effect on learning from two methodological approaches. Front. Psychol. **10**, 2678:1–2678:19 (2019). https://doi.org/10.3389/fpsyg.2019.02678

2. Baker, R., D'Mello, S., Rodrigo, M.M., Graesser, A.C.: Better to be frustrated than bored: The incidence, persistence, and impact of learners' cognitive–affective states during interactions with three different computer-based learning environments. Int. J. Hum.-Comput. Stud. **68**, 223–241 (2010). https://doi.org/10.1016/j.ijhcs.2009.12.003

3. Woolf, B., Burleson, W., Arroyo, I., Dragon, T., Cooper, D., Picard, R.: Affect-aware tutors: recognising and responding to student affect. Int. J. Learn. Technol. **4**, 129–164 (2009). https://doi.org/10.1504/ijlt.2009.028804

4. Grawemeyer, B., Mavrikis, M., Holmes, W., Gutierrez-Santos, S., Wiedmann, M., Rummel, N.: Affecting off-task behaviour: how affect-aware feedback can improve student learning. In: Proceedings of the Sixth International Conference on Learning Analytics & Knowledge. pp. 104–113. ACM, Edinburgh (2016). https://doi.org/10.1145/2883851

5. Lallé, S., Conati, C., Azevedo, R.: Prediction of student achievement goals and emotion valence during interaction with pedagogical agents. In: Proceedings of the 17th International Conference on Autonomous Agents and Multiagent Systems, pp. 1222–1231. IFAAMAS, Stockholm (2018). https://doi.org/10.1145/2883851

6. Salmeron-Majadas, S., Santos, O.C., Boticario, J.G.: An evaluation of mouse and keyboard interaction indicators towards non-intrusive and low cost affective modeling in an educational context. Procedia Comput. Sci. **35**, 691–700 (2014)

7. Jaques, N., Conati, C., Harley, J.M., Azevedo, R.: Predicting affect from gaze data during interaction with an intelligent tutoring system. In: Trausan-Matu, S., Boyer, K.E., Crosby, M., Panourgia, K. (eds.) ITS 2014. LNCS, vol. 8474, pp. 29–38. Springer, Cham (2014). https://doi.org/10.1007/978-3-319-07221-0_4

8. Paquette, L., et al.: Sensor-free affect detection for a simulation-based science inquiry learning environment. In: Trausan-Matu, S., Boyer, K.E., Crosby, M., Panourgia, K. (eds.) ITS 2014. LNCS, vol. 8474, pp. 1–10. Springer, Cham (2014). https://doi.org/10.1007/978-3-319-07221-0_1

9. Sabourin, J., Mott, B., Lester, J.C.: Modeling learner affect with theoretically grounded dynamic bayesian networks. In: D'Mello, S., Graesser, A., Schuller, B., Martin, J.-C. (eds.) ACII 2011. LNCS, vol. 6974, pp. 286–295. Springer, Heidelberg (2011). https://doi.org/10.1007/978-3-642-24600-5_32

10. Baker, R.S., et al.: Towards sensor-free affect detection in cognitive tutor algebra. In: Proceedings of the 5th International Conference on Educational Data Mining, pp. 126–133. IEDMS, Montréal (2012)

11. Wixon, M., Arroyo, I., Muldner, K., Burleson, W., Rai, D., Woolf, B.: The opportunities and limitations of scaling up sensor-free affect detection. In: Proceedings of the International Conference on Educational Data Mining, pp. 145–152. IEDMS, London (2014)

12. Litman, D.J., Forbes-Riley, K.: Predicting student emotions in computer-human tutoring dialogues. In: Proceedings of the Annual Meeting on Association for Computational Linguistics, pp. 351–358, Barcelona, Spain (2004). https://doi.org/10.3115/1218955.1219000

13. Bosch, N., D'Mello, S.: Co-occurring affective states in automated computer programming education. In: Proceedings of the Workshop on AI-supported Education for Computer Science (AIEDCS) at the 12th International Conference on Intelligent Tutoring Systems, pp. 21–30 (2014)

14. Dillon, J., et al.: Student emotion, co-occurrence, and dropout in a MOOC context. In: Proceedings of the 9th International Conference on Educational Data Mining, pp. 353–357. IEDMS, Raleigh (2016)
15. Harley, J.M., Bouchet, F., Azevedo, R.: Measuring learners' co-occurring emotional responses during their interaction with a pedagogical agent in MetaTutor. In: Cerri, S.A., Clancey, W.J., Papadourakis, G., Panourgia, K. (eds.) ITS 2012. LNCS, vol. 7315, pp. 40–45. Springer, Heidelberg (2012). https://doi.org/10.1007/978-3-642-30950-2_5
16. Gutica, M., Conati, C.: Student emotions with an edu-game: a detailed analysis. In: Proceedings of the Humaine Association Conference on Affective Computing and Intelligent Interaction. pp. 534–539. IEEE, Geneva (2013). https://doi.org/10.1109/acii.2013.94
17. Sinclair, J., Jang, E.E., Azevedo, R., Lau, C., Taub, M., Mudrick, N.V.: Changes in emotion and their relationship with learning gains in the context of MetaTutor. In: Nkambou, R., Azevedo, R., Vassileva, J. (eds.) ITS 2018. LNCS, vol. 10858, pp. 202–211. Springer, Cham (2018). https://doi.org/10.1007/978-3-319-91464-0_20
18. Azevedo, R., et al.: Using trace data to examine the complex roles of cognitive, metacognitive, and emotional self-regulatory processes during learning with multi-agent systems. In: Azevedo, R., Aleven, V. (eds.) International Handbook of Metacognition and Learning Technologies. SIHE, vol. 28, pp. 427–449. Springer, New York (2013). https://doi.org/10.1007/978-1-4419-5546-3_28
19. Petrovica, S., Anohina-Naumeca, A., Ekenel, H.K.: Emotion recognition in affective tutoring systems: collection of ground-truth data. Procedia Comput. Sci. **104**, 437–444 (2017). https://doi.org/10.1016/j.procs.2017.01.157
20. Ekman, P.: Basic emotions. In: Handbook of Cognition and Emotion. pp. 45–60. Wiley (1999)
21. Pekrun, R., Frenzel, A.C., Goetz, T., Perry, R.P.: The control-value theory of achievement emotions: An integrative approach to emotions in education. In: Emotion in Education, pp. 13–36. Elsevier (2007)
22. Pekrun, R., Vogl, E., Muis, K.R., Sinatra, G.M.: Measuring emotions during epistemic activities: the epistemically-related emotion scales. Cogn. Emot. **31**, 1268–1276 (2017). https://doi.org/10.1080/02699931.2016.1204989
23. Ocumpaugh, J., Baker, R.S., Rodrigo, M.M.: Baker rodrigo ocumpaugh monitoring protocol (BROMP) 2.0 technical and training manual. Technical Report. Teachers College, Columbia University, New York. Ateneo Laboratory for the Learning Sciences, Manila (2015)
24. Malekzadeh, M., Mustafa, M., Lahsasna, A.: A review of emotion regulation in intelligent tutoring systems. Educ. Technol. Soc. 18, 435–445. https://www.jstor.org/stable/10.2307/jeductechsoci.18.4.435
25. Jarrell, A., Harley, J.M., Lajoie, S., Naismith, L.: Success, failure and emotions: examining the relationship between performance feedback and emotions in diagnostic reasoning. Educ. Tech. Res Dev. **65**(5), 1263–1284 (2017). https://doi.org/10.1007/s11423-017-9521-6
26. Paquette, L., et al.: Sensor-free or sensor-full: a comparison of data modalities in multi-channel affect detection. In: Proceedings of the 8th International Conference on Educational Data Mining, pp. 93–100. IEDMS, Madrid (2016)
27. Kim, J., Seo, J., Laine, T.H.: Detecting boredom from eye gaze and EEG. Biomed. Sig. Process. Control **46**, 302–313 (2018). https://doi.org/10.1016/j.bspc.2018.05.034
28. Lallé, S., Conati, C., Carenini, G.: Predicting confusion in information visualization from eye tracking and interaction data. In: Proceedings on the 25th International Joint Conference on Artificial Intelligence, pp. 2529–2535. AAAI Press, New York (2016)
29. Henderson, N., Emerson, A., Rowe, J., Lester, J.: Improving sensor-based affect detection with multimodal data imputation. In: Proceedings of the 8th International Conference on Affective Computing and Intelligent Interaction, pp. 669–675. IEEE, Cambridge (2019)

30. Hutt, S., Mills, C., White, S., Donnelly, P.J., D'Mello, S.K.: The eyes have it: gaze-based detection of mind wandering during learning with an intelligent tutoring system. In: Proceedings of the 9th International Conference on Educational Data Mining, pp. 86–93. IEDMS, Raleigh (2016)
31. Kardan, S., Conati, C.: Comparing and combining eye gaze and interface actions for determining user learning with an interactive simulation. In: Carberry, S., Weibelzahl, S., Micarelli, A., Semeraro, G. (eds.) UMAP 2013. LNCS, vol. 7899, pp. 215–227. Springer, Heidelberg (2013). https://doi.org/10.1007/978-3-642-38844-6_18
32. Pekrun, R., Bühner, M.: Self-report measures of academic emotions. In: International Handbook of Emotions in Education. Routledge, London (2014)
33. Tan, P.-N., Kumar, V., Srivastava, J.: Selecting the right interestingness measure for association patterns. In: Proceedings of the 8th ACM International Conference on Knowledge Discovery and Data Mining, pp. 32–41. ACM, Edmonton (2002). https://doi.org/10.1145/775047.775053
34. Villarica, R., Richards, D.: Intelligent and empathic agent to support student learning in virtual worlds. In: Proceedings of the Conference on Interactive Entertainment, pp. 1–9. ACM, Newcastle (2014). https://doi.org/10.1145/2677758.2677761
35. Moridis, C.N., Economides, A.A.: Affective learning: empathetic agents with emotional facial and tone of voice expressions. IEEE Trans. Affect. Comput. **3**, 260–272 (2012). https://doi.org/10.1109/t-affc.2012.6
36. Craig, S., Graesser, A., Sullins, J., Gholson, B.: Affect and learning: an exploratory look into the role of affect in learning with AutoTutor. J. Educ. Media. **29**, 241–250 (2004). https://doi.org/10.1080/1358165042000283101
37. Liu, Z., Pataranutaporn, V., Ocumpaugh, J., Baker, R.: Sequences of frustration and confusion, and learning. In: Proceedings of the International Conference on Educational Data Mining, pp. 114–120. IEDMS, Memphis (2013)
38. D'Mello, S., Graesser, A.: The half-life of cognitive-affective states during complex learning. Cogn. Emot. **25**, 1299–1308 (2011). https://doi.org/10.1080/02699931.2011.613668
39. Huang, X., Mayer, R.E.: Benefits of adding anxiety-reducing features to a computer-based multimedia lesson on statistics. Comput. Hum. Behav. **63**, 293–303 (2016). https://doi.org/10.1016/j.chb.2016.05.034
40. Meyer, D.K.: Emotion regulation in K–12 classrooms. In: Handbook of Social Influences in School Contexts: Social-Emotional, Motivation, and Cognitive Outcomes. Routledge (2016)
41. Kardan, S., Lallé, S., Toker, D., Conati, C.: EMDAT: eye movement data analysis toolkit (1.x). The University of British Columbia (2021). https://doi.org/10.5281/zenodo.4699774
42. Bouchet, F., Harley, J.M., Trevors, G.J., Azevedo, R.: Clustering and profiling students according to their interactions with an intelligent tutoring system fostering self-regulated learning. J. Educ. Data Min. **5**, 104–146 (2013). https://doi.org/10.5281/zenodo.3554613
43. Pedregosa, F., et al.: Scikit-learn: machine learning in Python. J. Mach. Learn. Res. **12**, 2825–2830 (2011)
44. Zeng, Z., Pantic, M., Roisman, G.I., Huang, T.S.: A survey of affect recognition methods: audio, visual, and spontaneous expressions. IEEE Trans. Pattern Anal. Mach. Intell. **31**, 39–58 (2009). https://doi.org/10.1109/TPAMI.2008.52
45. Chawla, N.V., Bowyer, K.W., Hall, L.O., Kegelmeyer, W.P.: SMOTE: synthetic minority over-sampling technique. J. Artif. Intell. Res. **16**, 321–357 (2002). https://doi.org/10.1613/jair.953
46. Holm, S.: A simple sequentially rejective multiple test procedure. Scand. J. Stat. 65–70 (1979)

A Fairness Evaluation of Automated Methods for Scoring Text Evidence Usage in Writing

Diane Litman[1]([⊠]), Haoran Zhang[1], Richard Correnti[1],
Lindsay Clare Matsumura[1], and Elaine Wang[2]

[1] University of Pittsburgh, Pittsburgh, PA 15260, USA
{dlitman,colinzhang,rcorrent,lclare}@pitt.edu
[2] RAND Corporation, Pittsburgh, PA 15213, USA
ewang@rand.org

Abstract. Automated Essay Scoring (AES) can reliably grade essays at scale and reduce human effort in both classroom and commercial settings. There are currently three dominant supervised learning paradigms for building AES models: feature-based, neural, and hybrid. While feature-based models are more explainable, neural network models often outperform feature-based models in terms of prediction accuracy. To create models that are accurate and explainable, hybrid approaches combining neural network and feature-based models are of increasing interest. We compare these three types of AES models with respect to a different evaluation dimension, namely algorithmic fairness. We apply three definitions of AES fairness to an essay corpus scored by different types of AES systems with respect to upper elementary students' use of text evidence. Our results indicate that different AES models exhibit different types of biases, spanning students' gender, race, and socioeconomic status. We conclude with a step towards mitigating AES bias once detected.

Keywords: Automated essay scoring · Fairness · Argumentation

1 Introduction

With the deployment of automated essay scoring (AES) systems in both summative and formative scenarios (e.g., high-stakes testing and classroom instruction, respectively), it is important that a student's membership in a demographic group does not impact AES accuracy. While the study of AES fairness/bias has been of increasing interest, prior work has often focused on simulated rather than actual student data [22]. Also, an open question is whether AES fairness results generalize across different AI methods commonly used to build AES systems.

The research reported here was supported, in whole or in part, by the Institute of Education Sciences, U.S. Department of Education, through Grant R305A160245 to the University of Pittsburgh. The opinions expressed are those of the authors and do not represent the views of the Institute or the U.S. Department of Education.

© Springer Nature Switzerland AG 2021
I. Roll et al. (Eds.): AIED 2021, LNAI 12748, pp. 255–267, 2021.
https://doi.org/10.1007/978-3-030-78292-4_21

Table 1. RTA source article, writing prompt, and an essay (evidence score of 3).

Source Excerpt: Today, Yala Sub-District **Hospital has medicine, free of charge, for all of the most common diseases. Water is connected to the hospital,** which also has a **generator for electricity. Bed nets are used** in every sleeping site in Sauri
Essay Prompt: The author provided one specific example of how the quality of life can be improved by the Millennium Villages Project in Sauri, Kenya. Based on the article, did the author provide a convincing argument that winning the fight against poverty is achievable in our lifetime? Explain why or why not with 3–4 examples from the text to support your answer
Essay: In my opinion I think that they will **achieve it in lifetime.** During the years threw **2004 and 2008 they made progress.** People didn't have the money to buy the stuff in 2004. **The hospital was packed with patients** and they didn't have a lot of treatment in 2004. In 2008 it changed the **hospital had medicine, free of charge,** and **for all the common diseases. Water** was connected to the hospital and has a **generator for electricity.** Everybody has net in their site. **The hunger crisis has been addressed** with **fertilizer and seeds,** as well as the **tools needed to maintain the food. The school has no fees** and **they serve lunch.** To me that's sounds like it is going achieve it in the lifetime

Currently three supervised learning methods dominate the AES field. *Feature-based* models require hand-crafted features for essay representation and off-the-shelf learning algorithms for model training [1, 10, 24, 26]. While feature-based models are typically explainable and can be tightly tied to a scoring rubric, *neural network* models are increasingly popular as they often outperform feature-based models in terms of scoring accuracy and furthermore do not require any human feature engineering [9, 11, 23, 32, 37]. To create models that are both accurate and transparent, *hybrid* models combining neural network and feature-based models are also being developed [8, 17, 33].

In this paper, we compare these AES model types with respect to a different evaluation dimension than scoring accuracy or model transparency, namely *algorithmic fairness*. We apply three fairness measures tailored to AES [19] that have previously been used to analyze whether native language [19] or wearing face masks [18] introduces bias when English speaking proficiency is scored in an ETS testing context. We instead use these measures to analyze whether gender, socioeconomic status, and race introduce bias when essays produced by upper elementary school students are automatically scored for text evidence usage in a classroom context. Our results indicate that when evaluated using the same fairness measure, the feature-based, neural, and hybrid AES models exhibit different types of biases. We conclude with a simple example illustrating how certain AES models make it easier to mitigate AES bias once detected.

2   Essay Corpus

All AES models are trained using 2970 essays written by students in upper elementary school classrooms, using the response-to-text assessment (RTA) protocol [6]. After reading an article from *Time for Kids* about a United Nations effort to end poverty in a Kenyan village, students wrote an essay in response to a prompt encouraging them to use evidence from the article to support their claims. Table 1 shows a source article excerpt, the RTA prompt, and a student essay. After collection, essays were manually scored on a scale of 1 to 4 (low to

Table 2. Student Demographics (left)/Essay Scores (right) as "count (%)" (n = 818).

Male	Black	Free/Reduced	Score = 1	Score = 2	Score = 3	Score = 4
389 (47.6)	556 (68.0)	451 (55.1)	242 (29.6)	315 (38.5)	165 (20.2)	96 (11.7)

high) on five dimensions[1]. In particular, a team of undergraduates independently scored randomly ordered student essays from the corpus after extensive training by experts and guided by a rubric [21,30]. Here we focus only on the evidence dimension (inter-rater reliability ICC = 0.656, n = 735 essays [7]). The evidence dimension evaluates students' ability to find and use evidence from the source article (e.g., bolded phrases in the table) to support their ideas.

For our fairness evaluation, we report test results using only the sample of 818 student essays from the full corpus where we have information on student demographic characteristics (collected from the school district) in addition to the evidence scores. We focus specifically on whether the AES models might disadvantage particular groups, specifically African Americans, males, and students receiving free or reduced-price lunch. Table 2 shows the distributions of the student demographic characteristics to be investigated and the evidence scores for this sample.[2] Note that the demographics of students in our sample are roughly similar to that of the larger school district, where about 80% of students identified as Black and about 56% received free or reduced-price lunch.

3   AES Models

To score the essays in our corpus for text-based evidence usage, we use three different approaches to AES: 1) a feature-based supervised learning approach, which we refer to as AES_{rubric}, 2) a neural network approach, which we refer to as AES_{neural}, and 3) a hybrid approach combining a neural network and hand-crafted features, which we refer to as AES_{hybrid}.

AES_{rubric} uses traditional supervised machine learning (a random forest classification algorithm with max-depth = 5, implemented in Weka) with features hand-designed to align with the RTA evidence grading rubric. As detailed in [29,36], the features are automatically computed using natural language processing:

Number of Pieces of Evidence: the number of topics in the source article that are (semantically) mentioned in the essay.

Concentration: whether an essay elaborates on the source article topics.

Specificity: for each article topic, the number of specific examples (semantically) mentioned in the essay.

Word Count: the number of words in the essay.

---

[1] Analysis, Evidence, Organization, Style, Mechanics/Usage/Grammar/Spelling.

[2] Students in our sample also identified as Hispanic (22.0%), Native American (11.5%), Asian (4.3%), Hawaiian (2.0%) and White (12.1%). These categories are not mutually exclusive. We focus on African American students in our study as this was the only subgroup that was large enough (had sufficient data) for our analyses.

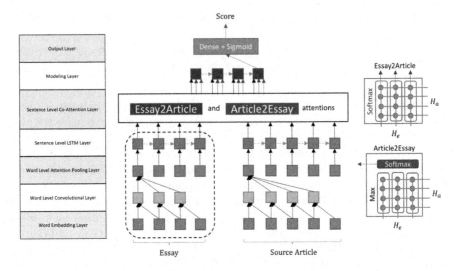

Fig. 1. Architecture of AES_{neural}, a co-attention based neural network [37].

Although the hand-crafted features of AES_{rubric} provide useful information for generating formative feedback in an accompanying automated writing evaluation (AWE) system [38], in order to improve stand-alone AES performance, a neural approach requiring no manual feature engineering and not restricted to the RTA was later developed [37]. As shown in Fig. 1, this model (AES_{neural}) uses a hierarchical neural network with a self-attention mechanism (in the dashed rounded box, originally designed for holistic scoring [9]), and adds a co-attention mechanism to support source-based scoring [37].[3]

To achieve high scoring performance yet provide some model transparency, in this paper we introduce AES_{hybrid},[4] a variant of AES_{neural} that enables the combination of hand-crafted features on any level of the hierarchical self-attention model. AES_{hybrid} offers the neural network the ability to model the features, and also no longer requires a source article. Figure 2 shows the combination of a hand-crafted feature at the word-level of the neural hierarchy. Since the released code computes hand-crafted linguistic features applicable to many AES tasks [13], we use feature selection to pick the following subset of 4 features:[5]

---

[3] https://github.com/Rokeer/co-attention.

[4] https://github.com/Rokeer/hybrid.

[5] We select one subset of features (from the set computed by the code release) that works for general AES purposes. Specifically, we introduce data from more prompts, including a second RTA prompt and eight prompts from the ASAP dataset (https://www.kaggle.com/c/asap-aes/). Then, we train models with only one combined hand-crafted feature for each prompt. Last, we select features that significantly improve the base neural model on the development set for at least 6 (out of 10) prompts. The intuition is that we want to select multiple features and combine each into the best level of the model hierarchy to create a version of AES_{hybrid} that is robust, while still preserving a reasonable number of features for our experiment.

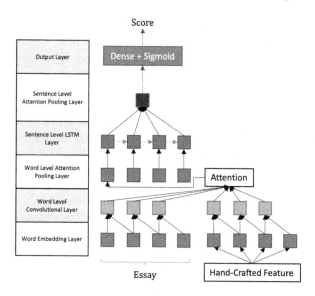

Fig. 2. Architecture of AES_{hybrid}, a self-attention based neural network that can be combined with hand-crafted features.

Discourse Connectives: Word categories rather than words are often used to reduce feature space dimensionality. This feature labels each word as to whether it belongs to a PDTB discourse connective category [28].

Readability: This feature computes an essay's readability using the Flesch Reading Ease Test [14].

Essay and Sentence Word Counts: These features count words at both the essay level (as in AES_{rubric}) and at the sentence level.

4   AES Fairness Measures

While a variety of measures can be used to examine algorithmic fairness in education [15], the measures chosen for our evaluation are recommended for automated scoring systems [19]. In particular, Loukina et al. [19] advocate for evaluating AES fairness along multiple dimensions, arguing that total algorithmic fairness may not be achievable and that addressing fairness problems may require different mitigation strategies for different fairness dimensions. They propose three measures – overall score accuracy (OSA), overall score difference (OSD), and conditional score difference (CSD) – to capture different fairness dimensions applicable to AES. We will use these three measures to compare the fairness of our three AES models.[6]

---

[6] Comparing to the broader fairness literature, Loukine et al. [19] state that OSA is similar in spirit to predictive accuracy [31], OSD to standardized mean difference [34] and treatment equality [3], and CSD to conditional procedure equality [3] and differential feature functioning [39].

Overall score accuracy (OSA) measures whether AES scores are *equally accurate* across student groups compared to human scores. First, the difference in squared error between human (H) and AES (S) scores are computed: $(S-H)^2$. Fairness is evaluated by fitting a linear regression with the squared error as the dependent variable and student demographic (e.g., male) as the independent variable. The regression R^2 is used as the OSA fairness value, with statistical significance suggesting AES bias. Further, a larger R^2 indicates more impact of student group membership on score accuracy and thus less fairness/more bias.

Overall score difference (OSD) measures whether AES and human scores are *consistently different* across student groups. In order to maintain the sign of the difference, this computation uses the absolute (rather than squared) error: $S-H$. The absolute difference is now the dependent variable in the regression, with student group again the independent variable. This regression model's R^2 is the OSD fairness value, with larger R^2 again indicating less AES fairness.

Conditional score difference (CSD) is similar to OSD, but first controls for student proficiency which is approximated using the human score H. This measure is computed by fitting a regression model with absolute difference $S-H$ as the dependent variable, first with only H as the independent variable, then with both H and student group. If the difference in R^2 between the two models is statistically significant, then student group membership is having an impact on AES accuracy beyond student proficiency.

5   Evaluating AES_{rubric}, AES_{neural}, and AES_{hybrid}

We first evaluate scoring performance. Based on Sects. 1 and 3, we hypothesize (H1) that AES_{rubric}, which is purely feature-based, will be outperformed by the other two models involving neural networks. We then evaluate the same models for fairness. Based on Sect. 4, we hypothesize (H2a) that for each AES model, different fairness measures will expose different biases. We in addition hypothesize (H2b) that using the same fairness measure, different biases for each type of AES algorithm will be identified. Next, we evaluate a simple method for mitigating detected bias in models involving hand-crafted features, and hypothesize (H3) that while mitigation can indeed improve fairness, there is a scoring tradeoff. Finally, we discuss the implications of our evaluations.

Evaluating Scoring Performance. We evaluate performance using QWK (Quadratic Weighted Kappa), a standard AES evaluation measure. All reported results are obtained by training each AES model on the full corpus of 2970 essays using a 5-fold cross-validation experimental setting. While AES_{rubric} uses 4 folds for training and 1 fold for testing in each round, both AES_{neural} and AES_{hybrid} use 3 folds for training, 1 fold for development and 1 fold for testing. All neural network models are built with TensorFlow 2.2.0, and trained on an RTX 5000 GPU. Table 3 shows the neural network hyper-parameters for both AES_{neural} and AES_{hybrid}, which are based on the original self-attention model [9].

Table 3. Hyper-parameters for neural training.

Layer	Parameter	Value	Layer	Parameter	Value
Embedding	Embedding dimension	50	Dropout	Dropout rate	0.5
Sent-LSTM	Hidden units	100	Modeling	Hidden units	100
Others	Epochs	50	Word-CNN	Kernel size	5
	Batch size	16		Number of filters	100
	Initial learning rate	0.001			
	Momentum	0.9			

Table 4. Quadratic weighted Kappa between AES and human gold-standard scores.

	AES_{rubric}	AES_{neural}	AES_{hybrid}
Full corpus (n = 2970)	0.653	0.697	0.692
Demographic sample (n = 818)	0.665	0.719	0.718

Table 4 shows that the results for all AES models support hypothesis H1, whether reporting test results using all essays or only those where we have associated demographics. AES_{neural} outperforms AES_{rubric}, while AES_{hybrid} is able to maintain AES_{neural}'s QWK while increasing model transparency. Model transparency will be exploited for bias mitigation as discussed below.

Evaluating Fairness. Table 5 shows the fairness results. Support for hypothesis H2a can be seen by comparing the 3 columns under each AES model, while keeping the row constant. For example, for AES_{rubric}, CSD significantly identifies (and OSD more weakly suggests) a bias in scoring males. While OSA is unable to detect any gender bias, it is instead the only measure to (weakly) identify a problem with AES_{rubric} and socioeconomic status (free/reduced in Table 5). For AES_{neural}, only OSA suggests a problem with scoring males, while only CSD suggests a problem with scoring students based on the other types of demographics. Finally, for AES_{hybrid}, OSA is the only fairness measure to identify any bias, here for males. In addition to the R^2 values shown in the table, the sign of the coefficients in each regression (not in the table) further indicate the direction of the bias. The male and free/reduced variables all have negative coefficients, while the black variable has a positive coefficient. This means, for example, that for OSD and CSD, the results suggest lower overall AES scores for male and free/reduced lunch students compared to the human scores. Our results support the need to evaluate a given AES model for a given demographic of interest using multiple dimensions of fairness, as each yields different insights [19].

Support for hypothesis H2b can be seen by comparing the 3 columns representing the same fairness measure across the three AES models. For example, evaluations along the single dimension measured by CSD show that while AES_{hybrid} is fair, the error of AES_{rubric} is impacted by a student's gender, while

Table 5. Fairness evaluation for each AES model, using the three measures representing different fairness dimensions. Cells for OSA and OSD contain adjusted R^2 values, while CSD cells contain ΔR^2 values. The values in each row show the percentage of variance for each AES model attributed to the membership of a student in the row's demographic (e.g. Male or Not). Larger values correspond to a greater impact of the demographic on scoring error. Cells marked 'ns' mean that the effect of the student demographic is not significant at $p < .05$. Cells with values in parentheses mean that while not significant, the demographic effect is a trend at $p < .1$.

	AES_{rubric}			AES_{neural}			AES_{hybrid}		
	OSA	OSD	CSD	OSA	OSD	CSD	OSA	OSD	CSD
Male	ns	(.002)	.009	(.003)	ns	ns	.009	ns	ns
Black	ns	ns	ns	ns	ns	.004	ns	ns	ns
Free/Reduced	(.002)	ns	ns	ns	ns	.005	ns	ns	ns

the error in AES_{neural} is instead impacted by the two other demographics. Overall, our results show that while all three AES models exhibit some dimension of bias, which fairness measures detect a bias, and for which student demographic varies for each model. AES_{hybrid} seems to be our fairest AES model, with only 1 of its nine cells suggesting a problem. This is also interesting since AES_{hybrid} evaluates best with respect to balancing QWK and model explainability.

Mitigating Detected Bias. Since Table 5 suggests that gender is the most significant bias issue for our models (in terms of number of cells as well as their values), we attempt to mitigate gender bias in our models, then examine the impact of this mitigation on both the scoring and fairness measures.

One source of model bias is often a very unequal demographic distribution in the training data. While this can potentially be mitigated by resampling to create more balance, Table 2 shows that imbalance is not the case for our gender demographic. Training demographic-specific models is another approach to handling bias, but we do not have a large enough training dataset to support splitting the data in half to train two separate models.

As an alternative to resampling training data or training demographic-specific models, Loukina et al. [19] also propose manipulating the feature representation of the data, by creating a 'fairer' feature subset. To be included in this subset, a feature's values should not differ across demographics of interest, even for the same proficiency level. Such features can be identified using the CSD computation from Sect. 4, but with the feature as the regression's dependent variable. We use this method to attempt to mitigate the gender biases detected above, by creating fairer feature subsets for AES_{rubric} and AES_{hybrid}. Note that we can not apply this mitigation to AES_{neural}, as no hand-crafted features are involved.

To create our 'fairer' feature subsets, we remove all features based on word counts. Although word count is often highly positively correlated with essay

Table 6. Effect of a simple gender bias mitigation on scoring (QWK) and fairness (OSD, CSD, OSA) for AES models allowing feature removal (n = 818).

	AES_{rubric} (QWK)	AES_{hybrid} (QWK)	AES_{rubric} (OSD)	AES_{rubric} (CSD)	AES_{hybrid} (OSA)
Original	0.665	0.718	(.002)	.009	.009
Mitigated	0.663	0.704	ns	.006	.008

quality and thus used by many feature-based AES systems [2,5,25,27,35], in our corpus, word count is not a 'fair' feature. In particular, essay word count is significantly smaller for students who are male (141.2) versus not (175.9), even after controlling for proficiency (145.2 vs 172.3). Essay word count is thus removed from both the AES_{rubric} and AES_{hybrid} feature sets; sentence word count (only used in the AES_{hybrid} feature set) is similarly removed.

After removing the word count features, we retrain the two models that use them, with the results shown in Table 6. As hypothesized (H3), although a simple mitigation method based on using a fairer feature subset indeed slightly reduces the previously detected gender bias across AES models and fairness measures, the use of fewer features also reduces each model's scoring performance.

6   Discussion

While the identified biases in Table 5 are small (although significant), they are similar in size to those found by Loukina et al. [19]. Specifically, the percentage of variance in AES error attributed to our investigated demographics is roughly similar to the percentage of variance in automated speech scoring error attributed to native language (with OSA, OSD, and CSD values of .002, .017, and .062, respectively [19]). Aligned in some respects to our research, other studies also have identified small, but significant algorithmic bias with respect to race and gender. As described in Bridgeman [4], for example, African American men tended to receive slightly lower scores from e-rater than from human raters.

While any level of algorithmic bias is concerning and undesirable, when a detected bias is large enough to warrant mitigation is an open question, particularly if there are tradeoffs. For example, one tradeoff could be between fairness and other evaluation dimensions such as AES reliability and validity (e.g., as in our work where increasing fairness reduced reliability). A different tradeoff could be between model interpretability (transparency) and fairness. If the purpose for using AES is to generate formative feedback to improve teaching and learning, then understanding how a score was derived is critical. In this case, the more transparent rubric-based scoring model would have an advantage over the neural net model. Similar explorations of model selection have been conducted outside of AES. For example, Kung and Yu [16] examined tradeoffs between accuracy, interpretability, and fairness when using different (non-neural) machine learning models to predict college success. While they did not find that their more interpretable models compromised accuracy or fairness, like us, they did find some (small) level of bias against student groups in even the fairest models. We emphasize that if AES is used for summative evaluation purpose, for example, to assign a course grade or make a more generalized inference about a student's skill and knowledge, then it would be important to include other measures, such as human evaluation, as a check to ensure that students in a particular group whose scores might show bias are evaluated fairly [4].

The 'fairer' feature approach to bias mitigation highlights the potentially limited utility of a given mitigation method across AES paradigms. For AES_{rubric} and AES_{hybrid}, some features might have high construct validity. For example, each of the AES_{rubric} features 'number of pieces of evidence', 'concentration', and 'specificity' capture scoring rubric criteria. 'Specificity' is in fact identified as unfair, but is undesirable to remove due to its construct validity; reconstituting the algorithm or mitigating some underlying component used to operationalize 'specificity' may be possible, but this suggests a more nuanced approach than removing the feature altogether. In contrast, the unfair features based on word counts that we did remove do not correspond to any explicit rubric criteria. Finally, for AES_{neural}, creating a fairer feature subset is not even applicable as the essay representation is learned rather than based on hand-crafted features.

7 Summary and Future Work

Our main contribution is to use a multi-dimensional approach to evaluating AES fairness as the basis of a systematic *fairness comparison across three prominent machine learning-based AES methods*. A secondary contribution is the introduction of new hybrid model architecture for AES. Our AES methods vary both with respect to whether they use hand-crafted features (AES_{nubric}, AES_{hybrid}) or not (AES_{neural}), and when features are used, whether the features primarily encode rubric-specific (AES_{rubric}) or more general linguistic (AES_{hybrid}) constructs. Comparing results across AES models demonstrates that 1) all three AES models suffer from a small but significant bias on at least one fairness dimension with respect to at least one demographic, 2) when evaluated along a single fairness dimension, the biases vary across the AES models, and 3) the utility of a fairer feature strategy for bias mitigation also varies across the AES models. Also, by comparing results within a single AES model while varying fairness measures, we generalize prior findings (namely, that multiple fairness dimensions are needed as they provide different insights) from speech scoring in a testing context [19] to the very different context of evidence scoring in elementary school classrooms.

As with similar studies of algorithmic fairness, our bias conceptualization assumed that human scores represent the gold standard by which to compare AES models. We note, however, that human ratings are not necessarily bias free and may also warrant investigation. Past research, for example, has noted that trained raters react differently to the linguistic features in the essays of African American, English learners, and standard American English writers and to student characteristics such as gender and socioeconomic background (e.g., [12, 20]).

An interesting future direction would be to flip the conceptualization, by exploring whether differences with a consistent and replicable AES might be a useful method for identifying bias in human scores.

References

1. Amorim, E., Cançado, M., Veloso, A.: Automated essay scoring in the presence of biased ratings. In: Proceedings of the 2018 Conference of the North American Chapter of the Association for Computational Linguistics: Human Language Technologies, (Long Papers), vol. 1, pp. 229–237 (2018)
2. Attali, Y., Burstein, J.: Automated essay scoring with e-rater® v. 2. J. Technol. Learn. Assess. 4(3) (2006)
3. Berk, R., Heidari, H., Jabbari, S., Kearns, M., Roth, A.: Fairness in criminal justice risk assessments: the state of the art. Sociol. Methods Res. 0049124118782533 (2018)
4. Bridgeman, B.: 13 human ratings and automated essay evaluation. In: Handbook of Automated Essay Evaluation: Current Applications and New Directions, p. 221 (2013)
5. Chen, H., He, B.: Automated essay scoring by maximizing human-machine agreement. In: Proceedings of the 2013 Conference on Empirical Methods in Natural Language Processing, pp. 1741–1752 (2013)
6. Correnti, R., Matsumura, L.C., Hamilton, L., Wang, E.: Assessing students' skills at writing analytically in response to texts. Elem. Sch. J. 114(2), 142–177 (2013)
7. Correnti, R., Matsumura, L.C., Wang, E., Litman, D., Rahimi, Z., Kisa, Z.: Automated scoring of students' use of text evidence in writing. Read. Res. Q. 55(3), 493–520 (2020)
8. Dasgupta, T., Naskar, A., Dey, L., Saha, R.: Augmenting textual qualitative features in deep convolution recurrent neural network for automatic essay scoring. In: Proceedings of the 5th Workshop on Natural Language Processing Techniques for Educational Applications, pp. 93–102 (2018)
9. Dong, F., Zhang, Y., Yang, J.: Attention-based recurrent convolutional neural network for automatic essay scoring. In: Proceedings of the 21st Conference on Computational Natural Language Learning (CoNLL 2017), pp. 153–162 (2017)
10. Ghosh, D., Khanam, A., Han, Y., Muresan, S.: Coarse-grained argumentation features for scoring persuasive essays. In: Proceedings of the 54th Annual Meeting of the Association for Computational Linguistics (Short Papers), vol. 2, pp. 549–554 (2016)
11. Jin, C., He, B., Hui, K., Sun, L.: TDNN: a two-stage deep neural network for prompt-independent automated essay scoring. In: Proceedings of the 56th Annual Meeting of the Association for Computational Linguistics (Long Papers), vol. 1, pp. 1088–1097 (2018)
12. Johnson, D., VanBrackle, L.: Linguistic discrimination in writing assessment: how raters react to African American "errors," ESL errors, and standard English errors on a state-mandated writing exam. Assess. Writ. 17(1), 35–54 (2012)
13. Ke, Z., Ng, V.: Automated essay scoring: a survey of the state of the art. In: Proceedings of the 28th International Joint Conference on Artificial Intelligence, pp. 6300–6308. AAAI Press (2019)
14. Kincaid, J.P., Fishburne Jr, R.P., Rogers, R.L., Chissom, B.S.: Derivation of new readability formulas (automated readability index, fog count and flesch reading ease formula) for navy enlisted personnel (1975)

15. Kizilcec, R.F., Lee, H.: Algorithmic fairness in education. In: Holmes, W., Porayska-Pomsta, K. (eds.) Ethics in Artificial Intelligence in Education. Taylor and Francis (forthcoming)
16. Kung, C., Yu, R.: Interpretable models do not compromise accuracy or fairness in predicting college success. In: Proceedings of the Seventh ACM Conference on Learning@ Scale, pp. 413–416 (2020)
17. Liu, J., Xu, Y., Zhao, L.: Automated essay scoring based on two-stage learning. arXiv preprint arXiv:1901.07744 (2019)
18. Loukina, A., Evanini, K., Mulholland, M., Blood, I., Zechner, K.: Do face masks introduce bias in speech technologies? The case of automated scoring of speaking proficiency. In: Meng, H., Xu, B., Zheng, T.F. (eds.) Interspeech 2020, 21st Annual Conference of the International Speech Communication Association, Virtual Event, Shanghai, China, 25–29 October 2020, pp. 1942–1946. ISCA (2020)
19. Loukina, A., Madnani, N., Zechner, K.: The many dimensions of algorithmic fairness in educational applications. In: Proceedings of the Fourteenth Workshop on Innovative Use of NLP for Building Educational Applications, pp. 1–10. Association for Computational Linguistics, Florence (2019)
20. Malouff, J.M., Thorsteinsson, E.B.: Bias in grading: a meta-analysis of experimental research findings. Aust. J. Educ. **60**(3), 245–256 (2016)
21. Matsumura, L.C., Correnti, R., Wang, E.: Classroom writing tasks and students' analytic text-based writing. Read. Res. Q. **50**(4), 417–438 (2015)
22. Mayfield, E., Black, A.W.: Should you fine-tune BERT for automated essay scoring? In: Proceedings of the Fifteenth Workshop on Innovative Use of NLP for Building Educational Applications, pp. 151–162 (2020)
23. Nadeem, F., Nguyen, H., Liu, Y., Ostendorf, M.: Automated essay scoring with discourse-aware neural models. In: Proceedings of the Fourteenth Workshop on Innovative Use of NLP for Building Educational Applications, pp. 484–493 (2019)
24. Nguyen, H.V., Litman, D.J.: Argument mining for improving the automated scoring of persuasive essays. In: Thirty-Second AAAI Conference on Artificial Intelligence (2018)
25. Östling, R., Smolentzov, A., Hinnerich, B.T., Höglin, E.: Automated essay scoring for Swedish. In: Proceedings of the Eighth Workshop on Innovative Use of NLP for Building Educational Applications, pp. 42–47 (2013)
26. Persing, I., Ng, V.: Modeling argument strength in student essays. In: Proceedings of the 53rd Annual Meeting of the Association for Computational Linguistics and the 7th International Joint Conference on Natural Language Processing (Long Papers), vol. 1, pp. 543–552 (2015)
27. Phandi, P., Chai, K.M.A., Ng, H.T.: Flexible domain adaptation for automated essay scoring using correlated linear regression. In: Proceedings of the 2015 Conference on Empirical Methods in Natural Language Processing, pp. 431–439 (2015)
28. Pitler, E., Nenkova, A.: Using syntax to disambiguate explicit discourse connectives in text. In: Proceedings of the ACL-IJCNLP 2009 Conference Short Papers, pp. 13–16 (2009)
29. Rahimi, Z., Litman, D., Correnti, R., Wang, E., Matsumura, L.C.: Assessing students' use of evidence and organization in response-to-text writing: using natural language processing for rubric-based automated scoring. Int. J. Artif. Intell. Educ. **27**(4), 694–728 (2017). https://doi.org/10.1007/s40593-017-0143-2
30. Rahimi, Z., Litman, D.J., Correnti, R., Matsumura, L.C., Wang, E., Kisa, Z.: Automatic scoring of an analytical response-to-text assessment. In: Trausan-Matu, S., Boyer, K.E., Crosby, M., Panourgia, K. (eds.) ITS 2014. LNCS, vol. 8474, pp. 601–610. Springer, Cham (2014). https://doi.org/10.1007/978-3-319-07221-0_76

31. Ramineni, C., Williamson, D.M.: Automated essay scoring: psychometric guidelines and practices. Assess. Writ. **18**(1), 25–39 (2013)

32. Tay, Y., Phan, M.C., Tuan, L.A., Hui, S.C.: SkipFlow: incorporating neural coherence features for end-to-end automatic text scoring. In: Thirty-Second AAAI Conference on Artificial Intelligence (2018)

33. Uto, M., Xie, Y., Ueno, M.: Neural automated essay scoring incorporating handcrafted features. In: Proceedings of the 28th International Conference on Computational Linguistics, pp. 6077–6088 (2020)

34. Williamson, D.M., Xi, X., Breyer, F.J.: A framework for evaluation and use of automated scoring. Educ. Meas. Issues Pract. **31**(1), 2–13 (2012)

35. Zesch, T., Wojatzki, M., Scholten-Akoun, D.: Task-independent features for automated essay grading. In: Proceedings of the Tenth Workshop on Innovative Use of NLP for Building Educational Applications, pp. 224–232 (2015)

36. Zhang, H., Litman, D.: Word embedding for response-to-text assessment of evidence. In: Proceedings of ACL 2017, Student Research Workshop, pp. 75–81 (2017)

37. Zhang, H., Litman, D.: Co-attention based neural network for source-dependent essay scoring. In: Proceedings of the Thirteenth Workshop on Innovative Use of NLP for Building Educational Applications, pp. 399–409 (2018)

38. Zhang, H., et al.: eRevise: using natural language processing to provide formative feedback on text evidence usage in student writing. In: Proceedings of the AAAI Conference on Artificial Intelligence, vol. 33, pp. 9619–9625 (2019)

39. Zhang, M., Dorans, N., Li, C., Rupp, A.: Differential feature functioning in automated essay scoring. In: Test Fairness in the New Generation of Large-Scale Assessment, pp. 185–208 (2017)

The Challenge of Noisy Classrooms: Speaker Detection During Elementary Students' Collaborative Dialogue

Yingbo Ma[1]($\boxtimes$), Joseph B. Wiggins[1], Mehmet Celepkolu[1],
Kristy Elizabeth Boyer[1]($\boxtimes$), Collin Lynch[2], and Eric Wiebe[2]

[1] University of Florida, Gainesville, FL 32601, USA
{yingbo.ma,jbwiggi3,mckolu,keboyer}@ufl.edu
[2] North Carolina State University, Raleigh, NC 27606, USA
{cflynch,wiebe}@ncsu.edu

Abstract. Adaptive and intelligent collaborative learning support systems are effective for supporting learning and building strong collaborative skills. This potential has not yet been realized within noisy classroom environments, where automated speech recognition (ASR) is very difficult. A key challenge is to differentiate each learner's speech from the background noise, which includes the teachers' speech as well as other groups' speech. In this paper, we explore a multimodal method to identify speakers by using visual and acoustic features from ten video recordings of children pairs collaborating in an elementary school classroom. The results indicate that the visual modality was better for identifying the speaker when in-group speech was detected, while the acoustic modality was better for differentiating in-group speech from background speech. Our analysis also revealed that recurrent neural network (RNN)-based models outperformed convolutional neural network (CNN)-based models with higher speaker detection F-1 scores. This work represents a critical step toward the classroom deployment of intelligent systems that support collaborative learning.

Keywords: Adaptive and intelligent collaborative learning support · Classroom environment · Speaker detection · Multimodal learning

1 Introduction

Adaptive and intelligent collaborative learning support (AICLS) systems [25] provide personalized feedback [45] to individual students working in pairs or groups. An AICLS system not only analyzes the group interaction [27] and provides tailored supports during the problem-solving process [36], but also adapts its content presentation or navigation support according to the learners' collaboration activity. This technology has been shown to be effective for improving students' learning outcomes [1], increasing their engagement in learning [46] and helping students build strong collaboration skills [26]. Early results have shown

© Springer Nature Switzerland AG 2021
I. Roll et al. (Eds.): AIED 2021, LNAI 12748, pp. 268–281, 2021.
https://doi.org/10.1007/978-3-030-78292-4_22

that adaptive supports are better than non-adaptive supports for providing flexible guidance [17] and improving learning outcomes [21].

Despite this promise, AICLS cannot currently support real-time collaboration between children speaking together in noisy classrooms. Instead, most current AICLS systems are designed for remote/distributed collaboration settings where an individual's speech and actions can easily be isolated [31,41] and where students' individual learning activities are often identified through analyzing students' log actions [37] or the group discourse through textual chat [41,44,45]. This is in part because classrooms are noisy: they feature multiple overlapping audio sources, and deploying ASR in these environments is difficult due to the challenges of handling background noise and detecting/isolating speech and speakers [3]. This problem could be mitigated with students wearing their own microphone with noise cancelling capabilities; however, most schools are unable to afford deploying these devices en masse. In addition, headsets detract from the fluid interplay of individual, small group, and whole class discourse.

To address these challenges and move toward AICLS systems that are viable for use in noisy classrooms, one task that must be addressed is detecting which child from a collaborating pair is speaking at a given moment. This paper reports on a novel speaker detection method that uses visual and acoustic features from video recordings of learners collaborating, with the goal of identifying which child is speaking. The proposed approach analyzes a single mixed audio source from two students in the group, which does not require their audios to be recorded into separate channels. In addition, the approach utilizes visual features detected from two children's faces, which could act as supplementary indicators to acoustic features. To the best of our knowledge, this paper presents the first empirical evaluation combining visual and acoustic features on the challenging task of identifying the speaker within student pairs in noisy classroom contexts.

2   Related Work

Recently, AICLS systems have been deployed for various learning domains, such as computer science learning [47], medical training [9], and music learning [24]. In this section we focus on AICLS systems within the context of computer science education. Current systems have used a variety of methods to identify each student's activity during collaboration. SIENA [29] tracked individual's learning progress by calculating the learner's posterior knowledge after he/she answered a question. NUCLEO [37] built an adaptation model for each learner based on the individual score obtained among team partners and the system-user interaction process, such as number of files created and answered messages. SCEPPSys [41] and Peer Tutor [45] analyzed group discourse from students' textual chat history. CycleTalk Chat [21] identified individuals by assigning each student an audio-based chat client and collecting their dialogues separately.

The aforementioned systems were all designed for remote/distributed collaboration where students were not co-located. There have been very few systems that analyze student dialogues while they are working collaboratively in person. Harsley et al. [12] designed Collab-ChiQat for analyzing student activity during collaboration; yet, the system required students to self-report who authored each line of code. Yett et al. [47] analyzed individual log actions of co-located students participating in a collaborative programming environment. The authors suggested that future work should combine log-based analysis and discourse analysis, which relies on the accurate differentiation of speech between individuals within the group. In another classroom study, Celepkolu et al. [5] designed a visualization tool to help individual students reflect on their collaborative dialogues. Even though the tool automatically analyzed the dialogue and generated the visualizations based on the transcriptions, it still required the dialogue to be manually transcribed. Blanchard et al. [3] tested and compared five ASR engines such as Google Speech and Bing Speech with audio data collected in middle school classrooms, but their focus was on teachers who wore individual wireless microphones. Li et al. [22] designed a Siamese neural network to detect dialogues for teachers and students in both *online* and *offline* classroom audio recordings. Although a promising level of speaker detection was achieved, the authors suggested that future work should combine both audio and video data.

Our study differs from these studies in three ways: First, our dataset consisted of pairs of students sitting next to each other, sharing the computer, with background noise from other students and the teacher. Such a research context makes distinguishing the speakers much more challenging. Second, we identify speakers by using video recordings (audio and video images) of the students' collaborative interaction process collected from the built-in computer webcam (without any headsets). Third, we applied recent machine learning techniques and compared the performance between CNN-based models and RNN-based models. Prior work by Hu et al. [15] has shown promise using CNN-based models to localize and identify each speaking character in a TV/movie/live show video, but did not consider the natural temporal connections within the sequential data. In contrast, RNN-based models represent a novel approach to solving this problem and have been used by Soleymani et al. [39] to analyze a speaker's verbal and nonverbal behaviors associated with self-disclosure with multimodal features extracted from video, audio and text data.

3   Data

3.1   Collection and Preprocessing

Our dataset was collected from 20 children (10 pairs) in 4th/5th grade classrooms in an elementary school in the southeastern United States in 2019. Among the children, 9 identified themselves as females and 11 as males. The students collaborated on a series of coding activities, in which they learned fundamental CS concepts such as variables, conditionals, and loops using Netsblox [30], a block-based learning environment. Each group's collaboration process was videotaped by the front-facing camera of their computer; meanwhile, the audio was recorded by the computer microphone without any additive noise cancellation equipment. The corpus contained a total of 7 h and 22 min of video recordings; raw audio recordings were then extracted from video recordings using FFmpeg [10], an open-source video converter.

Since noise sensitivity is a significant challenge for speech-related tasks, we approximated the quality of our audio recordings by following the method used by Tan et al. [40] to compute the *posterior* signal-to-noise ratio (SNR), the logarithmic ratio of the energy of the noisy speech to the energy of the noise. The average estimated SNR over ten recordings was +2.20 dB (as shown in Table 1), indicating a *fair* audio quality. Howard et al. [14] reported that the typical classroom SNRs range from −7 dB to +5 dB, while an SNR of +15 dB or above indicates *good* speech quality.

3.2 Annotation

We used ELAN [7] to synchronize video and audio clips and annotate them. The data was tagged at a one-second granularity, a time window previously used in similar acoustic classification tasks [42]. We tagged each one-second clip in one of three ways: Left Child (the child sitting in the left of the video was speaking), Right Child (the child sitting on the right was speaking), and Silence (neither Left Child nor Right Child was speaking). No children switched position during the activity. When the clip contained overlapping speech, we tagged the clip based on which child's speech was more audible. Table 1 shows the details of the corpus. The first author annotated the first four of ten videos, and the remaining six videos were annotated by three other annotators. To measure the labeling reliability, the first author then independently tagged 10% continuous video excerpts from the data tagged by other annotators. The Cohen's kappa scores between the first author and each of our three annotators were 0.8521, 0.7109, 0.7526 respectively, indicating substantial inner-annotator agreement [4].

Table 1. Details of the collected classroom recording corpus

Video ID	Duration (second)	Left child (second)	Right child (second)	Silence (second)[a]	SNR (dB)
1	2574	569	386	1619	+2.60
2	2199	394	498	1307	+1.24
3	2550	397	605	1548	+1.57
4	2693	416	485	1792	+3.17
5	3019	617	314	2088	+3.35
6	2665	165	302	2198	+2.67
7	2940	311	426	2203	+2.48
8	2804	526	275	2003	+2.12
9	2350	344	509	1497	+1.40
10	2673	377	604	1692	+1.39
In total	26467	4116 (15.55%)	4404 (16.64%)	17947 (67.81%)	+2.20

[a] Silence class also includes the clips in which the in-group children were silent but background speech was detected from the teacher and other children in the classroom. Background speech was irrelevant to in-group interaction and should not be taken into consideration for further in-group interaction analysis by the AICLS system

4   Features

4.1   Visual Feature: Dense Optical Flow

Facial movements, especially around the lip area, are critical to detect speakers [8,35]. In this paper, we extracted visual features using the dense optical flow [38] from children's faces in each pair (see Fig. 1). Dense optical flow uses the variation of pixels to calculate the object motion gradient along time. To compute the dense optical flows for two children in the video, we first extracted their faces using the deep learning-based face detector [33] from OpenCV [32] (a real-time computer vision library). Then, we re-scaled all faces into the same image size and used the *cv2.calcOpticalFlowFarneback()* [34] function from OpenCV to calculated one dense optical flow on their faces for each second. We applied dense optical flow on the whole face instead of the mouth region because whole-face optical flows were more robust to instances in which the child was not directly facing the camera, or in the case of low-resolution recording. Dense optical flow images were generated in grey-scale because the color in dense optical flow denotes the movement direction, which was not needed to identify speakers.

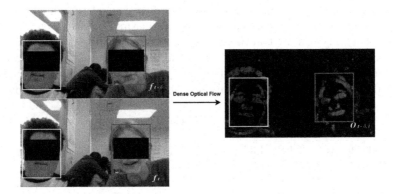

Fig. 1. *Left*: two sample frames ($f_{t-\delta}$ and f_t) from a one-second video clip when the left child was not speaking and the right child was speaking. *Right*: dense optical flow $O_{t-\delta,t}$, which represents the motion detected between the two frames. In this case, more motion was detected from the right child's face: the intensity in the dense optical flow denotes movement speed.

4.2   Acoustic Feature: Mel Spectrogram

We converted each one-second audio clip into one mel spectrogram, an image representation that describes an audio's time-frequency distribution where the frequencies are converted in the mel scale—a perceptual scale of pitches judged by human listeners. One advantage of the mel spectrogram over traditional acoustic features [19] (pitch, energy, mfcc coefficients, etc.) is it shows the variance of acoustic frequency and energy over time, which is useful for analyzing sequential data. In an mel spectrogram, the x-axis represents time and the y-axis represents frequency. We generated mel spectrograms using *librosa* [28], a python library for audio analysis. Figure 2 shows four mel spectrograms generated from 4 different audio clips.

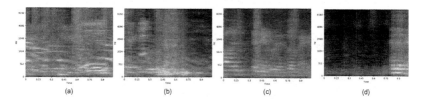

Fig. 2. Four mel spectrograms: *(a)*: The target child spoke over the whole audio clip; *(b)*: The speech from the target child only presented in the first 0.6 s of the audio clip; *(c)*: Silence, the target children were silent but background speech from the teacher or other children was audible; *(d)*: Silence, none speech detected over the whole audio clip

5   Methods: Speaker Detection

In this study, we conducted two experiments. First, to analyze the performance of different feature combinations, we compared the results of uni-modality (only visual or only acoustic features) with multi-modality (visual and acoustic features). Second, to compare the performance of different model architectures, we tested our dataset with two types of commonly used models (CNN-based and RNN-based).

Experiment 1: Comparing Uni-modality with Multi-modality. Figure 3 shows the high-level structure of the multimodal learning model, which was divided into three parallel streams (one visual stream for the left child, one visual stream for the right child, and one acoustic stream for both children). The model consisted of two parts: a modality encoding network and a sequence-based recurrent network. Since the visual and acoustic feature representations are both images, we used CNN-based models in the modality encoding network. We used ResNet-50 [13], a pre-trained CNN-based model that achieved the highest image classification accuracy on ImageNet [16], to map each image representation into a feature embedding. In the second sequence-based recurrent network, we used Bi-directional Long Short-Term Memory (Bi-LSTM) to learn temporal dependencies between sequential feature representations. We tested different time steps of the Bi-LSTM from 2 to 5. Each output of the Bi-LSTM is a feature embedding followed by a *softmax* layer [23] to calculate the class scores. Finally, we combined the class scores from three separate streams by averaging fusion [38]. The model (Code available on GitHub[1]) was implemented in Python with the Keras [18] API. Two visual streams were used for evaluating

---

[1] https://github.com/yingbo-ma/The-Challenge-of-Noisy-Classrooms-AIED2021.

the performance of the visual modality, and one acoustic stream was used for evaluating the performance of the acoustic modality.

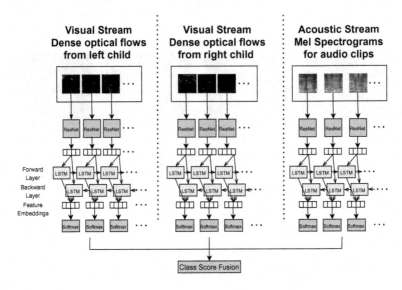

Fig. 3. Multimodal learning model

Experiment 2: Comparing CNN-Based Models with RNN-Based Models. We selected two types of commonly used models (CNN-based and RNN-based) that were proposed in the recent literature. Hu et al. [15] proposed a two-stream CNN-based learning framework for localizing and identifying each speaking character in a TV/movie/live show video. The model used convolutional layers as face feature extractors, then learned a unified multimodal classifier with fusion features combined from visual and acoustic features. Soleymani et al. [39] proposed a ResNet + GRU (gated recurrent unit)-based method to analyze a speaker's verbal and nonverbal behaviors associated with self-disclosure. The model built three separate classifiers based on the visual features extracted with ResNet, the acoustic features extracted with VGGish [43] (a pre-trained acoustic feature extractor trained on audio spectrograms), and the language features extracted with BERT [6] (a pre-trained language model that can map the spoken utterances to feature representations). The model then performed late fusion by simply averaging the output from all modalities. Since the feature fusion strategy was not the focus of this work, we implemented the above-mentioned models followed by the description of the model architecture in the two papers, and still used late averaging fusion. The CNN model [15] consisted of three stacked convolution + pooling layers followed by a fully connected layer. The RNN model [39] consisted of the pre-trained ResNet-50 [13] followed by a single GRU layer with 128 hidden units.

During the model training process across the two experiments, we conducted experiments on each video recording and used ten-fold cross-validation to train and evaluate the model. The network updated weights with an Adam optimizer [20] with the learning rate of 0.0001. We evaluated the trained model with the F-1 score [11] combined from precision and recall for each one of the three classes. Although F-1 score can be used as a general measurement of model performance, including precision and recall provides additional information. The context of collaborative dialogue may shift the cost of false negatives versus false positives, so these additional scores allows us to weigh each case.

6   Results

Results for Experiment 1. Figure 4 shows the performance of uni-modality and multi-modality. In Fig. 4-Left, the acoustic modality outperformed the visual modality and the combined modality when identifying the Silent class. In Fig. 4-Middle and Fig. 4-Right, the visual modality outperformed the acoustic modality and the combined modality when identifying one of the speech classes. Table 2 compares the different modalities with averaged precision, recall and F-1 score for each class. Table 3 displays results for the multimodal learning model's performance with different time steps. The time step of 3 performed the best for classifying the Silence class and the time step of 3 and 4 both performed similarly well at classifying the Left and Right Child class.

Results for Experiment 2. Table 4 shows the performance of different models on our corpus. The CNN architecture [15] performed the best at classify-

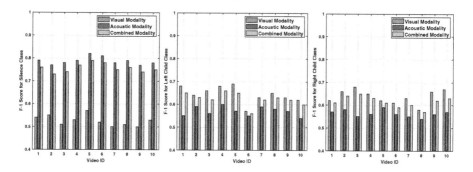

Fig. 4. F-1 score for three classes across corpus using different modalities. *Left*: Silence class—acoustic modality outperformed visual modality; *Middle*: Left Child class—visual modality outperformed acoustic modality; *Right*: Right Child class—visual modality outperformed acoustic modality

Table 2. Performance for each class under different modalities

	Silence			Left child			Right child		
	Precision	Recall	F-1 score	Precision	Recall	F-1 score	Precision	Recall	F-1 score
Visual modality	0.55	0.49	0.52	0.59	0.69	0.64	0.59	0.68	0.63
Acoustic modality	0.68	0.89	0.78	0.68	0.50	0.56	0.68	0.49	0.55
Combined modality	0.73	0.79	0.76	0.66	0.61	0.63	0.66	0.60	0.62

Table 3. Performance of the multimodal learning model with different time steps in Bi-LSTM

Time step	2			3			4			5		
	Precision	Recall	F-1 score	Precision	Recall	F-1 Score	Precision	Recall	F-1 score	Precision	Recall	F-1 score
Silence	0.72	0.84	0.76	0.72	0.84	0.77	0.72	0.84	0.77	0.71	0.83	0.76
Left child	0.63	0.58	0.60	0.66	0.60	0.63	0.66	0.59	0.62	0.64	0.58	0.61
Right child	0.64	0.59	0.61	0.66	0.60	0.62	0.67	0.60	0.63	0.67	0.60	0.63

ing Silence; Both the ResNet + GRU model [39] and the ResNet + Bi-LSTM model in our paper performed similarly, with better classification performance on Left Child and Right Child than the CNN architecture. ResNet + Uni-LSTM performed comparably with ResNet + Bi-LSTM, potentially indicating that whether a child intends to speak has stronger connection with his/her prior dialogues than latter dialogues.

Table 4. Performance of different models

Model	Class	Precision	Recall	F-1 score
CNN [15]	Silence	0.70	0.87	0.78
	Left child	0.65	0.53	0.58
	Right child	0.65	0.53	0.58
ResNet + GRU [39]	Silence	0.72	0.81	0.76
	Left child	0.67	0.58	0.62
	Right child	0.66	0.58	0.62
ResNet + Uni-directional LSTM	Silence	0.72	0.83	0.77
	Left child	0.66	0.60	0.63
	Right child	0.65	0.60	0.62
ResNet + Bi-directional LSTM	Silence	0.72	0.84	0.77
	Left child	0.66	0.60	0.63
	Right child	0.66	0.61	0.62

7   Discussion

This work evaluated several unimodal and multimodal learning frameworks' performance on identifying the speaker within pairs of children in a noisy elementary school classroom. Our results show the effectiveness of using visual optical flow and acoustic mel spectrogram for this task, and achieved averaged F-1 scores of 0.76 for Silence, 0.63 for Left Child, and 0.62 for Right Child.

These results have several implications for developing AICLS systems that can be utilized for personalized supports during collaborative learning in noisy classrooms. In the experiment investigating the contribution of each modality, the results showed that only using the visual modality yielded a higher F-1 score on detecting speakers compared to using the combined visual and acoustic modality. However, only using the visual modality has potential drawbacks due to lower Precision and higher Recall, meaning the model falsely reported more irrelevant background speech samples as in-group speech samples. This could potentially be misleading for an AICLS system. For example, the system might provide support when students are listening to teacher's lecture because the system would falsely classify the teacher's dialogues as the students' dialogues. Therefore, the feature modality should be carefully selected based on the noise level of a classroom. If the classroom is relatively quiet, using the visual modality may provide better speaker detection performance and report more true in-group speech samples. However, if a classroom is noisy and the in-group speech is overwhelmed by the background speech, the results suggest using the combined visual and acoustic modality may help. The experiment of comparing CNN-based models and RNN-based models showed that the CNN-based model performed better in differentiating in-group speech from background noise, and RNN-based models performed better for distinguishing between in-group speakers. Compared to silence, speech tends to have a more temporal connection, which was better modeled by the sequential neural network of the RNN. Therefore, CNN-based models would be better to use when the proportion of speech is much lower than the proportion of silence in students' dialogues, and RNN-based models would be more appropriate to use when in-group children interact with partners more frequently.

There are important limitations of the present approach. First, although our framework achieved promising results, the generalizability of the model has not been shown. Each learned model depends on the unique audio characteristics of children in the training set. In addition, the effectiveness of visual features largely relies on the correct setup of the video data collection process. The speaker detection performance on videos 6 and 8 was much lower than the averaged results across because in both videos, the front-facing camera was not positioned correctly. On the other hand, the effectiveness of acoustic feature depends on the group members' voices and the audio quality. If the frequency range of two children's voices is narrow (this often happens when two children in the group are of the same gender), the performance of using acoustic features would deteriorate.

8   Conclusions and Future Work

AI to support collaborative learning in classrooms holds great promise, but the tasks of identifying who is speaking, and what they are saying, present great challenges. This paper investigated the task of speaker detection. By utilizing features from the visual modality and the acoustic modality, our RNN-based model achieved encouraging speaker detection performance. The results indicated that the acoustic modality performed better at differentiating in-group speech and background noise; and the visual modality performed better in identifying in-group speakers. We also compared the performance of different models on this task and found that RNN-based models outperformed CNN-based models in modeling the temporal connection within the speech.

These results highlight several directions for future work. First, while the features used in this paper were promising, other features should be investigated (e.g., lip motion tracking, linguistic features). In addition, performance of cloud-based ASR services needs to be tested as well as the use of other popular face detection toolkits (e.g., Openface 2.0 [2]), and the results of learning models with different fusion strategies (feature versus class score fusion) needs further analysis. The work reported in this paper was a first step toward building an intelligent collaboration support system that can detect interactions between a pair of children and provide adaptive supports during learning within the noisy classroom environment. As we move toward this goal, we will be able to build and investigate systems that can significantly improve children's collaborative learning experience in classrooms.

Acknowledgments. This research is supported by the National Science Foundation through grant DRL-1721160. Any opinions, findings, conclusions, or recommendations expressed in this report are those of the participants, and do not necessarily represent the official views, opinions, or policy of the National Science Foundation.

References

1. Ahmed, I., et al.: Investigating help-giving behavior in a cross-platform learning environment. In: Isotani, S., Millán, E., Ogan, A., Hastings, P., McLaren, B., Luckin, R. (eds.) AIED 2019. LNCS (LNAI), vol. 11625, pp. 14–25. Springer, Cham (2019). https://doi.org/10.1007/978-3-030-23204-7_2
2. Baltrusaitis, T., Zadeh, A., Lim, Y.C., Morency, L.P.: Openface 2.0: facial behavior analysis toolkit. In: Proceedings of the International Conference on Automatic Face & Gesture Recognition, pp. 59–66. IEEE (2018)
3. Blanchard, N., et al.: A study of automatic speech recognition in noisy classroom environments for automated dialog analysis. In: Conati, C., Heffernan, N., Mitrovic, A., Verdejo, M.F. (eds.) AIED 2015. LNCS (LNAI), vol. 9112, pp. 23–33. Springer, Cham (2015). https://doi.org/10.1007/978-3-319-19773-9_3
4. Brack, A., D'Souza, J., Hoppe, A., Auer, S., Ewerth, R.: Domain-independent extraction of scientific concepts from research articles. In: Jose, J.M., et al. (eds.) ECIR 2020. LNCS, vol. 12035, pp. 251–266. Springer, Cham (2020). https://doi.org/10.1007/978-3-030-45439-5_17
5. Celepkolu, M., Wiggins, J.B., Galdo, A.C., Boyer, K.E.: Designing a visualization tool for children to reflect on their collaborative dialogue. Int. J. Child-Comput. Interact. **27**, 100232 (2021)
6. Devlin, J., Chang, M.W., Lee, K., Toutanova, K.: Bert: pre-training of deep bidirectional transformers for language understanding. arXiv preprint arXiv:1810.04805 (2018)
7. ELAN. https://archive.mpi.nl/tla/elan
8. Ellamil, M., Susskind, J.M., Anderson, A.K.: Examinations of identity invariance in facial expression adaptation. Cogn. Affect. Behav. Neurosci. **8**(3), 273–281 (2008). https://doi.org/10.3758/CABN.8.3.273
9. Fadljević, L., Maitz, K., Kowald, D., Pammer-Schindler, V., Gasteiger-Klicpera, B.: Slow is good: the effect of diligence on student performance in the case of an adaptive learning system for health literacy. In: Proceedings of the Tenth International Conference on Learning Analytics & Knowledge, pp. 112–117 (2020)

10. FFmpeg. https://github.com/FFmpeg/FFmpeg
11. Goutte, C., Gaussier, E.: A probabilistic interpretation of precision, recall and F-score, with implication for evaluation. In: Losada, D.E., Fernández-Luna, J.M. (eds.) ECIR 2005. LNCS, vol. 3408, pp. 345–359. Springer, Heidelberg (2005). https://doi.org/10.1007/978-3-540-31865-1_25
12. Harsley, R., Green, N., Di Eugenio, B., Aditya, S., Fossati, D., Al Zoubi, O.: Collab-ChiQat: a collaborative remaking of a computer science intelligent tutoring system. In: Proceedings of the 19th ACM Conference on Computer Supported Cooperative Work and Social Computing Companion, pp. 281–284 (2016)
13. He, K., Zhang, X., Ren, S., Sun, J.: Deep residual learning for image recognition. In: Proceedings of the IEEE Conference on Computer Vision and Pattern Recognition, pp. 770–778 (2016)
14. Howard, C.S., Munro, K.J., Plack, C.J.: Listening effort at signal-to-noise ratios that are typical of the school classroom. Int. J. Audiol. **49**(12), 928–932 (2010)
15. Hu, Y., Ren, J.S., Dai, J., Yuan, C., Xu, L., Wang, W.: Deep multimodal speaker naming. In: Proceedings of the 23rd ACM International Conference on Multimedia, pp. 1107–1110 (2015)
16. ImageNet. http://www.image-net.org/
17. Karakostas, A., Demetriadis, S.: Enhancing collaborative learning through dynamic forms of support: the impact of an adaptive domain-specific support strategy. J. Comput. Assist. Learn. **27**(3), 243–258 (2011)
18. Keras. https://keras.io/api/
19. Kiktova, E., Lojka, M., Pleva, M., Juhar, J., Cizmar, A.: Comparison of different feature types for acoustic event detection system. In: Dziech, A., Czyżewski, A. (eds.) MCSS 2013. CCIS, vol. 368, pp. 288–297. Springer, Heidelberg (2013). https://doi.org/10.1007/978-3-642-38559-9_25
20. Kingma, D., Ba, J.: Adam: a method for stochastic optimization. In: Proceedings of the International Conference on Learning Representations (2014)
21. Kumar, R., Rosé, C.P., Wang, Y.C., Joshi, M., Robinson, A.: Tutorial dialogue as adaptive collaborative learning support. Front. Artif. Intell. Appl. **158**, 383 (2007)
22. Li, H., Wang, Z., Tang, J., Ding, W., Liu, Z.: Siamese neural networks for class activity detection. In: Bittencourt, I.I., Cukurova, M., Muldner, K., Luckin, R., Millán, E. (eds.) AIED 2020. LNCS (LNAI), vol. 12164, pp. 162–167. Springer, Cham (2020). https://doi.org/10.1007/978-3-030-52240-7_30
23. Liu, W., Wen, Y., Yu, Z., Yang, M.: Large-margin softmax loss for convolutional neural networks. In: Proceedings of the International Conference on Machine Learning, pp. 507–516 (2016)
24. Lyu, F., et al.: EnseWing: creating an instrumental ensemble playing experience for children with limited music training. In: Proceedings of the CHI Conference on Human Factors in Computing Systems, pp. 4326–4330 (2017)
25. Magnisalis, I., Demetriadis, S., Karakostas, A.: Adaptive and intelligent systems for collaborative learning support: a review of the field. IEEE Trans. Learn. Technol. **4**(1), 5–20 (2011)
26. Marcos-García, J.A., Martínez-Monés, A., Dimitriadis, Y.: DESPRO: a method based on roles to provide collaboration analysis support adapted to the participants in CSCL situations. Comput. Educ. **82**, 335–353 (2015)
27. Martínez-Monés, A., Harrer, A., Dimitriadis, Y.: An interaction-aware design process for the integration of interaction analysis into mainstream cscl practices. In: Puntambekar, S., Erkens, G., Hmelo-Silver, C. (eds.) Analyzing Interactions in CSCL. Computer-Supported Collaborative Learning Series, pp. 269–291. Springer, Boston (2011). https://doi.org/10.1007/978-1-4419-7710-6_13

28. McFee, B., et al.: librosa: audio and music signal analysis in python. In: Proceedings of the 14th Python in Science Conference, vol. 8, pp. 18–25 (2015)
29. Moreno, L., Popescu, B., Groenwald, C.: Teaching computer architecture using a collaborative approach: the Siena tool tutorial sessions and problem solving. Learning **2**, 10 (2013)
30. Netsblox https://netsblox.org/
31. Nguyen, V., Dang, H.H., Do, N.K., Tran, D.T.: Enhancing team collaboration through integrating social interactions in a web-based development environment. Comput. Appl. Eng. Educ. **24**(4), 529–545 (2016)
32. OpenCV. https://github.com/opencv/opencv
33. OpenCV-Face-Detector. https://github.com/opencv/opencv/tree/master/samples/dnn/face_detector
34. OpenCV-Optical-Flow. https://opencv-python-tutroals.readthedocs.io/en/latest/py_tutorials/py_video/py_lucas_kanade/py_lucas_kanade.html
35. Ren, J., et al.: Look, listen and learn—a multimodal LSTM for speaker identification. In: Proceedings of the AAAI Conference on Artificial Intelligence, pp. 3581–3587 (2016)
36. Rodríguez, F.J., Boyer, K.E.: Discovering individual and collaborative problem-solving modes with hidden Markov models. In: Conati, C., Heffernan, N., Mitrovic, A., Verdejo, M.F. (eds.) AIED 2015. LNCS (LNAI), vol. 9112, pp. 408–418. Springer, Cham (2015). https://doi.org/10.1007/978-3-319-19773-9_41
37. Sancho, P., Fuentes-Fernández, R., Fernández-Manjón, B.: NUCLEO: adaptive computer supported collaborative learning in a role game based scenario. In: Proceedings of the IEEE International Conference on Advanced Learning Technologies, pp. 671–675. IEEE (2008)
38. Simonyan, K., Zisserman, A.: Two-stream convolutional networks for action recognition in videos. In: Advances in Neural Information Processing Systems, vol. 27, pp. 568–576 (2014)
39. Soleymani, M., Stefanov, K., Kang, S.H., Ondras, J., Gratch, J.: Multimodal analysis and estimation of intimate self-disclosure. In: Proceedings of the International Conference on Multimodal Interaction, pp. 59–68 (2019)
40. Tan, Z.H., Lindberg, B.: Low-complexity variable frame rate analysis for speech recognition and voice activity detection. IEEE J. Sel. Topics Sig. Process. **4**(5), 798–807 (2010)
41. Tsompanoudi, D., Satratzemi, M., Xinogalos, S.: Evaluating the effects of scripted distributed pair programming on student performance and participation. IEEE Trans. Educ. **59**(1), 24–31 (2015)
42. Varatharaj, A., Botelho, A.F., Lu, X., Heffernan, N.T.: Supporting teacher assessment in Chinese language learning using textual and tonal features. In: Bittencourt, I.I., Cukurova, M., Muldner, K., Luckin, R., Millán, E. (eds.) AIED 2020. LNCS (LNAI), vol. 12163, pp. 562–573. Springer, Cham (2020). https://doi.org/10.1007/978-3-030-52237-7_45
43. VGGish. https://github.com/tensorflow/models/tree/master/research/audioset/vggish
44. Vizcaíno, A., Contreras, J., Favela, J., Prieto, M.: An adaptive, collaborative environment to develop good habits in programming. In: Gauthier, G., Frasson, C., VanLehn, K. (eds.) ITS 2000. LNCS, vol. 1839, pp. 262–271. Springer, Heidelberg (2000). https://doi.org/10.1007/3-540-45108-0_30
45. Walker, E., Rummel, N., Koedinger, K.R.: Adaptive intelligent support to improve peer tutoring in algebra. In: Proceedings of the International Conference on Artificial Intelligence in Education, vol. 24, no. 1, pp. 33–61 (2014)

46. Walker, E., Rummel, N., Koedinger, K.R., et al.: Modeling helping behavior in an intelligent tutor for peer tutoring. In: Proceedings of the International Conference on Artificial Intelligence in Education, pp. 341–348 (2009)
47. Yett, B., Hutchins, N., Snyder, C., Zhang, N., Mishra, S., Biswas, G.: Evaluating student learning in a synchronous, collaborative programming environment through log-based analysis of projects. In: Bittencourt, I.I., Cukurova, M., Muldner, K., Luckin, R., Millán, E. (eds.) AIED 2020. LNCS (LNAI), vol. 12164, pp. 352–357. Springer, Cham (2020). https://doi.org/10.1007/978-3-030-52240-7_64

Extracting and Clustering Main Ideas from Student Feedback Using Language Models

Mihai Masala[1,2], Stefan Ruseti[1], Mihai Dascalu[1,3(✉)], and Ciprian Dobre[1]

[1] University Politehnica of Bucharest, 313 Splaiul Independentei,
060042 Bucharest, Romania
{mihai_dan.masala,stefan.ruseti,mihai.dascalu,ciprian.dobre}@upb.ro
[2] Institute of Mathematics of the Romanian Academy,
21 Calea Grivitei, 010702 Bucharest, Romania
[3] Academy of Romanian Scientists, Str. Ilfov, Nr. 3, 050044 Bucharest, Romania

Abstract. Feedback mechanisms for academic courses have been widely used to measure students opinions and satisfaction towards different components of a course; concurrently, open-text detailed impressions enable professors to continually improve their course. However, the process of reading through hundreds of student feedback responses across multiple subjects, followed by the extraction of important ideas is very time consuming. In this work, we propose an automated feedback summarizer to extract the main ideas expressed by all students on various components for each course, based on a pipeline integrating state-of-the-art Natural Language Processing techniques. Our method involves the usage of BERT language models to extract keywords for each course, identify relevant contexts for recurring keywords, and cluster similar contexts. We validate our tool on 8,201 feedback responses for 168 distinct courses from the Computer Science Department of University Politehnica of Bucharest for the 2019–2020 academic year. Our approach achieves a size reduction of 59% on the overall volume of text, while only increasing the mean average error when predicting course ratings from student open-text feedback by an absolute value of 0.06.

Keywords: Extraction of main ideas · Open-text student feedback · Natural Language Processing · Language models

1 Introduction

Student feedback is widely used as a tool of continual improvement in the teaching process, by directly and anonymously connecting the teacher with the students' opinions [1,2]. Feedback from students is, or should be, a key point in evaluating all course related aspects (e.g., curriculum, teaching capabilities, homework difficulty), both from the teacher's perspective and from an administrative point of view [3,4]. Student feedback is always acted upon, whether it

© Springer Nature Switzerland AG 2021
I. Roll et al. (Eds.): AIED 2021, LNAI 12748, pp. 282–292, 2021.
https://doi.org/10.1007/978-3-030-78292-4_23

involves small changes, like focusing more on a particular topic, or even for significant changes. As an extreme showcase presented later on in detail, a lecturer of a course in our university was changed in the 2020–2021 academic year when the collected feedback used in our work, alongside additional other evidences, were indicative of poor performance and improper attitude towards students. Moreover, student feedback can be used to identify mismatches between faculty perceptions and student expectations [5], with the strive for better alignment on the longer run.

Nevertheless, reading and understanding student feedback expressed as detailed text is a time consuming and tedious task for courses involving more than a few students. An automated method of analysing feedback becomes invaluable for all parties involved in the process: teaching staff, administrative staff, and students.

Our objective is to create an automated pipeline for summarizing and aggregating student feedback, while relying on state-of-the-art Natural Language Processing (NLP) techniques. Moreover, we propose an evaluation methodology that does not require any human annotation by assessing the prediction performance of the summaries versus the full responses in terms of course ratings. As such, our system allows both teaching and administrative staff to more easily read and interpret student viewpoints, by significantly reducing the overall feedback size.

The paper is structured as follows. The next section introduces related work, mostly centered on summarizing student open-text feedback, followed by details on our method. The fourth section introduces qualitative and quantitative evaluations of our model. The last section presents conclusions and directions of future work.

2   Related Work

Text summarization is a well studied problem in Natural Language Processing that can be broadly categorized in two large classes, namely extractive or abstractive summarization. The former is limited to words, sentences of phrases from the given text that are selected as the most relevant fragments. In contrast, abstractive summarization is more akin to human summarization in the sense that it has the ability to abstract and reason about key concepts in a text. Our method represents an extractive method of summarization, as we lack enough data (both in terms of sheer size and in terms of annotations) to tackle an abstractive approach.

Nevertheless, feedback summarization is a slightly different task, since the original content that needs to be summarized is composed of individual fragments of text. Luo et al. [6] propose a phrase-based highlighting scheme that is partially akin to keyword extraction, followed by the grouping of candidate phrases. Similarly, Unankard and Nadee [7] propose the usage of Latent Dirichlet Allocation (LDA) [8] for detecting and visualizing topics in online course feedback.

Luo and Litman [9] also propose to summarize student feedback by extracting phrases, instead of full sentences, to ease reading and visualization. Their approach is based on three steps, namely a) candidate phrase extraction, b) phrase clustering, and c) phrase ranking. In their subsequent work, Luo et al. [10] explore the usage of an integer linear programming framework to solve the summarization problem. Student feedback represents a great source of lexical variety, in the sense that there exists a high number of different expressions that represent the same meaning. Handling this challenge is done by allowing different sentences to share the same co-occurrence matrix, even though the sentences might not have the same author.

When considering state-of-the-art language models, Miller [11] proposes the usage of BERT [12] models to automatically generate a lecture summary to support student understanding. All paragraphs of a given lecture are passed through a BERT model, followed by a K-Means clustering algorithm on the paragraph embeddings. In our work, we use a similar mechanism, but at a different level of granularity, as applying clustering on entire feedback responses is not the best idea when considering that feedback usually contains more than one important aspect. Thus, our approach applies clustering on local contexts centered on specific keywords in order to group certain related aspects of the course.

One key difference to previous summarization work is the new paradigm we propose for evaluation that considers the overall aggregation of feedback. While previous methods used a labeled dataset and compared the original text with the summarized version using text overlap metrics (i.e., ROUGE [13]), we decide to steer away from this approach. The main reason is that our aim consists of selecting representative phrases for each considered feedback; as such, we want to measure the predictive power of our phrases in terms of the overall course rating given by the students.

3   Method

3.1   Corpus

The corpus used for the following experiments consists of student feedback in Romanian for all courses of the Computer Science Department from University Politehnica of Bucharest for the 2019–2020 academic year. After selecting only courses with more than ten feedback responses from students, we are left with a total of 8,201 responses on 168 distinct courses. Out of the considered courses, we set aside 33 courses (accounting for about 20% of courses) solely for the purpose of evaluating our approach.

The 8,201 feedback open-text responses consist of a total of 345,503 words, leading to an average of 42 words per feedback. The average rating given by students is 3.74, while the median rating is 3.94. The median value of responses per course is 39, while the average is 48.8. The histograms for all relevant statistics are presented in Fig. 1.

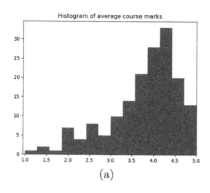
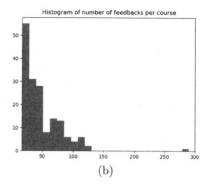

(a)   (b)

Fig. 1. Histograms for the average course rating (a) and for the number of feedback responses per course (b).

3.2   Automated Feedback Processing Pipeline

Figure 2 introduces the overall workflow of our proposed method. First, the text is preprocessed; second, keywords relevant for the current course are detected, followed by the extraction of contexts where the keywords occurred. Fourth, an additional clustering step is performed to separate the different ideas related to that keyword, if too many contexts are extracted for the same keyword.

Fig. 2. Conceptual diagram of our method.

Feedback Preprocessing. From each student feedback, three key components were extracted: the general evaluation of the course (as given by the student) in the form of a rating from 0 to 5, the student responses to the open-text question "What are the positive aspects of this course?" and to the open-text question "What should be improved in this course?". In the following experiments, the responses to the first question are referred as positive feedback, while negative feedback relates to the second question. Before running the keyword extraction, a diacritics restoration model based on RoBERT introduced by Masala et al. [14] is applied on all student responses.

Keyword Extraction. KeyBERT [15] is used for keyword extraction, including a Romanian BERT model – RoBERT model [14] – to compute keyword/document representations. The most relevant keywords are identified by comparing the representation of all candidate keywords with the document representation. For each course, the most relevant 10 keywords are extracted from the set of all nouns present in the respective student feedback responses. The

Maximal Marginal Relevance method [16] is used to ensure the diversity of the selected keywords. For this step, two KeyBERT approaches were considered: a simple pre-trained RoBERT-base and a finetuned RoBERT-base (more details about the process of finetuning are presented in Sect. 4).

Context Extraction. After keywords are extracted from student feedback for each individual course, the next step is to extract the contexts relevant for each keyword. For this, two methods for extracting the contexts were used: a) picking the sentence in which the keyword appears, and b) traversing the dependency tree of each sentence to extract only the information related to the keyword. The second method was implemented because sentences may contain information on more than one aspect; however, separating different aspects is not trivial. Our tree search approach started from the keyword and considered only a predefined list of universal dependency tags (i.e., "nsubj", "nmod", "det", "amod", "cop", "advmod", "case", "aux", "acl", "obl", "aux:pass", "mark" and "cc"). Conjunctions were only taken into account when going down in the tree, and rules were used to exclude tags that introduce subordinate clauses in specific cases. Examples are presented in the results section. The dependency tree is built with the "ro_core_news_lg" model[1] from the spaCy framework[2].

Clustering. The number of contexts can be very high for frequent topics (e.g., keywords can have over 80 contexts). As our goal is to ease reading, understanding, and acting upon student feedback, a clustering algorithm was applied for keywords with more than five contexts. The clustering was performed in the embedding space generated by BERT (i.e., the same model from the keyword extraction step), using the K-Means algorithm with five clusters; this value for k was empirically set as more clusters for a given keyword would have been difficult to follow. For each cluster, we select the point closest to the centroid as the representative context.

4 Evaluation

This section contains a qualitative assessment exemplifying all steps in the Natural Language Processing pipeline, followed by quantitative results for different configurations of the proposed method.

The RoBERT-base model was fine-tuned with a feedback text and its polarity (whether it originated as a positive or negative aspect of the course; this information was readily available from the preprocessing step) as input, and the given rating as target. After removing the added layers needed for fine-tuning, we are left with a classic RoBERT-base architecture with tweaked weights. This "fine-tuned" model is further used in the keyword extraction and classification steps, where applicable (see Table 4).

---

[1] https://spacy.io/models/ro#ro_core_news_lg. Retrieved April 15, 2021.

[2] https://spacy.io/. Retrieved April 15, 2021.

4.1   Qualitative Assessment

Given our task, a qualitative analysis provides valuable insights to understand the value of the presented method. This subsection is centered on real examples for each major step from the pipeline: keyword extraction, context extraction, and clustering steps.

Keyword Extraction. The following examples were extracted from three courses selected to be as representative as possible. One of the lowest ranked courses was picked, with an average rating of 1.21 and 290 feedback responses (highest number of responses out of all considered courses). The course was centered on project management (PM), outside of the core Computer Science curriculum, but mandatory for all students. After picking the worst rated course, the next selected one was highly rated, with a decent number of feedback responses – a freshman course centered on introducing logic circuits design (LC), with an average rating of 4.75 and 78 responses. Finally, a fundamental course for the Computer Science domain focused on algorithms (ALG) was selected, with a decent number of responses (42) and an average rating of 2.86. Extracted keywords for the three mentioned courses are presented in Table 1. We note that, for brevity, all keywords were manually translated to their English counterparts.

Table 1. Qualitative examples for keyword extraction.

Course	Keywords
PM	professor, seminar, attitude, situation, half, him, clarification, requirement, teaching, students
LC	professor, curriculum, work, seminar, circuit, laboratory, application, exercise, book, example
ALG	algorithm, seminar, exercise, subject, solution, complexity, test, student, attendance, Wednesday

The list of extracted keywords triggers tell-tale signs. For the low rated course (PM), the most relevant keywords are not directly related to the curriculum. This already hints that, for this course, there are very strong opinions (either good or bad) about aspects regarding mostly the teaching staff. For the other two courses, we can observe keywords directly related to the curriculum (e.g., "circuit", "algorithm", or "complexity") and general keywords related to a course (e.g., "professor", "laboratory", "seminar", "test", or "attendance"). Also notable are rather odd keywords, such as "half", "Wednesday", or "him". Some of these keywords stem from limitations of the current POS tagging model, especially for a low resource language such as Romanian. While it certainly seems that "Wednesday" is a poor choice for a keyword as it is highly specific, after a closer inspection, it turns out that it is a highly recurrent concept as the half-semester test took place on a Wednesday and this event generated a lot of discussions on the corresponding schedule. Extracting and clustering context for keywords becomes even more important for these seemingly odd appearances.

Context Extraction. We introduce only examples that use the dependency tree for context extraction, since the first method of selecting entire sentences is trivial. Here, the context and its dependency tree were kept in Romanian with corresponding translations in the visual representations (i.e., the dependency trees from Fig. 3 and 4 where the keyword is marked with a red bounding box and the extracted context in black), whereas the original and extracted contexts were manually translated to English in Table 2. For brevity, spelling errors were also manually corrected and irrelevant parts were omitted (marked by "[...]").

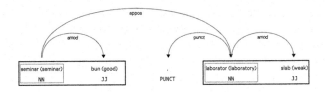

Fig. 3. Example of a simple context extraction.

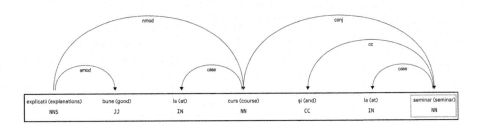

Fig. 4. Example of a complex context extraction.

Clustering. Table 3 introduces three examples of clusters (one feedback per line) in which the clustering step manages to group similar contexts; the feedback picked to represent the centroid of the cluster is marked with **bold**). We note that the first cluster is extracted from the problematic course mentioned in the Introduction. In addition to the representative context for each cluster, a critical piece of information is the size of such cluster - for example, having only three negative feedback responses is different to having over 10 such responses.

Table 2. Qualitative examples for context extraction.

Keyword	Feedback	Extracted context
Seminar	Interactive and interesting course, good explanations both at course and at seminar	Good explanations both at course and at seminar
Seminar	Not enough learning resources and the fact that the last part of the course is not taught in seminar is a problem of thoroughly understanding the curriculum the laboratory is [...]	Not enough learning resources and the fact that the last part of the course is not taught in seminar
Complexity	I learned important aspects about algorithm complexity and analysis by better understanding both aspects	I learned important aspects about algorithm complexity and analysis

4.2 Quantitative Analysis

The proposed method was evaluated on a holdout dataset containing 33 courses. As our goal is to automatically summarize feedback texts, it was important to measure how much information is retained after extracting the main ideas. The corresponding train and test datasets were built for each summarization method, while enforcing a static assignment (i.e., all train datasets consistently contain the same courses; all test datasets consistently contain the same courses). Each BERT-based model is trained using 4-fold cross-validation and grid search for hyper-parameters (i.e., batch size, number of epochs, dropout values). At evaluation time, the trained model was run on all feedback responses corresponding to a given course from the holdout dataset, and averaged across predictions to obtain the predicted average rating of a course.

The validation consists of measuring the predictive power of the summarized feedback in determining the general rating of a given course. Therefore, a Mean Course Average Error (MCAE) is computed as the average absolute error between the real average rating of each course and the average predicted ratings based on all feedback (see Formula 1).

$$MCAE = \sum_{c \in C} |real_c - \frac{1}{|F_c|} * \sum_{f \in F_c} pred_f| \qquad (1)$$

where C is the set of considered courses, $real_c$ is the real average course rating for course c, F_c is the set of feedback responses associated with course c, and $pred_f$ is our models prediction for feedback response.

Table 4 reports the summarization performance, both in term of size reduction and summary relevance. A lower value is better for MCAE, whereas a higher value is better for word reduction. The baseline is represented by training a RoBERT-base model on the original feedback responses with no extraction of main ideas (first line of Table 4). As expected, a significant size reduction (both

Table 3. Qualitative examples for clustering.

Cluster
The attitude of the supervisor [...]
The professor had an aggressive attitude towards the students especially [...]
The attitude towards the students and course and seminar attendance
but his attitude is totally inappropriate
Their attitude was more than excessive at the multiple choice test
Mocking attitude and
He had a defiant attitude
Teaching staff attitude is not appropriate
Resource for the laboratory should be improved
Resources from the laboratory are not functional
The wires and PCBs are a little faulty [...]
Laboratory resources and better laboratory explanations
Ease of understanding
Relaxed teaching style that is very useful for understanding
The professor is very thoughtful, answers all questions asked [...]
The professor is interested and involved
The course is hard but well taught

in terms of number of responses and in terms of total number of words) can be observed after clustering similar feedback responses. The same phenomenon can be observed when comparing the dependency tree method of extracting contexts with using the entire sentence as context, in favor of the former. In case of dependencies, the overall word count can be slightly higher than the initial count, as responses are divided into multiple contexts that can overlap.

In terms of size reduction, the best configurations manage to reduce the number of words by 85%, while only increasing MCAE by about 0.17. Even though the performance decrease is slightly high at 44%, we believe this is still a very strong result. If more predictive power is needed, the best performing model has only a 16% MCAE decrease (absolute value difference of only 0.06), while reducing the size of feedback by 59%.

Table 4. Results on the test set.

Keywords	Context	Clusters	# Feedback	# Words	MCAE
Full feedback	–	–	8,201	345,503	0.397
Base	Sentence	–	7,542 (−8%)	214,364 (−38%)	0.516 (+0.119)
Base	Sentence	5	4,935 (−40%)	139,604 (−60%)	0.529 (+0.132)
Base	Dependencies	–	8,297 (+1%)	87,547 (−75%)	0.627 (+0.230)
Base	Dependencies	5	5,027 (−39%)	53,104 (−85%)	0.572 (+0.130)
Fine-tuned	Sentence	–	7,818 (−5%)	224,152 (−32%)	0.501 (+0.104)
Fine-tuned	Sentence	5	4,974 (−39%)	142,027 (−59%)	0.457 (+0.060)
Fine-tuned	Dependencies	–	8,639 (+5%)	90,542 (−78%)	0.566 (+0.169)
Fine-tuned	Dependencies	5	5,065 (−38%)	52,873 (−85%)	0.565 (+0.168)

A smart size reduction scheme also increases the predictive power of the remaining feedback responses. In almost all cases, clustering increases performance (i.e., the MCAE metric is lower for the clustered contexts), while greatly reducing feedback size. The dependency tree method performs worse than the method that extracts the entire sentence as context. This is somehow expected because the former method is not infallible, as extracted contexts can be either too short or miss important aspects. Finally, the methods using the finetuned RoBERT model in the keyword extraction and clustering phase consistently outperform their counterparts that use RoBERT-base.

5   Conclusions and Future Research Directions

A fully automated method is introduced to extract and aggregate main ideas from student feedback responses in order to ease the reading and understanding of key aspects regarding academic courses. It is important to note that this approach requires no human intervention or annotation, and its results are readily available for each individual course. Our method was evaluated indirectly by estimating the amount of information kept in the generated summaries - i.e., the extent to which keyword contexts are predictive of the course rating. Our approach obtains an MCAE increase of only .06, while reducing the size of the feedback responses by 59%.

If more data becomes available, sentiment analysis tools can be considered to predict the polarity of each context. This information can be also integrated in the clustering step, separating positive and negative aspects for a specific keyword. Additionally, we envision creating 2D visualizations of the feedback embeddings with corresponding clusters using Tensorboard[3] and t-SNE [17]. The extension of the dataset to multi-year feedback responses will enable additional analyses to be performed, like extracting emerging keywords and topics over time using BERTopic [18].

Acknowledgments. This research was supported by a grant of the Romanian National Authority for Scientific Research and Innovation, CNCS – UEFISCDI, project number TE 70 PN-III-P1-1.1-TE-2019-2209, ATES – "Automated Text Evaluation and Simplification".

References

1. Seldin, P.: Using student feedback to improve teaching. Improve Acad. **16**(1), 335–345 (1997)
2. Flodén, J.: The impact of student feedback on teaching in higher education. Assess. Eval. High. Educ. **42**(7), 1054–1068 (2017)
3. Leckey, J., Neill, N.: Quantifying quality: the importance of student feedback. Qual. High. Educ. **7**(1), 19–32 (2001)

---

[3] https://www.tensorflow.org/tensorboard. Retrieved April 15, 2021.

4. Moore, S., Kuol, N.: Students evaluating teachers: exploring the importance of faculty reaction to feedback on teaching. Teach. High. Educ. **10**(1), 57–73 (2005)
5. Perera, J., Lee, N., Win, K., Perera, J., Wijesuriya, L.: Formative feedback to students: the mismatch between faculty perceptions and student expectations. Med. Teach. **30**(4), 395–399 (2008)
6. Luo, W., Liu, F., Litman, D.: An improved phrase-based approach to annotating and summarizing student course responses. In: Proceedings of COLING 2016, the 26th International Conference on Computational Linguistics: Technical Papers, pp. 53–63. The COLING 2016 Organizing Committee, Osaka (2016)
7. Unankard, S., Nadee, W.: Topic detection for online course feedback using LDA. In: Popescu, E., Hao, T., Hsu, T.-C., Xie, H., Temperini, M., Chen, W. (eds.) SETE 2019. LNCS, vol. 11984, pp. 133–142. Springer, Cham (2020). https://doi.org/10.1007/978-3-030-38778-5_16
8. Blei, D.M., Ng, A.Y., Jordan, M.I.: Latent Dirichlet allocation. J. Mach. Learn. Res. **3**, 993–1022 (2003)
9. Luo, W., Litman, D.: Summarizing student responses to reflection prompts. In: Proceedings of the 2015 Conference on Empirical Methods in Natural Language Processing, pp. 1955–1960 (2015)
10. Luo, W., Liu, F., Liu, Z., Litman, D.: Automatic summarization of student course feedback. In: Proceedings of the 2016 Conference of the North American Chapter of the Association for Computational Linguistics: Human Language Technologies, pp. 80–85 (2016)
11. Miller, D.: Leveraging BERT for extractive text summarization on lectures. arXiv preprint arXiv:1906.04165 (2019)
12. Devlin, J., Chang, M.W., Lee, K., Toutanova, K.: BERT: pre-training of deep bidirectional transformers for language understanding. In: Proceedings of the 2019 Conference of the North American Chapter of the Association for Computational Linguistics: Human Language Technologies, NAACL-HLT 2019, pp. 4171–4186 (2019)
13. Lin, C.Y.: ROUGE: a package for automatic evaluation of summaries. In: Text Summarization Branches Out, pp. 74–81. Association for Computational Linguistics, Barcelona (2004)
14. Masala, M., Ruseti, S., Dascalu, M.: RoBERT - a Romanian BERT model. In: Proceedings of the 28th International Conference on Computational Linguistics, pp. 6626–6637 (2020)
15. Grootendorst, M.: KeyBERT: minimal keyword extraction with BERT (2020). https://github.com/MaartenGr/KeyBERT
16. Carbonell, J., Goldstein, J.: Use of MMR, diversity-based reranking for reordering documents and producing summaries. In: SIGIR Forum (ACM Special Interest Group on Information Retrieval), pp. 335–336 (1998)
17. Van der Maaten, L., Hinton, G.: Visualizing data using t-SNE. J. Mach. Learn. Res. **9**(11), 2579–2605 (2008)
18. Grootendorst, M.: BERTopic: leveraging BERT and c-TF-IDF to create easily interpretable topics (2020). https://github.com/MaartenGr/BERTopic

Multidimensional Team Communication Modeling for Adaptive Team Training: A Hybrid Deep Learning and Graphical Modeling Framework

Wookhee Min[1](✉), Randall Spain[1], Jason D. Saville[1], Bradford Mott[1], Keith Brawner[2], Joan Johnston[2], and James Lester[1]

[1] North Carolina State University, Raleigh, NC 27695, USA
{wmin,rdspain,jdsavill,bwmott,lester}@ncsu.edu
[2] U.S. Army Combat Capabilities Development Command, Orlando, FL 32826, USA
{keith.w.brawner.civ,joan.h.johnston.civ}@mail.mil

Abstract. Team communication modeling offers great potential for adaptive learning environments for team training. However, the complex dynamics of team communication pose significant challenges for team communication modeling. To address these challenges, we present a hybrid framework integrating deep learning and probabilistic graphical models that analyzes team communication utterances with respect to the intent of the utterance and the directional flow of communication within the team. The hybrid framework utilizes conditional random fields (CRFs) that use deep learning-based contextual, distributed language representations extracted from team members' utterances. An evaluation with communication data collected from six teams during a live training exercise indicate that linear-chain CRFs utilizing ELMo utterance embeddings (1) outperform both multi-task and single-task variants of stacked bidirectional long short-term memory networks using the same distributed representations of the utterances, (2) outperform a hybrid approach that uses non-contextual utterance representations for the dialogue classification tasks, and (3) demonstrate promising domain-transfer capabilities. The findings suggest that the hybrid multidimensional team communication analysis framework can accurately recognize speaker intent and model the directional flow of team communication to guide adaptivity in team training environments.

Keywords: Team communication analytics · Probabilistic graphical models · Deep learning · Distributed language representations · Natural language processing

1 Introduction

There is broad recognition that team training can improve team effectiveness across a wide range of domains [1]. It can improve team knowledge, team coordination, and team leadership behaviors, which can in turn minimize errors, enhance productivity, and

© Springer Nature Switzerland AG 2021
I. Roll et al. (Eds.): AIED 2021, LNAI 12748, pp. 293–305, 2021.
https://doi.org/10.1007/978-3-030-78292-4_24

help ensure teams are successful. Adaptive team training holds significant potential for providing effective learning experiences by delivering tailored remediation and feedback that support the development of teamwork and taskwork skills and dynamically address a team's training needs [2, 3].

A key challenge posed by team training is developing approaches to reliably assessing and diagnosing team processes in real time. Team training theory and research shows team communication provides a rich source of evidence about team processes that can support team training experiences [3–5]. Team members communicate with one another to develop a shared understanding of goals, tasks, and responsibilities [4], to coordinate actions [6], and to regulate social and cognitive processes associated with team performance [1, 7]. Accurate analyses of team communication can therefore provide deep insight into team cognition, collaboration, and coordination, which can ultimately be used to adaptively support team training needs.

Work on team communication modeling has explored a variety of methods. For instance, latent semantic analysis (LSA) has been used to devise team communication analysis models and assess team discourse using team communication content, sequence, and structure [8]. However, LSA does not adequately account for the dynamically changing dialogue context and semantics of the utterances that could be used for in-depth team discourse analysis. More recently, approaches based on deep neural networks [9] and probabilistic graphical models [10] have demonstrated significant potential for performing fine-grained dialogue analyses using multi-level language data (e.g., characters, words, paragraphs, documents), as well as other discourse and context features (e.g., dialogue sequence, turn taking, task sequences, environmental events). These techniques offer considerable promise for producing more accurate representations of team communication. Thus, a key question is how we can most effectively leverage these recent advances to accurately analyze team discourse, assess team communication, predict team performance and, ultimately, provide adaptive training experiences for learners.

In this paper, we present a hybrid, multidimensional team communication analysis framework supporting adaptive team training (Fig. 1). The framework leverages conditional random fields' structured prediction and deep neural networks' contextual language representation learning capabilities to classify team communication data with respect to the intent of utterances (i.e., speech acts [11]) and how information is conveyed to a team (i.e., team development categories). We investigate the hybrid team communication framework on transcripts of spoken utterances captured from six U.S. Army squads during a live capstone training exercise [12]. We evaluate the predictive performance of the hybrid framework optimized through cross-validation on a held-out test set and compare them to bidirectional long short-term memory networks, which are optimized through multiple configurations of multi-task learning and fusion methods, across the two classification tasks.

2   Related Work

Natural language processing techniques have been used in a wide range of learning analytics tasks to assess student knowledge and competencies, analyze student and teacher dialogue, and provide individualized feedback [13, 14]. Previous work has investigated automated essay scoring [15], short answer grading [16], discourse analysis in class-rooms for both students [17] and teachers [18], text difficulty classification [19], and tutorial dialogues [20]. More recently, deep learning-based natural language processing has been explored for learning analytics tasks [e.g., 15, 16, 21], taking advantages of deep neural networks' capabilities on distributed linguistic representation learning [22, 23] and highly accurate modeling in an end-to-end trainable manner [24, 25]. Closely related to team training and performance, deep learning-based methods have been investigated for *computer-supported collaborative learning* (CSCL). In CSCL environments, group members work collaboratively towards a shared goal and solve problems as they learn [26], and deep neural network-based methods have been used in CSCL environments for detecting disruptive talk [27] and off-task behavior [28] with the goal of engaging in dialogues that are most conducive to learning.

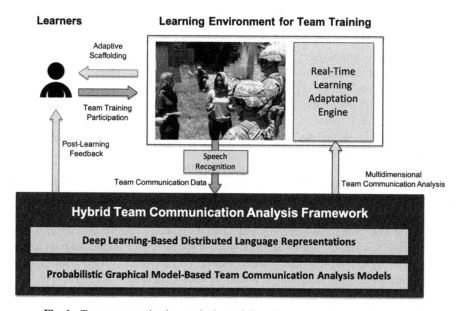

Fig. 1. Team communication analysis modeling for team training environments.

While the majority of previous work on natural language processing in learning analytics has focused on tasks centered on individual learners, analyzing team dialogue could offer significant value to support adaptive team training experience and improve team performance. Team communication provides a window into how teams collabo-rate, coordinate, and distribute information in order to achieve a shared goal during team training and improve team performance [3, 29]. Consequently, many approaches have been investigated for analyzing team dialogue to obtain insight into teamwork, team performance, coordination processes, and training needs, including a growing body of work on computational approaches to team communication analysis [30]. For instance, LSA has been used to detect socio-cognitive roles in multiparty interactions [31] and team communication content analysis [8]. Researchers have also successfully utilized

Markov models [32] and support vector machines utilizing multi-party dialogue embeddings [33] to analyze temporal patterns of team communication, as well as hierarchical regression models to investigate relationships between linguistic entrainment and team social outcomes [34].

Our work focuses on computational modeling of sequential communication patterns in actual team dialogue data collected from a set of live capstone training exercises. The hybrid, multidimensional team communication analysis framework shows considerable potential to support creating effective team training environments that adaptively facilitate teamwork and improve team performance.

3 Dataset

We investigate the hybrid team communication framework with transcribed audio logs captured from six U.S. Army squads as they each completed a 45-min live training scenario (Fig. 1) [12]. The training scenario included a scripted set of training objectives and events (e.g., contacting key local leaders, providing combat casualty care) that were designed to elicit team development behaviors among squad members. Throughout the mission, squad members were required to develop a baseline of advanced situation awareness, identify and report tactical threats, and accomplish mission objectives. Each squad consisted of 10 team members wearing individual microphones, and each team member assumed a designated role and communicated with other key role players to collectively complete the mission.

The audio logs were transcribed and annotated using a coding scheme of 27 speech acts, 18 team development labels, and the speaker's role by domain experts, where speech acts represented the basic purpose of a given utterance, such as requesting information or stating an action being taken, team development labels reflected how different forms of information were being transferred up and down the chain of command in a squad, and speaker roles indicated the role of the team member speaking (six speaker roles including one squad leader and two sub-team leaders). While every utterance was assigned a speech act label, utterances were only assigned team development label when applicable.

Balancing the granularity of dialogue labels, their impact on the predictive accuracy of the models, and the potential utility of their predictions for training, we developed a mapping to reduce the number of speech acts from 27 down to 9 distinct labels consisting of ACKNOWLEDGEMENT, ACTION REQUEST, ACTION STATEMENT, COMMAND, ATTENTION, GREETING, PROVIDE INFORMATION, REQUEST INFORMATION, and OTHER statements. Team development communication behavior labels consisted of 19 labels (e.g., COMMAND COMING FROM THE SQUAD LEADER, PROVIDE INFORMATION UP THE CHAIN OF COMMAND, REQUEST INFORMATION FROM DOWN THE CHAIN OF COMMAND), including one extra label ("N/A") to account for the utterances whose team development labels are not applicable. Overall, the dataset included 4,315 tagged utterances made by the team members from the six squads (Table 1). Frequency analyses showed PROVIDE INFORMATION ($n = 1,109$) was the most prevalent speech act in the dataset, followed by COMMAND ($n = 805$). For team development labels, the most frequent labels were N/A ($n = 1,978$) followed by PROVIDE INFORMATION UP THE CHAIN OF COMMAND ($n = 550$) and COMMAND COMING FROM THE SQUAD LEADER ($n = 362$).

Pearson correlation analyses of the dataset found that squads who provided information statements ($r = .862$, $p = .027$) and issued acknowledgement statements ($r = .864$, $p = .027$) more frequently received higher ratings of team performance during the training event [35]. Results also showed that ratings of team performance were positively correlated with the number of commands that squad leaders issued during the training event ($r = .848$, $p = .033$). Given the critical role communication plays in team effectiveness, being able to accurately classify team communication content in terms of speech act and team development labels could provide significant value for assessing team performance and developing adaptive training environments for teams.

Table 1. Example utterances and their speech act (SA) and team development (TD) labels.

Speaker	Example utterances	SA	TD
Team leader	Where are we moving?	REQUEST INFORMATION	REQUEST INFORMATION FROM UP THE CHAIN OF COMMAND
Team leader	Hey, we're getting ready to move.	PROVIDE INFORMATION	PASS INFORMATION DOWN THE CHAIN OF COMMAND
Squad leader	Six four be advised we're going to make contact with Romanov.	ACTION STATEMENT	PROVIDE INFORMATION UP THE CHAIN OF COMMAND
Squad leader	Hey two alpha, hold right there at those trees.	COMMAND	COMMAND COMING FROM THE SQUAD LEADER

4 Multidimensional Team Communication Analysis Framework

We first devise linear-chain conditional random fields (CRFs) and deep neural network (DNN)-based predictive models that could classify team communication utterances into speech acts and team development labels. CRFs are discriminative models for structured prediction and sequence modeling [36]. CRFs utilize the probabilistic graphical modeling for multivariate data classifications and have been found to be particularly effective for modeling interdependencies in predictive features (e.g., pixels in an image, words in a sentence) along with the class labels associated with the features. While they have proven useful for a variety of tasks, recent work has produced significant advances by incorporating CRFs with deep learning techniques for dialogue act classification [37] and sentiment analysis [38]. These approaches suggest that higher-level features, such as team communication metrics, could be modeled accurately with CRFs.

To effectively model dialogue interactions that have a sequential structure, we investigate linear-chain CRFs (Fig. 2). As shown in Eq. 1, the posterior probability of a

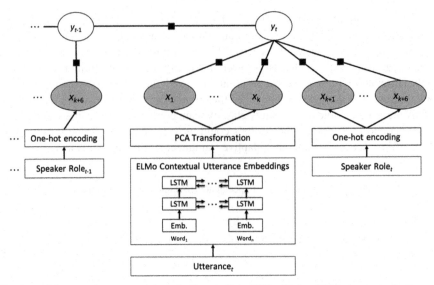

Fig. 2. A factor graph representation of a linear-chain CRF utilizing ELMo contextual utterance embeddings (CRF-ELMo). The gray shaded nodes denote input features (x) that are a concatenation of k-dimensional utterance features and 6 one-hot encoded speaker role features within a time step (t). The white nodes denote a target variable (y) such as speech act. The black shaded boxes indicate factor nodes.

sequence of classes (y) given a sequence of input feature vectors (x) from time 1 to T is computed using a weighted sum of K feature functions (f) that are parameterized with y at times t and t-1, and x at time t, where Z is an instance-specific normalization function [39]. To train the model, we sub-sampled sequences using a sliding window of length 100 (i.e., each subsequence with 100 utterances) from each team's communication data, considering both the context to capture from the dialogue sequence and potential data sparsity issues. In this way, we create a set of sub-sampled sequences equal to the number of utterances in each team's communication (for the sequences shorter than 100, we applied zero padding). The outputs y, which are the labels associated with the given input sequence, are generated for both training and testing. We use a block-coordinate Frank-Wolfe optimization technique [40] to train linear-chain CRFs with the maximum iteration number of 100.

$$p(y|x) = \frac{1}{Z(x)} \prod_{t=1}^{T} \exp\left\{ \sum_{k=1}^{K} \theta_k f_k(y_t, y_{t-1}, x_t) \right\} \tag{1}$$

To represent the speaker utterance, we employ a DNN-based contextual, distributed representation method using an ELMo language model [23]. In contrast to static, distributed representation methods such as GloVe [41], which provide fixed dictionary-based embeddings, contextual embedding approaches support inducing dynamic representations of text by utilizing a language model that takes as input a sequence of words. Consequently, ELMo-based approaches might be able to generate more accurate representations of utterances included in dialogues. In this work, we use a pre-trained ELMo model to generate utterance-level embeddings with 1,024-dimensional vectors through a mean pooling of all contextualized word representations. This ELMo model was built with stacked bidirectional LSTMs trained on the 1 Billion Word Benchmark, approximately 800M tokens of news crawl data from WMT 2011. Since the 1,024-dimensional vector representation per utterance is prohibitive for models to be effectively trained considering the dataset size examined in this work, we apply principal component analysis (PCA) to reduce the 1,024 dimensions down to one of 32, 64, or 128 dimensions, identifying the optimal reduced dimension through cross-validation. In summary, this hybrid model, referred to as *CRF-ELMo*, takes advantage of CRF's strong structure prediction capacity as well as ELMo's contextual language representation capability.

To identify the best performing CRF-ELMo, we examined two hyperparameters, including the regularization parameter from {0.1, 0.5, 1} and the optimizer convergence tolerance from {0.01, 0.001}. We used PyStruct [42], a Python-based off-the-shelf CRF modeling library, to train the models, while the optimal set of hyperparameters is identified through a cross-validation process.

We also construct bidirectional long short-term memory networks (BLSTMs) [43], deep learning-based sequence model baselines, that use the same ELMo contextual language embeddings (*BLSTM-ELMo*). Specifically, we adopt a two-layer BLSTM architecture, as we anticipated both forward and backward propagations of hidden representations of the input streams would more effectively capture bidirectional, sequential patterns in the streams of speaker role changes and utterances and thus more accurately model dynamics characterized in team communication behaviors. A preliminary analysis conducted with the training set indicated that the stacked BLSTM architecture's speech act classification approach outperformed both single-layer standard LSTMs and two-layer standard LSTMs.

Multi-task neural models offer distinct advantages over single-task variants when performing multiple classification tasks [44]. First, multi-task neural models are more cost-effective for training than single-task models because they use one network architecture with multiple output layers accounting for different classification tasks instead of training multiple models. Second, when multiple tasks are correlated, multi-task models can potentially improve their generalization performance through effective regularization, especially when training data is limited. For this reason, we investigate both multi-task and single-task versions of BLSTM-ELMos in this work.

We also explore two fusion methods, early fusion and late fusion, in terms of the input feature sets (utterance-based feature set and speaker role-based feature set) for optimal BLSTM-ELMo modeling. For early fusion, the PCA-applied, ELMo representations of the speaker utterance and the corresponding speaker role passed through an embedding layer are concatenated into a vector, which is fed into the BLSTM layer. For late fusion, two BLSTMs are created to deal with two input feature sets separately, and the two BLSTM outputs are concatenated to perform classifications in a softmax layer. In both cases, we explore the same set of reduced dimensions (i.e., 32, 64, or 128) by PCA for the utterances as done in the CRF-ELMo.

For the speaker role, we use a trainable embedding layer with the embedding size of 4 to represent the speaker role in a continuous vector space. We use 32 hidden units for the two BLSTM layers with a dropout rate of 0.25 for regularization of the trained

models, the softmax activation function for the output layers, and the Adam optimizer
[45]. Similar to CRF-ELMo, we set the maximum input sequence length to 100 and the
maximum training epochs to 100. Also, we train the models with the same sub-sampled
sequential dialogue data and adopt early stopping with the patience duration of 10 epochs
using the validation loss computed with 10% of the training set for effective training.

5   Evaluation

To evaluate the hybrid team communication framework, we split the team communication dataset into two sets: one contained data from 5 squads for performing cross-
validation and the other data from 1 squad for held-out testing. First, we performed
5-fold cross-validation using data from 1 squad as a test set and data from 4 squads
as a training set for each fold. The optimal set of model hyperparameters was identified through cross-validation by choosing the one that achieved the highest average
cross-validation accuracy rate. It should be noted that the held-out test data was completely unseen from the cross-validation and its hyperparameter optimization process
for fair generalization evaluation across models. The majority class baselines for the 9
speech acts and 19 team development labels were 25.7% and 45.8%, respectively. Table
2 shows the cross-validation results of the speech acts and team development labels.
CRF-ELMo uses the format of hyperparameters, {*optimizer regularization parameter,
optimizer convergence tolerance, reduced PCA dimensions*}, and BLSTM-ELMo uses
the format of {*task modeling type, fusion mode, reduced PCA dimensions*}.

Table 2. Averaged cross-validation accuracy rates (%) for CRF-ELMo and BLSTM-ELMo. The
highest predictive accuracy rates for speech act (SA) and team development labels (TD) per
modeling technique are marked in bold.

CRF-ELMo	SA	TD	BLSTM-ELMo	SA	TD
{0.1, 0.001, 32}	68.80	58.38	{Multi-task, Early, 32}	61.44	**55.79**
{0.1, 0.001, 64}	67.88	56.16	{Multi-task, Early, 64}	**62.07**	53.88
{0.1, 0.001, 128}	64.85	52.67	{Multi-task, Early, 128}	61.97	53.43
{0.1, 0.01, 32}	**68.88**	58.31	{Multi-task, Late, 32}	60.22	53.96
{0.1, 0.01, 64}	67.87	56.20	{Multi-task, Late, 64}	60.19	54.51
{0.1, 0.01, 128}	64.87	52.62	{Multi-task, Late, 128}	59.77	53.22
{1.0, 0.001, 32}	68.76	**58.84**	{Single-task, Early, 32}	62.04	55.13
{1.0, 0.001, 64}	67.45	56.03	{Single-task, Early, 64}	61.16	54.47
{1.0, 0.001, 128}	65.72	53.36	{Single-task, Early, 128}	61.84	53.93
{1.0, 0.01, 32}	68.83	58.77	{Single-task, Late, 32}	61.48	52.64
{1.0, 0.01, 64}	67.45	55.93	{Single-task, Late, 64}	60.53	53.54
{1.0, 0.01, 128}	65.62	53.29	{Single-task, Late, 128}	61.96	50.98

Overall, the CRF-ELMo model achieved higher predictive accuracy compared to BLSTM-ELMo model based on cross-validation results. Both CRF-ELMo and BLSTM-ELMo generally showed higher accuracy when adopting the smallest number of language features (32 dimensions), which could be attributed to model overfitting issues. For BLSTM-ELMo, the early fusion method often outperformed late fusion. Further results showed multi-task learning and single-task learning were competitive, with the highest cross-validation results for both the classification tasks being attained by multi-task learning.

Next, we chose the best performing model hyperparameter configurations for the speech act and team development communication behavior predictions for the CRF-ELMo and BLSTM-ELMo models (marked in bold in Table 2), re-trained the models with the hyperparameters using all available training data (i.e., 5 squad training data), and evaluated the trained models' predictive performance using the held-out test set, which involved a separate squad's communication data. Table 3 reports model test performance across the re-trained models using the best performing hyperparameter configurations identified by cross-validation.

Table 3. Test accuracy rates (%) for best performing CRF-ELMo and BLSTM-ELMo models.

	SA	TD		SA	TD
CRF-ELMo	**69.42**	**64.92**	BLSTM-ELMo	64.61	61.88

The held-out test set-based evaluation results in Table 3 suggest that the hybrid CRF-ELMo approach outperformed the BLSTM-ELMo method with sizable differences for both the classification tasks, as seen in the cross-validation evaluation (Table 2). It is notable that the test accuracy rates are slightly higher than the average cross-validation accuracy rates. The five-fold cross-validation accuracy rates for the best performing CRF-ELMo models vary from 67.24% to 72.41% across the folds for speech act classification (average: 68.88%) and from 56.40% to 64.26% for team development classification (average: 58.84%), and these indicate that the held-out test set evaluation results are in a similar range. Both CRF-ELMo and BLSTM-ELMo models trained with the *entire training data* (i.e., 5 squad communication data rather than 4 in cross-validation) could help capture the test set data distribution thereby exhibiting high generalization performance.

We also trained alternating CRF models using a bag-of-words (BoW)-based static representation for utterances (CRF-BoW). To train the models, we first transformed all of the words that appeared in the training set to lower case and created a dictionary only using the top 80% of the most frequently observed words included in the training set, while treating the remaining 20% of the least commonly occurring words as *unseen* (a special token). This decision was made to effectively deal with an out-of-vocabulary problem (e.g., idiosyncratic words, typographical errors) in the test set. To create a BoW representation for each utterance, we created a vector with the dimension of 1,089, which is *the size of the dictionary* + 1 (the *unseen* special token), and set the word bit to 1 for the words included in the utterance, while setting the *unseen* special token bit to 1 for any undefined words. A CRF-BoW model is trained using the same model architecture used for the best performing CRF-ELMo. This CRF-BoW achieves 59.37% and 56.54% for speech act classification and team development, respectively, for the test set evaluation.

The results indicate that combining CRF's sequence modeling capabilities with ELMo, which uses a deep learning-based contextual, distributed utterance representation learning technique, achieves considerably higher predictive performance for both of the team communication modeling tasks. Together, these results suggest the following: (1) CRF can serve as a high-fidelity, sequence modeling technique for team communication, even with a corpus that is perhaps too small to effectively train LSTMs; and (2) the ELMo deep learning-based contextual language model trained with a large, general natural language dataset can effectively extract context and semantics from team dialogue and improve the predictive accuracy of the CRF models.

To build on these results, we next evaluated the team communication framework's *domain-transfer* capabilities. To facilitate this analysis, we explored how well the models trained with the mission data examined in this work (M_{org}) could classify squad communication that was collected during another training mission (M_{new}) [12]. Results showed that the best performing CRF-ELMo model trained with M_{org} achieved 67.35% predictive accuracy on speech act classification for utterances from M_{new}. These results show promise for developing scalable NLP-based models that can effectively transfer its predictive capacity to data collected from a related training exercise.

6   Conclusion

Adaptive team training is critical for effectively developing teamwork skills, facilitating team processes, and improving team performance. A key challenge posed by creating adaptive training environments is reliably analyzing team communication, which is a crucial source of evidence about team interaction. To address this challenge, we have introduced a hybrid, multidimensional team communication analysis framework incorporating CRF-ELMo, which integrates a high-fidelity, hybrid model that utilizes a probabilistic graphical model with a deep learning-based contextual language representation model. Evaluations conducted with cross-validation followed by a held-out test set showed that CRF-ELMo team communication analysis models achieved the highest predictive accuracy with respect to both speech acts and team development labels by effectively dealing with noisy team communication data captured from a live training exercise, and they significantly outperformed stacked, bidirectional long short-term memory network classifiers as well as majority class baselines. This hybrid approach was also found to have shown promising domain-transfer capabilities when applied to a different training event.

Future research in team communication analytics should investigate other contextual embedding approaches, model architectures, and model optimization and regularization techniques that can support generalizability and further improve the classification accuracy of team communication. Accurately classifying team communication utterances would allow team training researchers to identify if teams are pushing and pulling information at optimal rates and identify if critical pieces of information are being passed to relevant team members. In addition, future research should also conduct error analysis on misclassified instances and investigate the sequential patterns of team communication to facilitate team cognition and team performance. Finally, it will be important for future work to investigate the relationships between team communication and team performance and explore dialogue dynamics that can serve as key team performance indicators with the ultimate goal of creating adaptive team training environments.

Acknowledgements. The research was supported by the U.S. Army Research Laboratory under cooperative agreement #W912CG-19-2-0001. Any opinions, findings, and conclusions expressed in this paper are those of the authors and do not necessarily reflect the views of the U.S. Army.

References

1. Salas, E., et al.: Does team training improve team performance? Meta-Anal. Hum. Factors **50**(6), 903–933 (2008)
2. Johnston, J.H., Burke, C.S., Milham, L.A., Ross, W.M., Salas, E.: Challenges and propositions for developing effective team training with adaptive tutors. In: Johnston, J., Sottilare, R., Sinatra, A., Burke, C. (eds.) Building Intelligent Tutoring Systems for Teams, vol. 19, pp. 75–97. Emerald Publishing Limited (2018)
3. Sottilare, R.A., Burke, C.S., Salas, E., Sinatra, A.M., Johnston, J.H., Gilbert, S.B.: Designing adaptive instruction for teams: a meta-analysis. Int. J. Artif. Intell. Educ. **28**(2), 225–264 (2018)
4. Smith-Jentsch, K.A., Johnston, J.H., Payne, S.C.: Measuring team-related expertise in complex environments. In: Cannon-Bowers, J.A., Salas, E. (eds.). Making Decisions Under stress: Implications for Individual and Team Training, pp. 61–87. American Psychological Association (1998)
5. Rousseau, V., Aubé, C., Savoie, A.: Teamwork behaviors: a review and an integration of frameworks. Small Group Res. **37**(5), 540–570 (2006)
6. Marks, M.A., Mathieu, J.E., Zaccaro, S.J.: A temporally based framework and taxonomy of team processes. Acad. Manage. Rev. **26**(3), 356–376 (2001)
7. Stout, R.J., Cannon-Bowers, J.A., Salas, E.: The role of shared mental models in developing team situational awareness: Implications for training. In: Salas, E. (ed.) Situational Awareness, pp. 287–318. Routledge (2017)
8. Gorman, J.C., Foltz, P.W., Kiekel, P.A., Martin, M.J., Cooke, N.J.: Evaluation of latent semantic analysis-based measures of team communications content. In: Proceedings of the Human Factors and Ergonomics Society Annual Meeting, vol. 47, no. 3, pp. 424–428. SAGE Publications (2003)
9. Deng, L., Liu, Y.: Deep learning in natural language processing. Springer (2018)
10. Yu, B., Fan, Z.: A comprehensive review of conditional random fields: variants, hybrids and applications. Artif. Intell. Rev. **53**(6), 4289–4333 (2019). https://doi.org/10.1007/s10462-019-09793-6
11. Stolcke, A., et al.: Dialogue act modeling for automatic tagging and recognition of conversational speech. Comput. Linguist. **26**(3), 339–373 (2000)
12. Johnston, J.H., et al.: A team training field research study: extending a theory of team development. Front. Psychol. **10**, 1480 (2019)
13. McNamara, D., Allen, L., Crossley, S., Dascalu, M., Perret, C.A.: Natural language processing and learning analytics. In: Handbook of Learning Analytics, pp. 93–104 (2017)
14. Litman, D.: Natural language processing for enhancing teaching and learning. In: AAAI Conference on Artificial Intelligence, pp. 4170–4176. AAAI (2016)

15. Kumar, V.S., Boulanger, D.: Automated essay scoring and the deep learning black box: how are rubric scores determined? Int. J. Artificial Intell. Educ. 1–47 (2020). https://doi.org/10.1007/s40593-020-00211-5

16. Sung, C., Dhamecha, T.I., Mukhi, N.: Improving short answer grading using transformer-based pre-training. In: International Conference on Artificial Intelligence in Education, pp. 469–481. Springer, Cham (2019). https://doi.org/10.1007/978-3-030-23204-7_39

17. Clarke, S.N., Resnick, L.B., Rosé, C.P.: Discourse analytics for classroom learning. In: Learning Analytics in Education, vol. 139 (2018)

18. Jensen, E., Dale, M., Donnelly, P.J., Stone, C., Kelly, S., Godley, A., D'Mello, S.K.: Toward automated feedback on teacher discourse to enhance teacher learning. In: 2020 CHI Conference on Human Factors in Computing Systems, pp. 1–13. ACM (2020)

19. Balyan, R., McCarthy, K.S., McNamara, D.S.: Applying natural language processing and hierarchical machine learning approaches to text difficulty classification. Int. J. Artif. Intell. Educ. 30(3), 337–370 (2020)

20. Katz, S., Albacete, P., Chounta, I.A., Jordan, P., McLaren, B.M., Zapata-Rivera, D.: Linking dialogue with student modelling to create an adaptive tutoring system for conceptual physics. Int. J. Artif. Intell. Educ. 1–49 (2021). https://doi.org/10.1007/s40593-020-00226-y

21. Stone, C., Quirk, A., Gardener, M., Hutt, S., Duckworth, A.L., D'Mello, S.K.: Language as thought: using natural language processing to model noncognitive traits that predict college success. In: International Conference on Learning Analytics & Knowledge, pp. 320–329. ACM (2019)

22. Devlin, J., Chang, M.W., Lee, K., Toutanova, K.: Bert: pre-training of deep bidirectional transformers for language understanding. arXiv preprint arXiv:1810.04805 (2018)

23. Peters, M.E., Neumann, M., Iyyer, M., Gardner, M., Clark, C., Lee, K., Zettlemoyer, L.: Deep contextualized word representations. arXiv preprint arXiv:1802.05365 (2018)

24. Hirschberg, J., Manning, C.D.: Advances in natural language processing. Science 349(6245), 261–266 (2015)

25. Young, T., Hazarika, D., Poria, S., Cambria, E.: Recent trends in deep learning based natural language processing. IEEE Comput. Intell. Mag. 13(3), 55–75 (2018)

26. Sullivan, F.R., Keith, P.K.: Exploring the potential of natural language processing to support microgenetic analysis of collaborative learning discussions. Br. J. Edu. Technol. 50(6), 3047–3063 (2019)

27. Park, K., Sohn, H., Mott, B., Min, W., Saleh, A., Glazewski, K., Hmelo-Silver, C., Lester, J.: Detecting disruptive talk in student chat-based discussion within collaborative game-based learning environments. In: International Learning Analytics and Knowledge Conference, pp. 405–415. ACM (2021)

28. Carpenter, D., Emerson, A., Mott, B.W., Saleh, A., Glazewski, K.D., Hmelo-Silver, C.E., Lester, J.C.: Detecting off-task behavior from student dialogue in game-based collaborative learning. In: International Conference on Artificial Intelligence in Education, pp. 55–66. Springer, Cham (2020). https://doi.org/10.1007/978-3-030-52237-7_5

29. Marlow, S., Lacerenza, C., Paoletti, J., Burke, C., Salas, E.: Does team communication represent a one-size-fits-all approach? a meta-analysis of team communication and performance. Organ. Behav. Hum. Decis. Process. 144, 145–170 (2018)

30. Foltz, P.W.: Automating the assessment of team collaboration through communication analysis. Design Recommendations for Intell. Tutor. Syst. 6, 179–185 (2018)

31. Dowell, N.M.M., Nixon, T.M., Graesser, A.C.: Group communication analysis: a computational linguistics approach for detecting sociocognitive roles in multiparty interactions. Behav. Res. Methods 51(3), 1007–1041 (2018). https://doi.org/10.3758/s13428-018-1102-z

32. Ayala, D.F.M., Balasingam, B., McComb, S., Pattipati, K.R.: Markov modeling and analysis of team communication. IEEE Trans. Syst. Man Cybern.: Syst. 50(4), 1230–1241 (2020)

33. Enayet, A., Sukthankar, G.: Analyzing team performance with embeddings from multiparty dialogues. arXiv preprint arXiv:2101.09421 (2021)
34. Yu, M., Litman, D., Paletz, S.: Investigating the relationship between multi-party linguistic entrainment, team characteristics, and the perception of team social outcomes. In: International Florida Artificial Intelligence Research Society Conference, pp. 227–232. AAAI (2019)
35. Saville, J.D., Spain, R., Johnston, J., Lester, J.: Exploration of team communication behaviors from a live training event. In: The 12th International Conference on Applied Human Factors and Ergonomics (2021, to appear)
36. Lafferty, J., McCallum, A., Pereira, F.C.: Conditional random fields: probabilistic models for segmenting and labeling sequence data (2001)
37. Kumar, H., Agarwal, A., Dasgupta, R., Joshi, S.: Dialogue act sequence labeling using hierarchical encoder with CRF. In: AAAI Conference on Artificial Intelligence, pp. 3440–3447 (2018)
38. Tran, T.U., Hoang, H.T.T., Huynh, H.X.: Bidirectional independently long short-term memory and conditional random field integrated model for aspect extraction in sentiment analysis. In: Frontiers in Intelligent Computing: Theory and Applications, pp. 131–140. Springer (2020). https://doi.org/10.1007/978-981-13-9920-6_14
39. Sutton, C., McCallum, A.: An introduction to conditional random fields for relational learning. In: Introduction to Statistical Relational Learning, vol. 2, pp. 93–128 (2006)
40. Lacoste-Julien, S., Jaggi, M., Schmidt, M., Pletscher, P.: Block-coordinate Frank-Wolfe optimization for structural SVMs. In: International Conference on Machine Learning, pp. 53–61. PMLR (2013)
41. Pennington, J., Socher, R., Manning, C.D.: GloVe: global vectors for word representation. In: Conference on Empirical Methods in Natural Language Processing (EMNLP), pp. 1532–1543 (2014)
42. Müller, A.C., Behnke, S.: PyStruct: learning structured prediction in python. J. Mach. Learn. Res. **15**(1), 2055–2060 (2014)
43. Graves, A., Schmidhuber, J.: Framewise phoneme classification with bidirectional LSTM and other neural network architectures. Neural Netw. **18**(5–6), 602–610 (2005)
44. Zhang, Y., Yang, Q.: A survey on multi-task learning. arXiv preprint arXiv:1707.08114 (2017)
45. Kingma, D.P., Ba, J.: Adam: A method for stochastic optimization. arXiv preprint arXiv: 1412.6980 (2014)

A Good Start is Half the Battle Won: Unsupervised Pre-training for Low Resource Children's Speech Recognition for an Interactive Reading Companion

Abhinav Misra[✉], Anastassia Loukina, Beata Beigman Klebanov,
Binod Gyawali, and Klaus Zechner

Educational Testing Service (ETS), Princeton, NJ 08540, USA
{amisra001,aloukina,bbeigmanklebanov,bgyawali,KZechner}@ets.org

Abstract. Children's speech recognition is a challenging task because of the inherent speech production characteristics of children's articulatory structure as well as their linguistic usage. In the context of developing automated reading companions, the problem is compounded by lack of training data. Most of the available data is recorded under clean and controlled conditions leading to a performance degradation in presence of uncontrolled and realistic acoustic environments. In this study, we address these challenges by leveraging a publicly available large unlabeled read speech corpus to learn generalized audio representations. These learned representations are then employed to augment the features used for training the acoustic model of limited in-domain children's speech. The representations are learned via a deep convolutional architecture optimized on a noise contrastive binary classification task to distinguish a true future audio sample from negatives. We obtain upto 24.87% relative improvement in the Word Error Rate (WER) of our speech recognition system using these generalized audio embeddings and show the effectiveness of using a pre-trained model when training data is limited.

Keywords: Speech recognition · Low resource speech recognition · Children's speech recognition · Unsupervised pre-training · Reading companion

1 Introduction

Artificial Intelligence (AI) systems including those in education, usually require training data. This can lead to a chicken-and-egg problem when building and deploying a new application: user data is necessary to train AI models but AI models are necessary to put together even a minimally functional prototype that the users can interact with. Furthermore, the initial amount of training data collected in pilot studies and beta releases is likely to be relatively small for training modern AI systems. In this paper, we show how representational

© Springer Nature Switzerland AG 2021
I. Roll et al. (Eds.): AIED 2021, LNAI 12748, pp. 306–317, 2021.
https://doi.org/10.1007/978-3-030-78292-4_25

learning [3] can be used to address this problem in the context of training an automated speech recognition system for an interactive reading application.

The most recent National Assessment of Educational Progress (NAEP) reading assessment of U.S. fourth graders show that 34% of students read even below the basic level[1]. It has been shown that one-on-one tutoring can provide significant improvement in raising reading fluency levels as compared to the one-to-many classroom instruction [30]. However, human tutoring is expensive and speech technology can be used to provide an impactful and cost-effective solution.

Many existing commercial and research applications already use automated speech recognition (ASR) and other speech processing technologies to assess oral reading fluency and assist with its development. Reviews of earlier systems can be found in [12,35] among many others; [6] provides an overview of some of more recent developments in the area of technology-based literacy instruction. VersaReader [2] and Project LISTEN [18] are two of the most mature systems in this area, while Moby.Read [5] is the latest addition to the list. All these systems rely on ASR to process children's speech and then use the hypothesis to compute various oral fluency measures and report promising results in terms of agreement with human ratings. Since the reliability of speech technology based measurements in education is closely related to the audio quality of the recording, most of these systems are tailored to support reading in a controlled acoustic environment. Moby.Read requires its readers to be in a quiet environment while Flora [4] recommends to use noise-canceling microphones. In most of the previous studies, students were instructed to be in a quiet area and were supervised by trained facilitators monitoring the session [2,19]. Although this ensures good quality audio recordings, it restricts the usage of these systems to specialized scenarios.

In this study, we attempt to build an interactive reading companion that can be used in naturalistic acoustic environments to provide a sustained reading experience with continuous and unobtrusive measurement of oral reading fluency. Unlike most of the systems mentioned in the previous paragraph which are tailored to support reading in a controlled acoustic environment, our application needs to support speech recorded in the presence of background noise, using poor recording equipment and containing mumbling or unclear speech. Furthermore, automatic recognition of children's speech is a particularly challenging task due to its different spectral and temporal characteristics as compared to adult speech [7,24].

These requirements make it difficult to find an existing data set that could be used to train the models necessary for automated speech recognition. There is not much publicly available acoustic data to train models for children's speech. Collecting data from minors is not as straightforward as collecting adult speech data. In fact, to the best of our knowledge, there is no children's speech data available that is collected for estimating reading fluency in naturalistic scenarios.

---

[1] https://nces.ed.gov/nationsreportcard/reading/.

In this paper, we show how representational learning can be used to lever-age publicly available datasets along with a relatively small amount of data collected through our application to achieve an improvement in performance of automated speech recognition. We also show that representational learning is particularly useful when the amount of in-domain training data is very small, a likely situation during early deployment of educational applications.

The remainder of this paper is organized as follows: Sect. 2 provides an overview of ASR for children; Sect. 3 describes the representational learning method used to improve the performance of limited data ASR; Sect. 4 provides details about the interactive reading app we built for supporting the development of oral reading fluency; Sect. 5 presents the data and experimental set-up used in our study; Sect. 6 presents and analyzes the results of our study; Sect. 7 concludes the paper and discusses future work.

2   ASR for Children

ASR aims to convert raw audio into a sequence of corresponding words [21,34]. It consists of a complex interplay of acoustic modeling [14], pronunciation dictio-nary and language modeling [31]. Acoustic modeling maps an audio signal into linguistic units that make up speech (such as syllables or phonemes). A pronun-ciation dictionary converts words to these linguistic units and a language model assigns probability estimate to word sequences. A speech recognition engine sim-ply generates a word sequence that is most likely to be produced given the acoustic model, dictionary and language model.

Children's speech has different spectral characteristics compared to adult speech. Due to their smaller vocal tracts, children have higher fundamental and formant frequencies [7,29]. In addition, children tend to speak at a more variable rate and modify their vocal effort considerably during the duration of their speech [24]. All these factors make children's speech recognition a challenging problem. Training children-specific acoustic models has been proven to be highly beneficial [24]. In [7], authors show that training language models on children's speech also provides improvement over using adult speech language models. This is mainly because of different grammatical constructs used by children. However, for the application of reading assessment, children are constrained to read a pre-determined passage and hence, obtaining children's language model is at a lower priority than obtaining children's acoustic data. There is not much publicly available acoustic data to train models for children's speech. In this paper, we have attempted to collect such data and then use representational learning to boost the performance of acoustic models trained on such limited data.

3   Unsupervised Pre-training

In fields such as Computer Vision (CV) and Natural Language Processing (NLP), representational learning has proven to be very helpful in reaching state-of-the-art results on a variety of tasks. For example, in CV, representations learned

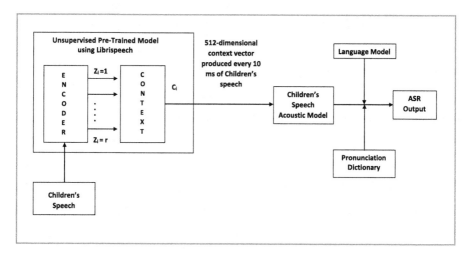

Fig. 1. A block diagram representing unsupervised pre-training used in our system. Each z_i corresponds to 30 ms of children's speech and $z_i...z_r$ correspond to a receptive field of 210 ms. A context vector c_i encompassing this receptive field is produced for every 10 ms of Children's speech. These context vectors are used to train the children's speech acoustic model. In other words, these context vectors are the representations of children's speech learned with the help of the pre-trained model and thereby improving the performance of children's ASR.

from ImageNet [9] have provided significant improvements in several tasks such as object detection, captioning or video recognition. In NLP, pre-trained language models like Bidirectional Encoder Representations from Transformers (BERT) [10], XLNet [33] or Robustly Optimized BERT Pretraining Approach (RoBERTa) [16] have been shown to capture important facets of language useful in most of the language understanding tasks that are part of the General Language Understanding Evaluation (GLUE) benchmark [32]. Speech processing is yet to witness such a widespread use of representations learned from pre-trained models. In [20], authors explore representational learning to classify phonemes and speakers in Librispeech dataset [22]. In [15], the authors learn representations from English to recognize German speech. In [27], the authors show improvement on a speech recognition task by replacing the log-mel filterbanks by pre-trained embeddings. In this study, we extend the work done by authors in [27] by exploring its usefulness in recognizing children's speech for assessing reading fluency.

The basic idea behind training an unsupervised universal model is to extract useful representations from it that are less specialized towards solving a single speech task such as ASR, but rather contains underlying information of the signal that is shared amongst other speech tasks as well such as voice biometrics, language recognition or emotion recognition. One of the biggest advantages of such unsupervised pre-training is that it can be applied to domains where training data is small and annotations are not available. For example, in our application, there is limited availability of labeled training data and consequently the Deep Neural Network (DNN) based acoustic model does not have enough examples to learn all the relevant speech signal characteristics. Furthermore, presence of background noise and reverberation corrupts the speech signal and some relevant signal characteristics might be lost altogether. By doing unsupervised pre-training on a large and readily available dataset, we expect to learn representations that encode basic speech signal features common across all speech tasks. These representations could then be used to augment speech features in any downstream task. In this paper, we have used 960 h of Librispeech data that consists of adult read speech. It is expected that the representations learned from Librispeech would provide some prior knowledge to the DNN based acoustic model and thereby help it in recognizing read children's speech. Since the model is pre-trained using unsupervised learning, there is no need to transcribe the Librispeech dataset.

Most of the unsupervised learning strategies have been based on predicting missing, future or contextual information [10,11]. In speech processing, correlation between consecutive samples has been widely utilized in applications such as speech coding. [1,28]. Hence, it follows naturally to exploit this inter-dependence between samples and learn some generalized features about speech signal.

Similar to [27], we first take the raw audio signal and project it onto a latent embedding space using a five layer convolutional encoder network. The latent vector z represents a lower dimensional compact embedding space that we assume is shared between the correlated samples of the speech signal. We obtain a latent representation z_i for every 10 ms and each representation encodes around 30 ms of speech. Next, a context network consisting of nine convolutional layers combines all the latent vectors within 210 ms of speech into a single context vector c_i. The context network can be thought of as an autoregressive model that produces a context representation by summarizing the encoded latent representations. We assume 210 ms is enough to capture most of the relevant context from the past.

Both the encoder and context networks are jointly trained to optimize a loss function based on Noise Contrastive Estimation (NCE) [13]. This essentially means that the model is trained to learn to distinguish between true data and a set of distractor or negative samples. Let z_{i+k} be a sample that is k steps ahead from the distractor samples z' drawn from the same audio file and conforming to a uniform distribution p such that $p(z) = 1/l$, where l is the sequence length. The model learns to distinguish z_{i+k} from the distractor samples by minimizing the following loss function for each step k:

$$L_k = -\sum_{i=1}^{l-k}(log\sigma(z_{i+k}^t(W_kc_i + b_k)) + \lambda \mathop{\mathbb{E}}_{z'\in p} [log\sigma(-z'^t(W_kc_i + b_k))]) \quad (1)$$

where, l is the sequence length and $(W_kc_i + b_k)$ is the linear transformation used for the prediction. σ stands for sigmoid function and λ is set equal to the number of distractor samples. It was observed that choosing distractor samples from a different audio file degrades the overall performance. The final loss is optimized by summing over all the different step sizes as:

$$L = \sum_{k=1}^{K} L_k \tag{2}$$

All this training is done using a large publicly available dataset known as the Librispeech corpus [22]. Once the training is complete, children's speech is input to this model to obtain the context vector c_i for every 10ms of the audio file. Figure 1 shows the block diagram representing the system used in this study.

4   App Design

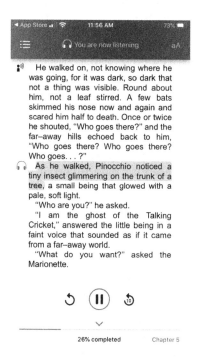

Fig. 2. A screenshot of the iOS version of Relay Reader.

We developed a reading and listening app called Relay Reader™ that is designed to help developing readers improve their reading fluency while enjoying a good story. Figure 2 shows a screenshot of the iOS version of the app.[2] Figure 3 shows an example of how children used our app in a fairly laid back and informal

---

[2] The app is freely available at relayreader.org as well as in Google Play and App Stores.

Fig. 3. Children reading a book using our app.

atmosphere. The user takes turns reading out loud from a long book with a pre-recorded model narrator (audiobook). Each reading turn is approximately 70 to 200 words long; the turn length can be configured by the user. The user's reading turns are recorded and processed, as described in the next section. The app also includes comprehension questions to further support the reading experience, as well as functionality to re-record the user's turn to promote self-teaching. Currently, the app does not provide the user any feedback based on their oral reading. The goal of the work described in this paper is to further develop the speech recognition technology that would support such feedback in later versions of the app. For more information about the app, see [17]. To alleviate any privacy and ethical concerns regarding data collection and usage, we followed our institutions's privacy policy[3] and Institutional Review Board (IRB) guidelines.

5   Experiments

5.1   Data

We use the audio recordings collected through the app to train and evaluate the system. The majority of the recordings were collected from US elementary school children belonging to grades 3–5. Most of them read with the app either during summer camp or as part of the school instruction. In addition, a small subset of data comes from adults and children who took part in pilot studies. The students read one of two books: "Harry Potter and the Sorcerer's Stone" by J.K. Rowling (HP1) or "The Adventures of Pinocchio" by Carlo Collodi, translation by Carol Della Chiesa ("Pinocchio").

The fact that recordings were collected in natural educational settings where children read on their own with minimal teacher involvement, means that the data contains a lot of behavioral and acoustic noise. Some of the previously identified issues include students not attempting to read during their turn; recordings

---

[3] ETS privacy policy can be found here: https://www.ets.org/legal/privacy.

with almost no audible speech due to high background noise; silent reading; or a student being distracted by other activities while their speech is being recorded.

The test set contains 645 recordings (14.6 h) collected from 33 children reading as part of the school programming. The reading was conducted entirely under teacher supervision and monitored remotely by the project staff through the analysis of the app logs. Children read in their regular classroom, with some care taken to disperse them as much as possible in the classroom; in some cases, teachers also sent some students to read in the corridor adjacent to the classroom. The children used consumer-grade in-ear headphones with built-in microphone. All recordings in the test set were transcribed by a professional transcription agency. The transcribers were provided with the text of the passage and were asked to indicate any deletions, substitutions, and insertions as well as provide timestamps for the beginning and end of on-task speech. All children read HP1.

The training set includes 6,545 recordings (133.3 h). Of these, 6,201 recordings (125 h) are from 129 children who read as part of summer camp programming.

The reading was done in regular classrooms and monitored by the teachers or camp instructors. The children used the app on tablets with consumer-grade in-ear headphones. In addition, a small set of recordings were collected during pilot studies conducted in quieter office environments: these include 158 recordings (4.4 h) from 43 kids as well as 186 recordings (3.9 h) from 12 adults (6 teachers and 6 adult literacy students). Pilot study users used either tablets or laptops and professional-grade headphones with built-in mics. Of the recordings in the training set, 111 h (83%) are from users reading HP1, same book as used for the test set, and 22 h from users reading Pinocchio. Only a small subset of recordings in the training set is transcribed: 764 responses, all from users reading HP1.

5.2   Experimental Set-Up

We train an acoustic model consisting of both Time Delay Neural Network (TDNN) and Long Short Term Memory (LSTM) layers using Kaldi toolkit [25]. The network consists of interleaving TDNN and LSTM layers, thereby combining the advantages of temporal convolution with recurrence [23]. This is done since both convolution as well as LSTM networks have shown improvement over DNNs for a wide variety of speech recognition tasks, and since both of them are complementary in their modeling capabilities, we wanted to take advantage of both through a unified architecture. Bi-directional LSTM (Bi-LSTM) networks and simple TDNN networks with fifteen layers did provide similar performance, however, that was at the expense of high latency and risk of overfitting respectively. There are seven TDNN and three LSTM layers containing 1024 neurons each in our architecture. Lattice-Free Maximum Mutual Information (LF-MMI) criterion is used for training along with reduced output frame rate, which helps in decreasing the latency [26]. Reducing the overall latency is important for an interactive system that seeks to provide live feedback to children.

Since we did not have transcriptions for most of the recordings in the training set, a 3-gram language model is trained mostly on the book passages that were read by the children. For a small number of cases when transcriptions are available (764 files), the language model is trained on transcriptions instead of the book passages. A baseline ASR system is developed using 13-dimensional Mel-Frequency Cepstral Coefficients (MFCCs) extracted from children's speech. A 100 dimensional i-vector [8] is added to each MFCC feature that provides useful information to the network to perform some form of feature normalization. Table 1 shows the performance of our baseline system.

The unsupervised model with encoder and context networks as discussed in Sect. 3, is trained using 960 h of Librispeech corpus. This choice was motivated by the fact that it is the largest publicly available English read speech corpus derived from audiobooks. After the model is trained, we input children's speech to the trained encoder network. The output of the encoder network is summarized by the context network that produces a 512 dimensional representation every 10 ms of the audio file. These representations are fed to the TDNN-LSTM acoustic model in four different ways: i) replace the MFCCs and i-vectors by context vectors; ii) replace only the MFCCs and add context vectors to the i-vectors; iii) replace the i-vectors and add context vectors to the MFCCs; iv) add context vectors to MFCCs and i-vectors.

6   Results

Table 1 shows the performance of the ASR system with all the four configurations according to which the representations from the context network were fed to the system. It can be observed that although there is a general trend of Word Error Rate (WER) reduction due to the addition of context vector, maximum improvement is obtained in the case of the context vector being added to the i-vector. Simply replacing the traditional MFCC features by the context vector does not provide any significant improvement. Augmenting the feature space by combining context vector and i-vector provides 7.13% relative improvement in WER. This might indicate that i-vectors and context vectors contain complementary information that together enhances the overall performance.

Next, we reduced the amount of children's data by randomly sampling 50% and 25% of the responses in the original training set to evaluate low resource scenarios where enough audio recordings are not present. It was observed that as the training data size decreases, the improvement obtained using context vectors over traditional features increases. Table 2 shows that when the training data is only 25% of its original size, the WER for the baseline model increased from 10.24% to 17.89%, while the WER for context model trained on this smaller data set was 13.44%, leading to a 24.89% relative improvement from using context representations. Hence, pre-training is really useful when in-domain training data is difficult to obtain which is usually the case while deploying an AI application. Having a model that is trained on a large publicly available dataset can be very helpful in such cases in providing a good starting point to any application.

Table 1. Effect of unsupervised pre-training on children's speech recognition

System configuration	WER (%)
MFCC + i-vector (baseline)	10.24
context vector	10.03
context vector + MFCC	10.08
context vector + i-vector + MFCC	10.09
context vector + i-vector	**9.51**

Table 2. Relationship between ASR WER (%) and size of children's data used to train the acoustic model. The less data is available for training, the more relative improvement is obtained using context representations over MFCC + i-vector features.

% Training Data used	MFCC + i-vector	context vector + i-vector	Relative Improvement (%)
100%	10.24	9.51	7.13
50%	13.30	11.03	17.07
25%	17.89	13.44	24.87

7   Conclusions

In this study, we conducted a systematic analysis of using unsupervised pre-training to enhance acoustic modeling of children's speech. We showed that using a pre-trained model can significantly boost the performance of an ASR system that doesn't have enough training data. We conducted experiments and observed that simply replacing the traditional features by representations learned from a universal model does not provide any substantial improvement. The maximum improvement was obtained by combining representations learned from a Librispeech trained universal model and i-vectors trained on in-domain children's speech. The improvement was even greater under low resource scenarios where limited amount of in-domain training data is available. In the context of deploying a real-life reading companion, collecting sufficient in-domain training data is one of the primary bottlenecks for training accurate models and providing users with useful speech-based feedback. Our proposed method offers a feasible solution in this regard by providing substantial gains over the baseline model that was trained with limited train data. This allows our reading companion application to provide more accurate feedback sooner after deployment. In future, we intend to further improve our app's speech recognition by exploring pre-training for language modeling. We plan to release a new version of our app in the summer of 2021 that will contain new books to provide more reading choices to readers. Employing pre-trained models become even more important in such scenarios as it is likely that a newly added book would not have reading samples available for training a book-specific acoustic model.

References

1. Atal, B., Schroeder, M.: Predictive coding of speech signals and subjective error criteria. In: ICASSP '78. IEEE International Conference on Acoustics, Speech, and Signal Processing, vol. 3, pp. 573–576 (1978)
2. Balogh, J., Bernstein, J., Cheng, J., Moere, A.V., Townshend, B., Suzuki, M.: Validation of automated scoring of oral reading. Educ. Psychol. Measur. **72**(3), 435–452 (2012)
3. Bengio, Y., Courville, A., Vincent, P.: Representation learning: a review and new perspectives. IEEE Trans. Pattern Anal. Mach. Intell. **35**(8), 1798–1828 (2013)
4. Bolaños, D., Cole, R., Ward, W., Tindal, G., Hasbrouck, J., Schwanenflugel, P.: Human and automated assessment of oral reading fluency. J. Educ. Psychol. **105**, 1142 (2013). https://doi.org/10.1037/a0031479
5. Cheng, J.: Real-time scoring of an oral reading assessment on mobile devices. In: INTERSPEECH (2018)
6. Crossley, S.A., McNamara, D.: Educational technologies and literacy development. In: Crossley, S.A., Mcnamara, D. (eds.) Adaptive Educational technologies for literacy instruction, pp. 1–12. Routledge, New York (2016)
7. Das, S., Nix, D., Picheny, M.: Improvements in children's speech recognition performance. In: Proceedings of IEEE ICASSP (1998)
8. Dehak, N., Kenny, P.J., Dehak, R., Dumouchel, P., Ouellet, P.: Front-end factor analysis for speaker verification. IEEE Trans. Audio Speech Lang. Process. **19**(4), 788–798 (2011)
9. Deng, J., Dong, W., Socher, R., Li, L., Li, K., Fei-Fei, L.: ImageNet: a large-scale hierarchical image database. In: 2009 IEEE Conference on Computer Vision and Pattern Recognition, pp. 248–255 (2009)
10. Devlin, J., Chang, M.W., Lee, K., Toutanova, K.: BERT: pre-training of deep bidirectional transformers for language understanding. ArXiv abs/1810.04805 (2019)
11. Doersch, C., Gupta, A., Efros, A.A.: Unsupervised visual representation learning by context prediction. In: 2015 IEEE International Conference on Computer Vision (ICCV), pp. 1422–1430 (2015)
12. Eskenazi, M.: An overview of spoken language technology for education. Speech Commun. **51**(10), 832–844 (2009). https://doi.org/10.1016/j.specom.2009.04.005
13. Gutmann, M., Hyvärinen, A.: Noise-contrastive estimation: a new estimation principle for unnormalized statistical models. J. Mach. Learn. Res. - Proc. Track **9**, 297–304 (2010)
14. Hinton, G., et al.: Deep neural networks for acoustic modeling in speech recognition: the shared views of four research groups. IEEE Sig. Process. Mag. **29**(6), 82–97 (2012). https://doi.org/10.1109/MSP.2012.2205597
15. Kunze, J., Kirsch, L., Kurenkov, I., Krug, A., Johannsmeier, J., Stober, S.: Transfer learning for speech recognition on a budget. In: ACL (2017)
16. Liu, Y., et al.: RoBERTa: a robustly optimized BERT pretraining approach. ArXiv abs/1907.11692 (2019)
17. Madnani, N., et al.: MyTurnToRead: an interleaved e-book reading tool for developing and struggling readers. In: Proceedings of the 57th Conference of the Association for Computational Linguistics: System Demonstrations, pp. 141–146. Association for Computational Linguistics, Florence (2019). https://www.aclweb.org/anthology/P19-3024
18. Mostow, J.: Why and how our automated reading tutor listens. In: Proceedings of the International Symposium on Automatic Detection of Errors in Pronunciation Training, pp. 43–52 (2012)

19. Mostow, J., et al.: Evaluation of an automated reading tutor that listens: comparison to human tutoring and classroom instruction. J. Educ. Comput. Res. **29**, 61–117 (2003). https://doi.org/10.2190/06AX-QW99-EQ5G-RDCF

20. van den Oord, A., Li, Y., Vinyals, O.: Representation learning with contrastive predictive coding. ArXiv (2018)

21. O'Shaughnessy, D.: Invited paper: automatic speech recognition: history, methods and challenges. Pattern Recognit. **41**(10), 2965–2979 (2008). https://doi.org/10.1016/j.patcog.2008.05.008. https://www.sciencedirect.com/science/article/pii/S0031320308001799

22. Panayotov, V., Chen, G., Povey, D., Khudanpur, S.: Librispeech: an ASR corpus based on public domain audio books. In: 2015 IEEE International Conference on Acoustics, Speech and Signal Processing (ICASSP), pp. 5206–5210 (2015)

23. Peddinti, V., Wang, Y., Povey, D., Khudanpur, S.: Low latency acoustic modeling using temporal convolution and LSTMs. IEEE Sig. Process. Lett. **25**(3), 373–377 (2018)

24. Potamianos, A., Narayanan, S., Lee, S.: Automatic speech recognition for children. In: Proceedings of Eurospeech (1997)

25. Povey, D., et al.: The Kaldi speech recognition toolkit. In: IEEE 2011 Workshop on Automatic Speech Recognition and Understanding (2011)

26. Povey, D., et al.: Purely sequence-trained neural networks for ASR based on lattice-free mmi, pp. 2751–2755 (2016). https://doi.org/10.21437/Interspeech. 2016–595

27. Schneider, S., Baevski, A., Collobert, R., Auli, M.: wav2vec: unsupervised pre-training for speech recognition. In: INTERSPEECH (2019)

28. Schroeder, M., Atal, B.: Code-excited linear prediction (CELP): high-quality speech at very low bit rates. In: ICASSP '85. IEEE International Conference on Acoustics, Speech, and Signal Processing, vol. 10, pp. 937–940 (1985)

29. Shivakumar, P.G., Potamianos, A., Lee, S., Narayanan, S.: Improving speech recognition for children using acoustic adaptation and pronunciation modeling. In: Proceedings of the INTERSPEECH Workshop on Child, Computer, and Interaction (2014)

30. Snow, C.E., Burns, M.S., Griffin, P.: Preventing Reading Difficulties in Young Children. National Academy Press, Washington, D.C. (1998)

31. Souto, N., Meinedo, H., Neto, J.P.: Building language models for continuous speech recognition systems. In: Ranchhod, E., Mamede, N.J. (eds.) PorTAL 2002. LNCS (LNAI), vol. 2389, pp. 101–110. Springer, Heidelberg (2002). https://doi.org/10.1007/3-540-45433-0_16

32. Wang, A., Singh, A., Michael, J., Hill, F., Levy, O., Bowman, S.R.: GLUE: a multi-task benchmark and analysis platform for natural language understanding. In: EMNLP (2018)

33. Yang, Z., Dai, Z., Yang, Y., Carbonell, J., Salakhutdinov, R., Le, Q.V.: XlNet: generalized autoregressive pretraining for language understanding (2019). http://arxiv.org/abs/1906.08237. cite arxiv:1906.08237 Comment: Pretrained models and code are available at https://github.com/zihangdai/xlnet

34. Yu, D., Deng, L.: Automatic Speech Recognition. Springer, Heidelberg (2016). https://doi.org/10.1007/978-1-4471-5779-3

35. Zechner, K., Sabatini, J., Chen, L.: Automatic scoring of children's read-aloud text passages and word lists. In: Proceedings of the NAACL-HLT Workshop on Innovative Use of NLP for Building Educational Applications, pp. 10–18 (2009)

Predicting Knowledge Gain During Web Search Based on Multimedia Resource Consumption

Christian Otto[1]([✉])[iD], Ran Yu[2][iD], Georg Pardi[3][iD], Johannes von Hoyer[3][iD], Markus Rokicki[4], Anett Hoppe[1][iD], Peter Holtz[3][iD], Yvonne Kammerer[3][iD], Stefan Dietze[2,4], and Ralph Ewerth[1,4][iD]

[1] TIB – Leibniz Information Centre for Science and Technology, Hannover, Germany
{christian.otto,anett.hoppe,ralph.ewerth}@tib.eu
[2] GESIS – Leibniz Institute for the Social Sciences, Cologne, Germany
{ran.yu,stefan.dietze}@gesis.org
[3] IWM – Leibniz-Institut für Wissensmedien, Tübingen, Germany
{g.pardi,j.hoyer,p.holtz,y.kammerer}@iwm-tuebingen.de
[4] L3S Research Center, Hannover, Germany
rokicki@l3s.de

Abstract. In informal learning scenarios the popularity of multimedia content, such as video tutorials or lectures, has significantly increased. Yet, the users' interactions, navigation behavior, and consequently learning outcome, have not been researched extensively. Related work in this field, also called *search as learning*, has focused on behavioral or text resource features to predict learning outcome and knowledge gain. In this paper, we investigate whether we can exploit features representing multimedia resource consumption to predict the knowledge gain (KG) during Web search from in-session data, that is without prior knowledge about the learner. For this purpose, we suggest a set of multimedia features related to image and video consumption. Our feature extraction is evaluated in a lab study with 113 participants where we collected data for a given search as learning task on the formation of thunderstorms and lightning. We automatically analyze the monitored log data and utilize state-of-the-art computer vision methods to extract features about the seen multimedia resources. Experimental results demonstrate that multimedia features can improve KG prediction. Finally, we provide an analysis on feature importance (text and multimedia) for KG prediction.

Keywords: Knowledge gain · Multimedia information extraction · Document layout analysis · Search as learning · Learning resources

---

C. Otto and R. Yu—Authors contributed equally to this work.

Part of this work is financially supported by the Leibniz Association, Germany (Leibniz Competition 2018, funding line "Collaborative Excellence", project SALIENT [K68/2017]).

© Springer Nature Switzerland AG 2021
I. Roll et al. (Eds.): AIED 2021, LNAI 12748, pp. 318–330, 2021.
https://doi.org/10.1007/978-3-030-78292-4_26

1   Introduction

The research field *search as learning* (SAL) focuses on Web searches with an *informational* intent, as opposed to *transactional* or *informational* [4], and explores how they can be supported by information retrieval (IR) systems [5,21]. This entails, for example, the detection of a user's learning intent, the prediction of knowledge state and knowledge gain during search, as well as the adaption of search results according to the learning goals. Thereby, search as learning goes clearly beyond relevance scoring of documents.

Previous work has studied the relationship between learning progress and text content or behavioral features collected from search sessions. For instance, Collins-Thompson et al. [6] studied the influence of distinct query types on knowledge gain, and found that intrinsically diverse queries are correlated with knowledge gain. On the other hand, Syed and Collins-Thompson [24] explored a range of text and resource-based features and their impact on short-term and long-term learning outcome, but did not investigate multimedia content. Moraes et al.'s [19] work compared the learning outcome of instructor-designed learning videos against three instances of search ("single-user", "search as support tool", "collaborative search") to find the most efficient approach for their learning scenario. Other work investigated the learning outcomes associated with the consumption of multimedia resources [20,23]. Pardi et al. [20] found that the time users spent on text-dominated websites associates with better learning outcomes compared to videos. Vakkari [25] provided a structured survey of features indicating learning needs as well as users' knowledge and knowledge gain throughout the search process. Gadiraju et al. [9] described the use of knowledge tests to measure the knowledge of users before and after the search sessions, and investigated the impact of search intent and search behavior on the knowledge gain of users. In follow-up work, Yu et al. [26] utilized interaction features to predict users' knowledge gain in search sessions using supervised machine learning.

In this paper, we investigate the impact of multimedia features on users' knowledge gain in a SAL scenario, but on a larger scale and with an extended set of behavioral and resource features. We conducted a user study that recorded the pre- and post-knowledge states of the participants through multiple-choice questionnaires. After the search session, we analyzed all visited Web pages to gather a set of features regarding consumed multimedia content, e.g., document layout, image size and type. This novel feature set allows us to investigate the role of multimedia features for knowledge prediction in this SAL scenario. Therefore, we train a supervised learning model (random forest) to predict knowledge gain based on text and multimedia features. Experimental results demonstrate the feasibility of the approach. A feature importance analysis shows that features related to image and video content slightly improve knowledge gain prediction compared to textual and behavioral features in terms of overall accuracy.

The remainder of the paper is structured as follows: Sect. 2 introduces the setup of our user study, while Sect. 3 presents our methodology for multimedia feature extraction. Section 4 reports the results for knowledge gain prediction. Section 5 concludes the paper and outlines areas for future research.

2   User Study and Data Collection

The participants (N = 113, 22.86 ± 2.92 years old, 96 females) of our lab study were asked to solve a realistic learning task: understand the principles of thunderstorms and lightning. This topic has been used in many studies that investigated learning with multimedia (e.g., [17,22]). This topic is related to natural sciences and has been chosen since it requires learners to gain knowledge about different physical and meteorological concepts and their interplay. The learning task itself can be classified as a causal task [10] in which learners need to learn about the causal chains of events. Therefore, they need to acquire declarative as well as procedural knowledge [2] about different concepts to gain comprehensive knowledge. We believe that this task is a suitable representative for a class of various and similar tasks. For example, comparable causal tasks would be learning about the greenhouse effect or photosynthesis. The acquisition of information about causal tasks can be accomplished through studying different representation formats like text, pictures, videos, or their combined presentation on Web pages.

Technical Setup: All search and learning activities of participants were conducted within a two-layer tracking framework. The SMI (SensoMotoric Instruments) ExperimentCenter (3.7) software enabled us to track participants' activities during Web search through screen recordings and navigation log files. We implemented a second tracking layer in the browser using plugins. These plugins saved all visited HTML files and tracked additionally navigation and interaction data (e.g., mouse movements) in local log files. The local and external tracking was realized through JavaScript code integrated into the plugin "Greasemonkey" (3.11) running in the browser. To track HTML files, we used the plugin "ScrapBook" (1.5.14) to automatically and simultaneously save all visited HTML pages (HTML files and folders) seen by the participants.

Knowledge Test: Based on previous work [22] we developed a 10-item multiple-choice knowledge test on the formation of thunderstorm and lightning. To measure participants' pre-knowledge state (pre-KS), the same test had to be completed at two different points in time: First, two days before the Web search task, and second time after the Web search task to measure the post-knowledge state (post-KS). Pre- and post-knowledge states were represented by the score of correct answers (out of 10). Knowledge gain (KG) is the difference between the two scores. Further information on the experimental setup are described in previous work [14].

3   Multimedia Feature Extraction

In this section, we outline how we generated the multimedia features based on text, but mainly for image and video content that serve as input for knowledge gain prediction. The output of the data logging per user is the input for our feature extraction process. The data logging output consists of a screen recording (MPEG-4 video format (*.mp4)), a timeline of visited Web pages, as well as

HTML and CSS files of every visited Web page. In a first step, Web pages are segmented into regions of headlines, (normal) text, images, etc. using a state-of-art method for document layout analysis (Sect. 3.1). The image regions are further processed through image type classification to infer the kind of seen content (Sect. 3.2). In Sect. 3.3 we describe the feature extraction process for text content. Both feature types are then utilized to predict knowledge gain using a random forest classifier.

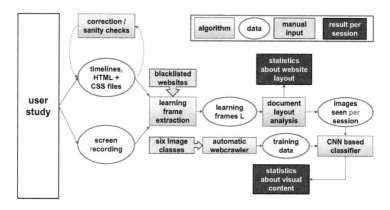

Fig. 1. Our multimedia feature extraction pipeline: The only manual inputs are the list of blacklisted websites and the set of image classes. The multimedia features per user (red boxes) as well as textual information described in Sect. 3.3 are the input for our knowledge gain predictor (Sect. 4). (Color figure online)

To reconstruct the visited Web pages, we exploit the screen recordings and segment them according to the timeline of the search session. The timeline should reflect the order of Web pages getting into focus, rather than the points in time URLs were opened in their respective browser tabs. In this way, we circumvent the problem of participants opening multiple links from the search result page at once in new tabs, leading to a flawed timeline. An overview of the framework is displayed in Fig. 1. As shown in Fig. 1, the first step separates the total number of F video frames into L learning relevant and N navigation-related frames, with $N + L = F$. We extract a frame every second of the video ($|F| = 173\,787$), but only keep those where the participant spent time on Web pages related to learning (and not navigating the browser or procrastinating). Thus, we excluded (study-specific) URLs containing *Google*, *TripAdvisor* and *adblock*. This procedure resulted in a total of $119\,164$ (average: 1268 frames per session) learning relevant frames which have to be segmented into pictorial, textual, and background information as described in the next section.

3.1 Document Layout Analysis

The goal of this step is to derive features on document layout by automatically dividing each frame $l \in L$ into coherent regions that represent the structure of the page. Additionally, the regions should be classified according to their content, e.g., image, text, menu, etc. This procedure is crucial for the image content analysis later but also challenging since the layout and design of the Web pages vary heavily. To address this challenge, we utilize the Mask R-CNN [1] network architecture, originally implemented for instance (object) segmentation, and fine-tune the provided pre-trained weights of the network. We annotated 300 randomly chosen frames from our user study using the browser-based "VGG Image Annotator". Six region classes are distinguished:

1. Heading: any headlines or titles that divide the page into sections;
2. Menu bar: buttons or lists of buttons displayed for navigational purposes;
3. Content list: enumerations like table of contents or bullet point lists;
4. Text: any coherent text block that is not part of headlines or button labels;
5. Images/Frames: All types of images (no size constraints) from small thumbnails to fullscreen video frames;
6. Background: everything that does not fit into the five other classes.

These classes are supposed to reflect the core parts of a Web page. The JSON (JavaScript Object Notation) style output of the manual annotations was then split into 90% training and 10% test data, which we used to fine-tune the fully-connected layers after the pre-trained bounding box detector (i.e., network heads) for 30 epochs with a learning rate of $lr = 0.001$. This option is predefined (by the Mask R-CNN authors) by creating the model with parameter $layers =$ "heads" and subsequently only retrains the region proposal network (RPN), the classifier, and the mask heads. The resulting network is able to segment our screen recording frames appropriately. An example output is depicted in Fig. 2 that also includes a picture-in-picture effect with two overlapping bounding boxes. This was resolved by computing pairwise Intersection over Union (IoU) and discarding the smaller bounding boxes if the overlap was above 80%.

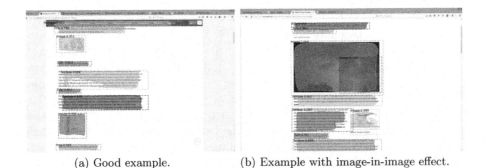

(a) Good example.   (b) Example with image-in-image effect.

Fig. 2. Two example outputs of the Document Layout Analysis.

In addition to our six classes we also compute the average image size per frame since we want to differentiate if a Web page with 20% visual content contained five small images or a single large one. Another merit of this feature is its ability to also indirectly measure the viewing time of videos since it is difficult to measure this feature directly with satisfactory accuracy. For instance, embedded videos on Web pages other than YouTube cannot always be captured. Our document layout features per frame i are represented as a vector d_i containing six percentages (summing up to 100%) and a scalar.

$$d_i = (head_i, menu_i, conlist_i, text_i, img_i, bg_i, \overline{imgsize_i}), \forall i \in L. \qquad (1)$$

Lastly, the results per frame in Eq. 1 are summed up for all seen learning frames $i \in L$ and divided by $|L|$ yielding seven features per participant p.

$$d_p = (\sum_{i=0}^{|L|} \frac{head_i}{|L|}, \sum_{i=0}^{|L|} \frac{menu_i}{|L|}, ..., \sum_{i=0}^{|L|} \frac{\overline{imgsize_i}}{|L|}) \qquad (2)$$

We identified a total of 755 756 bounding boxes that belonged to the "Images/Frames" class, which has around five samples per frame on average. This appears to be a lot at first, but has a simple explanation. Every (Web page) frame that is recorded when watching a (non-maximized) YouTube video contains 10 thumbnails of other recommended videos. In order to not skew the results heavily towards this large number of irrelevant images, we filtered them out if their height or width is below 100 pixels (full image resolution was 1280×800). The remaining samples will be further examined regarding their shown content.

3.2   Image Type Classification

This section briefly outlines how the images detected in the document layout analysis are examined regarding their content. We aim to predict the given **type** of an image. To the best of our knowledge, there is no comprehensive and task-specific taxonomy of image types that can be directly applied to the learning task of our study. Therefore, we focused on covering all topic-relevant categories to learn which type of images a learner saw when searching for the formation of thunderstorms. As a result, our set of image type classes consists of Infographics, Indoor Photo, Maps, Outdoor Photo, Technical Drawings, and Information Visualization. The class *Information Visualization* has a specific role. Images that are composites or hybrids of common visualization types are hard to assign to a unique class. For this reason, we merge all forms of *Information Visualizations* into one class and use it as a fallback class to gather all frames that are otherwise hard to assign.

The implementation was done in Keras, using a MobileNet [13] architecture with default parameters. We utilized a Google image crawler to gather 18 773 unique training samples which we split into 90% training and 10% test data. Three volunteers manually labeled the test data and achieved an intercoder agreement of $\alpha = 0.85$ (across all annotators, samples, and classes) according to Krippendorff's alpha [16]. Finally, the classifier achieved an accuracy of 87.15%

on this human-verified test set. The accuracy is sufficient for our task of knowl-edge gain prediction, as it is confirmed by the experimental results in Sect. 4.

The features do not represent the number of images seen per class, because a consequence of our frame-wise extraction is that the same image gets extracted multiple times. Instead we analyse the image in every frame again and report the fraction of the image types as a percentage. The idea is to weight the content according to the duration the images have been seen by the learner. The feature vector v_p representing the image types seen by participant p is defined as follows:

$$v_p = (\sum_{l=0}^{|L|} \sum_{n=0}^{N_l} p(Info. - Vis.), ..., \sum_{l=0}^{|L|} \sum_{n=0}^{N_l} p(Techn. Draw.)) \qquad (3)$$

Feature vector for the six image types seen per participant. $p(< class >)$ is the pseudo-probability given by the softmax layer. N_l is the number of images detected in frame l.

3.3 Text Features

In total, we used a set of 110 features to represent textual information[1], taking into account document complexity, HTML structure, and linguistic aspects.

Document Complexity Features. Based on the assumption that the docu-ment complexity is correlated with the user's knowledge state on a topic, we have extracted several features related to document complexity. Motivated by previous work [8] and our investigation of the data, we extracted the number of words (c_word), length of words (c_char), and length of sentences ($c\_sentence$) as features. Related work [11] suggests that the syntactic structure of a document, which can be represented by the ratio of the number of nouns, verbs, adjectives, or *other words* to the total number of words ($c\_\{noun, verb, adj, oth\}$) is likely to imply the complexity of its content.

There are several widely used metrics for assessing the readability or com-plexity of a textual document, which have been studied to be correlated with user's knowledge level [12]. We used Gunning Fog Grade[2](c_gi), SMOG [18] (c_smog) and Flesch-Kincaid Grade [15] (c_fk) as features.

HTML Structural Features. A possible explanation of the finding, that there is a negative association between the number of hyperlinks embedded in a Web page and users' KG [7], is that people may not focus on the content in the presence of too many embedded links. Hence, we extract the feature h_link by quantifying the number of outbound links (i.e., the $< a >$ elements in our case). Furthermore, we extract features that might indicate the readability of a Web page based on HTML tags, namely, the average length of each paragraph (h_p), the $< ul >$ elements embedded (h_oth_ul), and the number of scripts (h_script).

---

[1] Full feature list at: Dropbox-Link.

[2] http://gunning-fog-index.com/.

Linguistic Features. Related work [12] suggests that the number of words on Web pages that are correlated with different psychological processes and basic sentiment can influence a learner's cognitive state. The writing style could also affect the readability of a learning resource and the engagement of readers. Motivated by the above observations, we used the 2015 Linguistic Inquiry and Word Count (LIWC) dictionaries[3] to compute linguistic features that reflect the psychological processes, sentiment, and the writing style of Web page content. The features of this type are prefixed with l_- in the remainder of the paper.

4 Experimental Results for Knowledge Gain Predcition

In this section, we report experimental results for the task of knowledge gain prediction utilizing the features from Sect. 3. Our experimental dataset consists of 113 search sessions. On average, users have issued 11.1 queries and browsed 25.4 Web pages in each session. There was a significant increase in learners' knowledge on average (KG = 2.15 ± 1.84 for a full score of 10) after the search phase. The effect size for knowledge gain was large (Cohen's d = 1.29). The average pre-knowledge score was 5.22 ± 1.76 and post-knowledge was 7.37 ± 1.6.

4.1 Experimental Setup

The goal of our study is to predict knowledge gain in informal search sessions and to investigate the impact of text and multimedia resource features. We model KG prediction as a classification task and use random forest as a supervised learning approach. We aim for a fair comparison with the state of the art in users' knowledge gain prediction in Web search. Thus, we follow the same experimental setup as used by Yu et al. [26], in particular for the assignment of labels, the applied classifier, and its parameter tuning, unless other settings are denoted.

Ground Truth Data: We group a search session into one of three KG classes according to the measured knowledge gain X based on the *Standard Deviation (σ) Classification* approach. The classes are defined as follows: 1.) *Low* KG, if $X < \overline{X} - \frac{\sigma}{2}$; 2.) *Moderate* KG, if $\overline{X} - \frac{\sigma}{2} < X < \overline{X} + \frac{\sigma}{2}$; and 3.) *High* KG, if $X > \overline{X} + \frac{\sigma}{2}$. According to this approach, our dataset consists of 44 low, 42 moderate, and 27 high knowledge gain sessions.

Classifier: Random forest has shown to be the most effective classifier for knowledge gain prediction [26] and it allows for the analysis of feature importance. Hence, we adopt a random forest classifier and tune the hyperparameters for accuracy using grid search. For our experiments, we used the *scikit-learn* library for Python (https://scikit-learn.org/).

Metrics: After tuning the hyper-parameters of each classifier, we run 10 repetitions of 10-fold cross-validation (90% train, 10% test) and evaluate the classification results of each classifier according to the following metrics:

---

[3] http://liwc.wpengine.com/compare-dictionaries/.

- **Accuracy (*Accu*) across all classes:** percentage of search sessions that were classified with the correct class label.
- **Precision (*P*), Recall (*R*), F1 (*F*1) score of class *i*:** the standard precision, recall and F1 score on the prediction result of each class *i*.
- **Macro average of precision (*P*), recall (*R*), and F1 (*F*1):** the average of the corresponding scores across three classes.

Classification Results. The performance of the random forest classifier using textual features (TI), multimedia features (MI), as well as their combination is shown in Table 1. We also present the performance of the random forest classifier using behavioral features (the approach used by [26]) on our ground truth dataset in Table 1 for reference. We extract a subset of the user behavior features for all categories as described in the original paper, namely, session (e.g., session duration), query (e.g., number of queries), search engine result page (SERP, e.g., time spend on SERP), browsing (e.g., ratio of revisited pages), and partially, mouse (e.g., total scroll distance in session). The features regarding click behavior on the search results pages were not recorded. We adapt this approach as baseline as it is the state-of-the-art approach for the same task, and it is possible to compute the features used by their model based on our dataset. The results for all four test feature types are in a comparable range. When using only textual features (TI) or multimedia features (MI), results are slightly worse than the state-of-the-art approach [26], which uses behavioral features. Our approach utilizing features from both categories (MI&TI) has achieved the best performance concerning overall accuracy, indicating that the combination of textual and multimedia features has the potential to improve knowledge gain prediction. Comparing the performance for the different classes, the classifier performs better on low and moderate knowledge gain classes when using features from both categories. A potential reason for this result is that the high knowledge gain class has the least amount of training data in our ground truth dataset.

Please note that we have achieved comparable performance to the state of the art [26] with less training data (113 sessions versus 468 sessions) and more unbalanced classes. As shown in Table 1 the combination of multimedia and textual information (MI&TI) is able to outperform using behavior features at 85% confidence level in terms of accuracy. Since we focus on understanding the influence of textual and multimedia resource content on users' knowledge gain during the search, the classification model and the analysis of user behavior features are out of the scope of this work. We list the results of the classifier trained on user behavior features as evidence that our classification has reached satisfying performance.

Table 1. Results of knowledge gain prediction (in %) using text (TI) and multimedia features (MI), and comparing them with the state of the art [26].

Features	Low			Moderate			High			Macro average			All
	P	R	F1	P	R	F1	P	R	F1	P	R	F1	Accu
MI& TI	**41.5**	**52.0**	**46.1**	**39.1**	**40.0**	**39.5**	28.4	14.8	19.1	36.4	35.6	34.9	**38.7**
TI	39.9	**52.0**	45.0	36.6	33.8	35.0	28.9	17.4	21.5	35.1	34.4	33.8	37.0
MI	38.0	38.0	37.9	38.0	38.1	38.0	30.8	**31.1**	**30.8**	35.6	35.7	35.6	36.4
[26]	39.7	47.0	43.0	37.4	39.5	38.4	**34.9**	21.1	26.0	**37.3**	**35.9**	**35.8**	38.1

Feature Importance. To analyze the usefulness of individual features, we make use of the *Mean Decrease in Impurity (MDI)* metric based on the random forest model. The metric MDI is defined as the total decrease in node impurity (weighted by the probability of reaching that node) averaged over all trees of the ensemble [3]. Due to the space limitation, we only list and discuss the 20 features (Table 2) having the highest and lowest MDI values in the paper.

We observe that six out of 10 features with the highest importance are textual features. This is to be expected because, first, there are more textual features (110) than multimedia features (13), and, second, with recent advances in natural language processing techniques, we were able to design more sophisticated textual features such as the complexity of language and sentiment behind words. In contrast, it is still more challenging to analyze the semantics of multimedia data. Nevertheless, results indicate that the 13 multimedia features have shown promising importance for the classification, with *Heading, $\overline{imgsize}$, Menu Bar, Infographic, Technical Drawing* and *Outdoor* rank at 4, 5, 8, 9, 13, 15, respectively, among the 123 features in total. None of the multimedia features falls into the 10 least important features according to MDI. Among the six textual features with the highest importance, five are linguistic-based, while the remaining one is related to document complexity (SMOG Readability).

Table 2. Features with highest and lowest MDI importance scores.

Rank	Highest		Lowest	
	Feature	MDI	Feature	MDI
1	l_home	0.039	l_affect	0.004
2	l_relig	0.030	l_Tone	0.004
3	l_certain	0.018	l_power	0.004
4	Heading	0.018	l_AllPunc	0.003
5	*imgsize*	0.016	h_vid	0.003
6	c_smog	0.015	l_filler	0.003
7	l_focuspresent	0.015	l_sad	0.003
8	Menubar	0.015	h_aud	0.003
9	Infographic	0.014	l_Authentic	0.002
10	l_netspeak	0.014	h_obj	0.001

5   Conclusions

In this paper, we have investigated whether features describing multimedia resource content can help predict users' knowledge gain in a SAL task. Our results are based on a large lab study with $N = 113$ participants, where we recorded the individuals' behavior and the accessed Web resources. We extracted the textual and multimedia features to classify the knowledge gain of the participants. Finally, we provided a comprehensive analysis of feature importance.

It was shown that the combination of our feature categories can serve for knowledge gain prediction based on viewed resource content, which potentially can help improve a learning-oriented search result ranking (if content features are used accordingly). Although the classification accuracy is on a moderate level in terms of recall and precision, they suggest that knowledge gain is predictable. Particularly image and video features improved the classification notably when used jointly with text-based features.

To the best of our knowledge, that was the first study that analyzed the importance of multimedia features in a SAL scenario. Although the number of participants in our study is already higher than in the majority of previous studies in controlled lab settings, our current dataset is limited by the fact that only one learning task has been studied. In the future, we aim to conduct additional studies on diverse learning topics, to receive further insights into the relationship between features of learning resources used and knowledge gain.

References

1. Abdulla, W.: Mask R-CNN for object detection and instance segmentation on Keras and TensorFlow (2017). https://github.com/matterport/Mask_RCNN
2. Anderson, L.W., et al.: A taxonomy for learning, teaching and assessing: a revision of bloom's taxonomy. Educ. Horizons **9**(2), 137–175 (2001)
3. Breiman, L., Friedman, J.H., Olshen, R.A., Stone, C.J.: Classification and Regression Trees. Wadsworth (1984)
4. Broder, A.Z.: A taxonomy of web search. SIGIR Forum **36**(2), 3–10 (2002)
5. Collins-Thompson, K., Hansen, P., Hauff, C.: Search as learning (Dagstuhl seminar 17092). Dagstuhl Reports, vol. 7, no. 2, pp. 135–162 (2017)
6. Collins-Thompson, K., Rieh, S.Y., Haynes, C.C., Syed, R.: Assessing learning outcomes in web search: a comparison of tasks and query strategies. In: Proceedings of the 2016 ACM on Conference on Human Information Interaction and Retrieval, pp. 163–172. ACM (2016)
7. DeStefano, D., LeFevre, J.: Cognitive load in hypertext reading: a review. Comput. Hum. Behav. **23**(3), 1616–1641 (2007)
8. Eickhoff, C., Teevan, J., White, R., Dumais, S.T.: Lessons from the journey: a query log analysis of within-session learning. In: Carterette, B., Diaz, F., Castillo, C., Metzler, D. (eds.) Seventh ACM International Conference on Web Search and Data Mining, WSDM 2014, New York, NY, USA, 24–28 February 2014, pp. 223–232. ACM (2014)

9. Gadiraju, U., Yu, R., Dietze, S., Holtz, P.: Analyzing knowledge gain of users in informational search sessions on the web. In: Shah, C., Belkin, N.J., Byström, K., Huang, J., Scholer, F. (eds.) Proceedings of the 2018 Conference on Human Information Interaction and Retrieval, CHIIR 2018, New Brunswick, NJ, USA, 11–15 March 2018, pp. 2–11. ACM (2018)

10. van Genuchten, E., Scheiter, K., Schüler, A.: Examining learning from text and pictures for different task types: does the multimedia effect differ for conceptual, causal, and procedural tasks? Comput. Hum. Behav. **28**(6), 2209–2218 (2012)

11. Heilman, M., Collins-Thompson, K., Callan, J., Eskénazi, M.: Combining lexical and grammatical features to improve readability measures for first and second language texts. In: Sidner, C.L., Schultz, T., Stone, M., Zhai, C. (eds.) Human Language Technology Conference of the North American Chapter of the Association of Computational Linguistics, Proceedings, 22–27 April 2007, Rochester, New York, USA, pp. 460–467. The Association for Computational Linguistics (2007)

12. Horne, B.D., Adali, S.: This just. In: Fake News Packs a Lot in Title, Uses Simpler, Repetitive Content in Text Body, More Similar to Satire than Real News (2017)

13. Howard, A.G., et al.: Mobilenets: efficient convolutional neural networks for mobile vision applications. CoRR abs/1704.04861 (2017). http://arxiv.org/abs/1704.04861

14. von Hoyer, J., Pardi, G., Kammerer, Y., Holtz, P.: Metacognitive judgments in searching as learning (SAL) tasks: insights on (mis-) calibration, multimedia usage, and confidence. In: Proceedings of the 1st International Workshop on Search as Learning with Multimedia Information, SALMM 2019, pp. 3–10. Association for Computing Machinery, New York (2019). https://doi.org/10.1145/3347451.3356730

15. Kincaid, J.P., Fishburne Jr., R.P., Rogers, R.L., Chissom, B.S.: Derivation of new readability formulas (automated readability index, fog count and flesch reading ease formula) for navy enlisted personnel (1975)

16. Krippendorff, K.: Estimating the Reliability, Systematic Error and Random Error of Interval Data, vol. 30, no. 1. Longman, New York (1970)

17. Mayer, R.E., Moreno, R.: A split-attention effect in multimedia learning: evidence for dual processing systems in working memory. J. Educ. Psychol. **90**(2), 312 (1998)

18. Mc Laughlin, G.H.: Smog grading-a new readability formula. J. Read. **12**(8), 639–646 (1969)

19. Moraes, F., Putra, S.R., Hauff, C.: Contrasting search as a learning activity with instructor-designed learning. In: Cuzzocrea, A., et al. (eds.) Proceedings of the 27th ACM International Conference on Information and Knowledge Management, CIKM 2018, Torino, Italy, 22–26 October 2018, pp. 167–176. ACM (2018). https://doi.org/10.1145/3269206.3271676

20. Pardi, G., von Hoyer, J., Holtz, P., Kammerer, Y.: The role of cognitive abilities and time spent on texts and videos in a multimodal searching as learning task. In: O'Brien, H.L., Freund, L., Arapakis, I., Hoeber, O., Lopatovska, I. (eds.) CHIIR 2020: Conference on Human Information Interaction and Retrieval, Vancouver, BC, Canada, 14–18 March 2020, pp. 378–382. ACM (2020). https://doi.org/10.1145/3343413.3378001

21. Rieh, S.Y., Collins-Thompson, K., Hansen, P., Lee, H.: Towards searching as a learning process: a review of current perspectives and future directions. J. Inf. Sci. **42**(1), 19–34 (2016)

22. Schmidt-Weigand, F., Scheiter, K.: The role of spatial descriptions in learning from multimedia. Comput. Hum. Behav. **27**(1), 22–28 (2011)

23. Shi, J., Otto, C., Hoppe, A., Holtz, P., Ewerth, R.: Investigating correlations of automatically extracted multimodal features and lecture video quality. In: Proceedings of the 1st International Workshop on Search as Learning with Multimedia Information, SALMM 2019, pp. 11–19. Association for Computing Machinery, New York (2019). https://doi.org/10.1145/3347451.3356731

24. Syed, R., Collins-Thompson, K.: Exploring document retrieval features associated with improved short- and long-term vocabulary learning outcomes. In: Shah, C., Belkin, N.J., Byström, K., Huang, J., Scholer, F. (eds.) Proceedings of the 2018 Conference on Human Information Interaction and Retrieval, CHIIR 2018, New Brunswick, NJ, USA, 11–15 March 2018, pp. 191–200. ACM (2018)

25. Vakkari, P.: Searching as learning: a systematization based on literature. J. Inf. Sci. **42**(1), 7–18 (2016). https://doi.org/10.1177/0165551515615833

26. Yu, R., Gadiraju, U., Holtz, P., Rokicki, M., Kemkes, P., Dietze, S.: Predicting user knowledge gain in informational search sessions. In: Collins-Thompson, K., Mei, Q., Davison, B.D., Liu, Y., Yilmaz, E. (eds.) The 41st International ACM SIGIR Conference on Research & Development in Information Retrieval, SIGIR 2018, Ann Arbor, MI, USA, 08–12 July 2018, pp. 75–84. ACM (2018)

Deep Performance Factors Analysis for Knowledge Tracing

Shi Pu[1]([✉])[ID], Geoffrey Converse[2][ID], and Yuchi Huang[3]

[1] ETS Canada Inc., 240 Richmond St W, Toronto, ON M5V1V6, Canada
spu@etscanada.ca
[2] The University of Iowa, Iowa City, IA 52242, USA
[3] ACT, Inc., 500 ACT Drive, Iowa City, IA 52245, USA
yuchi.huang@act.org

Abstract. Knowledge tracing is the task of dynamically tracking a student's mastery of skills based on their assessment performances and learning-related information (e.g., time spent answering a particular question). Traditional approaches (e.g., Bayesian knowledge tracing [BKT] and performance factors analysis [PFA]), are easy to interpret. Modern approaches (e.g., deep knowledge tracing [DKT] and dynamic key-value memory networks [DKVMN]) usually produce superior performance on certain datasets, but their model complexity causes difficulty in scaling and linking them to existing educational measurement studies. In this paper, we present a simple but effective model, deep performance factors analysis (DPFA) (Source code is available at https://github.com/scott-pu-pennstate/dpfa), to resolve this problem. DPFA consistently outperforms PFA and DKT and has results comparable to those of DKVMN when tested on widely used public datasets. In addition, DPFA's light weight in parameters makes it easy to scale. Finally, we demonstrate a straightforward approach to enhance the base DPFA by incorporating features from the educational measurement literature. The enhanced DPFA showed superior performance than DKVMN.

Keywords: Deep knowledge tracing · Knowledge tracing · Performance factors analysis

1 Introduction

Knowledge tracing plays a central role in many personalized education strategies, particularly in an online learning environment. The task is to dynamically assess a target student's mastery of skills so that downstream algorithms can optimize learning materials for that student. For example, after a student answers the item "1 + 2 = 3", a knowledge-tracing model is used to assess how likely it is that the student has mastered the "addition skill." This probability is then used by a downstream algorithm to determine whether the student should move

---

S. Pu—The work is done before this author joined ETS Canada, Inc.

© Springer Nature Switzerland AG 2021
I. Roll et al. (Eds.): AIED 2021, LNAI 12748, pp. 331–341, 2021.
https://doi.org/10.1007/978-3-030-78292-4_27

on to the next math skill or review the addition skill. In this paper, we use the term "item" to refer to a question or exercise that a student completes via a learning platform, and "item response" or "item correctness" to indicate whether an item is correctly or incorrectly answered. We use the term "skill" to refer to the concept or knowledge component associated with an item.

A knowledge-tracing model is learned from a student's past item responses, and its performance is evaluated based on how well it can predict a student's future responses. Two well-established models of knowledge tracing are Bayesian knowledge tracing (BKT) [3] and performance factors analysis (PFA) [11]. BKT models a student's mastery of a particular skill as a hidden dichotomous variable that is either learned or unlearned. The model assumes a student will correctly answer the next question if they have either mastered the corresponding skill and applied it successfully, or if the student makes a lucky guess. PFA models a student's probability of correctly answering a future item as a logistic regression based on the student's frequency of success and failure on previous items that required the same skill.

Both BKT and PFA assume a student's performance on an item is affected by the student's mastery of the corresponding skill. This assumption hinders each model from utilizing the student's item responses that are associated with other skills. However, in reality, a student's mastery of Skill A may be correlated to their mastery of Skill B. Figure 1 visualizes the correlation between different skill masteries in a real-world dataset. As shown in the graph, if a student correctly answers an item associated with the "area" skill, then they are also likely to correctly answer an item associated with the "equation-solving" skill.

Moreover, BKT and PFA use the frequency of success or failure on past skills to predict the probability of a student's correctly answering the next question. However, using skills as input units prohibits the models from utilizing item-specific information. For example, when items have different levels of difficulty, success on a difficult item may be a stronger indicator of future success than success on an easy item.

Building on modern developments in deep learning, recent work on knowledge tracing tackle this task as a sequence-to-sequence problem. Piech et al. [12] used a recurrent neural network (RNN) to predict the probability of a student's answering the next question correctly. The model, referred as deep knowledge tracing (DKT), demonstrated some advantage over more traditional (e.g., BKT, PFA) methods, even after controlling data processing errors [19]. Zhang et al. [20] used a modified memory augmented neural network (MANN) [5] for knowledge tracing. Their model, dynamic key-value memory networks (DKVMN), moves away from RNNs entirely and instead opts for external memory to capture long-term dependencies. This yields a increase in accuracy across both real and simulated datasets.

A group of recent models explored novel ways of incorporating attention into knowledge tracing. Some early works used attention as a mechanism to find the past items that are most relevant to the next question [6,15]. Their intuition was that performance on similar items holds more predictive power for future items

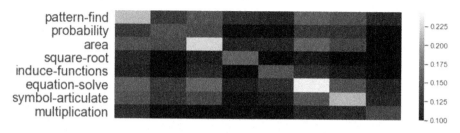

Fig. 1. Heat map visualizing the average likelihood that a student will answer an item related to Skill B correctly or incorrectly when the student answers an item related to Skill A correctly or incorrectly. Data are from the ASSISTments math tutoring system. Only the 10 most common skills were used.

than performance on dissimilar items. Others assumed an item's embedding is affected by its context (other items answered by the student) and experimented with the self-attention approach [10]. More recent studies have combined next item to past item attention and past item self-attentions [2, 4, 13]. These studies typically have reported improved model performance compared to DKT and DKVMN.

Compared to traditional methods, deep learning models for knowledge tracing take an end-to-end approach and rely on the flexibility of neural networks to extract meaningful features from inputs. This allows the models to use all past skill and item information to predict the correctness of a future item response. As a result, deep learning models for knowledge tracing often have better performance than traditional models.

However, deep learning models for knowledge tracing shed little light on which features are extracted from the inputs and how these features contribute to the models' performances. This creates obstacles for researchers who seek to understand and improve these models. To this end, we introduce deep performance factors analysis (DPFA), which combines the simple, interpretable nature of PFA with the strength of learning complex representations from deep learning models. DPFA can be summarized as a logistic regression based on the affinity of previous items and future items. This design allows DPFA to draw evidence directly from interdependence on item performance. Our experiments show that when tested on widely used public datasets, this simple architecture performs better than either PFA or DKT and is comparable to DKVMN. Furthermore, we demonstrate that DPFA can be straightforwardly enhanced by incorporating features from the existing literature. Lastly, DPFA has considerable fewer parameters than DKVMN, making it easier to train and deploy.

2   Model Description

We formally describe the knowledge-tracing problem. Given a sequence of student item responses $x_t = (q_t, c_t)$, $1 \leq t \leq T$, where q_t represents an item answered at step t and $c_t \in \{0, 1\}$ represents an incorrect or correct response,

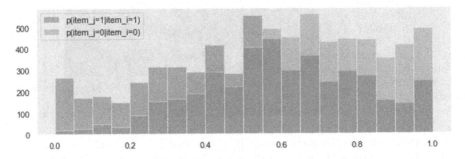

Fig. 2. Probability of correctly or incorrectly answering an item given a previous same-skill item response. Data are from ASSISTments 2017 and limited to a sample of the most common item pairs.

we aim to infer c_{t+1} from the previous interactions. In other words, we wish to approximate $P(c_{t+1} = 1 | q_1, c_1, ..., q_t, c_t, q_{t+1})$.

2.1   Performance Factors Analysis

In the simplest case where each item is associated with a single skill, PFA models a student's probability of correctly answering a question as

$$p_{t+1} = \sigma(\beta_k + \gamma_k s_k + \rho_k f_k) \tag{1}$$

where σ is the sigmoid function and k is the skill associated with the next item q_{t+1}. β_k is a skill bias, s_k records the number of previous successes with respect to skill k, and f_k records the number of previous failures with respect to skill k. More specifically,

$$s_k = \sum_{i<=t} \mathbf{I}(c_i = 1)\mathbf{I}(q_i \in k) \quad and \quad f_k = \sum_{i<=t} \mathbf{I}(c_i = 0)\mathbf{I}(q_i \in k) \tag{2}$$

where $\mathbf{I}(x)$ is the indicator function that equals 1 when x is true and equals 0 otherwise. PFA is a logistic regression in which the evidence supporting or against $p_{t+1} = 1$ is drawn from previous successes or failures associated with q_{t+1}'s corresponding skill.

PFA has three obvious shortcomings. First, it only draws evidence from same-skill items. As shown in Fig. 1, a student's success or failure in one skill is often correlated with their success or failure in other skills. This is likely to be the case if the skills have shared subcomponents or if they are siblings in a hierarchical skill tree. Second, PFA treats an item correctness as the corresponding skill correctness. However, as shown in Fig. 2, the influence between items varies dramatically within a skill. Given that items usually have different levels of difficulty, success on a difficult item should provide more evidence of skill mastery than success on an easy item. Third, PFA considers recent and less recent item responses equally. Because individuals learn and forget, recent item responses should be assigned more weight than less recent item responses. Using DPFA, we are able to overcome the first two shortcomings by drawing direct evidence of success and failure on all previous items. To solve the last problem, we give higher weight to recent evidence than we do to older evidence.

2.2   Deep Performance Factors Analysis

DPFA assumes each item has its own specific skill components; thereby, each item should have its own representation. For example, though both "13 + 29" and "13 + 26" may be tagged as addition problems in a learning system, the former item requires a student to understand the skill of carrying while the latter does not. Models [12] that use labeled skills to represent items lack this nuance. DPFA uses a h dimensional embedding vector e_i to represent an item q_i. The embedding vectors e_i are trainable.

When predicting whether a student can correctly answer the next item, DPFA draws evidence from the student's past item interactions and gives more weight to items that are similar to the next item and are more recent. The similarity between two items is modeled by the attention function:

$$A_{i,t+1} = e_i^\top e_{t+1} \tag{3}$$

e_i is the aforementioned h-dimensional embedding of item q_i. The similarity between the two items could be interpreted as the overlap of their underlying skills. Previous studies [2,10,13] have used asymmetric attentions to model the similarity between item interactions. For example, a popular choice is to set attention logits equal to $\frac{(Ke_i)^T Qe_j}{\sqrt{h}}$ where K and Q are two $h \times h$ matrices. The asymmetric attentions allow the similarity between the two items to depend on their answering order. We find this property counterintuitive for knowledge tracing: since the similarity between items represents the overlap of their underlying skills, the answering order should not affect the similarity. Furthermore, the extra parameters make a larger sample size necessary. As a result, we choose to use the dot product attention that ignores the answering order of items.

We use positional distance to model the recency of a past item:

$$d_{i,t+1} = -a(t - i + 1) + b \tag{4}$$

$t - i + 1$ is the positional difference between item response x_i and the next item response x_{t+1}, and a and b are trainable parameters.

The relevance, or weight, of a past item is jointly determined by its similarity to the next item and its recency:

$$w_i = softmax(A_{i,t+1} + d_{i,t+1}) \tag{5}$$

DPFA models the mastery of skills demonstrated after a item interaction (q_i, c_i) with a two-dimensional vector:

$$v_i = \begin{cases} v_i^0 \in R, & \text{if} \quad c_i = 0 \\ v_i^1 \in R, & \text{if} \quad c_i = 1, \end{cases} \tag{6}$$

v_i^0 could be interpreted as the expected mastery of skill for item i if it is answered incorrectly, and v_i^1 could be interpreted as the expected mastery of skill for item i if it is answered correctly.

Now we present the entire DPFA model:

$$p_{t+1} = \sigma\left(\beta_{t+1} + \sum_{c_i=0} w_i v_i^0 + \sum_{c_i=1} w_i v_i^1\right) \quad \forall i \leq t \tag{7}$$

In this model, σ is the sigmoid function and $\beta_{t+1} \in R$ is item-level bias. Similar to PFA, DPFA can be understood as a logistic regression in which the logit is the next item's difficulty plus all the evidence of mastery of skills gathered from past item responses. Since DPFA draws direct evidence from past items, it does not need the item-skill association to be provided in the data as PFA does. $\sum w_i v_i^1$ in DPFA replaces $\gamma_k s_k$ in PFA to provide evidence supporting p_{t+1}. $\sum w_i v_i^0$ in DPFA replaces $\rho_k f_k$ to provide evidence against p_{t+1}.

To train the model, we use the binary cross-entropy loss function:

$$\mathcal{L} = -\sum_{t=0}^{T-1} c_{t+1} \log(p_{t+1}) + (1 - c_{t+1}) \log(1 - p_{t+1}) \tag{8}$$

3   Experiments

We first compare DPFA with common benchmark models in knowledge tracing by testing the various models on four widely used public datasets. For each dataset, we evaluate a model with student-stratified five-fold cross validation and use the average test area under the curve (AUC) as the evaluation metric. We utilize 10% of the training data as the validation data for tuning hyper-parameters. Then we compare the comeplexity of different models and show a general approach for enhancing DPFA.

3.1   Data

All datasets used in this study are publicly available. Table 1 records the descriptive statistics for each dataset. In each case, we only keep a student's first attempt at an item.

Synthetic-5[1]. This simulated dataset was created by Piech et al. [12]. There are 4,000 synthetic students that answer the same 50 exercises in the same order.

NeurIPS 2020 Education Challenge[2]. This real-world dataset is comprised of K-12 students' answers to math questions using an online learning platform. Items in this dataset have a hierarchical skill structure so we use the leaf (most specific) skill for models that take skills as inputs. If an item is associated with multiple leaf skills, we treat the combination as a new skill.

---

[1] https://github.com/chrispiech/DeepKnowledgeTracing/tree/master/data/synthetic.
[2] https://competitions.codalab.org/competitions/25449#.

Table 1. Data statistics and average test AUC on all datasets.

Datasets	Statistics				Average Test AUC				
	Attempts	Stu	Items	Skills	BKT	PFA	DKT	DKVMN	DPFA
Syn-5	20k	4,000	50	5	N/A	N/A	0.8239	0.8267	**0.8348**
NeurIPS	15.8M	119K	27K	1078	0.6890	0.7249	0.7771	**0.7973**	0.7965
ASSIST	392.8K	1,709	4,117	102	0.7091	0.6624	0.7317	0.7958	**0.7964**
STAT	135.3K	316	987	279	0.7298	0.7435	0.7928	0.8046	**0.8061**

Table 2. Number of model parameters for different hidden sizes. For DKVMN, we set the memory key and value size to 10 and set the summary vector size to 50.

Models	Synthetic-5			NeurIPS 2020			Assist 2017			Stat F2011		
	h:16	32	64	h:16	32	64	h: 16	32	64	h: 16	32	64
DKT	8.3K	19K	45K	**0.2M**	**0.3M**	**0.6M**	**16K**	**34K**	**75K**	0.1M	0.3M	0.6M
DKVMN	5K	11K	26K	1.3M	2.6M	5.3M	0.2M	0.4M	0.8M	50K	101K	0.2M
DPFA	**1K**	**1.8K**	**3.4K**	0.5M	1.0M	1.8M	78K	0.1M	0.3M	**19K**	**35K**	**66K**

ASSISTments 2017[3]. This real-world dataset tracks middle and high school students' answers to math problems on the ASSISTments tutoring system. It is available through the 2017 ASSISTments Datamining Competition.

STATICS 2011[4]. This real-world dataset is from a college engineering course offered during fall 2011. The data include student attempts in tutor mode and assessment mode. All of a student's timestamps in the assessment mode are identical so we cannot properly order the attempts. We thus follow [16] to exclude the assessment mode from our experiments, which results in the elimination of 29.08% of student attempts. We follow [20]'s processing step to concatenate a problem name and a problem step as an item and use a problem name as a skill.

3.2 Settings

The input sequences in all datasets except Synthetic-5 have different lengths. We set the maximum length of the response sequence to be 200. Student response sequences shorter than 200 are padded with 0 to the left, and sequences longer than 200 are folded. We keep the original sequence length of 50 in Synthetic-5.

We implement DPFA in Tensorflow [1] and train the models with the Adam optimizer [7]. The initial learning rate is set to 0.001. We set the batch size to 256, and the model is trained for 100 epochs. During cross-validation, we use 10% of the training data to tune the learning decay rate, drop-out rate, and hidden size $h \in \{16, 32, 64\}$. For DKT (the long short-term memory version) and DKVMN, we use the optimal hyper-parameters reported in the literature when available. Otherwise, we tune the hyper-parameters as described above.

---

[3] https://sites.google.com/view/assistmentsdatamining.
[4] https://pslcdatashop.web.cmu.edu/DatasetInfo?datasetId=507.

Table 3. Enhancing DPFA by adding the item response time. The results for Syn-5 and NeurIPS2020 are not available due to a lack of item response time.

	Synthetic-5	NeurIPS 2020	Assist 2017	Stat 2011
DPFA Base	0.8348	0.7965	0.7964	0.8061
DPFA + Item Response Duration	N/A	N/A	**0.7991**	**0.8095**

4   Results

Model Performance. Table 1 compares the performance of DPFA with the performances of the traditional and deep learning methods. Since both BKT and PFA require skills as inputs, they are not relevant to the Synthetic-5 dataset. In all situations, DPFA outperforms traditional knowledge-tracing models; namely, BKT and PFA. DPFA also significantly outperforms DKT on the ASSISTments 2017 datasets. The gaps, however, are narrower for the other dataset comparisons. In all datasets, DPFA and DKVMN yield comparable performances.

Note that the performance of DKVMN on STAT 2011 is worse than the reported 0.828 in the original paper [20]. We believe this is due to data processing difference: we only include the "tutor" mode while the original paper include both "tutor" and "assessment" mode.

Model Complexity. Table 2 compares the complexity of DKT, DKVMN, and DPFA under different hidden size configurations. In all configurations and datasets, DPFA is significantly smaller than DKVMN. The size advantage of DPFA increases with the hidden size: when $h = 16$, the size of DPFA is around 20%–38% of DKVMN, and when $h = 64$, the size of DPFA decreases to 13%–33% of DKVMN. Since we have shown that DPFA and DKVMN have comparable performances across multiple datasets, we can conclude that DPFA is preferable to DKVMN. DPFA's size advantage makes DPFA less demanding in terms of memory and thus faster to train and less expensive to deploy than DKVMN.

DPFA is smaller than DKT in the Synthetic-5 and Stat F2011 datasets, but it is considerably larger than DKT in the NeurIPS 2020 and ASSISTments 2017 datasets. However, this increased complexity helps DPFA to perform better than DKT on these two datasets: when it comes to the NeurIPS 2020 and the ASSISTments 2017 datasets, respectively, DPFA has 2.49% and 8.84% higher AUCs than DKT. It is thus necessary to consider the use case before deciding which one is more suitable.

Enhancing DPFA. The simplicity of the DPFA model makes it easy to enhance by utilizing past findings in the educational measurement literature. For example, previous studies [17,18] have shown that item response time are correlated with student mastery of skills. DPFA can easily incorporate these past findings by extending the value function in Equation 6 to

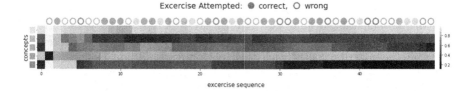

Fig. 3. A student's knowledge state in Synthetic-5 dataset. Each skill (concept) is marked with its own color on the left. After 50 questions, the student has shown mastery of Skills 1 and 4 but has failed to master Skills 2, 3, and 5.

Fig. 4. Clustering of items in Synthetic-5 dataset using t-SNE. Each node represents an item, and each color represents a ground-true skill. Items associated with the same skill are perfectly clustered together.

$$
v_i = \begin{cases} f_0(v_i^0, t_i), & \text{if } c_i = 0 \\ f_1(v_i^1, t_i) & \text{if } c_i = 1, \end{cases} \tag{9}
$$

where $v_i \in R$ is interpreted as the expected mastery of a skill for an item response (q_i, c_i, t_i) and $[v_i^0, v_i^1]$ is the two-dimensional value embedding for each item q_i, as shown in Eq. 6. $t_i \in R$ is the item response time. f_0 and f_1 are two 3-layer neural networks. More specifically,

$$
f_* = W_2(tanh(W_1[v_i^* \oplus t_i] + b_1)) + b_2 \tag{10}
$$

Table 3 shows that the extended DPFA has a slightly better performance than the base DPFA. More importantly, this approach allows us to readily incorporate more useful features into DPFA by replacing $[v_i^* \oplus t_i]$ with $[v_i^* \oplus features_i]$.

Tracking a Student's Knowledge State. We approximate a student's knowledge state according to their average probability of correctly answering all items associated with a given skill.

$$
S_{kt} = \frac{1}{n_k} \sum_{q_i \in k} p(c_t = 1 | q_1, c_1, ..., q_t) \tag{11}
$$

$S_{kt} \in [0, 1]$ represents a student's mastery of skill k at timestep t. n_k represents the number of items associated with skill k. Each probability $p(c_t = 1 | q_1, c_1, ..., q_t)$ is estimated with the DPFA model.

Figure 3 visualizes a student's knowledge state in the Synthetic-5 dataset using the aforementioned approach. After a student answers an item correctly (or incorrectly), the corresponding skill's mastery level increases (or decreases). Note that the contribution of each item response to a student's mastery of a particular skill is different and proportional to the item's difficulty. Therefore, sometimes we observe a sharp change in skill mastery level after an item response. At other times, the change is only mild.

Visualization of Item Embeddings. DPFA models the similarity between two items as the dot product of their embedding vectors. This design implies that items associated with the same skills are "close" to each other. We use t-SNE [9] to reduce the embedding vectors to a two-dimensional space. Figure 4 presents the learned item embedding from the Synthetic-5 dataset after dimension reduction. Since we know how the data are simulated, we use different colors to annotate the true skill labels associated with the various items. It is evident that items associated with the same skills are perfectly clustered together. This proves that DPFA is capable of learning the similarity between items.

5   Conclusion

In this paper, we presented a simple but effective model, DPFA, for knowledge tracing. Our model consistently outperformed traditional models and achieved results comparable with those of state-of-the-art deep learning models on public available datasets. Moreover, while DPFA performed on par with DKVMN on multiple datasets, it has only 13% to 33% of DKVMN's parameters. The advantage in size makes DPFA easier to train, experiment, and deploy than DKVMN.

We also demonstrated a general approach for enhancing DPFA: incorporating features that have been battle-tested in the psychometric literature through the *value* function. We showed that when item response time was added to DPFA using this approach, the enhanced model outperformed the base DPFA. Last but not least, we showed that DPFA is capable of learning a meaningful representation of a student's knowledge state and the similarities between items.

In future work, we plan to dive more deeply into the representation of items. A few studies have shown that text [14,15] and skill [8,16] informed item embedding works better than random item embedding learned from scratch for knowledge tracing. We are eager to see how this line of work can further enrich DPFA.

References

1. Abadi, M., et al.: TensorFlow: large-scale machine learning on heterogeneous systems (2015). https://www.tensorflow.org/, software available from tensorflow.org
2. Choi, Y., et al.: Towards an appropriate query, key, and value computation for knowledge tracing. arXiv preprint arXiv:2002.07033 (2020)
3. Corbett, A.T., Anderson, J.R.: Knowledge tracing: modeling the acquisition of procedural knowledge. In: User Model User-Adapted Interaction, vol. 4 (1995)

4. Ghosh, A., Heffernan, N., Lan, A.S.: Context-aware attentive knowledge tracing. In: Proceedings of the 26th ACM SIGKDD International Conference on Knowledge Discovery & Data Mining, pp. 2330–2339 (2020)

5. Graves, A., et al.: Hybrid computing using a neural network with dynamic external memory. Nature **538**(7626), 471–476 (2016)

6. Huang, Z., Yin, Y., Chen, E., Xiong, H., Su, Y., Hu, G., et al.: Ekt: exercise-aware knowledge tracing for student performance prediction. IEEE Trans. Knowl. Data Eng. **33**(1), 100–115 (2019)

7. Kingma, D.P., Ba, J.: Adam: a method for stochastic optimization. arXiv preprint arXiv:1412.6980 (2014)

8. Liu, Y., Yang, Y., Chen, X., Shen, J., Zhang, H., Yu, Y.: Improving knowledge tracing via pre-training question embeddings. arXiv preprint arXiv:2012.05031 (2020)

9. Maaten, L.V.d., Hinton, G.J.: Visualizing data using t-SNE. Mach. Learn. Res. **9**(Nov), 2579–2605 (2008)

10. Pandey, S., Karypis, G.: A self-attentive model for knowledge tracing. arXiv preprint arXiv:1907.06837 (2019)

11. Pavlik Jr., P.I., Cen, H., Koedinger, K.R.: Performance factors analysis-a new alternative to knowledge tracing. Online Submission (2009)

12. Piech, C., et al.: Deep knowledge tracing. In: Advances in Neural Information Processing Systems, pp. 505–513 (2015)

13. Pu, S., Yudelson, M., Ou, L., Huang, Y.: Deep knowledge tracing with transformers. In: Bittencourt, I.I., Cukurova, M., Muldner, K., Luckin, R., Millán, E. (eds.) AIED 2020. LNCS (LNAI), vol. 12164, pp. 252–256. Springer, Cham (2020). https://doi.org/10.1007/978-3-030-52240-7_46

14. Su, Y., et al.: Exercise-enhanced sequential modeling for student performance prediction. In: Proceedings of the AAAI Conference on Artificial Intelligence, vol. 32 (2018)

15. Tong, H., Zhou, Y., Wang, Z.: HGKT: introducing problem schema with hierarchical exercise graph for knowledge tracing. arXiv preprint arXiv:2006.16915 (2020)

16. Wang, T., Ma, F., Gao, J.: Deep hierarchical knowledge tracing. In: Proceedings of the 12th International Conference on Educational Data Mining (2019)

17. Wang, T., Hanson, B.A.: Development and calibration of an item response model that incorporates response time. Appl. Psychol. Meas. **29**(5), 323–339 (2005)

18. Wise, S.L., Kong, X.: Response time effort: a new measure of examinee motivation in computer-based tests. Appl. Meas. Educ. **18**(2), 163–183 (2005)

19. Xiong, X., Zhao, S., Van Inwegen, E.G., Beck, J.E.: Going deeper with deep knowledge tracing. International Educational Data Mining Society (2016)

20. Zhang, J., Shi, X., King, I., Yeung, D.Y.: Dynamic key-value memory networks for knowledge tracing. In: Proceedings of the 26th International Conference on World Wide Web, pp. 765–774 (2017)

Gaming and Confrustion Explain Learning Advantages for a Math Digital Learning Game

J. Elizabeth Richey[1]([⊠]) [iD], Jiayi Zhang[2], Rohini Das[2], Juan Miguel Andres-Bray[2], Richard Scruggs[2] [iD], Michael Mogessie[1] [iD], Ryan S. Baker[2] [iD], and Bruce M. McLaren[1] [iD]

[1] Carnegie Mellon University, Pittsburgh, PA 15213, USA
`jelizabethrichey@cmu.edu`
[2] University of Pennsylvania, Philadelphia, PA 19104, USA

Abstract. Digital learning games are thought to support learning by increasing enjoyment and promoting deeper engagement with the content, but few studies have empirically tested hypothesized pathways between digital learning games and learning outcomes. *Decimal Point*, a digital learning game that teaches decimal operations and concepts to middle school students, has been shown in previous studies to support better learning outcomes than a non-game, computer-based instructional system covering the same content. To investigate the underlying causes for *Decimal Point*'s learning benefits, we developed log-based detectors using labels from text replay coding of the data from an earlier study. We focused on gaming the system, a form of behavioral disengagement that is frequently associated with worse learning outcomes, and confrustion, an affective state that combines confusion and frustration that has shown mixed results related to learning outcomes. Results indicated that students in the non-game condition engaged in gaming the system at nearly twice the level of students in the game condition, and gaming the system fully mediated the relation between learning condition and learning outcomes. Students in the game condition demonstrated higher levels of confrustion during the self-explanation phase of the game, and while confrustion was not related to learning outcomes in the game condition, it was associated with better learning outcomes in the non-game condition. These results provide evidence that digital learning games may support learning by reducing behavioral disengagement, and that the effects of confusion and frustration may vary depending on digital learning context.

Keywords: Digital learning games · Affect detector · Ed. data mining

1 Introduction

1.1 Digital Learning Games and Learning Outcomes

Most American children play digital games. The Common Sense Census [18] found that 66% of U.S. tweens and 56% of teens report playing digital games on any given day, with an average time of two or more hours per day among those who play. Recognizing

© Springer Nature Switzerland AG 2021
I. Roll et al. (Eds.): AIED 2021, LNAI 12748, pp. 342–355, 2021.
https://doi.org/10.1007/978-3-030-78292-4_28

this enthusiasm for games, more than half of U.S. teachers ask their students to use digital learning games in class at least once a week [22, 25]. Although data are still emerging on how digital learning game use has changed during the COVID-19 pandemic, Internet search intensity for online learning resources doubled in the early months of the pandemic [4] and interactive learning environment usage has increased [10]. The increased reliance on digital learning tools is not likely to abate even when face-to-face instruction can consistently be resumed, and the importance of digital learning games in educational settings seems likely to continue to grow in the future.

A number of studies have found improved learning outcomes for digital learning games compared to non-game learning conditions [16, 58]. Several meta-analyses have also revealed motivational benefits of digital learning games, including benefits to self-efficacy and attitudinal outcomes compared to more traditional instruction [54, 59]. Prior research has shown learning and engagement benefits from digital learning games in a variety of academic domains, including mathematics [27, 47, 53], science [13, 14], and language learning [57, 62]. However, designing games that teach academic topics is still a challenging task that is not always successful, and the educational effectiveness of digital learning games varies depending on a number of circumstances [19, 33, 37, 60]. For instance, educational benefits are more likely to occur when games are specifically designed based on cognitive theories of learning [44].

In particular, there has been limited empirical evidence about what is effective for mathematics games, with a recent review finding only six methodologically sound experiments that compared learning mathematical material in a game versus more conventional media [37]. Of those six experiments, four produced positive results favoring game playing. In this paper, we focus on one of those games, *Decimal Point* [23, 38], which was designed in consultation with a mathematics education expert and based on theory and evidence about common student misconceptions regarding decimal mathematics [26, 31, 56]. Like many digital learning games, *Decimal Point* was designed to support students' learning after initial instruction on the relevant topics by providing engaging opportunities for additional practice. In a study involving more than 150 5th and 6th grade students, *Decimal Point* led to significantly more learning and was rated by students as significantly more engaging than a more conventional but still effective computer-based tutoring approach [38].

Experimental comparisons between digital learning games and conventional learning technology can establish digital learning games as effective (or not) at producing desired learning outcomes, but these methods do not get at the underlying *reasons* for the effects. Very few studies have tested specific cognitive or affective processes as potential mediators of learning from games compared to non-games. There is a general lack of understanding about how digital learning games support learning, and digital game designers often must work without empirical guidance for how to make learning games more effective. In some cases, this results in uninformed adoption of extrinsic rewards such as points, badges, and competition, which often do not foster productive learning processes [40, 41, 51]. Understanding how digital learning games support learning is essential for informing better digital learning game design. Additionally, teachers have limited class time available, and greater evidence of when and how students learn from digital learning games—and especially how they might learn *differently* from games compared to non-games—will help inform teachers' choices about which digital learning games to incorporate into their teaching and how to enhance their students' learning.

This suggests a need to take a more detailed look at the underlying cognitive and affective mechanisms that lead to learning with games. The field of learning analytics provides tools to help in identifying the cognitive and affective processes that educational technology supports [6, 24, 28, 52, 55]. In the current study, we use behavioral data and learning analytics to examine the cognitive and affective pathways through which digital learning games operate to support learning outcomes. Specifically, we reanalyze an existing dataset [38] to assess two potential paths—gaming the system and confrustion— that might explain differences in learning processes and outcomes.

1.2 Gaming the System and Confrustion

The last few decades have seen a surge in scholarship around student behaviors and emotions or affect while learning [6, 11, 42, 61]. Gaming the system—attempting to succeed in an interactive learning environment by exploiting properties of the system rather than by learning the material—has been a behavior of particular interest within computer-based game and tutoring contexts due to its negative relation with learning outcomes [5, 7, 17, 39]. Gaming the system has both an immediate and long-term impact on learning and academic performance. One study investigating the effects of gaming using log data from a middle-school Cognitive Tutor mathematics curriculum found that gaming the system was associated with immediate poorer learning *and* an aggregate negative impact on learning [7]. In addition, students who game the system in middle school mathematics are less likely to enroll in higher education [49] or to take a STEM job after college [3].

Several studies have also found evidence that differences in learner emotions or affect are associated with learning outcomes in both the short term [46] and long term [49]. Two affective states that have been of interest in affective computing research are confusion and frustration, which have both been found to be associated with student learning. Some studies have found strong positive correlations between confusion or frustration and learning [20, 35], while others have found strong negative correlations to learning [48, 50]. Whether confusion and frustration support or hinder learning may be related to whether the student has support or metacognitive skills to resolve their confusion and frustration [21, 36]. Learning context may also affect the relation between confusion or frustration and learning outcomes. Previous research that identified positive relations between confusion or frustration and learning was conducted in non-game digital learning environments [20, 35]. Fewer studies have examined the relation between affect and learning in the context of digital learning games, where confusion and frustration may be more disruptive to game play, but at least one recent study using *Decimal Point* found a negative relation [39]. Confusion and frustration are often difficult to distinguish when judging only based on students' interactions with educational technology. Due to this and to their similar relation with learning, a number of previous studies have investigated a combination of the two states instead, called "confrustion" [36, 39, 45].

2 Method

We obtained interaction and outcome data collected through *Decimal Point* in an experiment first reported in [38]. We developed log-based detectors using labels from text replay coding of the data [8, 34]. We briefly describe the methods of the previous study; for a more detailed description of both the game and study, see [23] and [38].

2.1 Participants

Students participated in the study as part of their normal math instruction at two middle schools in a northeastern major metropolitan area. A total of 213 students participated in the study, but 39 students (19 in the game condition and 20 in the non-game condition) were dropped from analyses for failing to complete the pretest, posttest, or delayed posttest. Of the remaining 174 students (97 female students, 76 male students, and 1 missing gender information), 81 students were assigned to play *Decimal Point*, while 93 students completed a non-game, computer-based instructional system covering the same content.

2.2 Materials and Procedure

Decimal Point is a single-player game with an amusement park metaphor targeting 5th and 6th grade students learning about decimal numbers. *Decimal Point* runs on the web, within a standard browser, and was developed using HTML/JavaScript and the Cognitive Tutor Authoring Tools, or CTAT [2]. The materials are deployed on the web-based learning management system TutorShop [1], which logs all student actions. *Decimal Point* is composed of a series of 24 "mini-games" within a larger amusement park map. Forty-eight decimal problems (two problems for each of the 24 mini-games) were implemented for the game.

  Decimal Point presents students with five types of mini-game problems: (1) ordering decimals; (2) number line placement; (3) decimal sequences; (4) sorting decimals into less-than and greater-than "buckets"; and (5) adding decimals (Fig. 1). After solving each problem, students are prompted to self-explain their answer by selecting from a multiple-choice list of possible explanations. For example, after an ordering problem, the student might see the following: "To order these decimals from smallest to largest, start by finding: a) the longest decimal; b) the decimal with the smallest tenths place value; c) the shortest decimal; or d) the decimal with the smallest hundredths place value." This employs a well-established learning science principle that can promote deeper learning [15, 32]. To develop the game problem types, the developers surveyed problems students currently encounter in popular math curricula and designed mini-games and tests to probe for decimal misconceptions [56].

  Decimal Point has six characters that serve as guides and cheerleaders for the player throughout the game. These game elements provide fantasy [9], as well as giving the player a narrative context for why they are performing various problem-solving activities. The interface and feedback design presents students with problem-solving activities embedded playfully in the mini-game context. Students are prompted by the characters to correct mistakes after an initial attempt.

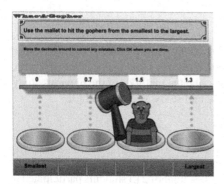
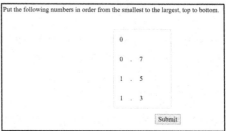

Fig. 1. & 2. *Decimal Point* "Whac-A-Gopher" (left), an example of an ordering mini-game, and the non-game equivalent (right).

The non-game control condition (Fig. 2) presented the same mathematical content, including both problem-solving and self-explanation elements, without the game features or narrative. Problems were presented on a plain background in a manner consistent with many intelligent tutoring systems. As with *Decimal Point*, students had to complete all problems in a predetermined sequence. In both the game and non-game versions, students were told immediately if their answers on the problem-solving and self-explanation questions were incorrect, and they could not advance to the next problem until they correctly answered the current problem.

Students completed three isomorphic versions of a test on decimal number operations and concepts. Tests were administered before students completed the materials (pretest), immediately after completion (posttest), and a week after completion (delayed posttest). Versions of the test were counterbalanced across time points to control for any unintended variations in the tests. Each test contained 24 problems, including some problems with similar decimal number content to what was presented in the game and non-game systems and other problems that targeted underlying concepts related to decimal number operations but not explicitly taught within the game and non-game. Students could earn multiple points on some problems, with a total of 61 points possible for correctly answering all questions on the test.

2.3 Detector Construction

Text replay coding has been used to identify learner behaviors and affect [8, 34]. In this method, coders base their affect coding on log data gathered on the students' interaction with the learning environment. Text replay coding involves breaking down the existing data set into text replays, or clips, each either spanning a specific amount of time, a specific number of transactions, or delineated by start or end events.

Whereas our previous detectors were built using problem-level labels, the current study broke each problem or game level down into their two steps during the labeling process: problem solving and self-explanation. As such, text replay coding had to be conducted in four iterations: once each for gaming and confrustion in the problem-solving step; and once each again for gaming and confrustion in the self-explanation step.

In each iteration, text replay coding was conducted in three phases. In phase 1, two human coders coded a set of clips together in order to establish a labeling rubric. In phase 2, both coders coded another set of clips separately, in order to assess inter-rater reliability. If the coders attained acceptable reliability, the coders moved on to phase 3. If not, the coders discussed the differences in their labeling, and then did another round of phase 2 coding, repeating this process until they attained acceptable reliability. Two rounds of phase 2 coding were conducted for confrustion in the problem-solving clips, and one round of phase 2 coding was conducted for the other three detectors. For the problem-solving clips, the inter-rater reliability (IRR) kappa was 0.74 for both confrustion and gaming. Kappa was 0.62 and 0.88 for confrustion and gaming, respectively, in the self-explanation clips. Once in phase 3, the two coders divided the remaining clips and coded them separately. Since less confrustion was observed in the self-explanation clips, almost twice as many self-explanation clips as problem-solving clips needed to be coded to have enough data to build the model. In total, 800 problem-solving clips and 1,500 self-explanation clips were coded and used to construct the automated affect detectors. Furthermore, clips were stratified to equally represent schools, problem type, and experiment condition.

Table 1. Detector performance for gaming and confrustion detectors in the problem-solving and self-explanation steps.

	Problem Solving	Self-Explanation
Gaming	AUC=0.889, k=0.504	AUC=0.999, k=0.952
Confrustion	AUC=0.915, k=0.565	AUC=0.956, k=0.645

The labeled data were input into machine learning algorithms to emulate the coders' judgments, based on prior studies that showed it was feasible to detect gaming [43] and confrustion [34] using this approach. The gaming and confrustion detectors were all built using the Extreme Gradient Boosting (XGBoost) classifier [12]. The classifier uses an ensemble technique that trains an initial, weak decision tree and calculates its prediction errors. It then iteratively trains subsequent decision trees to predict the error of the previous decision tree, with the final prediction representing the sum of the predictions of all the trees in the set. Four automated detectors were built in total, i.e., gaming in the problem-solving step, confrustion in the problem-solving step, gaming in the self-explanation step, and confrustion in the self-explanation step. Based on 10-fold student-level cross-validation, we determined that the models could reliably predict the two constructs in both the problem-solving and self-explanation steps. Detector performance can be found in Table 1. The detectors were then applied to predict gaming and confrustion in the rest of the data set.

3   Results

Results were previously reported regarding the effect of the game compared to the non-game on posttest and delayed posttest performance [38]. Specifically, analyses of covariance (ANCOVAs) revealed that students in the game condition outperformed.

Table 2. Average probabilities of gaming the system and confrustion by condition for problem-solving (PS) and self-explanation (SE) activities.

	Gaming (PS) M (SD)	Gaming (SE) M (SD)	Confrustion (PS) M (SD)	Confrustion (SE) M (SD)
Game	.14 (.099)	.22 (.11)	.18 (.086)	.041 (.035)
Non-game	.27 (.12)	.30 (.14)	.15 (.056)	.066 (.055)

students in the non-game condition on posttest, $F(1,172) = 11.50$, $p = .001$, $\eta_p^2 = .063$, and delayed posttest performance, $F(1, 172) = 11.86$, $p = .001$, $\eta_p^2 = .065$.

To understand the effect of the game on students' cognitive and affective processes, we compared predicted rates of gaming the system and confrustion among students playing the game against those completing the non-game version. We examined rates during problem solving and rates while completing the self-explanation questions separately (Table 2). Students using the non-game demonstrated almost double the levels of gaming the system while problem solving as students playing the game, and this difference was significant, $F(1, 173) = 57.64$, $p < .001$, $\eta_p^2 = .25$. On self-explanation questions, students in the non-game also showed significantly higher levels of gaming the system, $F(1, 173) = 17.87$, $p < .001$, $\eta_p^2 = .09$, and confrustion, $F(1, 173) = 12.40$, $p = .001$, $\eta_p^2 = .07$. In contrast, students using the non-game condition show significantly *lower* levels of confrustion during the problem-solving portion, $F(1, 173) = 5.77$, $p = .017$, $\eta_p^2 = .03$.

To understand how these cognitive and affective processes related to posttest performance, we assessed a regression model predicting posttest scores with pretest scores, gaming probabilities for problem solving and self-explanation, and confrustion probabilities for problem solving and self-explanation (Table 3). The resulting model predicted 68.9 percent of the variance. Within the model, pretest scores, gaming the system for problem-solving questions, and gaming the system for self-explanation questions were all significant predictors of posttest scores. We assessed the same model predicting delayed posttest scores. The resulting model predicted 66.1 percent of the variance and, within the model, pretest scores and gaming the system on problem-solving were again significant predictors of delayed posttest scores; additionally, confrustion on self-explanation emerged as a significant predictor.

Finally, we wanted to understand whether differences in cognitive or affective processes explained the effect of the game on learning outcomes. Given that gaming the system on problem-solving questions predicted learning outcomes at posttest and delayed posttest and that levels of gaming differed across conditions, we examined gaming the system on problem-solving questions as a mediator between condition and each test (posttest and delayed posttest; Fig. 3). We used the PROCESS macro for SPSS statistical software [30], which applies 5000 bootstrap estimates to create confidence intervals, to test the indirect effect of condition (game = 0, non-game = 1) on posttest and delayed posttest with gaming the system on problem-solving questions as the mediator. Pretest scores were included as a covariate. Results indicated that students in the non-game condition had significantly greater probabilities of gaming the system, $a = .70$, $p <$

Table 3. Regression models predicting posttest and delayed posttest scores with pretest scores, gaming probabilities, and confrustion probabilities.

	Posttest	Delayed posttest
Overall model	$R^2 = .70$, $F(5,168) = 77.60$, $p < .001$	$R^2 = .67$, $F(5,168) = 68.54$, $p < .001$
Pretest	$\beta = .48$, $p < .001$	$\beta = .45$, $p < .001$
Gaming (PS)	$\beta = -.30$, $p < .001$	$\beta = -.42$, $p < .001$
Gaming (SE)	$\beta = -.16$, $p = .005$	$\beta = -.077$, $p = .19$
Confrustion (PS)	$\beta = -.017$, $p = .77$	$\beta = .062$, $p = .20$
Confrustion (SE)	$\beta = .042$, $p = .36$	$\beta = .12$, $p = .012$

.001. Gaming the system was negatively associated with performance on the posttest regardless of condition, $b = -.37$, $p < .001$, and there was no direct effect of condition on posttest performance when controlling for gaming the system, $c = -.07$, $p = .48$. Consistent with our mediation prediction, the indirect effect of condition on posttest through gaming the system was significantly different than zero, $ab = -.26$, 95% CI $[-.12, -.064]$. Similar results were found for the delayed posttest: gaming the system was negatively associated with performance on the delayed posttest, $b = -.42$, $p < .001$, and there was no direct effect of condition on delayed posttest performance when controlling for gaming the system, $c = -.062$, $p = .56$. Again, the indirect effect of condition on delayed posttest through gaming the system was significantly different than zero, $ab = -.29$, 95% CI $[-.44, -.18]$.

Given the mixed results regarding confrustion in prior literature and in our findings, we examined whether the relation between confrustion and learning might differ between the game and non-game contexts. To do this, we tested game condition as a moderator of the relation between confrustion and each test (posttest and delayed posttest) while controlling for pretest. Moderation analyses in PROCESS showed no significant interaction between confrustion on problem-solving questions and condition when predicting posttest, $b = -15.70$, $p = .26$, 95% CI $[-43.24, 11.84]$, or delayed posttest, $b = -22.29$, $p = .13$, 95% CI $[-51.44, 6.85]$. However, there was a significant interaction between confrustion on self-explanation questions and condition when predicting posttest, $b = 69.66$, $p = .003$, 95% CI $[23.73, 115.58]$, and inclusion of the interaction term explained significantly more variance in the model, $\Delta R^2 = .018$, $F(1, 169) = 8.97$, $p = .003$. While confrustion was not related to posttest performance in the game condition ($b = -18.90$, $p = .34$), it was positively related to posttest performance in the non-game condition ($b = 50.76$, $p < .001$; Fig. 4). There was a similar interaction predicting delayed posttest, $b = 47.63$, $p = .049$, 95% CI $[.32, 94.94]$, and inclusion of the interaction term again explained significantly more variance in the model, $\Delta R^2 = .009$, $F(1, 169) = 3.95$, $p = .049$. As with the posttest, confrustion was not related to delayed posttest performance in the game condition ($b = 10.16$, $p = .62$), but it was positively related to delayed posttest performance in the non-game condition ($b = 57.79$, $p < .001$; Fig. 5).

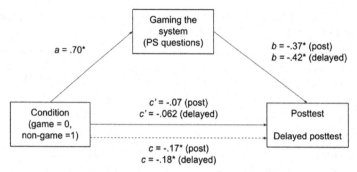

Fig. 3. The mediation model showing path standardized coefficients for a mediation analysis of learning condition on posttest through gaming the system on problem-solving questions.

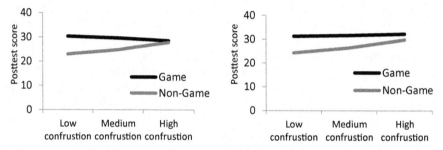

Fig. 4. & 5. Interaction of confrustion (SE) items and condition predicting posttest (left) and delayed posttest score (right). Scores were calculated using the regression equation for low (16th percentile), medium (50th percentile), and high (84th percentile) values of confrustion.

4   Discussion and Conclusion

Although digital learning games continue to grow in use, relatively few studies have empirically assessed differences in cognitive and affective processes between games and non-game, computer-based systems covering the same content. This paper presents a promising approach using educational data mining to build log-based detectors that can capture such differences. Results showed that the positive effect of learning with the game was fully mediated by students' lower levels of gaming the system when playing the game. Gaming the system has been consistently associated with negative short-term and long-term outcomes, ranging from lower achievement in the task where gaming is measured to reduced likelihood of enrolling in college or choosing a STEM-related job [3, 7, 49]. While it is not surprising that gaming the system was associated with worse performance in *Decimal Point,* it is an important and novel finding that the game reduced students' tendencies to game the system compared to the non-game version and that this reduction in gaming explained differences in learning outcomes. Gaming the system is considered a form of behavioral disengagement, and digital learning games are thought to increase students' engagement through game features such as fantasy and narrative context. Results appear to support the idea that introducing engaging features can reduce students' disengaged behaviors and thereby enhance learning, though causality cannot be inferred from these data.

Confrustion did not consistently predict learning outcomes, but these results are similar to prior research finding conflicting relations between confusion or frustration and learning. We found that confrustion on self-explanation questions played a different role in learning depending on whether students were working in the game or non-game context. In the game, confrustion did not predict learning outcomes, while in the non-game, greater levels of confrustion on self-explanation questions were associated with better learning outcomes. When students experience confusion or frustration while learning, it can trigger productive cognitive and metacognitive processes such as trying a different strategy and monitoring progress [21]. Students experiencing confrustion in the non-game may have engaged in these productive strategies to resolve their confrustion and ultimately gain more from the self-explanation process. On the other hand, confrustion may be less beneficial in a game setting because it feels disruptive to the engaging, playful interactions students expect from a game.

This work suggests several fruitful avenues for further advancing researchers' and developers' understanding of how digital learning games support learning. While our results suggest that differences in gaming the system could explain many of the benefits of games, there are a variety of other cognitive and affective processes that might also play a role. Developing additional detectors for constructs such as boredom, delight, engaged concentration, and carelessness could identify additional pathways that mediate the effect of digital learning games on learning. These detectors should also be applied to log data from other digital learning games and, ideally, non-game, computer-based controls. Given the large number of game features present across the diversity of digital learning games [9], it is important to explore whether gaming the system is reduced by a variety of games or if this mechanism is related to specific game features present in *Decimal Point*. Future research could explore how manipulating other game features, such as agency, might influence students' behavioral interactions and affective states [29]. Ultimately, understanding the connection between specific game features, cognitive and affective learning processes, and learning outcomes will provide digital learning game designers and teachers with a much more robust set of tools for determining when and how to implement digital learning games to best support students' learning. For example, if particular game features are especially effective at reducing problematic behaviors and affect (e.g., gaming, anxiety), a game with those features could be deployed when the context or content is likely to elicit those behaviors and affective states.

Acknowledgements. This work was supported by the National Science Foundation Award #DRL-1661121. The opinions expressed are those of the authors and do not represent the views of NSF. Thanks to Jimit Bhalani, John Choi, Kevin Dhou, Darlan Santana Farias, Rosta Farzan, Jodi Forlizzi, Craig Ganoe, Rick Henkel, Scott Herbst, Grace Kihumba, Kim Lister, Patrick Bruce Gonçalves McLaren, and Jon Star for important contributions to the development and early experimentation with *Decimal Point*.

References

1. Aleven, V., McLaren, B.M., Sewall, J.: Scaling up programming by demonstration for intelligent tutoring systems development: an open-access website for middle school mathematics learning. IEEE Trans. Learn. Technol. **2**(2), 64–78 (2009)
2. Aleven, V., et al.: Example-tracing tutors: Intelligent tutor development for non-programmers. Int. J. Artif. Intell. Educ. **26**(1), 224–269 (2016)
3. Almeda, M.V., Baker, R.S.: Predicting student participation in STEM careers: the role of affect and engagement during middle dchool. J. Educ. Data Mining **12**(2), 33–47 (2020)
4. Bacher-Hicks, A., Goodman, J., Mulhern, C.: Inequality in household adaptation to schooling shocks: covid-induced online learning engagement in real time. Natl. Bureau Econ. Res. **193**, w27555 (2020)
5. Baker, R.S.: Gaming the system: a retrospective look. Philippine Comput. J. **6**(2), 9–13 (2011)
6. Baker, R.S., De Carvalho, A.M.J.A., Raspat, J., Aleven, V., Corbett, A.T., Koedinger, K.R.: Educational software features that encourage and discourage "gaming the system". In: Proceedings of the 14th International Conference on Artificial Intelligence in Education, pp. 475–482 (2009)
7. Baker, R.S., Corbett, A.T., Koedinger, K.R., Wagner, A.Z.: Off-task behavior in the cognitive tutor classroom: when students "game the system." In: Proceedings of the SIGCHI Conference on Human Factors in Computing Systems, pp. 383–390 (2004)
8. Baker, R.S., Corbett, A.T., Wagner, A.Z.: Human classification of low-fidelity replays of student actions. In: Proceedings of the Educational Data Mining Workshop at the 8th International Conference on Intelligent Tutoring Systems, pp. 29–36 (2006)
9. Bedwell, W.L., Pavlas, D., Heyne, K., Lazzara, E.H., Salas, E.: Toward a taxonomy linking game attributes to learning: an empirical study. Simul. Gaming **43**(6), 729–760 (2012)
10. BrightBytes, Inc.: 2020 Remote learning survey research results (2020). https://www.bright bytes.net/rls-research. Accessed 12 Feb 2021
11. Calvo, R.A., D'Mello, S.: Affect detection: an interdisciplinary review of models, methods, and their applications. IEEE Trans. Affect. Comput. **1**(1), 18–37 (2010)
12. Chen, T., Guestrin, C.: Xgboost: a scalable tree boosting system. In: Proceedings of the 22nd ACM SIGKDD International Conference on Knowledge Discovery and Data Mining, pp. 785–794 (2016)
13. Cheng, M.T., Chen, J.H., Chu, S.J., Chen, S.Y.: The use of serious games in science education: a review of selected empirical research from 2002 to 2013. J. Comput. Educ. **2**(3), 353–375 (2015)
14. Cheng, M.T., Rosenheck, L., Lin, C.Y., Klopfer, E.: Analyzing gameplay data to inform feedback loops in the radix endeavor. Comput. Educ. **111**, 60–73 (2017)
15. Chi, M.T., De Leeuw, N., Chiu, M.H., LaVancher, C.: Eliciting self-explanations improves understanding. Cogn. Sci. **18**(3), 439–477 (1994)
16. Clark, D.B., Tanner-Smith, E., Killingsworth, S.: Digital games, design, and learning: a systematic review and meta-analysis. Rev. Educ. Res. **86**(1), 79–122 (2016)
17. Cocea, M., Hershkovitz, A., Baker, R.S.: The impact of off-task and gaming behaviors on learning: immediate or aggregate? In: Proceeding of the 2009 Conference on Artificial Intelligence in Education: Building Learning Systems that Care: From Knowledge Representation to Affective Modelling, pp. 507–514. IOS Press (2009)
18. Common Sense Media. The common sense census: Media use by tweens and teens. https://www.commonsensemedia.org/research/the-common-sense-census-media-use-by-tweens-and-teens. Accessed 12 Feb 2021
19. Crocco, F., Offenholley, K., Hernandez, C.: A proof-of-concept study of game-based learning in higher education. Simul. Gaming **47**(4), 403–422 (2016)

20. D'Mello, S., Lehman, B., Pekrun, R., Graesser, A.: Confusion can be beneficial for learning. Learn. Instr. **29**, 153–170 (2014)
21. Di Leo, I., Muis, K.R., Singh, C.A., Psaradellis, C.: Curiosity… Confusion? Frustration! the role and sequencing of emotions during mathematics problem solving. Contemp. Educ. Psychol. **58**, 121–137 (2019)
22. Fishman, B., Riconscente, M., Snider, R., Tsai, T., Plass, J.: Empowering Educators: Supporting Student Progress in the Classroom with Digital Games. University of Michigan, Ann Arbor. gamesandlearning.umich.edu/agames (2014)
23. Forlizzi, J., McLaren, B., Ganoe, C., McLaren, P., Kihumba, G., Lister, K.: Decimal point: designing and developing an educational game to teach decimals to middle school students. In: Busch, C. (ed.) Proceedings of the 8th European Conference on Games Based Learning (ECGBL-2014), pp. 128–135 (2014)
24. Gagnon, D. J., Harpstead, E., Slater, S.: Comparison of off the shelf data mining methodologies in educational game analytics. In: Proceedings of EDM, pp. 38–43 (2019)
25. Gamesandlearning.org.   http://www.gamesandlearning.org/2014/06/09/teachers-on-using-games-in-class/. Accessed 15 Feb 2021
26. Glasgow, R., Ragan, G., Fields, W.M., Reys, R., Wasman, D.: The decimal dilemma. Teach. Child. Math. **7**(2), 89-93 (2000)
27. Habgood, M.P.J., Ainsworth, S.E.: Motivating children to learn effectively: exploring the value of intrinsic integration in educational games. J. Learn. Sci. **20**(2), 169–206 (2011)
28. Harpstead, E., MacLellan, C.J., Aleven, V., Myers, B.A.: Using extracted features to inform alignment-driven design ideas in an educational game. In: Proceedings of the SIGCHI Conference on Human Factors in Computing Systems, pp. 3329–3338. ACM (2014)
29. Harpstead, E., Richey, J.E., Nguyen, H., McLaren, B.M.: Exploring the subtleties of agency and indirect control in digital learning games. In: Proceedings of the 9th International Conference on Learning Analytics Knowledge, pp. 121–129. ACM (2019)
30. Hayes, A.F.: Introduction to Mediation, Moderation, and Conditional Process Analysis: a Regression-Based Approach. Guilford Publications (2017)
31. Irwin, K.C.: Using everyday knowledge of decimals to enhance understanding. J. Res. Math. Educ. **32**(4), 399–420 (2001)
32. Johnson, C.I., Mayer, R.E.: Adding the self-explanation principle to multimedia learning in a computer-based game-like environment. Comput. Hum. Behav. **26**, 1246–1252 (2010)
33. Ke, F.: Designing and integrating purposeful learning in game play: a systematic review. Educ. Tech. Research Dev. **64**(2), 219–244 (2016)
34. Lee, D.M.C., Rodrigo, M.M. T., Baker, R.S., Sugay, J.O., Coronel, A.: Exploring the relationship between novice programmer confusion and achievement. In: International conference on affective computing and intelligent interaction, pp. 175–184. Springer, Heidelberg (2011). https://doi.org/10.1007/978-3-642-24600-5_21
35. Lehman, B., et al.: Inducing and tracking confusion with contradictions during complex learning. Int. J. Artif. Intell. Educ. **22**(1–2), 85–105 (2013)
36. Liu, Z., Pataranutaporn, V., Ocumpaugh, J., Baker, R.: Sequences of frustration and confusion, and learning. In: Educational Data Mining (2013)
37. Mayer, R.E.: Computer games in education. Ann. Rev. Psychol. **70**, 531–549 (2019)
38. McLaren, B.M., Adams, D.M., Mayer, R.E., Forlizzi, J.: A computer-based game that promotes mathematics learning more than a conventional approach. Int. J. Game-Based Learn. (IJGBL) **7**(1), 36–56 (2017)
39. Mogessie, M., Richey, J.E., McLaren, B.M., Andres-Bray, JM.L., Baker, R.S.: Confrustion and gaming while learning with erroneous examples in a decimals game. In International Conference on Artificial Intelligence in Education, pp. 208–213, Springer, Cham (2020). https://doi.org/10.1007/978-3-030-52240-7_38

40. Nicholson, S.: A user-centered theoretical framework for meaningful gamification, vol. 8, no. 1, pp. 223–230. Games+ Learning + Society (2012)
41. Nicholson, S.: Two paths to motivation through game design elements: reward-based gamification and meaningful gamification. In: Proceedings of the iConference 2013, pp. 671-672 (2013)
42. Paquette, L., Baker, R.S., Moskal, M.: A system-general model for the detection of gaming the system behavior in CTAT and LearnSphere. In: International Conference on Artificial Intelligence in Education, pp. 257–260, Springer, Cham (2018). https://doi.org/10.1007/978-3-319-93846-2_47
43. Paquette, L., de Carvahlo, A., Baker, R., Ocumpaugh, J.: Reengineering the feature distillation process: a case study in detection of gaming the system. In: Educational Data Mining (2014)
44. Parong, J., Wells, A., Mayer, R.E.: Replicated evidence towards a cognitive theory of game-based training. J. Educ. Psychol. **112**(5), 922–937 (2020)
45. Richey, J.E., et al.: More confusion and frustration, better learning: the impact of erroneous examples. Comput. Educ. **139**, 173–190 (2019)
46. Richey, J.E., et al.: Confrustion in learning from erroneous examples: does type of prompted self-explanation make a difference? In International Conference on Artificial Intelligence in Education, pp. 445–457, Springer, Cham (2019b). https://doi.org/10.1007/978-3-030-23204-7_37
47. Riconscente, M.M.: Results from a controlled study of the iPad fractions game motion math. Games Cult. **8**(4), 186–214 (2013)
48. Rodrigo, M.M.T., et al.: Affective and behavioral predictors of novice programmer achievement. In: Proceedings of the 14th ACM-SIGCSE Annual Conference on Innovation and Technology in Computer Science Education, pp. 156–160 (2009)
49. San Pedro, M.O.Z., Baker, R.S.J.D., Bowers, A.J., Heffernan, N.T.: Predicting college enrollment from student interaction with an intelligent tutoring system in middle school. In: Proceedings of the 6th International Conference on Educational Data Mining, pp. 177–184 (2013)
50. Schneider, B., Krajcik, J., Lavonen, J., Salmela-Aro, K., Broda, M., Spicer, J., et al.: Investigating optimal learning moments in U.S. and finnish science classes. J. Res. Sci. Teach. **53**(3), 400–421 (2015)
51. Seaborn, K., Fels, D.I.: Gamification in theory and action: a survey. Int. J. Hum Comput Stud. **74**, 14–31 (2015)
52. Serrano-Laguna, Á., Torrente, J., Moreno-Ger, P., Fernández-Manjón, B.: Application of learning analytics in educational videogames. Entertainment Comput. **5**(4), 313–322 (2014)
53. Siew, N.M., Geofrey, J., Lee, B.N.: Students' algebraic thinking and attitudes towards algebra: the effects of game-based learning using Dragonbox 12+ app. Electron. J. Math. Technol. **10**(2), 66–79 (2016)
54. Sitzmann, T.: A meta-analytic examination of the instructional effectiveness of computer-based simulation games. Pers. Psychol. **64**, 489–528 (2011)
55. Slater, S., Ocumpaugh, J., Baker, R., Scupelli, P., Inventado, P.S., Heffernan, N.: Semantic features of math problems: relationships to student learning and engagement. In: Proceedings of the 9th International Conference on Educational Data Mining, pp. 223–230 (2016)
56. Stacey, K., Helme, S., Steinle, V.: Confusions between decimals, fractions and negative numbers: a consequence of the mirror as a conceptual metaphor in three different ways. In: Heuvel-Panhuizen, M.V.D. (ed.) Proceedings of the 25th Conference of the International Group for the Psychology of Mathematics Education, pp. 217–224. Utrecht, PME (2001)
57. Suh, S., Kim, S.W., Kim, N.J.: Effectiveness of MMORPG-based instruction in elementary English education in Korea. J. Comput. Assist. Learn. **26**, 370–378 (2010)
58. Tokac, U., Novak, E., Thompson, C.G.: Effects of game-based learning on students' mathematics achievement: a meta-analysis. J. Comput. Assist. Learn. **35**(3), 407–420 (2019)

59. Vogel, J.J., Vogel, D.S., Cannon-Bowers, J., Bowers, C.A., Muse, K., Wright, M.: Computer gaming and interactive simulations for learning: a meta-analysis. J. Educ. Comput. Res. **34**(3), 229–243 (2006)
60. Wouters, P., van Oostendorp, H. (eds.): Instructional Techniques to Facilitate Learning and Motivation of Serious Games. Springer, New York (2017)
61. Wu, C.H., Huang, Y.M., Hwang, J.P.: Review of affective computing in education/learning: trends and challenges. Br. J. Edu. Technol. **47**(6), 1304–1323 (2015)
62. Yip, F.W.M., Kwan, A.C.M.: Online vocabulary games as a tool for teaching and learning English vocabulary. Educ. Media Int. **43**, 233–249 (2006)

Tackling the Credit Assignment Problem in Reinforcement Learning-Induced Pedagogical Policies with Neural Networks

Markel Sanz Ausin[✉][iD], Mehak Maniktala, Tiffany Barnes, and Min Chi[iD]

North Carolina State University, Raleigh, NC 27695, USA
{msanzau,mmanikt,tmbarnes,mchi}@ncsu.edu

Abstract. Intelligent Tutoring Systems (ITS) provide a powerful tool for students to learn in an adaptive, personalized, and goal-oriented manner. In recent years, Reinforcement Learning (RL) has shown to be capable of leveraging previous student data to induce effective pedagogical policies for future students. One of the most desirable goals of these policies is to maximize student learning gains while minimizing the training time. However, this metric is often not available until a student has completed the entire tutor. For this reason, the reinforcement signal of the effectiveness of the tutor is *delayed*. Assigning credit for each intermediate action based on a delayed reward is a challenging problem denoted the temporal *Credit Assignment Problem* (CAP). The CAP makes it difficult for most RL algorithms to assign credit to each action. In this work, we develop a general Neural Network-based algorithm that tackles the CAP by *inferring* immediate rewards from delayed rewards. We perform two empirical classroom studies, and the results show that this algorithm, in combination with a Deep RL agent, can improve student learning performance while reducing training time.

Keywords: Pedagogical agent · Credit assignment problem · Deep reinforcement learning

1 Introduction

Recent advances in Machine Learning have enabled the creation of algorithms that allow us to optimize certain desired metrics, for a large and diverse pool of users. Reinforcement Learning (RL), in particular, has shown great promise in the last few years, due to its effectiveness in inducing a policy to maximize a reward function while interacting with a non-stationary environment. In recent years, the combination of RL with deep neural networks has enabled solving very complex tasks. Deep RL (DRL) has achieved notable successes in a variety of complex tasks such as robotic control [2] and the game of Go [31]. Despite DRL's great success, there are still many challenges preventing DRL from being

© Springer Nature Switzerland AG 2021
I. Roll et al. (Eds.): AIED 2021, LNAI 12748, pp. 356–368, 2021.
https://doi.org/10.1007/978-3-030-78292-4_29

applied more broadly in practice, including applying it to educational systems such as Intelligent Tutoring Systems (ITSs).

ITSs and other educational software tools have gained popularity in recent years. These systems allow educators to provide a personalized learning process to each student, without needing to personally supervise the process. These e-learning environments often rely on *pedagogical policies* to decide how each problem or each part of the system is going to be displayed for a given user. The sequential decision-making nature of DRL, combined with its ability to learn from a reward function, makes it a perfect fit to induce pedagogical policies for ITSs and optimize the learning process for each student individually. However, most ITSs have a *delayed reward function* by design. These systems need to assess the overall learning process of each student, and they generally follow a standard structure of pre-test, training on the ITS, and post-test, where the learning improvement is measured. In this situation, discovering which of the tutor's actions are responsible for the delayed outcome can present a challenge. Because of this, the ability of DRL to be broadly effective in real-world applications is still unproven. In such delayed reinforcement tasks, a reward r_t obtained at time t, may have been affected by all the actions leading to that time-step: a_0, a_1, ..., a_{t-1}, and a_t. Assigning credit or blame for each of those actions individually is known as the *(temporal) Credit Assignment Problem (CAP)* [19]. The CAP is particularly relevant for real-world tasks, where we need to learn effective policies from small, limited training datasets. In prior work, one way to mitigate the impact of the CAP is to use model-based RL [6,32] or simulations, which allow collecting vast amounts of data. However, in many real-life domains such as healthcare and education, building accurate simulations is especially challenging because disease progression and student learning are rather complex processes.

The most appropriate rewards to use in education are the student learning outcomes, which are typically unobservable until the entire training process or trajectory is complete. This is because, in human learning progressions, it is difficult to assess student knowledge moment by moment, and more importantly, many instructional interventions that boost short-term performance may not be effective over the long term. To address the CAP, we present a general neural network-based algorithm to infer the immediate rewards from the delayed reward, and then use those inferred immediate rewards for pedagogical policy induction. In this work, we used an ITS that is designed to teach students how to solve logic proofs. We applied DRL to induce a pedagogical policy on one of the most widely studied types of tutorial decisions: whether to present a problem as a **Problem Solving** (PS) or a **Worked Example** (WE) [12,13,16,21,23,24,26,27,29,30,34,39].

In this work, we compared two DRL-based pedagogical policies against an Expert baseline policy and a PS-only policy, in two empirical classroom studies with college students. During the Spring 2019 semester, the DRL pedagogical policy first inferred the immediate rewards from the delayed rewards using a Gaussian Processes approach introduced by Azizsoltani et al. [5], and then a DQN agent [20] used those rewards to induce a pedagogical policy, referred to as InferGP in the future. InferGP is compared against an Expert-crafted policy that alternates between PS and WE. Next, during the Spring 2020 semester, we inferred the immediate rewards using InferNet, the algorithm we present in this paper, and then trained a Dueling-DQN agent [38] to induce a policy; InferNet is compared against a PS-only policy because most conventional ITSs are PS only. *As the two DQN-based policies used different scores as reward functions for training, they cannot be directly compared with one another.* Rather, we compare each of those RL-induced policies to the two control groups: Expert and PS-only. Our results show that while no significant difference was found between InferGP, Expert and PS-only in terms of learning gains or learning efficiency, InferNet outperforms the Expert group in terms of learning performance, and InferNet also outperforms the PS-only group in terms of learning efficiency. In short, our proposed InferNet in conjunction with a Dueling-DQN policy results in better and more efficient learning than traditional pedagogical strategies such as Expert-crafted policies or PS-only policies.

2   Background and Related Work

Prior research has applied both online RL and offline RL to induce data-driven pedagogical policies. In *online RL*, the agent learns a policy while interacting with either real or simulated student data, while offline RL approaches "use previously collected samples, and generally provide robust convergence guarantees" [25] and thus, the success of these offline RL approaches depends heavily on the quality of the training data. Furthermore, prior work can be divided into traditional RL vs. DRL approaches. In the former, for instance, Iglesias et al. applied Q-learning to induce policies for efficient learning [10, 11]. More recently, Rafferty et al. applied an online partially observable Markov decision process (POMDP) to induce policies for faster learning [22]. Shen et al. employed offline value iteration and least square policy iteration to induce a pedagogical policy that improved student learning [28, 29]. Chi et al. applied offline policy iteration to induce a pedagogical policy aimed at improving students' learning gain [7]. Mandel et al. [15] used an offline POMDP to induce a policy which aims to improve student performance in an educational game. All the models described above were evaluated in classroom studies and were found to yield certain improved student learning or performance relative to a baseline policy.

The DRL approaches have been motivated by the recent growth in using Deep Neural Networks as function approximation. For instance, the Deep Q-Network (DQN) algorithm [20] takes advantage of convolutional neural networks to learn to play Atari games observing the pixels directly. Since then, DRL has achieved success in various complex tasks such as the games of Go [31], Chess/Shogi [32], Starcraft II [36], and robotic control [2]. One major challenge of these methods is *sample inefficiency*, where RL policies need large sample sizes to learn optimal, generalizable policies. DRL has also been applied to ITSs. Wang et al. applied an online DRL approach to induce a policy for adaptive narrative generation in an educational game using simulations [37]; the resulting DRL-induced policies were evaluated via simulations only. Sanz Ausin et al. used offline DRL to induce

---

Algorithm 1. InferNet + DRL Offline

1: **Input**: Training dataset D, Number of training steps K
2: **for** $step \leftarrow 1$ to K **do**
3:    Sample mini-batch of episodes $B \sim D$ with Delayed Rewards R_{del}
4:    Train InferNet on B: $L(\theta) = (R_{del} - \sum_{t=0}^{T-1} f(s_t, a_t)|\theta))^2$
5: **end for**
6: **for** $ep \leftarrow 1$ to $|D|$ **do**
7:    Use the trained InferNet to infer immediate rewards for episode ep
8:    Replace original rewards with the new InferNet rewards
9: **end for**
10: Train DRL agent

---

pedagogical policies and showed that they can improve student learning, and can be more effective than expert-designed baseline policies [3,4]. Much prior work has induced a pedagogical policy by using DRL directly, while this work combines a mechanism that tackles the CAP, and a DRL algorithm to induce more effective policies.

3   InferNet

The ultimate goal of InferNet is to tackle the temporal CAP by inferring the immediate rewards from the delayed rewards. We model the environment as a standard Markov Decision Process. At time-step t, the environment is in some state s_t, the agent takes an action a_t, and receives a scalar reward r_t, which in the case of delayed rewards is zero unless it is the last reward in the episode, i.e., at the end of the entire trajectory (the delayed reward). We denote the immediate rewards as r and the delayed rewards as R_{del}.

The idea behind InferNet is rather straightforward. It uses a deep neural network to predict the immediate reward at each time-step, for an episode that contains T steps. At each time step t, InferNet receives a state s_t and its corresponding action a_t as inputs, and it outputs the predicted scalar reward r_t for that time-step: $r_t = f(s_t, a_t|\theta)$, where θ indicates the neural network parameters (weights and biases). To train the neural network, InferNet distributes the final delayed reward among all the states in the episode. More precisely, the neural network is trained to predict the immediate rewards from the delayed reward with a constraint: *the sum of all the predicted immediate rewards in each episode must be equal to the delayed reward of that episode:* $R_{del} = f(s_0, a_0|\theta) + f(s_1, a_1|\theta) + ... + f(s_{T-1}, a_{T-1}|\theta)$. By doing so, the network is tasked with modeling the reward function, conditioned on the state and actions that were passed as inputs. InferNet is trained by minimizing the loss between the sum of predicted rewards and the delayed reward.

For the implementation, the TimeDistributed layer available on TensorFlow Keras [1,8] was employed. This layer allows repeating the same neural network operation across multiple time-steps, sharing weights across time, and we use it to pass the entire episode at once to the neural network, as a sequence of states and action pairs. It should be noted that there is no internal state in InferNet, despite sharing weights across time as in a recurrent neural network. Each predicted reward is only dependent on the state and action passed as inputs at that timestep. The loss function that is used to train InferNet is shown in Eq. 1. Algorithm 1 shows the pseudo-code for training InferNet offline in conjunction with a DRL algorithm.

$$Loss(\theta) = (R_{del} - \sum_{t=0}^{T-1} f(s_t, a_t|\theta))^2 \tag{1}$$

4   GridWorld with Delayed Reinforcement

The effectiveness of InferNet is investigated on a simple GridWorld task where the immediate rewards are known. This allows us to compare the predicted inferred rewards to the true immediate rewards, and measure the error. This environment consists of a 14×7 grid, with five positive rewards $(+1)$ and four negative rewards (-1), located randomly, but always in the same locations. All other states have a reward of zero. The initial state is located at the bottom-right corner of the grid, and the agent's goal is to reach the terminal state, located at the top-left corner while collecting the positive rewards and avoiding the negative ones. The three available actions are to move up, left, and down. The highest total return that can be collected is $+5$, while the lowest one is -4.

We compare four reward settings: 1) *Immediate rewards:* when available, they are the gold standard. 2) *Delayed rewards:* these rewards are used as a baseline; here all the intermediate rewards will be zero and the delayed reward that indicates how good or bad the intermediate actions are is provided at the end of the episode. In other words, we simulate the delayed rewards by "hiding" the immediate rewards and providing the sum of all the immediate rewards at the end of the episode. 3) *InferGP rewards:* the inferred immediate rewards using the GP algorithm proposed in [5]. 4) *InferNet rewards:* the inferred immediate rewards through InferNet.

In this experiment, we compared different reward settings using both online and offline RL. InferNet can be trained online and offline, while InferGP can only be applied for offline RL. For online RL, we used an online RL algorithm known for being capable of solving the CAP, the TD(λ) algorithm; while for offline RL, we used Q-learning, which is one of the best known RL approaches.

Online TD(λ): TD(λ) is known to be one of the strongest methods to solve the CAP [33] in that it takes advantage of the benefits of Temporal Difference (TD) learning methods, and includes eligibility traces, which allows the agent to look at all the future rewards to estimate the value of each state. Here we compared InferNet against the delayed and immediate rewards because InferGP cannot be applied for online RL. Figure 1(Left) shows that by minimizing the training error in Eq. 1 (the difference between the delayed reward and the sum of inferred immediate rewards) (red line), InferNet minimizes the true error (the difference

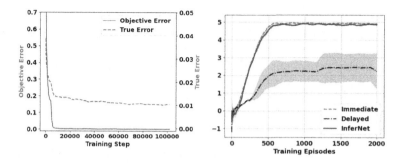

Fig. 1. Online Training. Left: Training InferNet online. Right: Performance of a TD(λ) agent on the GridWorld environment. (Color figure online)

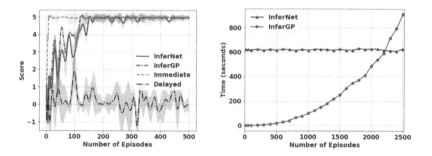

Fig. 2. Offline Training. Left: Performance of Q-Learning agents as a function of the number of training episodes. Right: Empirical time complexity comparison between InferNet and InferGP.

between the inferred immediate rewards and the true immediate rewards) (blue line) when trained online. This shows that our method can effectively approximate the true immediate rewards from the delayed reward.

Figure 1(Right) shows that when the rewards are delayed, TD(λ) is not able to learn as effectively as the agent with the true immediate rewards. However, by applying InferNet first on the delayed rewards, the InferNet agent achieves the same performance as using the immediate rewards; both converge to the optimal policy. Each experiment is repeated five times with different random seeds, and Figure 1(Right) shows the mean and standard deviation of those runs.

Offline Q-Learning: In this experiment, we compared all four reward settings. We first generate random gameplay data with immediate rewards from the GridWorld; then sum the immediate rewards in each episode to get its corresponding delayed reward; and finally, apply InferGP and InferNet to infer the corresponding rewards from the delayed reward. To compare the four reward settings, we train a tabular Q-learning agent offline for 5000 iterations on the dataset corresponding to each reward setting. For each of the four reward settings, once its corresponding RL policy is induced, its effectiveness is evaluated by interacting with the GridWorld environment directly for 50 episodes. Figure 2 (left) shows the mean and standard deviation of the performance of the agent, as a function of the number of episodes available in the training dataset. It shows that, as expected, the delayed policy performs poorly, while the Immediate policy can converge to the optimal policy after only 10 episodes of data; additionally, Infer-Net and InferGP are comparable and both can converge to the optimal policy but they need more training data (around 150 episodes) than the Immediate policy.

Time Complexity: Despite the fact that the performance of InferNet and InferGP is comparable for offline RL, Fig. 2(Right) shows that the training time of InferGP increases cubically $O(n^3)$ as the training data increases, while Infer-Net has a time complexity of $O(n)$, where n is the amount of training data. This is because InferNet only needs to be trained for a constant number of epochs. Furthermore, InferGP has an asymptotic space complexity of $O(n^2)$, while Infer-Net has a space complexity of $O(f * l)$, where f is the number of features in the state and action that are passed as inputs, and l is the length of the episode that is passed as input.

In short, InferNet is equivalent to InferGP in performance (as shown by the results in the GridWorld), but its time and space complexity are much better than those of InferGP. InferNet can be applied for both offline and online RL, which makes it much more effective and general, and RL algorithms can benefit greatly from using it to tackle the CAP.

5   Pedagogical Policy Induction

Next we describe how we use InferNet to induce pedagogical policies for an intelligent tutor. We focus on training a pedagogical policy to decide how to show a problem in one of two ways: Problem-Solving (PS) vs. Worked Example (WE). If PS is chosen, students are shown a problem, which they need to complete. In WE, the students are provided with an expert, step-by-step solution to the problem. A great deal of prior research has investigated the effectiveness of PS vs. WE as educational interventions [16–18, 21, 23, 24, 26, 34]. In general, evidence indicates that showing WEs can significantly reduce the total time on task while not hurting the learning performance too much [16–18]. On the other hand, alternating between PS and WE can be more effective than PS only [16, 21, 23, 24, 26, 34]. Despite all the prior studies, there is no clear consensus about how or when these two interventions should be combined to optimize student learning. As a result, most existing ITSs always choose PS [14, 35].

Training Corpus: Our training dataset contains 786 student trajectories, collected over five different semesters. Students spend around 2–3 h on the ITS completing problems. To represent the state of the learning environment, 142 features from five categories are extracted. We have 10 Autonomy features describing the amount of work done by the student; 29 Temporal features including total time spent, time spent on PS, time spent on WE, and so on; 35 Problem-Solving features describing the difficulty of the problem, the number of easy and difficult problems solved, and so on; 57 Performance features such as the number of incorrect steps; and 11 Hint-related features including the total number of hints requested, among others.

Reward Functions: Our goal is to create an RL-induced pedagogical policy to improve student Learning Gain while minimizing the training time. In other words, we want to maximize learning efficiency. In our empirical studies with students, we used two different reward functions and both rewards are only calculated for the post-test problems. The first one, which we will denote as S19 (due to the semester and year when it was used, Spring 2019), uses the number of incorrect rule applications made by the students, as well as the speed, measured by the time spent on the post-test problems. The second reward function, denoted S20, uses the solution length (number of logic statements in the solution), the solution accuracy (proportion of correct rule applications), and the speed. In this work, we applied InferGP to infer the immediate rewards from the delayed rewards using the S19 scoring metric; and InferNet to infer the immediate rewards from the delayed rewards using the S20 scoring metric. Once the inferred immediate rewards are inferred, we train a DQN-based agent [20] to induce the corresponding policies.

Deep Q-Network (DQN): [20] is a version of Q-Learning which uses neural networks for function approximation. DQN uses two neural networks with identical architectures. The main network (represented by the weights θ) is used to estimate the Q-values of the current state s; while the target network (represented by the weights θ^-) is used to estimate the Q-values of the next state s' in the Bellman Equation: $Q(s, a|\theta) = r + \gamma \max_{a'} Q(s', a'|\theta^-)$.

Dueling-DQN: [38] is an improved version of DQN that splits the Q-value estimation into a value function and an advantage function, and then sums both of them to get the final Q-values. The relation between the value $V(s)$, advantage $A(s, a)$ and Q-value $Q(s, a)$ is defined as A(s, a) = Q(s, a) - V(s). We combined the Dueling-DQN algorithm with a Long Short-Term Memory (LSTM) [9] neural network, which is suitable for tasks with long temporal dependencies.

6   Empirical Experiments

Our ITS teaches how to solve logic proofs. It is used as a graded homework assignment in the undergraduate Discrete Mathematics class at NC State University. To complete a problem, students must iteratively apply rules to logic statement nodes in order to derive the conclusion node. The system automatically checks the correctness of each step and provides immediate feedback on any rule that is applied incorrectly. The ITS consists of a pre-test section, a training phase, and a post-test. The pre-test is used to evaluate the incoming knowledge of the students, and it contains four problems. The pedagogical policy does not take any decisions here. The training phase contains five levels, with four problems per level. The pedagogical policy decides whether to show PS or WE to each student during this phase. However, the policy must follow some constraints determined by the course instructor, who is a professor with over 15 years of experience in the field, to guarantee that every student sees at least one PS and one WE per level. Finally, the post-test consists of six problems, which are used to evaluate the improvement in each student's performance, after undergoing the training stage. The post-test is designed to evaluate the skills of each student, following the requirements of the course. In the end, a score is assigned to each student using one of the two reward functions described in Sect. 5.

We performed two empirical experiments with college students, one in Spring of 2019 (S19) and the other one in Spring of 2020 (S20). For the S19 study, our pedagogical policy was determined by a DQN agent, and the immediate rewards in the training dataset were inferred using InferGP. In the S20 study, we used a Dueling-DQN agent, with immediate rewards inferred using the InferNet algorithm. Both agents used the exact same neural network architecture and hyper-parameters. *It is important to note that the reward functions of S19 and S20 are not directly comparable to each other and thus the induced InferGP and InferNet policies cannot be directly compared to each other, because they were trained to maximize different metrics.*

In the S19 study, we denote our groups as *InferGP*, and *Expert* (for the expert-designed policy that alternates between PS and WE); 64 students were randomly assigned to the two groups and 53 students completed the tutor, with $N = 30$ for InferGP and $N = 23$ for Expert. For the S20 study, we denote our groups as *InferNet*, and *PS-only* (for the policy that always provides PS). 84 students were randomly assigned to the two groups and 74 students completed the tutor, with $N = 36$ for InferNet and $N = 38$ for PS-only. A χ^2 test showed no significant difference between the completion rates of the four different groups: $\chi^2(3, N = 148) = 0.598, p = 0.896$.

7   Results

We analyzed two key metrics that allow us to evaluate the performance of the students and measure their learning: *post-test performance* and *learning efficiency*. Post-test performance evaluates how much the students have learned after using the ITS during the training phase. The learning efficiency also accounts for the time spent in the training phase; it divides the post-test score by the training time, which results in a measurement of how much time they needed to reach a certain knowledge level. We want our policies to help the students learn as much as possible in as little training time as needed.

InferGP: In this analysis, we compared the performance of the *InferGP* policy against the *Expert* and the *PS-only* policies using the S19 scoring metric. A one-way ANOVA test showed no significant difference in the pre-test scores among the three groups: $F(2, 88) = 0.202, p = 0.650$. That is, our pre-test analysis shows that all three groups were balanced in incoming competence.

Next, we analyzed the post-test score performance. A one-way ANCOVA test using the group as a factor and the pre-test score as a covariate showed no significant difference in the post-test scores: $F(2, 87) = 0.019, p = 0.889$. When analyzing the learning efficiency, a one-way ANCOVA test using the group as a

Table 1. Results by group for the InferNet study.

	Pre-test score	Post-test score	Learning efficiency
InferNet	**0.73** (0.27)	**0.72** (0.09)	**0.34** (0.27)
PS-only	0.67 (0.25)	0.70 (0.12)	0.18 (0.16)
Expert	0.67 (0.27)	0.51 (0.10)	0.23 (0.17)

factor and the pre-test score as a covariate, also showed no significant difference in the post-test learning efficiency: $F(2, 87) = 2.017, p = 0.159$. In short, our analysis found no significant differences between the students in the InferGP group and the PS-only and Expert groups.

InferNet: Table 1 shows the mean and SD of the performance of the *InferNet* policy against the *Expert* and the *PS-only* policies using the S20 scoring metric. A one-way ANOVA test showed no significant difference in the pre-test scores among the three groups: $F(2, 93) = 1.099, p = 0.297$. Again, our pre-test analysis shows that all three groups were balanced in incoming competence.

We analyzed the post-test score performance. A one-way ANCOVA test using the group as a factor and the pre-test score as a covariate showed a marginal difference in the post-test scores: $F(2, 92) = 3.182, p = 0.077$. Subsequent pairwise one-way ANCOVA tests showed a significant difference between the PS-only and the Expert groups ($F(1, 57) = 42.336, p < 0.001, d = 1.720$) as well as between the InferNet group and the Expert group ($F(1, 55) = 58.200, p < 0.001, d = 2.207$); no significant difference was found between InferNet and PS-only ($F(1, 69) = 0.331, p = 0.567$). Finally, we analyze the learning efficiency. A one-way ANCOVA test using the group as a factor and the pre-test score as a covariate showed a significant difference in the post-test learning efficiency: $F(1, 92) = 8.839, p = 0.003$. Subsequent pairwise one-way ANCOVA tests showed a significant difference in the learning efficiency between the InferNet and PS-only groups ($F(1, 69) = 7.910, p = 0.006, d = 0.721$) and no significant difference was found between InferNet and Expert ($F(1, 55) = 2.340, p = 0.132$) or between PS-only and Expert ($F(1, 57) = 1.489, p = 0.227$).

To summarize, our results show that the students in the InferNet group achieved a significantly superior post-test score performance than the students in the Expert group, and they were also significantly more efficient than the students in the PS-Only group. This means that they learned more than the students in the Expert group, and they learned more in less time than the students in the PS-only group.

8   Conclusion

In this work, we developed a new method, InferNet, to solve the temporal CAP and help RL agents learn more effectively in delayed reinforcement tasks. We compared our method to immediate and delayed rewards, as well a previous method denoted InferGP, in a simulated GridWorld task, both online and offline, and showed that InferNet can effectively infer the true immediate rewards from the delayed rewards. We also showed that the InferNet rewards can be more effective than the delayed rewards in all cases. Furthermore, we evaluated the effectiveness of the InferNet rewards in two empirical classroom studies with real students, and the results showed that when combining a Deep RL agent with InferNet, the students in the InferNet group achieved a significantly superior post-test score performance than the students in the Expert group, and they were also significantly more efficient than the students in the PS-Only group. These empirical results indicate that our method is effective at helping students learn more in less time. Our method provides a robust and general way to induce a pedagogical policy that can improve student learning.

Acknowledgements. This research was supported by the NSF Grants: #1726550, #1651909, #1937037 and #2013502.

References

1. Abadi, M., Agarwal, A., Barham, P., Brevdo, E.: TensorFlow: arge-scale machine learning on heterogeneous systems (2015). https://www.tensorflow.org/, software available from tensorflow.org
2. Andrychowicz, M., Baker, B., et al.: Learning dexterous in-hand manipulation. arXiv:1808.00177 (2018)
3. Ausin, M.S.: Leveraging deep reinforcement learning for pedagogical policy induction in an intelligent tutoring system. In: Proceedings of the 12th International Conference on Educational Data Mining (EDM 2019) (2019)
4. Sanz Ausin, M., Maniktala, M., Barnes, T., Chi, M.: Exploring the impact of simple explanations and agency on batch deep reinforcement learning induced pedagogical policies. In: Bittencourt, I.I., Cukurova, M., Muldner, K., Luckin, R., Millán, E. (eds.) AIED 2020. LNCS (LNAI), vol. 12163, pp. 472–485. Springer, Cham (2020). https://doi.org/10.1007/978-3-030-52237-7_38
5. Azizsoltani, H., et al.: Unobserved is not equal to non-existent: using gaussian processes to infer immediate rewards across contexts. In: Proceedings of the 28th IJCAI (2019)
6. Chen, B., Xu, M., Li, L., Zhao, D.: Delay-aware model-based reinforcement learning for continuous control. arXiv preprint arXiv:2005.05440 (2020)
7. Chi, M., VanLehn, K., Litman, D., Jordan, P.: Empirically evaluating the application of reinforcement learning to the induction of effective and adaptive pedagogical strategies. User Model. User-Adapted Interact. **21**(1–2), 137–180 (2011)
8. Chollet, F.: Keras. https://keras.io (2015)
9. Hochreiter, S., Schmidhuber, J.: Long short-term memory. Neural Comput. **9**(8), 1735–1780 (1997)
10. Iglesias, A., Martínez, P., Aler, R., Fernández, F.: Learning teaching strategies in an adaptive and intelligent educational system through reinforcement learning. Appl. Intell **31**(1), 89–106 (2009)
11. Iglesias, A., Martínez, P., Aler, R., Fernández, F.: Reinforcement learning of pedagogical policies in adaptive and intelligent educational systems. Knowl.-Based Syst. **22**(4), 266–270 (2009)

12. Ju, S., Chi, M., Zhou, G.: Pick the moment: identifying critical pedagogical decisions using long-short term rewards. In: Rafferty, A.N., Whitehill, J., Romero, C., Cavalli-Sforza, V. (eds.) Proceedings of the 13th International Conference on Educational Data Mining, EDM 2020, Fully Virtual Conference, 10–13 July 2020. International Educational Data Mining Society (2020). https://educationaldatamining.org/files/conferences/EDM2020/papers/paper_167.pdf

13. Ju, S., Zhou, G., Azizsoltani, H., Barnes, T., Chi, M.: Identifying critical pedagogical decisions through adversarial deep reinforcement learning. In: EDM International Educational Data Mining Society (IEDMS) (2019)

14. Koedinger, K.R., Anderson, J.R., Hadley, W.H., Mark, M.A.: Intelligent tutoring goes to school in the big city. Int. J. Artif. Intell. Educ. (IJAIED) **8**, 30–43 (1997)

15. Mandel, T., Liu, Y.E., Levine, S., Brunskill, E., Popovic, Z.: Offline policy evaluation across representations with applications to educational games. In: Proceedings of the 2014 International Conference on Autonomous Agents and Multi-agent Systems, pp. 1077–1084. International Foundation for Autonomous Agents and Multiagent Systems (2014)

16. McLaren, B.M., van Gog, T., Ganoe, C., Yaron, D., Karabinos, M.: Exploring the assistance dilemma: comparing instructional support in examples and problems. In: Trausan-Matu, S., Boyer, K.E., Crosby, M., Panourgia, K. (eds.) ITS 2014. LNCS, vol. 8474, pp. 354–361. Springer, Cham (2014). https://doi.org/10.1007/978-3-319-07221-0_44

17. McLaren, B.M., Isotani, S.: When is it best to learn with all worked examples? In: Biswas, G., Bull, S., Kay, J., Mitrovic, A. (eds.) AIED 2011. LNCS (LNAI), vol. 6738, pp. 222–229. Springer, Heidelberg (2011). https://doi.org/10.1007/978-3-642-21869-9_30

18. McLaren, B.M., Lim, S.J., Koedinger, K.R.: When and how often should worked examples be given to students? New results and a summary of the current state of research. In: Proceedings of the 30th Annual Conference of the Cognitive Science Society, pp. 2176–2181 (2008)

19. Minsky, M.: Steps toward artificial intelligence. Proc. IRE **49**, 8–30 (1961)

20. Mnih, V., Kavukcuoglu, K., Silver, D., et al.: Human-level control through deep reinforcement learning. Nature **518**(7540), 529 (2015)

21. Najar, A.S., Mitrovic, A., McLaren, B.M.: Learning with intelligent tutors and worked examples: selecting learning activities adaptively leads to better learning outcomes than a fixed curriculum. User Model. User-Adapted Interact. **26**(5), 459–491 (2016). https://doi.org/10.1007/s11257-016-9181-y

22. Rafferty, A.N., Brunskill, E., et al.: Faster teaching via pomdp planning. Cognit. Sci. **40**(6), 1290–1332 (2016)

23. Renkl, A., Atkinson, R.K., et al.: From example study to problem solving: smooth transitions help learning. J. Exp. Educ. **70**(4), 293–315 (2002)

24. Salden, R.J., Aleven, V., Schwonke, R., Renkl, A.: The expertise reversal effect and worked examples in tutored problem solving. Instr. Sci. **38**(3), 289–307 (2010)

25. Schwab, D., Ray, S.: Offline reinforcement learning with task hierarchies. Mach. Learn. **106**(9), 1569–1598 (2017). https://doi.org/10.1007/s10994-017-5650-8

26. Schwonke, R., Renkl, A., Krieg, C., Wittwer, J., Aleven, V., Salden, R.: The worked-example effect: not an artefact of lousy control conditions. Comput. Hum. Behav. **25**(2), 258–266 (2009)

27. Shen, S., Ausin, M.S., Mostafavi, B., Chi, M.: Improving learning & reducing time: a constrained action-based reinforcement learning approach. In: UMAP, pp. 43–51. ACM (2018)

28. Shen, S., Chi, M.: Aim Low: Correlation-based Feature Selection for Model-based Reinforcement Learning. International Educational Data Mining Society (2016)

29. Shen, S., Chi, M.: Reinforcement learning: the sooner the better, or the later the better? In: UMAP, pp. 37–44. ACM (2016)

30. Shen, S., Mostafavi, B., Lynch, C., Barnes, T., Chi, M.: Empirically evaluating the effectiveness of pomdp vs. mdp towards the pedagogical strategies induction. In: Penstein Rosé, C., et al. (eds.) AIED 2018. LNCS (LNAI), vol. 10948, pp. 327–331. Springer, Cham (2018). https://doi.org/10.1007/978-3-319-93846-2_61

31. Silver, D., Huang, A., Maddison, C.J., et al.: Mastering the game of go with deep neural networks and tree search. Nature **529**(7587), 484 (2016)

32. Silver, D., Hubert, T., Schrittwieser, J., et al.: A general reinforcement learning algorithm that masters chess, shogi, and go through self-play. Science **362**(6419), 1140–1144 (2018)

33. Sutton, R.S.: Learning to predict by the methods of temporal differences. Mach. Learn. **3**(1), 9–44 (1988)

34. Sweller, J., Cooper, G.A.: The use of worked examples as a substitute for problem solving in learning algebra. Cognit. Instr. **2**(1), 59–89 (1985)

35. VanLehn, K., Graesser, A.C., et al.: When are tutorial dialogues more effective than reading? Cognit. Sci. **31**(1), 3–62 (2007)

36. Vinyals, O., Babuschkin, I., Czarnecki, W., et al.: Grandmaster level in StarCraft ii using multi-agent reinforcement learning. Nature **575**, 350 (2019)

37. Wang, P., Rowe, J., Min, W., Mott, B., Lester, J.: Interactive narrative personalization with deep reinforcement learning. In: IJCAI (2017)

38. Wang, Z., Schaul, T., Hessel, M., Van Hasselt, H., Lanctot, M., De Freitas, N.: Dueling network architectures for deep reinforcement learning. arXiv:1511.06581 (2015)

39. Zhou, G., Azizsoltani, H., Ausin, M.S., Barnes, T., Chi, M.: Hierarchical reinforcement learning for pedagogical policy induction (extended abstract). In: IJCAI, pp. 4691–4695. ijcai.org (2020)

TARTA: Teacher Activity Recognizer from Transcriptions and Audio

Danner Schlotterbeck(✉), Pablo Uribe, Abelino Jiménez, Roberto Araya,
Johan van der Molen Moris, and Daniela Caballero

Center for Advanced Research in Education, University of Chile, Santiago, Chile

Abstract. Classroom observation methods are fundamental tools for improving the quality of education and students' academic achievement. However, they traditionally require participation of trained observers, making them expensive, prone to rater bias and time consuming. Hence, to address these challenges we present a cost-effective and non-intrusive method that automatically detects different teaching practices. In particular, we extracted acoustic features and transcriptions from teachers' talk recordings to train a multimodal learning model called Teacher Activity Recognizer from Transcriptions and Audio (TARTA), which detects three categories derived from the Classroom Observation Protocol for Undergraduate STEM (COPUS), namely *Presenting, Administration,* and *Guiding.* We found that by combining acoustic features and transcriptions, our model outperforms separate acoustic- and transcription-based models at the task of predicting teachers' activities along the lessons. In fact, TARTA can predict with high accuracy and discriminative power the presence of these teaching practices, achieving over 88% of accuracy and 92% AUC for all three categories. Our work presents improvements with respect to previous studies since (1) we focus on classifying what teachers do according to a validated protocol instead of discerning whether they or their students are speaking and (2) our model does not rely on expensive or third party equipment, making it easier to scale to large volumes of lessons. This approach represents a useful tool for stakeholders and researchers who intend to analyze teaching practices on a large scale, but also for teachers to receive effective and continuous feedback.

Keywords: Multimodal learning · Teaching practices detection ·
BERT · Spectral audio features

1 Introduction

Classroom observation is a primary tool for improving the quality of education in several ways. First, it allows us to measure how improvement efforts regarding

Support from ANID/ PIA/ Basal Funds for Centers of Excellence FB0003 and ANID-FONDECYT grant N° 3180590 are gratefully acknowledged.

ⓒ Springer Nature Switzerland AG 2021
I. Roll et al. (Eds.): AIED 2021, LNAI 12748, pp. 369–380, 2021.
https://doi.org/10.1007/978-3-030-78292-4_30

teachers' practices affect their behaviors [13]. Second, through observation it is possible to capture aspects of teaching that cannot be measured by surveys or test scores [10]. Third, it is a very useful tool for developing research about the quality of teaching due to the vast amount of information that it can retrieve [9]. However, many traditional tools used for teacher evaluation are designed to qualify teachers with respect to general domains such as planning, instruction, or assessment. This has generated a need for new instruments which are able to account for particular teaching practices like posing active learning instances or generating a positive classroom climate [17].

Regarding the observation of Science, Technology, Engineering, and Mathematics (STEM) lessons, one widely used instrument is the Classroom Observation Protocol for Undergraduate STEM (COPUS) [22]. COPUS aims to fulfill three objectives: characterizing the general state of teaching, providing feedback to instructors who desire information about how they and their students spend class time, and identify faculty professional development needs. Although this tool was developed for observing undergraduate STEM lessons, it has also been proven to be suitable for analyzing teaching practices in middle and high school [2]. Besides, since COPUS only focuses on teachers and students' plain actions without judging the cognitive level of the activities, and because these actions are also present in elementary school environments [23], we deemed it sufficient for our classification purposes. Moreover, one of the advantages of this tool is the minimal amount of training time that observers needs to ensure high values of Inter Rater Reliability when classifying teacher and student actions, which is around 1.5 h of training [22].

Nonetheless, despite the advantages of COPUS, the observation procedure presents several detriments. First, the observer effect affects teachers' development of a lesson, making the observation procedure biased [20], [18]. Second, since observers need to watch the whole lesson, potentially multiple times, to annotate it, this procedure becomes heavily time consuming. In addition, even when using validated instruments, multiple observers are required to achieve high reliability for a single lesson [3]. Third, the observers need to go through a training period before using this tool, which on top makes the procedure inherently expensive. These considerations make traditional classroom observation unfeasible for analyzing large volumes of lessons or providing teachers timely and continuous feedback.

The observation procedure is usually accompanied with video or audio recordings. Considering this, many researchers have tried to automate the analysis of teachers' talk using machine learning approaches and features extracted from these recordings. For example, [25] used the Learning Environment Analysis (LENA) system [8] and a Random Forest (RF) model to classify elementary school recordings as teacher lecturing, whole-class discussion, and student group work. [7] used linguistic, acoustic, and prosodic features in combination with multiple supervised models to automate the detection of teacher questions. [19] developed an automated model for decibel analysis using decision trees and identified different teaching patterns related to active learning situations by analyzing the mean volume and its standard deviation along the lessons. [5] used log Mel filterbanks along with the signal energy to train several Neural Networks for the task of labelling segments of the lessons as single voice, multiple voice, no voice or noise. Later, [16] proposed a multimodal attention mechanism for recognizing speaker roles (either teacher or student) in classrooms that combines speech and language information.

These studies have shown the potential of Machine Learning methods to automate the detection of different aspects of teaching. However, many of these approaches do not classify classroom practices according to a validated protocol, or they just focus on discerning whether teachers or students are speaking. Additionally, most of previous work relies on expensive equipment, which makes scaling these approaches to a large population of teachers, while giving them continuous feedback, more difficult. These considerations give rise to our main research question:

RQ: To what extent can we infer important characteristics of teachers' practices using a non-intrusive and scalable multimodal approach?

To answer this question, we studied how to effectively combine separately proposed acoustic-based and transcription-based approaches to improve their accuracy and discriminative power, while maintaining their scalability and cost-effectiveness. The acoustic-based approach consisted on a Random Forest (RF) model that used the mean and standard deviation of spectral representations from recordings to classify the three collapsed COPUS categories (*Presenting, Guiding*, and *Administration*) which are derived from the teacher section of COPUS [23]. On the other hand, the transcription-based method consisted of a deep network that is able to extract latent features from lesson transcriptions to recognize teacher activities.

To combine these approaches, we developed the multimodal learning model Teacher Activity Recognizer from Transcriptions and Audio (TARTA), a multimodal approach that detects the three COPUS collapsed categories. TARTA has a deep network architecture which is able to obtain latent features from transcriptions, while incorporating descriptive statistics of spectral representations from audio in an early fusion fashion to detect teacher's activities. We compared the performance of TARTA against different baselines including the acoustic- and text-only approaches, and a late fusion multimodal model of these two. We applied our methodology to 41 mathematics lessons from 18 fourth grade teachers. Our results reveal that TARTA outperforms models trained on each separate source and their late fusion. Moreover, we found that using this approach it is also possible to detect the underrepresented *Administration* category in our dataset, while other models systematically reject it. This way, TARTA is able to automatically capture different teaching practices derived from COPUS in a cost-effective way. Thus, we expect that our work can be useful for teachers and stakeholders, as our model is capable of analyzing multiple lessons in short periods of time in a non-intrusive and effortless way with high accuracy and discriminative power.

2   Methodology

2.1   Dataset

Our dataset consists of 41 fourth grade mathematics lessons from low Socio-Economic Status schools in Chile. The implementation involved a total of 18 teachers, where the number of recordings per teacher varied from one to 11, while their length ranged from 18 to 77 min. Audio was recorded using Rode SmartLav+ microphones connected to teachers' smartphones at a bit rate of 44.1 kHz. Additionally, a smartphone application developed for helping observers register classroom observations [15] was used by them to annotate teachers' activities along the lessons according to COPUS protocol in a continuous way. The observers had a training session on both the app usage and protocol and each lesson was annotated by one observer. Afterward, each observation was tagged with the ID of the corresponding recording, its code of the COPUS protocol, and the timestamps for the beginning and the end, both with respect to the start of the observation. Later, the original 12 COPUS codes related to teaching practices were compiled into the four categories proposed by [23]: *Presenting, Guiding/Feedback, Administration,* and *Other* (see Table 2 in [23] for details). Thus, the initial dataset consisted of 41 recordings corresponding to 34 h of audio with their respective and synchronized COPUS observations. Due to the lack of representation of *Other* (2.3%) in the dataset and because 10 (out of the 12) COPUS codes related to teaching practices were covered by the other three categories, we decided to drop this category from the following analyses.

2.2   Preprocessing and Feature Engineering

To prepare the data, the 41 lesson recordings were chunked into 15-second segments, obtaining a total of 8107. Subsequently, text and acoustic features were extracted for each segment from transcriptions and recordings, respectively.

Text Features. First, to obtain the text features of each segment these were automatically transcribed using the Google Speech API [1] and synchronized with the observations. Next, in order to provide the models contextualized information, each transcribed segment is concatenated with the 3 previous and 3 next transcribed segments of the lesson. In the cases where some of the segments in the context window do not exist (e.g.: at the beginning or end of the lesson) the context window is filled with the last available one. In this way, the models were provided a longer input sequence with previous and future context that we denote $\mathbf{X}_T$. This sequence was later tokenized using the BERT tokenizer from HuggingFace's [26] Spanish BERT model [4], and padded to a maximum of 120 tokens. Additionally, for each segment in our data set we calculated the number of words n_{words} and its relative position r across the transcription.

Acoustic Features. To represent the audio, we calculated two widely used spectral representations for each segment, which have been considered the state-of-the-art for several audio processing tasks: a 64-band Mel-scaled spectrogram and the first 13 components of the Mel Frequency Cepstral Coefficients (MFCC).

Next, several descriptive statistic are computed along each band of the Mel spectrogram and each component of the MFCC. Related approaches have been proven to achieve good performance in similar audio processing tasks [12,19,21]. The statistics include minima and maxima along every band/component; first, second, and third quartiles; mean and standard deviation; and a vectorization of the covariance matrix across the different bands/components. Finally, we add context by concatenating these same features calculated for the previous and next segments. We denote the set of acoustic features as $\mathbf{X}_A$.

Table 1. COPUS categories and examples in our dataset of segments transcriptions belonging to each category, obtained through Google Speech API.

Category	Segment transcription example (translated)
Presenting	"Mixed number is made up of a whole number plus a proper fraction these numbers allow us to express quantities greater than an integer How it was"
Guiding	"Ready you saw that it was easy someone still has doubts Matías What happened"
Administration	"They have to go for lunch it is 11 o'clock with 2 min that you have to give away please"

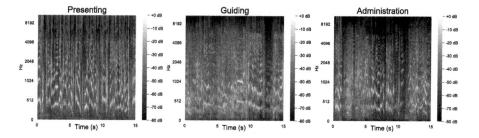

Fig. 1. Mel spectrograms of the segment examples presented in Table 1.

Once the features were calculated, each segment was tagged with boolean labels corresponding to the COPUS categories by synchronizing the timestamps of the observations and the recordings at a 15-second resolution. It is important to mention that one segment can belong simultaneously to more than one category, or not belong to any of them. Moreover, the segments that presented none of the categories were not considered for the models as those should have at least been marked as *Other* instances. Therefore, we could not trust these as true negative samples for any category. Thus, the final dataset consisted of 7682 samples with positive sample ratios of 30.1%, 63.4%, and 10.7% for *Presenting*, *Guiding*, and *Administration*. Table 1 and Fig. 1 show examples of transcribed segments and their respective Mel spectrograms that were classified by the observers as *Presenting*, *Guiding*, and *Administration*; respectively.

2.3 Framework

In this work we explored two different techniques for combining multimodal information: early and late fusion. Since the compiled categories are not disjoint along the lessons, we formulate this problem as a binary classification problem for each category: *Presenting*, *Guiding* and *Administration*. Both techniques, together with unimodal baseline models, are explained with more detail below:

Early Fusion Model. In this approach acoustic ($\mathbf{X}_A$) and text features ($\mathbf{X}_T$) are used as inputs for a classification model. Mathematically, an early fusion model corresponds to a function $\hat{f}$ such that:

$$\hat{f}(\mathbf{X}_A, \mathbf{X}_T) = y_E \tag{1}$$

where y_E is, again, a score estimating the presence of the COPUS category in the respective segment. In this work we proposed to model $\hat{f}$ through a deep network model to which we refer as Teacher Activity Recognizer from Transcriptions and Audio (TARTA). TARTA possesses an embedding, encoding and attention layer that automatically obtain latent futures from the text input features $\mathbf{X}_T$, which are later combined with the acoustic features $\mathbf{X}_A$ to recognize categories from the segments. Figure 2 summarizes the procedure for developing and assessing TARTA's performance. We give a brief explanation of its layers below:

1. **Embedding Layer**: This layer maps each token of the tokens sequence obtained from $\mathbf{X}_T$ into a high dimensional embedding vector. We initialized this layer with the word embeddings given by Spanish BERT's [4] first embedding layer weights (of dimension 768). We set this layer's weights to be non-trainable to reduce the number of parameters of the model.
2. **Encoder Layer**: This encoder reduces the embedding vectors' dimensionality from 768 to 10 by applying a linear function modeled by a Single Layer Perceptron (SLP) with output dimension 10 and linear activation to each of the previous word embeddings.
3. **Attention Layer**: This layer performs a soft-selection of the relevant vectors in the sequence by applying SLP with output dimension 1 and linear activation to each of output vectors of the encoder layer, and thus obtaining a sequence unidimensional weights. A softmax layer is applied to this sequence to obtain a probability distribution, which can be interpreted as the attention probability of each token of the original text input sequence $\mathbf{X}_T$. Later, a weighted sum of the encoded vectors is performed, where the weight of each vector corresponds to the respective attention probability. The result is then a single vector of dimension 10, noted as $\mathbf{h}_T$.
4. **Batch Normalization Layer**: after the action of previous layers, the last vector is concatenated with the acoustic features $\mathbf{X}_A$. Moreover, the respective number of words n_{words} and relative position r features are also added at this point, resulting into the vector $[\mathbf{h}_T, \mathbf{X}_A, n_{words}, r]$. Subsequently, this vector is fed into a Batch Normalization (BN) layer that aims to regularize the model by re-centering and re-scaling the features [11].

5. **Fully Connected Layers**: Once the last vector is passed through the BN, the output is fed into a Feed Forward Neural Network (FFNN) consisting of one fully connected layer with 64 neurons, ReLu activation function and dropout regularization [24] with 0.2 rate, followed by an output layer with sigmoid activation function. The output corresponds to the score (y_E) that the model gives to an input for belonging to the COPUS category in question.

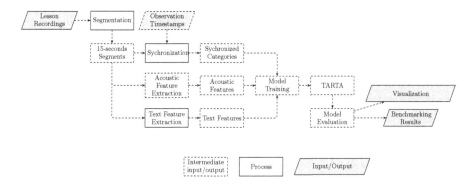

Fig. 2. Pipeline explaining the procedure for developing TARTA.

Unimodal Baselines. In order to compare the results of our early fusion model, separate acoustic- and transcription-based baselines were used. A previous acoustic-based model presented in [21] based on acoustic features and a RF to which we refer in this work as AUDIO+RF was used for this purpose. Additionally, a deep network that follows the same architecture of TARTA with the exception of the acoustic features was also considered. More explicitly, this model only uses $\mathbf{X}_T$, n_{words} and r as inputs, and differs from TARTA at the BN layer, in which it concatenates $\mathbf{h}_T$ only with n_{words} and r.

We accordingly named this model as Teacher Activity Recognizer from Transcriptions (TART). Furthermore, we used a BERT model [6] fine tuned for text classification with input $\mathbf{X}_T$ and BOW+LR, a bag-of-words and Logistic Regression (LR) approach with input $\mathbf{X}_T$ as unimodal transcription-based baselines.

Late Fusion Model. This approach consists in using score outputs from an acoustic- and a transcription-based models as features for predicting the presence of COPUS categories. More precisely, let y_A and y_T be the score outputs of previously trained acoustic- and transcription-based models respectively, for a particular segment and COPUS category. A late fusion model corresponds to a function f such that:

$$f(y_A, y_T) = y_L \tag{2}$$

where y_L is another score estimating the presence of the COPUS category in the respective segment. In this work we used AUDIO+RF [21] to obtain the acoustic-based score outputs y_A, and TART for obtaining the transcription-based score outputs y_T, as well as a LR for modeling f. We called this late fusion model Late-LR and we used it as a multimodal baseline.

3   Results

3.1   Benchmarking of the Different Models

To train and evaluate our models, we partitioned our data set in three sections: training, validation and test sets, selecting the target values according to the COPUS category we aim to predict. As the test set, we selected two teachers, one male and one female, each one with only one recording in our dataset. This way no other lecture of these teachers is present in the training or validation set. We made this to avoid biasing the models on a particular teacher's behavior and evaluating the models' generalization power on unseen teachers. For the validation set we randomly selected one of the remaining lectures, while for the training set we used all the rest. In total, the training set consisted in 7185 instances, while the validation and test sets in 153 and 344 instances respectively. Next, we trained TARTA with binary cross-entropy as a loss function. In addition, we used an early stopping regularization method, monitoring the loss on the validation set during the training process. On the other hand, the late fusion model was trained using training and validation sets through a 10-fold stratified cross-validation for hyper-parameter tuning [14]. Finally, we looked for a threshold level t so that any instance with a predicted score above this level ($y_{score} \geq t$) will be considered as a positive prediction, whereas all instances with a lower predicted score ($y_{score} < t$) will be considered negative predictions. Using the model's scores over the training and validation set, we determined an optimal threshold t_{opt} which maximizes the accuracy over these sets through a grid search. This same threshold level was used for the test set predictions to obtain the accuracy, precision and recall metrics for each COPUS category. Table 2 shows the performance metrics of these models over the test set. Results show that TARTA outperforms all other models in AUC and accuracy across the three categories, while obtaining relatively high precision and recall values. Particularly, for the underrepresented *Administration* category, TARTA achieved high AUC, precision and recall values, while most of other models are not able to effectively recognize this category (see Fig. 3 for a graphical intuition).

3.2   Prediction Score Curves

Figure 3 illustrates the scores of TARTA for the first lesson in our test set, as well as the scores of AUDIO+RF, TART, and Late-LR. In particular, Fig. 3c shows that TARTA's scores for *Administration* presents peaks at the beginning and at the end of the lesson, where this category was observed. In contrast, other models predict nearly constant scores along the lesson. This illustrates the high AUC of TARTA (0.95) compared to other models. Moreover, Fig. 3a represents how the multimodal approaches (TARTA and Late-LR) outperform separate acoustic-

Table 2. Performance metrics (AUC: Area Under Curve, Acc: accuracy, P: Precision, R: Recall) for each category over the test set.

Model	Presenting				Guiding				Administration			
	AUC	Acc	P	R	AUC	Acc	P	R	AUC	Acc	P	R
TARTA	**0.93**	**0.88**	0.64	**0.86**	**0.92**	**0.88**	0.93	0.90	**0.95**	**0.96**	**0.50**	**0.60**
Late-LR	0.92	**0.88**	**0.69**	0.77	0.90	0.83	**0.97**	0.81	0.69	**0.96**	0.00	0.00
TART	0.88	0.81	0.52	0.78	0.90	0.78	**0.97**	0.73	0.64	**0.96**	0.00	0.00
BERT	0.81	0.78	0.47	0.70	0.83	0.69	0.94	0.64	0.66	0.94	0.00	0.00
BOW+LR	0.68	0.74	0.40	0.57	0.68	0.70	0.87	0.71	0.55	0.94	0.18	0.13
AUDIO+RF	0.88	0.86	0.52	0.78	0.81	0.83	0.87	**0.91**	0.61	**0.96**	0.00	0.00

and transcription-based models in *Presenting*. In fact, TARTA's and Late-LR's scores are generally higher than those of TART and AUDIO+RF during the observed blocks of the category, while being relatively lower after minute 30, where *Presenting* was not observed. Again, this is reflected on the high AUC scores of multimodal models (over 0.92) compared to the rest.

4   Discussion

In summary, we have presented the development and assessment of TARTA, a multimodal model that combines acoustic features and teachers' talk transcriptions to classify their activities into three collapsed categories (*Presenting*, *Guiding* and *Administration*) from the COPUS protocol. In particular, we have shown that our model is able detect these categories with high accuracy and discriminative power (over 0.88 of accuracy and 0.92 of AUC), outperforming acoustic- and text-only models. TARTA can also recognize an underrepresented category (*Administration*), while other models systematically reject it. In addition, we have shown that a simple late fusion approach, such as Late-LR, also achieves better performance than separate acoustic- and transcription-based models.

Nonetheless, our approach is not exempt of limitations. One important caveat we found it was the limited amount of annotated data available to build a Deep Network model like TARTA, which makes it difficult to accurately estimate its generalization potential as in [19] or [5]. However, we carefully selected a test set to estimate the potential of TARTA to classify unseen teachers. Furthermore, we think on applying the presented method to other educational levels and STEM subjects as future research. In addition, we seek to explore other multimodal approaches for teacher activity recognition, such as attention mechanisms, as they have been shown to achieve high performance in a coarser task [16].

Finally, our work sets forth two key contributions. First, our models are trained using annotations from a validated protocol, which allows us to classify different teacher activities instead of detecting only their voices or their students'. Secondly, our approach only relies on inexpensive lavalier microphones connected to teachers' smartphones, which makes it cost-effective and feasible for large

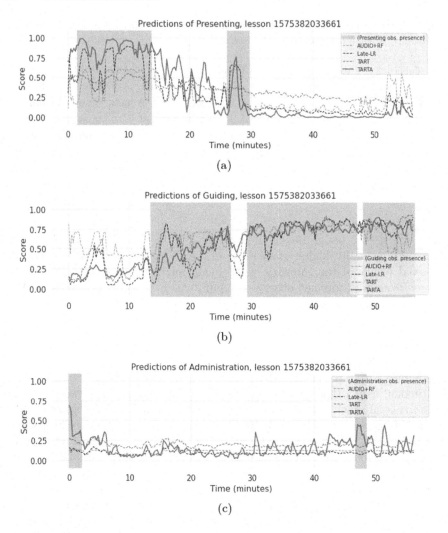

Fig. 3. Prediction scores of our models for each category in the first lesson of the test set. Blue segments indicate the presence of the category according to the observer. The red line indicates the evolution of TARTA's score along the lesson, while dashlines correspond to other models. (Color figure online)

scale studies and processing large amounts of data. We expect this work can serve in the future as a tool for teachers to get timely and continuous feedback regarding their time management during the lessons, but also to a variety of stakeholders and researchers who would like a quick general view about how teachers distribute time according to particular practices.

References

1. Speech-to-text: automatic speech recognition; google cloud, https://cloud.google.com/speech/
2. Akiha, K., et al.: What types of instructional shifts do students experience? Investigating active learning in science, technology, engineering, and math classes across key transition points from middle school to the university level. Front. Educ. **2**, 68 (2018)
3. Brian, K.: OECD Insights Human Capital How what you know shapes your life: how what you know shapes your life. OECD publishing (2007)
4. Canete, J., Chaperon, G., Fuentes, R., Pérez, J.: Spanish pre-trained bert model and evaluation data. PML4DC at ICLR **2020** (2020)
5. Cosbey, R., Wusterbarth, A., Hutchinson, B.: Deep learning for classroom activity detection from audio. In: ICASSP 2019–2019 IEEE International Conference on Acoustics, Speech and Signal Processing (ICASSP), pp. 3727–3731. IEEE (2019)
6. Devlin, J., Chang, M.W., Lee, K., Toutanova, K.: Bert: Pre-training of deep bidirectional transformers for language understanding. arXiv preprint arXiv:1810.04805 (2018)
7. Donnelly, P.J., Blanchard, N., Olney, A.M., Kelly, S., Nystrand, M., D'Mello, S.K.: Words matter: automatic detection of teacher questions in live classroom discourse using linguistics, acoustics, and context. In: Proceedings of the Seventh International Learning Analytics & Knowledge Conference, pp. 218–227 (2017)
8. Ford, M., Baer, C.T., Xu, D., Yapanel, U., Gray, S.: The lenatm language environment analysis system (2008)
9. Hill, H., Grossman, P.: Learning from teacher observations: challenges and opportunities posed by new teacher evaluation systems. Harv. Educ. Rev. **83**(2), 371–384 (2013)
10. Hill, H.C., Charalambous, C.Y., Kraft, M.A.: When rater reliability is not enough: teacher observation systems and a case for the generalizability study. Educ. Res. **41**(2), 56–64 (2012)
11. Ioffe, S., Szegedy, C.: Batch normalization: accelerating deep network training by reducing internal covariate shift. In: International conference on machine learning, pp. 448–456. PMLR (2015)
12. James, A., et al.: Automated classification of classroom climate by audio analysis. In: D'Haro, L.F., Banchs, R.E., Li, H. (eds.) 9th International Workshop on Spoken Dialogue System Technology. LNEE, vol. 579, pp. 41–49. Springer, Singapore (2019). https://doi.org/10.1007/978-981-13-9443-0_4
13. Kelly, S., Olney, A.M., Donnelly, P., Nystrand, M., D'Mello, S.K.: Automatically measuring question authenticity in real-world classrooms. Educ. Res. **47**(7), 451–464 (2018)
14. Kohavi, R., et al.: A study of cross-validation and bootstrap for accuracy estimation and model selection. In: Ijcai, vol. 14, pp. 1137–1145. Montreal, Canada (1995)
15. Kronholm, H., Caballero, D., Araya, R., Viiri, J.: A smartphone application for ASR and observation of classroom interactions. In: Finnish Mathematics and Science Education Research Association (FMSERA) Annual Symposium (2016)
16. Li, H., et al.: Multimodal learning for classroom activity detection. In: ICASSP 2020–2020 IEEE International Conference on Acoustics, Speech and Signal Processing (ICASSP), pp. 9234–9238. IEEE (2020)
17. McDonald, M., Kazemi, E., Kavanagh, S.S.: Core practices and pedagogies of teacher education: a call for a common language and collective activity. J. Teach. Educ. **64**(5), 378–386 (2013)

18. McIntyre, D.J.: Teacher evaluation and the observer effect. NASSP Bull. **64**(434), 36–40 (1980)
19. Owens, M.T., et al.: Classroom sound can be used to classify teaching practices in college science courses. Proc. Natl. Acad. Sci. **114**(12), 3085–3090 (2017)
20. Samph, T.: Observer effects on teacher behavior (1968)
21. Schlotterbeck, D., Uribe, P., Araya, R., Jimenez, A., Caballero, D.: What classroom audio tells about teaching: a cost-effective approach for detection of teaching practices using spectral audio features. In: LAK21: 11th International Learning Analytics and Knowledge Conference, pp. 132–140 (2021)
22. Smith, M.K., Jones, F.H., Gilbert, S.L., Wieman, C.E.: The classroom observation protocol for undergraduate stem (COPUS): a new instrument to characterize university stem classroom practices. CBE-Life Sci. Educ. **12**(4), 618–627 (2013)
23. Smith, M.K., Vinson, E.L., Smith, J.A., Lewin, J.D., Stetzer, M.R.: A campus-wide study of stem courses: new perspectives on teaching practices and perceptions. CBE-Life Sci. Educ. **13**(4), 624–635 (2014)
24. Srivastava, N., Hinton, G., Krizhevsky, A., Sutskever, I., Salakhutdinov, R.: Dropout: a simple way to prevent neural networks from overfitting. J. Mach. Learn. Res. **15**(1), 1929–1958 (2014)
25. Wang, Z., Pan, X., Miller, K.F., Cortina, K.S.: Automatic classification of activities in classroom discourse. Comput. Educ. **78**, 115–123 (2014)
26. Wolf, T., et al.: Huggingface's transformers: State-of-the-art natural language processing (2019). arXiv preprint arXiv:1910.03771

Assessing Algorithmic Fairness in Automatic Classifiers of Educational Forum Posts

Lele Sha[1,3], Mladen Rakovic[1,3], Alexander Whitelock-Wainwright[1,2],
David Carroll[1,2], Victoria M. Yew[1,2,3], Dragan Gasevic[1,3],
and Guanliang Chen[1,3(✉)]

[1] Centre for Learning Analytics at Monash, Faculty of Information Technology,
Monash University, Melbourne, Australia
{lele.sha1,mladen.rakovic,alex.wainwright,david.carroll,
dragan.gasevic,guanliang.chen}@monash.edu
[2] Deputy Vice-Chancellor Education, Monash University, Melbourne, Australia
[3] Department of Data Science and Artificial Intelligence, Faculty of Information
Technology, Monash University, Melbourne, Australia

Abstract. Automatic classifiers of educational forum posts are essential in helping instructors effectively implement their teaching practices and thus have been widely investigated. However, existing studies mostly stressed the *accuracy* of a classifier, while the *fairness* of the classifier remains largely unexplored, i.e., whether the posts generated by a group of students are more likely to be correctly labeled than those generated by other groups of students. Undoubtedly, any unfairness based on student performance, sex, or other subjective views can have a detrimental effect on a student's learning experience and performance. Therefore, this study aimed to assess the algorithmic fairness of six popular models used in building automatic classifiers of educational forum posts. Here, we measured the algorithmic fairness displayed (i) between students of different sex (female vs. male) and (ii) between students of different first languages (English-as-first-language speakers vs. English-as-second-language speakers). Besides, we investigated whether a classifier's fairness could be enhanced by applying data sampling techniques. Our results demonstrated that: 1) traditional Machine Learning models slightly outperformed up-to-date Deep Learning models in delivering fair predictions; 2) students of different first languages faced more unfair predictions than students of different sex, and most of the classifiers tended to favor English-as-first-language students; and 3) with equal numbers of posts generated by different groups of students in the training data, the fairness of a classifier could be greatly enhanced.

Keywords: Educational forum post · Text classification · Algorithmic fairness

© Springer Nature Switzerland AG 2021
I. Roll et al. (Eds.): AIED 2021, LNAI 12748, pp. 381–394, 2021.
https://doi.org/10.1007/978-3-030-78292-4_31

1   Introduction

Students in online courses are afforded opportunities to earn university credentials while learning remotely in a self-directed manner. Unlike traditional in-person classes, regular communication between course instructors and individual students in online courses is often sparse [26,27], despite the documented benefits of instructor's presence [23]. For this reason, many students in online classes feel deprived of necessary guidance and support [22]. This often hinders students' satisfaction and learning performance in an online course [24]. Communication among students themselves in an online learning environment has been considered a remedy for an instructor's absence [47,49]. A sense of community that students build in online discussion forums boosts their engagement and satisfaction in a course [36,43,49]. Importantly, productive forum discussions that unfold throughout a semester have been shown to benefit learning gains [44]. It is, therefore, critical for online students to create course-relevant discussion posts. To this end, educators need to continuously monitor discussion boards, identify posts that require instructors' urgent attention (e.g., posts asking questions related to the course learning content) and provide timely support to students. This is, however, a time-consuming task in many online courses, given an abundant number of posts typically created on discussion boards.

To address this challenge, educational researchers have developed a number of classifiers to automatically identify content-relevant and content-irrelevant discussion posts (whether the post content is related to knowledge taught in a course). To our knowledge, both traditional Machine Learning (ML) models, e.g., Random Forests, and up-to-date Deep Learning (DL) models, e.g., Long Short-Term Memory Neural Network (LSTM), have been exploited for this classification task [2,6,9,13,17,18,21,42,50,52,54]). While many of these models have demonstrated attractive classification accuracy, none of them has reported classification performance evaluated relative to different demographic groups in the student sample. Given the raising concerns about algorithmic unfairness of predictive models in educational research [19] and widely documented discrepancies in retention between female and male students, particularly in STEM courses [16,40], and cognitive and social barriers that many English-as-second-language speakers face when communicating about topics taught in English [20,32,34,39], we posit that the development of more inclusive educational technologies grounded in fair classification models that perform equally well across all groups of students, including their sex and first-language backgrounds, should be an important next step in the educational research agenda.

With this in mind, this study set out to assess not only the accuracy but also the fairness of popular models used to construct automatic classifiers of educational forum posts, including four ML models and two DL models. In particular, the fairness of these models was measured by distinguishing students of different sex and first-language backgrounds. Through extensive evaluations, we demonstrated that classifiers of educational forum posts were prone to algorithmic unfairness in classifying posts created by students of different sex and first languages. To address model unfairness, we explored the viability of equal sampling of the observed demographic groups in the model training process. Our results indicated that most of the models improved their fairness, suggesting that equal sampling can be an important step in the future development of fair classifiers of educational forum posts.

2 Related Work

Educational Forum Post Classification. Research efforts in predictive modeling for educational forum posts have generally relied upon traditional ML or DL models. Among traditional ML models, researchers have frequently used Random Forests [2,5,18,30,35,37], Support Vector Machine (SVM) [5,13,17,28,35,38,42, 53], Logistic Regression [1,2,35,52,56,58], and Naïve Bayes [4,5,35]. It should be noted that these models were often based on features engineered by experts. For instance, when applying Random Forests to classify forum posts by levels of cognitive presence, researchers in [18] designed 87 different features as proxies for cognitive presence, e.g., the length of a post, the semantic similarity between posts, number of replies a post received, and frequency of words indicative of different psychological processes. All together, these features enabled the Random Forest classifier to achieve a Cohen's κ score of 0.72. As another example, Cui et al. [13] engineered post features including unigrams and bigrams of a post text, the number of views and votes a post attracted, part-of-speech tags; they used these features to create an SVM classifier to distinguish content-relevant posts from content-irrelevant ones to assist instructors to identify posts that require urgent attention in MOOC discussion forums. With the SVM classifier, about 86% of forum posts were accurately identified.

In recent years, driven by the great success achieved by DL models in tackling various prediction tasks, a growing number of researchers has opted for DL models to classify educational forum posts [3,9,11,12,21,50,54]. Compared to traditional ML models, DL models do not require domain experts to carefully design features as input. Instead, DL models can take the raw text of a post as input and make use of the powerful affordances of deep neural networks to implicitly capture features that are important to correctly classify a post. For example, one of the pioneering studies that applied DL models was reported in [50]. Specifically, the authors in [50] developed ConvL, a DL classifier that identifies different levels of urgency, confusion, and sentiment in educational forum posts. The classifier development involved two important steps. Firstly, the researchers applied CNN to derive contextual features related to a post and, secondly, used LSTM to capture sequential relationships between these features for classification. Evaluated on the dataset with more than 30 thousand educational forum posts, ConvL achieved accuracy between 81% and 87%. Other relevant studies that applied DL models for post classifications tasks, typically, relied on CNN, LSTM, or variants of these two models [54]. Moreover, a recent study reported in [12] demonstrated that, even when the size of annotated data is insufficient to support the training of DL models, pre-trained language models, e.g., BERT [14], could be exploited to empower those DL models for post classification. Specifically, the researchers in [12] showed that, by simply coupling only one classification neural network layer on top of the output of BERT, the classification accuracy could be boosted up to to 92%. Though researchers have achieved great advances in constructing accurate classifiers of educational forum posts, it remains largely unknown whether these classifiers generate equally accurate predictions to different groups of students. To our knowledge, our study is the first to investigate the problem of fairness in constructing post classifiers. To this end, we assessed the capability of a total of six different models in generating both accurate and fair classification results for different groups of students, which were created as per their sex (female and male) and first-language background (English-as-first-language vs English-as-second-language speakers).

Fairness-Aware Machine Learning Models in Education. As witnessed by the establishment of the ACM Conference on Fairness, Accountability, and Transparency in 2018, one of the recent foci in the broader ML community is to assess algorithmic unfairness of different intelligent systems and investigate approaches for alleviating the negative impacts brought by such algorithmic unfairness. In the educational research field, a few studies have been carried out to investigate the fairness of existing predictive modeling techniques used to support educational practices [15,19,48,55]. Typically, these studies have focused on evaluating the fairness of predictive models that modeled student performance [19,25,31]. For example, Gardner et al. [19] proposed the Absolute Between-ROC Area (ABROCA) metric to measure the unfairness of a predictive model as its differential prediction accuracy between different groups of students. Compared to other group fairness metrics (e.g., a demographic parity measure), ABROCA was designed based on equalized odds which ensures equal false and true positive rates among baseline and comparison classes, and therefore avoids individual unfair outcomes in the group fairness measure. By applying ABROCA, Gardner et al. [19] evaluated the unfairness of five mainstream models developed to predict the likelihood of a student to complete a Massive Open Online Course (MOOC). In addition to MOOC education, a group of similar studies has been conducted in other educational settings like higher education [25,29,31,57] and virtual learning environments [41]. In a different vein, Doroudi and Brunskill [15] investigated whether the existing models used for knowledge tracing generate inequitable results for different groups of students and found that the additive factor model was superior to the Bayesian knowledge tracing algorithm and the N-Consecutive Correct Responses heuristic algorithm in delivering fair predictions. Besides, Loukina et al. [32] first discussed different types of fairness that could be applied to evaluate ML models used in educational research, and then utilised both simulated and real datasets to depict how models used for automated scoring of English language proficiency tests might disadvantage students whose first language was not English.

3   Method

3.1   Dataset

The dataset used in this study comprised 3,703 randomly-selected discussion posts created by students in the Learning Management System Moodle at Monash University. The topics covered by these posts included arts, design, business, economics, computer science, and mechanical engineering. Here, we differentiated posts as *content-relevant* (e.g., "What is poly-nominal regression?") and *content-irrelevant* (e.g., "When is the due date to submit the second assignment?"). All posts were first manually labeled by a junior teaching staff and then reviewed by two senior teaching staff to ensure the reliability of the derived labels. The dataset contains 2,339 (63%) content-relevant posts and 1,364 (37%) content-irrelevant posts. Additionally, we obtained for each post a student's demographic information, i.e., sex (female or male) and first language (any language). Inspired by [32], which demonstrated that English-as-second-language speakers could be disadvantaged by algorithms used for assessing their learning performance, we transformed the first language categorical variable to a binary form, i.e., English-as-first-language speakers vs. English-as-second-language speakers. The descriptive statistics of the dataset are given in Table 1, based on which we can observe that female students tended to generate more elaborated posts than male students and, similarly, the posts generated by English-as-first-language students were likely to compose more words than those generated by English-as-second-language students.

Table 1. The descriptive statistics of the dataset used in this study. The columns **Male**, **Female**, **First language**, and **Second language** show the number of forum posts generated by students who are male, female, English-as-first-language speakers, and English-as-second-language speakers, respectively.

	All	Male	Female	First language	Second language
# Posts	3,703	1,478	2,225	1,585	2,112
# Words	485,737	171,768	308,087	230,806	254,931
# Avg. words/post	131.39	116.77	138.90	145.62	120.71
# Unique words	268,824	97,004	170,171	125,297	143,527
# Avg. unique words/post	72.71	65.94	76.72	79.05	67.96

3.2   Model Selection

As summarized in Sect. 2, both traditional ML models and up-to-date DL models have been exploited to construct automatic classifiers of educational forum posts.

Therefore, to enable a comprehensive evaluation, we selected the representative models from both of the two categories in this study.

Traditional ML Models. Four traditional ML models were evaluated in this study, namely Naïve Bayes, SVM, Random Forests, and Logistic regression. These models have been widely applied in the context of educational forum classification in previous studies [2,10,18,33,53]. Relying upon an extensive feature engineering, these models achieved high classification accuracy. To ensure the ML models in our study were comparable with models reported in previous studies, we replicated the feature engineering process used in previous models, including (i) the top-1000 most frequent unigrams and bigrams contained in the discussion posts [2,13,38,46,51,52,58]; (ii) the length of a post [35,42,53,58]; (iii) the TF-IDF (term frequency-inverse document frequency) score related to each selected unigram [2,5]; (iv) the frequency of words indicating different psychological processes along with each post (e.g., affects and cognitive process), which were extracted with the aid of LIWC [2,10,18,30,33,37,53]; (v) scores extracted by applying Coh-Metrix to indicate text coherence, linguistic complexity, text readability, and lexical category [30,37], and (vi) the LSA score indicating the average sentence similarity within a post [30]. In total, 3180 features were engineered as input to the four traditional ML models.

DL Models. Existing studies based on DL models typically made use of two types of deep neural networks, i.e., Bi-directional LSTM (Bi-LSTM) [9,21,54] and CNN-LSTM [21,50,54]. However, it should be noted that the training of these complex neural networks often requires a large amount of annotated data (tens of thousands at least). In recent years, the development of pre-trained language models (e.g., BERT [14]) enabled researchers to exploit the power of these complex neural networks even when there is only a small amount of annotated data available. In more details, a widely-adopted method is to couple a task model (e.g., Bi-LSTM and CNN-LSTM in our case) on top of the output layer of BERT and then use the annotated data to co-train BERT and the task model as a whole to produce the classification results. Given the limited number of annotated posts in our dataset, we also used BERT to empower Bi-LSTM and CNN-LSTM for our classification task.

3.3 Evaluation Metrics

Accuracy Metrics. In line with previous studies on constructing automatic classifiers of educational forum posts, we adopted the following four metrics to measure the prediction accuracy of a classifier: Accuracy, Cohen's κ, AUC, and F1 score.

Fairness Metrics. To our knowledge, [19] was the first study which attempted to investigate appropriate metrics to evaluate the fairness of predictive models in the field of educational research. Specifically, a metric called Absolute Between-ROC Area (ABROCA) was presented in [19] to measure the prediction unfairness of a predictive model against different demographic groups, which is calculated by finding the definite integral between the ROC curves of the two observed groups. Noticeably, ABROCA has two advantages: 1) ABROCA accounts for performance difference across the entire range of thresholds, which is superior over other fixed-threshold approaches; and 2) ABROCA can be easily computed from prediction results with no need for collecting additional data or computing additional metrics. Therefore, we also used this metric in our study. Notice here, the lower an ABROCA value is, the less algorithmic unfairness a predictive model has.

3.4   Study Setup

Text Pre-Processing. We pre-process the text contained in a post by performing the following steps: 1) removing invalid characters; 2) removing stopwords; and 3) applying word stemming with the help of the Python package NLTK [8].

Model Implementation. We used the Python package scikit-learn to implement the traditional ML models. To develop DL models, we first generated text embeddings by using the tool Bert-as-service[1]. Next, we implemented CNN-LSTM and Bi-LSTM by replicating model parameters reported in previous studies [9,21,50,54]. In CNN-LSTM, we used 128 convolution filters with the width of 5. For both CNN-LSTM and Bi-LSTM, (i) we set the number of hidden units used in the final classification layer to 1 and L2 regularization lambda to 0.001, and utilised sigmoid as the activation function; (ii) the LSTM layer was set to have 128 hidden states and 128 cell states; (iii) we set the batch size to 32 and the maximum input text to 512; (iv) we applied the one cycle policy for training and set the maximum learning rate to 2e-05; (v) the dropout probability was set to 0.5; and (vi) we opted for 50 maximum training epochs with shuffling performed at the end of each epoch together with early stopping mechanism.

Model Training. Prior to training a model, we first randomly selected 20% of the available posts as the testing data, and then prepared the training data from the remaining posts. It is worth noting that, as reported in Table 1, the number of posts generated by female and male students are unequal (same for those generated by students with English as first/second language). Previous studies (e.g., [55]) suggested that the algorithmic unfairness of a predictive model may be partially attributed to the unequal amount of training data related to different demographic groups. Therefore, we trained the six classifiers with two different training data samples, namely (i) *original training sample*, i.e., all of the remaining posts (after selecting the testing data) were used as the training data; and (ii) *equal training sample*, i.e., an equal number of posts for each demographic group were randomly selected from the remaining posts and then combined as the training data. It should be pointed out that the same testing data was used to evaluate classification performance in the two training data samples, and thus the results were comparable. While training the models, 10%

---

[1] https://github.com/hanxiao/bert-as-service.

of the training data was randomly selected as the validation data and the best model was selected based on the error reported in the validation data.

4   Results

Results on Original Training Sample. Table 2 presents the performance of the six classifiers when using original training sample. Based on Table 2, we can have several important observations. When measuring the accuracy of the classification results, DL models were universally superior to traditional ML models, which was in line with the findings presented in previous works [11,54]. However, when scrutinizing the fairness of these models, traditional ML models tended to slightly outperform DL models. For instance, SVM displayed lowest level of unfairness to students of different sex and Logistic Regression achieved the best level of fairness towards students of different first-language backgrounds. These findings suggested that prediction accuracy should not be the only criterion when selecting a predictive model, and more importantly, the fairness of the model should also be evaluated and taken into account. Overall, CNN-LSTM achieved the best prediction accuracy (ranked 1st in both AUC and Cohen's κ) while maintaining acceptable level of fairness to different demographic groups of students (ranked 3rd in both ABROCA (Sex) and ABROCA (Language)). In fact, this implied that a strict accuracy-for-fairness trade-off was not evident in our study. Due to the limited space, the results of Accuracy and F1 score are omitted here, though similar findings can be drawn on those results.

Table 2. Results on original training sample. The top 3 best results are in bold.

Models	AUC	Cohen's κ	ABROCA (Sex)	ABROCA (Language)
Random Forests	0.763	0.525	0.038	**0.033**
Naïve Bayes	0.752	0.502	0.062	0.084
Logistic Regression	0.758	0.516	**0.014**	**0.032**
SVM	**0.786**	**0.577**	**0.007**	0.069
CNN-LSTM	**0.795**	**0.584**	**0.014**	**0.063**
Bi-LSTM	**0.786**	**0.565**	**0.010**	0.068

As showed before, there was no indication that DL models produced fairer results than the traditional ML models did. This was not expected given that feature engineering in traditional ML models involved more manual work than the automatic embedding generation in DL models, and therefore might be more susceptible to bias. This indicates that feature engineering may be only marginally related to the unfairness in classification models. However, we also note that in this study we utilised the features extensively engineered in previous studies to address the same classification task, which may have reduced bias. We also observe that the mean ABROCA value for sex (0.024) is only about a half of the mean ABROCA value for language (0.058), which means that the language group (English-as-first-language vs. English-as-second-language speakers) had far more unfair prediction than the sex group. This indicates that linguistic difference of different demographic groups of students may play an important role in improving model fairness. In Fig. 1, we also note that, except for Naïve Bayes, all other models provided better classification performance (measured by ROC) to English-as-first-language students. One possible explanation is that these models relied heavily on students' English proficiency to make accurate prediction and therefore posed strong unfairness to students whose first language was not English. Also, this may be partially due to the fact that popular feature and embedding extraction tools were typically trained by using standard English corpus (e.g., LIWC and BERT). Therefore, it may be worthy allocating further research efforts to scrutinize whether there exist any algorithmic unfairness in these tools and further improve these tools.

Original training sample vs. equal training sample. In Table 3, we summarized the results of using equal training sample. While the prediction accuracy remained comparable to those of using the original training sample, most of the classifiers (except for Logistic Regression) became fairer in both of the Sex and Language groups after including an equal number of posts related to each demographic group in the training data. In particular, Naïve Bayes had over 61% reduction in ABROCA between male and female, which shows a non-trivial role of data sampling in reducing the algorithmic unfairness of classification models. Therefore, we note that future model training should take demographic balancing into account to encourage fairer classification.

Table 3. Results on equal training sample. The top 3 best results are in bold.

Models	Sex			Language		
	AUC	Kappa	ABROCA	AUC	Kappa	ABROCA
Random Forests	0.760	0.518	0.030	0.773	0.545	**0.023**
Naïve Bayes	0.763	0.531	0.024	0.766	0.537	0.052
Logistic Regression	0.783	0.568	**0.003**	0.775	0.547	**0.043**
SVM	0.788	**0.581**	**0.004**	0.772	0.548	**0.012**
CNN-LSTM	**0.792**	**0.579**	0.009	**0.802**	**0.601**	0.062
Bi-LSTM	**0.791**	0.575	**0.007**	**0.784**	**0.559**	0.066

5   Discussion and Conclusion

This paper investigated both the accuracy and fairness of six popular automatic classifiers of educational forum posts. For each classifier, we evaluated the

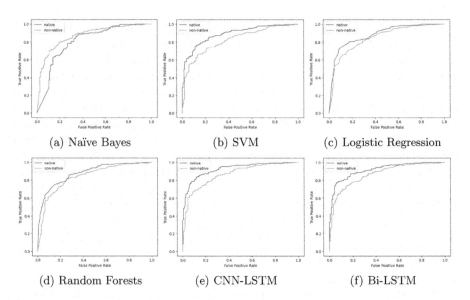

Fig. 1. ROC plots by first-language backgrounds (i.e., English-as-first-language vs. English-as-second-language speakers) on original training sample.

algorithmic fairness between students of different sex and first languages. Our results showed that while classification accuracy varied slightly, the difference of the model unfairness (measured by ABROCA) was more evident. Besides, we observed that, compared to the posts generated by English-as-second-language students, posts generated by English-as-first-language students were overwhelmingly predicted with higher accuracy by most of the classifiers (except for Naïve Bayes). Our results indicated that existing classifiers and feature engineering approaches, originally developed to process standard English, might be prone to discrimination against English-as-second-language students. This finding supported the recent initiatives in the NLP research community to expand the language varieties in the training text corpora to mitigate biases that emerged when researchers designed a prediction model in one context (e.g., texts written by English-as-first-language users) and applied it in another context [7,45]. As an attempt to address model unfairness, we applied equal sampling to model training. The results were promising with most of the models showing improved fairness. Since it did not require a complex alternation to existing model training, equal sampling can be incorporated with a minimal cost in the future versions of educational forum post classifiers.

Implications. Our findings suggested that a strict performance-for-fairness trade-off is not evident, and by utilising techniques such as equal sampling, researchers can help alleviate the problem of model unfairness without sacrificing classification performance. Moreover, existing model evaluation should take fairness metrics into consideration and avoid models that display a high level of unfairness. We also note that limited work has been done to evaluate bias in feature engineering and embedding extraction in educational research. Future work thus can investigate the possibility of extracting fairer features and evaluating feature fairness before evaluating model fairness, to prevent models from receiving discriminating input, particularly as this information is usually hard to detect later in the model implementation. Additionally, pre-trained language models such as BERT should incorporate a variety of base textual data into their training sets, rather than just using standard English corpus (e.g., Wikipedia).

Limitations. We acknowledged the following limitations of our study. First, the analysis involved only one prediction task, i.e., classifying content-relevant and content-irrelevant forum posts. To further increase the generalizability of our findings, additional prediction tasks using different datasets need to be investigated. Second, the analysis reported in this paper focused only on two types of demographic groups of students. In future studies, we will investigate the algorithmic fairness of different models with respect to other demographic groups, e.g., students of different educational backgrounds and minority students.

References

1. Agrawal, A., Venkatraman, J., Leonard, S., Paepcke, A.: YouEDU: addressing confusion in MOOC discussion forums by recommending instructional video clips (2015)
2. Almatrafi, O., Johri, A., Rangwala, H.: Needle in a haystack: identifying learner posts that require urgent response in MOOC discussion forums. Comput. Educ. **118**, 1–9 (2018)
3. Alrajhi, L., Alharbi, K., Cristea, A.I.: A multidimensional deep learner model of urgent instructor intervention need in MOOC forum posts. In: Intelligent Tutoring Systems, pp. 226–236. Springer International Publishing, New York City (2020)
4. Atapattu, T., Falkner, K., Tarmazdi, H.: Topic-wise classification of MOOC discussions: a visual analytics approach. International Educational Data Mining Society (2016)
5. Bakharia, A.: Towards cross-domain MOOC forum post classification. In: Learning@Scale, pp. 253–256 (2016)
6. Barbosa, G., et al.: Towards automatic cross-language classification of cognitive presence in online discussions. In: LAK, pp. 605–614 (2020)
7. Bender, E.M., Friedman, B.: Data statements for natural language processing: toward mitigating system bias and enabling better science. Trans. Assoc. Comput. Linguist. **6**, 587–604 (2018)
8. Bird, S.: Nltk: the natural language toolkit. In: Proceedings of the COLING/ACL 2006 Interactive Presentation Sessions, pp. 69–72 (2006)
9. Brahman, F., Varghese, N., Bhat, S.: Effective Forum Curation via Multi-task Learning, p. 8 (2020)
10. Caines, A., Pastrana, S., Hutchings, A., Buttery, P.J.: Automatically identifying the function and intent of posts in underground forums. Crime Sci. **7**(1), 19 (2018)
11. Chen, J., Feng, J., Sun, X., Liu, Y.: Co-training semi-supervised deep learning for sentiment classification of MOOC forum posts. Symmetry **12**(1), 8 (2020)

12. Clavié, B., Gal, K.: Edubert: Pretrained deep language models for learning analytics (2019). arXiv preprint arXiv:1912.00690
13. Cui, Y., Wise, A.F.: Identifying content-related threads in MOOC discussion forums. In: Learning@Scale, pp. 299–303 (2015)
14. Devlin, J., Chang, M.W., Lee, K., Toutanova, K.: Bert: Pre-training of deep bidirectional transformers for language understanding (2018). arXiv preprint arXiv:1810.04805
15. Doroudi, S., Brunskill, E.: Fairer but not fair enough on the equitability of knowledge tracing. In: Proceedings of the 9th International Conference on Learning Analytics & Knowledge, pp. 335–339. LAK19, Association for Computing Machinery, New York, NY, USA (2019). https://doi.org/10.1145/3303772.3303838
16. Duran, R., Haaranen, L., Hellas, A.: Gender differences in introductory programming: comparing MOOCs and local courses. In: Proceedings of the 51st ACM Technical Symposium on Computer Science Education, pp. 692–698 (2020)
17. Feng, L., Liu, G., Luo, S., Liu, S.: A transferable framework: classification and visualization of MOOC discussion threads. In: International Conference on Neural Information Processing, pp. 377–384. Springer (2017)
18. Ferreira, M., Rolim, V., Ferreira Mello, R., Lins, R.D., Chen, G., Gašević, D.: Towards automatic content analysis of social presence in transcripts of online discussions. In: LAK, pp. 141–150 (2020)
19. Gardner, J., Brooks, C., Baker, R.: Evaluating the fairness of predictive student models through slicing analysis. In: LAK, pp. 225–234 (2019)
20. Guo, P.J.: Non-native English speakers learning computer programming: barriers, desires, and design opportunities. In: Proceedings of the 2018 CHI conference on human factors in computing systems, pp. 1–14 (2018)
21. Guo, S.X., Sun, X., Wang, S.X., Gao, Y., Feng, J.: Attention-based character-word hybrid neural networks with semantic and structural information for identifying of urgent posts in MOOC discussion forums. IEEE Access **7**, 120522–120532 (2019)
22. Hew, K.F., Cheung, W.S.: Students' and instructors' use of massive open online courses (MOOCs): motivations and challenges. Educ. Res. Rev. **12**, 45–58 (2014)
23. Hew, K.F., Hu, X., Qiao, C., Tang, Y.: What predicts student satisfaction with MOOCs: a gradient boosting trees supervised machine learning and sentiment analysis approach. Comput. Educ. **145**, 103724 (2020)
24. Hone, K.S., El Said, G.R.: Exploring the factors affecting MOOC retention: a survey study. Comput. Educ. **98**, 157–168 (2016)
25. Hutt, S., Gardner, M., Duckworth, A.L., D'Mello, S.K.: Evaluating fairness and generalizability in models predicting on-time graduation from college applications. International Educational Data Mining Society (2019)
26. Jacobs, A.: Two cheers for web u. New York Times **162**(56113), 1–7 (2013)
27. Jansen, R.S., van Leeuwen, A., Janssen, J., Conijn, R., Kester, L.: Supporting learners' self-regulated learning in massive open online courses. Comput. Educ. **146**, 103771 (2020)
28. Khan, A., et al.: Machine learning approach for answer detection in discussion forums: an application of big data analytics. Sci. Program. **2020**, (2020)
29. Kizilcec, R.F., Lee, H.: Algorithmic fairness in education (2020)
30. Kovanović, V., Joksimović, S., Waters, Z., Gašević, D., Kitto, K., Hatala, M., Siemens, G.: Towards automated content analysis of discussion transcripts: a cognitive presence case. In: LAK, pp. 15–24 (2016)
31. Lee, H., Kizilcec, R.F.: Evaluation of fairness trade-offs in predicting student success (2020)

32. Loukina, A., Madnani, N., Zechner, K.: The many dimensions of algorithmic fairness in educational applications. In: Proceedings of the Fourteenth Workshop on Innovative Use of NLP for Building Educational Applications, pp. 1–10. Association for Computational Linguistics, Florence, Italy (August 2019). https://doi.org/10.18653/v1/W19-4401, https://www.aclweb.org/anthology/W19-4401
33. Lui, M., Baldwin, T.: Classifying user forum participants: separating the gurus from the hacks, and other tales of the internet. Proc. Australas. Lang. Technol. Assoc. Workshop **2010**, 49–57 (2010)
34. Mitra, S.K.: Internationalization of education in India: emerging trends and strategies. Asian Soc. Sci. **6**(6), 105 (2010)
35. Moreno-Marcos, P.M., Alario-Hoyos, C., Muñoz-Merino, P.J., Estévez-Ayres, I., Kloos, C.D.: Sentiment analysis in MOOCs: a case study. In: 2018 IEEE Global Engineering Education Conference (EDUCON), pp. 1489–1496. IEEE (2018)
36. Morris, L.V., Finnegan, C., Wu, S.S.: Tracking student behavior, persistence, and achievement in online courses. Internet High. Educ. **8**(3), 221–231 (2005)
37. Neto, V., Rolim, V., Ferreira, R., Kovanović, V., Gašević, D., Dueire Lins, R., Lins, R.: Automated analysis of cognitive presence in online discussions written in portuguese. In: Pammer-Schindler, V., Pérez-Sanagustín, M., Drachsler, H., Elferink, R., Scheffel, M. (eds.) EC-TEL 2018. LNCS, vol. 11082, pp. 245–261. Springer, Cham (2018). https://doi.org/10.1007/978-3-319-98572-5_19
38. Ntourmas, A., Avouris, N., Daskalaki, S., Dimitriadis, Y.: Comparative study of two different MOOC forums posts classifiers: analysis and generalizability issues. In: 2019 10th International Conference on Information, Intelligence, Systems and Applications (IISA), pp. 1–8. IEEE (2019)
39. Probyn, M.: Teachers voices: teachers reflections on learning and teaching through the medium of English as an additional language in South Africa. Int. J. Biling. Educ. Biling. **4**(4), 249–266 (2001)
40. Rayyan, S., Seaton, D.T., Belcher, J., Pritchard, D.E., Chuang, I.: Participation and performance in 8.02 x electricity and magnetism: The first physics MOOC from mitx (2013). arXiv preprint arXiv:1310.3173
41. Riazy, S., Simbeck, K., Schreck, V.: Fairness in learning analytics: student at-risk prediction in virtual learning environments. In: CSEDU (1), pp. 15–25 (2020)
42. Rossi, L.A., Gnawali, O.: Language independent analysis and classification of discussion threads in Coursera MOOC forums. In: Proceedings of the 2014 IEEE 15th International Conference on Information Reuse and Integration (IEEE IRI 2014), pp. 654–661. IEEE (2014)
43. Rovai, A.P.: Sense of community, perceived cognitive learning, and persistence in asynchronous learning networks. Internet High. Educ. **5**(4), 319–332 (2002)
44. Rovai, A.P.: Facilitating online discussions effectively. Internet High. Educ. **10**(1), 77–88 (2007)
45. Shah, D., Schwartz, H.A., Hovy, D.: Predictive biases in natural language processing models: A conceptual framework and overview (2019). arXiv preprint arXiv:1912.11078
46. Sun, C., Li, S., Lin, L.: Thread structure prediction for MOOC discussion forum. In: Che, W., Han, Q., Wang, H., Jing, W., Peng, S., Lin, J., Sun, G., Song, X., Song, H., Lu, Z. (eds.) ICYCSEE 2016. CCIS, vol. 624, pp. 92–101. Springer, Singapore (2016). https://doi.org/10.1007/978-981-10-2098-8_13
47. Toven-Lindsey, B., Rhoads, R.A., Lozano, J.B.: Virtually unlimited classrooms: pedagogical practices in massive open online courses. Internet High. Educ. **24**, 1–12 (2015)

48. Tsai, Y.S., Perrotta, C., Gašević, D.: Empowering learners with personalised learning approaches? Agency, equity and transparency in the context of learning analytics. Assess. Eval. High. Educ. **45**(4), 554–567 (2020). https://doi.org/10.1080/02602938.2019.1676396

49. Verstegen, D., Dailey-Hebert, A., Fonteijn, H., Clarebout, G., Spruijt, A.: How do virtual teams collaborate in online learning tasks in a MOOC? Int. Rev. Res. Open Distrib. Learn. **19**(4), 1–18 (2018)

50. Wei, X., Lin, H., Yang, L., Yu, Y.: A convolution-LSTM-based deep neural network for cross-domain MOOC forum post classification. Information **8**(3), 92 (2017)

51. Wise, A.F., Cui, Y., Jin, W., Vytasek, J.: Mining for gold: identifying content-related MOOC discussion threads across domains through linguistic modeling. Internet High. Educ. **32**, 11–28 (2017)

52. Wise, A.F., Cui, Y., Vytasek, J.: Bringing order to chaos in MOOC discussion forums with content-related thread identification. In: LAK, pp. 188–197 (2016)

53. Xing, W., Tang, H., Pei, B.: Beyond positive and negative emotions: looking into the role of achievement emotions in discussion forums of MOOCs. Internet High. Educ. **43**,100690 (2019)

54. Xu, Y., Lynch, C.F.: What do you want? Applying deep learning models to detect question topics in MOOC forum posts? In: Wood-stock 2018: ACM Symposium on Neural Gaze Detection, pp. 1–6 (2018)

55. Yan, S., Kao, H.t., Ferrara, E.: Fair class balancing: Enhancing model fairness without observing sensitive attributes. In: Proceedings of the 29th ACM International Conference on Information & Knowledge Management, pp. 1715–1724 (2020)

56. Yang, D., Wen, M., Howley, I., Kraut, R., Rose, C.: Exploring the effect of confusion in discussion forums of massive open online courses. In: Learning@Scale, pp. 121–130 (2015)

57. Yu, R., Li, Q., Fischer, C., Doroudi, S., Xu, D.: Towards accurate and fair prediction of college success: evaluating different sources of student data. In: EDM. pp. 292–301. ERIC (2020)

58. Zeng, Z., Chaturvedi, S., Bhat, S.: Learner affect through the looking glass: characterization and detection of confusion in online courses. International Educational Data Mining Society (2017)

"Can You Clarify What You Said?": Studying the Impact of Tutee Agents' Follow-Up Questions on Tutors' Learning

Tasmia Shahriar[✉] and Noboru Matsuda[✉]

North Carolina State University, Raleigh, NC 27695, USA
{tshahri,noboru.matsuda}@ncsu.edu

Abstract. Students learn by teaching others as tutors. Advancement in the theory of learning by teaching has given rise to many pedagogical agents. In this paper, we exploit a known cognitive theory that states if a tutee asks deep questions in a peer tutoring environment, a tutor benefits from it. Little is known about a computational model of such deep questions. This paper aims to formalize the deep tutee questions and proposes a generalized model of inquiry-based dialogue, called the constructive tutee inquiry, to ask follow-up questions to have tutors reflect their current knowledge (aka knowledge-building activity). We conducted a Wizard of Oz study to evaluate the proposed constructive tutee inquiry. The results showed that the constructive tutee inquiry was particularly effective for the low prior knowledge students to learn conceptual knowledge.

Keywords: Learning by teaching · Deep questions · Teachable agents · Tutor learning · Knowledge-building · Wizard of Oz

1 Introduction

Students often learn by teaching others. This type of learning is called *tutor learning* [1–10]. Although learning by teaching is impactful for the tutors, some researchers argue about the consistency and effect size of the tutor learning [3]. Roscoe [11] sought to understand how the tutors learn in the learning by teaching environment to leverage the benefits of tutoring more consistently. In one study, Roscoe *et al.* [12] found that tutor learning happens when students (who are *tutors*) engage in instructional activities like reflecting on their understanding [13], revisiting the concepts, providing correct and complete explanations to make sense of solution steps [14, 15], and recovering from their misconceptions or knowledge gaps [15] while tutoring. These instructional activities are called knowledge-building activities. When students perform knowledge-building activities to answer a question, those answers are known as knowledge-building responses that elicit learning [12]. One of our motivations for the current study is to evaluate the impact of knowledge-building responses on tutor learning in an Intelligent Tutoring System (ITS) setting.

Students infrequently engage in knowledge-building activities when they act as tutors in a peer-tutoring environment. Instead of developing their knowledge, students seem

© Springer Nature Switzerland AG 2021
I. Roll et al. (Eds.): AIED 2021, LNAI 12748, pp. 395–407, 2021.
https://doi.org/10.1007/978-3-030-78292-4_32

more inclined to deliver what they already know or directly dictate solution steps with little elaboration to their tutees [11, 16, 17]. Researchers found that *deep* tutee questions made tutors generate more knowledge-building responses while tutoring [16–23]. Although different types of *deep* tutee questions have been observed, they all agreed that not all tutee questions are equally helpful for tutor learning. Despite the advancement in developing effective teachable agents [24–29], a computational model of *deep* tutee questions beneficial for tutor learning is yet to be developed.

In the current study, we develop a synthetic tutee that asks questions to promote tutors' knowledge-building responses. We hypothesize that letting the synthetic tutee ask follow-up questions to remind the tutor to provide knowledge-building responses facilitates tutor learning. For example, the synthetic tutee may ask tutors to elaborate their shallow response. We shall call this kind of question asking the *Constructive Tutee Inquiry* (CTI). We propose a model of CTI for a tutee to ask follow-up questions. This is the first attempt to model a synthetic tutee's follow-up questions to facilitate tutor learning to the best of our knowledge. As an initial step, we evaluate the effectiveness of CTI through a Wizard of Oz study (WoZ). In the study, a synthetic tutee embedded into an artificial peer learning environment called APLUS was controlled by a researcher who manually typed the tutee questions as if a machine generated them. The study participants were told that the synthetic tutee was artificial intelligence.

In the traditional APLUS (which does not have CTI), students interactively teach a synthetic tutee named SimStudent [30] to solve linear algebraic equations. In WoZ, an extended version of the traditional APLUS, called AskMore APLUS, was used. In AskMore APLUS, a synthetic tutee named Gabby instantiated follow-up questions according to the CTI. The result showed that the proposed CTI model helped the low prior students generate more knowledge-building responses, facilitating their learning of conceptual knowledge. Our contributions are summarized as follows: (1) We propose a domain-independent Constructive Tutee Inquiry model that encourages tutors to provide more knowledge-building responses. (2) We present rigorous analysis to understand how and why Constructive Tutee Inquiry facilitates tutor learning.

2 Related Work

Many researchers have tested the effectiveness of varying tutee prompts in facilitating tutor learning. Prior studies revealed a controversial impact of *explanation prompt* on tutor learning. While some studies found asking for explanation effective [31, 32], some studies showed that asking a tutor to explain at all times has a detrimental effect on tutor learning [23, 33, 34]. In another study, Rittle-Johnson *et al.* [22] argued that despite the general effectiveness of explanation prompt for improved learning, explanatory questions divide tutors' attention to different types of information, negatively impacting tutor learning. These studies highlight that *deep* tutee questions are more than just asking for explanations from the tutor.

More recently, Baker *et al.* [35] found a positive impact of asking *contrasting prompts* to draw tutors' attention towards identifying similarities or dissimilarities between contradictory scenarios on tutor learning. On the contrary, Sidney *et al.* [36] claimed that contrasting questions alone on their own was not beneficial for tutor learning; instead, it was both the *explanation* and *contrasting prompts* that together facilitated tutor learning [36]. This analysis indicates that any question type alone is insufficient for tutor learning.

Looi *et al.* [37] investigated the design of the synthetic tutee's question prompts to engage the tutors in knowledge-building activities on an online learning environment named Betty's Brain. These questions were one-sided questions with no follow-up regime in case of failure to engage tutors in knowledge-building activities. We hypothesize that *deep* questions are not just a single one-sided question; rather, it is an accumulation of subsequent follow-up questions on a certain topic. On the other hand, their proposed method requires the synthetic tutee to be equipped with a complete expert model, making it a domain-dependent question generation model. Our proposed model is domain-independent because no path of the CTI algorithm requires specific knowledge about the domain to generate the subsequent follow-up questions. Our model also does not assume that the synthetic tutee needs to be more knowledgeable than the tutor to engage them in knowledge-building activities. Therefore, our model arguably captures the naturalistic scenarios for tutee inquiries in a classroom setting.

3 The Traditional APLUS with SimStudent

Our study extends the SimStudent project [38], which we call traditional APLUS. Traditional APLUS is an intelligent learning environment where students (who are *tutors*) teach SimStudent how to solve linear algebraic equations. SimStudent learns through demonstration. When the tutor teaches a step, SimStudent learns generalized production rules that look like, "if [*preconditions*], perform [*transformation*]". In APLUS, *transformation* allows four basic math operations: *add, subtract, divide,* and *multiply* by a *number.* SimStudent keeps adding or modifying the production rules in its knowledge base according to the tutor's feedback. Besides demonstrating solution steps, tutors can interact with SimStudent and give textual explanations using the chat panel. In traditional APLUS, SimStudent only asks why questions in some particular scenarios. For example, "*Why did you perform [transformation] here?*" or "I performed this *[transformation] due to a previously taught production rule. Why do you think I am wrong?*". SimStudent never follow-up after the tutor's response to the why questions. Additionally, tutors can quiz SimStudent anytime they want to check its knowledge status. Quiz topics include equations with one-step, two-steps, variables on both sides, and a final challenge containing variables on both sides. Traditional APLUS also has resource tabs like problem bank, unit overview, and worked-out examples for tutors to review at any time.

4 Overview of the Constructive Tutee Inquiry

4.1 Motivation

Prior studies have highlighted that tutors learn most effectively when they engage in *knowledge-building activities* [12, 16, 39]. In this paper, we call the tutors' responses to the tutee's questions that required them to engage in knowledge-building activities the *knowledge-building responses* (KBR). As an example, suppose the tutee asked, "*Why do we perform a transformation on both sides?*". Tutor's reply, "*An equation is like a balanced weight scale. You do the same thing on both sides to keep it balanced at all times,"* is KBR because the tutor provided a complete and correct explanation to make sense of a solution step, which is a *knowledge-building* activity.

Roscoe *et al.* [12] grouped KBR broadly into two categories: elaboration and sense-making (Table 1). The elaboration response provides extended explanations or novel examples to clarify a concept of interest. For example, the tutor's answer *"one needs to undo all the operations performed on the variable term to solve an equation"* when asked how to know an equation is solved is KBR because the tutor provides an extended explanation to clarify the concept of equation solving. On the other hand, the sense-making response reflects that the tutor realized their errors or realized new inferences based on their prior knowledge. For example, the tutor may mention that he has just learned that *"subtracting a positive number is the same as adding a negative number."*

Table 1. A summary of knowledge-building response category and its sub-categories. The types of prompt Gabby uses as follow-up tutee inquiry is also shown.

KBR category	KBR Sub-category	Follow-up Tutee Inquiry prompts
Elaboration	Providing extended clarification for a concept of interest	Explanation prompt [Pumping] *"Can you elaborate?"*
	Providing more examples for clarification	Example prompt [Pumping] *"I know little about [x], tell me more?"*
Sense-making	Realizing own errors or misconceptions	Error realization prompt [Splicing] *"I acted according to the rule I have learnt from you. Why am I wrong?"*
	Realizing new inferences based on prior knowledge	Inference prompt [Pumping] *"How to convert the unfamiliar form to the familiar one you've taught me before?"*

We hypothesize that when a tutee's inquiry did not induce the tutors' KBR, having the tutee ask a follow-up question will increase the tutors' chance of committing KBR. We, therefore, propose Constructive Tutee Inquiry (CTI) as a sequence of follow-up inquiries to guide the tutor to KBR. CTI consists of an initial tutee inquiry followed by a chain of follow-up inquiries based on tutors' responses to the previous inquiry. The initial inquiries are the same as the ones that SimStudent asks in traditional APLUS.

4.2   Mechanism of the Follow-Up Tutee Inquiry

A follow-up tutee inquiry can be one of the following prompts: (1) explanation, (2) example, (3) error realization, and (4) inference, as shown in Table 1.

The mechanism of the follow-up tutee inquiry is inspired by how the teacher and students jointly improve the quality of an answer in the classroom proposed by Graesser *et al.* [10]. Teachers follow *pumping, splicing* and, *summarization* techniques introduced in [10] to improve the quality of their students' answers. Teacher asking for more information when students' answer is not informative or vague is *pumping*. If students' answer is error-ridden, a teacher may split the answer into correct and incorrect parts and ask for information about the incorrect part, called *splicing*. Finally, a teacher summarizes the gathered information to the students, called *summarization.*

CTI implements pumping, splicing and, summarization to operate the follow-up tutee inquiries. The follow-up tutee inquiry starts after tutors' response to an initial tutee inquiry and ends with the tutee's *summarization*. The following algorithm operates the subsequent follow-up tutee inquiries:

IF [tutor's response is vague] THEN [use the *explanation prompt* (which is pump)]
ELSE IF [tutor's response contradicts with already perceived knowledge] THEN [use the *error realization prompt* (which is splice)]
ELSE IF [tutor's response agrees with already perceived knowledge] THEN [use *example generation prompt* (which is pump)]
ELSE IF [tutor's response reveals tutor is stuck] THEN [use the *inference generation prompt* (which is pump)]
ELSE [summarize and move to the next scenario]

Figure 1 shows an example of CTI. It starts with an initial tutee inquiry, like traditional APLUS. Since the tutor provided a vague answer to the initial tutee inquiry, Gabby pumps using the *explanation prompt*. Gabby ends the follow-up tutee inquiry by summarizing because tutor's response to the *explanation prompt* was not vague and did not contradict any perceived knowledge.

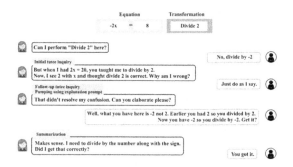

Fig. 1. An example of Constructive Tutee Inquiry

5 Method

This paper explores the following research questions: (1) Does Constructive Tutee Inquiry (CTI) inspire tutors to generate more knowledge-building responses while tutoring? (2) If so, do increased knowledge-building responses facilitate tutor learning?

We conducted a Wizard of Oz experiment (WoZ) to gather early-stage evidence of our proposed Constructive Tutee Inquiry (CTI) effectiveness as a randomized controlled trial with two conditions: AskMore APLUS as the experimental and Traditional APLUS as the control condition. In WoZ, a human researcher controlled Gabby in AskMore APLUS and manually typed questions according to the CTI model as if a machine generated them. To save the cost of system implementation, AskMore APLUS was built as a chat app running on a standard Web browser by mimicking the appearance of traditional APLUS. We used the same interface to simulate traditional APLUS to avoid any confounding issue due to the difference in the appearance of the interface and system interaction. When participants were using simulated traditional APLUS, the human researcher controlled SimStudent and manually typed questions the same way SimStudent would ask in traditional APLUS. Participants were redirected to another screen containing traditional APLUS whenever they clicked the quiz tab in the chat application. A session manager fed all the tutor demonstrated steps to traditional APLUS to ensure that the quiz reflects the synthetic tutee's knowledge status.

5.1 Structure of the Study

30 middle school students (11 male and 19 female) of 6th–8th grade from various middle schools participated in the study. Participants visited our lab individually and received $15/h as monetary compensation for their participation.

Participants took a pre-test for 15 min before the intervention. Then they were randomly assigned to one of the conditions ensuring an equal balance of the average pre-test scores between two conditions. 16 participants were assigned to AskMore and 14 to the Traditional APLUS condition. A two-tailed unpaired t-test on the pre-test score confirmed no condition difference between the mean pre-test scores; $M_{AskMore} = 9.9 \pm 5.4$ vs. $M_{Traditional} = 10.6 \pm 4.1$; $t(28) = -0.44$, $p = 0.66$. Participants watched a 10-min video tutorial on the given intervention before using the assigned app. In the video, participants were informed that their goal was to have SimStudent / Gabby pass the quiz. A single intervention session took about 90 min, depending on how quickly the participants achieved their goals. Most of our participants (23 out of 30) came in for the second-day intervention session. Only 18 out of 30 participants met the goal of having their synthetic tutee pass the quiz: 10 for AskMore and 8 for Traditional APLUS. Our data analysis considered all 30 participants irrespective of their synthetic tutee pass the overall quiz. Upon completion of the intervention, participants took 15 min post-test. The tutoring sessions were audio and video recorded, and students were asked to think aloud in both conditions. All interface actions taken by participants and the tutee inquiries and participant responses were logged.

5.2 Measures

The pre- and post-test questions were isomorphic. Both pre- and post-tests consist of 2 tests: (1) The Conceptual Knowledge Test (CKT) contains 9 questions - 2 multiple choice questions and 7 single-choice questions that address various misconceptions of linear algebraic equation solving. An example of a single-choice question that addresses the misconception of zero while solving equations is "The equation $7x + 14 = 0$ is same as $7x = 14$ because the RHS is 0" with Agree/Neutral/Disagree as options. (2) The Procedural Skill Test (PST) contains 10 questions – solving one-step (1 question), two steps (3 questions), and with variables on both sides (6 questions) equations. An example of two steps equation is "Solve for x: 4x + 15 = 3". The answers were scored as either 1 for overall correctness or 0 for incorrect or incomplete answers. The highest score any participants could achieve in CKT is, therefore, 9 and in PST is 10.

The participants entered a total of 4605 responses while tutoring the synthetic tutee. Two human coders categorized those responses into "knowledge-building" and "non-knowledge-building" responses. Based on Cohen's Kappa coefficient, the inter-coder reliability for this coding showed $\kappa = 0.81$.

6 Results

6.1 Test Scores

Table 2 shows a summary of average test scores—overall, procedural skill test (PST), and conceptual knowledge test (CKT)—both for Traditional and AskMore APLUS.

We ran a mixed design analysis for both CKT and PST with test-time (pre vs post) as within subject variable and condition (AskMore vs Traditional) as a between subject variable. There was no condition difference for post-test scores in CKT ($M_{AskMore} = 5.9 \pm 1.8$, $M_{Traditional} = 6.0 \pm 2.0$, $F(1,28) = 0.30$, $p = 0.60$) and PST ($M_{AskMore} = 6.3 \pm 3.8$, $M_{Traditional} = 7.0 \pm 2.2$, $F(1, 28) = 0.14$, $p = 0.71$). However, test-time (pre vs. post) was a main effect for both CKT ($M_{Pre} = 4.7 \pm 2.1$, $M_{Post} = 6.0 \pm 2.0$, $F(1,28) = 9.56$, $p < 0.01$) and PST ($M_{Pre} = 5.5 \pm 3.3$, $M_{Post} = 6.6 \pm 3.1$, $F(1, 28) = 5.53$, $p < 0.05$). *Tutors in both conditions showed an equal amount of learning from pre to post tests on both CKT and PST.*

Table 2. Average pre- and post-test scores in AskMore and Traditional APLUS condition.

Condition	Overall (pre)	Overall (post)	PST (pre)	PST (post)	CKT (pre)	CKT (post)
AskMore	9.9 ± 5.4	12.2 ± 5.3	5.4 ± 3.7	6.3 ± 3.8	4.4 ± 2.2	5.9 ± 1.8
Traditional	10.6 ± 4.1	13.0 ± 3.5	5.6 ± 3.0	7.0 ± 2.2	5.1 ± 2.0	6.0 ± 2.0

An aptitude treatment interaction (ATI) found for the conceptual knowledge test (CKT). Figure 2 shows a scattered plot with the centered conceptual pre-test score on the x-axis and conceptual post-test score on the y-axis. In the plot, *among those who scored below average on the pre-test, AskMore tutors outperformed Traditional tutors on the post-test.* We ran a two-way ANOVA with the conceptual post-test as the dependent variable, conceptual pre-test and condition (AskMore vs. Traditional APLUS) as the independent variables. The interaction between conceptual pre-test and condition was statistically significant; $F(1, 26) = 5.70$, $p < 0.05$. However, an ATI was not observed for the procedural skill test. The same two-way ANOVA, as shown above, did not show a statistically significant interaction term among the procedural pre-test score and condition; $F(1, 26) = 0.05$, $p = 0.83$. *Tutors with lower prior competency (below-average pre-test score) learned more conceptual knowledge when using AskMore APLUS than Traditional APLUS.*

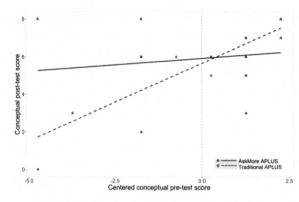

16 datapoints in triangle represent AskMore APLUS tutors and 14 datapoints in circle represent Traditional APLUS tutors. There are many overlapping datapoints due to more than one tutors achieving the same test scores.
For tutors with the below-average pre-test score (left on the dotted vertical line), AskMore tutors outperformed Traditional tutors on the post-test.

Fig. 2. Centered pre- vs. post-test score for CKT between AskMore vs. Traditional tutors.

6.2 Effect of Responding to the Follow-Up Tutee Inquiries

We hypothesized that simply answering more tutee inquiries (regardless it induced knowledge-building responses or not) facilitated conceptual learning. A simple regression model with the normalized learning gain on CKT, i.e., (posttest – pretest)/(1 – pretest), as a dependent variable and the number of inquiries tutor answered as an independent variable did not reveal the number of inquiries answered as a reliable predictor for the learning gain on CKT; $F(1,14) = 0.21$, $p = 0.66$. *Simply answering more tutee inquiries did not predict conceptual learning.*

6.3 Learning to Generate Knowledge-Building Responses

We investigated if generating more KBR promoted conceptual learning. A regression analysis fitting the conceptual post-test with the conceptual pre-test and normalized KBR count confirmed that normalized KBR is a reliable predictor; $F(1, 27) = 14.11$, $p < 0.01$. The regression model suggests that if *tutors committed one more knowledge-building response than the average, they would have ended up with a 1.0% increase in their conceptual post-test score.* However, the equivalent regression analysis suggests that *committing to more knowledge-building responses did not help procedural learning;* $F(1, 27) = 1.55$, $p = 0.22$.

Fig. 3. Boxplot of average % knowledge-building responses generated by tutors due to initial tutee inquiries and follow-up tutee inquiries in both conditions.

We also found a significant positive correlation between the number of follow-up tutee inquiries asked and KBR generated by tutors; $r = 0.51$, $p < 0.01$. *About 24% of the follow-up tutee inquiries yielded knowledge-building responses.*

To further understand the process of generating KBR between the conditions, we divided total tutee inquiries into two parts (1) initial tutee inquiries (ITI) and (2) follow-up tutee inquiries (FTI). ITI was available in both conditions where FTI was only available in AskMore APLUS. We tagged the KBR generated by AskMore APLUS tutors into two categories (1) KBR due to initial tutee inquiries (KBR-ITI) and (2) KBR due to follow-up tutee inquiries (KBR-FTI).

The boxplot in Fig. 3 shows that 12% of the total responses by the AskMore tutors were KBR, whereas, for the Traditional tutors, it is only 4%. A *t*-test confirmed that AskMore tutors had a higher ratio of generating KBR than the Traditional tutors; $t(21) = -4.89$, $p < .01$. The boxplot also revealed that the percentage of KBR-ITI was fairly equal in both conditions. A t-test confirmed that there was no difference between the average percent KBR ($M_{AskMore} = .04$, $M_{Traditional} = .04$) due to initial tutee inquiry between conditions $t(28) = .09$, $p = .93$.

The above observations suggest that the follow-up tutee inquiry resulted in increased knowledge-building responses (i.e., KBR-FTI) generated by AskMore tutors, which further facilitated conceptual learning.

Table 3 shows that the AskMore low prior tutors were asked 26 initial tutee inquiries on average, whereas Traditional low prior tutors were asked 25. A t-test revealed low prior tutors in both conditions ($M_{AskMore} = 2$, $M_{Traditional} = 3$) generated equal number of KBR-ITI on average; $t(9) = 1.60$, $p = 0.14$. However, AskMore low prior tutors were additionally asked 49 follow-up tutee inquiries on average that resulted in an additional 5 more KBR (i.e., KBR-FTI) during the entire tutoring session.

Table 3. Average number of initial tutee inquiries (ITI) and follow-up tutee inquiry (FTI); and the average number of resultant KBR due to ITI (KBG-ITI) and KBR due to FTI (KBR-FTI)

Prior	Condition	Total inquiries		Total KBR	
		ITI	FTI	KBR-ITI	KBR-FTI
Low	AskMore	26	49	2	5
	Traditional	25	–	3	–
High	AskMore	21	30	2	4
	Traditional	28	–	2	–

In sum, it was the follow-up tutee inquiries in AskMore APLUS that assisted the low prior tutors to generate more knowledge-building responses, which in turn facilitated their conceptual learning.

However, the same finding does not apply to the high prior tutors even though they generated 6 KBR on average while tutoring. We hypothesized that different types of KBR (Table 1) affect tutor learning differently. However, the current study was not designed to collect data to test this hypothesis. A future investigation is needed.

6.4   Learning to Review Resources

Our study revealed that reviewing the resources positively impacts conceptual learning regardless of the condition. A regression analysis with conceptual gain as the dependent variable and resource usage as the independent predictor confirmed that resource usage is a reliable predictor; $F(1, 28) = 4.39, p < 0.05$.

Did follow-up tutee inquiries inspire the low prior tutors to review the resources more, and did more frequent resource reviews result in better conceptual learning? Follow-up tutee inquiries inspired the AskMore low prior tutors to review the resource tabs 11.9 times, whereas Traditional low prior tutors reviewed the resources 8.8 times on average while tutoring. However, the t-test revealed no condition difference in resource review count; $t(13) = -1.01, p = .33$. A qualitative analysis of dialog data disclosed that the low prior tutors in AskMore APLUS tended to review the resources more often to better answer Gabby's inquiries. Figure 4 shows an example conversation in which an AskMore low prior tutor reviewed the resources while answering follow-up tutee inquiries. The tutor reviewed *UNIT OVERVIEW*, one of the resources available for tutors in APLUS. Although *UNIT OVERVIEW* does not contain a direct answer to Gabby's inquiry, it contains information like *"To solve an equation you need to do mathematical transformations until at the end you have "x = a number"* The tutor elaborated on this information to come up with a better answer to Gabby's inquiry.

7   Discussion

Our current data showed an interesting ATI—generating more knowledge-building responses (KBR) in AskMore APLUS facilitated learning conceptual knowledge only for the low prior tutors. Our hypothesis that CTI encouraged low prior tutors to generate more KBR was supported. *About 24% of the follow-up tutee inquiries (asked by Gabby) yielded knowledge-building responses (by the tutors).*

Our data also revealed that conceptual learning is highly correlated with reviewing the resources in the application. We further hypothesized that CTI inspired the low prior tutors to review the resources more often, which is another reason for the ATI we found. This hypothesis was not supported. However, conversational data showed low prior tutors frequently reviewed the resources to come up with a better answer to the follow-up tutee inquiry.

All these findings apply to the low prior tutors only. The number of KBR did not have a notable impact on the high prior tutors' learning. We hypothesize that different types of KBR (Table 1) have different contributions to learning. The current data do not allow us to conduct rigorous analysis on this hypothesis due to the limited number of participants. We aim to investigate this hypothesis at length in our future work.

8   Conclusion

We found that Constructive Tutee Inquiry (CTI) helped low prior students provide more knowledge-building responses (KBR) by prompting them to elaborate the confusing explanations and motivating them to commit sense-making reflections. The data also

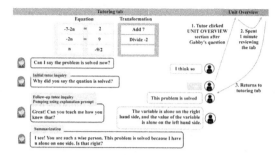

Fig. 4. Example of reviewing resources after follow-up tutee inquiries

showed that the KBR further facilitated learning conceptual knowledge. Understanding how CTI could assist in procedural skills learning is within the scope of our future work. Our focus of interest also goes to the high prior students who did not get the advantage of CTI as effectively as the low prior students. We believe that learning by teaching, with the advanced teachable agent technology, can offer rich learning opportunities to diverse students. Understanding how KBR types affect tutor learning differently would allow us to investigate how to make the CTI more effective.

Acknowledgment. This research was supported by the Institute of Education Sciences, U.S. Department of Education, through Grant No. R305A180319 and National Science Foundation Grant No. 1643185 to North Carolina State University. The opinions expressed are those of the authors and do not represent views of the Institute or the U.S. Department of Education.

References

1. Annis, L.F.: The processes and effects of peer tutoring. Hum. Learn. **2**(1), 39–47 (1983)
2. Bargh, J.A., Schul, Y.: On the cognitive benefits of teaching. J. Educ. Psychol. **72**(5), 593–604 (1980)
3. Cohen, P.A., Kulik, J.A., Kulik, C.L.C.: Education outcomes of tutoring: a meta-analysis of findings. Am. Educ. Res. J. **19**(2), 237–248 (1982)
4. Renkl, A.: Learning for later teaching: an exploration of mediational links between teaching expectancy and learning results. Learn. Instr. **5**(1), 21–36 (1995)
5. Roscoe, R.D., Chi, M.T.H.: Understanding tutor learning: knowledge-building and knowledge-telling in peer tutors' explanations and questions. Rev. Educ. Res. **77**(4), 534–574 (2007)
6. Chi, M.T.H., et al.: Learning from human tutoring. Cogn. Sci. **25**, 471–533 (2001)
7. Cohen, E.G.: Restructuring the classroom: conditions for productive small groups. Rev. Educ. Res. **64**(1), 1–35 (1994)
8. Devin-Sheehan, L., Feldman, R.S., Allen, V.L.: Research on children tutoring children: a critical review. Rev. Educ. Res. **46**(3), 355–385 (1976)
9. Gartner, A., Kohler, M., Riessman, F.: Children Teach Children: Learning by Teaching. Harper & Row, New York (1971)
10. Graesser, A.C., Person, N.K., Magliano, J.P.: Collaborative dialogue patterns in naturalistic one-to-one tutoring. Appl. Cogn. Psychol. **9**(6), 495–522 (1995)

11. Roscoe, R.D.: Opportunities and barriers for tutor learning: knowledge-building, metacognition, and motivation. University of Pittsburgh (2008)
12. Roscoe, R.D., Chi, M.: Tutor learning: the role of explaining and responding to questions. Instr. Sci. **36**(4), 321–350 (2008)
13. Butler, D.L.: Structuring instruction to promote self-regulated learning by adolescents and adults with learning disabilities. Exceptionality **11**(1), 39–60 (2003)
14. Hong, H.-Y., et al.: Advancing third graders' reading comprehension through collaborative Knowledge Building: a comparative study in Taiwan. Comput. Educ. **157**, 103962 (2020)
15. Cohen, J.: Theoretical considerations of peer tutoring. Psychol. Sch. **23**(2), 175–186 (1986)
16. Roscoe, R.D., Chi, M.T.H.: The influence of the tutee in learning by peer tutoring. In: Forbus, K., Gentner, D, Regier, T. (eds.) Proceedings of the 26th Meeting of the Cognitive Science Society, pp. 1179–1184. Erlbaum, Mahwah (2004)
17. Roscoe, R.D.: Self-monitoring and knowledge-building in learning by teaching. Instr. Sci. **42**(3), 327–351 (2013). https://doi.org/10.1007/s11251-013-9283-4
18. Chin, C., Osborne, J.: Students' questions: a potential resource for teaching and learning science. Stud. Sci. Educ. **44**(1), 1–39 (2008)
19. Watts, M., et al.: Prompting teachers' constructive reflection: pupils' questions as critical incidents. Int. J. Sci. Educ. **19**(9), 1025–1037 (1997)
20. Graesser, A.C., Person, N.K.: Question asking during tutoring. Am. Educ. Res. J. **31**(1), 104–137 (1994)
21. Van den Boom, G., Paas, F., Van Merrienboer, J.J.: Effects of elicited reflections combined with tutor or peer feedback on self-regulated learning and learning outcomes. Learn. Instr. **17**(5), 532–548 (2007)
22. Rittle-Johnson, B., Loehr, A.M.: Eliciting explanations: constraints on when self-explanation aids learning. Psychon. Bull. Rev. **24**(5), 1501–1510 (2016). https://doi.org/10.3758/s13423-016-1079-5
23. Matsuda, N., et al.: Studying the effect of tutor learning using a teachable agent that asks the student tutor for explanations. In: Sugimoto, M., et al. (eds.) Proceedings of the International Conference on Digital Game and Intelligent Toy Enhanced Learning (DIGITEL 2012), pp. 25–32. IEEE Computer Society, Los Alamitos (2012)
24. Biswas, G., et al.: Learning by teaching: a new agent paradigm for educational software. J. Appl. Artif. Intell. **19**(3 & 4), 363–392 (2005)
25. Bredeweg, B., et al.: DynaLearn - engaging and informed tools for learning conceptual system knowledge. In: Pirrone, R., Azevedo, R., Biswas, G. (eds.) Cognitive and Metacognitive Educational Systems (MCES 2009), AAAI Fall Symposium, pp. 46–51. AAAI Press, Arlington (2009)
26. Ketamo, H., Kiili, K.: Conceptual change takes time: game based learning cannot be only supplementary amusement. J. Educ. Multimed. Hypermedia **19**(4), 399–419 (2010)
27. Nichols, D.M.: Intelligent Student Systems: an Application of Viewpoints to Intelligent Learning Environments. Lancaster University, Lancaster (1993)
28. Pareto, L., Arvemo, T., Dahl, Y., Haake, M., Gulz, A.: A teachable-agent arithmetic game's effects on mathematics understanding, attitude and self-efficacy. In: Biswas, G., Bull, S., Kay, J., Mitrovic, A. (eds.) AIED 2011. LNCS (LNAI), vol. 6738, pp. 247–255. Springer, Heidelberg (2011). https://doi.org/10.1007/978-3-642-21869-9_33
29. Reif, F., Scott, L.A.: Teaching scientific thinking skills: students and computers coaching each other. Am. J. Phys. **67**(9), 819–831 (1999)
30. Matsuda, N.: Applying machine learning to cognitive modeling for cognitive tutors. [Technical report]. Carnegie Mellon University. School of Computer Science. Machine Learning Dept. (2006). Carnegie Mellon University, School of Computer Science, Machine Learning Dept., Pittsburgh [15] p.

31. Chi, M.T.H., et al.: Eliciting self-explanations improves understanding. Cogn. Sci. **18**(3), 439–477 (1994)
32. Kwon, K., Kumalasari, C.D., Howland, J.L.: Self-explanation prompts on problem-solving performance in an interactive learning environment. J. Interact. Online Learn. **10**(2), 1–17 (2011)
33. Rosé, C.P., Torrey, C.: Interactivity versus expectation: eliciting learning oriented behavior with tutorial dialogue systems. In: Proceedings of Interact 2005 (2005)
34. DeCaro, M.S., Rittle-Johnson, B.: Exploring mathematics problems prepares children to learn from instruction. J. Exp. Child Psychol. **113**(4), 552–568 (2012)
35. Baker, R.S., Corbett, A.T., Koedinger, K.R.: Learning to distinguish between representations of data: a cognitive tutor that uses contrasting cases. In: Proceedings of the 6th International Conference on Learning Sciences (2004)
36. Sidney, P.G., Hattikudur, S., Alibali, M.W.: How do contrasting cases and self-explanation promote learning? Evidence from fraction division. Learn. Instr. **40**, 29–38 (2015)
37. Looi, C.K., Wu, L.: Design of agent tutee's question prompts to engage student's role-playing as tutor in a learning-by-teaching agent environment. In: Proceedings of the 8th International Conference on International Conference for the Learning Sciences-Volume International Society of the Learning Sciences (2008)
38. Matsuda, N., et al.: Learning by teaching SimStudent – an initial classroom baseline study comparing with cognitive tutor. In: Biswas, G., Bull, S., Kay, J., Mitrovic, A. (eds.) AIED 2011. LNCS (LNAI), vol. 6738, pp. 213–221. Springer, Heidelberg (2011). https://doi.org/10.1007/978-3-642-21869-9_29
39. Berghmans, I., et al.: A typology of approaches to peer tutoring. Unraveling peer tutors' behavioural strategies. Eur. J. Psychol. Educ. **28**(3), 703–723 (2013)

Classifying Math Knowledge Components via Task-Adaptive Pre-Trained BERT

Jia Tracy Shen[1]([✉]), Michiharu Yamashita[1], Ethan Prihar[2], Neil Heffernan[2], Xintao Wu[3], Sean McGrew[4], and Dongwon Lee[1]

[1] Penn State University, University Park, PA 16802, USA
jqs5443@psu.edu
[2] Worcester Polytechnic Institute, Worcester, MA 01609, USA
[3] University of Arkansas, Fayetteville, AR 72701, USA
xintaowu@uark.edu
[4] K12.com, Herndon, VA 20170, USA
smcgrew@k12.com

Abstract. Educational content labeled with proper knowledge components (KCs) are particularly useful to teachers or content organizers. However, manually labeling educational content is labor intensive and error-prone. To address this challenge, prior research proposed machine learning based solutions to auto-label educational content with limited success. In this work, we significantly improve prior research by (1) expanding the input types to include KC descriptions, instructional video titles, and problem descriptions (i.e., three types of prediction task), (2) doubling the granularity of the prediction from 198 to 385 KC labels (i.e., more practical setting but much harder multinomial classification problem), (3) improving the prediction accuracies by 0.5–2.3% using Task-adaptive Pre-trained BERT, outperforming six baselines, and (4) proposing a simple evaluation measure by which we can recover 56–73% of mispredicted KC labels. All codes and data sets in the experiments are available at: https://github.com/tbs17/TAPT-BERT

Keywords: BERT · Knowledge component · Text classification · NLP

1 Introduction

In the math education community, teachers, Intelligent Tutoring Systems (ITSs) and Learning Management Systems (LMSs) have long focused on bringing learners to the target mastery over a set of skills, also known as **Knowledge Components (KCs).** Common Core State Standards (CCSS)[1] is one of the most common categorizations of knowledge components skills in mathematics from kindergarten to high school in the United States with a full set of 385 KCs. For example, in the CCSS code *7.NS.A.1*, *7* stands for 7-th grade, *NS* stands for the domain *Number system*, *A.1* stands for the standard number of the code [5].

---

[1] www.corestandards.org.

© Springer Nature Switzerland AG 2021
I. Roll et al. (Eds.): AIED 2021, LNAI 12748, pp. 408–419, 2021.
https://doi.org/10.1007/978-3-030-78292-4_33

Table 1. Examples of three data types, all having the KC label "8.EE.A.1"

Data Type	Text
Description Text	Know and apply the properties of integer exponents to generate equivalent numerical expressions
Video Title	Apply properties of integer exponents to generate equivalent numerical expressions
Problem Text	Simplify the expression: (z2)2 *Put parentheses around the power if next to coefficient, for example: $3 \times 2 = 3(x^2)$, x5=x^5

In the process of using KCs, the aforementioned stakeholders often encounter the challenges in three scenarios: (1) teachers need to know what KCs a student is unable to master by describing the code content (S_1), (2) ITSs need to tag instructional videos with KCs for better content management (S_2), and (3) LMSs need to know what KCs a problem is associated with in recommending instructional videos to aid problem solving (S_3).

The solutions to these scenarios typically framed the problem as the *multi-nominal classification*–i.e., given the input text, predicts one most relevant KC label out of many KCs: $I(nput) \mapsto text$ and $O(utput) \mapsto KC$. Prior research solutions included SVM-based [12], Non-negative Matrix Factorization (NMF) [6], Skip-gram Representation [17], Neural Network [18] or even cognitively-based knowledge representation [20]. Existing solutions, however, used relatively small number of labels (e.g., 39 or 198) from CCSS with the input of problem text only (similar to Table 1-Row 3) [12,17,18].

Toward this challenge, in this work, we significantly improve existing methods in auto-labeling educational content. First, based on three scenarios of S_1, S_2, and S_3, we consider three types of input, including KC descriptions, instructional video titles, and problem text (as shown in Table 1). Second, we solve the multinomial classification problem with 385 KC labels (instead of 198). Note that the problem becomes much harder. Third, we adopt the *Task-adpative Pre-trained* (TAPT) BERT [9] in solving the multinomial classification problem. Our solution outperforms six baselines, including three classical machine learning (ML) methods and two prior approaches, improving the prediction accuracies by 0.5–2.3% for the tasks of S_1, S_2, and S_3, respectively. Finally, we propose a new evaluation measure, *TEXSTR*, that enables 56–69% more KC labels to be correctly predicted than using the classical measure of *accuracy*.

2 Related Work

KC Models. Rose et al. [20] is one of the earliest work predicting knowledge components, which took a cognitively-based knowledge representation approach. The scale of KCs it examined was small with only 39 KCs. Later research extended the scale of KCs using a variety of techniques. For example, Desmariais [6] used non-negative matrix factorization to induce Q-matrix [3] from simulated data and obtained an accuracy of 75%. The approach did not hold when applying to real data and only got an accuracy of 35%. The two aforementioned studies shared the same drawback: not using the texts from the problems. Karlovcec et al. [12] used problem text data from the ASSISTments platform [10] and created a 106-KC model using 5-fold cross validation via ML approach SVM, achieving top 1 accuracy of 62.1% and top 5 accuracy of 84.2%. Pardos et al. [17] predicted for 198 labels and achieved 90% accuracy via Skip-gram word embeddings of problem id per user (no problem text used). However, Patikorn et al. [18] did a generalizability study of Pardos et al. [17]'s work and only achieved 13.67% accuracy on a new dataset. They found that was because Pardos et al. [17]'s model was over-fitting due to memorizing the question templates and HTML formatting as opposed to encoding the real features of the data. Hence, Patikorn et al. [18] removed all the templates and HTML formatting and proposed a new model using Multi-Layer-Perceptron algorithm, which achieved 63.80% testing accuracy and 22.47% on a new dataset. The model of Patikon et al. [18] became the highest performance for the type of problem text. The preceding research is only focused on problem related content (ID or texts) whereas our work uses not only the problem text but also the KC descriptions and video title data covering a broad range of data.

Pre-Trained BERT Models. The state-of-the-art language model BERT (Bidirectional Encoder Representations From Transformer) [7] is a pre-trained language representation model that was trained on 16 GB of unlabeled texts including Books Corpus and Wikipedia with a total of 3.3 billion words and a vocabulary size of 30,522. Its advantage over other pre-trained language models such as ELMo [19] and ULMFiT [11] is its bidirectional structure by using the *masked language model* (MLM) pre-training objective. The MLM randomly masks 15% of the tokens from the input to predict the original vocabulary id of the masked word based on its context from both directions [7]. The pre-trained model then can be used to train from new data for tasks such as text classification, next sentence prediction.

Users can also further pre-train BERT model with their own data and then fine-tune. This combining process has become popular in the past two years as it can usually achieve better results than fine-tuning only strategy. Sun et al. [21] proposed a detailed process on how to further pre-train new texts and fine-tune for classification task, achieving a new record accuracy. Models such as FinBERT [16], ClinicalBERT [1], BioBERT [15], SCIBERT [2], and E-BERT [23] that were further pre-trained on huge domain corpora (e.g. billions of news articles, clinical texts or PMC Full-text and abstracts) were referred as *Domain-adaptive Pre-trained* (DAPT) BERT and models further pre-trained on task-specific data are referred as *Task-adaptive Pre-trained* (TAPT) BERT by Gururangan et al. [9] such as MelBERT [4] (Methaphor Detection BERT). Although DAPT models usually achieve better performance (1–8% higher), TAPT models also demonstrated competitive and sometimes even higher performance (2% higher) accord-

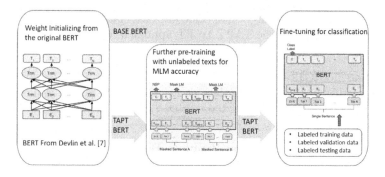

Fig. 1. An illustration of training and fine-tuning process of BASE vs. TAPT

ing to Gururangan et al. [9]. In Liu et al. [16], FinBERT-task was 0.04% higher than domain FinBERT in accuracy. In addition, TAPT requires less time and resource to train. In light of this finding, we use the task-specific data to further pre-train the BERT model.

3 The Proposed Approach

To improve upon existing solutions to the problem of auto-labeling educational content, we propose to exploit recent advancements by BERT language models. Since BERT can encode both linguistic structures and semantic contexts in texts well, we hypothesize its effectiveness in solving the KC labeling problem. By effectively labeling the KCs, we expect to solve the challenges incurred from three scenarios in Sect. 1.

3.1 Task-Adpative Pre-Trained (TAPT) BERT

In particular, we propose to adopt the Task-adaptive Pre-trained (TAPT) BERT and fine-tune it for three types of data. The "pre-training" process is unsupervised such that unlabeled task-specific texts get trained for MLM objective whereas the "fine-tuning" process is supervised such that labeled task-specific texts get trained for classification (see Fig. 1). We call a BERT model that only has a fine-tuning process as BASE. For TAPT, we first initialize the weights from the original BERT (i.e., BERT-base-uncased model). Then, we further pre-train the weights using the unlabeled task-specific texts as well as the combined task texts (see detail in Sect. 4.1) for MLM objective, a process of randomly masking off 15% of the tokens and predict their original vocabulary IDs. The pre-training performance is measured by the accuracy of MLM. Once TAPT is trained, we fine-tune TAPT with the task-specific labeled texts by splitting them into training, validation and testing datasets and feed them into the last softmax layer for classification. We measure the performance of fine-tuning via the testing data accuracy. For BASE, we do not further train it after initializing the weights but directly fine-tune it with the task-specific data for classification (see Fig. 1). To show the effectiveness of the TAPT BERT approach, we compare it against six baselines including BASE BERT for three tasks:

- T_d: to predict K-12 KCs using dataset D_d (description text) based on S_1
- T_t: to predict K-12 KCs using dataset D_t (video title text) based on S_2
- T_p: to predict K-12 KCs using dataset D_p (problem text) based on S_3.

3.2 Evaluating KC Labeling Problem Better: *TEXSTR*

In the regular setting of multinomial classification to predict KC labels, the evaluation is done as binary–i.e., exact-match or non-match. For instance, if a method predicts a KC label to be *7.G.B.6*, but its ground truth is *7.G.A.5*, *7.G.B.6* is considered to be a non-match. However, the incorrectly predicted label of *7.G.B.6* could be closely related to *7.G.A.5* and thus still be useful to teachers or content organizers. For example, in Fig. 2, the input to the classification problem is a video title "Sal explains how to find the volume of a rectangular prism fish tank that has fractional side lengths." Its ground truth label is *7.G.B.6* (7-th grade geometry KC), described as "Solve real world problem involving ... volume ... composed of ... prisms." When one looks at three non-match labels, however, their descriptions do not seem to be so different (see in Fig. 2). That is, all of the three non-match labels (*6.G.A.2, 5.MD.C.5,* and *5.MD.C.3*) mention "volume solving" through "fine/relate/recognize with operations and concepts," which is quite similar to the KC description of the ground truth. However, due to the nature of exact-match based evaluation, these three labels are considered wrong predictions. Further, domain experts explain that some skills are prerequisites to other skills, or that some problems have more than one applicable skills (thus multiple labels) and they could all be correct.

Therefore, we argue that using a strict exact-matching based method in evaluating the quality of the predicted KC labels might be insufficient in practical settings. We then propose a method that considers both semantic and structural similarities among KC labels and their descriptions to be an additional measure to evaluate the usability of the predicted labels.

- Semantic Similarity (C_t): We adopt the Doc2Vec algorithm [14] to capture the similarity between KC labels. Doc2Vec, derived from word-vector algorithm, generates similarity scores between documents instead of words and is proved to have lower error rate (7.7–16%) than the word vector approach [14].
- Structural Similarity (C_s): We exploit prerequisite relationships among skills (KC labels) and capture such as edges and KC labels as nodes in a graph. The prerequisite relationships are extracted from a K-G8 math coherence map by Jason Zimba [24] and a high school (G9-G12) coherence map by UnboundEd Standard Institue [22]. Then, we adopt Node2Vec algorithm [8] that is efficient and flexible in exploring nodes similarity and achieved a new record performance in network classification problem [8].

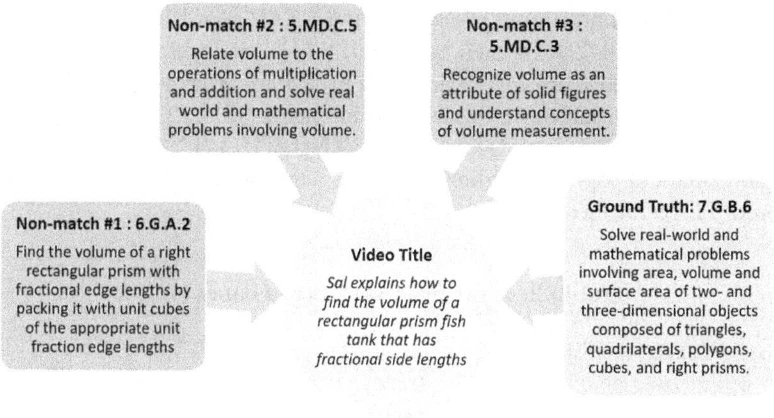

Fig. 2. An illustration of multiple possibilities of a correct label for a given video title text

In the end, we craft a new evaluation measure, named as *TEXSTR* (Λ), by combining both C_t and C_s as follows: $\Lambda = \alpha \cdot C_t + (1 - \alpha) \cdot C_s$, where α controls the weight between C_t and C_s as an oscillating parameter.

4   Empirical Validation

4.1   Datasets and Evaluation Measure

Table 2 summarizes the details of the datasets for pre-training and fine-tuning processes. D_d contains 6,384 description texts (84,017 tokens) and 385 math KCs (an example shown in Fig. 1-a). Part of D_d are extracted from Common Core Standards website[2] and part are provided by k12.com[3], an education management organization that provides online education to American students from kindergarten to Grade 12. D_t contains 6,748 video title texts (62,135 tokens) and 272 math KCs (an example shown in Fig. 1-b) Part of D_t are extracted from *Youtube.com* (via youtube DataAPI[4]) and part are provided by k12.com. D_p contains 13,722 texts (589,549 tokens) and 213 math KCs provided by ASSIST-ments[5] (an example shown in Fig. 1-c). Further, D_{d+t}, D_{d+p}, D_{t+p}, and D_{all} are different combinations of the unlabeled texts from D_d, D_t, and D_p. They are only used in the TAPT pre-training process. We pre-process all aforementioned texts by removing all the templates and HTML markups to avoid over-fitting, suggested by the prior highest accuracy method [18]. In the TAPT pre-training process, 100% of the unlabeled texts from the aforementioned datasets are used

---

[2] http://www.corestandards.org/math.

[3] http://www.k12.com.

[4] http://developers.google.com/youtube/v3.

[5] http://www.assistments.org/.

for pre-training. In fine-tuning process for both TAPT and BASE , only D_d, D_t, and D_p are used and 72% of their texts and labels are used for training, 8% are for validation and 20% are for testing (see in Table 2 Row 1–3 and Col. 6–8).

As an evaluation measure, following prior research [6,12,17,18,20] for direct comparison, we use Accuracy@k as (TP + TN)/(TP + TN + FP + FN), when a method predicts top-k KC labels. Further, we evaluate our method using the proposed *TEXSTR* measure.

Table 2. A summary statistics of datasets.

Name	# Labels	# Texts	# Tokens	Fine-tuning partition		
				Training (72%)	Validation (8%)	Testing (20%)
D_d	385	6,384	84,017	4,596	511	1,277
D_t	272	6,748	62,135	4,858	540	1,350
D_p	213	13,722	589,549	9,879	1,098	2,745
D_{d+t}	/	13,132	146,152	/	/	/
D_{d+p}	/	20,106	673,566	/	/	/
D_{t+p}	/	20,470	651,684	/	/	/
D_{all}	/	26,854	735,701	/	/	/

4.2   Pre-training and Fine-Tuning Details

To further pre-train, we follow the same pre-training process of original BERT with the same network architecture (12 layers, 768 hidden dimensions, 12 heads, 110M parameters) but on our own unlabeled task-specific texts (see Col. 4 in Table 2). With an 8-core v3 TPU, we further train all our models with 100k steps, achieving MLM accuracy of above 97% that lasts about 1–4 hours. We experiment hyper-parameters such as learning rate (lr) $\in$ $\{1e-5, 2e-5, 4e-5, 5e-5, 2e-4\}$, batch size (bs) $\in \{8, 16, 32\}$, and max-sequence length (max-seq-len) $\in \{128, 256, 512\}$. The highest MLM accuracy was achieved when lr $\leftarrow$ 2e-5, bs $\leftarrow$ 32, and max-seq-len $\leftarrow$ 128 (for D_d and D_t) and max-seq-len $\leftarrow$ 512 with the same lr and bs (for D_p, D_{d+p}, D_{t+p}, D_{all}). To fine-tune, we also follow the original BERT script by splitting D_d, D_t, D_p into 72% for training, 8% for validation and 20% for testing per task. We experiment ep $\in \{5, 10, 25\}$ due to the small size of the data size and retain the same hyper-parameter search for lr, bs, max-seq-len. We find that the best testing accuracy is obtained when ep $\leftarrow$ 25, lr $\leftarrow$ 2e-5, bs $\leftarrow$ 32, and max-seq-len $\leftarrow$ 128 for D_d, D_t whereas the best testing accuracy for D_p is obtained when ep $\leftarrow$ 25, lr $\leftarrow$ 2e-5, bs $\leftarrow$ 32, and max-seq-len $\leftarrow$ 512. We find that after ep $\leftarrow$ 25, it is difficult to gain significant increase on the testing accuracy. Hence, the optimal hyper-parameters while task-dependent seem to have very minimal change across tasks. This finding is consistent with SCIBERT reported [2].

4.3   Result #1: TAPT BERT vs. Other Approaches

Table 3 summarizes the experimental results of six baseline approaches and TAPT for each task. For baseline methods, we group them into categories (see in Table 3) (1) classical ML, (2) prior work, and (3) BASE BERT. By including popular ML methods such as Random Forest and XGBoost, we aim to compare its performance to the one from prior ML work (SVM) proposed by Karlovec et al. [12] in the literature review. As to comparing to the prior highest accuracy method [18], we applied the same 5-fold cross-validation on our own problem texts and obtain Acu@1 and Acu@3. Overall, we see that TAPT models outperform all other methods at both Acu@1 and Acu@3 across three tasks. Note TAPT models here are simply trained on the unlabeled texts from D_d, D_t, and D_p. Compared to the best method in baseline, TAPT has an increase of 0.70%, 1.72%, 0.07% at Acu@1 and 0.51%, 2.28%, 1.52% at Acu@3 across three tasks. Compared to BASE, TAPT shows an increase of 2.30%, 1.72%, 0.70% at Acu@1 and 0.51%, 2.28%, 1.52% at Acu@3 across three tasks. Acu@1 and Acu@3 from both TAPT and BASE models are the average performance over five random seeds with significant difference (see last row in Table 3). BERT variants such as FinBERT [16], SCIBERT [2], BioBERT [15] and E-BERT [23] were able to achieve a 1–4% increase when further trained on much larger domain knowledge corpus (i.e. 2–14 billion tokens). Our corpus although comparatively small with D_d (84,017 tokens), D_t (62,135 tokens), and D_p (589,549 tokens) still result in a decent improvement of 0.51–2.30%.

Table 3. Accuracy comparison (best and 2nd best accuracy in blue bold and underlined, respectively, $BL\dagger$ for baseline best, and * for statistical significance with p-value < 0.001)

Approach Type	Algorithm	D_d		D_t		D_p	
		Acu@1	Acu@3	Acu@1	Acu@3	Acu@1	Acu@3
Classical ML	SVM [12]	44.87	70.40	48.15	70.30	78.07	87.69
	XGBoost	43.07	71.34	45.33	66.15	77.63	87.94
	Random Forest	49.26	78.78	49.33	74.37	78.03	88.23
Prior Work	Skip-Gram NN [17]	34.07	34.15	43.00	43.52	76.88	77.06
	Sklearn MLP [18]	50.53	74.41	48.22	57.95	80.70	81.13
BERT	BASE	48.30	76.40	50.99	76.55	81.73	90.99
	TAPT	**50.60**	**79.29**	**52.71**	**78.83**	**82.43**	**92.51**
Improvement	$|TAPT - BL\dagger|$	0.07	0.51	1.72	2.28	0.70	1.52
	$|TAPT - BASE|$	2.30*	0.51*	1.72*	2.28*	0.70*	1.52*

4.4   Result #2: Augmented TAPT and TAPT Generalizability

In addition to the simply trained TAPTs (referred as simple TAPT) in Table 3, we augment the pre-training data and form another four TAPTs ($TAPT_{d+t}$,

$TAPT_{d+p}$, $TAPT_{t+p}$ and $TAPT_{all}$). We call them augmented TAPT. Table 4 showcases the differences in Acu@3 between simple and augmented TAPT. For D_d, augmented $TAPT_{d+p}$ outperforms all simple TAPT models (Acu@3 = 79.56%) and augmented $TAPT_{d+t}$ achieves the second best Acu@3 (79.40%). For D_t, all the augmented TAPT models only outperform simple $TAPT_p$. For D_p, augmented $TAPT_{t+p}$ outperforms all simple TAPTs with Acu@3 of 92.64%. To sum up, augmenting the pre-training data for TAPT seems to help increase the accuracy further.

Table 4. Acu@3: BASE vs. TAPT. (best and 2nd best per row in bold and underlined, and subscripts indicate outperformance over BASE)

Data	BASE	Simple			Augmented			
		$TAPT_d$	$TAPT_t$	$TAPT_p$	$TAPT_{d+t}$	$TAPT_{d+p}$	$TAPT_{t+p}$	$TAPT_{all}$
D_d	76.40	$79.29_{2.89}$	$78.78_{2.38}$	$77.84_{1.44}$	$\underline{79.40}_{3.00}$	$\mathbf{79.56}_{3.16}$	$79.01_{2.61}$	$79.01_{2.61}$
D_t	76.55	$\underline{77.85}_{1.30}$	$\mathbf{78.83}_{2.28}$	$76.30_{-0.25}$	$77.56_{1.01}$	$77.56_{1.01}$	$77.70_{1.15}$	$77.78_{1.23}$
D_p	90.99	$91.22_{0.23}$	$91.44_{0.45}$	$\underline{92.51}_{1.52}$	$92.06_{1.07}$	$92.50_{1.51}$	$\mathbf{92.64}_{1.65}$	$92.35_{1.36}$

Furthermore, we compare the generalizability of TAPT to BASE over different datasets. We define the *generalizability* as task accuracy (specifically Acu@3) that a model can obtain when applied to a different dataset. Both BASE and TAPT are pre-trained models and obtain task accuracy via fine-tuning on a different task data. The subscripts in Table 4 present the difference in Acu@3 between TAPT and BASE, showcasing who has stronger generalizability ($-$ sign indicates weak generalizability). For D_d, all simple and augmented TAPT models generalize better than BASE, especially augmented TAPTs have an average of about 3% increase. For D_t, all TAPT models have better generalizability than BASE with over 1% average increase except for $TAPT_p$. For D_p, we also see all the TAPTs generalize better than BASE model with the augmented $TAPT_{t+p}$ having the best generalizability.

4.5   Result #3: TEXSTR Based Evaluation

Following the definition of *TEXSTR* ($=\Lambda$) in Sect. 3.2, we vary the values of α by {0, 0.5, 1} and generate three variations of Λ for top-3 predictions. We then decide the percentage of miss-predictions to be reconsidered based on Λ value by three cut-off thresholds {0.5, 0.75, 0.9}. Before that, we make sure that the predicted labels are not subsequent to the ground truth, i.e., if the ground truth is *7.G.A.2*, a predicted label such as *8.G.A.3* shall not be reconsidered as correct because it is the skill to be learned subsequently "after" *7.G.A.2*. In such a case, we exclude predicted labels that have subsequent relations to the ground truth and calculate Λ. Table 5 presents the percentage of miss-predictions after removing the subsequent-relation labels by three Λ thresholds when $\alpha \in$

$\{0, 0.5, 1\}$. Across three values of α and datasets, note that 56–73% of miss-predictions could be reconsidered as correct if $\Lambda > 0.5$, 5–53% of them could be reconsidered if $\Lambda > 0.75$, and 0–32% could be reconsidered if $\Lambda > 0.9$. The wide percentage range for $\Lambda \in \{0.75, 0.9\}$ infers that higher thresholds of Λ are more sensitive to the change of α.

To further ensure the *TEXSTR* measure to be useful in practice, we conduct an empirical study where eight experienced K-12 math teachers rate each pair of top-3 KC labels and the corresponding text (e.g., description, video title, or problem text) on a scale of 1 to 5. The Fleiss' kappa value to assess the multi-rater agreement among eight teachers is 0.436, which is considered as moderate agreement by Landis et al. [13]. We ensure that none of top-3 miss-predicted KCs are subsequent to ground truths and have Λ score at least 0.5. Then, we quantify the *relevance* (Υ) score as either Λ score (when $\alpha = 0.5$) or teachers' rating of [1,5] range divided by 5 (to be on the same scale as *TEXSTR*'s [0,1]). Table 6 summarizes three varying relevance scores ($\Upsilon \in \{0.5, 0.75, 0.9\}$) on the pair of top-3 predictions and the texts. For Top-1 predictions, *TEXSTR* considers all of them to have $\Upsilon > 0.5$ (due to the pre-selection) and 37.93% of all have $\Upsilon > 0.75$ and 3.45% have $\Upsilon > 0.9$. Teachers, on the other hand, think that only 54.31% of the texts have $\Upsilon > 0.5$ ($\downarrow$ 45.69% from Λ) but 43.53% have $\Upsilon > 0.75$ ($\uparrow$ 5.6% from Λ) and 31.03% have $\Upsilon > 0.9$ ($\uparrow$ 27.58% from Λ). We also find a similar pattern for Top-2 and Top-3 predictions where teachers find 6.47–6.89% more cases than *TEXSTR* that have $\Upsilon > 0.75$ and 9.48–13.79% more cases than *TEXSTR* that have $\Upsilon > 0.9$. This indicates that *TEXSTR* is more conservative than teachers in judging the relevance of KC labels to texts when $\Upsilon \in \{0.75, 0.9\}$, suggesting *TEXSTR* is effective in reassessing miss-predictions and "recover" them as correct labels in practice.

Table 5. % of miss-predictions recovered by *TEXSTR* (Λ)

Data	# Miss-predictions	$\Lambda > 0.5$			$\Lambda > 0.75$			$\Lambda > 0.9$		
		$\alpha = 0$	$\alpha = 0.5$	$\alpha = 1$	$\alpha = 0$	$\alpha = 0.5$	$\alpha = 1$	$\alpha = 0$	$\alpha = 0.5$	$\alpha = 1$
D_d	248	70.16	68.95	72.98	52.82	24.19	8.87	32.26	2.42	0.81
D_t	240	58.33	55.83	57.5	37.92	17.08	6.67	17.08	0	1.25
D_p	166	60.84	56.63	58.43	38.55	16.27	5.42	18.67	1.2	1.2

Table 6. % of top-3 predictions by relevance (Υ) level when $\alpha = 0.5$

Υ	Top 1			Top 2			Top 3		
	Λ	Teachers	Δ	Λ	Teachers	Δ	Λ	Teachers	Δ
>0.5	100	54.31	−45.69	100	40.95	−59.05	100	21.98	−78.02
>0.75	37.93	43.53	5.60	20.69	27.16	6.47	6.9	13.79	6.89
>0.9	3.45	31.03	27.58	0	13.79	13.79	0	9.48	9.48

5 Conclusion

The paper classified 385 math knowledge components from kindergarten to 12th grade using three data sources (e.g., KC descriptions, video titles, and problem texts) via the *Task-adaptive Pre-trained* (TAPT) BERT model. TAPT has achieved a new record by outperforming six baselines by up to 2% at Acu@1 and up to 2.3% at Acu@3. We also compared TAPT to BASE and found the accuracy of TAPT increased by 0.5–2.3% with a significant p-value. Furthermore, the paper discovered that TAPT trained on the augmented data by combining different task-specific texts had better Acu@3 than TAPT simply trained on the individual datasets. In general, TAPT has better generalizability than BASE by up to 3% at Acu@3 across different tasks. Finally, the paper proposed a new evaluation measure *TEXSTR* to reassess the predicted KCs by taking into account semantic and structural similarity. *TEXSTR* was able to reconsider 56–73% of miss-predictions as correct for practical use.

Acknowledgement. The work was mainly supported by NSF awards (1940236, 1940076, 1940093). In addition, the work of Neil Heffernan was in part supported by NSF awards (1917808, 1931523, 1917713, 1903304, 1822830, 1759229), IES (R305A170137, R305A170243, R305A180401, R305A180401), EIR (U411B190024) and ONR (N00014-18-1-2768) and Schmidt Futures.

References

1. Alsentzer, E., et al.: Publicly available clinical BERT embeddings. In: Proceedings of the 2nd Clinical Natural Language Processing Workshop, pp. 72–78 (2019). https://www.aclweb.org/anthology/W19-1909.pdf
2. Beltagy, I., Lo, K., Cohan, A.: SCIBERT: a pretrained language model for scientific text. In: Proceedings of the Conference on Empirical Methods in Natural Language Processing and 9th International Joint Conference on Natural Language Processing, pp. 3615–3620 (2019)
3. Birenbaum, M., Kelly, A.E., Tatsuoka, K.K.: Diagnosing knowledge states in algebra using the rule-space model. J. Res. Math. Educ. **24**(5), 442–459 (1993). https://www.jstor.org/stable/749153?seq=1&cid=pdf-
4. Choi, M., et al.: MelBERT : metaphor detection via contextualized late interaction using metaphorical identification theories. In: Proceedings of NAACL (2021)
5. corestandards.org: Coding the Common Core State Standards (CCSS). Technical report.http://www.corestandards.org/wp-content/uploads/Math_Standards.pdf
6. Desmarais, M.C.: Mapping question items to skills with non-negative matrix factorization. ACM SIGKDD Explor. News. **13**(2) (2012). https://doi.org/10.1145/2207243.2207248
7. Devlin, J., Chang, M.W., Lee, K., Toutanova, K.: BERT: pre-training of deep bidirectional transformers for language understanding. In: 2019 Conference of the North American Chapter of the Association for Computational Linguistics: Human Language Technologies, vol. 1, pp. 4171–4186 (2019)
8. Grover, A., Leskovec, J.: Node2vec: scalable feature learning for networks. Proc. ACM SIGKDD Int. Conf. Knowl. Discovery Data Min. **13–17**, 855–864 (2016). https://doi.org/10.1145/2939672.2939754

9. Gururangan, S., et al.: Allen: Don't stop pretraining: adapt language models to domains and tasks. In: Proceedings of the 58th Annual Meeting of the Association for Computational Linguistics (2020)

10. Heffernan, N.T., Heffernan, C.L.: The ASSISTments ecosystem: building a platform that brings scientists and teachers together for minimally invasive research on human learning and teaching. Int. J. Artif. Intell. Educ. **24**(4), 470–497 (2014). https://doi.org/10.1007/s40593-014-0024-x

11. Howard, J., Ruder, S.: Universal language model fine-tuning for text classification. In: Proceedings of the 56th Annual Meeting of the Association for Computational Linguistics, pp. 328–339 (2018)

12. Karlovčec, M., Córdova-Sánchez, M., Pardos, Z.A.: Knowledge component suggestion for untagged content in an intelligent tutoring system. In: Cerri, S.A., Clancey, W.J., Papadourakis, G., Panourgia, K. (eds.) ITS 2012. LNCS, vol. 7315, pp. 195–200. Springer, Heidelberg (2012). https://doi.org/10.1007/978-3-642-30950-2_25

13. Landis, J.R., Koch, G.G.: The measurement of observer agreement for categorical data. Biometrics **33**(1), 159 (1977). https://doi.org/10.2307/2529310

14. Le, Q., Mikolov, T.: Distributed representations of sentences and documents. In: Proceedings of the 31st International Conference on International Conference on Machine Learning, pp. II-1188-II-1196 (2014)

15. Lee, J., et al.: Data and text mining BioBERT: a pre-trained biomedical language representation model for biomedical text mining. Bioinformatics p. 1234–1240 (2020). https://doi.org/10.1093/bioinformatics/btz682

16. Liu, Z., Huang, D., Huang, K., Li, Z., Zhao, J.: FinBERT: a pre-trained financial language representation model for financial text mining. In: Proceedings of the Twenty-Ninth International Joint Conference on Artificial Intelligence Special Track on AI in FinTech (2020)

17. Pardos, Z.A.: Imputing KCs with representations of problem content and context. In: Proceedings of the 25th Conference on User Modeling, Adaptation and Personalization. pp. 148–155 (2017). https://doi.org/10.1145/3079628.3079689

18. Patikorn, T., Deisadze, D., Grande, L., Yu, Z., Heffernan, N.: Generalizability of methods for imputing mathematical skills needed to solve problems from texts. In: Isotani, S., Millán, E., Ogan, A., Hastings, P., McLaren, B., Luckin, R. (eds.) AIED 2019. LNCS (LNAI), vol. 11625, pp. 396–405. Springer, Cham (2019). https://doi.org/10.1007/978-3-030-23204-7_33

19. Peters, M.E., Neumann, M., Gardner, M., Clark, C., Lee, K., Zettlemoyer, L.: Deep contextualized word representations. In: Proceedings of NAACL-HLT, pp. 2227–2237 (2018)

20. Rosé, C., Donmez, P., Gweon, G., Knight, A., Junker, B., Cohen, W., Koedinger, K., Heffernan, N.: Automatic and semi-automatic skill coding with a view towards supporting on-line assessment. In: Proceedings of the conference on Artificial Intelligence in Education, pp. 571–578 (2005)

21. Sun, C., Qiu, X., Xu, Y., Huang, X.: How to fine-tune BERT for text classification? In: Sun, M., Huang, X., Ji, H., Liu, Z., Liu, Y. (eds.) CCL 2019. LNCS (LNAI), vol. 11856, pp. 194–206. Springer, Cham (2019). https://doi.org/10.1007/978-3-030-32381-3_16

22. UnboundEd: A "Coherence Map" for the High School Standards. Technical report (2017). https://www.unbounded.org/other/8610

23. Zhang, D., et al.: E-BERT: Adapting BERT to E-commerce with Adaptive Hybrid Masking and Neighbor Product Reconstruction (2020)

24. Zimba, J.: A graph of the content standards. Technical report (2012). https://achievethecore.org/page/844/a-graph-of-the-content-standards

A Multidimensional Item Response Theory Model for Rubric-Based Writing Assessment

Masaki Uto[(⊠)] [iD]

The University of Electro-Communications, Tokyo, Japan
uto@ai.lab.uec.ac.jp

Abstract. When human raters grade student writing assignments, writing assessment often involves the use of a scoring rubric consisting of multiple evaluation items in order to increase the objectivity of evaluation. However, even when using a rubric, assigned scores are known to be influenced by the characteristics of both the rubric's evaluation items and the raters, thus decreasing the reliability of student assessment. To resolve this problem, these characteristic effects have been considered in many recently proposed item response theory (IRT) models for estimating student ability. Such IRT models assume unidimensionality, meaning that a rubric measures one latent ability; in practice, however, this assumption might not be satisfied because a rubric's evaluation items are often designed to measure multiple sub-abilities that constitute a targeted ability. To address this issue, this study proposes a multidimensional extension of such an IRT model for rubric-based writing assessment. The proposed model improves the assessment reliability. Furthermore, the model is useful for objective and detailed analysis of rubric quality and its construct validity. This study demonstrates the effectiveness of the proposed model through simulation experiments and application to real data.

Keywords: Educational/psychological measurement · Writing assessment · Analytic rubrics · Test theory · Statistical/probabilistic model

1 Introduction

In various assessment fields, writing assessment has attracted much attention as a way to measure practical and higher-order abilities, such as logical thinking, critical reasoning, and creative thinking [1,2,13,20,32,34,42]. In writing assessments, human raters often use a scoring rubric that consists of multiple evaluation items when grading student writing assignments to increase the objectivity of evaluation. However, even when using a rubric, assigned scores are known to depend on the characteristics of both the rubric's evaluation items and the raters, which decreases the reliability of the assessment of student ability [6,12,25,27,30,41,44]. Therefore, to improve measurement accuracy, ability

© Springer Nature Switzerland AG 2021
I. Roll et al. (Eds.): AIED 2021, LNAI 12748, pp. 420–432, 2021.
https://doi.org/10.1007/978-3-030-78292-4_34

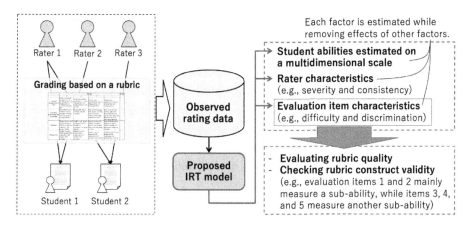

Fig. 1. Outline of an application of the proposed model.

estimation that considers the effects of the abovementioned characteristics is required.

For this reason, item response theory (IRT) models have been proposed that can estimate student abilities while considering the characteristics of both the rubric's evaluation items and the raters [15,18,35,44,48]. One representative model is the many-facet Rasch model (MFRM) [18], which has been used in various performance assessments, including writing assessments [5,6,12,16,19,39]. The MFRM, however, makes strong assumptions that rarely hold in practice [15,25,28,36,46]. Thus, several extensions of the MFRM that relax these assumptions have been recently proposed [15,35,44,46]. These IRT models are known to measure abilities with higher accuracy than that of simple scoring methods based on point totals or averages [43,46].

Such IRT models assume *unidimensionality*, meaning that a rubric measures one latent ability. However, this assumption might not hold in practice because evaluation items in a rubric are often designed so that multiple sub-abilities that comprise a targeted ability are measured. Applying unidimensional IRT models to data with multidimensional ability scales deteriorates model fitting and ability measurement accuracy [14].

IRT models that can estimate multidimensional ability scales have been proposed for traditional objective testing scenarios [31]. Such multidimensional IRT models, however, have no rater parameters, which prevents not only estimation of student ability while considering the effects of rater characteristics, but also direct application to rubric-based writing assessment data.

To resolve the abovementioned problems, the present study proposes a new multidimensional IRT model that incorporates parameters for the characteristics of both the rubric's evaluation items and the raters. The outline of an application of the proposed model to rubric-based writing assessment data is shown in Fig. 1. The use of the proposed model has the following advantages.

1. The proposed model allows for estimation of student abilities while considering the effects of the rubric's evaluation items and the raters simultaneously, which improves the model fitting and ability measurement accuracy.
2. Student abilities can be assessed on an appropriate multidimensional ability scale that is assumed under the rubric's evaluation items.
3. The model provides the characteristic parameters for the rubric's evaluation items while removing the effects of the raters and students. According to the parameters, we can conduct an objective and detailed analysis of the rubric's characteristics and its construct validity, and therefore obtain useful information to evaluate the rubric's quality and to develop a better rubric.

This study demonstrates the effectiveness of the proposed model through simulation experiments and application to actual data.

2 Rating Data from Rubric-Based Writing Assessment

In this study, we assume situations where each student's writing assignment is graded by multiple raters who use a scoring rubric consisting of multiple evaluation items. Obtained rating data are defined as $\boldsymbol{X} = \{x_{ijr} | x_{ijr} \in \mathcal{K} \cup \{-1\}, i \in \mathcal{I}, j \in \mathcal{J}, r \in \mathcal{R}\}$, where x_{ijr} is a rating assigned to a writing outcome of student $j \in \mathcal{J} = \{1, 2, \cdots, J\}$ by rater $r \in \mathcal{R} = \{1, 2, \cdots, R\}$ based on the rubric's evaluation item $i \in \mathcal{I} = \{1, 2, \cdots, I\}$. Here, $\mathcal{K} = \{1, 2, \cdots, K\}$ represents rating categories, and $x_{ijr} = -1$ represents missing data. This study aims to estimate student ability from rating data $\boldsymbol{X}$ using IRT.

3 Item Response Theory

IRT [21] is a test theory based on mathematical models and has been widely used in various educational assessments. IRT represents the probability of a student response to a test item as a function of latent student ability and item characteristics such as difficulty and discrimination. Traditional IRT models are applicable to two-way data (*students* × *test items*), consisting of student test item scores. Well-known IRT models that are applicable to ordered-categorical data, such as writing assessment data, include the generalized partial credit model (GPCM) [24] and the graded response model [33]. Such traditional models, however, cannot be directly applied to rubric-based writing assessment data comprising *students* × *raters* × *evaluation items*. To address this problem, IRT models that can consider the characteristics of both the rubric's evaluation items and the raters have been proposed [15,18,35,44,48]. Note that some such IRT models originally consider characteristics of test items and raters assuming three-way data consisting of *students* × *raters* × *test items*. However, we apply such IRT models by regarding the facet of *test items* as the *rubric's evaluation items*.

3.1   IRT Models in Writing Assessment

The most widely used IRT model with characteristic parameters of a rubric's evaluation items and raters is the MFRM [18]. However, the MFRM makes strong assumptions that all raters are consistent in how they rate, and that the discriminatory power of all evaluation items is the same, even though these assumptions do not hold in practice [15,25,28,36,46]. To relax these assumptions, various extensions of the MFRM have recently been proposed [7,15,35,44,46]. The present study introduces the generalized MFRM [45,46], which is one of the latest MFRM extensions that relaxes these assumptions. This model provides the probability that $x_{ijr} = k$ as

$$P_{ijrk} = \frac{\exp \sum_{m=1}^{k} [1.7\alpha_r \alpha_i (\theta_j - \beta_i - \beta_r - d_{rm})]}{\sum_{l=1}^{K} \exp \sum_{m=1}^{l} [1.7\alpha_r \alpha_i (\theta_j - \beta_i - \beta_r - d_{rm})]} , \tag{1}$$

where θ_j is the latent ability of student j, α_i is a discrimination parameter for evaluation item i, α_r is the consistency of rater r, β_i is a difficulty in evaluation item i, β_r is the severity of rater r, and d_{rm} is a step parameter denoting the severity of rater r in transition from evaluation category $m-1$ to m. The constant 1.7 is used to make the model similar to the normal ogive function. For model identification, $\prod_{i=1}^{I} \alpha_i = 0$, $\sum_{i=1}^{I} \beta_i = 0$, $d_{r1} = 0$, $\sum_{m=2}^{K} d_{rm} = 0$, and a normal prior for ability θ_j are assumed.

The model parameters can be estimated from the rating data $\boldsymbol{X}$. IRT models, such as the model described above, are known to measure student abilities with higher accuracy than simple scoring, such as point averages, because the abilities can be estimated while removing bias effects [43,46]. However, as described in Sect. 1, conventional models assume *unidimensionality*, which might not hold in practice. Applying unidimensional models to data with multidimensional ability scales deteriorates model fitting and ability measurement accuracy [14].

3.2   Multidimensional IRT Models

In objective testing contexts, multidimensional IRT models that can measure student ability in multidimensional space have widely been used [31]. A representative multidimensional IRT model for ordered-categorical data is the non-compensatory multidimensional GPCM [50]. When test item parameters are regarded as evaluation item parameters, the model gives the probability that student j obtains score k for evaluation item i as

$$P_{ijk} = \frac{\exp \sum_{m=1}^{k} \left[1.7 \left(\sum_{l=1}^{L} \alpha_{il}\theta_{jl} - \beta_i - d_{im}\right)\right]}{\sum_{l=1}^{K} \exp \sum_{m=1}^{l} \left[1.7 \left(\sum_{l=1}^{L} \alpha_{il}\theta_{jl} - \beta_i - d_{im}\right)\right]} , \tag{2}$$

where L indicates the number of assumed ability dimensions, θ_{jl} is the ability of student j for dimension $l \in \mathcal{L} = \{1, \cdots, L\}$, α_{il} indicates the discriminatory power of evaluation item i for the l-th ability dimension, and d_{im} is a step parameter denoting difficulty in transition between scores $m - 1$ and m for evaluation item i. In model identification, $d_{i1} = 0$, $\sum_{m=2}^{K} d_{im} = 0$, and a normal prior for the ability of each dimension θ_{jl} are assumed.

Such conventional multidimensional IRT models, however, have no rater parameters, which prevents not only estimation of student ability while considering the effects of rater characteristics, but also direct application to rubric-based writing assessment data. To address this limitation, this study proposes a new multidimensional IRT model that considers the characteristics of both the rubric's evaluation items and the raters.

4   Proposed Model

The proposed model is formulated as an extension of the non-compensatory GPCM. Specifically, this model gives the probability that $x_{ijr} = k \in \mathcal{K}$ as

$$P_{ijrk} = \frac{\exp \sum_{m=1}^{k} \left[1.7\alpha_r \left(\sum_{l=1}^{L} \alpha_{il}\theta_{jl} - \beta_i - \beta_r - d_{im} \right) \right]}{\sum_{l=1}^{K} \exp \sum_{m=1}^{l} \left[1.7\alpha_r \left(\sum_{l=1}^{L} \alpha_{il}\theta_{jl} - \beta_i - \beta_r - d_{im} \right) \right]} . \tag{3}$$

In model identification, this study implements the restrictions $\prod_{r=1}^{R} \alpha_r = 0$, $\sum_{r=1}^{R} \beta_r = 0$, $d_{i1} = 0$, and $\sum_{k=2}^{K} d_{ik} = 0$, and assumes the standard normal prior for the ability of each dimension θ_{jl}.

Application of the proposed model to the rubric-based writing assessment data provides the various characteristics of each evaluation item and rater, which helps in interpreting the quality of the evaluation items and the raters. Also, the evaluation item's discrimination parameters α_{il} offers information for interpreting what each ability dimension measures, which makes an objective analysis of rubric construct validity possible. The model, thus, can be viewed as an artificial intelligence model that extracts a latent structure in rating data. We show an example of such analysis in the actual data experiment section.

Furthermore, the proposed model can estimate student ability on a multidimensional scale while considering the characteristics of both the evaluation items and the raters, although the conventional models cannot consider rater characteristics nor estimate ability on a multidimensional scale. Thus, the proposed model is expected to provide better model fitting and appropriate ability measurement compared with the conventional models.

To estimate the proposed model parameters, we use an expected a posteriori (EAP) estimation, which is a type of Bayesian estimation, using the No-U-Turn (NUT) sampler-based Markov chain Monte Carlo (MCMC) algorithm [11]. The EAP is known to provide more robust estimations than a maximum likelihood estimation [8,43] and the NUT sampler is highly efficient compared with the Metropolis-Hastings-within-Gibbs sampling method [29], which is a common MCMC algorithm for IRT models [3]. The estimation program was implemented in RStan [4,37]. We used the standard normal distribution $N(0.0, 1.0)$ as a prior distribution for θ_{jl}, $\log \alpha_{il}$, $\log \alpha_r$, β_i, β_r, and d_{ik}. The EAP estimates were calculated using parameter samples obtained from 2,000 to 4,000 periods.

In the proposed model, the number of ability dimensions, L, is a hand-tuned parameter. In IRT studies, the optimal number of dimensions is generally explored based on principal component analysis. However, this analysis method is not applicable to the three-way data assumed in the present study. Dimensionality selection, which is well-known in machine learning, can also be considered as a model selection task. The model selection is typically conducted using information criteria. This study uses the widely applicable information criterion (WAIC) [47] because it can be used with Bayesian estimation based on a MCMC method and is applicable regardless of the true distribution. Specifically, we select the number of dimensions that minimizes the WAIC.

5   Simulation Experiments

5.1   Parameter Recovery Experiment

In this subsection, we describe a parameter recovery experiment for the proposed model through simulations. Specifically, the following experiments were conducted while the number of students J, evaluation items I, raters R, and ability dimensions L were varied (where the number of categories K was fixed at 4 to match the condition of the actual data used in a later section).

1) Generate true model parameters randomly for θ_{jl}, $\log \alpha_{il}$, $\log \alpha_r$, β_i, β_r, and d_{im} from the standard normal distribution. To maintain the identifiability of the dimensions, we set skewed discrimination values to the first L evaluation items $i \in \{1, \ldots, L\}$ according to related experiments that used conventional multidimensional IRT models [22]. 2) Given the true parameters, sample rating data from the proposed model randomly. 3) Estimate the model parameters using the data by the MCMC algorithm. 4) Calculate the root mean square error (RMSE) between the estimated and true parameters. 5) Repeat the above procedure 30 times, then calculate the average values of the RMSEs.

The *RMSE* column in Table 1 shows the results, which confirm the following tendencies: 1) The RMSEs for ability values tend to decrease as the number of evaluation items and/or raters increases. Similarly, the RMSEs for raters and evaluation item parameters tend to decrease as the number of students increases. These tendencies are caused by the increase in the amount of data per parameter, which is consistent with previous studies [43,44]. 2) An increase in the number of dimensions tends to lead to an increase in the RMSEs because the ability and discrimination parameters increase without an increase in the amount of data. This tendency is also consistent with previous research [17,22,38].

We also confirmed the bias and the Gelman–Rubin statistic $\hat{R}$ [9,10], which is a well-known convergence diagnostic index. The average bias was nearly zero in all cases, indicating no overestimation or underestimation of parameters. The $\hat{R}$ statistic was less than 1.1 in all cases, indicating that the MCMC runs converged.

From the above, we conclude that the parameter estimation for the proposed model can be appropriately conducted through use of the MCMC algorithm.

Table 1. Results of simulation experiments.

J	I	R	L	RMSE						Average rank		
				θ_{jl}	α_{il}	α_r	β_i	β_r	d_{im}	$L^e=1$	$L^e=2$	$L^e=3$
100	5	5	1	0.22	0.11	0.09	0.07	0.06	0.13	**1.57**	2.07	2.37
			2	0.32	0.16	0.08	0.10	0.05	0.15	2.93	1.77	**1.30**
			3	0.36	0.16	0.09	0.12	0.07	0.16	3.00	2.00	**1.00**
		15	1	0.13	0.08	0.09	0.04	0.06	0.08	**1.30**	1.93	2.77
			2	0.22	0.10	0.09	0.07	0.05	0.09	3.00	**1.33**	1.67
			3	0.25	0.12	0.08	0.09	0.06	0.09	3.00	1.93	**1.07**
	15	5	1	0.13	0.09	0.04	0.06	0.03	0.15	**1.20**	1.90	2.90
			2	0.24	0.11	0.05	0.09	0.03	0.16	3.00	**1.20**	1.80
			3	0.29	0.12	0.04	0.10	0.03	0.16	3.00	2.00	**1.00**
		15	1	0.09	0.06	0.04	0.04	0.03	0.10	**1.17**	1.87	2.97
			2	0.17	0.09	0.05	0.07	0.03	0.10	3.00	**1.13**	1.87
			3	0.20	0.09	0.05	0.09	0.03	0.09	3.00	2.00	**1.00**
50	15	15	1	0.11	0.10	0.07	0.06	0.04	0.12	**1.13**	1.97	2.90
			2	0.20	0.12	0.08	0.10	0.04	0.13	3.00	**1.07**	1.93
			3	0.22	0.13	0.08	0.10	0.05	0.14	3.00	2.00	**1.00**

5.2   Validity of Dimensionality Selection

In this subsection, we describe a simulation experiment that evaluates the appropriateness of the dimensionality selection using the WAIC as an information criterion. The following experiments were conducted while the number of students J, evaluation items I, raters R, and ability dimensions L were varied.

1) Generate rating data from the proposed model given randomly generated true model parameters. 2) Estimate the parameters for the proposed models assuming $L^e \in \{1, 2, 3\}$ number of dimensions using the data by the MCMC algorithm. 3) Rank the WAIC values for each L^e, such that the L^e with the lowest WAIC value is ranked first place. 4) Repeat the above procedure 30 times, then calculate the average rank.

The *Average rank* column in Table 1 displays the results, with the highest ranks shown in bold. The results show that the true dimensionality was selected in all cases except when the number of evaluation items and raters was small. These results verify the appropriateness of using the WAIC to select the optimal number of dimensions.

6   Actual Data Experiments

In this section, we describe the performance of the proposed model in experiments based on actual data. In the experiment, we collected actual rubric-based writing assessment data according to the following procedure: 1) We gathered

134 Japanese university students majoring in various STEM fields. 2) The students were asked to complete an essay-writing task. 3) The written essays were evaluated by 18 raters who used a rubric consisting of nine evaluation items divided into four rating categories. We assigned four raters to each essay based on a systematic links design [35, 40, 49] to decrease the raters' assessment workload. The *Evaluation items* column in Table 2 lists the abstracts of the evaluation items.

Table 2. Evaluation items and their characteristic parameters.

Evaluation items	$\hat{\alpha}_{i1}$	$\hat{\alpha}_{i2}$	$\hat{\beta}_i$	$\hat{d}_{i2}$	$\hat{d}_{i3}$	$\hat{d}_{i4}$
1. Appropriateness of problem setting	0.203	**0.381**	−0.631	−0.920	−0.250	1.170
2. Consistency between claims and conclusions	0.222	**0.473**	−0.629	−0.731	−0.291	1.022
3. Presentation of evidence	0.137	**0.451**	−0.595	−1.472	0.219	1.254
4. Consideration of opposing viewpoints	0.111	**0.274**	−0.297	−0.399	−0.246	0.645
5. Appropriateness of logical structure	0.296	**0.495**	−0.795	−0.901	−0.212	1.113
6. Consideration of readers	0.314	**0.442**	−0.673	−0.651	−0.460	1.112
7. Typographical accuracy	**0.517**	0.109	−1.345	−0.814	−0.380	1.194
8. Stylistic consistency	**0.421**	0.177	−0.815	−0.659	−0.247	0.907
9. Usage of conjunctions	**0.449**	0.243	−1.250	−0.762	−0.282	1.044

6.1   Model Comparison Using Information Criteria

As explained above, the proposed model can estimate student ability on a multidimensional scale while considering the characteristics of both the raters and the rubric's evaluation items. To evaluate the effectiveness of the consideration of the multidimensionality and rater characteristics, we conducted a model fitting evaluation based on information criteria. Specifically, we calculated the WAIC for the proposed model using the actual data for each dimensionality $L \in \{1, \cdots, 5\}$. We conducted the same procedure for the proposed model without rater parameters, which is the model constrained $\alpha_r = 1$ and $\beta_r = 0$ for all r. We designated the model without rater parameters as the *conventional model* because it is consistent with the equation of the multidimensional GPCM defined in Eq. (2).

Table 3. Model comparison using actual data.

	# of dimensions L				
	1	2	3	4	5
Proposed model	11741.78	**11642.76**	11652.29	11654.60	11661.45
Conventional model	12279.44	12201.60	12206.06	12220.16	12226.76

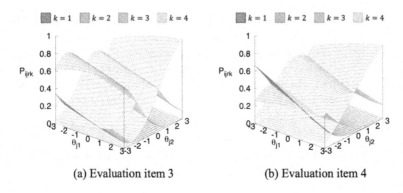

(a) Evaluation item 3   (b) Evaluation item 4

Fig. 2. Score distributions for two evaluation items with different step difficulty.

Table 3 shows the results. The table indicates that the WAIC is minimized when $L = 2$ in both the proposed model and the conventional model. This means that the unidimensionality assumption is not satisfied in the data, suggesting the requirement of the multidimensional models. Furthermore, comparison of the two models shows that the proposed model provides a better fitting than the conventional model in all cases. The results suggest that consideration of rater characteristics is effective in improving model fitting, which verifies the effectiveness of the proposed model.

6.2   Characteristic Interpretation of the Rubric's Evaluation Items

In this subsection, we show the interpretation of the characteristics of the evaluation items. Table 2 shows the parameters of the evaluation items, which were estimated by the proposed model under $L = 2$. Here, $L = 2$ was used because it provided the highest model fitting, as shown in the experiment describe above.

According to Table 2, the evaluation items reveal different patterns of discrimination parameters. For example, evaluation items 1–6 have larger discrimination values in the second dimension, whereas evaluation items 7–9 have larger discrimination values in the first dimension. Moreover, evaluation item 4 has relatively low discrimination values in both dimensions, meaning that it might not be suitable for distinguishing student ability. In contrast, evaluation item 6 has moderate discrimination values in both dimensions, meaning that it measures two-dimensional ability concurrently.

The discrimination parameters of each evaluation item enable us to interpret what is mainly measured by each ability dimension. Specifically, as described above, Table 2 shows that evaluation items 1–6 have larger discrimination values in the second dimension, and evaluation items 7–9 have larger values in the first dimension. These results suggest that the first ability dimension reflects a common ability underlying evaluation items 7–9, and the second dimension reflects a common ability underlying evaluation items 1–6. According to the contents of the evaluation items, we can see that evaluation items 7–9 relate to *stylistic skills*

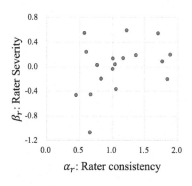
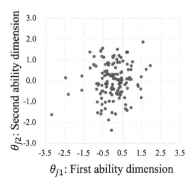

Fig. 3. Rater parameters   **Fig. 4.** Ability estimates

(such as typological errors and word choice), whereas evaluation items 1–6 relate to *logical skills* (such as augmentation and organization). Indeed, the rubric was designed such that evaluation items 1–6 mainly measure argumentative skills, and evaluation items 7–9 measure stylistic skills [23, 26]. These results suggest that the rubric developer's expectation is supported by the analysis based on the proposed model.

Furthermore, Table 2 shows that the level of difficulty differs among the evaluation items. For example, evaluation item 4 is the most difficult, and evaluation item 7 is the easiest. These are reasonable judgments because evaluation item 4 requires sufficient discussion about opposing opinions, whereas evaluation item 7 requires only superficial typological correctness.

The step difficulty parameters, d_{im}, also show different patterns, meaning that the score distribution differs among the evaluation items. As examples, Fig. 2 depicts the score distribution (plot of P_{ijrk}) for evaluation items 3 and 4, which have different step difficulty parameter patterns as well as relatively similar discrimination and difficulty. The figure shows that a score of 2 tends to be avoided in evaluation item 4. See [7, 44, 46] for further details on interpretation of step difficulty parameters.

6.3   Raters Parameter Estimates and Ability Estimates

To confirm whether rater characteristics differed, we plotted characteristic parameters for each rater, as shown in Fig. 3. In that figure, each plot represents a rater, and horizontal and vertical axes respectively show the rater consistency α_r and severity β_r values. According to Table 2, severity and consistency differed among the raters. This is the reason why the proposed model provided a higher model fitting than the conventional multidimensional GPCM model.

Moreover, Fig. 4 shows the two-dimensional ability estimates for each student. The horizontal axis indicates the first-dimensional ability value θ_{j1}; the vertical axis indicates the second-dimensional ability value θ_{j2}; and each dot represents a student. The figure shows that the students have different ability patterns.

Such multidimensional ability measurement cannot be realized by conventional unidimensional IRT models.

7   Conclusion

This study proposes a new multidimensional IRT model with characteristic parameters of raters and a rubric's evaluation items for rubric-based writing assessment. Through simulation experiments and actual real data application, we demonstrated the effectiveness of the proposed model. The proposed model not only improves assessment reliability, but also is useful for objective and detailed analysis of rubric characteristics and its construct validity. In the educational domain, a scoring rubric is widely used in various performance assessment scenarios. In such situations, the proposed method is helpful to evaluate the rubric's quality and to develop a better rubric. We plan to evaluate the effectiveness of the proposed method using various and more massive datasets in future studies.

References

1. Abosalem, Y.: Beyond translation: adapting a performance-task-based assessment of critical thinking ability for use in Rwanda. Int. J. Second. Educ. **4**(1), 1–11 (2016)
2. Bernardin, H.J., Thomason, S., Buckley, M.R., Kane, J.S.: Rater rating-level bias and accuracy in performance appraisals: the impact of rater personality, performance management competence, and rater accountability. Hum. Resour. Manag. **55**(2), 321–340 (2016)
3. Brooks, S., Gelman, A., Jones, G., Meng, X.: Handbook of Markov Chain Monte Carlo. Chapman & Hall/ CRC Handbooks of Modern Statistical Methods, CRC Press, Boca Raton (2011)
4. Carpenter, B., Gelman, A., Hoffman, M., Lee, D., Goodrich, B., Betancourt, M., Brubaker, M., Guo, J., Li, P., Riddell, A.: Stan: a probabilistic programming language. J. Stat. Softw. Art. **76**(1), 1–32 (2017)
5. Chan, S., Bax, S., Weir, C.: Researching participants taking IELTS Academic Writing Task 2 (AWT2) in paper mode and in computer mode in terms of score equivalence, cognitive validity and other factors. Technical report, IELTS Research Reports Online Series (2017)
6. Deng, S., McCarthy, D.E., Piper, M.E., Baker, T.B., Bolt, D.M.: Extreme response style and the measurement of intra-individual variability in affect. Multivar. Behav. Res. **53**(2), 199–218 (2018)
7. Eckes, T.: Introduction to Many-Facet Rasch Measurement: Analyzing and Evaluating Rater-Mediated Assessments. Peter Lang Pub. Inc., New York (2015)
8. Fox, J.P.: Bayesian Item Response Modeling: Theory and applications. Springer, Heidelberg (2010)
9. Gelman, A., Carlin, J., Stern, H., Dunson, D., Vehtari, A., Rubin, D.: Bayesian Data Analysis, Third Edition. Chapman & Hall/CRC Texts in Statistical Science, Taylor & Francis, London (2013)
10. Gelman, A., Rubin, D.B.: Inference from iterative simulation using multiple sequences. Stat. Sci. **7**(4), 457–472 (1992)

11. Hoffman, M.D., Gelman, A.: The No-U-Turn sampler: adaptively setting path lengths in Hamiltonian Monte Carlo. J. Mach. Learn. Res. **15**, 1593–1623 (2014)
12. Hua, C., Wind, S.A.: Exploring the psychometric properties of the mind-map scoring rubric. Behaviormetrika **46**(1), 73–99 (2019)
13. Hussein, M.A., Hassan, H.A., Nassef, M.: Automated language essay scoring systems: a literature review. PeerJ Comput. Sci. **5**, e208 (2019)
14. Hutten, L.R.: Some Empirical Evidence for Latent Trait Model Selection. ERIC Clearinghouse (1980)
15. Jin, K.Y., Wang, W.C.: A new facets model for rater's centrality/extremity response style. J. Educ. Meas. **55**(4), 543–563 (2018)
16. Kaliski, P.K., Wind, S.A., Engelhard, G., Morgan, D.L., Plake, B.S., Reshetar, R.A.: Using the many-faceted Rasch model to evaluate standard setting judgments. Educ. Psychol. Measur. **73**(3), 386–411 (2013)
17. Kose, I.A., Demirtasli, N.C.: Comparison of unidimensional and multidimensional models based on item response theory in terms of both variables of test length and sample size. Procedia. Soc. Behav. Sci. **46**, 135–140 (2012)
18. Linacre, J.M.: Many-faceted Rasch Measurement. MESA Press, San Diego (1989)
19. Linlin, C.: Comparison of automatic and expert teachers' rating of computerized English listening-speaking test. Engl. Lang. Teach. **13**(1), 18 (2019)
20. Liu, O.L., Frankel, L., Roohr, K.C.: Assessing critical thinking in higher education: current state and directions for next-generation assessment. ETS Res. Rep. Ser. **1**, 1–23 (2014)
21. Lord, F.: Applications of item response theory to practical testing problems. Erlbaum Associates, Mahwah (1980)
22. Martin-Fernandez, M., Revuelta, J.: Bayesian estimation of multidimensional item response models. a comparison of analytic and simulation algorithms. Int. J. Methodol. Exp. Psychol.**38**(1), 25–55 (2017)
23. Matsushita, K., Ono, K., Takahashi, Y.: Development of a rubric for writing assessment and examination of its reliability [in Japanese]. J. Lib. Gen. Educ. Soc. Japan **35**(1), 107–115 (2013)
24. Muraki, E.: A generalized partial credit model. In: van der Linden, W.J., Hambleton, R.K. (eds.) Handbook of Modern Item Response Theory, pp. 153–164. Springer (1997)
25. Myford, C.M., Wolfe, E.W.: Detecting and measuring rater effects using many-facet Rasch measurement: part I. J. Appl. Meas. **4**, 386–422 (2003)
26. Nakajima, A.: Achievements and issues in the application of rubrics in academic writing: a case study of the college of images arts and sciences [in Japanese]. Ritsumeikan High. Educ. Stud. **17**, 199–215 (2017)
27. Nguyen, T., Uto, M., Abe, Y., Ueno, M.: Reliable peer assessment for team project based learning using item response theory. In: Proceedings of the International Conference on Computers in Education, pp. 144–153 (2015)
28. Patz, R.J., Junker, B.W., Johnson, M.S., Mariano, L.T.: The hierarchical rater model for rated test items and its application to large-scale educational assessment data. J. Educ. Behav. Stat. **27**(4), 341–384 (2002)
29. Patz, R.J., Junker, B.: Applications and extensions of MCMC in IRT: multiple item types, missing data, and rated responses. J. Educ. Behav. Stat. **24**(4), 342–366 (1999)
30. Rahman, A.A., Hanafi, N.M., Yusof, Y., Mukhtar, M.I., Yusof, A.M., Awang, H.: The effect of rubric on rater's severity and bias in TVET laboratory practice assessment: analysis using many-facet Rasch measurement. J. Tech. Educ. Train. **12**(1), 57–67 (2020)

31. Reckase, M.D.: Multidimensional Item Response Theory Models. Springer, New York (2009). https://doi.org/10.1007/978-0-387-89976-3_4
32. Rosen, Y., Tager, M.: Making student thinking visible through a concept map in computer-based assessment of critical thinking. J. Educ. Comput. Res. **50**(2), 249–270 (2014)
33. Samejima, F.: Estimation of latent ability using a response pattern of graded scores. Psychometrika Monogr. **17**, 1–100 (1969)
34. Schendel, R., Tolmie, A.: Assessment techniques and students' higher-order thinking skills. Assess. Eval. High. Educ. **42**(5), 673–689 (2017)
35. Shin, H.J., Rabe-Hesketh, S., Wilson, M.: Trifactor models for multiple-ratings data. Multivar. Behav. Res. **54**(3), 360–381 (2019)
36. Soo Park, Y., Xing, K.: Rater model using signal detection theory for latent differential rater functioning. Multivar. Behav. Res. **54**(4), 492–504 (2019)
37. Stan Development Team: RStan: the R interface to stan. R package version 2.17.3. http://mc-stan.org (2018)
38. Svetina, D., Valdivia, A., Underhill, S., Dai, S., Wang, X.: Parameter recovery in multidimensional item response theory models under complexity and nonnormality. Appl. Psychol. Meas. **41**(7), 530–544 (2017)
39. Tavakol, M., Pinner, G.: Using the many-facet Rasch model to analyse and evaluate the quality of objective structured clinical examination: a non-experimental cross-sectional design. BMJ Open **9**(9), 1–9 (2019)
40. Uto, M.: Accuracy of performance-test linking based on a many-facet Rasch model. Behavior Research Methods p. In press (2020)
41. Uto, M., Duc Thien, N., Ueno, M.: Group optimization to maximize peer assessment accuracy using item response theory and integer programming. IEEE Trans. Learn. Technol. **13**(1), 91–106 (2020)
42. Uto, M., Okano, M.: Robust neural automated essay scoring using item response theory. In: Proceedings of the International Conference on Artificial Intelligence in Education, pp. 549–561 (2020)
43. Uto, M., Ueno, M.: Item response theory for peer assessment. IEEE Trans. Learn. Technol. **9**(2), 157–170 (2016)
44. Uto, M., Ueno, M.: Empirical comparison of item response theory models with rater's parameters. Heliyon **4**(5), 1–32 (2018)
45. Uto, M., Ueno, M.: Item response theory without restriction of equal interval scale for rater's score. In: Proceedings of the International Conference on Artificial Intelligence in Education, pp. 363–368 (2018)
46. Uto, M., Ueno, M.: A generalized many-facet Rasch model and its Bayesian estimation using Hamiltonian Monte Carlo. Behaviormetrika **47**(2), 469–496 (2020)
47. Watanabe, S.: Asymptotic equivalence of Bayes cross validation and widely applicable information criterion in singular learning theory. J. Mach. Learn. Res. **11**(12), 3571–3594 (2010)
48. Wilson, M., Hoskens, M.: The rater bundle model. J. Educ. Behav. Stat. **26**(3), 283–306 (2001)
49. Wind, S.A., Jones, E.: The effects of incomplete rating designs in combination with rater effects. J. Educ. Meas. **56**(1), 76–100 (2019)
50. Yao, L., Schwarz, R.D.: A multidimensional partial credit model with associated item and test statistics: an application to mixed-format tests. Appl. Psychol. Meas. **30**(6), 469–492 (2006)

Towards Blooms Taxonomy Classification Without Labels

Zichao Wang[1(✉)], Kyle Manning[1], Debshila Basu Mallick[2],
and Richard G. Baraniuk[1,2]

[1] Rice University, Houston, TX, USA
{jzwang,ksm9,richb}@rice.edu
[2] OpenStax, Houston, TX, USA
debshila@rice.edu

Abstract. In this work, we explore weakly supervised machine learning for classifying questions into distinct Bloom's Taxonomy levels. Bloom's levels provide important information that guides teachers and adaptive learning algorithms in selecting appropriate questions for their students. However, manually providing Bloom labels is expensive and labor-intensive, which motivates a machine learning approach. Current automated Bloom's level classification methods employ *supervised learning* that relies on large *labeled* datasets that are difficult and costly to construct. In this paper, we propose a *weakly supervised learning* method that performs binary Bloom's level labeling *without any a priori known Bloom's taxonomy labels*. The key idea behind BLACBOARD (for *B*loom's *L*evel cl*A*ssifi*C*ation *B*ased *O*n we*A*kly supe*R*vise*D* learning) is to appropriately incorporate human domain knowledge into the modeling process to produce a *weakly labeled* dataset on which discriminative models can then be trained. We compare BLACBOARD to fully supervised learning methods and show that it achieves little to no performance compromise while *using entirely unlabeled data*.

Keywords: Bloom's level classification · Weakly supervised learning

1 Introduction

Educational assessments, e.g., homework and quiz questions, are important pedagogical instruments that help assess students' knowledge retention and foster higher-order cognitive processing such as thinking and reasoning [1]. To effectively use such questions to improve learning, it is important to know which ones are appropriate for which students and maximize the alignment between the course content and assessments [2]. To this end, teachers often utilize the *Bloom's Taxonomy* of educational objectives [3,4] as a framework to categorize questions based on the specific cognitive functions that they exercise. This framework provides practical guidelines on how to characterize existing questions such that they facilitate specific cognitive processes and how to author *new* questions. However, teachers often do not assign Bloom's labels when authoring new

© Springer Nature Switzerland AG 2021
I. Roll et al. (Eds.): AIED 2021, LNAI 12748, pp. 433–445, 2021.
https://doi.org/10.1007/978-3-030-78292-4_35

questions, making it difficult for other teachers to reuse them. The reason is that manually assigning Bloom's level labels is incredibly time-consuming, expensive, and error prone [5,6].

To reduce the cost of manually labeling questions with Bloom's levels, researchers have developed various automatic labeling methods that almost universally formulate the task as a supervised learning classification problem [6–15]. The resulting models must learn using *supervised training data*, i.e., a large collection of questions already labeled with Bloom's levels, in order to accurately predict Bloom's levels [6]. Gathering such data involves the expensive and problematic process of manually collecting Bloom's level labels outlined above. Likely due to the high cost of collecting labeled data, previous works have used very small labeled datasets, which raises concerns about their robustness and generalizability [6]. In contrast, it is straightforward to collect questions that *do not* have Bloom's level labels. The abundance of unlabeled data and the high cost of collecting labeled data calls for methods *other than supervised ones* for Bloom's level classification.

1.1   Contributions

In this paper, we develop a new framework for Bloom's level classification based on *weakly supervised learning* (WSL) that accurately classifies questions into Bloom's levels *without requiring labeled training data*. The fundamental idea behind BLACBOARD (for *B*loom's *L*evel cl*A*ssifi*C*ation *B*ased *O*n we*A*kly supe*R*vise*D* learning) is to codify experts' domain knowledge in Bloom's Taxonomy into a set of *labeling functions* (LFs) and then programmatically generate Bloom's level labels using these functions to form a *weakly* labeled dataset. In this way, we create a labeled dataset using entirely unlabeled data and human experts' domain knowledge.

Our framework consists of three main components. The first component is a novel set of *LFs* carefully crafted from domain experts' knowledge of Bloom's Taxonomy, which generates a set of (noisy) Bloom's level labels for each question. The second component is a *probabilistic graphical model* that infers the most appropriate (weak) Bloom's level label for each question from the set of (noisy) labels. The third and last component is a *supervised classifier* that we train on the inferred weakly labeled dataset and use for the final Bloom's level assignment. We experimentally evaluate our framework on a large, real-world question bank spanning a variety of subjects such as calculus, physics, sociology, and history. Preliminary results on a binary Bloom's level classification task demonstrate that our proposed WSL framework achieves competitive classification performances compared to fully supervised learning methods. Notably, our framework obtains such results *without any a priori known labels*.

2   Preliminaries and Related Work

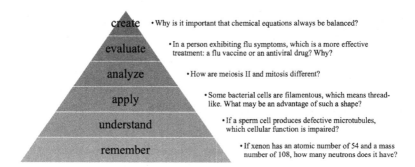

Fig. 1. Illustration of the Bloom's Taxonomy levels from level 1 (bottom) to level 6 (top), with an example question corresponding to each level from a biology textbook.

Bloom's Levels and Classification. The Bloom's Taxonomy [4] that we use in this work consists of 6 levels, each aiming to evaluate cognitive processes that increase in difficulty. Figure 1 illustrates each Bloom's level. The 6 Bloom's levels have in several instances been re-categorized into *two levels* to reflect lower-order cognitive skills (LOCS) and higher-order cognitive skills (HOCS) [1,3,16–18], where higher-order cognitive skills refers to cognitive processes that require more than merely retrieving information [19,20]. Aligned with this perspective, in this work we consider this LOCS and HOCS binary Bloom's level categorization, where LOCS contains Bloom's level 1 and HOCS contains Blooms level 2 – 6.

Existing research has developed methods for Bloom's level classification based on supervised learning. Most of the prior work is based on support vector machines (SVMs) [7,8,12,13] with a few others using naïve Bayes [14] and ensemble methods [6,9]. Other work explores text representation methods such as augmenting the TF-IDF representation [10] or integrating linguistic features [11,15]. However, as mentioned earlier, all of the above rely on fully labeled datasets, which are difficult and expensive to obtain in practice. Indeed, most of the above works use very small datasets of only a few hundred or fewer questions, which severely limits their practical and research impacts.

Weakly Supervised Learning. Weakly supervised learning (WSL) [21] is an emerging machine learning paradigm that enables one to solve classification problems *without using any labeled data*. We refer readers interested in WSL to [21] for a thorough introduction and focus on its notable features here. Compared to traditional supervised learning, WSL requires no a priori known labels; the labels are created during the modeling process. This overcomes supervised learning methods' reliance on labeled data, which is often limited in quantity

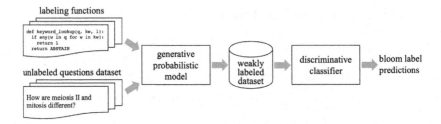

Fig. 2. An illustration of BLACBOARD, our proposed weakly supervised learning framework for Bloom's level classification of questions.

and difficult to collect. Thus, WSL makes it possible to solve classification problems using only unlabeled data, which in some applications is massive and cheap to collect. WSL also has rigorous theoretical foundations [21–24] and has had promising empirical success in a wide range of real-world, high-stakes applications. For example, in medical applications, WSL has contributed to medical entity recognition [25], MRI image classification [26], medical device surveillance [27], and genomic information compilation [28]. WSL has not yet been applied in education except for one work that proposes a weak supervision-based conversational agent for teacher education [29] (Fig. 2).

3   Methodology

We now describe our BLACBOARD framework. We introduce our novel LFs, explain how to incorporate LFs into a graphical model to infer the weak Bloom's level label for each question, and finally show how to combine the weakly labeled questions dataset with a supervised classifier. As mentioned in Sect. 2, in this work we tackle the *binary* Bloom's level classification problem, where one class LOCS includes Bloom's level 1 and the other class HOCS includes Bloom's level 2–6. Extension to all 6 Bloom's levels is left for future work.

3.1   Human Expert-Inspired Labeling Functions (LFs)

An LF $f_j(\boldsymbol{x}_i) : \mathbb{R}^D \to |\boldsymbol{y}| \cup \{\emptyset\}$ assigns a Bloom's level label to each question. $\boldsymbol{x}_i \in \mathbb{R}^D$ is the D-th dimensional vector representation of question i. $\boldsymbol{y} = \{y_i\}_{i=1}^N$ is the set of labels and $y_i \in \{0, 1\}$ is the label for each of the N question. We assume LOCS and HOCS are class 0 and 1, respectively. $j \in \{1, \ldots, L\}$ indexes the LFs. $|\cdot|$ is the cardinality of $\boldsymbol{y}$, which in our case is 2 because $\boldsymbol{y}$ is binary. We include the empty set as a potential output of an LF, because an LF can abstain, i.e., give no label to a question.

To effectively design these critical LFs, we conducted semi-structured interviews of 3 education experts investigating how they utilize Bloom's taxonomy in their general pedagogy while creating tests, authoring questions, and labeling existing questions. We used the findings from these interviews to design

Table 1. Description of labeling functions (LFs). "Bloom 1 – 6 kw" collapses 6 similar LFs.

LF	Description	Output
Short	Check the number of words in the question	LOCS if # characters less than 75, $\emptyset$ otherwise
Why	Check whether the word "why" is in the question	HOCS if the word "why" is in question, $\emptyset$ otherwise
Bloom 1–6 kw	Each checks whether keywords (kw) specific to each Bloom's level is in the question	LOCS if the keyword is in question, $\emptyset$ otherwise
Glossary	Check whether glossary terms is in the question	HOCS if the more than 3 terms are in question, $\emptyset$ otherwise
Readability	Computes a question's Flesch readability score	HOCS if the score < 50, $\emptyset$ otherwise

11 simple labeling functions that represent Bloom's level characteristics and domain knowledge, which we believe to be useful for determining the appropriate Bloom's level for a given question. Table 1 describes all of our LFs, which we categorize into 3 groups. The first group ("short", "why", "readability") focuses on question properties. Our intuition is that HOCS questions tend to be longer, less readable, and ask more "why" questions. The second group ("Bloom 1 – 6 kw") looks for keywords (kw) indicative of each Bloom's level. We collect these keywords from teachers' rubrics and instructions for writing questions at a specific Bloom's level. The third group ("glossary") looks for keywords specific to *subject domains*, i.e., biology. Our intuition is that HOCS questions tend to contain more subject domain keywords, which potentially reflects increased question complexity and demands higher level skills. We collect these keywords from the textbooks' glossaries.

3.2 Graphical Model for Weak Label Inference

With the LFs, each data point now has a set of noisy labels. However, to train a classifier, each data point must have a label. Therefore, we must learn the most likely (weak) label given a set of labels for each data point. To do so, we leverage a generative model following [21], which we include here for completeness. Concretely, let $y \in \mathbb{R}^N$ be the ground-truth labels and $\Upsilon \in (y \cup \{\emptyset\})^{N \times M}$ be the weak label matrix obtained from the LFs where N is the number of data points and L is the number of LFs. Then, we model the joint distribution of the weak and the true labels for all data points using the following generative model:

$$p_\theta(\Upsilon, y) = A_\theta^{-1} \exp \left(\sum_{i=1}^M \theta^\top f_i(\Upsilon, y_i) \right),$$

where A_θ is a normalizing constant. $f_i(\cdot)$ is a function that combines three LF properties including labeling propensity f^{pro}, accuracy f^{acc} and correlation f^{cor}:

$$f_{i,j}^{\mathrm{pro}}(\Upsilon, \boldsymbol{y}) = \mathbf{1}\{\Upsilon_{i,j} \neq \emptyset\}, \tag{1}$$

$$f_{i,j}^{\mathrm{acc}}(\Upsilon, \boldsymbol{y}) = \mathbf{1}\{\Upsilon_{i,j} = y_i\}, \tag{2}$$

$$f_{i,j,k}^{\mathrm{cor}}(\Upsilon, \boldsymbol{y}) = \mathbf{1}\{\Upsilon_{i,j} = \Upsilon_{j,k}\}, \tag{3}$$

where θ is the model parameters and $\mathbf{1}\{\cdot\}$ is an indicator function. These three properties are important for understanding LFs' effectiveness and thus are incorporated into the generative model. Notably, computing LF properties using Eqs. 1 and 3 do not require any ground-truth data. We will leverage these unsupervised LF analytics in Sect. 4.3 and validate LF effectiveness. Because we assume ground-truth labels $\boldsymbol{y}$ are unavailable in our setting, we optimize the model and learn the model parameters $\widehat{\theta}$ using the marginal log likelihood which eliminates $\boldsymbol{y}$. Concretely, the optimization objective is

$$\widehat{\theta} = \arg\min_\theta - \log \sum_{\boldsymbol{y}} p_\theta(\Upsilon, \boldsymbol{y}).$$

More details on labeling correlation computation and model optimization are available in [21].

3.3 Bloom's Level Classifier

To obtain the final Bloom classification results, we leverage a classifier trained on the weakly labeled dataset in which each data point has a label inferred by the generative model using our LFs. Note that we may simply use the inferred labels as the final Bloom taxonomy label for each question without training a supervised classifier. However, a classifier brings more modeling capability and is beneficial for classification performance. In Sect. 4.2, we empirically confirm the advantage of additionally training a classifier on the weak labels.

4 Experiments

We now empirically show the power of BLACBOARD that uses questions without any Bloom's level labels for Bloom's level classification.[1] We first compare BLACBOARD with the selected LFs to supervised learning methods that use fully labeled data. We then present LF analytics that our framework enables and that help us understand the effectiveness of each LF. Notably, this LF evaluation step is unsupervised, i.e., without access to the ground-truth labels.

---

[1] A demonstration and associated code of BLACBOARD are available at https:// github.com/manningkyle304/edu-research-demo.

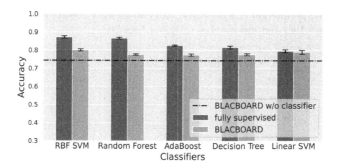

Fig. 3. Quantitative Bloom's level classification results comparing BLACBOARD to fully supervised methods. We see that for all classifiers used, BLACBOARD achieves classification accuracies very close to supervised methods using *fully unlabeled* data.

4.1 Dataset

We use a new, closed-source, large-scale, real-world dataset from OpenStax[2] of 17,719 multiple-choice questions that are actively used in practice and have expert-tagged Bloom's levels ranging from level 1 to 6. The dataset includes questions from multiple subjects, including natural sciences (biology, physics) and social sciences (economics, history, sociology), and is representative of high-school and college-level courses. These properties make our dataset the largest and most diverse one to be used for Bloom's level classification to our knowledge. For our binary Bloom's level classification problem, we reassign the Bloom labels, resulting in 11,190 LOCS questions and 6,529 HOCS questions. A naïve majority classifier gives a classification accuracy of 63.15%, which serves as one of our baselines. We encode each question into a numeric feature vector using TF-IDF that is commonly used in text mining and information retrieval [30].[3]

4.2 Comparing BLACBOARD to Fully Supervised Methods

In this experiment, we compare BLACBOARD, which uses entirely unlabeled data, against supervised learning methods that use fully labeled data. This experiment will demonstrate the capability of WSL in effectively performing classification tasks in the absence of human-provided ground-truth labels. We randomly split the data into 80% training and 20% test sets. For BLACBOARD, we learn the weak labels for all questions in the training set and then train a classifier on the weakly labeled training set. For supervised learning, we simply train a classifier on the training set with ground-truth labels. To verify the results in different settings, we use a variety of classifiers for both BLACBOARD and supervised learning, including linear support vector machine (SVM), radial Basis function

---

[2] https://openstax.org.

[3] We also experimented with other featurization methods, but the results were similar to TF-IDF. We thus use TF-IDF for all experiments in this paper.

Table 2. Labeling function (LF) analysis. We can identify 2 weak LFs, because of low coverage ("why" LF) and low overlap ("Bloom 5 kw" LF).

Labeling functions	Coverage	Overlap	Conflict
Short	0.435	0.326	0.111
Why	0.007	0.006	0.003
Bloom 1 kw	0.321	0.308	0.133
Bloom 2 kw	0.218	0.211	0.163
Bloom 3 kw	0.286	0.250	0.185
Bloom 4 kw	0.166	0.163	0.101
Bloom 5 kw	0.142	0.006	0.003
Bloom 6 kw	0.142	0.142	0.091
Glossary	0.104	0.085	0.053
Readability	0.329	0.271	0.197

(RBF) SVM, random forest, adaboost, and decision trees [31,32]. We perform each experiment 5 times and report the average accuracies on the test set.

Figure 3 visualizes the average test accuracies (with standard deviation) comparing BLACBOARD to fully supervised learning methods for each classifier. We observe that BLACBOARD achieves classification performance close to fully supervised methods. In particular, for linear SVM, BLACBOARD achieves statistically the same performance as its fully supervised counterpart. This result showcases that, with entirely unlabeled data and by creatively incorporating domain expertise, BLACBOARD approaches the performance of supervised learning methods using fully labeled data with minimal performance degradation. We also see that removing the classifier in BLACBOARD leads to lower accuracy, implying that a classifier trained on weak labels can improve performance.

4.3 Unsupervised Labeling Function Analysis

In this experiment, we show how we can perform LF analysis in an unsupervised manner, i.e., without the ground-truth labels. This analysis reveals insights about the effectiveness of each LF and helps us retain or discard certain LFs.

Metrics. Recall that the generative model in BLACBOARD leverages three LF properties including propensity, accuracy, and correlation. We now leverage these properties to define 3 types of statistics for each LF. The first statistic is **coverage**, which computes the number of questions that an LF assigns a label, i.e., $\Upsilon_{ij} \neq \emptyset$ for LF f_j. The second statistic is *overlap*, which computes the portion of questions with at least 2 weak labels. The third statistic is *conflict*, which computes a portion of questions for which at least 1 other LF yields a label different from the LF under examination.

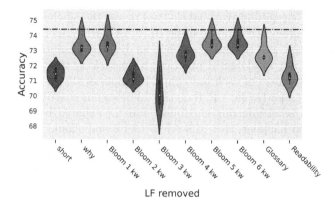

Fig. 4. Post-hoc leave-one-LF-out analysis results. We show the average and density of the accuracies for the experiment with each excluded LF. The horizontal line is the best accuracy with all LFs. We can see that none of the LFs, if removed, statistically improve the labeling accuracy, suggesting that each individual LF contributes to the labeling inferring capability and all should be kept.

Results, Interpretation and Significance. Table 2 reports the analysis results, averaged over 5 random runs. We first see that the conflict scores are low for all LFs. This is an encouraging signal because each LF agrees with the other LFs in general. The opposite situation, in which LFs tend to give contrasting labels, would cause much trouble for the graphical model to infer the most likely weak label. Therefore, having a sizable number of LFs that do not conflict much suggests that all LFs are reasonable. However, some LFs have low coverage (e.g., "why" LF) and low overlap (e.g., "why" and "Bloom 5 kw" LFs). An LF with low coverage and overlap suggests that this LF influences only a very small fraction of all data points and contributes little to improving the modeling capacity. For example, for the "why" LF (indexed by j), its corresponding row in the weak label matrix Υ_j would have mostly -1 representing abstain (e.g., no label). This row thus has limited influence for the graphical model inference.

In this work, we choose to keep all LFs because conflicts are low. Even for the LFs with low coverage and overlap, they have lower conflicts and thus do not appear to cause negative effects on the weak label inference process. Through these analyses, we show that by examining the LF statistics in an unsupervised manner (e.g., without using any ground-truth labels), we can verify the validity of our LFs and identify LFs that have limited contribution to the weak label inference process.

Post-hoc Analysis with Ground-truth Labels. To illustrate the conclusions from our unsupervised LF analysis using coverage, overlap, and conflict statistics, we additionally perform a post-hoc, leave-one-LF-out experiment. Specifically, we remove one LF and use the remaining LFs to train the generative model in BLACBOARD. We perform this training step for every LF using the training data (again without ground-truth labels) and report the labeling accuracy on the test set. This accuracy is computed using BLACBOARD's inferred labels and the ground-truth labels and is thus a post-hoc analysis because we assume ground-truth labels are not available in practice. Nevertheless, this post-hoc analysis reveals the effectiveness of each individual LF. Specifically, if the test accuracy improves *without* a particular LF, then this LF does not contribute to improving BLACBOARD's label inferring capability and thus should be removed. If the opposite situation happens, then this LF is useful and should be retained.

Figure 4 shows the post-hoc analysis results for each LF, averaged over 5 runs with different train-test splits. The horizontal line is the best labeling accuracy with all LFs. We can see that most of the LFs, if removed, significantly decrease the accuracy, suggesting that these are important LFs and should be kept. Some LFs, such as the "knowledge keywords" (Bloom 1 kw), sometimes improve performance if removed. However, the improvement is not statistically significant; in most of the 5 runs, the accuracy decreases when these LFs are removed. Thus, all LFs are useful in BLACBOARD and none should be removed. This result is consistent with and confirms the conclusion in the preceding unsupervised LF analysis.

5   Conclusions and Future Work

In this paper, we have introduced BLACBOARD, a WSL framework for Bloom's level classification. To the best of our knowledge, this is the first work to investigate WSL for Bloom's level classification. Our framework, unlike existing supervised methods for Bloom's level classification, requires no labeled dataset. Instead, it incorporates instructional and domain expertise into modeling to create weak labels for classification. We report promising preliminary results on a large, real-world question dataset, demonstrating that, compared to conventional fully supervised methods, BLACBOARD suffers little to no decline in performance.

The modular framework of our weak supervision approach coupled with our new procedures to perform unsupervised model diagnostics enables iterative and intuitive adjustments for improvements. In the future, we intend to extend our framework from binary to full 6-level Bloom's level labeling. One promising avenue of research is to investigate more sophisticated LFs based on linguistic and heuristic characteristics of Bloom's levels. More advanced models that leverage recently developed deep probabilistic methods can also contribute to improving the weak label inference capability. The essential value of a WSL approach is that it does not rely on massive, high-quality, labeled data, therefore resulting in a scalable solution to a previously unscalable problem. Our present work forecasts the exciting promise of transferring the WSL approach for solving a wide range of problems in Artificial Intelligence in Education beyond Bloom's level classification including question generation [33], educational conversational agents [34], forum posts sentiment analysis [35], and knowledge graph construction [36].

Acknowledgements. This work was supported by NSF grants 1842378 and 1937134 and by ONR grant N0014-20-1-2534. We thank Prof. Colleen Countryman (Ithaca College), Prof. Lauren Rast (The University of Alabama at Birmingham), Joyce Spangler (Six Red Marbles), and Andrew Giannakakis (OpenStax) for helpful discussions on the Labeling Functions. Thanks to Fred Sala for insights on WSL. Thanks to anonymous reviewers and CJ Barberan for suggestions on the manuscript.

References

1. Swart, A.J.: Evaluation of final examination papers in engineering: a case study using Bloom's taxonomy. IEEE Trans. Educ. **53**(2), 257–264 (2010)
2. Blumberg, P.: Maximizing learning through course alignment and experience with different types of knowledge. Innovative High. Educ. **34**(2), 93–103 (2009)
3. Bloom, B., Engelhart, M., Furst, E., Hill, W., Krathwohl, D.: Taxonomy of educational objectives: the classification of educational goals. Handbook 1: cognitive domain. David McKay, New York (1956)
4. Krathwohl, D.R.: A revision of bloom's taxonomy : an overview. Theory Pract. **41**(4), 212–218 (2002)
5. Abduljabbar, D.A., Omar, N.: Exam questions classification based on Bloom's taxonomy cognitive level using classifiers combination. J. Theor. Appl. Inf. Technol. **78**(3), 447 (2015)
6. Osadi, K., Fernando, M., Welgama, W., et al.: Ensemble classifier based approach for classification of examination questions into Bloom's taxonomy cognitive levels. Int. J. Comput. Appl. **162**(4), 1–6 (2017)
7. Yahya, A.A., Osman, A.: Automatic classification of questions into Bloom's cognitive levels using support vector machines. In: International Arab Conference on Information Technology (2011)
8. Jayakodi, K., Bandara, M., Perera, I.: An automatic classifier for exam questions in engineering: a process for Bloom's taxonomy. In: IEEE International Conference on Teaching, Assessment, and Learning for Engineering (TALE), pp. 195–202 (2015)
9. Mohamed, O.J., Zakar, N.A., Alshaikhdeeb, B.: A combination method of syntactic and semantic approaches for classifying examination questions into bloom's taxonomy cognitive. J. Eng. Sci. Technol. **14**(2), 935–950 (2019)
10. Mohammed, M., Omar, N.: Question classification based on Bloom's taxonomy using enhanced TF-IDF. Int. J. Adv. Sci. Eng. Inf. Technol. **8**, 1679–1685 (2018)
11. Osman, A., Yahya, A.A.: Classifications of exam questions using natural language syntatic features: a case study based on Bloom's taxonomy. In: Proceedings of the International Arab Conference on Quality Assurance in Higher Education (2016)
12. Sangodiah, A., Ahmad, R., Ahmad, W.F.W.: A review in feature extraction approach in question classification using support vector machine. In: IEEE International Conference on Control System, Computing and Engineering, pp. 536–541 (2014)
13. Pota, M., Esposito, M., De Pietro, G.: A forward-selection algorithm for SVM-based question classification in cognitive systems. In: De Pietro, G., Gallo, L., Howlett, R.J., Jain, L.C. (eds.) Intelligent Interactive Multimedia Systems and Services 2016. SIST, vol. 55, pp. 587–598. Springer, Cham (2016). https://doi.org/10.1007/978-3-319-39345-2_52
14. Supriyanto, C., Yusof, N., Nurhadiono, B., et al.: Two-level feature selection for Naive Bayes with kernel density estimation in question classification based on

Bloom's cognitive levels. In: International Conference on Information Technology and Electrical Engineering, pp. 237–241 (2013)

15. Diab, S., Sartawi, B.: Classification of questions and learning outcome statements (LOS) into Blooms taxonomy (BT) by similarity measurements towards extracting of learning outcome from learning material. arXiv preprint (2017)

16. Zoller, U.: Are lecture and learning compatible? Maybe for LOCS: unlikely for HOCS. J. Chem. Edu. **70**(3), 195 (1993)

17. Karamustafaoğlu, S., Sevim, S., Karamustafaoğlu, O., Cepni, S.: Analysis of Turkish high-school chemistry-examination questions according to bloom's taxonomy. Chem. Educ. Res. Pract. **4**(1), 25–30 (2003)

18. Crowe, A., Dirks, C., Wenderoth, M.P.: Biology in Bloom: implementing bloom's taxonomy to enhance student learning in biology. CBE-Life Sci. Educ. **7**(4), 368–381 (2008)

19. Baker, E.L.: Developing comprehensive assessments of higher order thinking. Assess. High. Order Think. Math. **7**, 20 (1990)

20. Herrington, J., Oliver, R.: Using situated learning and multimedia to investigate higher-order thinking. J. Interact. Learn. Res. **10**(1), 3–24 (1999)

21. Ratner, A., et al.: Snorkel: rapid training data creation with weak supervision. VLDB J. **29**(2), 709–730 (2019). https://doi.org/10.1007/s00778-019-00552-1

22. Varma, P., Ré, C.: Snuba: automating weak supervision to label training data. Proc. VLDB Endow. **12**(3), 223–236 (2018)

23. Varma, P., He, B.D., Bajaj, P., Khandwala, N., Banerjee, I., Rubin, D., Ré, C.: Inferring generative model structure with static analysis. Adv. Neural. Inf. Process. Syst. **30**, 240–250 (2017)

24. Bach, S.H., He, B., Ratner, A., Ré, C.: Learning the structure of generative models without labeled data. In: Proceedings of the International Conference on Machine Learning, pp. 273–282 (2017)

25. Fries, J.A., et al.: Trove: ontology-driven weak supervision for medical entity classification. arXiv e-prints, August 2020

26. Fries, J.A., et al.: Weakly supervised classification of aortic valve malformations using unlabeled cardiac MRI sequences. Nature Commun. **10**(1), 3111 (2019)

27. Callahan, A., Fries, J.A., Ré, C., Huddleston, J.I., Giori, N.J., Delp, S., Shah, N.H.: Medical device surveillance with electronic health records. NPJ Digit. Med. **2**(1), 94 (2019)

28. Kuleshov, V., et al.: A machine-compiled database of genome-wide association studies. Nature Commun. **10**(1), 3341 (2019)

29. Datta, D., Phillips, M., Chiu, J., Watson, G.S., Bywater, J.P., Barnes, L., Brown, D.: Improving classification through Weak supervision in context-specific conversational agent development for teacher education. arXiv e-prints, October 2020

30. Salton, G., McGill, M.J.: Introduction to Modern Information Retrieval. McGraw-Hill Inc, New York, USA (1986)

31. Hastie, T., Tibshirani, R., Friedman, J.: The Elements of Statistical Learning. Springer New York Inc., New York, USA (2001)

32. Bishop, C.M.: Pattern Recognition and Machine Learning (information science and statistics). Springer-Verlag, Berlin, Heidelberg (2006)

33. Wang, Y., Zheng, J., Liu, Q., Zhao, Z., Xiao, J., Zhuang, Y.: Weak supervision enhanced generative network for question generation. arXiv preprint (2019)

34. Datta, D., et al.: Improving classification through weak supervision in context-specific conversational agent development for teacher education. arXiv preprint (2020)

35. Ramesh, A., Kumar, S.H., Foulds, J., Getoor, L.: Weakly supervised models of aspect-sentiment for online course discussion forums. In: Proceedings of the 53rd Annual Meeting of the Association for Computational Linguistics and the 7th International Joint Conference on Natural Language Processing, pp. 74–83 (2015)
36. Qiu, Y., Wang, Y., Jin, X., Zhang, K.: Stepwise reasoning for multi-relation question answering over knowledge graph with weak supervision. In: Proceedings of the 13th International Conference on Web Search and Data Mining, pp. 474–482 (2020)

Automatic Task Requirements Writing Evaluation via Machine Reading Comprehension

Shiting Xu, Guowei Xu, Peilei Jia, Wenbiao Ding$^{(\boxtimes)}$, Zhongqin Wu,
and Zitao Liu

TAL Education Group, Beijing, China
{xushiting,xuguowei,jiapeilei,dingwenbiao,
wuzhongqin,liuzitao}@tal.com

Abstract. Task requirements (TRs) writing is an important question type in Key English Test and Preliminary English Test. A TR writing question may include multiple requirements and a high-quality essay must respond to each requirement thoroughly and accurately. However, the limited teacher resources prevent students from getting detailed grading instantly. The majority of existing automatic essay scoring systems focus on giving a holistic score but rarely provide reasons to support it. In this paper, we proposed an end-to-end framework based on machine reading comprehension (MRC) to address this problem to some extent. The framework not only detects whether an essay responds to a requirement question, but clearly marks where the essay answers the question. Our framework consists of three modules: question normalization module, ELECTRA based MRC module and response locating module. We extensively explore state-of-the-art MRC methods. Our approach achieves 0.93 accuracy score and 0.85 F1 score on a real-world educational dataset. To encourage reproducible results, we make our code publicly available at https://github.com/aied2021TRMRC/AIED_2021_TRMRC_code.

Keywords: Task requirements writing · Machine reading comprehension · Pre-training language model · Neural networks

1 Introduction

Key English Test[1] (KET) and Preliminary English Test[2] (PET) are examinations to assess the communication ability of the test taker in practical situations. In PET and KET, there are a variety of question types, including speaking, reading, listening, and writing. In writing questions, examinees are not only required to write an essay precisely and correctly but need to make responses to the **Task Requirements (TRs)**. According to official scoring instructions, an essay with poor task achievements should be assigned a low grade. Some examples of TR writing questions are shown in Table 1.

---

[1] https://www.cambridgeenglish.org/exams-and-tests/key.
[2] https://www.cambridgeenglish.org/exams-and-tests/preliminary.

© Springer Nature Switzerland AG 2021
I. Roll et al. (Eds.): AIED 2021, LNAI 12748, pp. 446–458, 2021.
https://doi.org/10.1007/978-3-030-78292-4_36

Table 1. Examples of TR writing questions in PET.

1	*A TV company came to your school yesterday to make film.*
	Write an email to your English friend Alice. In your email, you should
	* Explain why the TV company chose your school
	* Tell her who or what they filmed
	* Say when the programme will be shown on television.
2	*You arranged to meet your English friend Sally next Tuesday,*
	but you have to change the time.
	Write an email to Sally. In your email, you should
	* Suggest a new time to meet on Tuesday
	* Explain why you need to change the time
	* Remind Sally where you arranged to meet

[1] Lines begin with ***** are task requirement questions.

Timely and accurate evaluation on the performance of test-takers, especially informing them of TR achievements of their essays, is essential to improve their writing and communication skills. Such evaluation usually takes experienced teachers a large amount of time as each essay needs to be graded carefully. However, due to the limitation of teacher resources, most English learners cannot get timely assessments on the quality of their essays. Although many researchers studied how to automatically score an essay, most of the current approaches can only provide total scores without enriched supports [6, 26, 29]. This is not really helpful for students to improve their writing skills.

In natural language processing field, machine reading comprehension (MRC) has been studied for a long time and can be employed to provide details in terms of how well TRs have been achieved in students' essays. In MRC field, the second version of Stanford Question Answering Dataset (SQuAD 2.0) is the most widely used benchmark dataset to evaluate model performance [22]. However, our experiments prove that even a model that achieves the best performance on SQuAD 2.0 cannot be directly used on educational scenarios, as there is a significant performance degradation. The main reason is that SQuAD 2.0 is a general-purpose open-source dataset, but there is a huge difference between educational and general-purpose corpora.

To alleviate these problems, we construct a real-world educational dataset and propose an end-to-end framework based on MRC approach, which uses ELECTRA as a backbone, to detect whether students respond to TRs in their essays [3]. Our framework can clearly and accurately locate sentences in student essays that respond to the requirements. Experiments on an educational dataset show that the proposed framework achieves 0.93 accuracy score and 0.85 F1 score, outperforming many existing approaches. We believe that this research can help automatic essay scoring system provide interpretable grading results, thereby helping students improve their writing skills.

2   Related Work

2.1   Automated Writing Evaluation

Automated writing evaluation (AWE) has been studied for a long time in both industry and academia [1,13,20,30]. Since Page and Ellis B published their works in 1996, plenty of automated scoring products and applications, e.g., E-rater, have emerged. Based on AWE, lots of works on automatic essay scoring (AES) have been published [6,20,26,29]. However, these works mainly focused on giving a holistic score, which measures the overall quality of an essay. Taghipour explored several neural network models for AWE and outperformed strong baselines without requiring any feature engineering [26]. Dong proposed a reinforcement learning framework that incorporates quadratic weighted kappa as guidance to optimize the scoring system [6]. In recent years, a variety of researches focused on fine-grained essay evaluation [2,12,21]. In Persing's work, they presented a feature-rich approach to score prompt adherence of essays [21]. In Ke's work, they not only predicted a score of thesis strength but also provided more reasons [12]. Nevertheless, none of these works address the problem of detecting TR achievements in AES systems.

2.2   Machine Reading Comprehension

At document level, finding students' response to a TR is similar to extractive and abstractive MRC task in which given several reading materials, the model is expected to answer related questions based on the materials. The MRC models are expected to understand both the context and the question and be able to perform reasoning. In TR writing, we could regard student's essays as reading materials, and the model is supposed to find answers to TRs. If no answer is found, it indicates that the essay does not respond to the requirement.

The early trend of MRC used long short-term memory or convolutional neural network as an encoder of questions and contexts and blended a variety of attention mechanisms, e.g., attention sum, gated attention [5,8,11,19]. Approaches mimicking the process of how humans do reading comprehension were also proposed, such as multi-hop reasoning [16,24,25]. Recently, pre-trained language models, e.g., BERT, RoBERTa, ALBERT, BART, ELECTRA, became prevalent encoder architectures in MRC and achieved state-of-the-art performance [3,4,14,15,17]. Besides these improvements and optimizations on the encoder module, research about the decoder in the MRC model also starts to draw attention. Zhang al et. proposed an answer verification method and achieved state-of-the-art single model performance on SQUAD 2.0 benchmark with ELECTRA encoder module [22,23,31].

Another line of research on MRC is how to construct high-quality datasets and lots of works have been done [7,10,18,23,27]. Among them, SQuAD is one of the most widely-used reading comprehension benchmarks [23]. However, Rajpurkar et al. showed that the success on SQuAD does not ensure robustness to distracting sentences [9,22]. One reason is that SQuAD focuses on questions for which a correct answer is guaranteed to exist in the context document.

Therefore, models only need to select the span that seems most related to the question, instead of checking that the answer is actually entailed by the text. Based on SQuAD, Rajpurkar et al. proposed SQuAD 2.0. To do well on SQuAD 2.0, systems must not only answer questions when possible but determine when no answer is supported by the paragraph and abstain from answering [22].

Comparing with previous AWE works, to the best of our knowledge, we are the first to use a MRC approach to detect TR achievements in educational domain. We also construct a Student Essay Dataset (SED) which can be deemed as SQuAD 2.0 in the educational field and we explore the usage of a combination of SQuAD 2.0 and SED.

3   Problem Statement

In the TRs writing evaluation task, let Q denote a collection of task requirement questions and q denote a single question in Q. Let t_q^i denotes the i-th token in the question q such that $q = (t_q^1, t_q^2, t_q^3, \cdots, t_q^m)$. $E = (t_e^1, t_e^2, t_e^3, \cdots, t_e^n)$ is an essay written by a student where t_e^j denotes the j-th token in the essay E. Then the problem is defined as for each requirement q, is there a sequential text span $S = (t_e^j, t_e^{j+1}, \cdots, t_e^{j+s})$ in E that responds to the requirement q? If such span S exists, q is achieved and S needs to be extracted from the essay E, if not, q is not achieved by E.

4   Method

4.1   The Overall Workflow

The overview of our proposed framework is displayed in Fig. 1. Our approach is mainly composed of three principal modules, question normalization (QN) module, MRC module, and response locating (RL) module.

4.2   Question Normalization Module

Task requirement questions are proposed from the perspective of examiners, but essays are from examinees' perspective. This perspective gap brings difficulties to the MRC model. To eliminate the difference, we normalize texts of task requirements with two rule-based methods: switching personal pronouns and deleting redundant words.

Switch Personal Pronouns. We use pre-defined rules to replace personal pronouns in the sentence. For example, a question *"What will you do in the summer vacation ?"* may receive a student's answer *"I will travel to Japan"*. If we change personal pronouns "you" in the question, it will be normalized as *"What will I do in the summer vacation ?"*. The normalized question will decrease the difficulties of this task for the models.

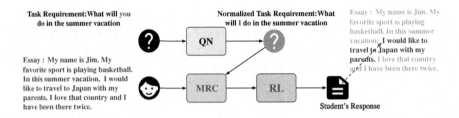

Fig. 1. The workflow of TRs evaluation framework.

Delete Redundant Words. We define question words such as *"what"*, *"how"*, etc., and then delete redundant words that appear before them. One example of deleting unnecessary words is that we omit the word *"explain"* in the question *"explain why you need to change the time"* and change it to *"why you need to change the time"*. Another instance is that we delete the words *"remind Sally"* in *"remind Sally where you arranged to meet"* and acquire the normalized question *"Where I arranged to meet"*.

4.3 Machine Reading Comprehension Module

In MRC module, normalized task requirement question q and the whole essay E are concatenated with a special symbol $[SEP]$. The entire input sequence to MRC model can be described as $T = ([CLS], t_q^1, t_q^2, t_q^3, \cdots, t_q^i, \cdots, t_q^m, [SEP], t_e^1, t_e^2, t_e^3, \cdots, t_e^j, \cdots, t_e^n)$, where the full length of T is $\tau = m + n + 2$.

ELECTRA Encoder. We use the discriminator module of ELECTRA to encode each token in T into a dense vector. The max length of T is 512 and tokens exceeding the max length will be truncated at the end. We use h_u^L to represent the final layer outputs of ELECTRA at position u which corresponds to the u-th token in T. We use $H^L = (h_1^L, ..., h_\tau^L)$ to denote the last-layer hidden states of the input sequence, where $H^L \in \mathbb{R}^{\tau \times 768}$. ELECTRA model is based on a multi-layer bidirectional Transformer encoder, and multi-head attention network [28]. Therefore, h_u^L is able to capture the context of the u-th token from q and E. The attention function in ELECTRA and the output of layer l are showed in Eq. (1). In layer l, inputs Q, K, V are computed by $H^{l-1}W_q$, $H^{l-1}W_k$, $H^{l-1}W_v$ respectively, where H^{l-1} denotes the output of the previous layer and $W_q \in \mathbb{R}^{768 \times d_k}$, $W_k \in \mathbb{R}^{768 \times d_k}$, $W_v \in \mathbb{R}^{768 \times d_k}$. Thus Q, K, V have the same dimensions $\mathbb{R}^{\tau \times d_k}$ where d_k is the dimension of vectors in K.

$$Attention(Q, K, V) = softmax(\frac{Q^T K}{\sqrt{d_k}})V$$

$$H^l = max(0, Attention(Q, K, V)W_1 + b_1)W_2 + b_2$$

$$(1)$$

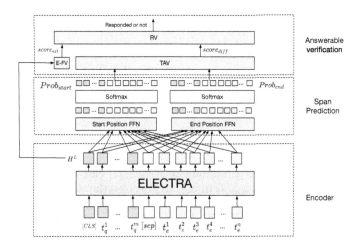

Fig. 2. The architecture of MRC model

Span Prediction. We employ a fully connected layer with softmax operation which takes H_L as input and outputs start and end probabilities of each token in T, as shown in Eq. (2). Let p^i_{start} and p^i_{end} represent the start and end probabilities of i-th token in T respectively, thus $Prob_{start} = p^i_{start}, i \in [1, \tau]$ is the start probability vector for all tokens in T and $Prob_{end} = p^i_{end}, i \in [1, \tau]$ is the end probability vector for all tokens in T.

$$Prob_{start} = softmax(H^L * W_{start} + b_{start})$$
$$Prob_{end} = softmax(H^L * W_{end} + b_{end})$$
(2)

Answerable Verification. Motivated by Zhang's work, we introduce the same answerable verification step to determine whether an essay responds to a task requirement [31].

We feed h^L_1 which is the representation vector of $[CLS]$ token encoded by ELECTRA into external front verification (E-FV) module. E-FV uses a fully connected layer followed by softmax operation to calculate classification logits $\hat{y}_i = (logit_{ans}, logit_{na})$ where $logit_{ans}$ is a scalar to indicate the answered logits and $logit_{na}$ is a scalar to indicate no-answer logits. We calculate the difference as the external verification score with Eq. 3a.

Threshold-based answerable verification (TAV) takes start and end probabilities as input and outputs the no-answer score $score_{diff}$ computed with Eq. 3b, 3c and 3d. p^1_{start} and p^1_{end} in Eq. 3c represents the start and end probabilities of the $[CLS]$ token in T.

Rear verification (RV) combines $score_{diff}$ and $score_{ext}$ to obtain the final answerable score $score_{final}$ as shown in Eq. 3e, where $\beta 1$ and $\beta 2$ are weights. MRC model predicts that question q is answered by E if $score_{final} > \zeta$, and not answered otherwise, where ζ is a hyper parameter.

$$score_{ext} = logit_{na} - logit_{ans} \tag{3a}$$

$$score_{has} = max(p^k_{start} + p^l_{end})\ k, l \in (1, \tau]\ and\ k \leq l \tag{3b}$$

$$score_{null} = p^1_{start} + p^1_{end} \tag{3c}$$

$$score_{diff} = score_{null} - score_{has} \tag{3d}$$

$$score_{final} = \beta_1 score_{diff} + \beta_2 score_{ext}, \tag{3e}$$

4.4   Response Locating Module

In RL module, it takes start probabilities $Prob_{start}$, end probabilities $Prob_{end}$ and answerable score $score_{final}$ as input, and decides the start and end positions according to these inputs. A naive path to achieve this goal is that positions that obtains the highest start and end probabilities are chosen as start and end positions respectively. All tokens between these two positions are extracted as the student's response to the task requirement. If the start or the end position is less than $m + 1$, in which case a span of question is marked, or their positions are contradictory, e.g., start position greater than end position, the module decides that the question is not responded. Finally, the framework outputs both the binary label indicating whether the student's essay does respond to the task requirement and the location of the responsive span if it is available.

5   Experiments

5.1   Datasets

SQuAD 2.0. SQuAD 2.0 is the most widely used benchmark in machine reading comprehension literature. It combines the first version of SQuAD with over 50,000 unanswerable questions written adversarially by crowd workers to look similar to answerable ones [23]. It contains 130,319 training examples from 442 Wikipedia articles and 11,873 development examples from 78 Wikipedia articles, where each example is made of a question and an article. This dataset requires that a model should not only answer the question when it is possible but also abstain from answering when there is no answer in the reading materials.

SED. This is a real-world student essay dataset that we collect from a third-party K-12 online learning platform. It consists of 9,450 examples in the training set and 3,357 examples in the test set, where each example contains an essay and a requirement question. There are 3,367 different essays and 593 different task requirement questions in the training set. In the test set, the number of essays and requirement questions are 1,655 and 185 respectively. In order to obtain labels, annotators need to firstly decide whether an essay does respond to the question and label it positive or negative accordingly. Secondly, for all positive essay examples, annotators need to mark the start and end positions of the span in the essay that responds to the question.

Despite that SQuAD 2.0 and SED share similarities in terms of task and structure, there are many differences between them. First of all, SED is in the educational domain and SQuAD 2.0 is from Wikipedia. Secondly, answers in SED are much longer than answers in SQuAD 2.0. Fig. 3 illustrates that most answers in SQuAD 2.0 are between 5 to 20 characters, while answers in SED are between 25 to 100 characters. The average length of answers in SQuAD 2.0 is 18.0 while the average length of answers in SED is 103.4. The last difference is that there are more grammatical errors in SED because essays in SED are written by second language learners. So a model that achieves the best performance on SQuAD 2.0 may not be directly deployed on educational scenarios.

5.2   Experimental Setting

In this section, we describe three sets of experiments as follows.

- Set 1. This set aims to prove that existing SOTA models on SQuAD 2.0 cannot be directly deployed on educational scenarios. In Set 1, all models are trained on SQuAD 2.0 but evaluated on the test set of SED. SAN was trained 50 epochs with learning rate $2e^{-3}$ on SQuAD 2.0 [16]. Pre-trained language models such as BERT, RoBERTa, ALBERT, and BART, were acquired from hugging face[3]. Our ELECTRA-based approach was trained 2 epochs with default parameters in this work [31].
- Set 2. This set is to prove that MRC approaches are effective solutions to TRs writing evaluation when trained on the educational corpus. The training parameters of the models are consistent with those in Set 1. The difference is that models are all trained on SED.
- Set 3. This set explores how can we utilize SQuAD 2.0 and further improve model performance on SED. Following the idea that models pre-trained on massive data can be a good warm-up for subsequent finetuning, we first train MRC models on SQuAD 2.0 so as to acquire basic models, and then finetune them on SED for optimal performance.

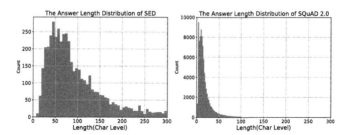

Fig. 3. Distributions of answer length (char level) in SED and SQuAD 2.0.

---

[3] https://huggingface.co.

$$Accuracy = \frac{N_{correct}}{N_{total}}$$

$$precision = \frac{Num_{overlap}}{Num_{predict}}$$

$$recall = \frac{Num_{overlap}}{Num_{gold}} \tag{4}$$

$$F1 = \frac{2 * precision * recall}{precision + recall}$$

In all experiments, we use two evaluation indicators. One is Accuracy (Acc.) which measures the performance of the model on the binary classification task of predicting whether the essay answers the TR. Another is Answer Overlap F1 score (F1) which measures the performance of the model to predict the location of the answer span. Accuracy and F1 metrics can be calculated by Eq. 4.

In Eq. 4, N_{total} indicates the number of examples in the test set, and $N_{correct}$ is the number of examples that are correctly predicted by the framework. $Num_{overlap}$ represents the number of identical tokens in both the predicted span and the gold span. $Num_{predict}$ is the total number of tokens in predicted span and Num_{gold} is the total number of tokens in the gold span.

5.3   Results and Evaluation

Results of Set 1. Table 2 shows that existing SOTA models on SQuAD 2.0 are suffered a significant performance degradation on SED. All models in Table 2 are well finetuned on SQuAD 2.0 and their F1 scores on SQuAD 2.0 dev set are all over 0.66. However, when evaluating them on SED test set, performances drop dramatically. For example, RoBERTa and our method achieve F1 score of 0.83 and 0.89 on SQuAD 2.0 dev set, but both drop to F1 score of 0.49 on SED test set.

Result of Sets 2&3. Table 3 shows results of Set 2 and Set 3. From the results of Set 2, we conclude that the MRC approaches can solve the TRs writing

Table 2. Performances of models trained on SQuAD 2.0

Training dataset	Methods	SQuAD 2.0 dev		SED test	
		ACC.	F1	ACC.	F1
SQuAD 2.0 (set 1)	SAN	0.70	0.66	0.57	0.31
	BERT	0.78	0.73	0.65	0.37
	ALBERT	0.85	0.81	0.58	0.37
	RoBERTa	0.86	0.83	0.69	0.49
	BART	0.87	0.81	0.62	0.42
	Ours	0.92	0.89	0.68	0.49

evaluation problem. Comparing with models trained on SQuAD 2.0 (Set 1), models trained on SED achieve significantly better results on SED test set. Our framework in Set 2 achieves the best F1 score of 0.84 and the best accuracy of 0.91, outperforms our framework in Set 1 by 23% Accuracy and 35% F1 score.

If we compare results in Set 2 and Set 3, we find that optimal performance can be obtained by firstly training models on SQuAD 2.0 and then finetuning on SED. Specifically, F1 score of SAN increases by 11%, and F1 score of BERT increases by 8%. Similarly, the accuracy also increases significantly in Set 3.

Table 3. Performances of models trained on SED and SQuAD 2.0&SED

Training dataset	Methods	SED test	
		Acc.	F1
SED (set 2)	SAN	0.67	0.58
	BERT	0.79	0.68
	ALBERT	0.84	0.77
	RoBERTa	0.81	0.71
	BART	0.82	0.73
	Ours	0.91	0.84
SQuAD 2.0& SED (set 3)	SAN	0.79 (+0.12)	0.69 (+0.11)
	BERT	0.84 (+0.05)	0.76 (+0.08)
	ALBERT	0.86 (+0.02)	0.80 (+0.03)
	RoBERTa	0.88 (+0.07)	0.80 (+0.09)
	BART	0.89 (+0.07)	0.82 (+0.09)
	Ours	**0.93 (+0.02)**	**0.85 (+0.01)**

Comparing with Set 2, the accuracy of BART and our framework increase by 7% and 2% respectively. Furthermore, our approach achieves the best performance in each of the three sets of experiments, and outperforms a variety of SOTA approaches.

6 Conclusion

In this paper, we proposed a MRC based approach which cannot only detect if an essay responds to a requirement question but find where the essay answers the question. From our experiments and analysis, we demonstrate that SQUAD 2.0 is very different from our educational dataset, so existing SOTA models on SQuAD 2.0 cannot be directly deployed on educational scenarios. Instead, we propose to firstly train a basic model on SQuAD 2.0 and then finetune the basic model on educational data for optimal performance. We believe this proposed framework is able to help automatic essay scoring systems provide detailed grading results, thereby helping students improve their writing skills.

Acknowledgment. This work was supported in part by National Key R&D Program of China, under Grant No. 2020AAA0104500 and in part by Beijing Nova Program (Z201100006820068) from Beijing Municipal Science & Technology Commission.

References

1. Klebanov, B.B., Madnani, N.: Automated evaluation of writing - 50 years and counting. In: Proceedings of ACL, pp. 7796–7810. Association for Computational Linguistics (2020). https://doi.org/10.18653/v1/2020.acl-main.697, https://www.aclweb.org/anthology/2020.acl-main.697

2. Carlile, W., Gurrapadi, N., Ke, Z., Ng, V.: Give me more feedback: annotating argument persuasiveness and related attributes in student essays. In: Proceedings of ACL, pp. 621–631. Association for Computational Linguistics (2018). https://doi.org/10.18653/v1/P18-1058, https://www.aclweb.org/anthology/P18-1058

3. Clark, K., Luong, M., Le, Q.V., Manning, C.D.: ELECTRA: pre-training text encoders as discriminators rather than generators. In: Proceedings of ICLR. OpenReview.net (2020). https://openreview.net/forum?id=r1xMH1BtvB

4. Devlin, J., Chang, M.W., Lee, K., Toutanova, K.: BERT: Pre-training of deep bidirectional transformers for language understanding. In: Proceedings of NAACL-HLT, pp. 4171–4186. Association for Computational Linguistics (2019). https://doi.org/10.18653/v1/N19-1423, https://www.aclweb.org/anthology/N19-1423

5. Dhingra, B., Liu, H., Yang, Z., Cohen, W., Salakhutdinov, R.: Gated-attention readers for text comprehension. In: Proceedings of ACL, pp. 1832–1846. Association for Computational Linguistics (2017). https://doi.org/10.18653/v1/P17-1168, https://www.aclweb.org/anthology/P17-1168

6. Dong, F., Zhang, Y., Yang, J.: Attention-based recurrent convolutional neural network for automatic essay scoring. In: Proceedings of the 21st Conference on Computational Natural Language Learning (CoNLL 2017), pp. 153–162. Association for Computational Linguistics (2017). https://doi.org/10.18653/v1/K17-1017, https://www.aclweb.org/anthology/K17-1017

7. Hewlett, D., et al.: WikiReading: a novel large-scale language understanding task over Wikipedia. In: Proceedings of ACL, pp. 1535–1545. Association for Computational Linguistics (2016). https://doi.org/10.18653/v1/P16-1145, https://www.aclweb.org/anthology/P16-1145

8. Hochreiter, S., Schmidhuber, J.: Long short-term memory. Neural Comput. **9**(8), 1735–1780 (1997)

9. Jia, R., Liang, P.: Adversarial examples for evaluating reading comprehension systems. In: Proceedings of EMNLP, pp. 2021–2031. Association for Computational Linguistics (2017). https://doi.org/10.18653/v1/D17-1215, https://www.aclweb.org/anthology/D17-1215

10. Joshi, M., Choi, E., Weld, D., Zettlemoyer, L.: TriviaQA: A large scale distantly supervised challenge dataset for reading comprehension. In: Proceedings of ACL, pp. 1601–1611. Association for Computational Linguistics (2017). https://doi.org/10.18653/v1/P17-1147, https://www.aclweb.org/anthology/P17-1147

11. Kadlec, R., Schmid, M., Bajgar, O., Kleindienst, J.: Text understanding with the attention sum reader network. In: Proceedings of ACL, pp. 908–918. Association for Computational Linguistics (2016). https://doi.org/10.18653/v1/P16-1086, https://www.aclweb.org/anthology/P16-1086

12. Ke, Z., Inamdar, H., Lin, H., Ng, V.: Give me more feedback II: annotating thesis strength and related attributes in student essays. In: Proceedings of ACL, pp. 3994–4004. Association for Computational Linguistics (2019). https://doi.org/10.18653/v1/P19-1390, https://www.aclweb.org/anthology/P19-1390

13. Ke, Z., Ng, V.: Automated essay scoring: a survey of the state of the art. In: Proceedings of the Twenty-Eighth International Joint Conference on Artificial Intelligence, IJCAI 2019, Macao, China, 10–16 August 2019, pp. 6300–6308. ijcai.org (2019). https://doi.org/10.24963/ijcai.2019/879

14. Lan, Z., Chen, M., Goodman, S., Gimpel, K., Sharma, P., Soricut, R.: ALBERT: a lite BERT for self-supervised learning of language representations. In: Proceedings of ICLR. OpenReview.net (2020). https://openreview.net/forum?id=H1eA7AEtvS

15. Lewis, M., et al.: BART: denoising sequence-to-sequence pre-training for natural language generation, translation, and comprehension. In: Proceedings of ACL, pp. 7871–7880. Association for Computational Linguistics (2020). https://doi.org/10.18653/v1/2020.acl-main.703, https://www.aclweb.org/anthology/2020.acl-main.703

16. Liu, X., Shen, Y., Duh, K., Gao, J.: Stochastic answer networks for machine reading comprehension. In: Proceedings of ACL, pp. 1694–1704. Association for Computational Linguistics (2018). https://doi.org/10.18653/v1/P18-1157, https://www.aclweb.org/anthology/P18-1157

17. Liu, Y., et al.: Roberta: a robustly optimized bert pretraining approach. arXiv preprint arXiv:1907.11692 (2019)

18. Nguyen, T., et al.: A human generated machine reading comprehension dataset. arXiv preprint ArXiv:1607.06275 (2016)

19. O'Shea, K., Nash, R.: An introduction to convolutional neural networks. arXiv preprint arXiv:1511.08458 (2015)

20. Page, E.B.: The imminence of... grading essays by computer. The Phi Delta Kappan **47**(5), 238–243 (1966)

21. Persing, I., Ng, V.: Modeling prompt adherence in student essays. In: Proceedins of ACL, pp. 1534–1543. Association for Computational Linguistics (2014). https://doi.org/10.3115/v1/P14-1144, https://www.aclweb.org/anthology/P14-1144

22. Rajpurkar, P., Jia, R., Liang, P.: Know what you don't know: Unanswerable questions for SQuAD. In: Proceedings of ACL, pp. 784–789. Association for Computational Linguistics (2018). https://doi.org/10.18653/v1/P18-2124, https://www.aclweb.org/anthology/P18-2124

23. Rajpurkar, P., Zhang, J., Lopyrev, K., Liang, P.: SQuAD: 100,000+ questions for machine comprehension of text. In: Proceedings of EMNLP, pp. 2383–2392. Association for Computational Linguistics (2016). https://doi.org/10.18653/v1/D16-1264, https://www.aclweb.org/anthology/D16-1264

24. Shen, Y., Huang, P., Gao, J., Chen, W.: Reasonet: Learning to stop reading in machine comprehension. In: Proceedings of the 23rd ACM SIGKDD International Conference on Knowledge Discovery and Data Mining, Halifax, NS, Canada, August 13–17, 2017, pp. 1047–1055. ACM (2017). https://doi.org/10.1145/3097983.3098177

25. Shen, Y., Liu, X., Duh, K., Gao, J.: An empirical analysis of multiple-turn reasoning strategies in reading comprehension tasks. In: Proceedings of the Eighth International Joint Conference on Natural Language Processing (Volume 1: Long Papers). pp. 957–966. Asian Federation of Natural Language Processing (2017). https://www.aclweb.org/anthology/I17-1096

26. Taghipour, K., Ng, H.T.: A neural approach to automated essay scoring. In: Proceedings of EMNLP, pp. 1882–1891. Association for Computational Linguistics (2016). https://doi.org/10.18653/v1/D16-1193, https://www.aclweb.org/anthology/D16-1193

27. Trischler, A., et al.: NewsQA: a machine comprehension dataset. In: Proceedings of the 2nd Workshop on Representation Learning for NLP, pp. 191–200. Association for Computational Linguistics (2017). https://doi.org/10.18653/v1/W17-2623, https://www.aclweb.org/anthology/W17-2623

28. Vaswani, A., et al.: Attention is all you need. In: Advances in Neural Information Processing Systems 30: Annual Conference on Neural Information Processing Systems 2017, December 4–9, 2017, Long Beach, CA, USA, pp. 5998–6008 (2017). https://proceedings.neurips.cc/paper/2017/hash/3f5ee243547dee91fbd053c1c4a845aa-Abstract.html

29. Wang, Y., Wei, Z., Zhou, Y., Huang, X.: Automatic essay scoring incorporating rating schema via reinforcement learning. In: Proceedings of EMNLP, pp. 791–797. Association for Computational Linguistics (2018). https://doi.org/10.18653/v1/D18-1090, https://www.aclweb.org/anthology/D18-1090

30. Wang, Z., Liu, H., Tang, J., Yang, S., Huang, G.Y., Liu, Z.: Learning multi-level dependencies for robust word recognition. Proc. AAAI Conf. Artif. Intell. **34**, 9250–9257 (2020)

31. Zhang, Z., Yang, J., Zhao, H.: Retrospective reader for machine reading comprehension. arXiv preprint arXiv:2001.09694 (2020)

Temporal Processes Associating with Procrastination Dynamics

Mengfan Yao[1]([✉]), Shaghayegh Sahebi[1], Reza Feyzi Behnagh[2], Semih Bursali[2], and Siqian Zhao[1]

[1] Department of Computer Science, University at Albany - SUNY, Albany, USA
myao@albany.edu
[2] Department of Educational Theory and Practice, University at Albany - SUNY, Albany, USA

Abstract. Procrastination, as an act of voluntarily delaying tasks, is particularly pronounced among students. Recent research has proposed several solutions to modeling student behaviors with the goal of procrastination modeling. Particularly, temporal and sequential models, such as Hawkes processes, have proven to be successful in capturing students' behavioral dynamics as a representation of procrastination. However, these discovered dynamics are yet to be validated with psychological measures of procrastination through student self-reports and surveys. In this work, we fill this gap by discovering associations between temporal procrastination modeling in students with students' chronic and academic procrastination levels and their goal achievement. Our analysis reveals meaningful relationships between the learning dynamics discovered by Hawkes processes with student procrastination and goal achievement based on student self-reported data. Most importantly, it shows that students who exhibit inconsistent and less regular learning activities, driven by the goal to outperform or perform not worse than other students, also reported a higher degree of procrastination.

Keywords: Hawkes process · Procrastination · Student modeling

1 Introduction

Student academic procrastination has been shown to be associated with negative consequential outcomes such as on academic performance [15], well-being [25], and emotions [22]. Consequently, it is important to model and understand the underlying dynamics of this behavior to be able to detect and manage procrastination in students. Since time-management and self-regulation skills are shown to be important factors in procrastination [27,33], many models try to use students' dilatory studying behaviors over time as a proxy for procrastination [1,4,21,29].

We divide these attempts into two main categories: static procrastination models and the temporal ones. Static procrastination models describe student behaviors using point estimates on time-related features such as students' average delays in starting coursework, average time spent on assignments, and

© Springer Nature Switzerland AG 2021
I. Roll et al. (Eds.): AIED 2021, LNAI 12748, pp. 459–471, 2021.
https://doi.org/10.1007/978-3-030-78292-4_37

average pace of studying [1,2,4,6,14]. On the other hand, temporal models describe student activity history via sequential model such as association pattern mining [17], Markov models [10,12], mixture Poisson [21], and Hawkes processes [11,16,29,30]. Such temporal models have become increasingly popular as, unlike the point estimates in static procrastination models, they can describe students' continuous behaviors within the studying time period.

Although successful in detecting dynamic behavioral patterns and clusters in students, such temporal procrastination models have not been validated by measures endorsed by procrastination theories [7,23,26]. In other words, these models can only infer students' learning patterns by using their interaction log data collected from online courses and do not consider students' self-reported data such as the ones collected using self-report surveys. Namely, the behavioral dynamics discovered by temporal models may not always be associated with chronic or academic procrastination in students, but with other reasons. For example, a student may delay in submitting an assignment because of having commitments to other concurrent tasks. As a result, the literature on temporal procrastination models lack experiments to show if the discovered patterns are actually associated with theory-supported procrastination measures. One of the potential reasons for this gap, can be the challenge of obtaining self-reported and survey data from students in massive online classes in which the temporal models are experimented on.

In this paper, we bridge this gap by studying the associations between the patterns discovered by temporal procrastination models and self-reported procrastination in students. We collect studying behaviors and survey responses from a study time management application Proccoli that provides a unique opportunity to access both sequential and self-report data from students. Due to the success of Hawkes processes in modeling students' behavioral dynamics in massive online courses [29,30] we apply this model on student learning activities in smaller university courses captured by Proccoli. Also, given the potential association between procrastination and goal-orientation in students [3,25], we evaluate the patterns discovered in relation to these two phenomena. In summary, we seek to answer the following research questions: Q1. Are Hawkes processes fit to characterize students' learning behavior dynamics captured in university courses? (Sect. 4.1) RQ2. Can Hawkes processes discover significant patterns among students' learning dynamics in university courses? (Sect. 4.2) RQ3. Are there associations between students' learning dynamics and their self-reported goal orientations? (Sect. 4.3) RQ4. Are there associations between students' learning dynamics and their self-reported procrastination? (Sect. 4.4)

Our findings show significant relations between Hawkes process procrastination model and students' goal orientation and noteworthy connections with student procrastination.

2 Dataset

The data in this paper is collected from Proccoli, a time management application for students, over Spring and Fall semesters 2020. In Proccoli, a student can create a study goal (e.g. studying for the final exam) and optionally decompose it into smaller subgoals (e.g. reviewing the first lecture for the exam). For each goal, a student can log their study sessions by setting and using a count-down timer (e.g. a 25-min study session) or by reporting their past study start and end time in the app. During study, the student can pause the timer anytime for a break and resume it later. Also, the timer can be manually stopped if the student wishes to finish the study session early. The following activities and their corresponding unix timestamps are collected: *GoalCreatedTime*: time when a goal is created, *SubGoalCreatedTime*: time when a subgoal is created, *TimerStartAt*: start time of the timer, *TimerBreakTime*: time when the timer is paused for a break, *TimerResumeTime*: resume time of the timer, *FinishTime*: time when the timer automatically runs out, *TimerStopTime*: time when the timer is manually stopped by the student, *ReportedStartTime*: reported start time of the study session, *ReportedFinishTime*: reported stop time of the study session, and *ReportTime*: time when a self-report is submitted. We include "active" students, who have more than five activities in the app, in our analysis. In total, the data includes 3339 activities with timestamps over 383 goals created by 47 students.

Besides student activities, this dataset contains three self-report surveys that measure students' goal orientations (Achievement Goal Questionnaire-Revised (AGQ-R)[7]), chronic procrastination (General Procrastination Scale (GPS-9) [24]), and academic procrastination (Academic Procrastination State Inventory (APSI) [23]). Each questionnaire is on a Likert 1–5 scale, with 1 representing strongly disagree and 5 representing strongly agree. AGQ-R, measures students' aim in terms of 4 groups of items, i.e. mastery-approach (e.g. learn as much as possible), mastery-avoidance (e.g. avoid learning less than possible), performance-approach (e.g. perform better than others), and performance-avoidance (e.g. to not perform worse than others). In GPS-9, students' trait-like chronic procrastination is measured by the average score of the nine questionnaire items. Finally, in APSI, the average score of 13 items is used to describe students' academic procrastination [23]. In both procrastination questionnaires, a higher score corresponds to a higher degree of procrastination.

3   Hawkes Processes for Student Behavioral Dynamics

Recently, several Hawkes process models have been proposed and customized for modeling student learning activities in large online courses to represent procrastination. These models have shown to be successful in effectively capturing the learning dynamics of students [29], finding clusters of student behaviors [30], and capturing various studying stimuli in student sequences [31]. In this section, we briefly introduce Hawkes process [13], and explain how we adopt it to model student activities in our dataset.

To apply Hawkes processes, the main assumption to adopt is the time-dependency assumption. According to this assumption, students' learning activities can be driven by two types of stimuli: (1) external stimuli such as student's studying routines or deadlines (e.g. a student habitually starts a study session every morning), and (2) internal stimuli, i.e. historical activities that have triggering effects on other activities (e.g. setting a goal on the App may consequently trigger the student to start a study session logged by the timer). To formulate procrastination modeling as Hawkes processes, suppose we are given a collection of N student sequences, denoted as $S := \{S_1, ..., S_N\}$. Suppose each sequence contains K^i activities (as described in Sect. 2), represented as $S_i := \{x_i^1, ..., x_i^{K_i}\}$, where x_i^τ is the timestamp of the τ-th activity in S_i. According to the formulation of Hawkes processes, we parameterize each student sequence S_i by the following intensity function, which models the number of activities that take place as a function of time:

$$\lambda(t|S_i) = \mu_i + \sum_{x_i^\tau < t} \alpha_i \beta_i e^{-\beta_i(t-x_i^\tau)}. \tag{1}$$

In this equation, μ (called base rate) represents the expected number of activities that are triggered by external stimuli; α (self-excitement rate) describes the number of activities that are self-excited by the previous activities, i.e. from internal stimuli; and β (decay rate) parameterizes the exponential function which captures the decaying influence of self-excitement with respect to time. A larger μ describes a higher activity rate triggered by external stimuli. A larger α value means a higher influence of historical activities on the future ones. Finally, a larger β value describes a faster decay of self-excitement, which means past activities have an influence on activities at current time t for a shorter period of time.

4   Experiments and Analyses

4.1   Testing the Goodness-of-Fit (RQ1)

As mentioned in Sect. 1, current Hawkes-based models for describing student procrastination are designed for Massive Open Online Courses (MOOCs). In addition to a large number of students, these courses need more self-regulation and time management from students. As a result, we need to re-analyze the fitness of Hawkes processes and their assumptions for our dataset, which includes a small number of students studying in a more structured university setting.

To address RQ1, we first apply Hawkes processes to our data as explained in Sect. 3 and then apply the Point Process Residual Theorem [20] to evaluate the fitness of external and internal stimuli assumptions of Hawkes processes. To fit Hawkes process on our data, we use stochastic gradient descent (SGD) to optimize a loss function built upon Eq. 1. Specifically, the loss is set to be the negative likelihood of observing all historical activities by T, i.e. $\{x_i^1, ... x_i^{K_i}\}$. To set a proper time-interval unit for activity intensities, we perform grid search on one-second, one-minute, five-minute and ten-minute intervals. Five-minute results in the smallest loss on our data. For the decay rate β, we follow the convention of traditional Hawkes process optimization [5,28,32] and perform a grid search between 1 and 120 (5 min to 2 h) with a step size of one. The β that gives the smallest negative likelihood within this range for each student sequence is used as the optimal β [1].

Next, we apply the Point Process Residual Theorem which aims to test if the defined intensity function $\lambda(t)$ fits the observed activity sequences well [20]. Particularly, Kolmogorov-Smirnov (KS) test is used in this theorem with the null hypothesis that a transformed sequence computed via Eq. 1 is drawn from exp(1). According to the theorem, the goodness-of-fit can be validated by not being able to reject this null hypothesis. As a result of this test, the averaged p-values of this test on all student sequences is 0.74. It demonstrates that the Hawkes model defined in Eq. 1 represents students' learning dynamics well.

4.2   Discovering Behavior Patterns Using Hawkes Processes (RQ2)

To answer RQ2 and study the presence of significant patterns among students' learning dynamics discovered by Hawkes processes, we first use the discovered three Hawkes parameters (base rate μ, self-excitement rate α, and decay rate β) to describe the learning dynamic of each student sequence. Then, we cluster the students according to these parameters to examine significant differences that can be discovered using these parameters. In this context, base rate μ can be viewed as the frequency of activities that a student plans to do that are driven by external stimuli, such as their reactions to deadlines. On the other hand, internally triggered activities characterized by self-excitement rate α and decay rate β can be interpreted as activities a student spontaneously initiates as a timely reaction to their recent activities. To this end, we represent all students as $S^d = \{S_1^d, ..., S_N^d\}$, where $S_i^d = (\mu_i, \alpha_i, \beta_i)$.

Next, we apply K-means on $S_1^d, ..., S_N^d$ to identify possible clusters of learning dynamics. We then compute the center of each cluster and test if the clusters have significant differences among them. To decide the optimal cluster number, we use the elbow method [18], where the distortion, i.e. the mean of the Euclidean distances from the cluster centers is compared against the cluster number k. Trying $k \in \{1, ..., 10\}$ we found that two clusters is optimal in our data. The two cluster centers parameterized by mean μ, α, and β are presented in Table 1. 26 students are grouped into cluster 1 and 21 are in cluster 2.

Table 1. Centers of the clusters identified by K-means.

Cluster	Base rate μ	Self-excitement rate α	Decay rate β	Cluster size
1	0.059	0.43	17.88	26
2	0.021	0.25	64.76	21

We first observe that the learning dynamics characterized by Hawkes parameters are very different across the clusters. To validate that this difference is

---

[1] The implementation can be found in https://github.com/persai-lab/AIED2021_Hawkes.

significant, we run a two-sample Kolmogorov–Smirnov (KS) test on each of the parameters from the two clusters, with the null hypothesis that the two samples are drawn from the same distribution. The p-values of KS test on base rate μ, self-excitement rate α, and decay rate β are all significantly <0.001 , which reject the null hypotheses. This observation validates the significance of statistical differences between the two clusters in terms of learning dynamics. It means that students grouped into these two clusters using Hawkes parameters have significantly different learning behavior dynamics.

To better compare the learning dynamics of the two clusters, we sample and visualize a sequence to represent each of the clusters. For the sampling, we use Ogata Thinning Algorithm [19], while setting the base rate μ, self-excitement rate α, and decay rate β to the centers of these two clusters. These two sampled sequences are shown in Fig. 1, where the x-axis is time t in hours and y-axis is the intensities of the sampled sequences computed via Eq. 1. We observe two very different learning dynamics, described as follows: In cluster 1, student sequences have more frequent and consistent learning activities (higher base rate μ), while at the same time, their historical activities have stronger internal triggering effects (higher self-excitement α) for a longer period (smaller decay rate β). On the other hand, students in cluster 2 have almost the opposite learning dynamics: a smaller studying frequency is driven by external stimuli (i.e. lower base rate μ) and less effect of previous activities, suggested by smaller self-excitement rate α and much higher β. In other words students in cluster 2 have less tendency to initiate follow-up activities and study less intensely.

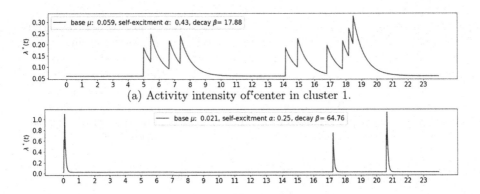

(a) Activity intensity of center in cluster 1.

Fig. 1. Learning dynamics of the cluster centers depict by Hawkes.

In sum, students in cluster 1 are more driven by both external and internal stimuli which leads to more consistent and regular studying towards the goals. Whereas in cluster 2, students are relatively less sensitive to external and internal stimuli. Furthermore, contrary to cluster 1's frequent and consistent learning pace, higher irregular intensity peaks within short time intervals are usually presented in cluster 2. This shows that Hawkes processes can discover significant patterns in students' learning dynamics for our dataset.

4.3   Learning Dynamics Associating with Goal Orientation (RQ3)

To answer RQ3, which is the association between the discovered students' learning dynamics and their goal orientation, we run two experiments: a correlation analysis and a cluster analysis.

Correlation Analysis. Here, we compute the Pearson correlation between each of the Hawkes parameters and each group of items of AGQ-R. The results are shown in Table 2. We first look at performance-approach and performance-avoidance measures, where students are asked if their goal is to respectively outperform or not perform worse than other students. We observe strong negative correlations between the base rate μ and both of these item groups. On the other hand, a positive correlation between the decay rate β and each of these item groups is observed. Combining these two observations shows that students who focus more on performance comparison with others study less regularly and less consistently using Proccoli and the influence from their past activities on current activities wears off faster. Altogether it suggests less sensitivity to both external and internal stimuli for these students[2]. This finding is in accordance with the literature that points to the relation between low motivation and performance attainment to the pursuit of performance-based goals [7,8].

Table 2. Correlation between each pair of a Hawkes parameter and AGQ-R item group that describes students' goal orientation. The significance level is denoted as follows: $p < 0.01$***, $p < 0.05$**, $p < 0.1$*.

	Base rate μ	Self-excitement rate α	Decay rate β
Performance-Approach	−0.540**	0.219	0.329*
Performance-Avoidance	−0.681***	0.145	0.285*
Mastery-Approach	0.256	0.198	−0.036
Mastery-Avoidance	−0.391**	0.267	0.061

Next, we see that there is a significant negative correlation between the frequency and regularity of students' studying (i.e. base rate μ) and their goal to avoid learning less than needed (i.e. mastery avoidance). Similarly, this is consistent with the finding that reveals the association of low self determination and disorganized study with a high emphasis on mastery-avoidance [7].

Cluster Analysis. Next, we examine if the clusters identified by the Hawkes Process are associated with students' goal orientation in the clusters. To do so, we check if there exists any difference between these clusters in terms of AGQ-R item groups. For each AGQ-R item group, we use the two-sample KS test on the two clusters. The null hypothesis is that students' scores on each AGQ-R item group from the two clusters follow the same distribution. So, a small p-value suggests a highly significant difference between students' goal achievement in the

---

[2] Please note that these are based on correlation, and are not causal effects.

two clusters. Checking performance-approach and performance-avoidance item scores, we observe that they are statistically significant differences in the two clusters, with p-values respectively to be 0.007 and 0.026. To have a better representation, we visualize the distributions of these two item groups in each of the two clusters in Fig. 2. This observation suggests that students in cluster 2 have a stronger focus on the performance comparison with their peers. Remember that these students studied less regularly with Proccoli (small base μ) and had less frequent and fewer spontaneous follow-up activities (high self-excitement α and decay β). For example in performance-avoidance, where a score of 5 shows that they strongly agree that their goal is to not perform worse than others, students in cluster 2 scored an average of 4.42 (between agree to strongly agree). Whereas in cluster 1, students scored an average of 3.4, suggesting an average response of neutral to agree. A similar observation can be made in performance-approach responses.

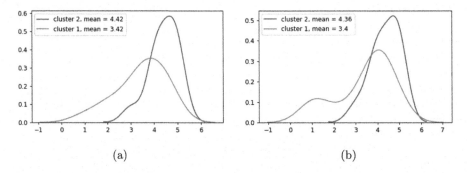

Fig. 2. Density distributions of performance approach (a) and performance avoidance (b) in two clusters.

On the other hand, KS test reveals little significant difference between the clusters in mastery-approach, with an average score of 4.08 and 4.14 in cluster 1 and cluster 2 respectively. Similarly, in mastery-avoidance (i.e. to avoid learning less than needed), students in cluster 1 have an average of 3.67 vs. 3.97 in cluster 2, with the difference shown to be not statistically significant across the two clusters. To this end, we find that in both clusters students have acknowledged their aim of task mastery (mastery-approach and mastery-avoidance) to the same degree. But, students in cluster 2 have a higher pursuit of performance comparison compared to cluster 1. Connecting the findings in this analysis to the observations made in correlation analysis, there might be factors that inhibit students in cluster 2 from being more driven by internal and external stimuli, such as low motivation that has been associated with the pursuit of performance-based goals in the literature [7]. To explore this topic further, in the following section, we examine students' chronic and academic procrastination scores and their possible association to the aforementioned differences.

4.4 Learning Dynamics Associating with Procrastination (RQ4)

To answer RQ4, which is on the association between learning dynamics and students' procrastination, we follow an analysis similar to the previous section, between learning dynamics characterized by Hawkes and students' self-reported procrastination described by GPS-9 and APSI.

Table 3. Correlation between each pair of a Hawkes parameter and students' chronic or academic procrastination. The significance level is denoted as follows: $p < 0.01$***, $p < 0.05$**, $p < 0.1$*.

	Base rate μ	Self-excitement rate α	Decay rate β
Chronic procrastination	-0.401*	0.208	-0.627*
Academic procrastination	-0.271	0.312	-0.327*

Correlation Analysis. As shown in Table 3, students' chronic procrastination is shown to have a significant negative correlation with the base rate μ. This suggests that students with less regular and less frequent studying sessions on Proccoli (smaller base rate μ), also report a higher degree of trait-like chronic procrastination. Furthermore, we also find that both chronic and academic procrastination are significantly negatively correlated with decay rate β, which may be caused by chunks of intensive studying activities close to the deadline [9]. By comparing chronic procrastination with academic procrastination, we see that both procrastination types are shown to have the same correlation coefficient signs with Hawkes parameters (negative for μ and β, and positive for α). However, the correlations in chronic procrastination are stronger and more significant, compared to the academic one. A possible reason is that chronic procrastination describes students' general procrastinatory behaviors (i.e. the extent of trait-like procrastination in daily life) similarly as Hawkes process, especially the base rate μ, describes students' overall learning regularity (i.e. via constant learned parameters per student). As a result, the correlation between chronic procrastination and Hawkes parameters tend to be more significant. However, in the academic procrastination questionnaire, factors related to academic tasks such as task difficulty are evaluated. For example, one question from APSI asks: "Gave up when studying was not going well". Students' answers to these kinds of task-specific questions may be associated with the academic nature of the task, rather than their general studying habits and regularity. This may lead to a less significant correlation between academic procrastination and the base study rate μ.

Cluster Analysis. To further examine the possible differences in terms of student procrastination between the two clusters discovered by Hawkes, similar to the previous section, we use two-sample KS tests on student procrastination scores across the clusters. We find that students in cluster 2 reported an average of 3.31 on chronic procrastination, which is significantly higher than

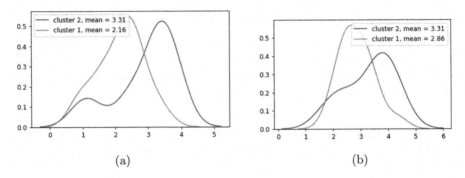

Fig. 3. Density distributions of (a) chronic procrastination measured by GPS-9 and (b) academic Procrastination measured by APSI in two clusters.

chronic procrastination of students in cluster 1, suggested by a p-value of 0.047 in the KS test. Figure 3 (a) shows the density distribution comparison of the clusters in terms of chronic procrastination. Similar significant difference can be observed in students' academic procrastination presented in Fig. 3 (b), supported by a p-value of 0.091. This finding suggests that the characteristic learning behaviors presented in cluster 2 (i.e. less frequent and less consistent studying towards goals, higher peaks within short time intervals) are highly associated with a higher degree of both chronic and academic procrastination reported by the students. Connecting this finding to the study of students' goal orientation (Sect. 4.3), possibly a higher degree of procrastination presented in cluster 2 inhibits students from having more regular and consistent studying activities, and the motivations of outperforming or at least not doing worse than peers are not strong enough to offset the effect of procrastination, which may be one reason that could explain the different learning dynamics exhibited in cluster 2 comparing with cluster 1.

5   Conclusions

In this paper we presented and evaluated four research questions in associating Hawkes process procrastination models, based on students' logged behavioral data, with the students' self-reported data. In summary, we concluded that Hawkes processes present a good fit for modeling students' procrastination-like behavioral dynamics, collected from study time management app Proccoli, even in small university courses (RQ1). We also discovered two significantly different behavioral clusters using the learned Hawkes parameters: cluster 1 with students who study more consistently and frequently and are triggered to study more as a result of their past studies with a lingering effect, and cluster 2 with an opposite behavior (RQ2). By finding significant relations between students' goal orientation and model results (RQ3), we discovered that, in correspondence with previous literature, performance-related goal orientations were associated with procrastination-like behaviors explained by model parameters and presented in cluster 2 students. Interestingly, mastery-related goal orientations did not show such a strong significant relation. Our analysis of procrastination questionnaires with model results (RQ4) showed that both academic and chronic procrastination are associated with behavioral dynamics presented in cluster 2 of students. However, we noted another unique observation: that chronic procrastination is more significantly related to lower regular study habits, compared to academic procrastination. In sum, a higher degree of procrastination was found in students of Hawkes-discovered cluster 2 with performance-oriented motivations that were not strong enough to offset the procrastination effect.

Acknowledgement. This paper is based upon work supported by the National Science Foundation under Grant Number 1917949.

References

1. Agnihotri, L., Baker, R.S., Stalzer, S.: A procrastination index for online learning based on assignment start time. In: 13th International Conference on Educational Data Mining (2020)
2. Asarta, C.J., Schmidt, J.R.: Access patterns of online materials in a blended course. Decis. Sci. J. Innov. Educ. **11**(1), 107–123 (2013)
3. Azevedo, R., Feyzi-Behnagh, R.: Dysregulated learning with advanced learning technologies. In: AAAI Fall Symposium: Cognitive and Metacognitive Educational Systems (2010)
4. Cerezo, R., Esteban, M., Sánchez-Santillán, M., Núñez, J.C.: Procrastinating behavior in computer-based learning environments to predict performance: a case study in Moodle. Front. Psychol. **8**, 1403 (2017)
5. Du, N., Farajtabar, M., Ahmed, A., Smola, A.J., Song, L.: Dirichlet-Hawkes processes with applications to clustering continuous-time document streams. In: Proceedings of the 21th ACM SIGKDD International Conference on Knowledge Discovery and Data Mining, pp. 219–228 (2015)
6. Dvorak, T., Jia, M.: Do the timeliness, regularity, and intensity of online work habits predict academic performance? J. Learn. Anal. **3**(3), 318–330 (2016)
7. Elliot, A.J., McGregor, H.A.: A 2 × 2 achievement goal framework. J. Pers. Soc. Psychol. **80**(3), 501 (2001)
8. Elliot, A.J., Murayama, K.: On the measurement of achievement goals: critique, illustration, and application. J. Educ. Psychol. **100**(3), 613 (2008)
9. Elvers, G.C., Polzella, D.J., Graetz, K.: Procrastination in online courses: performance and attitudinal differences. Teach. Psychol. **30**(2), 159–162 (2003)
10. Geigle, C., Zhai, C.: Modeling MOOC student behavior with two-layer hidden Markov models. In: Proceedings of the Fourth ACM Conference on Learning@ Scale, pp. 205–208 (2017)
11. Halpin, P.F., von Davier, A.A., Hao, J., Liu, L.: Measuring student engagement during collaboration. J. Educ. Meas. **54**(1), 70–84 (2017)
12. Hansen, C., Hansen, C., Hjuler, N., Alstrup, S., Lioma, C.: Sequence modelling for analysing student interaction with educational systems. arXiv preprint arXiv:1708.04164 (2017)
13. Hawkes, A.G.: Spectra of some self-exciting and mutually exciting point processes. Biometrika **58**(1), 83–90 (1971)

14. Kazerouni, A.M., Edwards, S.H., Hall, T.S., Shaffer, C.A.: DevEventTracker: tracking development events to assess incremental development and procrastination. In: Proceedings of the 2017 ACM Conference on Innovation and Technology in Computer Science Education - ITiCSE 2017, pp. 104–109. ACM Press, Bologna (2017)

15. Kim, K.R., Seo, E.H.: The relationship between procrastination and academic performance: a meta-analysis. Personality Individ. Diff. **82**, 26–33 (2015)

16. Lan, A.S., Spencer, J.C., Chen, Z., Brinton, C.G., Chiang, M.: Personalized thread recommendation for MOOC discussion forums. In: Berlingerio, M., Bonchi, F., Gärtner, T., Hurley, N., Ifrim, G. (eds.) ECML PKDD 2018. LNCS (LNAI), vol. 11052, pp. 725–740. Springer, Cham (2019). https://doi.org/10.1007/978-3-030-10928-8_43

17. Mirzaei, M., Sahebi, S., Brusilovsky, P.: SB-DNMF: a structure based discriminative non-negative matrix factorization model for detecting inefficient learning behaviors. In: 2020 IEEE/WIC/ACM International Joint Conference On Web Intelligence And Intelligent Agent Technology. WI-IAT (2020)

18. Ng, A.: Clustering with the k-means algorithm. Machine Learning (2012)

19. Ogata, Y.: On Lewis' simulation method for point processes. IEEE Trans. Inf. Theory **27**(1), 23–31 (1981)

20. Ogata, Y.: Statistical models for earthquake occurrences and residual analysis for point processes. J. Am. Stat. Assoc. **83**(401), 9–27 (1988)

21. Park, J., Yu, R., Rodriguez, F., Baker, R., Smyth, P., Warschauer, M.: Understanding student procrastination via mixture models. International Educational Data Mining Society (2018)

22. Pychyl, T.A., Lee, J.M., Thibodeau, R., Blunt, A.: Five days of emotion: an experience sampling study of undergraduate student procrastination. J. Soc. Behav. Pers. **15**(5), 239 (2000)

23. Schouwenburg, H.C.: Academic procrastination. In: Schouwenburg, H.C. (ed.) Procrastination and Task Avoidance. The Springer Series in Social Clinical Psychology, pp. 71–96. Springer, Heidelberg (1995). https://doi.org/10.1007/978-1-4899-0227-6_410.1007/978-1-4899-0227-6_4

24. Sirois, F.M., Yang, S., van Eerde, W.: Development and validation of the General Procrastination Scale (GPS-9): a short and reliable measure of trait procrastination. Personality Individ. Diff. **146**, 26–33 (2019)

25. Steel, P.: The nature of procrastination: a meta-analytic and theoretical review of quintessential self-regulatory failure. Psychol. Bull. **133**(1), 65 (2007)

26. Steel, P.: Arousal, avoidant and decisional procrastinators: do they exist? Personality Individ. Differ. **48**(8), 926–934 (2010)

27. Steel, P., König, C.J.: Integrating theories of motivation. Acad. Manag. Rev. **31**(4), 889–913 (2006)

28. Valera, I., Gomez-Rodriguez, M.: Modeling adoption and usage of competing products. In: 2015 IEEE International Conference on Data Mining, pp. 409–418. IEEE (2015)

29. Yao, M., Sahebi, S., Behnagh, R.F.: Analyzing student procrastination in MOOCs: a multivariate Hawkes approach. International Educational Data Mining Society (2020)

30. Yao, M., Zhao, S., Sahebi, S., Behnagh, R.F.: Relaxed clustered Hawkes process for procrastination modeling in MOOCs. arXiv preprint arXiv:2102.00093 (2020)

31. Yao, M., Zhao, S., Sahebi, S., Behnagh, R.F.: Stimuli-sensitive Hawkes processes for personalized student procrastination modeling. arXiv preprint arXiv:1608.05745 (2020)

32. Zhou, K., Zha, H., Song, L.: Learning triggering kernels for multi-dimensional Hawkes processes. In: International Conference on Machine Learning, pp. 1301–1309. PMLR (2013)
33. Zimmerman, B.J.: Investigating self-regulation and motivation: historical background, methodological developments, and future prospects. Am. Educ. Res. J. **45**(1), 166–183 (2008)

Investigating Students' Experiences with Collaboration Analytics for Remote Group Meetings

Qi Zhou[1](✉), Wannapon Suraworachet[1], Stanislav Pozdniakov[2],
Roberto Martinez-Maldonado[2], Tom Bartindale[2], Peter Chen[2], Dan Richardson[2],
and Mutlu Cukurova[1]

[1] University College London, London, UK
qtnvqz3@ucl.ac.uk
[2] Monash University, Melbourne, VIC, Australia

Abstract. Remote meetings have become the norm for most students learning synchronously at a distance during the ongoing coronavirus pandemic. This has motivated the use of artificial intelligence in education (AIED) solutions to support the teaching and learning practice in these settings. However, the use of such solutions requires new research particularly with regards to the human factors that ultimately shape the future design and implementations. In this paper, we build on the emerging literature on human-centred AIED and explore students' experiences after interacting with a tool that monitors their collaboration in remote meetings (i.e., using Zoom) during 10 weeks. Using the social translucence framework, we probed into the feedback provided by twenty students regarding the design and implementation requirements of the system after their exposure to the tool in their course. The results revealed valuable insights in terms of visibility (what should be made visible to students via the system), awareness (how can this information increase students' understanding of collaboration performance), and accountability (to what extent students take responsibility of changing their behaviours based on the system's feedback); as well as the ethical and privacy aspects related to the use of collaboration analytics tools in remote meetings. This study provides key suggestions for the future design and implementations of AIED systems for remote meetings in educational settings.

Keywords: Human-centred AI · Remote meetings · Collaboration analytics · Ethics

1 Introduction and Background

There is an increasing amount of research that shows the positive impact of using Artificial Intelligence (AI) applications to support students' academic performance [1, 2], their affective engagement [3–5], and metacognitive development [6–8]. In the design of effective AI in Education (AIED) tools, most available research highlights the significance of robust technical approaches and the use of learning sciences principles [9,

© Springer Nature Switzerland AG 2021
I. Roll et al. (Eds.): AIED 2021, LNAI 12748, pp. 472–485, 2021.
https://doi.org/10.1007/978-3-030-78292-4_38

10]. However, a range of other human factors related to AIED tools are often neglected, including students' preferences, why and how the tools will be used [11], the social contexts in which the tools will be used, and ethical [12] and societal implications related to fairness, accountability and transparency [13]. Understanding how human factors (i.e. the characteristics of students, educators, other relevant stakeholder and the environment) can shape the use of AIED tools is key for their successful adoption and the field's wider impact on Education. The value of research in human factors in the design and implementation of AI, in general, has now been established and is addressed in specific tracks of influential conferences including the ACM SIGCHI Conference on Human Factors in Computing Systems (CHI) [14] and the Association for the Advancement of Artificial Intelligence (AAAI) Conference on AI [15]. Yet, there is limited previous work addressing concerns with regards to the human factors of AIED.

Aiming to address such a gap, in a series of studies, Holstein et al., [16–19] investigated the iterative co-design of augmented reality glasses for an intelligent tutoring system (ITS) with K-12 teachers and students. The studies provided valuable insights into teachers' experiences and challenges in using an ITS in their classroom settings [18]. For instance, although teachers often preferred the automation of certain tasks to ease their teaching workload, over-automation of tasks in teaching environments was considered as a threat to their flexibility to choose and implement their own pedagogical goals. Similarly, Van Leeuwen and Rummel [20] documented the teachers' experiences after using three different AIED interfaces (aimed at mirroring, alerting and advising) and identified significant differences in the way teachers can use each of them [21]. Dillenbourg et al., also investigated teachers' experiences while orchestrating ITSs in collaborative learning contexts [22] and co-designed a series of multimodal analytics prototypes with educators [23]. Just a few studies have focused on the potential role that students may play in the design of a data-intensive educational tool. For instance, Prieto-Alvarez et al. [24] encouraged students to co-create a learner-data journey based on their particular needs and Chen and Zhu [25] investigated students' experience with a visualisation tool that analysed their engagement and interactions with others through social network analysis. Similarly, Chaleer [26] studied students' experience and perceived awareness and usefulness with an ambient group awareness tool. However, the tool was evaluated in a single class, so the students' exposure to it was very limited.

These studies have provided significant contributions to our understanding of teachers and students' experiences with AIED tools in real-world contexts, which then can be used to shape the design and implementation of AIED tools. However, prior work has focused on limited types of AIED tools (i.e., ITSs), limited instructional approaches and goals (i.e., monitoring student activities in classrooms), and mainly focused on the experiences of teachers rather than those of students. In this paper, we build on the emerging literature exploring students' experience of AIED implementations in real-world contexts. We contribute to this literature through the analysis of students' experiences with an AIED tool that monitors their collaboration in remote meetings (using Zoom) as part of a ten-week postgraduate course. The contribution of the paper is two-folded. First, the themes that emerged from the analysis of students' experiences can contribute to and shape the design features of similar systems and their further automation with AI. Second, since it focuses on a novel context for AIED systems -collaboration analytics in synchronous remote meetings using Zoom-, the findings of this study have significant implications for future pedagogical interventions. Remote meetings have become the norm for students studying synchronously at a distance during the coronavirus pandemic, which highlights the timeliness of these contributions.

1.1 Collaboration Analytics and AIED in Remote Meetings

The study presented in this paper was conducted in the context of the use of a collaboration analytics tool. The term Collaboration Analytics refers to AI and Analytics solutions aimed at scrutinising interaction group data to extract insights for supporting sense-making processes and the development of effective collaboration skills [27]. There are plenty of research studies in the literature that are explicitly or implicitly categorized under this umbrella. Some significant examples include but are not limited to AI assistants for scheduling group meetings [28], personal assistants for providing help in collaborative problem-solving [29], real-time gaze feedback with metacognitive supports from a pedagogical agent for dyads [30], utterance analytics of chats and discussion forums to support students' awareness in their involvement [31], feedback provision to groups of students based on their interaction patterns [32], external help-seeking support in collaboration contexts for students [33], and tools to provide summary information of student groups based on certain indicators to support teachers' class monitoring and control [21]. Most available studies describe the design of collaboration analytics in asynchronous online (e.g., [34]) or classroom settings (e.g., [35]). Whilst the virtual meetings have become crucial for remote education due to the need for synchronous collaboration, more work is needed to understand how AI innovations can support reflection and students' learning in such settings. For instance, Cornide-Reyes et al. [36] recently developed the NAIRA system, a real-time multimodal learning analytics tool that inspects students' level of participation within the remote meetings through an influence graph, a speech time distribution, and a silence bar. However, the study did not investigate the students' real-world experiences with the tool in detail.

2 The Context of the Study

The study was conducted in the context of a post-graduate course (covering the design and use of educational technology) that lasted ten weeks. A total of forty-four students completed the course. Students were divided into ten groups, ensuring each group was interdisciplinary (education, design, and technology graduate members) and mixed in terms of gender. Group sizes ranged from three to five. At the beginning of the course, each group was asked to identify an educational challenge. Then, they had to carry out an educational technology design case to solve the challenge and submit a design case solution in Week 10. Analytics generated from online group meetings were used to provide formative feedback on groups' behaviours.

Groups used Zoom during their regular classes to conduct their planning and design meetings. The ZoomSense system's "sensor" appeared as a participant in the Zoom meetings, recorded the verbal utterances of each student in Zoom, and stored them in

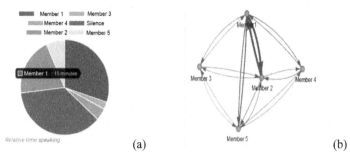

Fig. 1. (a) A pie chart represents the total speech time per student including the relative fraction of time a group has been silent. Each portion represents the relative speaking time of each student. (b) Turn-taking network represents conversational flows between students.

a cloud database. The actual content of the meetings was not recorded. Verbal utterances data were then used to model two constructs i) students' total speech time, ii) students turn-taking behaviours. Figure 1(a) presents the total speech time visualisation for group 8 in Week 3. This chart also includes the total silence time and relative speaking time of each student (i.e. the most verbally active group member spoke for 15 min). Figure 1(b) shows the turn-taking behaviours of students. This was presented as a network/sociogram, where the direction of the edges depicts the conversational flows from one student to another during the discussions. The thickness of the edges represents the mutuality of the conversation. After every remote meeting, these two visualisations and a written report were sent to each group separately via email. The report served to provide written feedback (a sample of email feedback) to students indicting how they could improve group interactions. In the later versions of the tool, the written feedback was also automatically provided via the Zoom chat to scaffold students' collaboration in *real-time*. In this study, the feedback was sent by teaching assistants every week after group meetings.

3 Methodology

In this paper, we addressed three research questions. i What are the specific needs of students' that can impact the *design features* of collaboration analytics in remote meetings? ii. What are the specific needs of students' that can impact the *educational implementation* of collaboration analytics in remote meetings? iii. What are the *ethical and privacy concerns* of students with regards to being monitored during remote meetings?

To address the research questions, we theoretically framed the student probes according to the components of the Social Translucence (ST) framework: Visibility, Awareness, and Accountability [37]. This framework was proposed to help investigate users' design needs for the particular purpose of computer-mediated, online group activities [23]. Based on ST, a total of twelve open-ended interview questions were used in retrospective semi-structured interviews at the end of the module. Interview questions covering the Visibility dimension (4 questions) focused on the significant aspects of students' online synchronous meetings and what features of their collaboration should be made visible to them. Awareness dimension's questions (3 questions) aimed at exploring to what extent the information provided by the analytics create a well-informed understanding of students' own and others' performance. Accountability questions focused on understanding to what extent the feedback provided by the analytics can help students take responsibility for improving their performance (2 questions). In addition to the ST framework, we added 3 questions to particularly explore privacy and ethics concerns of students with regards to the use of AIED tools in remote meetings.

In total twenty students (four male and sixteen female -representative of the cohorts' gender ratio) volunteered to participate in the interviews. At least one student from all ten groups was included in the sample. None of the participants had any experience of using collaboration analytics or similar AIED tools in the past. The study has received full ethics approval from the host institute of the lead author. All participants were clearly informed and signed consent forms accordingly.

The data analysis was conducted using Braun and Clarke's six phases of thematic analysis [38]. First, the data was transcribed verbatim. Initial thematic codes were generated by two independent researchers individually. After that, themes from two researchers were compared, discussed, and revised to make sure that emerging themes covered all the collected data and that they are auditable. This process led to an agreed final coding scheme. After this process was completed, the final coding scheme was applied to all transcriptions from scratch to ensure consistency.

4   Results

The thematic coding analysis described in the previous section led to the emergence of ten themes from the transcription data. The themes were then categorised into four dimensions: visibility (4.1), awareness (4.2), accountability (4.3), and the ethics (4.4).

4.1 Visibility

Comprehensibility of Collaboration Analytics. Thirteen participants responded positively with regards to the easiness to comprehend information and straightforward interpretation of the visualisations shown in Fig. 1. For example, P11 reacted positively as follows: *"This is the first time that I have seen such a straightforward way to show the interactions during our collaborative learning."* On the contrary, five participants partially agreed on this (P4, 10, 12, 14, 20), one firmly replied 'no' (P17) and one reported uncertainty to answer the question (P6). Overall, they pointed out that the definition of effective contribution was not clear to them and the analytics only covered partial contributions in speech time and turn-taking.

Accuracy of the Analytics Information. Fifteen participants reported that the graphs are accurate and "similar to their feelings" (P8, 15). P5 elaborated: *"I think it clearly shows the volume of contribution. So those who are talking the most, [what] it is showing is quite accurate in terms of calculating who was the person that was talking the most and ... [with whom he was having] conversations with."* However, four participants (P3, 6, 11, 19) reported differences between the analytics presented and their actual experiences. Notably, P3 and P6 thought their participation was higher than depicted, while P19 argued s/he contributed to the discussion less. There was also a report from P11 that there was always a higher amount of silence presented in the analytics than they experienced as a group.

Lack of Quality Evaluations and Partially Represented Contribution. However, all participants expressed concerns over the lack of quality evaluations of student contributions. Seven participants specifically raised concerns that their contributions were only quantitatively represented through speech time and turn-taking but it did not show the quality of their contributions which could be *"total rubbish"* (P1), *"off-topic"* (P12) or *"not useful"* (P16). Therefore, higher speech time did not always mean more actual contribution (P5, 11, 12, 13, 15, 17, 18, 20). On the contrary, lower speech time could also represent a key contribution to the further progress of their work (P5, 6, 13, 17). Generally, participants argued that the contributions in a group task are more about the quality of the content than its quantity (P1, 4, 5, 6, 10, 15). Similarly, the turn-taking lines shown in the collaboration analytics, which show conversational flows between group members, were argued to provide potentially misleading information as explained by P14, as follows: *"sometimes someone spoke after me but what he said was not related to what I have said. I think he diverted the topic and I could not reply to him."*

At the same time, six participants raised concerns over the limitation of unimodal data collection since the information represented with the analytics was only captured from the students' Zoom meetings. Students might be "recorded" as silent in the collaboration analytics, but they might have been focusing on completing their co-design tasks on another collaboration tool beyond what is captured by the system. Furthermore, participants also mentioned various group activities that were crucial to their group work but were excluded from the analytics including their chats via instant messaging platforms such as WhatsApp (P19), additional meetings of sub-groups or group as a whole (P16) that took place out of the module, the final presentation preparations (19) and other forms of preparation before the discussion (P12). To illustrate: *"During the meeting, we might express these points [prepared ideas] with a few sentences in a short time but we might have spent a significant amount of time and energy on preparing them. The speech time cannot represent these pre-meeting preparations."* – P12.

4.2 Awareness

The Value of Seeing One's Own Performance. Participants mutually agreed upon the value of the tool to make them aware of their performance (19 participants), yet their reasons varied. Some reported, thanks to analytics, they ensured a high level of participation (P10) or maintained continuous participation in their meetings (P14). Importantly, the tool appeared to prompt students to reflect on their performance. As P13 reported, *"I asked myself, why was I the person who spoke the least?"* On the other hand, P11, who was a regular high contributor, reported that *"sometimes I would ask myself: Did I speak such a lot?"* In general, collaboration analytics were considered as external objective measures that can help students be less "biased" from their own experience when evaluating their performance in the group activities. As P5 pointed out: *"Obviously about the* *whole thing about eyewitness testimony, it can be distorted by events that happen post the experience. So, what the graph does, it really helps you to have a clear data point to say, Okay, this is what happened in the group."*

The Value of Seeing Others' Performance. Not only the tool was considered as an enabler for students to reflect on their performance, but it was also considered as an enabler to reflect on others' performance. The majority of the participants (17) acknowledged that collaboration analytics can make them aware of their group members' contributions, and determine who is struggling or need help. P20 explained this as follows: *"[the analytics] can help you know others' contribution better or help you find their problem. We had a new member. He rarely participated in the group work in the last few weeks and he muted himself during the meeting."* This potential was also recognised by P1, 4 and 9. Surprisingly, such awareness of a struggling member was not that evident without the weekly reports sent to students, as P1 pointed out: *"I didn't know that one of our group members didn't spend a lot of time speaking. I mean, it took him about seven weeks before he told us 'I struggle with your accents'."*

4.3 Accountability

Collaboration Analytics to Foster Group Discussions. The collaboration analytics were considered as a medium for triggering discussions by almost half of the participants (9). While some groups reported having a specific discussion about the analytics occasionally (P3, 4, 5, 9, 13, 14, 19), some reported that constant discussions were going on in their weekly meetings about the previous weeks' feedback (P2, 7). For example, P5 explained that *"It did work because one week our meeting started when we were discussing the graphs. The persons who were showing to be contributing less, were talking about why they felt they were doing that. And one highlighted an issue where somebody felt that they didn't understand the material enough to contribute that week."*

Self-regulation and Socially Shared Regulation of Behaviours. At the individual level, nineteen participants tried to regulate their behaviours and adapt their level of interaction according to the collaboration analytics (i.e., if they had a high level of participation and dominated the discussion in one meeting, they tended to speak less in consecutive meetings). This was indicated by P1, as follows: *"...[after seeing analytics on their group behaviours] I shut up. I didn't talk for about half an hour."* Similar incidents were reported by P15. In contrast, if they had a low level of participation, they tried to speak more. As P13 described *"once I was detected to have less speech time, I would speak more in the next time. I would try my best to catch up with my teammates and have more interactions with them."* Some students also reflected on how their activity or lack of preparation outside of the meeting reflected their levels of interaction during the meeting. For instance, seven participants (P7, 8, 13, 16, 18, 19, 20) attributed their low level of interaction to lack of preparation for the meeting and hence, tried to prepare more in future meetings. To illustrate this, P19 explained that she could not contribute much if she did not finish the weekly readings. As a result, she aimed to finish the weekly readings, check the weekly tasks, and prepare contributions for the group discussions in advance.

Regulation of student behaviours appeared to occur also at a social level. Twelve participants reported various strategies they used to regulate their behaviours based on their understanding of others' needs. For instance, they were encouraging the less active speakers to speak more (P2,9,11,14,18); helping others diagnose their problems (P4); providing a further explanation and inviting struggling members to contribute (P19); and developing group strategies such as assigning a weekly host for the group discussions (P12). Some participants were also able to make informed strategic changes as P5 argued: *"for myself and another person in the group, we could see that we were talking back and forth quite a lot. So, one week, we made a pact to not keep responding to each other's points yet to open up the floor for others in the group to respond to questions."* However, whether regulated behaviours were beneficial for learning or not was not clear. For instance, P4 reported that the analytics directed her towards responding to people, not about discussing the contents: *"I was very much concerned with making sure I had good airtime and decent thick lines between the various people. And so, it became more about a response, less thinking about what that person said."*

Gaming the System. 'Gaming the system' refers to a situation where students attempt to accomplish a task within the system by not truthfully working on the tasks as intended but rather taking advantage from the gap within the system [39]. There were four reports of 'gaming the system' (P3, 12, 14, 17). P14 acknowledged that for the least active speakers to have more interaction, s/he performed the following action: *"[another member] discussed something not related to our tasks but easy for [the least active speaker] to talk in the meeting."* The same approach was followed in the group of P3, as she described: *"because we wanted to give space [to members spotted as less active] so that it would be more equal, we would end up letting someone talk about completely random subjects, just that they had enough time."*

Swinging Back to "Normal", the Tentative Nature of the Changes. Notably, the changes to the group discussions dynamics informed by the tool were not long-lasting. Seven participants reported swinging back their "normal" after a short while, whereas six participants noticed the tentative nature of the changes of other members' behaviours. Multiple reasons for the short-term nature of the changes were provided: including the lack of control during the heat of the discussions (P10, 11), the restriction on their speech-time giving unspontaneous flows of conversation (P3, 6), the lack of summative evaluations of their collaboration (P2, 7, 11, 12, 1316). Overall, one-third of participants argued for the value of integrating the tool and the assessment motives. As P7 elaborated: *"I am a behaviourist sort of thing. I feel like I don't really contribute much because I don't really focus there because I know this will not affect my final mark. Where if I was thinking maybe that is a 5% or 2% of our final marks will be affected. I think people would contribute more."*

4.4 Privacy and Ethics Concerns

Half of the participants reported that they did not have any concerns and claimed they ignored the fact of being monitored in their group meetings, with P5 explaining: *"I'd say we completely forgot the sensors were there, aside from them just appearing in the panel, and we were like presenting our screens anyway.*" P3 reasoned that this comfort in being monitored might be due to the course's subject area. As she explained: "*We came on this course to learn about educational technology. So, in that sense to do that, it wasn't shocking, you know? Not like if I'd come, maybe on a different course, maybe then I'd find it really weird.*" P12 also reported no concerns due to her interest in AIED. Moreover, two participants (P15, 18) argued their comfort was due to the formative use of the tool, as it was not for summative assessment: "*If they [the analytics] were only there for feedback but not assessment, I think that's alright to be monitored*" (P15). By contrast, one-quarter of participants said their concerns were rather fleeting and the other quarter added that they were significantly concerned. Four participants (P1, 2, 3, 15) asked to confirm whether the tool recorded their voices as P2 described their group concerns that "*there is one thing that we always discuss about... are you [the lecturers] listening to everything that we are talking about?... some information even though it's supposed to be private, it is not really private.*" Additionally, five participants revealed uncomfortable feelings upon being monitored, such as feeling "*uncomfortable*" (P3), "*strange*" (P4), "*super-concerned*" (P6), "*nervous*" (P15), and "*being spied on*" (P4, 15). Interestingly, these concerns were particularly observed from students with low contributions. As P6 stated: "*It was really, really challenging. So, knowing that something is monitoring how much time I speak, I had the pressure to do it and it went out of hand. The second week, I was under pressure. I think I spoke like two minutes or so.*" P3 reported that her group was more spontaneous when not being monitored: "*We had some sessions outside of the bots. And yeah, then we did not worry about that[being observed] anymore. Whoever needed to say something said it. If we wanted to have a chat, we had a chat....Personally, I was a bit different and I felt we were more spontaneous.*" This aligned with reports from P6, 7, 9, 15, 20 that they would have acted more openly if they were not being observed.

On the contrary, P4, 5, 7, 8, 14, 17 asserted that the being monitored helped them to act productively as their group was "supervised" indirectly through the tool. P4 explained that "*this small thing that sits in your head is echoed publicly, in some way is representative of who you are, and your teachers are seeing this, and you don't want to look bad to your professors.*" P17 reported that: "*To be honest, I have stayed here [the university] for three years. I had my undergraduate here, acted as an invisible man. I don't have confidence so I rarely express my opinions in the class. Since this year we had the [tool], I forced myself to express more about my opinions.*"

5   Discussion and Conclusion

The results presented above have significant implications for the design and implementation of AI tools for collaboration in educational remote meetings. With regards to our first research question on the design implications, results show that the collaboration analytics in remote meetings have the potential to make students aware of their own as well as their group members' collaborative behaviours. However, students argued that the tool only represented a small part of their actual contribution and so they did not always perceive the tool as significant for their success in the course. The main critiques were the lack of content analysis and unimodal nature of the tool. Due to these design drawbacks, students struggled to make connections between what the tool represents and what really 'mattered' for their learning. It was argued that content analysis of the discussion that would provide proxies on the quality of the contributions by group members -in addition to the quantity of contribution- is essential for the uptake of the tool. Therefore, we suggest that future designs of similar AIED tools should consider involving the content analysis and multiple modalities in their collaboration analytics. For instance, detection of off-topic discussions and introduction of data from writing analytics from chats as a second modality can increase the value of collaboration analytics in remote meetings. Similarly, perhaps at a more practical level, future iterations that involve data analysis from multiple platforms (i.e. collaborative docs, chats, presentation platforms) can lead to more holistic representations of student contributions in remote meeting settings. In turn, such representations are more likely to lead to a stronger relationship between students' awareness of their performance and to what extent they change their behaviours accordingly [23, 40, 41].

Results also indicated that the reflections driven through awareness can lead students to change their behaviours in remote meetings. As discussed in self-regulated learning (SRL) literature [42, 43], by providing means to students to support evaluation not only of the overall progress of the group but rather to make an accurate attribution of personal contribution to the group progress (reflection phase), students can plan their future learning and correct their expectations (forethought phase) [42]. Therefore, the awareness provided by the tool has the potential to improve students' learning in remote meetings. However, such changes in student behaviours were argued to be temporary and many students returned to their "normal" behaviours in remote meeting interactions. This is aligned with research investigating the effects of digital tools on behaviour change persistency in general [44]. Multiple reasons were presented by students for the observed phenomenon of "regressing to business as usual". This phenomenon is partly related to the incomplete representation of students' contributions which we have discussed above. Moreover, students reported that this "back to normal" may be caused by the lack of intervention. Since the tool did not provide guidance or suggestions to the students during the meeting, it is challenging for students to make a change on time. Therefore, the future design of collaboration analytics tools should not only focus on providing visualisations but should also include real-time automated feedback on what actionable steps they can take to improve their collaboration behaviours. On the other hand, the guidance may also be structured into the implementation of the collaboration analytics tool which is explored in the second research question.

Our second question investigated the suggestions for educational implementation of AIED tools with collaboration analytics in remote meetings. Firstly, students would benefit from instructions that would scaffold them on what sort of actions they could potentially take based on their reflections of the collaboration analytics. As some students noted, although they realised that they needed to change certain behaviours, they did not know exactly how to do this. This may be due to the feedback sent regarding students' participation which did not have strong elements on how students' can regulate their actions. Therefore, they struggled to adapt and change their behaviours accordingly [45]. Future implementations should involve clear instructions on what further actions can be taken to address the tool's suggestions. Secondly, the learning context in which the tool was implemented significantly affected to what extent students engaged with it. For instance, in this study, the analytics were not considered as part of the summative assessment, so some students were not motivated to take long-lasting actions based on them. This leads to the suggestion that teachers and AIED designers should carefully align the collaboration analytics and the learning design including assessment [46]. Thirdly, better instructions on what kind of analytics outcomes are expected for different group tasks were deemed as important. Some students regulated their behaviours to equalise the contribution in their group discussions, others purposely made no effort in this regard as they considered some of the group meetings as peer learning opportunities rather than collaboration. They wanted to learn from the students who have more experiences and knowledge. This may indicate that students have varied definitions of collaboration for different group tasks. Therefore, an alignment of group tasks' learning design, its collaboration analytics, and their consequent visualisations should ideally be shared with students in advance. As discussed in the literature, there are distinctions between collaborative learning, cooperative learning and peer learning [47] which may require students to present different behaviours [48].

Regarding our third research question, we explored students' privacy concerns about being monitored by the collaboration analytics tools. Most students did not report negative emotions towards being monitored and some reported motivational value in being observed. One possible reason may be that the analytics were not part of the summative assessment. It was also argued that students were behaving more comfortably as they knew the system could not record the content of their discussions. This highlights the importance of informing students about what the AIED tool can and cannot do and how it will be implemented. Yet, this also leads to a significant dilemma. On the one hand, students asked for more detailed investigations of their collaborative behaviours (i.e., content analysis) and argued that the tool would make them more accountable if the analytics involved summative assessments. On the other hand, students argued that they would have more significant privacy concerns had this has been the case.

5.1 Limitations and Future Research

Since the participants were postgraduate students and the course was in educational technology, it is challenging to generalise the results. Similar studies in diverse contexts are called for drawing a better picture of student experiences. Moreover, although there were indications about the value of the tool to help students regulate their behaviours, future work is needed to delineate to what extent the tool supports self-regulation (SRL) ("regulate oneself"), co-regulation ("supporting each other") or socially shared regulation (SSRL) ("regulating together") [43]. Based on the findings, a future version of the system may include the generation of fully automated real-time prompts, to be sent to students via the Zoom chat, to scaffold students' collaboration based on the discussion dynamics, including SRL (e.g., ask the student who demonstrated no verbal activity in the last 5 min to verbally summarise the current state of discussion) and SSRL (e.g., advice to the most active students to involve less active students). However, further co-design evaluations of prompts are needed before any potential AI-driven automation to understand what exact behaviours need to be prompted, when exactly, and how.

References

1. Li, H., Gobert, J., Dickler, R.: Evaluating the transfer of scaffolded inquiry: what sticks and does it last? In: Isotani, S., Millán, E., Ogan, A., Hastings, P., McLaren, B., Luckin, R. (eds.) AIED 2019. LNCS (LNAI), vol. 11626, pp. 163–168. Springer, Cham (2019). https://doi.org/10.1007/978-3-030-23207-8_31

2. VanLehn, K., Banerjee, C., Milner, F., Wetzel, J.: Teaching Algebraic model construction: a tutoring system, lessons learned and an evaluation. Int. J. Artif. Intell. Educ. **30**(3), 459–480 (2020). https://doi.org/10.1007/s40593-020-00205-3

3. Baker, R.S.J., D'Mello, S.K., Rodrigo, M.M.T., Graesser, A.C.: Better to be frustrated than bored: the incidence, persistence, and impact of learners' cognitive–affective states during interactions with three different computer-based learning environments. Int. J. Hum.-Comput. Stud. **68**, 223–241 (2010). https://doi.org/10.1016/j.ijhcs.2009.12.003

4. D'Mello, S., Graesser, A., Picard, R.: Toward an affect-sensitive autotutor. Intell. Syst. IEEE. **22**, 53–61 (2007). https://doi.org/10.1109/MIS.2007.79

5. Boulay, B.D.: Intelligence tutoring systems that adapt to learners motivation. Presented at the 1 October (2018)

6. Azevedo, R., Cromley, J.G., Seibert, D.: Does adaptive scaffolding facilitate students' ability to regulate their learning with hypermedia? Contemp. Educ. Psychol. **29**, 344–370 (2004). https://doi.org/10.1016/j.cedpsych.2003.09.002

7. Laru, J., Järvelä, S.: Integrated use of multiple social software tools and face-to-face activities to support self-regulated learning: a case study in a higher education context. In: Wong, L.-H., Milrad, M., Specht, M. (eds.) Seamless Learning in the Age of Mobile Connectivity, pp. 471–484. Springer Singapore, Singapore (2015). https://doi.org/10.1007/978-981-287-113-8_24

8. Winne, P.H.: Enhancing self-regulated learning for information problem solving with ambient big data gathered by nstudy. In: Adesope, O.O., Rud, A.G. (eds.) Contemporary Technologies in Education, pp. 145–162. Springer, Cham (2019). https://doi.org/10.1007/978-3-319-896 80-9_8

9. Luckin, R., Cukurova, M.: Designing educational technologies in the age of AI: a learning sciences-driven approach. Br. J. Educ. Technol. **50**, 2824–2838 (2019). https://doi.org/10.1111/bjet.12861

10. Rosé, C.P., McLaughlin, E.A., Liu, R., Koedinger, K.R.: Explanatory learner models: why machine learning (alone) is not the answer. Br. J. Educ. Technol. **50**, 2943–2958 (2019). https://doi.org/10.1111/bjet.12858

11. Shum, S.B., Ferguson, R., Martinez-Maldonado, R.: Human-Centred Learning Analytics. J. Learn. Anal. **6**, 1–9 (2019). https://doi.org/10.18608/jla.2019.62.1

12. Holmes, W., et al.: Ethics of AI in education: towards a community-wide framework. Int. J. Artif. Intell. Educ. (2021). https://doi.org/10.1007/s40593-021-00239-1

13. Sjödén, B.: When lying, hiding and deceiving promotes learning - a case for augmented intelligence with augmented ethics. In: Bittencourt, I.I., Cukurova, M., Muldner, K., Luckin, R., Millán, E. (eds.) AIED 2020. LNCS (LNAI), vol. 12164, pp. 291–295. Springer, Cham (2020). https://doi.org/10.1007/978-3-030-52240-7_53

14. Kuniavsky, M., Churchill, E., Steenson, M.W. (eds): Designing the user experience of machine learning systems. In: AAAI Spring Symposium Proceedings (Technical Report SS-17–04). The AAAI Press, Palo Alto, CA, U.S.A. (2017)

15. Amershi, S., et al.: Guidelines for Human-AI interaction. In: Proceedings of the 2019 CHI Conference on Human Factors in Computing Systems, pp. 1–13. ACM, Glasgow Scotland UK (2019)

16. Holstein, K., McLaren, B.M., Aleven, V.: Student learning benefits of a mixed-reality teacher awareness tool in AI-enhanced classrooms. In: Penstein Rosé, C., et al. (eds.) AIED 2018. LNCS (LNAI), vol. 10947, pp. 154–168. Springer, Cham (2018). https://doi.org/10.1007/978-3-319-93843-1_12

17. Holstein, K., McLaren, B.M., Aleven, V.: Informing the design of teacher awareness tools through causal alignment analysis. In: 13th International Conference of the Learning Sciences (ICLS 2018) (2018)

18. Holstein, K., McLaren, B.M., Aleven, V.: Designing for complementarity: teacher and student needs for orchestration support in AI-Enhanced classrooms. In: Isotani, S., Millán, E., Ogan, A., Hastings, P., McLaren, B., Luckin, R. (eds.) AIED 2019. LNCS (LNAI), vol. 11625, pp. 157–171. Springer, Cham (2019). https://doi.org/10.1007/978-3-030-23204-7_14

19. Holstein, K., McLaren, B.M., Aleven, V.: Co-designing a Real-time classroom orchestration tool to support teacher–AI complementarity. J. Learn. Anal. **6**, 27–52 (2019). https://doi.org/10.18608/jla.2019.62.3

20. van Leeuwen, A., Rummel, N.: Comparing teachers' use of mirroring and advising dashboards. In: Proceedings of the Tenth International Conference on Learning Analytics & Knowledge. pp. 26–34. ACM, Frankfurt Germany (2020)

21. van Leeuwen, A., Bos, N., van Ravenswaaij, H., van Oostenrijk, J.: The role of temporal patterns in students' behavior for predicting course performance: a comparison of two blended learning courses: Comparison of two blended learning courses. Br. J. Educ. Technol. **50**, 921–933 (2019). https://doi.org/10.1111/bjet.12616

22. Dillenbourg, P., Prieto, L.P., Olsen, J.K.: Classroom orchestration. In: International Handbook of the Learning Sciences. Routledge (2018)

23. Echeverria, V., Martinez-Maldonado, R., Shum, S. B.: Towards collaboration translucence: giving meaning to multimodal group data. In: Proceedings of the 2019 CHI Conference on Human Factors in Computing Systems - CHI 2019, pp. 1–16. ACM Press, Glasgow, Scotland UK (2019)

24. Prieto-Alvarez, C.G., Martinez-Maldonado, R., Shum, S.B.: Mapping learner-data journeys: evolution of a visual co-design tool. In: Proceedings of the 30th Australian Conference on Computer-Human Interaction, pp. 205–214. ACM, Melbourne Australia (2018)

25. Chen, B., Zhu, H.: Towards value-sensitive learning analytics design. In: Proceedings of the 9th International Conference on Learning Analytics and Knowledge, 343–352 (2019). https://doi.org/10.1145/3303772.3303798

26. Charleer, S., Klerkx, J., Duval, E.: Towards balanced discussions in the classroom using ambient information visualisations. Int. J. Technol. Enhanc. Learn. **9**, 27 (2017)

27. Martinez-Maldonado, R., Kay, J., Shum, S.B., Yacef, K.: Collocated collaboration analytics: principles and dilemmas for mining multimodal interaction data. Hum.-Comput. Interact. **34**, 1–50 (2019). https://doi.org/10.1080/07370024.2017.1338956

28. Cranshaw, J., et al.: Calendar.help: Designing a workflow-based scheduling agent with humans in the loop. In: Proceedings of the 2017 CHI Conference on Human Factors in Computing Systems, 2382–2393 (2017). https://doi.org/10.1145/3025453.3025780

29. Winkler, R., Bittner, E., Neuweiler, M.L., Söllner, M.: Hey Alexa, Please help us solve this problem! How interactions with smart personal assistants improve group performance. Presented at the Fortieth International Conference on Information Systems, Munich (2019)

30. Hayashi, Y.: Gaze awareness and metacognitive suggestions by a pedagogical conversational agent: an experimental investigation on interventions to support collaborative learning process and performance. Int. J. Comput.-Support. Collab. Learn. **15**(4), 469–498 (2020). https://doi.org/10.1007/s11412-020-09333-3

31. Trausan-Matu, S., Dascalu, M., Rebedea, T.: PolyCAFe—automatic support for the polyphonic analysis of CSCL chats. Int. J. Comput.-Support. Collab. Learn. **9**(2), 127–156 (2014). https://doi.org/10.1007/s11412-014-9190-y

32. Kim, T., McFee, E., Olguin, D.O., Waber, B., Pentland, A.: "Sandy": sociometric badges: using sensor technology to capture new forms of collaboration: sensor technology and collaboration in teams. J. Organ. Behav. **33**, 412–427 (2012). https://doi.org/10.1002/job.1776

33. Alavi, H.S., Dillenbourg, P.: An ambient awareness tool for supporting supervised collaborative problem solving. IEEE Trans. Learn. Technol. **5**, 264–274 (2012). https://doi.org/10.1109/TLT.2012.7

34. Kent, C., Cukurova, M.: Investigating collaboration as a process with theory-driven learning analytics. J. Learn. Anal. **7**, 59–71 (2020). https://doi.org/10.18608/jla.2020.71.5

35. Janssen, J., Erkens, G., Kirschner, P.A.: Group awareness tools: It's what you do with it that matters. Comput. Hum. Behav. **27**, 1046–1058 (2011). https://doi.org/10.1016/j.chb.2010.06.002

36. Cornide-Reyes, H., et al.: A multimodal real-time feedback platform based on spoken interactions for remote active learning support. Sensors. **20**, 6337 (2020). https://doi.org/10.3390/s20216337

37. Erickson, T., Kellogg, W.A.: Social translucence: an approach to designing systems that support social processes. ACM Trans. Comput.-Hum. Interact **7**, 59–83 (2000). https://doi.org/10.1145/344949.345004

38. Braun, V., Clarke, V.: Using thematic analysis in psychology. Qual. Res. Psychol. **3**, 77–101 (2006). https://doi.org/10.1191/1478088706qp063oa

39. Baker, R., Walonoski, J.A., Heffernan, N., Roll, I., Corbett, A., Koedinger, K.: Why students engage in "Gaming the system" behavior in interactive learning environments. J. Interact. Learn. Res. **19**, 185–224 (2008)

40. Prestigiacomo, R., et al.: Learning-centred translucence: an approach to understand how teachers talk about classroom data. In: Proceedings of the Tenth International Conference on Learning Analytics & Knowledge, pp. 100–105. ACM, Frankfurt Germany (2020)

41. Szostek, A.M., Karapanos, E., Eggen, B., Holenderski, M.: Understanding the implications of social translucence for systems supporting communication at work. In: Proceedings of the ACM 2008 Conference on Computer Supported Cooperative Work - CSCW 2008, p. 649. ACM Press, San Diego, CA, USA (2008)

42. Panadero, E.: A review of self-regulated learning: six models and four directions for research. Front. Psychol **8**, 142 (2017). https://doi.org/10.3389/fpsyg.2017.00422

43. Järvelä, S., Järvenoja, H., Malmberg, J.: Capturing the dynamic and cyclical nature of regulation: methodological progress in understanding socially shared regulation in learning. Int. J. Comput.-Support. Collab. Learn. **14**(4), 425–441 (2019). https://doi.org/10.1007/s11412-019-09313-2

44. Yanovsky, S., Hoernle, N., Lev, O., Gal, K.: One size does not fit all: a study of badge behavior in stack overflow. J. Assoc. Inf. Sci. Technol. n/a (2020). https://doi.org/10.1002/asi.24409

45. Sedrakyan, G., Malmberg, J., Verbert, K., Järvelä, S., Kirschner, P.A.: Linking learning behavior analytics and learning science concepts: designing a learning analytics dashboard for feedback to support learning regulation. Comput. Hum. Behav. **107**, 105512 (2020). https://doi.org/10.1016/j.chb.2018.05.004

46. Lockyer, L., Heathcote, E., Dawson, S.: Informing pedagogical action: aligning learning analytics with learning design. Am. Behav. Sci. **57**, 1439–1459 (2013). https://doi.org/10.1177/0002764213479367

47. Damon, W., Phelps, E.: Critical distinctions among three approaches to peer education. Int. J. Educ. Res. **13**, 9–19 (1989). https://doi.org/10.1016/0883-0355(89)90013-X

48. Cukurova, M., Luckin, R., Millán, E., Mavrikis, M.: The NISPI framework: analysing collaborative problem-solving from students' physical interactions. Comput. Educ. **116**, 93–109 (2018). https://doi.org/10.1016/j.compedu.2017.08.007

"Now, I Want to Teach It for Real!": Introducing Machine Learning as a Scientific Discovery Tool for K-12 Teachers

Xiaofei Zhou[✉], Jingwan Tang, Michael Daley, Saad Ahmad, and Zhen Bai

University of Rochester, Rochester, NY 14627, USA
{xzhou50,jtang21,sahmad11,zbai7}@ur.rochester.edu,
mdaley@warner.rochester.edu

Abstract. Machine Learning (ML) is a powerful tool to unveil hidden patterns in data, unearth new insights and promote scientific discovery (SD). However, expertise is usually required to actualize the potential of ML fully. Very little has been done to begin instructing the youth of society in ML, nor utilize ML as an SD tool for the K-12 age range. This research proposes SmileyDiscovery, an ML-empowered learning environment that facilitates SD for K-12 students and teachers. We conducted a 2-session preliminary study with 18 K-12 STEM teachers. Findings confirm the effectiveness of SmileyDiscovery in supporting teachers to (1) carry out ML-empowered SD, (2) design their own curriculum-aligned SD lesson plans, and (3) simultaneously obtain a rapid understanding of k-means clustering. Design implications distilled from our study can be applied to foster more effective learning support in future systems.

Keywords: K-12 Education · Machine learning · Scientific discovery learning · Technology-enhanced learning

1 Introduction

Scientific discovery (SD) learning plays a critical role in K-12 STEM education by mimicking how scientists study the world through data collection, experimental operations, and pattern interpretation [9,10]. SD naturally connects with Machine Learning (ML) which accelerates data analysis by systematically searching hypotheses and revealing complex patterns in big data [16]. With ML becoming increasingly fundamental in generating new findings in astronomy, biology, chemistry [21], and other STEM domains, it is essential to provide opportunities for K-12 students and teachers to apply ML as a new discovery tool.

Imagine a high-school biology teacher encouraging students to discover new knowledge about dynamic ecosystems. The teacher first introduces a dataset containing over 10 ecological attributes collected from hundreds of ecological field sites. By exploring a few field sites, students may raise questions/hypotheses on

© Springer Nature Switzerland AG 2021
I. Roll et al. (Eds.): AIED 2021, LNAI 12748, pp. 486–499, 2021.
https://doi.org/10.1007/978-3-030-78292-4_39

interactions between ecological attributes. Then students can begin probing these initial ideas using pattern recognition with the help of ML. This may, in turn, lead to a cycle of further inquiries with new hypotheses. Such processes would largely promote science practices required by national standards. These practices include asking questions, planning and carrying out investigations, analyzing and interpreting data, engaging in evidence-based argumentation, and so forth [46].

Despite those promising benefits, little effort has been made to understand ML as a data-driven discovery tool for K-12 science learning. One challenge is balancing the support in learning ML and applying ML for novice learners [2,52]. The other is the lack of curriculum-aligned learning activities for K-12 teachers to engage students in ML-empowered SD [29,48].

To address these challenges, we developed a learning environment, SmileyDiscovery, to support low-barrier ML-empowered SD without extra ML training for K-12 teachers and students. SmileyDiscovery integrates three major components aligned with SD learning phases [33]: (1) orientation & initial conceptualization with Smiley-Data mapping, (2) initial investigation with pairwise comparison and manual clustering, (3) further investigation & conceptualization with automatic clustering. Then we evaluated SmileyDiscovery with K-12 teachers due to their essential roles in integrating innovative technology for pedagogy [25]. Our research questions are: **RQ1.** Can SmileyDiscovery support K-12 teachers to carry out ML-empowered SD? **RQ2.** Can SmileyDiscovery support K-12 teachers to design SD learning activities? **RQ3.** Can SmileyDiscovery support learning ML? Our main contributions include:

1. SmileyDiscovery facilitating ML-empowered SD for K-12 STEM learning;
2. A set of ML-SD connections for K-12 teachers to design ML-empowered SD learning activities aligned with STEM curriculum;
3. Design implications for technology designers without SD background.

2   ML-Empowered SD and K-12 STEM Learning

Research shows that ML approaches empower data-driven discovery by enabling hypothesis generation, iterative experimentation with different parameters, and pattern recognition by gradually revealing more refined parameters [30,31]. Various ML techniques have been proposed to automate SD [27]. For example, k-means clustering, an unsupervised ML algorithm, is used to discover laws by grouping similar objects [13,14], identify dependencies of attributes [44], and form taxonomies [51]. Such methods, however, are applied in science at a professional level [16,21] and thus are inappropriate for K-12 teachers and students with limited CS/ML backgrounds. This points out a demand for designing an ML-empowered SD learning environment in K-12 contexts.

There are emerging research efforts to explore the opportunities of making ML concepts and methods accessible for K-12 students [14,28,49,53]. One study shows that data visualization supports students with limited computing knowledge to gain a basic understanding of cluster analysis [49]. Further, it indicates the potentials of applying ML methods for data interpretation by pattern generation. Another study facilitates youth to train and test ML models of their athletic activities [53]. It shows that ML enhances science learning by aligning ML modeling with modeling scientific phenomena, an essential practice of science recommended in curriculum standards [46]. Informed by these, our work aims to design a learning environment connecting ML components with SD practices. We incorporate design guidelines from existing research about introducing ML in K-12 STEM contexts, such as unveiling complex ML concepts step by step [14,28] and visualizing ML models for explainability [13,49,53].

3   The Design of SmileyDiscovery

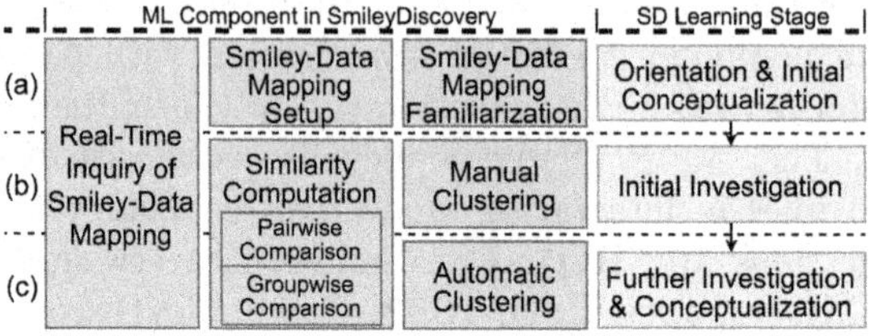

Fig. 1. SmileyDiscovery components: (a) orientation & initial conceptualization by Smiley-Data mapping; (b) initial investigation by pairwise comparison and manual clustering; (c) further investigation & conceptualization by automatic clustering.

We adopted *K-means clustering* to support SD due to its wide application in STEM domains [3,26,35,39]. Compared to supervised learning, unsupervised ML (e.g., clustering) more naturally connects with exploration leading to deeper learning in SD [43], and inductive reasoning through accumulative evidence [15,38], an accessible cognitive skill for young learners [30,40,42]. To make cluster analysis accessible for K-12 students, we used *Smiley* visualization [49], translating each data attribute to a facial feature, to take advantage of people's high processing capacity to human faces [6] and facilitate similarity computation with superposition comparative visualization [17].

SmileyDiscovery enables SD learning stages modified from well-established frameworks [1,5,33], including **orientation & initial conceptualization**, where learners get familiar with the topic and generate hypotheses based on prior knowledge; **initial investigation**, where learners explore dataset for preliminary analysis; **further investigation & conceptualization**, where learners iterate experiments and derive findings. Three components (Fig. 1) support scaffolding for SD [37] to instruct toward higher complexity [24]. This includes introducing from basic (e.g., pairwise comparison) to advanced ML components (e.g., automatic clustering) and from a small subset to the entire dataset. Further, we designed typing boxes to record the generation and refinement of hypotheses.

We collaborated with an experienced science educator and designed three ML-empowered SD learning activities: ecosystems [32], wine chemistry [8], and breast cancer diagnosis [11]. Two ML experts checked the appropriateness of applying k-means clustering in those SD activities. Below we present how SmileyDiscovery supports SD learning across stages with the ecosystem activity.

3.1 Orientation and Initial Conceptualization

First, learners are introduced to multidimensional data about ecological field sites (Fig. 2(a)). Second, they propose initial hypotheses and drag attributes of interest onto facial features (Fig. 2(b)). Such an active construction of Smiley can better engage learners [41]. Third, they manipulate sliders to understand how data attribute values influence corresponding Smiley facial features (e.g., a lower latitude of a field site leads to a smaller mouth). To reduce the cognitive load of memorizing mapping relationships through SD, learners can view Smiley-data mapping in real-time by hovering the cursor over facial features (Fig. 2(d)).

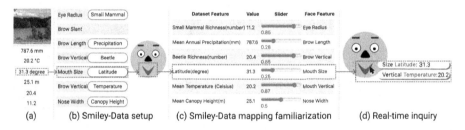

(a) (b) Smiley-Data setup   (c) Smiley-Data mapping familiarization   (d) Real-time inquiry

Fig. 2. SmileyDiscovery component supporting orientation & initial conceptualization.

3.2 Initial Investigation

First, learners use pairwise comparison to identify intriguing patterns between two pre-selected field sites representing two distinct ecosystem clusters. This design is informed by contrastive explanation [7] stimulating abductive reasoning [15,40]. E.g., the distinctions between two Smileys (Fig. 3(a)) may trigger learners to wonder if lower latitudes relate to higher temperatures, precipitation, canopy, beetle richness. Second, learners click on Smileys to overlay them on the representative field sites (Fig. 3(b)) to select similar ones. This trial-and-error process supports deeper reasoning [18,20,34] about (dis)similarities unveiled (e.g., some field sites share low latitudes and high canopy & beetle richness, while some share high latitudes and low canopy & beetle richness).

3.3 Further Investigation and Conceptualization

First, learners select a value of k (Fig. 3(c)). Second, learners conduct inductive cluster analysis by investigating (1) shared features within clusters (intra-cluster pattern) via visual inspection of the stack of Smileys belonging to the same group (Fig. 3(d)); (2) differentiating features between clusters (inter-cluster pattern) by overlaying the two average Smileys (centroid) (Fig. 3(e)). To still consider intra-cluster variations while using a centroid representing each cluster, learners can click on each cluster to switch the view between a stack (Fig. 3(d)) and a centroid (Fig. 3(e)). With variations and patterns introduced by the entire dataset, learners are expected to concentrate on fewer ecological attributes than initial investigation. Third, learners synthesize accumulative evidence from intra-&inter-cluster patterns for further conceptualization (Fig. 3(f)). E.g., the first two clusters show that a high canopy may lead to high beetle richness, and field sites with similar latitudes have similar precipitations and temperatures.

The components above naturally open up the black-box of ML by asking students to gradually apply similarity computation, centroid, evaluating values of k with intra-&inter-cluster patterns. The algorithmic process of the k-means clustering is also implicitly embedded in the scaffolding for manual clustering.

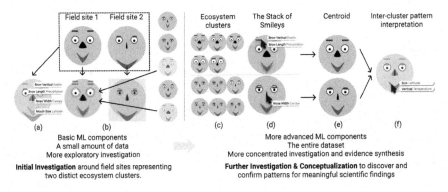

Fig. 3. SmileyDiscovery components supporting the initial investigation and further investigation & conceptualization.

4   Methods

4.1   Study Design

Eighteen in-service K-12 STEM teachers without CS/ML backgrounds were recruited from a teacher education course, *Integrating Technology with STEM*

Table 1. Participant information for each group.

Group	Teaching grades	Subjects
1	Elementary (N = 3), Middle school (N = 1)	Science (N = 2), Math (N = 2)
2	Middle school (N = 4)	Science (N = 3), Math (N = 1)
3	High school (N = 4), Middle school (N = 1)	Science (N = 1), Math (N = 4)
4	High school (N = 5)	Science (N = 5)

Teaching, at a research-based university. They were divided into four groups based on their teaching experience (grades & subjects) (Table 1) and participated in the study via an online meeting platform, Zoom. The study contains two sessions in two consecutive weeks. In the *Teacher-as-Learner (TaL)* session, teachers watched a tutorial video about completing an ML-empowered SD activity in SmileyDiscovery and performed another one with in-time help from researchers. In *Teacher-as-Designer (TaD)*, teachers collaboratively designed ML-empowered SD lesson plans via an online design canvas by specifying each instruction step and selecting SmileyDiscovery components to facilitate corresponding steps.

4.2   Data Collection and Analysis

RQ1. Can SmileyDiscovery Support K-12 Teachers to Carry Out ML-empowered SD? We collected log data of how teachers went through the example activity in TaL, including text input and clicking behaviors (Table 2). We measured successful completions with text input by examining (1) if all questions are answered based on proper ecological attributes, (2) if further conceptualization involves meaningful findings emerging from the data; we then counted clicking behaviors to see if teachers interacted elaborately with ML components. We measured patterns in successful completions by examining hypothesis development and comparing differences in clicking behaviors between successful and unsuccessful completions. Four participants who encountered technical issues were excluded.

Table 2. Log data (text input & clicking behaviors) collected for each SD stage.

Orientation & Initial conceptualization Text input: hypothesis of ecological interactions based on prior knowledge

Initial investigation Clicking behavior: (1) select field sites similar to the two representative field sites for manual clustering; (2) remove less similar field sites from a cluster. Text input: (3) interpretation of shared patterns identified manually; (4) interpretation of differentiating patterns between ecological field site subsets

Further investigation & conceptualization Clicking behavior: (1) conduct automatic clustering with different values of k; (2) switch between Smiley stacks and centroids; (3) compare centroids of ecosystem clusters. Text input: (4) interpretation of shared & differentiating patterns in ecosystem clusters; (5) findings of dynamic interactions between ecological attributes

RQ2. Can SmileyDiscovery Support K-12 Teachers to Design SD Learning Activities? We explored the pedagogical potentials of SmileyDiscovery by asking teachers to (1) post SmileyDiscovery-supported teaching ideas before TaD; (2) collaboratively design ML-empowered lesson plans in TaD; (3) reflect on applying

SmileyDiscovery in teaching in journals after TaD. First, we measured the diversity of teaching ideas. Two researchers independently assessed each teaching idea on whether it includes multidimensional datasets and applies cluster analysis to solve problems, then independently categorized teaching ideas into NGSS disciplinary core ideas [46]. Both achieve near-perfect agreement (Cohen's Kappas: 0.87, 0.91). Second, to measure teachers' fulfillment of ML-SD connections, we identified ML components selected to support each SD phase in teacher-designed lesson plans and counted each connection. Third, we measured teachers' perceptions toward ML-empowered STEM teaching. Two researchers independently coded teachers' reflection journals using thematic analysis, meeting regularly to address disagreements and refine codes.

RQ3. Can SmileyDiscovery Support Learning ML? We administered pre-post tests before and after the TaL to assess teachers' understanding of k-means clustering. Two researchers independently rated the tests, achieving near-perfect agreement with Cohen's Kappas of 0.85 (pre) and 0.83 (post). We measured learning gains by paired t-test as the data satisfies normal distribution. Then we measured the remaining misconceptions by thematic analysis on teachers' answers from post-tests. Two raters coded each incorrect answer independently, reaching near-perfect agreement (Cohen's Kappas above 0.86 for all items).

5   Results

5.1   RQ1. Can SmileyDiscovery Support K-12 Teachers to Carry Out ML-empowered SD?

Completion of ML-empowered SD Learning. 10 out of 14 teachers successfully completed all SD questions and generated meaningful findings of dynamic interactions between ecological attributes through cluster analysis. Two teachers needed to further articulate relationships identified, while the rest two didn't answer the last question for further conceptualization.

The numbers of ecological attributes involved in the investigation show that teachers naturally started with a more exploratory style by looking out attributes as much as possible. Then they reduced the scope as more evidence emerged from the entire dataset. During the initial investigation, 10 out of 14 teachers ended up with clusters sharing high similarity for more than four out of six ecological attributes. After automatic clustering, 10 out of 14 learners narrowed down to fewer attributes most strongly supported by data.

The numbers of different clicking behaviors show that teachers went through all ML components, with more frequent interactions for some of them than others. Specifically, teachers spent much time on manual clustering for initial investigation. On average, they selected 17.43 (SD = 10.21) field sites to compare with two representative field sites, removed 9.07 (SD = 10.54) field sites that are not similar enough, and reserved 8.36 (SD = 2.34) field sites for pattern interpretation. In comparison, teachers roughly played with different values of k for automatic clustering. They tried less than one new k-value (M = 0.71, SD = 0.99) in addition to the two rounds required by the instruction.

Patterns in Successful Completions. We identified two patterns in hypothesis development. (1) *Iterated initial hypotheses* (N = 7): Hypotheses became more specific or more inclusive from initial to further conceptualization. E.g., one teacher initially hypothesized that "latitude and mean temperature are related". In the end, she collected evidence for "different latitudes influence the rest of the ecological attributes a lot". (2) *Generating new findings* (N = 3): Original hypotheses were rejected, and new ones were proposed through investigation.

Teachers who successfully completed interacted more with manual clustering (selection: M = 17.70, removal: M = 8.70) than those who didn't (selection: M = 4.06, removal: M = 3.56). In further investigation & conceptualization, teachers who successfully completed switched between Smiley stacks and centroids (M = 9.5) more than those who didn't (M = 4) and compared centroids (M = 5.2) more than those who didn't (M = 1.5). These indicate the importance of an extensive engagement with similarity computation and sufficient pattern interpretation for generating meaningful findings.

5.2 RQ2. Can SmileyDiscovery Support K-12 Teachers to Design SD Learning Activities?

Diversity of Teaching Ideas. 37 out of 46 teaching ideas were identified as qualified, across science (N = 31), mathematics (N = 4), and social studies (N = 2). For science subjects, we identified 11 out of 13 NGSS [45] core disciplinary ideas, such as biological evolution and engineering design. Three primary learning objectives are identified from the teaching ideas: (1) categorize complex phenomena into groups and describe the patterns (e.g., discover biological patterns in different organisms); (2) understand interactions between different attributes within a system (e.g., investigate relationships between temperatures, humidity, surface types, and bacteria found in different locations); (3) identify the factors most relevant to cause the change/development of a system (e.g., investigate organism traits in different environments and find out which are more critical for survival). These results suggest SmileyDiscovery's pedagogical potential to fulfill a variety of K-12 STEM learning objectives aligned with the curriculum.

Teachers' Fulfillment of ML-SD Connections. Topics of teacher-designed lesson plans are (1) construction materials for flood resistance, (2) biological characteristics & evolution, (3) influential factors to income, and (4) risk factors for heart disease. Two researchers applied the EQuIP rubric [45] and confirmed each lesson plan's alignment with NGSS standards [46]. Patterns in the ML-SD connections applied by teachers are analyzed (Fig. 4). First, similarity computation is used for conceptualization, different from example SD activities. Teachers preferred hypothesis generation through abduction based on a small amount of data rather than prior knowledge. E.g., group 4 asked students to generate initial hypotheses by observing factors' puzzling impacts on heart disease risk. However, accelerating hypothesis generation by ML-revealed patterns is missing from teachers' design. Second, automatic clustering is frequently used for investigation. Two groups designed iterative investigation from small to large datasets. Group 3 proposed to run clustering with different sets of attributes, then compare results from each trial to refine hypotheses of what factors influence a person's income the most [4,51]. Moreover, all groups added a new design for prediction, such as predicting heart disease risk to evaluate the refined hypothesis.

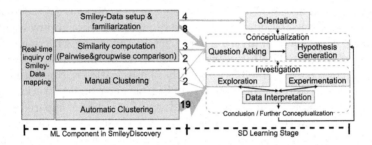

Fig. 4. ML-SD connections identified in four teacher-designed lesson plans.

Teachers' Perceptions Toward ML-empowered STEM Teaching. Teachers appreciated SmileyDiscovery's novelty as a teaching tool as it makes the large data accessible for K-12 students for pattern exploration and interpretation (N = 14), offers a playful learning experience to engage students (N = 10), low barrier to entry (N = 12), and can be applied in various STEM subjects (N = 13). After designing an SD learning activity on what factors influence a person's income, one teacher expressed her wish to conduct the learning activity with the Advancement Via Individual Determination (AVID) program she is teaching: *"If we do create it for real, I can do it with AVID!"* Nevertheless, teachers expected to gain a deeper understanding of ML methods (N = 5) and ML-empowered instruction design (N = 7) before implementing it in actual classrooms.

5.3   RQ3. Can SmileyDiscovery Support Learning ML?

The mean differences of all questions between pre- and post-tests were normally distributed at an alpha level of 0.05. A paired-sample t-test showed significant increases (Table 3) from pre- to post-test for four k-means clustering concepts: similarity computation, centroid, clustering process, evaluating values of k with intra-&inter-cluster pattern interpretation. This suggested that SmileyDiscovery successfully supported teachers to gain a rapid understanding of k-means clustering while applying it for SD. The answers indicate some misconceptions. For *similarity computation*, five teachers only addressed the subjectivity that the decision-making changes based on different criteria. For *evaluating values of k*, nine teachers didn't demonstrate comprehensive procedures, such as using a centroid to represent a cluster without considering intra-cluster variations.

Table 3. Paired t-test results for pre- and post-tests (N = 18)

Questions (Scores range 0–3)	Pre-test		Post-test		t-test	p
	M	SD	M	SD		
What makes two multidimensional datapoints similar or dissimilar?	0.31	0.49	1.50	1.23	−4.26	0.001
What is the centroid of a cluster of data points?	0.89	1.08	1.75	1.19	−2.67	0.031
Order the major steps for the K-means clustering algorithm	0.97	0.60	1.56	0.78	−3.58	0.002
How to decide which value of k gives better clustering results?	0.25	0.49	1.14	1.04	−4.05	0.001

6 Discussion and Future Work

SmileyDiscovery aims to bridge the gaps in ML-enhanced & curriculum-aligned STEM learning [29,48] for K-12 students and teachers with limited computing backgrounds [2,52]. Results show that K-12 teachers applied ML to discover meaningful scientific findings and simultaneously understood related ML concepts and methods. Teaching ideas and lesson plans show SmileyDiscovery's pedagogical potential in diverse K-12 STEM subjects. Teachers also reported that SmileyDiscovery is an innovative and playful way with a low entry barrier to *"explore data and draw connections with visualization"*.

Informed by the study findings, we identified three key design implications for more effective ML-empowered SD. First, it's critical to design efficient scaffolding for ML visual analytics [12,36], as teachers novice to ML tended to carry out less sufficient investigation and synthesis of ML-generated patterns. For example, immediate feedback [23] can be designed to address common challenges in analyzing ML-generated results, such as outlier interpretation and considering intra-cluster variations while interpreting inter-cluster patterns. Second, advanced design to support converting visual representation (e.g., Smiley) to data is needed to support efficient sense-making in the context of subject matter, as teachers reported that the frequent manual Smiley-data translation was overwhelming when interpreting the ML-generated patterns. The advanced design may involve automating such non-salient & routine tasks [37] to reduce cognitive load for SD, which already requires high working memory [22]. Third, trial-and-error should be encouraged by a more inviting design for exploratory ML-enhanced investigation [20], as teachers with better SD performance experimented with more Smileys for similarity computation during manual clustering.

In the teacher-designed learning activities, no teacher applied automatic clustering for conceptualization, indicating certain biases introduced by example SD activities. A customizable authoring system can be designed to provide personalized recommendations of a list of potential ML-SD connections for teachers to select from based on their teaching objectives. Besides, teachers' after-study reflection shows a need to reveal more advanced mathematical knowledge about ML methods: *"While I can conceptualize the process, the mathematical computations in the analytic is a bit abstract to me."* Technical tutorials, such as an interactive workbook [47], can be embedded as supplementary supports.

Limitations and Future Work. As a preliminary study to explore an innovative system [19], our work has several limitations. First, COVID-19 interruption and remote participation constrained data collection and undermined teachers' engagement. Second, the study didn't include a control condition. Thus, our next step is to evaluate the educational effectiveness of an improved SmileyDiscovery on students' learning of scientific knowledge and skills, compared to traditional computer-supported SD learning environments. For more effective and accurate science learning, a component to review the main takeaways can be added at the end of an ML-empowered SD learning activity. Besides, we plan to extend SmileyDiscovery with other similarity-based and supervised ML algorithms [50], engaging learners to derive evaluable scientific laws through SD.

References

1. Understanding science. http://www.understandingscience.org (2021). Accessed 15 Jan 2021
2. Agassi, A., Erel, H., Wald, I.Y., Zuckerman, O.: Scratch nodes ML: a playful system for children to create gesture recognition classifiers. In: Extended Abstracts of the 2019 CHI Conference on Human Factors in Computing Systems, pp. 1–6 (2019)
3. Ay, M., Kisi, O.: Modelling of chemical oxygen demand by using ANNs, ANFIs and k-means clustering techniques. J. Hydrol. **511**, 279–289 (2014)
4. Boutsidis, C., Drineas, P., Mahoney, M.W.: Unsupervised feature selection for the k-means clustering problem. In: Advances in Neural Information Processing Systems, pp. 153–161 (2009)
5. Bybee, R.W., et al.: The BSCS 5E instructional model: origins and effectiveness. In: BSCS, vol. 5, pp. 88–98. Colorado Springs, Co. (2006)
6. Chernoff, H.: The use of faces to represent points in k-dimensional space graphically. J. Am. Statist. Assoc. **68**(342), 361–368 (1973)
7. Chin-Parker, S., Bradner, A.: A contrastive account of explanation generation. Psychon. Bull. Rev. **24**(5), 1387–1397 (2017)
8. Cortez, P., Cerdeira, A., Almeida, F., Matos, T., Reis, J.: Modeling wine preferences by data mining from physicochemical properties. Decis. Support Syst. **47**(4), 547–553 (2009)
9. National Research Council: National Science Education Standards. National Academies Press (1996)
10. De Jong, T., Sotiriou, S., Gillet, D.: Innovations in STEM education: the Go-Lab federation of online labs. Smart Learn. Environ. **1**(1), 1–16 (2014)
11. Dua, D., Graff, C.: UCI Machine Learning Repository. School of Information and Computer Science, University of California, Irvine, CA (2019)
12. Endert, A., et al.: The state of the art in integrating machine learning into visual analytics. In: Computer Graphics Forum. vol. 36, pp. 458–486. Wiley Online Library (2017)

13. Essinger, S.D., Rosen, G.L.: An introduction to machine learning for students in secondary education. In: 2011 Digital Signal Processing and Signal Processing Education Meeting (DSP/SPE), pp. 243–248. IEEE (2011)
14. Evangelista, I., Blesio, G., Benatti, E.: Why are we not teaching machine learning at high school? a proposal. In: 2018 World Engineering Education Forum-Global Engineering Deans Council (WEEF-GEDC), pp. 1–6. IEEE (2018)
15. Folger, R., Stein, C.: Abduction 101: reasoning processes to aid discovery. Hum. Resource Manage. Rev. **27**(2), 306–315 (2017)
16. Gil, Y., Greaves, M., Hendler, J., Hirsh, H.: Amplify scientific discovery with artificial intelligence. Science **346**(6206), 171–172 (2014)
17. Gleicher, M., Albers, D., Walker, R., Jusufi, I., Hansen, C.D., Roberts, J.C.: Visual comparison for information visualization. Inf. Visual. **10**(4), 289–309 (2011)
18. Hitron, T., Orlev, Y., Wald, I., Shamir, A., Erel, H., Zuckerman, O.: Can children understand machine learning concepts? The effect of uncovering black boxes. In: Proceedings of the 2019 CHI Conference on Human Factors in Computing Systems, pp. 1–11 (2019)
19. IES: Common guidelines for education research and development. https://www.nsf.gov/pubs/2013/nsf13126/nsf13126.pdf (2013)
20. Käser, T., Schwartz, D.L.: Modeling and analyzing inquiry strategies in open-ended learning environments. Int. J. Artif. Intell. Educ. **30**(3), 504–535 (2020)
21. Kitano, H.: Artificial intelligence to win the nobel prize and beyond: creating the engine for scientific discovery. AI Mag. **37**(1), 39–49 (2016)
22. Klahr, D., Dunbar, K.: Dual space search during scientific reasoning. Cognit. Sci. **12**(1), 1–48 (1988)
23. Van der Kleij, F.M., Feskens, R.C., Eggen, T.J.: Effects of feedback in a computer-based learning environment on students' learning outcomes: a meta-analysis. Rev. Educ. Res. **85**(4), 475–511 (2015)
24. Koedinger, K.R., Booth, J.L., Klahr, D.: Instructional complexity and the science to constrain it. Science **342**(6161), 935–937 (2013)
25. Koehler, M., Mishra, P.: What is technological pedagogical content knowledge (TPACK)? Contemp. Issues Technol. Teach. Educ. **9**(1), 60–70 (2009)
26. Kupfer, J.A., Gao, P., Guo, D.: Regionalization of forest pattern metrics for the continental united states using contiguity constrained clustering and partitioning. Ecol. Inform. **9**, 11–18 (2012)
27. Langley, P.: The computational support of scientific discovery. Int. J. Hum.-Comput. Stud. **53**(3), 393–410 (2000)
28. Lin, P., Van Brummelen, J., Lukin, G., Williams, R., Breazeal, C.: Zhorai: designing a conversational agent for children to explore machine learning concepts. In: AAAI, pp. 13381–13388 (2020)
29. Marques, L.S., Gresse von Wangenheim, C., Hauck, J.C.: Teaching machine learning in school: a systematic mapping of the state of the art. Inform. Educ. **19**(2), 283–321 (2020)
30. McAbee, S.T., Landis, R.S., Burke, M.I.: Inductive reasoning: the promise of big data. Hum. Resource Manage. Rev. **27**(2), 277–290 (2017)
31. Muller, M., Guha, S., Baumer, E.P., Mimno, D., Shami, N.S.: Machine learning and grounded theory method: Convergence, divergence, and combination. In: Proceedings of the 19th International Conference on Supporting Group Work, pp. 3–8 (2016)
32. NEON: National ecological observatory network data products: [neondp1.100220.001, dp1.10072.001]. http://data.neonscience.org (2020). Accessed 15 Jan 2021

33. Pedaste, M., et al.: Phases of inquiry-based learning: definitions and the inquiry cycle. Educ. Res. Rev. **14**, 47–61 (2015)
34. Penner, D.E., Giles, N.D., Lehrer, R., Schauble, L.: Building functional models: designing an elbow. J. Res. Sci. Teach.: Official J. Natl. Assoc. Res. Sci. Teach. **34**(2), 125–143 (1997)
35. Perini, F.: High-dimensional, unsupervised cell clustering for computationally efficient engine simulations with detailed combustion chemistry. Fuel **106**, 344–356 (2013)
36. Pike, W., et al.: The scalable reasoning system: lightweight visualization for distributed analytics. Inf. Visual. **8**(1), 71–84 (2009)
37. Quintana, C., et al.: A scaffolding design framework for software to support science inquiry. J. Learn. Sci. **13**(3), 337–386 (2004)
38. Rodrigues, C.T.: The method of scientific discovery in peirce's philosophy: deduction, induction, and abduction. Logica Universalis **5**(1), 127–164 (2011)
39. Romesburg, C.: Cluster Analysis for Researchers. Lulu (2004)
40. Ross, J.M.: Informatics creativity: a role for abductive reasoning? Commun. ACM **53**(2), 144–148 (2010)
41. Sawyer, R.K.: The Cambridge Handbook of the Learning Sciences. Cambridge University Press (2005)
42. Schulz, L.: The origins of inquiry: inductive inference and exploration in early childhood. Trends Cognit. Sci. **16**(7), 382–389 (2012)
43. Schwartz, D.L., Chase, C.C., Oppezzo, M.A., Chin, D.B.: Practicing versus inventing with contrasting cases: the effects of telling first on learning and transfer. J. Educ. Psychol. **103**(4), 759 (2011)
44. Skapa, J., Dvorsky, M., Michalek, L., Sebesta, R., Blaha, P.: K-mean clustering and correlation analysis in recognition of weather impact on radio signal. In: 2012 35th International Conference on Telecommunications and Signal Processing (TSP), pp. 316–319. IEEE (2012)
45. Achieve and National Science Teachers Association: EQuIP rubric for lessons and units: Science (2014)
46. NGSS Lead States: Next Generation Science Standards: For states, by states. National Academies Press, Washington, DC (2013)
47. Tang, D., et al.: Empowering novices to understand and use machine learning with personalized image classification models, intuitive analysis tools, and MIT App Inventor. Ph.D. thesis, Massachusetts Institute of Technology (2019)
48. Vazhayil, A., Shetty, R., Bhavani, R.R., Akshay, N.: Focusing on teacher education to introduce AI in schools: Perspectives and illustrative findings. In: 2019 IEEE Tenth International Conference on Technology for Education (T4E), pp. 71–77. IEEE (2019)
49. Wan, X., Zhou, X., Ye, Z., Mortensen, C.K., Bai, Z.: Smileycluster: supporting accessible machine learning in k-12 scientific discovery. In: Proceedings of the Interaction Design and Children Conference, pp. 23–35 (2020)
50. Wang, D., Yang, Q., Abdul, A., Lim, B.Y.: Designing theory-driven user-centric explainable AI. In: Proceedings of the 2019 CHI Conference on Human Factors in Computing Systems, pp. 1–15 (2019)
51. Wang, D., Nie, F., Huang, H.: Unsupervised feature selection via unified trace ratio formulation and K-means clustering (TRACK). In: Calders, T., Esposito, F., Hüllermeier, E., Meo, R. (eds.) ECML PKDD 2014. LNCS (LNAI), vol. 8726, pp. 306–321. Springer, Heidelberg (2014). https://doi.org/10.1007/978-3-662-44845-8_20

52. Zhang, Y., Wang, J., Bolduc, F., Murray, W.G., Staffen, W.: A preliminary report of integrating science and computing teaching using logic programming. In: Proceedings of the AAAI Conference on Artificial Intelligence, vol. 33, pp. 9737–9744 (2019)
53. Zimmermann-Niefield, A., Turner, M., Murphy, B., Kane, S.K., Shapiro, R.B.: Youth learning machine learning through building models of athletic moves. In: Proceedings of the 18th ACM International Conference on Interaction Design and Children, pp. 121–132 (2019)

Better Model, Worse Predictions: The Dangers in Student Model Comparisons

Jaroslav Čechák[(✉)] and Radek Pelánek[(✉)]

Masaryk University, Brno, Czech Republic
{xcechak1,pelanek}@fi.muni.cz

Abstract. The additive factor model is a widely used tool for analyzing educational data, yet it is often used as an off-the-shelf solution without considering implementation details. A common practice is to compare multiple additive factor models, choose the one with the best predictive accuracy, and interpret the parameters of the model as evidence of student learning. In this work, we use simulated data to show that in certain situations, this approach can lead to misleading results. Specifically, we show how student skill distribution affects estimates of other model parameters.

Keywords: Additive factor model · Student modeling · Simulation · Model comparison

1 Introduction

In order to make learning environments adaptive and personalized, we need to model the knowledge state of students [22]. Student modeling techniques are used for a variety of purposes. Models like Bayesian Knowledge Tracing or the Elo rating system are used for updating knowledge estimates after each answer, and this estimate is used for immediate personalization of the learning environment (e.g., the choice of the next question or evaluation of mastery criterion). Other types of student models are used to perform offline learning analytics, obtain actionable insights, and then use them to perform targeted interventions that improve the learning environment. This type of analysis is in literature sometimes described as "closing the loop" studies [6, 11, 13].

In this work, we focus on the second type of student model applications. A commonly used model for this purpose is the Additive Factor Model (AFM). The model's main aim is to evaluate and refine the domain model, specifically the mapping of items to concepts (knowledge components), which is often called Q-matrix. The term item refers to any simple task given to a student, i.e., solving a simple math problem. The concept refers to a general rule needed to correctly answer the item, i.e., the addition of natural numbers. The Q-matrix is then a binary matrix representing which items require which concepts. For each concept, AFM specifies two parameters: easiness and learning rate. Once the model

I. Roll et al. (Eds.): AIED 2021, LNAI 12748, pp. 500–511, 2021.
https://doi.org/10.1007/978-3-030-78292-4_40

is fitted to data, these parameters are interpreted as evidence of learning (or its absence). Concepts with low learning rates are natural candidates for revision.

AFM is a widely used model and has been used in a variety of previous studies. Studies [12,13,16,17,19] focus on domain model refinement, [2,15] give an overview of domain modeling using AFM, and [24] uses AFM to produce learning curves for further analysis. However, most of these studies do not pay much attention to methodological details of parameter fitting and model comparison. They often use off-the-shelf solutions like DataShop [10] without discussing implementation details and interpret the fitted model parameters as evidence of student learning. Unfortunately, in student modeling, even small methodological details can have a significant impact on the obtained results [23].

We use simulated data to explore potential problems in model comparison and interpretation of model parameters. With simulated data, we know the ground truth, and we can objectively assess the quality of fitted model parameters (which is a luxury we do not have for data coming from real students). We use our AFM implementation as well as DataShop's implementation that was used in many previous studies. We show how the treatment of student skill parameters, while rarely analyzed, can impact model comparison and values of the fitted learning rates. Specifically, we provide a concrete setting where a model with correct parameter values has worse predictive accuracy than other objectively worse models when the evaluation is done using a commonly used approach. The results show that using a black-box approach to evaluation, without proper attention to methodological details, can lead to misleading conclusions.

2   Additive Factor Model

2.1   Model Formulation

Here we formally define the additive factor model following the notation used in a recent review of the AFM [7] that is very similar across previous work. For a given group of students I and a group of items J (together with a Q-matrix mapping items to concepts), the additive factor model predicts the probability that a student i will answer an item j correctly, taking into account difficulties of concepts involved in the item j and practice history of the student i. The probability is described by the following equation:

$$P(Y_{ij}|\alpha,\beta,\gamma) = \sigma(z_{ij}) \qquad z_{ij} = \left(\alpha_i + \sum_{k=1}^{K} \beta_k q_{jk} + \sum_{k=1}^{K} \gamma_k q_{jk} t_{ik} \right) \qquad (1)$$

where:

- $i \in \{1,\dots,I\}$ is an index of a student, $j \in \{1,\dots,J\}$ is an index of an item,
- Y_{ij} is a binary response of a student i on an item j,
- $\sigma(x) = 1/(1+e^{-x})$ is a standard logistic function,
- z_{ij} is a logit of Y_{ij},

- K is a number of concepts,
- Q is a $J \times K$ binary matrix where q_{jk} is 1 if an item j uses a skill k and 0 otherwise,
- α_i is a proficiency (prior skill) of a student i and $\overline{\alpha} \stackrel{\text{def}}{=} 0$ to avoid non-identifiability problem
- β_k is an easiness of a skill k,
- γ_k is a learning rate for a concept k, and
- t_{ik} is a number of times a student i has practiced a skill k (practice opportunities).

2.2 Parameter Estimation

In a typical application of the AFM, the Q-matrix is provided by human experts, whereas parameter vectors α, β, and γ are fitted by a parameter estimation technique. For this work, we have implemented our custom parameter estimation based on descriptions in previous work [5,7,8]. We used the TensorFlow framework to create a computational graph model for Eq. 1. Parameter vectors α, β, and γ are initially set to zeros and iteratively optimized using gradient descent. Initializing parameters with zeroes has the benefits of not making any ad-hoc choices, giving more reproducible results than a random initialization, and having a natural interpretation of making all probabilities of correct answers 0.5. We use a penalized log-likelihood as a cost function to optimize and Adam optimizer for computing gradients. The learning rate is gradually lowered with an exponential decay to achieve convergence more reliably. An important detail of our implementation is per concept scaling of opportunity counts into the range $[0, 1]$ as suggested in [8] to correctly fit γ values. The implementation has an option not to fit α parameters at all (in that case, they remain zero).

Previous publications often do not provide a detailed description of parameter fitting procedures used to fit AFM. It seems likely, and some explicitly mention it, that they use AFM implemented in DataShop [10]. The DataShop's AFM implementation is described in detail in [5]. The general idea can be summarized as optimization of Penalized Maximum Likelihood Estimation that penalizes high absolute α values. Our implementation is very similar in this aspect. DataShop provides two implementations in its Tigris Workflow tool: AFM[1] and Python AFM[2] Since it has been widely used, we decided to use both DataShop implementations on our simulated data. Note that DataShop is typically used to analyze real data, yet we consider this a useful test of a commonly used tool.

2.3 Treatment of Student Parameters

The primary focus of an AFM application is on getting insight into the learning domain, i.e., on the values of β and γ parameters. Even though the student

---

[1] https://github.com/LearnSphere/WorkflowComponents/tree/dev/AnalysisAfm.
[2] https://github.com/LearnSphere/WorkflowComponents/tree/dev/AnalysisPyAfm.

parameters (prior skills α) are not necessary for the model application, they play a crucial role in proper evaluation.

We have reviewed some previous work on AFM to understand the typical treatment of the student parameters α. The majority of reviewed papers mention student parameters only in the formal definition of AFM. However, student parameter fitting details are often omitted, and thus their treatment in model evaluation and comparison is especially unclear.

The student parameters fitting is described in detail only in [7]; other works only hint at the general fitting method [2] or mention modeling technique for student parameters [9]. Most reviewed papers do not discuss any details of parameter fitting and probably rely on the available AFM implementation from DataShop, e.g., [12,13,19]. This claim is based on either explicit mentions of DataShop in these papers or on the visual style of learning curve figures closely matching figures produced by DataShop. Details of DataShop's AFM parameter estimation are discussed in Sect. 2.2. However, the treatment of student parameters in DataShop's model evaluation is unclear.

Commonly used evaluation metrics are Akaike information criterion (AIC) [1], Bayesian information criterion (BIC) [25], and cross-validated root mean square error (RMSE) that are used in [2,12–14,16,17,19]. These metrics require model predictions and, therefore, estimates of all model parameters, including the students' skills. Although it is not always reported on which dataset AIC and BIC were computed, we assumed it was done on the same data set used for training. Our experience with DataShop supports this assumption. In cross-validation, however, part of the dataset is held out during training, and it is only used later for evaluation. This poses a question, what parameters should be given to students not seen in the training data?

A straightforward solution is to use $\alpha = 0$ for unseen students, and this choice of α also makes sense for the intended use of AFM. AFM is mainly used in domain modeling (e.g., comparing Q-matrices, analyzing learning curves) and not for estimating student skills, which is typically done by other models (e.g., Bayesian Knowledge Tracing, Performance Factor Analysis). Also, estimated α parameters should be centered around zero, and so $\alpha = 0$ represents an average student. A possible alternative is to estimate α parameter after every attempt and iteratively refit the model and predict probabilities. Such an approach is, in principle, possible, but it is non-trivial, and it has not been described in previous research. For these reasons, we assume $\alpha = 0$ is used for unseen students, which is also true for our evaluations.

3   Experiments with Parameter Fitting

3.1   Data and Models

We employ simulated data in our analyses as they provide ground truth (i.e., true model parameters), otherwise not accessible for real-world datasets. The simulated datasets are generated by randomly sampling from Bernoulli distribution where the probability of a student answering an item correctly is given by

Table 1. Summary of AFM variants used in this work.

Name	Implementation	α	β	γ
AFM ground truth	Custom	Ground truth	Ground truth	Ground truth
AFM $\alpha\beta\gamma$	Custom	Fitted	Fitted	Fitted
AFM $\beta\gamma$	Custom	Zeros	Fitted	Fitted
AFM DataShop	DataShop AFM	Fitted	Fitted	Fitted
AFM DataShop P	DataShop Python AFM	Fitted	Fitted	Fitted

Eq. 1. Ground truth model parameters are either hand-picked or sampled from normal distributions. We refer to the simulation setting as a scenario.

In this work, we use three similar scenarios differing in the setting of student skill distributions. They are intentionally minimalistic to highlight the effects of student skill distribution on other model parameters estimates. There is only a single concept to remove any potential effects of concept combinations on the parameter estimation. There are ten items all practicing this single concept, so the Q-matrix is only a column of ones. Student parameters α are sampled from a normal distribution centered around zero with standard deviation σ_α. The three scenarios have $\sigma_\alpha = 1$, 2, and 3, respectively. So, for example, scenario $\sigma_\alpha = 2$ has $\alpha \sim \mathcal{N}(0, 2^2)$. Parameters β and γ for the single concept are fixed to values representing a common learning situation: $\beta = -0.5$ represents a bit harder concept, and $\gamma = 0.2$ is a moderate learning rate.

In all three scenarios, we let every student attempt every item. While this is unlikely to happen in the real world, it is the best-case scenario for the model parameter estimation. With this setting, we avoid potential biases, including attrition bias [18,20] or item ordering bias [4].

We compare multiple AFMs differing in what parameters the model uses, if they were estimated, and the actual implementation of parameter estimation. All models used in this work are summarized in Table 1. Our custom implementation refers to the TensorFlow implementation discussed in Sect. 2.2. The Item average model always predicts the mean success rate observed for an item for all students.

3.2 Experimental Setup

In the experiment, we explore simulated data sets generated using scenarios described in Sect. 3.1. These scenarios give us the least biased data where every student attempts every item in random order, and the main emphasis is on student parameters that we wish to explore. Using these scenarios, we have generated five training sets, each containing simulated answers of 2000 students and one testing set with simulated answers of 1000 students. Set sizes were chosen sufficiently large to reduce unwanted noise due to randomness in simulations. Note that students in the testing set do not appear in training sets. Therefore trained models have no estimate of their skills. This cross-validation setting corresponds to the real usage of student models in learning environments.

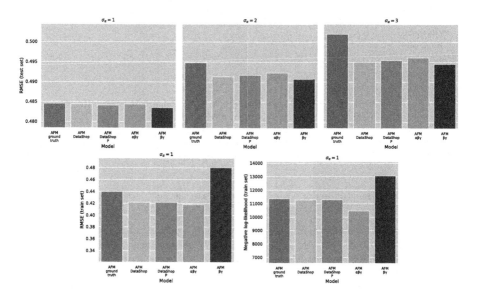

Fig. 1. Evaluation of models on training and testing sets using RMSE and negative log-likelihood. In all cases, a lower value means a better fit to data. Each bar represents the mean value of the given metric over five instances of the model fitted on five training sets. Note that y-scales do not start at zero to emphasize the relative ordering of models. Relative order based on some metric rather than the actual values is typically used in previous research to select the model that best explains the data.

In the evaluation, we compare AFMs with ground truth parameters and AFMs fitted on training sets in terms of the predictive ability and the actual fitted parameters values. We also include the Item average model as a naïve baseline. All models except the two with ground truth parameters were fitted five times on five training sets and evaluated on both training and testing sets. Fitting models multiple times allows us to average out evaluation results and obtain more representative results.

For the evaluation, we choose RMSE and negative log-likelihood as our metrics. Both were used in previous research and are fairly standard [21]. RMSE is a typical choice in machine learning, and it is better suited for binary data than mean absolute error. AIC and BIC, used in previous research, are log-likelihoods with an added term for the model complexity [3]. Since we are not interested in the model complexities , we ignore the complexity term and use plain log-likelihood. RMSE is computed both on testing and training sets and log-likelihood only on training sets. When computing RMSE on the testing set, we assume all students' parameters $\alpha = 0$. The same could be done for log-likelihood, but it is typically used to measure the fit to the training data.

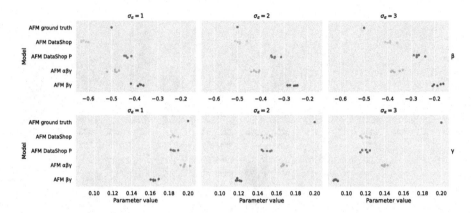

Fig. 2. Values of β and γ parameters for a single concept with increasingly wider student skill distributions. The first model uses true parameter values used in data generation. The other four models have been fitted five times on different training sets, and each dot represents an estimate from one training set. There is artificial vertical jitter to visually separate points with similar x coordinates.

3.3   Results

Figure 1 shows a comparison of models for different scenarios and different metrics. The top row of plots shows mean RMSE on the testing set, the bottom left plot shows mean RMSE on training sets, and the bottom right plot shows mean negative log-likelihood on training sets.

Predictive performance on the testing set is comparable across most models. AFMs with fitted parameters have better RMSE than AFM ground truth in all three scenarios despite their fitted parameters differing from ground truth ones. The differences in RMSE on the testing set between AFM ground truth and models with fitted parameters are more pronounced with increasing σ_α. This suggests that models are finding a more probable explanation of data than the actual ground truth model.

AFMs with fitted student parameters also achieve much better performance on training sets both in terms of RMSE and log-likelihood. Even better than the actual model AFM ground truth that has been used to generate the data. This might suggest a slight over-fitting of student parameters.

In Fig. 2, we also examine the fitted concept parameters β and γ and compare them to ground-truth parameters. We examine three scenarios with increasingly wider student skill distributions with standard deviations $\sigma_\alpha = 1$, 2, and 3, respectively. In all three scenarios, estimated values of both β and γ are shifted towards zero. In other words, the fitted model presents the learning material as easier and with a smaller impact on learning than it is. This effect becomes stronger for wider student skill distributions.

The results also show that although there are small differences between parameters obtained by different AFM implementations, the key aspect (shift towards zero) is consistent across implementations, i.e., it is not a purely techni-

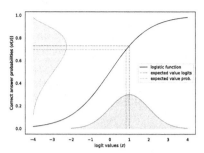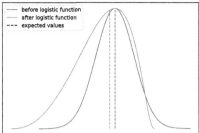

Fig. 3. An illustration of the logistic function transformation of normally distributed data and its effect on the distribution's expected value (mean). The original data follows $\mathcal{N}(1, 1)$. The left figure depicts how the distribution gets transformed, and the right figure depicts both distributions median aligned. Note that the distributions are scaled to the same height for better clarity.

cal idiosyncrasy of a specific parameter fitting procedure. The only exception to the consistency of results is the β parameter of AFM DataShop for the scenario with $\sigma_\alpha = 1$ that is estimated further from zero. Since this model's γ parameter is estimated roughly the same as in AFM DataShop P, this could indicate a problem in the implementation or data preprocessing. We were unable to pinpoint the exact source of this behavior.

3.4 Explanation

In Sect. 3.3, we observed fitted models outperforming models with ground truth parameters and estimated parameter values shifting towards zero. We believe both of these effects are caused by skewness introduced by applying the logistic function. To get probabilities of correct answers for a given item and students after a given amount of practice opportunities, normally distributed student skills are added together with concept difficulties and learning effect forming logits that are then projected using the logistic function. While logits still follow symmetric normal distribution only with shifted mean, the distribution of probabilities after applying logistic function is skewed. The median is no longer equal to the mean, as shown in Fig. 3.

The skew occurs because the logit values in one direction from the mean get projected closer together into a narrower range, and the logit values in the other direction are projected farther apart into a wider range. In Fig. 3, values to the right of the mean are squashed, and values to the left of the mean are stretched. In general, values closer to zero where the logistic function is the steepest get stretched. Values away from zero where the logistic function flattens are squashed. The skewing effect is more substantial as the mean of logits moves farther from zero, which happens for easier concepts or high opportunity counts.

When we use $\alpha = 0$ for evaluation on the testing set, we are, in effect, evaluating point estimates of correct answer probabilities (orange distribution in Fig. 3). The best point estimate with minimal RMSE is the expected value of the correct answer probability. However, due to skewness, the expected values are not the same for probabilities and logits. By estimating parameters closer to zero, models can achieve better RMSE when α is fixed to 0 and yet diverge from the true parameters simultaneously.

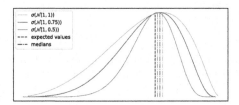

Fig. 4. An illustration of a shifting median when three normal distributions with different standard deviations get transformed by the logistic function and aligned on their expected values (means). Note that the distributions are scaled to the same height for better clarity.

The same also applies to log-likelihood if we were to evaluate it on testing set. However, we are evaluating log-likelihood on training sets with non-zero estimated α parameters, as does an optimizer during parameter fitting. After inspecting estimated values of α, we have made two observations. 1) There are only a few distinct α values, and 2) their distribution is narrower with a smaller standard deviation. The first observation is the artifact of a simple scenario with a single concept. All students with the same number of correct answers have similar estimated skills. The number of correct answers is the most differentiating factor between a student with high and low prior skill. The second observation is tied to the normalization of α parameters and explains why β and γ estimates are closer to zero. If the estimated distribution of α has a smaller standard deviation, the estimated probabilities of the correct answers are less skewed by the logistic function. After aligning expected values (means) of estimated and true probabilities of correct answers to optimize log-likelihood, we arrive at β and γ estimates closer to zero. Note that model AFM $\beta\gamma$, which keeps $\alpha = 0$, is equivalent to estimated distribution having zero standard deviation, i.e., the point estimate of expected value.

To better illustrate the effect of too strict α normalization, suppose the true probability of students answering a given item correctly after a given amount of practice follows logistic function transformed $\mathcal{N}(1,1)$. This situation occurs when students' prior skills follow $\mathcal{N}(0,1)$ and concept difficulties with the effect of learning sum to 1. The goal is to minimize the penalized log-likelihood. In case of too strict α normalization, the penalized log-likelihood will be optimal for α estimates with a smaller standard deviation than the true α distribution has, i.e., the standard deviation of 0.75 instead of 1, as in Fig. 4). To maximize the penalized log-likelihood, we must match the expected values of both true and estimated distributions (alignment on the black dashed line in Fig. 4). Since a narrower distribution is less skewed by the logistic function, it is necessary to shift the whole estimated distribution to make the expected values equal. The shifting of estimated distribution can only be done by changing β and γ as α parameters are constrained to be centered around zero. Thus, we have to bring β and γ parameters' estimates close to zero to maximize the penalized log-likelihood. The whole problem can be avoided by fine-tuning the penalization hyper-parameters. However, the true student population is unknown outside of simulations, making it impossible to properly tune the hyper-parameters without cross-validation using a proper methodology on the testing set.

4 Discussion

In the previous section, we have described a specific situation where an objectively better model can lead to worse predictions than alternatives. The described situation is not a single, artificial outlier. Using simulated data, we have detected similar behavior also in other cases. For example, we simulated the ordering and mastery attrition biases, which are common in many learning systems [4,18,20], e.g., when students solve items in order from easier to more difficult and there is systematic attrition (only a subset of students solves more advanced items). Under these circumstances, even a simple baseline item average model can achieve comparable performance (with respect to predictive accuracy) as the ground truth model. Models with misspecified Q-matrix can beat the model with ground truth parameters by using the fitted parameters to compensate for the mastery bias.

These results show that fitted models have to be interpreted carefully. In our review of previous works using AFM, we have identified a common practice consisting of four steps. 1) Define several models with different candidate Q-matrices. These Q-matrices can be either constructed by experts, refined versions of Q-matrices from previous analyses, or even generated with the help of machine learning from some base Q-matrix. 2) Fit the models' parameter values on training data. Typically the training data is the same real collected data that is to be analyzed. 3) Compare the performance of the models either on the training set or the held-out testing set. To maximally utilize all available data, the evaluation is done on the training set, and k-fold cross-validation is used. 4) Select a model with the best performance and interpret its β and γ parameters (easiness and learning rate). The interpretations range from the evidence of learning to proofs of the existence of new concepts.

Our experiment with simulated data shows how this approach can lead to misleading conclusions. We showed that the best performing model is not necessarily the correct one. Models with incorrectly estimated parameters beat model with ground truth parameters due to technical issues with the treatment of the α parameters (student skills). The problem can be avoided by tuning hyper-parameters of parameter estimation procedure using cross-validation with dynamic predictions in evaluation [23], i.e., recomputing α parameters after each observed attempt in the test set (which is, however, computationally demanding).

Let us make clear that we do not claim that previously reported results are necessarily misleading. In our experiments, we purposefully use scenarios that exaggerate a specific aspect of the situation in order to clearly show its effect. Real data often contain these effects, but probably not in such a clear manner. However, our results show that more care is needed.

References

1. Akaike, H.: A new look at the statistical model identification. IEEE Trans. Autom. Control **19**(6), 716–723 (1974)
2. Aleven, V., Koedinger, K.R.: Knowledge component (kc) approaches to learner modeling. In: Sottilare, R.A., Graesser, A., Hu, X., Holden, H. (eds.) Design Recommendations for Intelligent Tutoring Systems, vol. 1, pp. 165–182. US Army Research Laboratory (2013)
3. Bishop, C.M.: Pattern Recognition and Machine Learning. Springer, Heidelberg (2006)
4. Čechák, J., Pelánek, R.: Item ordering biases in educational data. In: Isotani, S., Millán, E., Ogan, A., Hastings, P., McLaren, B., Luckin, R. (eds.) AIED 2019. LNCS (LNAI), vol. 11625, pp. 48–58. Springer, Cham (2019). https://doi.org/10.1007/978-3-030-23204-7_5
5. Cen, H.: Generalized learning factors analysis: improving cognitive models with machine learning. Ph.D. thesis, Carnegie Mellon University (2009)
6. Cen, H., Koedinger, K.R., Junker, B.: Is over practice necessary?-Improving learning efficiency with the cognitive tutor through educational data mining. In: Proceedings of Artificial Intelligence in Education, pp. 511–518 (2007)
7. Durand, G., Goutte, C., Belacel, N., Bouslimani, Y., Leger, S.: Review, computation and application of the additive factor model (AFM). Technical report 23002483. National Research Council Canada (2017)
8. Effenberger, T., Pelánek, R., Čechák, J.: Exploration of the robustness and generalizability of the additive factors model. In: Proceedings of Learning Analytics & Knowledge, pp. 472–479 (2020)
9. Käser, T., Koedinger, K., Gross, M.: Different parameters-same prediction: an analysis of learning curves. In: Proceedings of Educational Data Mining (2014)
10. Koedinger, K.R., Baker, R.S., Cunningham, K., Skogsholm, A., Leber, B., Stamper, J.: A data repository for the EDM community: the PSLC DataShop. Handbook Educ. Data Mining **43**, 43–56 (2010)
11. Koedinger, K.R., McLaughlin, E.A.: Closing the loop with quantitative cognitive task analysis. In: Proceedings of Educational Data Mining (2016)
12. Koedinger, K.R., McLaughlin, E.A., Stamper, J.C.: Automated student model improvement. In: Proceedings of Educational Data Mining (2012)
13. Koedinger, K.R., Stamper, J.C., McLaughlin, E.A., Nixon, T.: Using data-driven discovery of better student models to improve student learning. In: Lane, H.C., Yacef, K., Mostow, J., Pavlik, P. (eds.) AIED 2013. LNCS (LNAI), vol. 7926, pp. 421–430. Springer, Heidelberg (2013). https://doi.org/10.1007/978-3-642-39112-5_43

14. Liu, R., Koedinger, K.R.: Variations in learning rate: student classification based on systematic residual error patterns across practice opportunities. In: Proceedings of Educational Data Mining (2015)

15. Liu, R., Koedinger, K.R.: Going beyond better data prediction to create explanatory models of educational data. In: The Handbook of Learning Analytics, pp. 69–76 (2017)

16. Liu, R., Koedinger, K.R., McLaughlin, E.A.: Interpreting model discovery and testing generalization to a new dataset. In: Proceedings of Educational Data Mining, pp. 107–113 (2014)

17. Long, Y., Holstein, K., Aleven, V.: What exactly do students learn when they practice equation solving?: Refining knowledge components with the additive factors model. In: Proceedings of Learning Analytics and Knowledge, pp. 399–408. ACM (2018)

18. Murray, R.C., et al.: Revealing the learning in learning curves. In: Lane, H.C., Yacef, K., Mostow, J., Pavlik, P. (eds.) AIED 2013. LNCS (LNAI), vol. 7926, pp. 473–482. Springer, Heidelberg (2013). https://doi.org/10.1007/978-3-642-39112-5_48

19. Nguyen, H., Wang, Y., Stamper, J., McLaren, B.M.: Using knowledge component modeling to increase domain understanding in a digital learning game. In: Proceedings of Educational Data Mining (2019)

20. Nixon, T., Fancsali, S., Ritter, S.: The complex dynamics of aggregate learning curves. In: Proceedings of Educational Data Mining, pp. 338–339 (2013)

21. Pelánek, R.: Metrics for evaluation of student models. J. Educ. Data Mining 7(2), 1–19 (2015)

22. Pelánek, R.: Bayesian knowledge tracing, logistic models, and beyond: an overview of learner modeling techniques. User Model. User-Adapted Interact. 27(3), 313–350 (2017). https://doi.org/10.1007/s11257-017-9193-2

23. Pelánek, R.: The details matter: methodological nuances in the evaluation of student models. User Model. User-Adapted Interact. 27, 1–29 (2018). https://doi.org/10.1007/s11257-018-9204-y

24. Rivers, K., Harpstead, E., Koedinger, K.: Learning curve analysis for programming: Which concepts do students struggle with? In: Proceedings of International Computing Education Research, pp. 143–151 (2016)

25. Schwarz, G.: Estimating the dimension of a model. Ann. Statist. 6(2), 461–464 (1978)

Author Index

Abdelshiheed, Mark I-215
Abdi, Solmaz II-11
Abhinav, Kumar I-3
Abou-Khalil, Victoria II-18
Adair, Amy II-134
Adams, Cathy II-24
Adeniran, Adetunji II-29, II-308
Adjei, Seth A. I-16
Afzaal, Muhammad II-37, II-395, II-433
Agarwal, Mansi II-98
Ahmad, Saad I-486
Ahmed, Ishrat II-43
Akhuseyinoglu, Kamil I-64
Alharbi, Khulood II-48
Alinejad-Rokny, Hamid II-384
AlKhuzaey, Samah I-29
Allesio, Danielle I-178
Almeda, Ma. Victoria II-60
Aly, Sherif G. II-145
Alyuz, Nese I-42
Amperayani, Venkata Naga Sai Apurupa
    I-190
Anany, Mohammed R. II-145
Andres, Juliana M. A. L. I-52, II-60
Andres-Bray, Juan Miguel I-342, II-427
Andrews, Anya II-109
Aomi, Itsuki II-54
Araya, Roberto I-369
Arora, Veenu I-3
Arroyo, Ivon I-178
Aslan, Sinem I-42
Ausin, Markel Sanz I-356
Azevedo, Roger I-241, II-109, II-129

Bae, Chan II-446
Baek, Jineon II-446
Bahel, Vedant I-16
Bai, Zhen I-486
Baker, Ryan S. I-16, I-52, I-342, II-60,
    II-427
Ballelos, Nikki Anne M. II-109
Banerjee, Ayan I-190
Banerjee, Chandrani II-367
Baraniuk, Richard G. I-433

Barnes, Tiffany I-215, I-356
Barria-Pineda, Jordan I-64
Bartindale, Tom I-472
Bashir, Ibrahim I-228
Bautista, Peter II-66
Bayer, Vaclav II-71, II-190
Beheshti, Amin II-384
Behnagh, Reza Feyzi I-459
Beigman Klebanov, Beata I-306
Belfer, Robert II-331
Bell, Timothy H. II-82
Bellas, Francisco II-88
Bellhäuser, Henrik II-168
Bengio, Yoshua II-331
Bergner, Yoav II-43
Beudt, Susan II-224
Bhardwaj, Nitish I-3
Biswas, Gautam I-52
Blais, Chris II-239
Boateng, George II-93, II-208
Boote, Bikram II-98
Botarleanu, Robert-Mihai I-77
Bounajim, Dolly II-355
Boyer, Kristy Elizabeth I-165, I-268, II-355
Brawner, Keith I-293
Bredeweg, Bert II-325
Brown, Chris II-48
Brusilovsky, Peter I-64
Buddemeyer, Amanda II-338
Burns, Nathan II-331
Bursali, Semih I-459
Bywater, James P. I-88

Caballero, Daniela I-369
Cao, Ruoqi II-417
Carroll, David I-381
Castiglioni, Analia II-109
Čechák, Jaroslav I-500
Celepkolu, Mehmet I-268
Charlin, Laurent II-331
Chaudhry, Muhammad Ali I-228
Chen, Guanliang I-381
Chen, Jiahao II-104
Chen, Peter I-472

Chi, Min   I-215, I-356
Ching, Ansona Onyi   II-331
Chiu, Jennifer L.   I-88
Chouhan, Ashish   II-234
Clark, Adam   II-43
Clevenger, Charis   II-344
Cloude, Elizabeth B.   II-109, II-129
Conati, Cristina   I-241
Converse, Geoffrey   I-331, II-114
Corlatescu, Dragos-Georgian   II-119, II-296
Correnti, Richard   I-255
Cosyn, Eric   II-124, II-451
Cristea, Alexandra I.   II-48, II-139
Crossley, Scott Andrew   I-77
Cukurova, Mutlu   I-228, I-472
Cunningham, James   II-124

D'Mello, Sidney K.   I-42
D'Souza, Meenakshi   I-3
Dai, Huan   II-417
Daley, Michael   I-486
Dartigues-Pallez, Christel   II-82
Darvishi, Ali   II-11
Das, Rohini   I-342
Dascalu, Maria-Dorinela   II-296
Dascalu, Mihai   I-77, I-282, II-119, II-296
Dever, Daryn A.   II-129
Dewan, M. Ali Akber   II-273
Dickler, Rachel   II-134
Dietze, Stefan   I-318
Ding, Wenbiao   I-446, II-104, II-183, II-251, II-256
Dobre, Ciprian   I-282
Drousiotis, Efthyvoulos   II-139
du Boulay, Benedict   I-228
Dubey, Alpana   I-3

Effenberger, Tomáš   I-101
Elbourn, Stephen   II-384
Elkins, Sabina   II-331
Elshafey, Ahmed E.   II-145
Emerson, Andrew   II-151, II-355
Esme, Asli Arslan   I-42
Ewerth, Ralph   I-318, II-196

Fahid, Fahmid Morshed   I-113, II-355
Falcão, Taciana Pontual   II-173
Fancsali, Stephen E.   II-441
Fang, Qiang   II-256

Faraji, Farid   II-331
Farrow, Elaine   I-125
Feek, Graham   II-482
Feichtenbeiner, Rolf   II-224
Fernandez, Miriam   II-71, II-190
Ferreira, Máverick   II-156
Fiorentino, Giuseppe   II-162, II-168
Fisher, Josh   II-441
Flanagan, Brendan   II-18
Floryan, Mark   I-88
Fontenla-Romero, Oscar   II-88
Fors, Uno   II-37
Frau, Antoine   II-331
Freeman, Jason   I-165
Furtado, Ana Paula   II-168

Galanis, Elizabeth   II-384
Gao, Yanjun   II-465
Garcia, Samantha   II-173
Gašević, Dragan   I-125, I-381, II-156, II-162, II-168, II-173
Genolini, Christophe   II-82
Ghosh, Aritra   I-137
Glenberg, Arthur M.   II-239
Gobert, Janice   II-134, II-476
Goldberg, Benjamin S.   I-113
Gomez, Ligia E.   II-239
Gorson, Jamie   I-150
Grasso, Floriana   I-29
Griffith, Amanda E.   I-165
Guerra, Carla   II-178
Guerreiro-Santalla, Sara   II-88
Guo, Junqi   II-378
Gupta, Ankit   I-178
Gupta, Sandeep K. S.   I-190
Gupta, Shivang   II-308
Gyawali, Binod   I-306

Hao, Yang   II-183, II-251
Harpstead, Erik   II-390
Hastings, Peter   II-202
Hatley, Leshell   II-338
Heffernan, Neil   I-408, II-290
Henderson, Nathan   II-151
Henderson-Singer, Sharon   II-338
Hernandez, Caridad   II-109
Herodotou, Christothea   II-190
Hlosta, Martin   II-71, II-190
Holtz, Peter   I-318

Hoppe, Anett   I-318, II-196
Hossain, Sameena   I-190
Hu, Cindy Hsinyu   I-150
Huang, Yuchi   I-331
Hussain-Abidi, Huma   II-134
Hutt, Stephen   I-52, II-60, II-427
Hwang, Chanyou   II-446

Inventado, Paul Salvador   II-66
Ismail, Daneih   II-202
Ivanovic, Mirjana   I-64

Jacobs, Jennifer   II-344
Jaillet, Florent   II-82
Jain, Rishabh Ranjit Kumar   II-124
Jain, Sakshi   I-3
Jajodia, Aditya   II-372
Jenkins, Chris   I-228
Jennings, Jay   I-203
Jia, Peilei   I-446
Jiménez, Abelino   I-369
John, Samuel   II-208
John, Varun   II-234
Johnston, Joan   I-293
Ju, Song   I-215

Kähler, Marco   II-224
Kammerer, Yvonne   I-318
Kamzin, Azamat   I-190
Kang, Yu   II-251
Karpurapu, Abhilash   II-372
Katuka, Gloria Ashiya   I-165
Kay, Judy   II-3
Kent, Carmel   I-228
Khazanchi, Rashmi   II-471
Khosravi, Hassan   II-11
Kim, Jung Hoon   II-446
Klebanov, Beata Beigman   II-76
Ko, Neroli   II-331
Kochmar, Ekaterina   II-331
Koedinger, Kenneth R.   II-308
Koedinger, Kenneth   II-390
Kothiyal, Aditi   II-267
Kragten, Marco   II-325
Kumar, Amruth N.   II-213, II-219

Lagmay, Ezekiel Adriel   II-229
LaGrassa, Nicholas   I-150

Lai, Vivian   II-344
Lallé, Sébastien   I-241
Lalwani, Riya   II-234
Lan, Andrew   I-137
LaRochelle, Jeffrey   II-109
Lee, Dongwon   I-408
Lee, Elise   I-150
Lee, William   I-178
Leite, Walter   II-245
Lekshmi Narayanan, Arun Balajiee   II-239
Lemermeyer, Gillian   II-24
Lester, James   I-113, I-293, II-151, II-355
Li, Chenglu   II-245
Li, Hang   II-104, II-183, II-251
Li, Xiu   II-37, II-395, II-433
Lim, Ju Eun   II-239
Lin, Fuhua   II-273
Lins, Rafael Dueire   II-156
Litman, Diane   I-255
Liu, Alex   II-361
Liu, Qiongqiong   II-256
Liu, Tianqiao   II-256
Liu, Zitao   I-446, II-104, II-183, II-251,
    II-256
Lobczowski, Nikki G.   II-308
Lopes, Manuel   II-178
Loukina, Anastassia   I-306, II-76
Lu, Jianchao   II-384
Lu, Yu   II-457
Luckin, Rose   II-183
Luckin, Rosemary   I-228
Lugrin, Birgit   II-314
Lynch, Collin   I-268
Lyu, Jiahao   II-378

Ma, Yingbo   I-268
Magerko, Brian   I-165
Mahajan, Aakash   II-234
Maharaj-Pariagsingh, Lurlynn   II-262
Majumdar, Rwitajit   II-267
Mallick, Debshila Basu   I-433
Maniktala, Mehak   I-356
Manning, Kyle   I-433
Marques, Elaine Cristina Moreira   II-173
Martin, James H.   II-344
Martinez-Maldonado, Roberto   I-472
Masala, Mihai   I-282
Masthoff, Judith   II-29

Matajova, Adela   II-331
Matayoshi, Jeffrey   II-124, II-451
Matsuda, Noboru   I-395, II-320
Matsumura, Lindsay Clare   I-255
McGrew, Sean   I-408
McKlin, Tom   I-165
McLaren, Bruce M.   I-342, II-60
McLaughlin, Elizabeth A.   II-308
McNamara, Danielle S.   I-77, II-119, II-296
Mello, Rafael Ferreira   II-156, II-162, II-168, II-173
Melo, Francisco S.   II-178
Menon, Neeraj   I-178
Merchant, Chirag   II-372
Metzger, Stefania   II-43
Milicevic, Aleksandra Klasnja   I-64
Milner, Fabio   II-367
Min, Wookhee   I-293, II-151
Minogue, James   II-151
Miranda, Péricles   II-162, II-168
Mishra, Shitanshu   II-267
Misra, Abhinav   I-306
Mitrović, Antonija   II-349
Moeini, Anissa   I-228
Mogessie, Michael   I-342, II-60
Mohamed, Amr S.   II-145
Mohammed, Phaedra S.   II-262
Moore, Alexander   II-290
Moore, Allison   I-52
Moore, Johanna   I-125
Morris, David   II-196
Mostow, Jack   II-98
Mott, Bradford   I-293, II-355
Mui, John   II-273
Mukhopadhyay, Raktim   II-124
Muldner, Kasia   I-203
Munshi, Anabil   I-52
Murali, Rohit   I-241
Murray, Tom   I-178

Nachman, Lama   I-42
Nascimento, André   II-168
Nasiar, Nidhi   I-52
Nguyen, Tri   II-239
Nogas, Jacob   II-422
Nouri, Jalal   II-37, II-395, II-433

O'Brien, Mariel   II-134
O'Rourke, Eleanor   I-150

Ocumpaugh, Jaclyn L.   I-52
Ogan, Amy   II-338
Ogata, Hiroaki   II-18
Oliveira, Hilário   II-162
Oliveira, Suely   II-114
Olney, Andrew M.   II-279, II-406
Olsen, Joe   II-134, II-476
Osman, Gihan   II-302
Ostrow, Korinn   II-427
Otto, Christian   I-318
Ouyang, Yuanxin   II-285

Pande, Prajakt   II-267
Papapetrou, Panagiotis   II-37
Paquette, Luc   I-52
Pardi, Georg   I-318
Park, Juneyoung   II-446
Passonneau, Rebecca J.   II-465
Paudyal, Prajwal   I-190
Pavelko, Martina   II-441
Pavero, Vincent   II-331
Payne, Terry R.   I-29
Pedro, Michael Sao   II-134
Pelánek, Radek   I-101, I-500
Pendyala, Naresh   II-234
Pentaliotis, Panagiotis   II-139
Pente, Patti   II-24
Petersen, Andrew   II-422
Pickard, Hannah   I-228
Pokorny, Robert   I-113
Potochny, Joseph   II-331
Pozdniakov, Stanislav   I-472
Prabhune, Ajinkya   II-234
Prihar, Ethan   I-408, II-290
Pu, Shi   I-331, II-114

Rafferty, Anna   II-422
Rakovic, Mladen   I-381
Raković, Mladen   II-162
Raspat, Jay   I-137
Rebelsky, William   I-178
Restrepo, M. Adelaida   II-239
Richardson, Dan   I-472
Richey, J. Elizabeth   I-342, II-60, II-308
Riedmann, Anna   II-314
Ritter, Steven   II-441
Robinson, Ava Marie   I-150
Rockwell, Geoffrey   II-24
Rodrigo, Ma. Mercedes T.   II-229

Rokicki, Markus   I-318
Rong, Wenge   II-285
Rowe, Elizabeth   II-60
Rowe, Jonathan P.   I-113
Rowe, Jonathan   II-151
Ruseti, Stefan   I-282, II-296

Sadiq, Shazia   II-11
Sahebi, Shaghayegh   I-459
Sakr, Nourhan   II-145, II-302
Salama, Aya   II-302
Saville, Jason D.   I-293
Schaldenbrand, Peter   II-308
Schaper, Philipp   II-314
Schlotterbeck, Danner   I-369
Schofield, Matthew   I-52
Scott, Kimberly   II-338
Scruggs, Richard   I-342
Serban, Iulian Vlad   II-331
Sha, Lele   I-381
Shahriar, Tasmia   I-395
Shaikh, Hammad   II-422
Shang, Xuequn   II-417
Sharvani, Vijaya   I-3
Shayan, Muhammad   II-331
Shen, Jia Tracy   I-408
Sheng, Quan Z.   II-384
Shi, Lei   II-48, II-139
Shimmei, Machi   II-320
Slater, Stefan   I-52
Smith, Andy   II-355
Smofsky, Ariella   II-331
Solyst, Jaemarie   II-338
Sonar, Prashant   II-234
Song, Jiachen   II-457
Sotardi, Valerie   II-349
Spain, Randall   I-293
Spain, Randall D.   I-113
Spitz, Loek   II-325
Srinivasan, Ravi   II-361
Stepanyan, Anush   II-331
Stewart, Angela E. B.   II-338
St-Hilaire, Francois   II-331
Streicher, Alexander   II-234
Sumner, Tamara   II-344

Suraworachet, Wannapon   I-472
Suresh, Abhijit   II-344

Tahir, Faiza   II-349
Tameesh, Nadeen   II-302
Tamma, Valentina   I-29
Tan, Chenhao   II-344
Tang, Jiliang   II-183, II-256
Tang, Jingwan   I-486
Tian, Xiaoyi   II-355
Trausan-Matu, Stefan   II-296
Tsutsumi, Emiko   II-54
Tyler, Marcus   II-361
Tymms, Peter   II-48

Ueno, Maomi   II-54
Uribe, Pablo   I-369
Uto, Masaki   I-420, II-54
Uzun, Hasan   II-124, II-451
van der Molen Moris, Johan   I-369

VanLehn, Kurt   II-367
von Hoyer, Johannes   I-318
Vu, Dung Do   II-331

Walker, Erin   II-43, II-239, II-338
Wang, Elaine   I-255
Wang, Ning   II-372
Wang, Ruhan   II-378
Wang, Shuang   II-384
Wang, Yufei   II-384
Wang, Zichao   I-433
Warriem, Jayakrishnan Madathil   II-267
Watanabe, Micah   I-77
Weegar, Rebecka   II-37, II-395, II-433
Weitekamp, Daniel   II-390
Wetzel, Jon   II-367
Wheeler, Leslie   II-441
Whitehill, Jacob   I-178
Whitelock-Wainwright, Alexander   I-381
Wiebe, Eric   I-268, II-355
Wiggins, Joseph B.   I-165, I-268, II-355
Williams, Joseph Jay   II-422
Woodruff, Matthew   II-482
Woolf, Beverly   I-178

Wu, Xintao   I-408
Wu, Yongchao   II-37, II-395, II-433
Wu, Zhongqin   I-446, II-183, II-251, II-256
Wylie, Ruth   II-43

Xia, Feng   II-256
Xing, Wanli   II-245
Xiong, Qingyun   II-378
Xiong, Zhang   II-285
Xu, Guowei   I-446
Xu, Shiting   I-446

Yamamoto Ravenor, R.   II-401
Yamashita, Michiharu   I-408
Yao, Mengfan   I-459
Yarbro, Jeffrey T.   II-406
Yew, Victoria M.   I-381
Yu, Jinglei   II-457
Yu, Ran   I-318

Yu, Shengquan   II-457
Yudelson, Michael   II-412
Yun, Yue   II-417
Zavaleta-Bernuy, Angela   II-422

Zechner, Klaus   I-306
Želem-Ćelap, Stefan   I-64
Zhang, Haoran   I-255
Zhang, Hongbo   II-285
Zhang, Jiayi   I-342
Zhang, Yupei   II-417
Zhao, Jiafu   II-256
Zhao, Siqian   I-459
Zheng, Qi Yin   II-422
Zhou, Guojing   I-215
Zhou, Qi   I-472
Zhou, Xiaofei   I-486
Zhou, Yiqiu   II-427
Zhou, Yucong   II-285
Zia, Aayesha   II-37, II-395, II-433f

Printed in the United States
by Baker & Taylor Publisher Services